Joseph Benjamin McCaul

The Epistle to the Hebrews, in Paraphrastic Commentary

With illustrations from Philo, the Targums, the Mishna and Gemara, the later

Rabbinical writers, and Christian annotators, etc.

Joseph Benjamin McCaul

The Epistle to the Hebrews, in Paraphrastic Commentary
With illustrations from Philo, the Targums, the Mishna and Gemara, the later Rabbinical writers, and Christian annotators, etc.

ISBN/EAN: 9783337386603

Printed in Europe, USA, Canada, Australia, Japan

Cover: Foto ©Lupo / pixelio.de

More available books at **www.hansebooks.com**

THE
EPISTLE TO THE HEBREWS,

IN A

PARAPHRASTIC COMMENTARY, WITH ILLUSTRATIONS

FROM

PHILO, THE TARGUMS,
THE MISHNA AND GEMARA, THE LATER RABBINICAL WRITERS,
AND CHRISTIAN ANNOTATORS, ETC., ETC.

לְמַעַן יָרוּץ קוֹרֵא בוֹ

"That he may run that readeth it."—Hab. ii. 2.

BY

THE REV. JOSEPH B. M'CAUL,

HONORARY CANON OF ROCHESTER CATHEDRAL; RECTOR OF ST. MICHAEL
BASSISHAW, LONDON; CHAPLAIN TO THE LATE LORD BISHOP OF ROCHESTER;
AND SOMETIME DIVINITY LECTURER AND CENSOR
IN KING'S COLLEGE, LONDON;
AUTHOR OF "*Bishop Colenso's Criticism Criticised;*" "*The Abbé Migne and the Bibliothèque Universelle du Clergé;*" "*The Ten Commandments the Christian's Spiritual Instructor.*"

LONDON:
LONGMANS, GREEN, AND CO., PATERNOSTER-ROW.

1871.

To the Bishops and Clergy

OF THE

Sister Churches of England and Ireland,

SEVERED, BUT STILL UNITED IN FAITH, HOPE, AND LOVE,

THESE FEW PAGES

ARE RESPECTFULLY DEDICATED BY

THEIR HUMBLE SERVANT,

THE AUTHOR.

SAINT MICHAEL BASSISHAW, LONDON, E.C.,
June, 1871.

Οὐ γὰρ εἰκῇ οἱ ἀρχαῖοι ἄνδρες ὡς Παύλου αὐτὴν παραδεδώκασι.—*Origen.*

PREFACE.

The present work is the result of many happy hours devoted to the instruction of Candidates for Holy Orders. My invariable practice was to commence our Greek Testament reading by the study of the Epistle to the Hebrews. Whereas the other epistles are addressed to separate Churches or individuals, and are devoted to special or *locally* interesting topics, the Epistle to the Hebrews presents us with no meagre epitome of those arguments and facts, drawn from the Old Testament Scriptures, upon which the superstructure of Christianity was laid. The first Christian Church at Jerusalem was built up of Jewish materials. In Acts vi. 7 we read, πολύς τε ὄχλος τῶν ἱερέων ὑπήκουον τῇ πίστει, "And a great company of the priests were obedi-"ent to the faith." In the Epistle to the Hebrews we listen again to the arguments which, by the converting power of God's Holy Spirit, were so potent to convince the very same men who rejected Jesus of Nazareth, and condemned Him to death, that they had been guilty of a grievous injustice, and that that same Jesus, whom the house of Israel crucified, God the Father "hath made both Lord and Christ." (Acts ii. 36.) We understand how St. Paul and his companions "reasoned" (διελέγετο) with the Jews, and how it is written concerning Apollos, εὐτόνως τοῖς Ἰουδαίοις διακατηλέγχετο δημοσίᾳ, ἐπιδεικνὺς διὰ τῶν γραφῶν, εἶναι τὸν Χριστὸν Ἰησοῦν. "For he mightily convinced the Jews, *and that* "publicly, showing BY THE SCRIPTURES that Jesus was the "Christ (*i.e.*, המשיח, *the Messiah*)." The expression CHRIST, or MESSIAH, is a phrase strictly Jewish, and the attempt to convince Jews that Jesus of Nazareth was the Messiah whom they expected, implies that the reasoners, and the reasoned with, had much in common. In other words, that the Professors of Christianity claimed to expound the well-grounded hopes of the Jewish people (as held out in the Old Testament Scriptures), according to their only legitimate interpretation and fulfilment. It was the custom with Voltaire and his imitators, English and foreign, to endeavour to bring Christianity into contemptuous disrepute by representing it to be the illegitimate offspring of Judaism. The Jews are caricatured by the "Philosopher of Verney" and his copyists, as being a nation utterly revolting and disgusting in their ethical antecedents, and their sacred books are scoffed at, as being a tissue of misstatements, of credulous inhumanity, of supernatural impossibilities, and of indecent puerilities. (See Voltaire's DICTIONNAIRE PHILOSOPHIQUE, Tom. V., Article JUIFS, pp. 349—357, "*Assassinats juifs. Les " Juifs ont ils été anthropophages? . . . Les pères et mères " ont-ils immolé leurs enfans ? Et de quelques autres belles " actions du peuple de Dieu.*" Amsterdam Edition, 1789, 12mo.) Modern propriety recoils, with conventional delicacy, from any glaring outrage upon the "religious persuasion" of any denomination or sect whatever. All history teaches that it has been an amiable and excusable foible of the human mind to believe in some system or other of religious belief. So definitely marked and universally prevalent (although utterly mistaken) a propensity is to be honoured with a kind of contemptuous respect. From the Moloch worship of the Canaanites up to the latest developments of Anglican ritualistic symbolism, all religions are viewed alike, viz., as the outcomings of an ineradicable tendency of the human mind towards superstition. This belief in supernaturalism is the idol to be overthrown. But the incredulity of to-day is well aware that to be listened to, she must be cautiously decent; yet she is as hostile, as ever were the Encyclopedists, to all definite creeds. She, therefore, spares no opportunity of sneering at credulity in general, and at the authenticity of the sacred writings in detail. Her patronising toleration is far more insidiously dangerous to ill-informed but well-disposed minds, than was the open and vulgar hostility of the professed Atheist and Deist of the last century. She has endeavoured to persuade men that belief and reverence for God's Word is synonymous with vulgarity and ignorance. Hence has arisen the modern figment of a "Higher Criticism." The professors of this boastful system of destructive theology have unfortunately succeeded in producing a vague but very widespread persuasion of the historical untrustworthiness of the Bible. The calumny has been reiterated with such loud and consistent pertinacity that a general sense of insecurity has been at last produced upon the minds of teachers and students alike. We see an unhappy tendency to a timid handling of the Word of God manifesting itself in the English theological literature of the present day. Men are afraid to speak with decision, lest they should be decried as unscholarly. The real cause of this unnecessary hesitation, I regret to believe, is to be found in the superficial standard of theological attainments, not only expected of candidates for the ministry of our Church, but accepted with complaisance by the reading public from those who profess to be teachers. Nearly all, if not all, the modern objections against, and supposed discrepancies in, the Holy Scriptures have been repeatedly and amply disposed of by the early Jewish writers, and also by Christian Divines of the last three centuries. To any one fairly acquainted with sacred literature, these pretended new discoveries present no novelty whatever. The bustling self-importance with which they are nowadays propounded, as the results of a new and "Higher Criticism," would provoke a smile, were not the results, already produced, so disastrous in unsettling the faith of many earnest and simpleminded inquirers after God's truth. Utterly inexcusable are such words of vague and indefinite mistrust as we find Dean Alford presenting to the mind of the young student (although he gives no illustrations of his real meaning) in his *Prolegomena* (sect. i., 191) to the Epistle to the Hebrews. They read very like a preliminary apology for any orthodox sentiments which may unavoidably or unintentionally be found in his treatment of the Epistle: "And he (the student) will bear in mind, that "the day is happily passing away with Biblical writers and "students, when the strong language of those, who were "safe in the shelter of a long-prescribed and approved "opinion, could deter any from humble and faithful re-"search into the various phenomena of God's Word itself: "when the confession of having found insoluble difficulties "was supposed (!) to indicate unsoundness of faith, and the "recognition of discrepancies (!) was regarded as affecting "the belief of Divine inspiration. We have at last in this "country began to learn that Holy Scripture shrinks not "from any tests, however severe, and requires not any "artificial defences, however apparently expedient." First of all, it is contrary to fact that "*the confession of having* "*found insoluble difficulties*" in GOD'S WORD, was ever "*supposed*" by theologians, whose opinion was worth having, "*to indicate unsoundness of faith.*" In a volume of such venerable antiquity as the Bible such difficulties must be expected to occur. The self-confident assumption *that such difficulties are necessarily mistakes*, is what all reverent minds have regarded with pain and indignation, as indicative of presumption, and not of scholarship, far less of faith. Secondly, wherever Dean Alford exemplifies what he is pleased to proclaim as a "discrepancy," the fault lies with the would-be expounder, and not with the sacred writer. Dean Alford has attempted in his exegesis, something far beyond his powers of discrimination, and, I might add, far beyond his reading. He (and his collaborateurs) deserve all praise for their industrious compilation and laborious collations, but in other respects this Greek Testament produces a feeling of profound disappointment. Dean Alford is, apparently, very partially acquainted with the Hebrew text of the Old Testament Scriptures. He is equally unfamiliar with Jewish habit of thought and expression, and the opinions of the Rabbinical authorities. And yet he professes to expound the writings of Jewish Apostles and Evangelists, not to mention our Blessed Lord Himself, who was also a Jew, and ministered exclusively to Jews, in a satisfactory manner for Christian readers! Can it be any matter for surprise if a Commentator on the Epistle to the Hebrews, furnished with such credentials of his preliminary fitness for his work, should perchance find "insoluble difficulties" and "discrepancies" in the course of his labours? The acceptance, by any number of the clergy of our Church, of such works as Dean Alford's Greek Testament, Dean Stanley's Lectures on the Jewish Church, of Bishop Colenso's inconceivably silly book on the Pentateuch, and of many (*not* all) of the articles in Smith's Dictionary of the Bible, as being representative specimens of the Anglican theological attainments of the present day, must have produced but a sorry impression on the Continent respecting the present state of Scriptural learning in that branch of Christ's Church, which in former days produced its Usshers, Waltons, Warburtons, Kidders, Lightfoots, Louths, Kennicotts, Blayneys, Hodys, &c., &c., not to mention a layman like Selden, the wonderful erudition of whose writings is unsurpassed by the writers of any country or any age. Verily, the advocates of the ancient and orthodox systems of interpretation have only to wait with patience, and Time, that most impartial trier of the value of all things, will avenge them of their adversaries. Meanwhile, I would earnestly exhort all students of Holy Writ not to be ashamed of being considered over-orthodox. It is not too "much learning" that has inspired the recent attacks upon God's Word. The accusations of ignorance come with an ill grace from the professors of the modern and diffident school of theology, whose special qualification, as a rule, is a contented

b

unacquaintance with the Old Testament Scriptures, even in
the English and Greek, not to speak of the Hebrew ver-
nacular.

The following trenchant words of the illustrious Heinrich
Ewald * of Gottingen are too important in their appreciation
of the modern style of German theological criticism, which
has unfortunately come recently so much into vogue in
England, not to be given in their integrity :—" Ich habe
" schon lange die Erfahrung gemacht dass, wie heute das
" Christenthum von den Gelehrten und Geistlichen unter
" uns meist verstanden und angewandt wird, die Bücher
" des N. T.'s vorherrschend noch weit oberflächlicher und
" gewissenloser behandelt werden als die des A. T.'s; was
" sonderbar, und auf den ersten Blick, nicht wohl möglich
" scheint, und doch nur zu wahr ist. Denn das A. T. wird
" zwar auf der einen Seite von den Liebhabern alter Irrthümer,
" auf der andern von den übeln Neuerern ebenfals noch
" immer so oft in genug eiteler Weise gelesen erklärt und
" angewandt: allein zum Theil entschuldigt sich das, wegen
" der grösseren Schwierigkeiten seines genügenden Verständ-
" nisses leichter, zum Theil kann dies nicht so offen und so
" schädlich betrieben werden. . . . Die seit 1866 neu auf-
" geblasene . . . Berlinische Zerstörung aller wahren Religion
" erkühnt sich zwar in neuer Weise auch über das A. T.
" ihren Selbstdünkel, und ihre Finsterniss zu ergiessen:
" allein das hat bis jezt wenig zu sagen, und ist nur eine
" einzelne der vielen Windblasen dieser an sich sebst vollko-
" menen hohlen neuester Nationalliberalen Windhose. Die
" Bücher des N. T.'s aber scheinen zu naheliegend, zu leicht
" verständlich, und zugleich zu unmittelbar nothwendig, und
" zu unbeweisbar von wichtigster und entscheidenster Bedeu-
" tung zu seyn, als das nicht jeder Windbeutel unserer Tage

* *Das Sendschreiben a.d. Hebräer und Jakobos' Rundschreiben
übersetzt und erklärt von H. Ewald.* (Vorwort, p. iv., &c.) *Göttingen*,
1870, 8vo. Dr. Ewald's book only came into my hands after a considerable portion of the present work was in type.

" mit ihnen alles zu versuchen, und alles in ihnen zu finden,
" sich ganz aufgelegt und wohlgemuth, vor allem auch nach
" den heutigen Staatsgesezen, ganz straflos fühlen sollte.
" Diese Spielereien mögen nun auch wol erträglich scheinen
" so lange sie bloss auf dem flüchtig vergänglichen Papiere
" bleiben, und sich am liebsten nur in den herumschwirren-
" den Tagesblättern jedem anbieten der an ihnen seinen
" Vergnügen findet: allein hat man nun wenigstens seit
" 1866 erkannt welches entsezliche Verderben hinter ihnen
" lauert? Ist es nicht endlich Zeit dass gerade de N. Tlichen
" Bücher überall am schärfsten und zugleich am richtigsten
" erkannt, und in dem Sinne angewandt werden der ihr
" eigener ist. Denn dieser braucht von uns nur so wie er
" ursprünglich und ewig derselbe ist sicher wiedererkannt
" zu werden, um uns jenem gesunden kräftigen Heilmittel
" zu dienen, welches wir nicht entbehren können, wenn nicht
" die allgemeine Zerstörung in Deutschland welche schon
" begonnen, ihr Werk vollenden soll. Zu diesem Zwecke
" bedarf es einer zwar völlig erschöpfenden, aber in sich
" ganz klaren und sich mit sich selbst begnügenden zuver-
" lässigen keuschen, vor allem auch leicht übersichtlichen
" Erklärung jedes einzelnen Buches. Bei dem Trosse der
" Erklärer unserer Zeit herrscht, soweit sie nicht etwa bloss
" erbaulich erklären, und diesen ganz einseitigen, aber für die
" meisten dennoch zu hohen Zweck verfolgen wollen, nur die
" Sucht vor andern Erklärern möglichst viele, sei es philolo-
" gische oder dogmatische Fehler vorzuwerfen, und damit
" entweder dicke Bände zu füllen, oder bei allem engern
" Raum den man etwa buchhändlerische Vortheile wegen
" einhalten will, dennoch nach allen Seiten hin mit dem
" Hacken auszuschlagen. Man hat diese Dinge allmälig
" immer mehr zu einer Art möglichst beliebter Kunst
" gemacht, und so herrschen sie jezt, haben aber deutlich
" nicht wenig zu dem höchst geringen Nuzen beigetragen wel-
" chen die Erklärung des N. T.'s bis jezt in der Kirche und im
" Volke gestiftet hat. Wie mir nun diese Art zu erklären

" von jeher widerstanden hat, so habe ich mich auch hier um
" sie nicht bekümmert, und nicht ein dickes, oder ein düstres
" Buch schreiben wollen. Aber ich hoffe dass auch die hier
" behandelten zwei Bücher des N. T.'s durch diese ihre Erklä-
" rung so wenig irgend etwas verloren haben dass ihre einge-
" borne Herrlichkeit aus ihr nur desto heller und unverkenn-
" barer hervorleuchtet. Kein einzelnes Biblisches Buch auch
" des N. T.'s soll uns zwar für sich allein genügen; es will
" dieses auch gar nicht, und weist uns immer auf etwas
" zurück was noch weit über ihm steht. . . . Die genauere
" Erklärung lässt uns dazu auf vieles einzelne scheinbar
" kleinere, und doch zulezt höchst bedeutsame richtig mer-
" ken, was, ausser ihr immer räthselhafter und unsicherer
" bleibt, als nöthig ist. Hinter allen N. Tlichen Büchern
" sehen wir alsdann zwar eine Menge Schriften stehen
" welche die Schriftsteller auch noch ausser den jezt im
" A. T. erhaltenen benuzten: was sich nirgends so im
" Grossen und Ganzen entdecken lässt, als bei dem Hebräer-
" briefe, wenn man diesen richtig zu verstehen weiss. Aber
" unsere beiden Bücher geben uns alsdann auch die sicher-
" sten Zeugnisse dass als sie geschrieben wurden, schon
" längst ein höchst thätiges neues Christliches Schriftthum
" von Evangelien und von Briefen gegründet war. Die zu
" Leipzig, bei Fues, in diesem Jahre herausgekommenen
" *Evangelien* des Zürischer Theologen Volkmar fallen schon
" dadurch zu Boden; und müssen in Deutschland zu Boden
" fallen, wenn man überhaupt unter uns noch ernstlich das
" Christenthum will. Was wollen nun dagegen alle die
" neueren und neuesten Faseleien welche noch immer den
" Ursprung der Evangelien weit später herabzusezen sich
" bemühen! Möchte man doch, auch dieser entfernteren
" Folgerungen wegen, in unseren Zeiten endlich sorgsamer
" werden, um nicht die Beute solcher faselnden Theologer
" und roher Philologen zu werden"!

So much, then, for the modern figment of a "Higher
Criticism," according to the opinion of one of the pro-

foundest thinkers, and most learned scholars of Germany, at the present moment. But in addition to the empirical pratings and crude guesses of a hybrid Anglo-German neology, we are threatened with an influx of unbelief from a very different quarter. According to the latest phase of the Anglo-French school of Antichristianism, Christianity, as we see it, is a somewhat recent outgrowth from the teaching of an illiterate Jewish peasant, half impostor, half enthusiast, who propounded a scheme of universal and philanthropic benevolence, but which, apart from its intrinsic excellence, has no substantial basis of authority whatever to rest upon. According to these newest lights, Christianity gradually came into vogue on account of the agreeable and comprehensive principles of humanitarianism which it inculcated. All its sharply defined dogmas, all its pretensions to be God's one way of salvation, all its appeals to genuineness, on account of its being the fulfilment of prophecy, are later interpolations, foisted by theologians upon the simple scheme of universal brotherhood which Jesus preached with a fervid simplicity, approaching to fanaticism.

The propounders of such a theory must either be very uncandid or very illiterate. To notice it would seem superfluous, were it not for the persistent endeavours made at the present moment to inculcate it, in a diluted, and less alarming form, from the pulpit and the press, by members of our own Communion. Any one who has read even a few pages of Philo, or Josephus, or of the Targums, or of the earlier Rabbinical writers, must be well aware that an elaborated system of theology, very nearly akin to Christianity, in some respects identical with it, even to its very phraseology, and absolutely depending for its existence upon the historical and prophetical genuineness of the Old Testament writings, was in existence at the very time that Jesus and his Apostles first promulgated his claims to be the Messiah of God. Let any one read, for example, the following passage of Philo, and, remembering the language professedly held by Christ

and his Apostles, as recorded in the Gospels and Epistles, pronounce judgment upon the validity of the theory that Christianity is a new religion—let him say whether they spoke a new and unintelligible jargon, or whether they adopted and sanctioned a manner of expression accepted and perfectly understood by that larger portion of the Jewish Church and nation which rejected the claims of Jesus to be the Son of God:—Οὕτως οὖν ἡ ψυχὴ γανωθεῖσα, πολλάκις εἰπεῖν οὐκ ἔχει, τί τὸ γανῶσαν αὐτὴν ἐστι· διδάσκεται δὲ ὑπὸ τοῦ ἱεροφάντου καὶ προφήτου Μωϋσέως, ὃς ἐρεῖ, οὗτός ἐστιν ὁ ἄρτος, ἡ τροφὴ ἣν ἔδωκεν ὁ Θεὸς τῇ ψυχῇ προσενέγκασθαι, τὸ ἑαυτοῦ ῥῆμα, καὶ τὸν ἑαυτοῦ λόγον· οὗτος γὰρ ὁ ἄρτος ὃν δέδωκεν ἡμῖν φαγεῖν, τοῦτο τὸ ῥῆμα Λέγει δὲ καὶ ἐν Δευτερονομίῳ, καὶ ἐκάκωσέ σε, καὶ ἐλιμαγχόνησέ σε, καὶ ἐψώμισέ σε τὸ μάννα, ὃ οὐκ ᾔδεισαν οἱ πατέρες σου, ἵνα ἀναγγείλῃ σοι, ὅτι οὐκ ἐπὶ ἄρτῳ μόνῳ ζήσεται ἄνθρωπος, ἀλλ' ἐπὶ παντὶ ῥήματι ἐκπορευομένῳ διὰ στόματος Θεοῦ .... Περιποιεῖ δ' ἡμῖν καὶ λιμὸν, οὐκ ἀρετῆς, ἀλλὰ τὸν ἐκ πάθους καὶ κακίας συνιστάμενον· τεκμήριον δὲ· διατρέφει γὰρ ἡμᾶς τῷ γενικωτάτῳ αὐτοῦ λόγῳ. Τὸ γὰρ μάννα ἑρμηνεύεται τί, τοῦτό ἐστι τὸ γενικώτατον τῶν ὄντων· καὶ ὁ λόγος δὲ τοῦ Θεοῦ ὑπεράνω παντός ἐστι τοῦ κόσμου, καὶ πρεσβύτατος καὶ γενικώτατος τῶν ὅσα γέγονε. Τοῦτον τὸν λόγον οὐκ ᾔδεισαν οἱ πατέρες. ..... Ἀναγγελλέτω οὖν ὁ Θεὸς τῇ ψυχῇ, ὅτι οὐκ ἐπ' ἀρτῷ μονῷ ζήσεται ὁ ἄνθρωπος κατ' εἰκόνα, ἀλλ' ἐπὶ παντὶ ῥήματι τῷ ἐκπορευομένῳ διὰ στόματος Θεοῦ· τουτέστι καὶ διὰ παντὸς τοῦ λόγου τραφήσεται, καὶ διὰ μέρους αὐτοῦ. Τὸ μὲν γὰρ στόμα σύμβολον τοῦ λόγου, τὸ δὲ ῥῆμα μέρος αὐτοῦ. Τρέφεται δὲ τῶν μὲν τελειοτέρων ἡ ψυχὴ ὅλῳ τῷ λόγῳ· ἀγαπήσαιμεν δ' ἂν ἡμεῖς, εἰ καὶ μέρει τραφείημεν αὐτοῦ. "So also the soul,
" when it rejoices, is oftentimes unable to describe the cause
" of its joy. But it is explained by Moses, the priest and
" prophet, who says: This is the bread, the food which God
" has given to the soul to appropriate to itself, viz., his own
" utterances and his own WORD. For this is the bread which
" He has given to us to eat, viz., his utterances. For he

"says in Deuteronomy, He afflicted thee, and suffered thee to hunger, and fed thee with manna, which thy fathers knew not, in order that He might inform thee that man does not live by bread only, but by every word that proceedeth out of the mouth of God. . . . . . He brings hunger upon us, not of virtue, but that which arises from our passions and evil dispositions. The proof of this is, that He nourishes us with his most general WORD. For the manna is interpreted *What is it?* That is, the most general of all things that exist. And the WORD of God is above the whole universe, and the eldest and most general of all things created whatsoever. This WORD our fathers did not know. . . . . . Let God therefore inform the soul, that man, who was created in his image, does not live by bread only, but by every word (or utterance) that proceedeth out of the mouth of God. That is to say, he shall be nourished by the whole WORD, and by his parts also. For the expression 'mouth' is symbolical of the WORD, but the utterance ($\rho\tilde{\eta}\mu\alpha$) is a part of it. The soul, then, of the more perfect sort of men is nourished by the whole WORD, but we should be desirous to be fed even with a part thereof." (Philo, *SS. Leg. Alleg.*, lib. iii., Works, Mangey's Edit., tom. i., pp. 121, 122.) What a train of reflections does the perusal of a passage like the above awaken! On first reading it, we might suppose that it proceeded from a Christian source, and that it contained repeated allusions to the very words of our Saviour himself. But it is not so. These are the words of an Alexandrian Jew, who, about A.D. 40, was sent on an embassy from his nation to Caligula at Rome, and who probably never heard the name of his Judæan compatriot and contemporary JESUS mentioned. How comes it, then, that the phraseology and teaching of Philo the Alexandrian, the accomplished and Greek-speaking Jew, and of Jesus the lowly-born prophet of Nazareth, are so striking in their resemblance to each other? But one answer can be given to the question. Their systems of Theology were in the main identical. Jesus taught no new religion. He taught the old one with Divine authority. He enforced it, He illustrated it, He adorned it with the authority and sanction of his spotless example and lifegiving doctrine. This, then, has been one main object which I have kept steadily before me in writing the present commentary, viz., to show that our Faith, as we profess it, is as ancient as the patriarchs; that it is the "one faith" of which the Apostle speaks; that our Lord Jesus Christ propounded no new religion, as is so often foolishly asserted; but that He and his followers claimed to rest upon the old foundation, and put no novel interpretations upon either the prophetical, or historical, or doctrinal writings of the Old Testament. Our Lord came not to innovate, but to restore. He came not to destroy, but to fulfil.

I have, therefore, endeavoured in this little work to point the student to the now sadly neglected and forgotten sources of the earliest Christian interpretations. I hope that I have succeeded in getting together a tolerable number of curious and conclusive proofs that, upon many, if not most religious topics, the Hebrew-speaking and the Greek-speaking branches of the early Jewish Church were at one with ourselves, in the first ages of Christianity. If this can be satisfactorily established, as I feel persuaded it can be, then all the mischievous and illiterate insinuations of the present day, respecting the gradual development of Christianity and her creeds, from such a source as I have described on p. vi., collapse at once.—Meanwhile we occupy this vantage-ground in reference to our controversy with our unbaptized and unbelieving Jewish brethren—we can say to them, "It is *we*
" who hold the doctrines entertained by the Pharisees and
" their disciples respecting the nature and Divinity of the
" Messiah. It is *you* who, in order to neutralize the pre-
" tensions of Jesus of Nazareth, have departed from the
" ancient Jewish Canon of Interpretation held by such
" Doctors of the Law as Gamaliel and his contemporaries,
" and which are preserved to us in the Targums, in the book

"Sohar, in the Mishna, in the Talmuds, and in a vast number of other ancient Hebrew writings."

One word in conclusion. I have, in various portions of this work, stated my conviction that the Epistle to the Hebrews is the work of St. Paul. The alleged discrepancies of style in this Epistle, and the style of the acknowledged writings of the great Apostle, present no insuperable difficulty to my mind. The difference of subject, the difference of handling, above all, the nature of the treatise itself, are quite sufficient to account for any dissimilarity of style. The composition of such an Epistle as the present would be to St. Paul indeed a labour of love. Upon it he would expend all the resources of his mighty and versatile genius. He who could write (Rom. ix. 1—5), " I say the truth in Christ, " I lie not, my conscience also bearing me witness in the " Holy Ghost, that I have great heaviness and continual " sorrow in my heart. For I could wish myself accursed " (ἀνάθεμα) from Christ, for my brethren, my kinsmen " according to the flesh, who are Israelites, to whom *per-* " *taineth* the adoption, and the glory, and the covenants, and " the giving of the law, and the service *of God*, and the " promises; whose are the fathers, and of whom, as con- " cerning the flesh, Christ *came*, who is over all, God, " blessed for ever. Amen."—He, I say, who could thus write, would spare no pains to lay before his kinsmen a treatise as persuasively attractive in style, as well as convincing in argument, as he was capable of producing. If he thus mourned over his brethren, who were yet strangers to Christ, doubly near to his heart would it be to reconvince the wavering, and, if possible, to reclaim the apostates. I cannot help believing that the Epistle was originally written in Greek, although Dean Alford's assertion that the author's citations are from the LXX. version, " even where no corre- " sponding terms are found in the Hebrew text," conveys an erroneous impression. First of all, the Writer does not slavishly copy from the LXX.; secondly, the "corresponding

c

"terms," although not the *exact words*, are always found in the Hebrew text.

I cannot believe, with Dean Alford, that the Writer was "*not a pure Jew*, speaking and quoting Hebrew, but a "Hellenist; a Jew brought up in Greek habits of thought, "and in the constant use of the LXX. version." A one-sided and partial, if not a second-hand acquaintance with the writings of Philo, without even a corresponding knowledge of the theological writings of the earlier Rabbinical authorities, has led to the elaboration of a baseless theory that the Hellenistic Jews differed widely from their Hebrew-speaking brethren in their religious opinions and modes of expression. Not only the Epistle to the Hebrews, but the other writings of the New Testament, exhibit a marked correspondence with (*not*, as I take it) the sentiments of Philo, but with the universal Jewish habit of thought which is to be found exemplified in Philo's writings. The Jews of Palestine, in our Lord's day, were not ignorant of the fact that the LXX. version proceeded from an unimpeachably Jewish source. The familiar use that is made of it by the New Testament writers would be unaccountable, if it were *then* held in such disrepute amongst the Hebrew-speaking Jews, as some would have us to believe. May it not have occupied, by toleration, if not by acceptance, in Palestine, the position of a Greek TARGUM of the original Scriptures? When, however, the Messianic controversy between Jews and Christians brought out into prominent relief a limited number of interpretations, which were authoritatively adopted from the LXX. by the Apostles, as giving the true mind of the Holy Ghost, *i.e.*, the inspired signification of the Hebrew text, then the LXX. version would be gradually disowned by the Rabbinical Jews. On p. 141 I have given an illustration from the *Chizzuk Emunah*, in which R. Isaac ignorantly accuses St. Paul of altering the text of Ps. xl., in Hebrews x. 8, to suit his own views, whereas he only accepted the interpretation of the Greek-speaking branch of the Jewish Church.

That the Jews of Jerusalem were not unaccustomed to the familiar and conversational use of the Greek language is plain from Acts xxii. 2. The populace of the Holy City expected that St. Paul was about to address them in Greek, but "when they heard that he spake in the Hebrew tongue "to them, they kept the more silence." As to the Writer to the Hebrews having imported the doctrine of the *Logos* into his Epistle from Philo, I have disposed of so unfounded an assertion in note 2, on pp. 174, 175. Furthermore, this doctrine of the *Logos* (דבר יהוה) was not borrowed from the Greek Philosophy by the Jews, but was derived, doubtless, from the Jewish Scriptures and the Jewish Theology by the heathen searchers after truth. When we consider that the seed of Abraham were, in turn, brought into contact with all the civilized and imperial nations of the old world, and that God, by SUPERNATURAL interposition (I am one of the old-fashioned that believe in miracles), repeatedly stamped their religion with his authoritative sanction, it is not difficult to perceive that their theological tenets and sacred books must have awakened a respectful curiosity in the philosophers of all times. (See Prideaux's *Connexion*, vol. ii., pp. 28, 29. Tegg's edition, 1845, 8vo.) Aristobulus, an Alexandrian Jew, and a Peripatetic philosopher (B.C. 125), asserts that the Scriptures had been, for the most part, translated into Greek *before the times of Alexander and the Persian monarchy*. He also states, what is indubitably true, "that Pythagoras, " Plato, and other Grecians, had taken most of their philo- " sophy from the Hebrew Scriptures." Be it also observed that Josephus, who was a priest, and originally a Pharisee (*Antiq.* xii. 2, 6), casts no slur on the LXX. version of the Scriptures, but-relates as authentic the story that it was made by men, *selected by Eleazar the high priest at Jerusalem*, who were sent by him, with a copy of the law, to Egypt, for the purpose of translating it into Greek. On p. 201 (and *passim*) I have also called attention to the correspondence between the opinions of Philo (quoted on p. 179 and elsewhere) and those of the earlier Talmudical and Rabbinical writers.—The Writer, then, of this Epistle, was a Hebrew of the Hebrews, writing to his Hebrew compatriots in Palestine. He was well versed in all the Pharisaic glosses upon the Sacred Text, as well as in the Alexandrian refinements upon the sentiments of their, perhaps, less polished and more downright Hebrew kinsmen. There is, moreover, apparent, in every line of the Epistle, that distinctive gravity and authoritative weight which distinguishes the Apostolic writings from all mere human compositions. Place it side by side with any portion of Holy Writ, either of the Old Testament or the New, and it will amply support its just claim to be considered a portion of the inspired WORD OF GOD. It speaks in no hesitating tones. It appeals not for corroboration to any human tribunal of opinion. In the master-tones of Divine authority, it claims reverential obedience, and whenever the distinctively human element comes out into prominent notice, the characteristic attributes of St. Paul are evermore apparent. But, whilst giving to the natural phenomena of any Scriptural composition their due weight, I would urge upon my readers, in this unbelieving age of cavils, and "philosophy falsely so called," not to forget that it is the teaching of the Church of England (whose Articles I have subscribed), that all Holy Scripture is written by inspiration of God. Holy men wrote, of old time, as they were moved by the Holy Ghost. Here, then, TO BELIEVERS, is a sufficient explanation of the exceptional phenomena of any separate portion of God's Word. Such an assertion will, doubtless, excite a derisive smile in those who are prudent in their own eyes, and learned in their own sight. But I am not ashamed of any ridicule which such an unphilosophic proposition may awaken. I look upon the Word of God as differing from all merely human compositions. Other books have been written, according to the caprice or limited information of their authors. With the Bible, if it be the Word of the GOD OF TRUTH, it is not so. To assert that there are "*discrepancies*" in the words dictated by the SPIRIT OF TRUTH, is nothing short of blasphemy. It is either a hypocritical assumption of reverential respect for writings which we believe to be erroneous, thus to speak of them as "the Word of God," or else it indicates a miserable conception of God's infallible knowledge. Would to God that the clergy of the Church of England would at last awake to a perception of the "heavenly treasure" committed to their custody! We are not expounders of a book (however venerable) replete with the peculiarities of human infirmity. We have in our hands the "ORACLES OF GOD," which have stood the test, and survived the hostile ingenuity of centuries of pretended "criticism." That "criticism," upon being brought to the test of real scholarship, resolves itself into the individual opinion of experimenters, more or less qualified for the task which they have undertaken. Nothing has ever been adduced in modern times, of sufficient authority to reverse the testimony of nearly nineteen centuries of fiery trial and patient investigation. The charge of ignorance against the old school of interpretation is singularly unsuitable in the mouths of pretended professors of a "HIGHER "CRITICISM," especially in England. They are ignorant not only of the elementary features of the Sacred Text of the Original Scriptures, but they demonstrate their unacquaintance with the fact that there exists a vast and profoundly learned literature in Hebrew, Latin, and English, in which all the real and supposed difficulties, which they complacently proclaim as *recent discoveries*, are treated of, and calmly discussed, with the dignified propriety of a real erudition, that is evermore distinguished by its MODESTY.

POSTSCRIPT TO THE PREFACE.

As it is important that it should be understood, how far the charge of Platonism, alleged against Philo, affects his belief in the Divine authority and inspiration of the Scriptures, I have thought it desirable to allow him to speak for himself, upon a matter of such paramount interest. The reader will see that he delivers his opinion in no faltering tones, as to the supernatural guidance, and prompting influences, under which the prophets of old discharged their embassage from God. He writes as follows (*Quis Rerum Divinarum Hæres*, Works, Mangey, tom. i., pp. 510, 511) :—

"The fourth form (of prophetic ecstasy) is exemplified in the passage which we are now examining (Gen. xv. 12), *And when the sun was going down, a deep sleep* (ἔκστασις) *fell upon Abraham*, i.e., the condition of one who is in a prophetic trance and under the Divine influence (ἐνθουσιῶντος καὶ θεοφορήτου τὸ πάθος). It is not, however, this circumstance alone that proves him to have been a prophet, but it is so written concerning him, in express terms, in the sacred books. For when one attempted to separate his natural virtue (*i.e.*, Sarah) from him (as if it were not the natural possession of a wise man alone, and could belong to every pretender to prudence), it is said (Gen. xx. 7), *Restore the man his wife, for he is a prophet, and he shall pray for thee, and thou shalt live.* Moreover, the Sacred Word ascribes prophecy to every good (ἀστείῳ) man.* For a prophet enunciates nothing of his own (ἴδιον μὲν οὐδὲν ἀποφθέγγεται), but entirely the things of another, who suggests them to him. But it is not in accordance with the eternal fitness of things that a wicked man should be one of God's interpreters; wherefore no bad man can be said to be Divinely inspired. Such an expression is applicable to none but a wise man.

---

* Philo's meaning, from the context, appears to be that Scripture restricts the gift of prophecy to good men.

" For he is only an instrument that emits the voice of God (ὄργανον
" Θεοῦ ἐστιν ἠχοῦν), being invisibly touched and played upon by Him.
" All, therefore, whom He has enrolled amongst the 'just' (ὁπόσους
" ἀνέγραψε δικαίους) are instanced as inspired and prophesying (κατεχο-
" μένους καὶ προφητεύοντας εἰσήγαγε). Noah was a 'just' man, and was
" he not also a prophet? Or did he pronounce the blessings and the
" curses which he uttered respecting future generations, and which
" were verified by the events, without inspiration? What of Isaac and
" of Jacob? They are admitted to have prophesied, for many reasons,
" but especially on account of their predictions concerning their pos-
" terity. For those words (Gen. xlix. 2), *Gather yourselves together,*
" *that I may tell you that which shall befall you in the last days,*
" were the words of one that was inspired (ἐνθουσιῶντος ἦν), for the
" perception of futurity is no natural attribute of a man. What again
" of Moses? Is he not celebrated everywhere as a prophet? For it is
" said (λέγει γὰρ—Numb. xii. 5), *If there be a prophet of the Lord among*
" *you, I will make myself known unto him in a vision: but to Moses I*
" *will speak, apparently, and not in dark speeches* (ἐν εἴδει καὶ οὐ δι᾽
" αἰνιγμάτων). And again (Deut. xxxiv. 10), *There arose not a prophet*
" *like Moses, whom the Lord knew face to face.* Excellently well, there-
" fore, He signifies that (Abraham) was under the prophetic afflatus,
" when he says (Gen. xv. 12), *When the sun was going down a deep sleep*
" (ἔκστασις) *fell upon him.* Under the figure of the sun, he symbolises
" the human mind (τὸν ἡμέτερον νοῦν). For our reasoning powers answer
" to the sun in the universe, inasmuch as they both are luminaries; the
" one emitting perceptible light to every one, the other giving us that
" illumination which is mentally discerned. As long, therefore, as our
" mind (νοῦς) shines forth, and sheds abroad a light like the noonday sun
" through our whole soul, we remain master of our faculties, and are
" not inspired (ἐν ἑαυτοῖς ὄντες, οὐ κατεχόμεθα). But when sunset
" approaches, as might be expected, the Divine ecstasy and the pro-
" phetical furor ensue. For when the Divine light shines in its bright-
" ness, the human light sets; but when the former wanes, the latter
" revives and rises again. But this is what is wont to happen to the
" race of the prophets. For our own reasoning faculty (νοῦς) departs
" from us when the Divine Spirit comes in, and when the latter takes
" its leave, the former resumes its indwelling. For it would be contrary
" to eternal fitness, that that which is mortal should dwell together with
" the immortal. Therefore the sunset of the reasoning faculty (τοῦ
" λογισμοῦ) and the accompanying darkness produced (in Abraham) the
" condition of ecstacy and Divine furor (θεοφόρητον μανίαν). But the
" consequence is intimated in the Scripture, inasmuch as it states, *It*

"was said to Abraham. For assuredly the prophet, when he apparently "speaks, in reality keeps silence; for another (*i.e.*, God's Spirit) "appropriates to his own use his vocal organs, his mouth and tongue, "to signify whatsoever it pleases Him. He strikes them, as it were, "with invisible and musical skill, and produces results replete with a "tuneful and harmonious symphony."

Consult also p. 483, and *De Migr. Abrahami*, ibid., p. 442, and also tom. ii., pp. 124, 222, 343, 417.

SUPPLEMENTARY NOTE TO CHAP. II. 6—9.

In John v. 26, 27, our Lord says, "For as the Father "hath life in himself, so hath he given to the Son to have "life in himself; and hath given him authority to execute "judgment also, because he is the SON OF MAN." It appears to me, that the Writer's application of the words of Ps. viii. 4—6, to the Lord Jesus Christ, gives the real clue to this difficult expression, "What is man that thou art mindful of "him, and the Son of man that thou visitest him. . . . . "Thou hast put all things under his feet," &c. Our Lord's words would then indicate, "Because he is the representative "SON OF MAN" spoken of by David in the 8th Psalm. Compare also, Dan. vii. 13.

THE EPISTLE TO THE HEBREWS.

The Epistle to the Hebrews, or more correctly according to the title, "the Epistle to Hebrews" or Jews, partakes of a twofold character. It is an *epistola consolatoria* and also an *epistola commonitoria*. It is addressed to Jewish converts. They were evidently suffering from the persecution of their unbelieving brethren, who also twitted them with having abandoned the religion of their ancestors, and, by so doing, voluntarily excluded themselves from participation in the consolations of the prophetic writings, in the glorious temple worship, the sacrifices, the Aaronic priesthood, and the covenanted privileges secured for ever to the children of Abraham. From the construction of the Epistle, it is plain that the Jewish polity had not yet come to an end. The writer speaks of the temple as still standing, of the priests as still performing their sacrificial functions, of the Mosaic law as being ἐγγὺς ἀφανισμοῦ, *i.e.*, near to disappearance, or "ready to vanish away." Had the case been otherwise, the arguments adduced would have been drawn from the fact of the ancient *régime* having been abolished. There would have been no occasion for the elaborate deductions drawn from the Scriptures to indicate the impending changes. But then, also, in all probability, the Christian controversialist would have been deprived of one of the most conclusive and subtle pieces of argumentation against Jewish cavils that ever was penned. The Epistle to the Hebrews is at the present moment a handbook, based upon ancient Rabbinic interpretation, of the points at issue between the believers in the claims of Jesus of Nazareth and those who suppose that the Mosaic dispensation is only temporarily suspended on account of the sins of the Jewish nation, and will yet be restored to its primitive splendour, with its august apparatus of sacrifice and temple-worship. The object of the writer is to show that the Christian Israelites had made no mistake; that they had gained everything, instead of losing by their acceptance of Jesus; that the Mosaic dispensation was only the type and prelude to the Christian. That it had had its day, and is now superseded by the "thing signified" with its "far more exceeding weight of glory." From the allusions to apostacy in the course of the Epistle, it is plain that the faith of some of the converts had not been proof against the arguments and entreaties and persecutions of their unbelieving kinsmen. To any one acquainted with the intensity of bitterness exhibited by the adherents of Judaism towards those who have embraced Christianity, this will awaken but little surprise. No sacrifices are deemed too costly to induce the "destroyed ones," for so the converts are termed, to abjure their new faith. If they continue steadfast, they are regarded by their relatives as socially dead. The mention of their names is forbidden in the family circle; personal violence is not unfrequently resorted to. Their very lives are in jeopardy from the bigoted and fanatical abhorrence wherewith they are regarded by their nearest kinsmen.[1]

Against such fiery trial the faith of certain of those mentioned in this Epistle had proved too weak. Many of those that remained unpersuaded, but not unmoved, were in a wavering and desponding frame of mind. The odium and obloquy which they daily endured had produced a most depressing

[1] The implacable persecutions which the celebrated Uriel Dacosta met with, and the disgraceful treatment which he experienced on the occasion of his public abjuration of Christianity in the synagogue at Amsterdam, so preyed upon his mind that he committed suicide by blowing out his brains with a pistol. The narrative of his sufferings and recantation is related in G. B. de Rossi's *Dizionario storico degli autori Ebrei e delle loro opere* (Vol. 1, p. 37. *Parma*, 1802. 8vo.) After undergoing a thousand indescribable insults and cruel injuries, and enduring two several excommunications, the second of which lasted for a period of seven years, he was finally persuaded to read a recantation in the synagogue. On the day appointed he presented himself, attired in mourning, with a lighted taper in his hand, and ascended the pulpit to read his renunciation of Christianity. This done, he was taken in a corner and stripped of his garments, all but his girdle, and tied to a pillar, when he was savagely scourged. He was then compelled to lie down in the doorway whilst the entire congregation passed over his body, trampling him under foot and spitting upon him. Stung to the quick by such unexpectedly barbarous and outrageous treatment, and the public infamy to which he had been subjected, he shortly after terminated his career by his own hand, as above described, in the month of April, 1647.

effect. The entreaties of parents and relatives, the scornful demeanour of their former acquaintances, the exclusions from the family circle, the perpetual annoyances and spiteful persecutions by which they were surrounded, rendered a letter such as the present Epistle particularly seasonable.

Exception has been taken against its Pauline authorship, from the omission of St. Paul's habitual statement of his apostleship. This circumstance, to my own mind, is a conclusive demonstration that the writer, whoever he may have been, knew perfectly how to adapt himself to the frame of mind and the peculiar position of those to whom he wrote. The question at issue was not whether the writer was an Apostle of Jesus Christ, but whether Jesus Christ had any claim to be heard as the Messiah of God. The very statement of such a commission, unless preliminarily enforced by the most valid and irrefragable proofs, drawn from accepted Hebrew expositions of the Old Testament writings, would be a fatal objection to the Jewish mind. The disciple of Rabbinism would take his stand upon the express injunctions of Moses contained in Deut. xiii. 1—5:—" If there arise among you a prophet, or a
" dreamer of dreams, and giveth thee a sign or a
" wonder, and the sign or the wonder come to pass,
" whereof he spake unto thee, saying, Let us go
" after other gods, which thou hast not known, and
" let us serve them; thou shalt not hearken unto
" the words of that prophet, or that dreamer of
" dreams: for the Lord your God proveth you, to
" know whether ye love the Lord your God with all

" your heart and with all your soul. Ye shall walk
" after the Lord your God, and fear him, and keep
" his commandments, and obey his voice, and ye
" shall serve him, and cleave unto him. And that
" prophet, or that dreamer of dreams, shall be put
" to death; because he hath spoken to turn you
" away from the Lord your God, which brought
" you out of the land of Egypt, and redeemed you
" out of the house of bondage, to thrust thee out of
" the way which the Lord thy God commanded thee
" to walk in. So shalt thou put the evil away from
" the midst of thee."

Now this was no mere ideal obstacle in the way of the Gospel of Christ. It exists to this very day, in all its original force and intensity, amongst the unbelieving Israelites. And this was what our Lord Himself referred to when He assured the disciples that the time should come in which those that killed them should think that they were doing God a service. St. Paul himself (Rom. x. 2) bears his Jewish kinsmen record that they " have a zeal for God, but not according to knowledge."[1] Such deep-seated and apparently well-founded prejudices could

---

[1] Viewed from a Rabbinic point of view (by the light of Deut. xiii.) the judicial murder of Stephen and of Christ and St. Paul's persecuting zeal against his converted brethren and sisters, were not only justifiable but meritorious; and on the authority of the above chapter of Deut. the *Nizzachon Vetus*, an ancient Jewish handbook of the points at issue between Jews and Christians, glories in the Saviour's crucifixion.

ותהה אין אמר ישו רק כי הוא נביא אבל עשה עצמו אלוה והסית אחיו ועל כן אמר אליו
משה לא תאבה לו ולא תשמע אליו כי הריג ההרגנו וכן עשו לו ותלוהו בעין

" Now not only did Jesus say that he was a prophet, but he also
" made himself God, and seduced his brethren. Therefore Moses spake

only be met and removed by arguments drawn from the Scriptures themselves to which the Jews appealed in vindication of their unbelief. To inquire into the religion of Jesus was considered a violation of the commandments of Moses. To hint that any portion of the ceremonial law would ever cease to be obligatory was not only high treason against God, but a grave insult to the national institution, upon the minute observance of which their political existence depended. The statement of his apostleship by the writer would, therefore, have been to place a preliminary obstacle in the way of obtaining a hearing. It would have been, so to speak, a *petitio principii*. To commence with a statement of the personal claims of Jesus of Nazareth would have been scarcely less objectionable. The controversy at issue rested upon a far broader basis, viz., the testimony of the Scriptures to the fact that the old dispensation would run its course, be superseded by a new and a better one, and thus altogether fall into abeyance. Before obtaining a hearing at all, therefore, the writer knew that he must distinctly establish Scriptural and prophetic declarations, and these according to accepted Rabbinic interpretations, of the coming transition from the covenant of Moses to the better covenant of Christ. The question was not, are the claims of Jesus to be the Messiah plausible? but, are they

---

" concerning him (Deut. xiii. 8), *Thou shalt not consent unto him, nor hearken unto him*, but shalt surely kill him. And this also they did, " hanging him upon a tree."—*Nizzachon Vetus*, p. 50, Wagenseil, *Tela Ignea Satanae*.

contained in, and proved by, the Old Testament Scriptures, whose inspired authority is, to Christians as well as Jews, an end of all controversy? In the first verse, therefore, in his opening words, he strikes the key-note of the strain that runs throughout the entire Epistle. He disposes of the question of authority.*

---

* The tone and mode of our Lord's teaching was totally different from that of the Scribes. He taught as one ἐξουσίαν ἔχων, *having authority;* e.g., "Verily, verily, I say unto you," and not "Rabbi 'So and So' says," or "our elders have taught." This decisive and infallible authority our Lord imparted to his Apostles. With us Christians their *dicta* ought to be the end of all controversy, as expressing the mind of the Holy Ghost; but with the unbelieving Jews, the case is altogether different. They must first be convinced that we are "not following cunningly devised fables," and that Jesus of Nazareth was neither an enthusiast, nor an impostor, but the Christ of God, the Divine Messiah, spoken of "by the mouth of all the holy Prophets, since the world began."

CHAPTER I.

Verses 1, 2.—In manifold apportionments, and in a variety of ways,[1] in the olden time (πάλαι), God having spoken to the fathers by (ἐν)[2] the prophets, in these last days[3] hath spoken to us by (ἐν υἱῷ) his Son, whom He hath appointed heir of all things (Ps. ii. 7, 8); by whom, also, he made the worlds.[4]

[1] Πολυμερῶς καὶ πολυτρόπως, *Multipliciter et Multis Modis.* J. C. Wolfius. *Curæ Phil et Crit.* Tom. iv. p. 596. The Writer contrasts the delegated authority with which the prophets spoke, as (and *at what time*) they were moved by the Holy Ghost, with the completeness and integrity of Christ's power to speak in his Father's name. They delivered their message as ambassadors when the Divine afflatus came upon them, and when the message was put into their mouths. In Christ, however, dwelt all the fulness of the Godhead bodily. He spoke as one having authority, and to whom all power in heaven and earth was committed. J. C. Wolfius observes, *ibid.*, p. 597, " τὸ " πολυτρόπως vero, varios revelationis divinæ modos infert. Horum " quinque nonulli appellant, nempe במראה *in visione,* בחלום *in somnis,* " בחידה *in ænigmate,* cum aliud apparet, aliud innuitur, בתמונה *in figura,* " cum rerum imagines apparent, ac denique בפה sive *allocutione divina.*" Schoettgen divides the τρόπους of prophecy as follows. The first the Patriarchal, supplemented later, by the Covenant of Circumcision. Secondly, that commencing at the Exodus, in which God spake by the additional medium of symbols and rites, *e.g.*, the Paschal Lamb, &c., to which, in the time of the Judges, a " μέρος quoddam " was added, viz., in the Schools of the Prophets. This τρόπος, he says, lasted, with intervals, up to the time of the Babylonish Captivity; but certain μέρη were withdrawn, *e.g.*, the Shechinah, the Urim and Thummim, as well as the gift of prophecy. Then followed the completed volume of the Old Testament Scriptures, after the gift of prophecy had ceased, to which, when needful, was added the Bath Kol (בת קול *daughter*

of a voice), *i.e.*, a voice from heaven, and which was sent, not to propound new doctrines, but to admonish the Jews as to what to do upon occasions of urgent emergency.

² ἐν τοῖς προφήταις, בנביאים, including the ministration of angels. Those were days of prediction, these are days of fulfilment.

³ ἐπ᾽ ἐσχάτων τῶν ἡμερῶν τούτων. Some MSS. read, ἐπ᾽ ἐσχάτου, κ.τ.λ. These words are equivalent to the Hebrew expression, באחרית הימים, *i.e.*, "*the latter days*," or, *the closing days of this earthly dispensation*. As Nachmanides observes on Genesis xlix. 1, כי לדברי הכל באחרית הימים ימות המשיח—" For by universal consent, *in the last days*, are the days of "Messiah." So, also, Kimchi and Abarbanel. (See further in *J. Rhenferdij Dissertat.* 1, *de Seculo Futuro*. Menschen, *N. Test. ex Talmude illustr.*, p. 1122, &c.) The Targum of Onkelos translates Gen. xlix. 10, " until Shiloh come," by " until Messiah come." So also the Targum of Jonathan, " until the king Messiah come," adding, " How beauteous " is the king, the Messiah, who will arise from the house of Judah ! "

⁴ Δι᾽ οὗ καὶ τοὺς αἰῶνας ἐποίησεν, and so the Jewish writers speak of God as בורא עולם, and בורא עולמים. See Schoettgen, *Horæ Hebraicæ*, tom. i., p. 911 ; Wolfius, tom. iv., p. 601, 602. Philo again and again asserts that the world was made by the Word of God, *e.g.*, Λόγος δέ ἐστιν εἰκὼν Θεοῦ δι᾽ οὗ σύμπας ὁ κόσμος ἐδημιουργεῖτο—" But the Word is the " image of God, by whom the whole world was framed."—*De Monarchia*, Works, Mangey's edit., vol. ii., p. 225.

Again, in reference to Gen. ii. 4, he observes (*S. S. Legum Allegor., lib.* i. ; Works, vol. i., p. 47), τῷ γὰρ περιφανεστάτῳ καὶ τηλαυγεστάτῳ ἑαυτοῦ λόγῳ, ῥήματι ὁ Θεὸς ἀμφότερα ποιεῖ—" For by his most illustrious and splendid Word, by a word, God created both," (sc. *ideam intellectûs*, which he compares to heaven, and *ideam sensûs*, which he likens to earth). Again, *ibid.*, p. 106, σκιὰ Θεοῦ δέ ὁ λόγος αὐτοῦ ἐστιν, ᾧ καθάπερ ὀργάνῳ προσχησάμενος, ἐκοσμοποίει—" But the shadow of God " is his Word, by which, having used it as an instrument, He made the " world." Again (*De Cherubim, ibid.*, p. 162), εὑρήσεις......ὄργανον...... λόγον Θεοῦ, δι᾽ οὗ κατεσκευάσθη· τῆς δὲ κατασκευῆς αἰτίαν, τὴν ἀγαθότητα τοῦ δημιουργοῦ—" But thou wilt find......the instrument by which it was " planned to be the Word of God, but the cause of its plan, the benevo- " lence of the Founder." So also (*de Migratione Abrahami, ibid.*, p. 437), Τίς ἂν οὖν εἴη, πλὴν ὁ λόγος ὁ πρεσβύτερος τῶν γένεσιν εἰληφότων, οὗ καθάπερ οἴακος ἐνειλημμένος ὁ τῶν ὅλων κυβερνήτης πηδαλιουχεῖ τὰ σύμπαντα. Καὶ ὅτε ἐκοσμοπλάστει, χρησάμενος ὀργάνῳ τούτῳ πρὸς τὴν ἀνυπαίτιον τῶν ἀποτελουμένων σύστασιν—" What else can it therefore be except the Word, " which is the eldest of things that received a being, of which He who " steers all things, having taken hold of, pilots all the universes, as with "a helm? And when He framed the worlds, He made use of this instrument to put together and complete his faultless work."

Again, the Jerusalem Targum reads in Gen. i. 27, "And the Word of the Lord created man in his likeness, in the likeness of the presence of the Lord He created him." So, also, in Gen. iii. 8, the Targum of Jonathan or Palestine has, "And they heard the voice of the Word of the Lord walking," &c. Whilst the Jerusalem Targum has, in verse 7, "And the Word of the Lord God called," &c. Again, in Gen. iii. 22, the Jerusalem Targum paraphrases, "And the Word of the Lord God said, Behold, Adam whom I have created," &c.

Verses 3, 4.—Who being the brightness of his glory[1] and the express image[2] of his person, and upholding[3] all things by the Word ($\tau\hat{\varphi}$ $\dot{\rho}\acute{\eta}\mu\alpha\tau\iota$) of his power, having by himself made purification of our sins, sat down (Ps. cx. 1) on the right hand of the majesty on high.[4] Being made so much better than the angels, in proportion as he has obtained, by inheritance, a more excellent name than they.

[1] ἀπαύγασμα τῆς δόξης. Schoettgen rightly refers this expression to the glory of the Shechinah, whereby the Second person of the ever Blessed Trinity manifested Himself on the mercy seat. (See Heb. ix. 5.) He says that the Hebrews have three modes of expression, which exactly answer to the above, viz., יוי יקרא *splendor gloriæ*, used in the Targum of Onkelos (Exod. xxxiv. 29, and Deut. xxxiv. 7) of the glory of Moses' face. Secondly, יוי איקונין *splendor imaginis* sive *faciei*, quod convenit cum voce ἀπαύγασμα. It occurs in *Bereshith Rabba* in reference to Gen. xxi. 2. מלמד שהיה ויו איקונין שלו דומה לו, *We learn that* he (Isaac) *was the splendor of his* (Abraham's) *face, and that he was like him*. Thirdly, קלסתר פנים, written also קלסתר, *similitudo cum splendore conjuncta, ex unius facie in alterius faciem derivata*, e.g., קלסתר פנים של שכינה, ἀπαύγασμα *Schechinæ*. (Midrasch Echa in Sohar Chadash, fol. 71, 4, &c.) Schoettgen observes that ἀπαύγασμα means, "splendorem ex alia quadam luce derivatum, qui tamen ejusdem cum illa est essentiæ," and shows how pregnant in meaning these four words of the writer to the Hebrews are respecting the divinity of Christ. First, as asserting that He emanated from the essence of the Father. 2. That Christ having been begotten of the essence of the Father, is of the same essence. 3. That He is a person distinct from the Father. 4. That He is coeternal with the Father. (*Horæ Hebraicæ*, tom. iii., pp. 911—919.) See also J. C. Wolfius, *Curæ Phil.*, tom. iv., pp. 603, 604.

CHAP. I., 3, 4.

[2] χαρακτὴρ τῆς ὑποστάσεως αὐτοῦ· Philo uses very similar language in reference to the Eternal Word, e.g., Ὁ δ' ὑπεράνω τούτων λόγος θεῖος εἰς ὁρατὴν οὐκ ἦλθεν ἰδέαν, ἅτε μηδενὶ τῶν κατ' αἴσθησιν ἐμφερὴς ὤν, ἀλλ' αὐτὸς εἰκὼν ὑπάρχων Θεόν, τῶν νοητῶν ἁπαξαπάντων ὃ πρεσβύτατος, ὁ ἐγγυτάτω, μηδενὸς ὄντος μεθορίου διαστήματος, τοῦ μόνου ὅ ἐστιν ἀψευδῶς, ἀφιδρυμένος. "But he who is above these, viz., the Divine Word, never comes into "visible shape ; since he is comparable to nothing perceptible with the "senses. But he is the image of God, the eldest of all things soever "which can be mentally discerned. The closest copy of Him who "alone truly is, since there is no separating interval between him."— *De Profugis*, Mang. Works, tom. i., p. 561. See also *De Mundi opificio*, *ibid.*, pp. 6, 7. *Deterius potiori insidiatur*, *ibid.*, p. 207.

Ὁ δὲ δὴ μέγας Μωϋσῆς οὐδενὶ τῶν γεγονότων τῆς λογικῆς ψυχῆς τὸ εἶδος ὁμοίως ὠνόμασεν, ἀλλ' εἶπεν αὐτὴν τοῦ θείου καὶ ἀοράτου Θεοῦ ἐκείνου εἰκόνα, δόκιμον εἶναι νομίσας ἧς εἴωθε καὶ τυπωθὲν σφραγῖδα Θεοῦ, ἧς ὁ χαρακτήρ ἐστιν ὁ ἀΐδιος λόγος. "Moses the Great has not, in like manner, "noticed the likeness of the reasonable soul to any one of created things. "On the contrary, he said that it was the image of the Divine and "Invisible God, accounting it a proof and impression struck by the "customary seal of God, the engraving whereof is the Eternal Word."— *De Mundo*, Works, vol. ii., pp. 605, 606.

See also in the Fragments from Eusebius, *ibid.*, p. 625, where a passage from Philo is quoted in which he says that man was not, and could not, be "made in the image" of the Father of all things, but that this expression means that he was made like "to the Second God, "which is his Word" (ἀλλὰ πρὸς τὸν δεύτερον Θεόν, ὅς ἐστιν ἐκείνου Λόγος).

[3] φέρων τε, κ.τ.λ. Schoettgen gives the following illustrations from the Rabbinical writers. In *Bereshith Rabba*, sect. 22, fol. 23, 2, Cain is represented as addressing God thus—לעליונים אתה סובל ולתחתונים "Thou "upholdest things above and beneath."

Schemoth Rabba, sect. 19, fol. 118, 3, שהוא סובל בריותיו "This is He "who upholds his creatures."

Ibid., sect. 36, fol. 133, 4, הקב"ה סבל עולמו "The Holy One, Blessed be "He, upholds his world."

Again in the מדרש הנעלם, in the Sohar Chadash, fol. 9, 1, "The Holy "One, Blessed be He, סובל כל העולמות בכוחו upholds all the worlds by his "strength."—*Schoettgen*, *ibid.*, p. 919.

The doctrine that the universes are upheld and governed by the Word of God is asserted again and again by Philo, e.g., ὁ πηδαλιοῦχος καὶ κυβερνήτης τοῦ παντὸς λόγος θεῖος. "The helmsman and pilot of all "things, viz., the Divine Word."—Philo *de Cherubim*, Works, vol. i., p. 145.

Again, when speaking of the rise and fall of nations, he attributes the administration of the world to God's Word. χορεύει γὰρ ἐν κύκλῳ λόγος ὁ θεῖος, ὃν οἱ πολλοὶ τῶν ἀνθρώπων ὀνομάζουσι τύχην. "The Divine "Word makes circuits (of the universes), whom the majority of men "designate Fortune."—*Quod Deus sit immutabilis, ibid.*, p. 298.

Further, on Gen. xxxi. 13, "I am the God of Bethel, where thou "anointedst the pillar," &c. Philo writes, τὸ δ' ἐπίγραμμα ἐμηνύεν, ὅτι μόνος ἔστηκα ἐγώ, καὶ τὴν πάντων φύσιν ἱδρυσάμην, τὴν ἀταξίαν καὶ ἀκοσμίαν εἰς τάξιν καὶ κόσμον ἀγαγών, καὶ τὸ πᾶν ὑπερείσας ἵνα στηριχθῇ βεβαίως τῷ κραταιῷ καὶ ὑπάρχῳ μου λόγῳ. The inscription signified, "*I stand alone,* "*and have founded the entire course of nature, reducing confusion and* "*disorder into order and harmony, and have supported the whole, in order* "*that it may be firmly secure, upon my powerful and representative Word.*" —*Quod a Deo Mittantur Somnia, ibid.*, p. 656.

The *Divine Word* is also described as God's ὕπαρχος or representative Lieutenant (*De Agricultura, ibid.*, p. 308), by whom the universes are administered. In commenting upon the words of Ps. xxiii. 1, Philo says, προστησάμενος τὸν ὀρθὸν αὐτοῦ λόγον, πρωτόγονον υἱόν, ὅς τὴν ἐπιμέλειαν τῆς ἱερᾶς ταύτης ἀγέλης, οἷα τις μεγάλου βασιλέως ὕπαρχος διαδέξεται. "He "has set over it his upright Word, his first begotten Son, who under- "takes the oversight of this sacred flock, as the lieutenant of some "great king."—*De Agricultura, ibid.*, p. 308.

Again, νόμος δὲ ὁ ἀΐδιος Θεοῦ τοῦ αἰωνίου, τὸ ὀχυρώτατον καὶ βεβαιότατον ἔρεισμα τῶν ὅλων ἐστίν. Οὗτος ἀπὸ πῶν μέσων ἐπὶ τὰ πέρατα, καὶ ἀπὸ τῶν ἄκρων ἐπὶ τὰ μέσα ταθεὶς, δολιχεύει τὸν τῆς φύσεως δρόμον ἀήττητον, συνάγων τὰ μέρη πάντα καὶ σφίγγων· δεσμὸν γὰρ αὐτὸν ἄρρηκτον τοῦ παντὸς ὁ γενήσας ἐποίει πατήρ. "But the eternal law (Word) of the everlasting God is the "most irrefragable and sure prop (stay) of all things. He pervades "from the centre to the extremest limits, and from the highest point to "the centre. He permeates the untiring course of nature, and thus "unites and draws together its several component parts, inasmuch as "the Father who begat Him has constituted Him the indissoluble bond "of all things."—*De Plantatione Noe, ibid.*, pp. 330, 331. The very same words are to be found.—*De Mundo, ibid.*, vol. ii., p. 604.

Further, Χαῦνα γὰρ τά τε ἄλλα ἐξ ἑαυτῶν, εἰ δέ που καὶ πυκνωθὲν εἴη, λόγῳ σφίγγεται θείῳ. Κόλλα γάρ ἐστι καὶ δεσμὸς οὗτος, τὰ πάντα τῆς οὐσίας ἐκπεπληρωκώς. For all things are constitutionally liable to go to pieces, but if they have any solidity they are held together by his Divine Word. For He is the principle of cohesion and the band, which supplements all things that subsist.—*Quis rerum Divinarum Hæres, ibid.*, tom. i., p 499. (Compare Eph. i. 23, iii. 19, iv. 10.)

"Ὅ, τε γὰρ τοῦ Ὄντος λόγος, δεσμός ὢν τῶν ἁπάντων, ὡς εἴρηται, καὶ "συνέχει τὰ μέρη πάντα, καὶ σφίγγει, καὶ κωλύει αὐτὰ διαλίεσθαι καὶ "διαρτᾶσθαι. For the Word of the Self-existent, as we have already "asserted, upholdeth each several part, and knits them together, and "prevents them from going to pieces and being disintegrated."—*De Profugis, ibid.,* p. 562.

¹ Ps. lxviii. 18 (Heb. 19) עלית למרום, "Thou hast ascended on high," &c. For the interpretation of this Psalm see *The Messiahship of Jesus*, by Alex. M'Caul, D.D., p. 164, and also *The Psalms in Hebrew*, with Commentary by G. Phillips, D.D., vol. ii., pp. 79—108. Schoettgen, *Horæ Hebr.*, tom. i., pp. 772—775. Surenhus. Βίβλ. Καταλλ, p. 584, &c.

Here, then, at one rapid and masterly stroke, in the short compass of four verses, the writer sketches out the Divine superiority of the Messianic dispensation over the Patriarchal as well as the Mosaic. He reminds his readers that when Christ speaks of the things of God, He speaks of his own; for that He is God's eternal Son—that the Father has designated Him heir of all things. (Ps. ii. 7, 8.) That He has omnipotent authority to demand our obedience, as well as power to enforce it. That in Him the prophecies which predicted his vicarious sufferings have been accomplished; and that now, inasmuch as his expiatory sacrifice is completed and his redeeming career of humiliation accomplished, He has ascended on high in fulfilment also of the prophetic declaration of Ps. cx. 1, and lxviii. 18, when he sits at the right hand of God expecting until his enemies be made his footstool. No prominent feature of the Messiah's character, as expected by the ancient Jewish Church, is left unnoticed. He is God because He is the Creator of the worlds, and upholds the universes. He is the legitimate exponent of the Divine will because He is of the same substance and essence with the Father. He has, by his sacrifice of himself once offered, abrogated the necessity for the Mosaic sacrifices, having by himself purged away our sins (as foretold by Isaiah liii.),[1] and now, at the right hand of God, He waits for the further and final accomplishment of the predicted reward, when his enemies shall have been made his footstool. Thus all the leading objections against the Messiahship and religion of Jesus are met and disposed of at the outset. The comparison of Christ's dignity with that of the angels, seems to be designed to meet the objection that in former ages the will of God was, from time to time, made known to the fathers by the ministry and embassage of the heavenly host. If Jesus were a mere human teacher, He would be inferior to them and without authority to repeal that which was by them delivered. But if He be "the Christ of God," *i.e.*, his Divine and Eternal Son,[2] then He is of necessity superior to them by the inheritance of his glorious name, as

[1] The most celebrated ancient Jewish interpreters, with one consent, have applied Isaiah liii. to the Messiah, *e.g.*, the Sohar, Targum of Jonathan, Babylonian Talmud, Yalkut Shimoni, R. Alshech, &c. See the late Dr. M'Caul's *Doctrine and Interpretation of Isaiah liii.*, pp. 16—21, who observes that, "Aben Ezra and Abarbanel both begin "their commentaries by mentioning the Christian exposition, and with "a confession that they depart from the ancient Jewish exposition." See also the learned Dr. Margoliouth's *Penitential Hymn of Judah and Israel after the Spirit. An Exposition of Isaiah liii.* Second Edition. 1856. 8vo.

[2] Schoettgen (*Horæ Hebraicæ*, tom. i., p. 905) supposes that St. Paul (whom he, in common with many of the other giants of theological erudition of former days, holds to be the author of the Epistle to the Hebrews) had in mind the ancient Jewish tradition, which declared that Messiah should be greater than Abraham and Moses, and the Patriarchs, and the Ministering Angels.

"Nullam vel Spiritui Sancto, hanc epistolam inspiranti, vel etiam

well as being their Creator, which idea is included in the assertion, "By whom He also made the worlds," for it is written in Gen. i. 1, "In (the) beginning God created the heavens and the earth." The creation of the heavens in remote ages, before our world was prepared for man's habitation, included the creation of the angels or heavenly host. The citation from Psalm cx. 1, "Jehovah said unto " my Lord, Sit thou on my right hand," &c., in verse 3, is especially noteworthy. It is the identical passage wherewith Jesus put the Pharisees (Mark xii. 35) to silence. The Scribes apparently interpreted the text, of Messiah the Son of David, even in our Lord's day, " And Jesus answered and said ... " How say the Scribes that Christ (*i.e.*, Messiah) is " the Son of David, for David himself said by the " Holy Ghost, The Lord said unto my Lord " (נאם יהוה לאדני, *Jehovah said unto my Lord*), Sit " thou on my right hand till I make thine enemies

"Apostolo injuriam facio, si dicam, Apostolum in mente habuisse "priscam hanc traditionem, quæ exstat in *Tanchuma*, citante *Jalkut* "*Simeoni*, part 2, fol. 53, 3, ad verba Jes. lii. 13. Ecce sapienter aget "servus meus : זה מלך המשיח. *Intelligitur Rex Messias*. Extolletur et "elevabitur valde. *Extolletur ultra Abrahamum, et elevabitur ultra* "*Mosen, et sublimis erit* כמלאכי השרת *præ Angelis Ministerialibus*. Aliter "exprimitur in *Jalkut Chadash*, fol. 144, 2. משיח גדול מן האבות ומן משה "ומן מלאכי השרת *Messias major est Patriarchis, Mose, et Angelis minis-* "*terialibus*."

R. Simeon ben Lakish in the Babylonian Gemara (*Sanhedrin*, col. 974, Ugolin. Thes., vol. xxv.) expresses the subordination and inferiority of the ministering angels as follows. When commenting on Isaiah lxiii. 4, *The day of vengeance is in my heart*, he says, ללבי גליתי למלאכי השרת לא גליתי, " I have revealed it to my own heart, to " the ministering angels I have not revealed it." This Rabbinical interpretation has a remarkable correspondence with the words of our Lord (Matt. xxiv. 36), " But of that day and hour knoweth no man, no, " not the angels of heaven, but my Father only."

"thy footstool. David therefore calleth him Lord, "and whence is he his Son?" So also a little later the Targum renders the same passage, "Jehovah said "in," or, "unto his Word." The writer moves, therefore, in an atmosphere of ancient Jewish[1] interpretation in his application of the Old Testament prophecies to the Messiah. And now he follows up his advantage, and shows conclusively that the words of Ps. ii. 7, 8, "I will declare the decree: "the Lord hath said unto me, Thou art my Son; "this day have I begotten thee. Ask of me, and I "shall give thee the heathen for thine inheritance, "and the uttermost parts of the earth for thy pos-"session," cannot apply to any angelic being. Nor yet the words of 2 Sam. vii. 14.

Verse 5.—For to which of the angels did He ever say, Thou art my Son; this day have I begotten thee? (Ps. ii. 7.) And again (2 Sam. vii. 14), I will be to him (for) a Father (εἰς πατέρα), and he shall be to me (for) a Son (εἰς υἱόν, אני אהיה לו לאב והוא יהיה לי לבן)?

True, that in Job i. 6, ii. 1, xxxvii. 7, the angels are called "*sons of God*" (בני אלהים, as also in Dan. iii. 25), the angelic being who appeared to Nebuchadnezzar in the furnace, was said by him to be "like a son of God" (לבר אלהין, υἱῷ Θεοῦ. LXX.) But these are only sons by creation and obedience. The passage does not exist in which Jehovah condescends to address any angelic servant of his, as His Son by generation, and thus to designate him as a partaker

---

[1] For an excellent account of the Rabbinic interpretations of Ps cx., see J. Jacobi Schudt *Comment. Philol. in Psalmum c.x.* Frankfort, 1718. 8vo.

of his Divine essence and nature; to proclaim his kinsmanship, and to invite him to share his throne and Eternal Sovereignty. This honour is reserved for the Messiah, whom Jehovah distinguishes as "the man who is my fellow." (גבר עמיתי, ἄνδρα πολίτην μου, LXX.) The Christian interpretation of these words of Zech. xiii. 7 was well known to the Rabbies.[1]

[1] See R. David Kimchi's Commentary on Zechariah, translated with Notes and Observations on the Passages relating to the Messiah, by the late Dr. M'Caul, pp. 167—177.

Verses 6, 7.—But, when He bringeth in again the First-begotten[1] into the world, he saith, "Let all the angels of God worship Him."[2] (Ps. xcvii. 7.) And yet, in reference to the angels (καὶ πρὸς μὲν τοὺς ἀγγέλους), he saith (λέγει, sc., ἡ γραφὴ, Ps. civ. 4), "Who maketh his angels spirits, and his ministers (משרתיו, λειτουργοὺς) a flame of fire."

[1] τὸν πρωτότοκον. Schoettgen quotes from R. Bechai to show that this appellation is in no way derogatory to Christ's divinity, inasmuch as the Jews were accustomed to call God the Father "*the Firstborn of all the whole world*," שהוא הוא בכורו של עולם. Also, from the *Shemoth Rabba*, sect. 19, fol. 118, 4. "R. Nathan said, The Holy One, blessed be He, said to Moses, *As I have made Jacob my firstborn* (Exod. iv. 22), *so also will I make King Messiah my firstborn* (Ps. lxxxix. 28)."—*Horæ Hebr.*, tom. i., p. 992.

Philo repeatedly calls the divine Word of God the firstbegotten (πρωτόγονος) and eldest son (πρεσβύτατος υἱός) of God. For a very remarkable example of this, see *De Confusione Linguarum* (Works, vol. i., p. 414), where, in reference to the LXX. version of Zech. vi. 12, Ἰδοὺ ἀνήρ, Ἀνατολὴ ὄνομα αὐτῷ (הנה איש צמח שמו Behold a man whose name is the BRANCH), Philo observes that Ἀνατολὴ, *Oriens, sunrising*, was a very unusual designation for a mortal man; but, if applied to the incorporeal image of God, it would be most suitable in every respect. Τοῦτον μὲν γὰρ πρεσβύτατον υἱὸν ὁ τῶν ὄντων ἀνέτειλε πατήρ, ὃν ἑτέρωθι πρωτόγονον ὠνόμασε, καὶ ὁ γεννηθεὶς μέντοι μιμούμενος τὰς τοῦ πατρὸς ὁδοὺς, πρὸς παραδείγματα ἀρχέτυπα ἐκείνου βλεπῶν, ἐμόρφου εἴδη. "Him the Father of all things caused to arise as his eldest Son, whom "he also called his Firstbegotten: and after he was begotten, he "presently imitated his Father's ways, and after the archetypal patterns "which he saw of His, he also formed other species." See also *De Confusione Linguarum*, ibid., p. 427; *De Profugis*, ibid, 563. So also *De Agricultura*, where Philo describes God the Father as regulating the universes as a Shepherd and King, according to justice and equity, over which He has set his upright Word, his firstbegotten Son, τὸν ὀρθὸν αὐτοῦ λογον, πρωτόγονον υἱὸν, who takes the oversight of the sacred flock as the lieutenant of a great king. Again, *Quod a Deo mittantur Somnia*, ibid., p. 653. Δύο γὰρ, ὡς ἔοικεν, ἱερὰ Θεοῦ, ἐν μὲν ὅδε ὁ κόσμος, ἐν ᾧ καὶ ἀρχιερεὺς, ὁ πρωτόγονος αὐτοῦ θεῖος λόγος. "There are, methinks, two "temples of God. The one is this world, whose High priest is his "Firstbegotten Divine Word." See also J. Wesselius' three very learned and elaborate dissertations, *De Christo Primogenito, De Secunda Primogeniti in Mundum Inductione, De Primogeniti Adoratione Angelis Imperata* (Dissertationes Academicæ, *Lugd. Bat.*, 1734, 4to., pp. 501-567). Wesselius handles the phrase ὅταν δὲ πάλιν εἰσαγ' in a masterly style.

Schoettgen says, without, however, adducing any Old Testament examples, in reference to ὅταν εἰσαγάγῃ κ.τ.λ., "Phrasis est hebraica "בא בעולם *venit in mundum*, i.e., natus est. . . . . . In Hiphil הביא בעולם "est, *facere ut quis nascatur*. Et sic verba hæc sensum satis com-"modum habebant: eo vero tempore quo Deus Pater filium suum "Messiam ex virgine natum in hunc mundum produxit, eumque inter "homines quasi introduxit, hæc verba Psalmistæ de eo impleta sunt: "Adorent ipsum omnes Angeli Dei." He sees the accomplishment in the Angels' Hymn at the Nativity.—*Horæ Hebr.*, tom. i., p. 921.

² Καὶ προσκ. κ.τ.λ. This quotation seems to be taken from Ps. xcvii. 7, and not from Deut. xxxii. 43, in which latter passage the words προσκυνησάτωσαν αὐτῷ πάντες ἄγγελοι Θεοῦ are found in the LXX., but not in the Hebrew, although St. Paul (Romans xv. 10) declares the words immediately following, "Rejoice, O ye nations, with his people," to be a prophetic invitation, addressed by Moses to the Gentiles, to come in and participate in the spiritual blessings of Israel. The real clue to the quotation is found in the words ὅταν δὲ πάλιν εἰσαγάγῃ τὸν πρωτότοκον εἰς τὴν οἰκουμένην. The subject in hand is the superiority of Christ's dispensation over the Mosaic. By his eternal Son God made the world. When He bringeth Him in the second time (ὅταν δὲ πάλιν) into the world, to set up his kingdom on earth, He calls upon his angels to worship Him. Psalm xcvii. is descriptive of Christ's kingdom, and commences, "Jehovah reigneth; let the earth rejoice, let the "multitude of the isles be glad thereof." The "isles" denote the remote Gentile nations. This thankful exultation of the nations is in exact accordance with the promise to Abraham (Gen. xxii. 18; xxvi. 4),

where the Hebrew signifies "shall account themselves blessed." The Hithpael, or reflective conjugation of the verb ברך is here used, instead of the Niphal, or passive, as in Gen. xii. 3; xviii. 18; xxviii. 14. Prof. Moses Stuart observes that, in Deut. xxxii. 43, "The Codex Alex. " reads, υἱοὶ Θεοῦ, instead of ἄγγελοι Θεοῦ, and one Codex at Oxford "omits the whole clause." The Hebrew in Ps. xcvii. 7 (Heb. 6) has השתחוו לו כל אלהים (worship Him all ye gods; Ps. viii. 5, cxxxviii. 1, LXX., angels). The writer to the Hebrews adduces the passage as showing that the angels, although sometimes, *honoris causâ*, as were the Judges of Israel (Exod. xxi. 6—13; xxii. 8, 9, 28; Ps. lxxxii. 1—6; 1 Sam. ii. 25), called "gods" and "sons of God," are yet required to render to the "only begotten Son," the Messiah, the worship that is alone due to Jehovah the Lord of Hosts. The LXX. read ἄγγελοι αὐτοῦ, instead of Θεοῦ, in Ps. xcvii. 7. (xcvi. 7 in the Greek.)

Verses 8—14.—But to the Son he saith (Ps. xlv. 6, 7), "Thy throne, O God (אלהים ὁ Θεός, *vocative*), is for ever and ever; a sceptre of righteousness is the sceptre of thy kingdom.¹ Thou hast loved righteousness and hated iniquity; therefore God, even thy God, hath anointed² thee with the oil of gladness above thy fellows." ³

And again, in Ps. cii. 25, 27, when the perpetuity of Messiah's kingdom is celebrated in consoling contrast to the brevity of human life:—

Thou, Lord, in the beginning hast laid the foundation of the earth, and the heavens are the work of thine hands.⁴ They shall perish, but thou remainest, and they all shall wax old, as doth a garment;⁵ and as a vesture shalt thou fold them⁶ up, and they shall be changed; but thou art the same, and thy years shall not fail. But to which of the angels said He at any time (as in Ps. cx. 1) Sit on my right hand until I make thine enemies thy footstool? Are they not all ministering spirits,⁷ sent forth to minister (εἰς διακονίαν *on an errand of service*) for (διὰ *on behalf* of) them who shall be heirs of salvation?

The writer appeals to his readers' acquaintance with Old Testament history, which relates numberless instances of the mission of angels on behalf of God's people. They always appear in the subordinate capacity of messengers, as, indeed, the word מלאך ἄγγελος signifies. To be an assessor of the Lord Jehovah upon his throne is a dignity reserved for Messiah alone. He has by inheritance obtained a more excellent name than they.

¹ This Psalm cii. looks forward to the time when the "heathen shall "fear the name of Jehovah, and all the kings of the earth" his glory (verse 15). And also, "When the peoples (עמים *plur.*) are gathered "together, and the kingdoms, to serve the Lord" (verse 22). In other words, it is Messianic in its consolatory exhortations. The application of verses 25—27 to the Divine Messiah is no forced interpretation. Jacob had foretold that to Him should "the gathering of the nations "be." The Targums of Onkelos, Jonathan, and Jerusalem, with one consent, interpret Jacob's prophecy concerning SHILO, of the Messiah; as also the Babylonian Gemara, *Sanhedrim*, col. 970 (Ugolin. Thes., vol. 25), where a variety of opinions are given as to Messiah's name, דבי רבי שילא אמרי שילא שמו שנאמר עד כי יבא שילה "The disciples of R. Sila "said, *Shiloh is his name, for it is said, 'until Shiloh come.'*" See also *The Messiaship of Jesus*, by Alexander M'Caul, D.D., pp. 142—145.

² Ἔχρισε. The word משיח, Messiah, means *anointed one*. The allusion to the Messiah is self-evident. The Targum applies this Psalm xlv. to the Messiah, as in verse 2. שפרך מלכא משיחא *thy beauty, O king Messiah, is more than that of the sons of men. The Spirit of Prophecy is given to thy lips.* And to the Messiah, Aben Ezra says, it is most fitly applicable. R. Joseph Ben Moshe also, in כתר תורה, fol. 36, 4, הפסוקים אלה מדברים נגד מלך משיח "These verses speak of King Messiah." See Schoettgen; *Horæ Hebr.*, p. 924; also, J. Wesselius' Six Dissertations on Ps. xlv., contained in his *Diss. Acad.*, published at Leyden 1734, pp. 177—319.

³ Παρὰ τοὺς μετόχους σου. Schoettgen well observes that, if Christ were God only, He would have no fellows or associates. Since, therefore, his fellows are spoken of, He must be either man or angel. But He is not an angel, because He took the seed of Abraham; and He is the son of David, and therefore human as well as divine. The superabundant unction of the Messiah is in reference to the special manner in which the High-priest was anointed with the holy oil. It was poured upon his head (Exod. xxix. 7; Levit. viii. 12; comp. Ps. cxxxiii. 2), and ran down upon his beard, even to the skirts of his garments,

whilst the ordinary priests were only anointed by sprinkling. Thomas Goodwin says, " Secundani Sacerdotes tantum adspergebantur oleo isto " unctionis admixto sanguine qui erat super altari (Levit. viii. 30). " Hinc *Sacerdos Summus* in fonte legitur *Sacerdos unctus* (Levit. iv. 5). " Jonathan habet ; *Sacerdos magnus vel summus*. Disserte Aben-Ezra ; " *Sacerdos magnus ipse est Sacerdos unctus*. Lyranus adhuc clarius ; " *Sacerdos unctus est Sacerdos magnus, quia inferiores Sacerdotes non* " *ungebantur*. Per hoc denotata fuit unctio nostri Salvatoris, *uncti oleo* " *alacritatis supra consortes suos* Ps. xlv. 8. Unctus fuit supra con- " sortes suos *extensive et intensive*. *Extensive*, nam etsi Aaron fuerit " Sacerdos unctus, Saul Rex unctus, Elisa propheta unctus, Melchizedek " et Rex et Sacerdos, Moses Sacerdos et propheta, David Rex et " Propheta ; nemo tamen nisi solus Christus Χριστός, משיח simul et Rex, " et Sacerdos et Propheta fuit. *Intensive ;* Ipse est *unctus*, nos ad- " *spersi ;* ipse plenus gratiâ et veritate, nos ex ipsius plenitudine " accipimus gratiam pro gratia, χάριν ἀντὶ χάριτος ; Joh. i. 14—16. Et " omnes Christiani, praeprimis *ministri*, sunt Χριστοῦ εὐωδία τῷ Θεῷ " *fragrantia Christi Deo ;* 2 Cor. ii. 15. (*Moses et Aaron*, pp. 77, 78. " *Francofurti ad Moenum*, 1710, 8vo.) " See also Reland's *Antiq. Sacr. vet. Hebr.* (*Traject. Bat.*, 1712), 8vo., pp. 140, 141 ; Cunaeus *de Rep. Hebr.* (*Lugd. Bat.*, 1632, 12mo.), lib. ii., cap. 7, pp. 206—209 ; also, J. Selden, *De Successionibus ad leges Ebraeorum* (De Success. in Pontificat., lib. ii., cap. 9), pp. 508—522. *Lugd. Bat.*, 1638, 12mo. ; and J. Wesselius' *Diss. de justitia Messiae vicaria, causa unctionis ejus supra consortes suos.* (Dissertationes Academicae. *Lugd. Bat.*, 1734, 4to., pp. 226—253.)

⁴ Καὶ Σὺ κατ' ἀρχὰς, κ.τ.λ. A citation by the Psalmist from Gen. i. 1. The creation of the heavens included the heavenly hosts, *i.e.*, the angels. " In this summing up of creation (Gen. ii 1) ' all the host of them ' is " mentioned to include angels .... to teach that they were not inde- " pendent beings, but creatures of God."— *Dr. M'Caul's Essay*, Mosaic Record of Creation, § 9 ; *Aids to Faith*, p 206. See also Philo, *De Mundi Opificio*, Works, *Mangey's* edit., vol. i., col. 6.

The Divine pre-eminence of Jesus over prophets and angels has now been established. If He be the Messiah, then his authority to speak in his own and in his Father's name is unquestionable. It is no departure from the ancient creed, nor infringement of the strictest letter of the Law of Moses, to give heed to his teaching. The converts to whom the Epistle is addressed had already convinced themselves that in Him the predictions of the prophets were minutely fulfilled. Unhesitating obedience, unswerving faith is therefore justly his due. To no purpose do the unbelieving Jews rest the immutability of the old dispensation upon "the disposition of angels." Messiah is Lord of the angels. It is his prerogative to limit and define the things already spoken, and also give such additional revelation as He pleases. God in these latter times speaks to us by his Son. He can revoke his own institutions when they have accomplished the ends for which He gave them.

⁵ Ἐνδύεται δ' ὁ μὲν πρεσβύτατος τοῦ ὄντως λόγος ὡς ἐσθῆτα τὸν κόσμον. "The eldest Word of the Self-Existent is clothed with the universe as "with a garment." (Philo, *De Profugis*, Works, Mangey's edition, vol. i., p. 562.) The passage will repay examination.

⁶ Καὶ ὡσεὶ περιβόλαιον ἑλίξεις αὐτούς. Ludovicus Cappellus writes on these words, " In Hebræo est תחליף, *immutabis eos*, sed videntur LXX. "scripsisse ἀλλάξεις, nam sequitur ἀλλαγήσονται, sed a sciolo aliquo "mutatum est ἀλλάξεις in ἑλίξεις" (Crit. Sacr., p. 62). And again (*ibid.*, p. 66), "Et in ipsa τῶν LXX. translatione videtur aliquando "esse lapsus etiam librarii, ut Heb. i. 16, ὡσεὶ περιβόλαιον ἑλίξεις "αὐτούς, ubi jam supra notavimus lapsu librarii ἑλίξεις scriptum videri "pro ἀλλάξεις, nam in Hebræo est תחלים h.e. ἀλλάξεις αὐτούς, immutabis "eos; deinde sequitur immediate καὶ ἀλλαγήσονται, *et immutabuntur*, ut "omninò videantur LXX. sic ex Hebræo reddidisse verbatim ὡσεὶ "περιβόλαιον ἀλλάξεις αὐτούς, καὶ ἀλλαγήσονται." Gesenius, however, seems to give the real clue to the adoption of ἑλίξεις by the LXX., and by the writer to the Hebrews, "מחלפות, plur. f., a rad. חלף, Pi. et Hiph. "*mutavit*, hincque *plexuit*, capillorum plexus, Haarflechten, Zöpfe. "Jud. xvi. 13—19." (Lex. Man., *Lips.*, 1847, p. 514.)

Be it further observed that the LXX. (in Is. xxxiv. 4) render the Hebrew ונגלו כספר השמים, "And the heavens shall be rolled together as "a scroll," by καὶ ἑλιγήσεται ὁ οὐρανὸς ὡς βιβλίον. Surenhusius (Βιβλ. Καταλλ.), p. 602, writes on Hebr. i. 12, "Sed observanda hic est varia "lectio in textu Græco, etenim quædam exemplaria legunt ἀλλάξεις "*commutabis*, quædam vero ἑλίξεις *convolves*, sed utraque bona est, et "ita quidem ut Judæorum oculi hac lectione offendi nequeant, cum "utraque sit biblica ; quæ legunt ἀλλάξεις, ea expressa sunt secundum "illud תחלים, quod in Psalmo extat ; quæ vero exemplaria legunt "ἑλίξεις *convolves, complicabis*, ea expressa sunt secundum illud Jes "xxxiv. 4, ונגלו כספר השמים *et complicati instar libri coeli isti*, jam vero "veteribus Hebræorum doctoribus in more positum est textui allegato "interdum verba quædam ex alio loco adjungere, in quo de eodem "subjecto agitur, quemadmodum constat ex thesi nostra V. de Modis "interpretandi Scripturas sacras. Præterea Raschi ad כלבוש תחלים notat, "se rem habere veluti cum eo ההופך לבושו לפשטו *qui convertit indumentum* "*suum ad exuendum illud.*"

CHAP. I., 8—14.

A very curious example of the *lapsus librarii* occurs in the LXX. of Jer. xxiii. 6 :—" Καὶ τοῦτο τὸ ὄνομα αὐτοῦ, ὃ καλέσει αὐτὸν Κύριος, Ιωσεδὲκ " ἐν τοῖς προφήταις." This verse in the Hebrew ends with יהוה צדקנו ; but the 9th verse of the Hebrew commences, לבאים נשבר לבי, " My heart "is broken because of the prophets"; whilst, in the LXX., the 9th verse begins, συνέτριβη ἡ καρδία μου ἐν ἐμοὶ, and the 7th and 8th verses of the Hebrew are left out.

[7] Λειτουργικὰ πνεύματα. The following quotations from Philo will serve to show the opinion of the Hellenistic portion of the ancient Jewish Church respecting the nature and ministrations of angels :—
Ἄγγελοι γὰρ στρατός εἰσι Θεοῦ, ἀσώματοι καὶ εὐδαίμονες ψυχαί—" For " the angels are the host of God, incorporeal and happy souls." Again, *de Sacrificiis Abelis et Caini*, Works, *Mangey's Edit*, vol. i., p. 164. So also *ibid*, p. 296, *Quod Deus sit immutabilis*. Οὐδὲ ἂν οὖν ἐκ λάκκου πίοι, ᾧ δίδωσιν ὁ Θεὸς τὰς ἀκράτου μεθύσματος πόσεις, τότε μὲν διά τινος ὑπηρετοῦντος τῶν ἀγγέλων, ὃν οἰνοχοεῖν ἠξίωσε, τότε δὲ καὶ δι' ἑαυτοῦ, μηδένα τοῦ διδόντος καὶ τοῦ λαμβάνοντος μεταξὺ τιθείς. " That man will never " drink from a cistern, to whom God supplies draughts of unmixed " wine, at one time by the hand of some ministering angel, whom He " hath appointed to pour it out, and at another time doing it Himself, " interposing no one between the giver and the receiver." Again, *ibid.*, p. 463, *De migratione Abrahami*, ὁ δὲ ἑπόμενος Θεῷ, κατὰ ἀναγκαῖον συνοδοιπόροις χρῆται τοῖς ἀκολούθοις αὐτοῦ λόγοις, οὓς ὀνομάζειν ἔθος ἀγγέλους. " He who follows God is necessarily accompanied by his words that " follow Him, which it is customary to call angels." *Ibid*, p. 577. *De Profugis*, Ἄγγελοι δ' οἰκέται Θεοῦ. "Angels are the servants (*famuli*) " of God." *Ibid.*, p. 642. *Quod a Deo mittuntur somnia*. Ἄλλαι δ' εἰσὶν καθαρώταται καὶ ἄρισται, μειζόνων φρονημάτων καὶ θειοτέρων ἐπιλαχοῦσαι, μηδενὸς μὲν τῶν περιγείων ποτὲ ὀρεχθεῖσαι τοπαράπαν, ὕπαρχοι δὲ τοῦ παηγεμόνος, ὥσπερ μεγάλου βασιλέως ὀφθαλμοὶ καὶ ὦτα, ἀφορῶσαι πάντα καὶ ἀκούουσαι. Ταύτας δαίμονας μὲν οἱ ἄλλοι φιλόσοφοι, ὁ δὲ ἱερὸς λόγος ἀγγέλους εἰωθὲ καλεῖν, προσφυέστερῳ χρώμενος ὀνόματι. Καὶ γὰρ τὰς τοῦ πατρὸς ἐπικελεύσεις τοῖς ἐγγόνοις, καὶ τὰς τῶν ἐκγόνων χρείας τῷ πατρὶ διαγγέλλουσι. " There are besides other most pure and excellent beings, " who partake of higher and diviner intelligences, and never in the " smallest degree are swayed by earthborn instincts. But they are " lieutenants of Him who is ruler of all things, and, as it were, the eyes " and ears of a mighty King, seeing and hearing all things. Philo- " sophers are wont to call them *genii*, but the Sacred Word usually " styles them angels, employing a designation more agreeable to their " nature. They announce the behests of their Father to his children,

"and also the necessities of his children to their Father." Again, p. 643, συγκαταβαίνοντες διὰ φιλανθρωπίαν καὶ ἔλεον τοῦ γένους ἡμῶν, ἐπικουρίας ἕνεκα καὶ συμμαχίας, ἵνα καὶ τὴν ἔτι ὥσπερ ἐν ποταμῷ, τῷ σώματι, φορουμένην ψυχὴν, τὰ σωτήρια ἀναπνέοντες, ἀνασώσωσι. "Descending out "of kindness and pity for our race, in order that they may render us "succour and assistance, they rescue the soul when it is borne along in "the body, as by a river, breathing into it things that accompany salva- "tion." On p. 642, Philo speaks of the angels as "mediators and inter- cessors." (See Coloss. ii. 18.) Schoettgen, *Horæ Hebraicæ*, tom. i., p. 906, cites the opinion of Joseph Ben Albo, that a qualified adoration of angels, in their capacity of ambassadors of God, was permissible, and redounded to the honour of their King, but for their own sakes, and in considera- tion of their inherent dignity as celestial beings, they might not be adored. Philo, *de Gigantibus* (*ibid.*, p. 263), declares that the angels spoken of by Moses are called by the philosophers *genii* (δαίμονας). He adds that they are "souls flying in the air," ψυχαὶ δ' εἰσὶ κατὰ τὸν ἀέρα πετόμεναι. The passage is well worth perusal from its striking resem- blance, in many respects, to the intimations of St. Paul in his Epistles, and of the other New Testament writers. On p. 264, *ibid.*, Philo says, ὑπηρέτεσι καὶ διακόνοις ὁ δημιουργὸς ἔιωθε χρῆσθαι πρὸς τὴν τῶν θνητῶν ἐπίστασιν. "The Creator is wont to employ them as ministers and "servants in superintending the affairs of mortals." And again, *ibid.*, he draws the distinction between these holy and happy ministering angels, and others who are undeserving of the name of good, confirming his opinion by the words of Psalm lxxviii. 49. Further, pp. 122, 409, he says that the angels are called λόγοι, *i.e.*, *Words* of God. Again, *de Abrahamo*, vol. ii. 17, ὑποδιάκονοι καὶ ὕπαρχοι τοῦ πρώτου Θεοῦ, "ministers and lieutenants of the supreme God." *De Humanitate*, p. 387, he speaks of men and ministering angels (ἄνθρωποί τε καὶ ἄγγελοι λειτουργοί) listening to Moses' Hymn. *De Mundo*, p. 604, he describes them as πρεσβευομέναις καὶ διαγγελλούσας τά τε παρὰ τοῦ ἡγεμόνος τοῖς ὑπηκόοις ἀγαθὰ, καὶ τῷ βασιλεῖ, ὧν εἰσιν ὑπήκοοι χρεῖοι, "acting as God's "ambassadors, and announcing good tidings to his subjects, and also "bringing word to their King what things his subjects have need of." On p. 605, he again speaks of the evil angels mentioned in Ps. lxxviii. 49. In the fragment *De Resurrectione Terribili*, tom. ii., p. 656, Philo says that the nature of angels is spiritual, but that they often assume human shape. *De Cherubim*, vol. i., p. 139, he asserts that Hagar was brought back by ὑπαντήσαντος ἀγγέλου, ὅς ἐστι θεῖος λόγος, "an angel that met "her, which is the Divine Word." So also, *De Cherubim*, *ibid.*, pp. 144, 145, he says that the sword of the cherubim, and also the angel that met Balaam, was the Word of God. Again, *De Confusione Linguarum*, *ibid.*, p. 427, Κἂν μηδέπω μέντοι τυγχάνῃ τις ἀξιόχρεως ὢν υἱὸς Θεοῦ προσαγορεύεσθαι, σπουδαζέτω κοσμεῖσθαι κατὰ τὸν πρωτόγονον αὐτοῦ λόγον, τὸν ἄγγελον πρεσβύτατον, ὡς ἀρχάγγελον πολυώνυμον ὑπάρχοντα, καὶ γὰρ ἀρχὴ, καὶ ὄνομα Θεοῦ, καὶ λόγος, καὶ ὁ κατ' εἰκόνα ἄνθρωπος, καὶ ὁρῶν 'Ισραὴλ προσαγορεύεται. "But if any one be not yet worthy to be designated " (see Heb. v. 10) a son of God, let him give diligence to be adorned " like his Firstbegotten Word, who is the oldest angel, being, so to " speak, an archangel of many names, for he is designated '*Beginning*,' " and the '*Name of God*,' and '*the Word*,' and '*He who is Man in his* " '*likeness*' (*Cujus homo factus est ad imaginem*, Mangey), and '*He who* " '*sees Israel.*'" This very striking declaration of Philo (so consistent with what is related in the Old Testament concerning the *Angel of Jehovah*, who is the Second Person in the Ever Blessed Trinity) he follows up with an explanation equally important in its significance :— Καὶ γὰρ εἰ μήπω ἱκανοὶ Θεοῦ παῖδες νομίζεσθαι γεγονάμεν, ἀλλά τοι τῆς ἀϊδίου εἰκόνος αὐτοῦ, λόγου τοῦ ἱερωτάτου· Θεοῦ γὰρ εἰκὼν λόγος ὁ πρεσβύτατος. "For if we be not, as yet, fit to be accounted sons of God, we " may be nevertheless of his eternal likeness (or image), viz., his Most " Sacred Word, for the image of God is the Eldest Word."

See J. Wesselii *De Rubo Mosis Diss*. (Dissertationes Acad. *Lugd. Bat.*, 1734, p. 1, &c.); J. Wesselii *De Angelo Jehovæ ab Hagara viso Diss*. (Dissertationes Sacræ Leidenses. *Lugd. Bat.*, 1721, pp. 1—54), and *De Angelo faciei Jehovæ, ibid.*, pp. 289—335; J. G. Surenhusii Βίβλος Καταλλαγῆς, pp. 591—595.

CHAPTER II.

Verses 1—4.—On this account (Διὰ τοῦτο) we ought, SAYS THE WRITER, to give the more earnest heed to (προσέχειν, *tenaciously adhere to*) the things which we have heard, lest at any time we should let them slip,[1] (or, perhaps, *lapse ourselves*, after the example of those who have already apostatized). For if the word spoken by angels[2] was stedfast (ἐγένετο βέβαιος, *was absolutely* confirmed in every particular), and every transgression and disobedience received a just recompense of reward, how shall we escape if we neglect so great a salvation? Which was, in the first instance, spoken by the Lord (Jesus Christ), and was confirmed to us by those who heard Him,[2]

God himself accompanying it (the preaching of the Gospel) by the ratifying testimony of signs, and portents, and various miraculous exhibitions of his power, and distributions of the Holy Spirit, according to his own will.

[1] παρραρυῶμεν. "Metaphora a navibus petita, quæ per fluxum et "refluxum maris, vel ventos etiam prohibeantur quominus adpellant "ad portum," &c. See J. C. Wolfius, *in loc.*

[2] Prof. Stuart understands ὁ δὶ ἀγγέλων λαληθεὶς λόγος of the giving of the law on Mount Sinai, as he also does the words of Stephen (Acts vii. 53), and of St. Paul (Gal. iii. 19), and cites Josephus and Philo in confirmation of his opinion. To my mind, the transition to the law exclusively is, in the present instance, somewhat abrupt. Does it not rather, also, refer to the ministrations of angels vouchsafed from time to time during the whole of the earlier dispensation, and to which allusion is made in the concluding verse of the first chapter?

[3] This admission, that the Gospel had been in part received from secondhand, seems to militate in some degree against St. Paul's invariable claim to a direct and special revelation from Christ himself. In Gal. i. 11, 12, ii. 6, he expressly disclaims any human sources of information. In 1 Cor. xi. 23 he asserts that Christ himself communicated to him the sacramental formula. The first person, which the writer employs on the present occasion, must not be too closely pressed. He probably speaks in the name of his readers.

Verses 5—9.—For God hath not put in subjection unto angels the world to come[1] of which we speak (chap. i., verse 6); but one, in a certain place (Ps. viii. 4—6), has explicitly asserted as follows (διεμαρτύρατο λέγων) :— "What is man that thou art mindful of him, and the son of man that thou visitest him? [2] Thou madest him a little lower (βραχύ τι might, perhaps, be fairly rendered "for a little season," *i.e.*, until, in our resurrection glory, we shall reign with Christ) than the angels (מאלהים παρ᾿ ἀγγέλους). Thou crownedst (or *wilt crown*) him with glory and honour, and didst set (or *wilt set*) him over the works of thy hands. Thou hast (or *wilt*) put all things in subjection under his feet." But, by that phrase of "subjecting all things to him," He hath left nothing unsubjected (*i.e.*, nothing in the universe can claim exemption from his authority). But now we do not yet see all things put under Him; but we do see Jesus, that was made a little (or, *for a little while*, βραχύ τι, מעט) lower than the angels³ by the suffering of death, crowned with glory and honour; so that, by the grace of God, he might taste death for every man.⁴

¹ Τὴν οἰκουμενην τὴν μέλλουσαν may fairly be understood of the supernatural world, viz., the signs and the wonders just spoken of, *i.e.*, the δυνάμεις μέλλοντος αἰῶνος (chap. vi. 5). It refers more probably, however, to the Christian dispensation hereafter, *in its final consummation*, during the reign of Christ over a ransomed Church and a regenerated nature. No such promise has been left to the angels, but to man (the second Adam—Christ) there has been, in the prophetic assertion, "Thou "hast put all things under his feet," and to us also who are joint heirs with him.

Stuart says that τὴν οἰκ. τὴν μέλλ. "is equivalent to ὁ αἰὼν ὁ μέλλων, "*i.e.*, the Christian dispensation, the world as it will be in future— "ὁ μέλλων, *i.e.*, the world under the reign of Christ." Now this interpretation of both phrases is contrary to the almost invariable Jewish interpretation of the phrase העולם הבא, *i.e., the world to come*, and of which the two Greek expressions are the exact equivalent. The Rabbins placed the days of Messiah in this world (עולם הזה *this present age*), expecting a reign upon earth, after which the general resurrection and judgment will take place. אחרית הימים "the latter days," were understood to be the closing days of Messiah's reign, and of the world's existence. Rhenferdius, in his first dissertation *De Seculo Futuro*, p. 1123, quotes as follows from the Gemara—"Cod. *Schabbat.*, fol. 63 (et alibi saepius), אמר ר׳ חייא בר אבא כל הנביאים כולם לא נתנבאו אלא לימות המשיח אבל לעולם הבא עין לא ראתה אלהים זולתך וגו׳"

"R. Chija Bar Abba has said, 'All the prophets, without exception, "have prophesied nothing except concerning the days of Messiah; but "concerning the "world to come" (לעלם הבא) *it is written* (Is. lxiv. 1), "Eye hath not seen except Thee, O God, &c.'" (Meuschen, *N. Test. ex Vet. illustr.*) For a multitude of other early Jewish authorities, see Rhenferdius' very learned and elaborate tract, as cited above.

The same passage occurs in the treatise *Sanhedrin*, Gem. Babyl., col. 974 (Ugol. *Thes.*, vol. xxv.), with some additions and slight variations.

תני אבימי בריה דרבי אבהו ימות המשיח לישראל שבעת אלפים שנה שנאמר כמשוש החתן על כלה כן ישיש עליך ה׳ אלהיך אמר רב יהודה אמ׳ שמואל ימות המשיח כמים

סבנרא העולם וצד עכשיו שנאמר כימי השמים על הארץ רב נחמן בר יצחק אמר כימי
נח עד עכשיו שנאמר כימי נח זאת לי אשר נשבעתי א״ר חייא בר אבא א״ר יוחנן כל
הנביאים כולן לא נתנבאו לימות המשיח אבל לעולם הבא עין לא ראתה אלהים זולתך וגו׳"

"R. Abimai, son of R. Abau, teaches:—The days of the Messiah of
"Israel are seven thousand years. For it is said (Is. lxii. 5), *And as a*
"*bridegroom rejoiceth over a bride, so will the Lord thy God rejoice over*
"*thee.* R. Judah says; Samuel says:—The days of Messiah are as the
"days in which the world was created, up to the present time. For it
"is said, *As the days of the heaven upon the earth.* (Deut. xi. 21.) R.
"Nachman bar Isaac says:—As the days of Noah up to the present
"time. For it is said, *For this is as the waters* [days] *of Noah unto me,*
"*as I have sworn.* (Is. liv. 9.) R. Chijah bar Aba says; R. Jochanan
"says:—All the prophets did not prophesy concerning the days of
"Messiah, but concerning the world to come; [as it is written] *Eye*
"*hath not seen, besides Thee, O God, what He hath prepared for him*
"*that waiteth for Him.* (Is. lxiv. 4.)"

² Professor Stuart would read "yet" or "but" ותחסרהו.

³ Professor Stuart suggests somewhat gratuitously, I would submit, that the unbelieving Jews urged "Two objections against the superiority "of Christ over angels. 1. Christ was a man. 2. He suffered an igno- "minious death." Now Christ's superiority over the angels is naturally introduced, not as a Jewish cavil, but in the course of the argument. The real point at issue was this, Had Christ any authority to set aside the civil and ceremonial laws given by the disposition of angels, or were his claims disposed of by his sufferings and death? The author of the Epistle has shown that Christ the Messiah is the Lord and Creator of the angels. (See note 3, on p. 14.) That it was He who sent them, and that his temporary inferiority to the angels, *i.e*, his manhood, had been predicted in Psalm viii., whilst an honour belonged to Him, by heredit- ary right and Divine generation, to which no angel could advance the slightest claim, viz., that of being designated by God as his "first- begotten Son," *i.e.*, his only son, and being saluted by the Father as his assessor on his throne. If, then, the revelations from time to time vouchsafed by the mediation of angels were deserving of reverent obedience, much more the revelations imparted in these latter times by the Divine Son of God.

⁴ This exaltation of Christ, as a reward of his voluntary sufferings, had been distinctly foretold by Isaiah lii. and liii., and was so under- stood by the ancient Rabbinical commentators. The following passage from the *Yalkut Shimoni* (quoted on p. 20 of the late Dr. M'Caul's *Doctrine and Interpretation of Isaiah liii.*) abundantly establishes the above assertion:—"Behold my servant shall deal prudently. This is "the King Messiah. He shall be exalted and extolled, and be very

"high. He shall be more exalted than Abraham......He shall be "extolled more than Moses......and he shall be higher than the "ministering angels......' But he was wounded for our transgressions, "'he was bruised for our iniquities: the chastisement of our peace was "'upon him, and with his stripes we are healed.' R. Huna, in the "name of R. Acha (says), 'The chastisements or afflictions were divided "'into three parts—one to David and the fathers, one to the rebellious "'generation, and one to King Messiah.'" Upon which Dr. M'Caul remarks, "This passage, the first part of which is a quotation from a "much more ancient book (see note 2, pp. 14, 15), plainly shows "that the Jews interpreted this prophecy of Messiah: it also con- "tains an important illustration of the character of the Messiah, "describing him as superior in dignity to the three patriarchs, "to Moses and the ministering angels, and yet a man of sorrows "and acquainted with grief. We would entreat our Jewish brethren "to compare this Rabbinical passage with the first two chapters of "the Hebrews. The next testimony is that of R. Moses Alshech, "who flourished about the middle of the sixteenth century, 'Behold, "'our Rabbies with one mouth have confirmed, and received "'by tradition, that King Messiah is here spoken of.'" Doubtless (in Phil. ii. 6—11) St. Paul had the prophecy of Isaiah's chapter liii. in his mind when he writes, "Who being in the form of God, thought "it not robbery to be equal with God, but made himself of no reputa- "tion (ἐκένωσε), and took upon him the form of a servant, and was "made in the likeness of men, and being found in fashion as a man, he "humbled (ἐταπείνωσεν) himself, and became obedient unto death, even "the death of the cross. Wherefore God also hath highly exalted him "(ὑπερύψωσε), and given him a name which is above every name, that at "the name of Jesus every knee shall bow, of things in heaven and "things in earth and things under the earth (ἐπουρανίων καὶ ἐπιγείων "καὶ καταχθονίων), and that every tongue should confess that Jesus "Christ is Lord, to the glory of God the Father." As a parallel to the above citation from Isaiah, I would adduce the last verse of the cxth Messianic Psalm, "He (Messiah) shall drink of the brook in the way, "therefore He (God the Father) shall lift up his head, *i.e.*, exalt him." (מנחל בדרך ישתה על כן ירים ראש) To "lift up the head" signifies to pro- mote to honour and triumph, and so it is used in Ps. xxvii. 6: "And now shall my head be lifted up above mine enemies" (ירום ראשי). The exaltation is consequent upon, and antithetic to, the act of stooping to drink of the wayside stream of humiliation and death. The word נהל *brook, stream, river, flood*, is used to denote persecution and affliction, in 2 Sam. xxii. 5, "the floods of ungodly men," and its cognate נחלה occurs in a similar sense in Ps. cxxiv. 4 (3), "the stream had gone over our soul." The author of *Nizzachon Vetus*, p. 184, gives the following sneering reply to the Christian application of this 7th verse of Ps. cx. to Jesus, but which singularly enough confirms the view I have taken of it.

אדרבה כל כן יבוש ויכנוש פניו לקרקע ולא ישא ראשו ויהי אבל והפוי ראש שצריך לשתות
פן ימות בצמא

"To this I will reply, He will be on the contrary ashamed, and com-"pelled to bow down with his face to the earth, so far from lifting it "up. He will rather have lamentation, and hang down his head, "because it is necessary for him to drink, lest he die of thirst." (See Wagenseil, *Tela ignea Satanæ*, where the above treatise is printed at length.)

Verses 10—13.—For it became Him (ἔπρεπε γὰρ αὐτῷ), for whom are all things, and by whom are all things (*i.e.*, God the Author and Creator of all things), to make the Captain of their salvation, when bringing many sons to glory (ἀγαγόντα, κ.τ.λ.), perfect,[1] on account of (his) sufferings. For both (Christ) who sanctifieth and they who are sanctified[2] (by Him) are all of one (*s.c.*, *human nature*, ἐξ ἑνὸς γενοῦς, Stuart), for which cause (δι᾽ ἣν αἰτίαν, *which being the case*) he is not ashamed to call them brethren, saying (Ps. xxii. 22), "I will declare thy name unto my brethren, in the "midst of the Church (קהל, ἐκκλησία) will I sing praise "unto thee."[3] And again (Isaiah viii. 17), "I will put "my trust in him"[4] (קויתי לו *I have firmly confided in him*, LXX, πεποιθὼς ἔσομαι ἐν αὐτῷ) and (Isaiah viii. 18), "Behold I and the children which God hath given me."

Having thus established from current Rabbinic interpretations of the above passages, that the Divine Messiah would claim kinsmanship with flesh and blood, the writer continues:—

Verse 14.—Forasmuch then as the children were partakers of flesh and blood, he also himself likewise (παραπλησίως is equivalent to ὁμοίως, *in the same manner, as well as*, Stuart) took part of (μετέσχε, *participated in*) the same;

CHAP. II., 14.   31

that through death he might destroy him that had the
power of death, that is, the devil.⁵

¹ Professor Stuart understands with Theophylact that "τελείωσις here
means δόξαν ἥν ἐδοξάσθη." He translates the verse thus, "It became
"him, also, for whom are all things, and by whom are all things, to
"bestow, on account of sufferings, the highest honours upon him who
"is the Captain of their salvation leading many sons to glory." Dean
Alford's objection to this arrangement seems faulty both in its
premises and deductions. The Dean says, "It would be contrary to all
"Scripture analogy to represent us as *sons*, in relation to Christ." How
does the Dean propose to explain 'Ἰδοὺ ἐγὼ καὶ τὰ παιδία (הילדים) ἅ μοι
ἔδωκεν ὁ Θεός, which words of Is. viii. 18 are applied by the writer to
Jesus in verse 13? Apart from this quotation, there is no need whatever to understand υἱοὺς out of its ordinary interpretation, viz., "Sons
"of God." Other commentators understand διὰ παθημάτων τελειῶσαι
"by the medium of sufferings to complete" the mediatorial qualifications of Christ, as without these a perfect sympathy could not have
existed between himself and his people. The authorised English version
apparently refers ἀγαγόντα to God the Father.
² "Both he who maketh expiation and they for whom expiation is
made," so Professor Stuart translates ὅ τε γὰρ ἁγιάζων, κ.τ.λ. He shows
how ἁγιάζω in the LXX (Levit. xxii. 2, 3; Exod. xiii. 2, &c.) corresponds to the Hebrew קדש and הקדיש *to make holy, consecrate, as an
offering*; also, as in Job i. 5, *to expiate* or *make atonement*, LXX
ἐκαθάριζεν αὐτούς. It also corresponds (Exod. xxix. 33) to כפר *to make
atonement, to expiate*. Probably the writer to the Hebrews had in his
mind the words of Isaiah liii. 11, 12, "By his knowledge shall my
"righteous servant justify (צדי *make righteous*) many, for he (הוא
"*emphat*.) shall bear their iniquities. Therefore will I divide him," &c.
³ Ἀπαγγελῶ τὸ ὄνομα, κ.τ.λ. The LXX translate אספרה by διηγήσομαι.
Schoettgen, in his treatise *de Messia* (*Horæ Hebr.*, tom. ii., pp. 232, 233),
gives the following ancient Jewish interpretations of Psalm xxii. :—
"*De cerva auroræ*. Midrasch Tehillim : *De eo qui salit sicut cervus, et
"illustrat mundum tempore tenebrarum*. Hierosol. Berachoth in Jalkut
"Simeoni ad h.l. et Schir haschirim rabba, fol. 28, 3. *R. Chija fil.
"Abba et R. Simeon fil. Chalpatha iverunt simul tempore diluculi in convalle
"ad urbem Arbela, et viderunt cervam auroræ, quæ* (sic vocatur quia
"quasi) *lucem ejus discindit. Dixit ipsi R. Chija : Dicito sic : hæc est
"redemptio Israelitarum, quæ sensim sensimque advenit. Respondit alter,
"Hoc ipsum est, quod Scriptura dicit* Michæ vii. 8. *Quando sedebo in
"tenebris, Dominus mihi lux est*. In Sohar Exod., fol. 49, col. 295,

"Cerva auroræ dicitur Schechina, quæ propter filios suos gemit, ex
"qua vero fit Leo matutinus, Messias filius David. (Locus integer
"exstat inferius, libro iii.)—v. 8. *Omnes videntes me subsannarunt me.*
"Pesikta rabbathi in Jalkut Simeoni ii., fol. 56, 4. *Eo tempore, quo*
"*Messias in carcere conclusus fuit, singulis diebus dentibus frenduerunt,*
"*oculis nictarunt, capitibus nutarunt et labia distenderunt,* q.d. Omnes
"videntes me.—v. 9. *Convolvat in Dominum.* Midrasch Tehillim :
"*Omnes species convolutionum ego porto. Peccata ipsorum devolve in me*
"*et ego portabo.*—v. 16. Lingua mea adhæsit faucibus. *Ibidem,* col. 3.
"*Dixit Deus S.B. O Messia, peccata illorum, qui reconditi sunt apud te,*
"*intrudent te in jugum ferreum, et reddent te similem vitulo, cujus oculi*
"*caligant, comprimentque spiritum tuum jugo, et propter illorum peccata*
"*adhærebit lingua tua palato tuo.*"

⁴ Much discussion has arisen amongst critics as to whether the words
ἐγὼ ἔσομαι πεποιθώς, κ.τ.λ., are a citation from Isaiah viii. 17 or from
some other passages of the Old Testament. Illustrious names are to be
found on both sides of the question. Grammius, however, has to my
mind, conclusively settled the question in favour of Isaiah viii. 17.
See J. C. Wolfius on Hebr. ii. 13 ; and, on the other side, Surenhusius,
Βιβλ. Καταλλ., pp. 607—609.

⁵ Apparently a citation from Hosea xiii. 14. "The power of the
grave," in the Hebrew, is יד שאול, *from the hand of Hades,* ἐκ χειρὸς
ᾅδου, LXX. See also Isaiah xxv. 8. The following curious legend
is quoted by Schoettgen in his treatise *De Messia (Hor. Hebr.,* tom. ii.,
p. 376), " Jesa. xxv. 8. Pesikta in Jalkut Simeoni ii., fol. 56, 3. *Dixit*
"*Satanas ad Deum Sanctum Benedictum: Domine totius mundi, Lux illa,*
"*quam sub throno gloriæ tuæ recondisti, ad quemnam spectat ? Respondit*
"*Deus, ad eum* פנים בבושת ולהבליכך להחוירך עתיד שהוא, *qui te repressurus et*
"*ignominia adfecturus est. Regessit Satanas : Domine, ostende mihi illum.*
"*Deus respondit : Veni et vide illum. Quum vero Satanas illum con-*
"*spiceret,* פניו על ונפל נורצוע, *exterritus est, et in faciem suam cecidit, dicens,*
"לי להסיל שעתיד משיח זה והו בוראי, *sane hinc est Messias, qui me et omnes*
"*gentiles in infernum præcipitaturus est,* q.d. Jesa. xxv. 8. Degluciet
"mortem in æternum." For Rabbinic explanations of Hos. xiii. 14,
in reference to the Messiah, see Schoettgen, *ibid.,* pp. 209 and 564.

Verses 15—18.—And set free those who, through fear of
death, were during their lifetime subject (ἔνοχοι *held by,*
bound by) to bondage. For verily (as you know) he
did not (οὐ γὰρ δήπου, *nimirum, certe, utique, profecto.*
Schrevel.) take upon him the nature of angels, but he

took upon him the seed of Abraham¹ (as it had been foretold he should do (Gen. xxii. 18), otherwise Christ could not have so perfectly sympathised with mortal nature, man being at present a little lower than the angels. This 16th verse seems to be parenthetic, and the subject is resumed in verse 17). Wherefore (ὅθεν, *whence*) in all things it behoved him to (ὤφειλε, *it was essential that he should*) be made like unto his brethren, in order that he might be a merciful (ἐλεήμων, *compassionate*) and reliable (πιστός, *trustworthy*)² High Priest³ in things pertaining to God, to make reconciliation (*Ut misericors fieret, et fidelis pontifex ad Deum ut repropitiaret.* Vulg. —εἰς τὸ ἱλάσκεσθαι) for the sins of the people. For in that (*in eo enim, in quo passus est.* Vulg.) he himself hath suffered being tempted, he is able to succour them that are tempted.⁴

¹ Stuart translates οὐ γὰρ δήπου ἀγγ. κ.τ.λ, "Besides he doth not at all help the angels, but he helpeth the seed of Abraham"; a rendering which appears quite inconsistent with the context, however it may be warranted by the occasional use of the verb ἐπιλαμβάνεται. The writer is alleging an all-sufficient reason why Christ took human nature, and did not, and could not, take upon him the nature of angels. First, it would have been in direct violation of the prophetic Scriptures. Secondly, he could not then, from actual experience, have sympathised with the infirmities of flesh and blood as he does now. He would not have been a πιστὸς ἀρχιερεύς, an high priest in whom we could confide, as we can now, seeing that he disdains not to call us brethren.

² Wolfius (*in loco*) writes :—" Theodorus Dassovius in Diss de Pontif.
" Hebr. Summi ingress. in Sanct. Sanctor., sec. 14, existimat, alludi hic
" ad fidelitatem, quam, interposito jurejurando, olim polliceri debebat
" Sacerdotibus aliis, facturum se, ne Sanctum Sanctorum ingressurus
" thus prunis injiceret, Salducæorum more, sed faceret illud post
" ingressum. *Vide Joma*, cap. i., sec. 5, et *Siphra* passim. Confer
" Cl. Schlichteri *Decimas Sacras*, p. 516, sqq., cui Apostolus respicere
" potius videtur Mosen, servum Dei, qui intercessione sua Deum populo
" rebelli benevolum reddiderit ac propitium, cujusque fidelitas capite iii.
" integro summis laudibus extollatur, quemadmodum Philo Mosen
" vocet ἄριστον βασιλέα, καὶ νομοθέτην, καὶ Ἀρχιερέα καὶ προφήτην δοκι-
" μώτατον. Confer Hebr. iii. 1, 2."

³ In verse 11 the writer has called attention to the fact that an earthly priest, who performs sanctificatory rites for the people, is of the same human nature. The like sympathetic tie exists between Christ and the believers, so that implicit confidence can subsist between our High Priest and his flock.

⁴ An allusion to Ps. lxxxix. 19 (20), "Then spakest thou in vision to thy holy one, and saidst, I have laid help upon one that is mighty (שויתי עזר על גבור); I have exalted one chosen out of the people." Is. lxiii. 1, "Who is this that cometh from Edom......? I that speak in righteousness, mighty to save" (רב להושיע). A number of ancient Jewish interpretations of Is. lxiii. 1 will be found in Schoettgen. Consult the Scripture index in both volumes.

CHAPTER III.

THE writer has now, whilst admitting the authority and inspiration of the prophets, established from their writings, the transcendent dignity of the Son of God. He has reminded his readers how He first purged our sins by his death and sufferings, and then, in fulfilment of the predictions of David and Isaiah, sat down at the right hand of the majesty on high. He is, by his eternal generation and by his Creatorship, Lord over the angels, who are required to render him Divine honours. If, then, the revelation given by prophets and angels demanded implicit and reverential obedience, much more the additional revelation imparted in these latter days by God's Son. God has "set to his seal" to the mission of Jesus, by a stupendous manifestation of miraculous credentials. These miraculous powers of the "world to come" had never been promised to angels, nor yet the ultimate sovereign Lordship over all things. They were promised to the Son of man, the Messiah, who for the time being, was to be made a little lower than the angels, on account of his manhood. Man at present is confessedly "a little lower than the angels." The object of the taking of the manhood, instead of the nature of angels, into God, is explained. It is, that the Messiah might be capable of death, as a propitiatory sacrifice, and so the declarations of all the prophets respecting a suffering Messiah might be fulfilled, and also, that he might be able to call us "brethren," and sympathise with the temptations and frailties incident to human nature. So it had been expressly declared by David and Isaiah. By his death and resurrection he has overcome death, and redeemed the souls of the believers from the slavish fear of death as well as from the power of the devil. The conditions of Christ's redemption are thus presented in miniature, so to speak. The irresistible inference to be drawn from all these minute fulfilments of the character of Christ the Messiah, as stipulated by the prophets from the beginning, is that Jesus is a faithful and reliable High Priest in things pertaining to God. His manhood, sufferings, and death, instead of awakening misgivings, are the irrefragable testimonies to the validity of his claims. Having thus particularly examined into the preliminary question, *What sort of a Christ or Messiah do the prophets lead us to expect?* the writer affectionately invites a more careful consideration of the personal apostleship (*i.e.*, mission) and High Priesthood of Jesus Christ, the profession of faith (ὁμολογία) in whose name his readers have adopted. The point insisted on is his exact conformity to the Divine intentions of God who appointed him (πιστὸν ὄντα τῷ ποιήσαντι αὐτόν), precisely as Moses was scrupulously exact in all his house, to carry out his instructions to the very letter.

Verses 1—4.—Wherefore, holy brethren, partakers of the heavenly calling, consider the Apostle and High Priest of our profession, Jesus Christ, that he was faithful to him who created him (a High Priest, *Qui ipsum constituit*, J. C. Wolfius), as Moses was in all his household (or œconomy). But the former (οὗτος, *Christ*) has been accounted worthy of (ἠξίωται, *i.e.*, *can claim as his due*) a greater glory than Moses; inasmuch as he who plans it has a greater honour than the house itself. For every house is planned by some person or other, but he who planned all things (τὰ πάντα, *the universes, and the scheme of man's redemption*) is God.

Now the writer has already shown (i. 10—12) that to Messiah is ascribed in Ps. cii. 25, &c., the glory of being the Eternal[1] Creator of all things, therefore Christ being God, is as immeasurably above Moses as the infinite over the finite, the Creator over the creature.

[1] Σὺ κατ' ἀρχὰς, κ.τ.λ., *i.e.*, *in primal ages.* In like manner Dr. M'Caul (*Mosaic Record of Creation*, *Aids to Faith*, sec. 7) observes how Onkelos in his Targum (Gen. i. 1) interprets בראשית by בקדמין, *in antiquities*, or *former times*, and also how the Hebrew ought properly (standing as it does without an article) to be translated "in beginning" in *Reshith*, and then adds, "The sum of all that has been said is, that "the words 'in the beginning' refer to 'time or duration,' not to *order*, "and thus, therefore, the first verse does not mean 'at first God created "'the heaven and the earth,' nor 'in the beginning of (our) creation he "'created the heavens and the earth,' but 'of old, in former duration, "'God created the heavens and the earth.' How long ago is not said. "The Hebrew word is indefinite, and can include millions or milliards "of years just as easily as thousands."

CHAP. III., 5—11.

Verses 5—11.—Moses, moreover, was faithful over all his house,[1] as a servant (he was only a steward of the things committed to him; his authority was a delegated one), to bear testimony to the things yet to be spoken (εἰς μαρτύριον τῶν λαληθησομένων).[2] But Christ as a Son over his own house (and therefore *with supreme authority*), whose house (or household) we are, if at least (ἐάνπερ, *provided that*) we hold fast the public profession and cheerful, frank avowal (τὴν παρρησίαν καὶ τὸ καύχημα) of our hope, unwaveringly (βεβαίαν) unto the end.[3] Wherefore (as the Holy Ghost saith, Ps. xcv. 7), To-day if ye will hear his voice, harden not your hearts, as in the provocation (παραπικρασμῷ, *embitterment*), as in the day of temptation in the wilderness.[4] (כמריבה כיום מסה במדבר *as at Meribah, as in the day of Massah in the wilderness*, where, by a rebellious want of faith in God's appointments, they provoked Him to wrath.) When (or *where*, οὗ, אשר) your fathers tempted me, proved me, and saw my works (פעלי *my work*, sing.) forty years.[5] Wherefore I was grieved (Διὸ προσώχθισα, *was indignant*) with that generation, and said,[6] They do always err in their heart, but they have not known my ways. So I sware in my wrath (Num. xiv. 28—30), They shall not enter into my rest. (מנוחתי *my rest*, this expression is not found in Numbers xiv., where the historical event is related, but is taken from the Inspired Commentary upon it, spoken by the Holy Ghost in Psalm xcv. 7—11.)

---

[1] Οἶκος here means *household, domestic economy*, in reference to the entire Mosaic dispensation. The Hebrew בית *house*, is repeatedly employed thus, e.g., Gen. xviii. 19, "his household after him" (ביתו, τῷ οἴκῳ αὐτοῦ, LXX.) Compare Num. xii. 6—8, which is here cited.

[2] That Moses did bear this testimony appears from Deut. xviii. 15—19:—" The Lord thy God will raise up unto thee a Prophet from "the midst of thee, of thy brethren, like unto me; unto him ye shall "hearken; according to all that thou desiredst of the Lord thy God "in Horeb in the day of the assembly (*i.e.*, a mediator to stand between

"God and man, and to speak in God's name), saying, Let me not hear "again the voice of the Lord my God, neither let me see this great fire "any more, that I die not. And the Lord said unto me, They have "well spoken that which they have spoken. I will raise them up a "Prophet from among their brethren, like unto thee, and I will put "my words in his mouth; and he shall speak unto them all that I shall "command him. And it shall come to pass, that whosoever will not "hearken unto my words which he shall speak in my name, I will "require it of him." (אנכי אדרש מעמו, ἐγὼ ἐκδικήσω ἐξ αὐτοῦ, LXX.) The personal pronoun is emphatic in this concluding clause, which in Acts iii. 23 is paraphrased, ἐξολοθρευθήσεται ἐκ τοῦ λαοῦ. The verb דרש *he required, sought after*, in Gen. ix. 5, xlii. 22, Deut. xxiii. 21 (22), Ps. ix. 12 (13), Ezek. xxxiii. 6, has the signification of *exacting the extreme penalty, punishing to the uttermost, enforcing a claim with rigorous severity*.

³ Any wavering, or false shame in the profession of Christianity would be next door to a denial of Christ, and but a step removed from apostasy, inasmuch as it would indicate a hesitating and halting faith. It was a time for decision, and not for compromise, even as Christ declared, "He that is not with me is against me; and he that gathereth not with me scattereth abroad." (Matt. xii. 30.)

⁴ "And he called the name of the place Massah, and Meribah, "because of the chiding of the children of Israel, and because they "tempted the Lord, saying, Is the Lord among us, or not?" (Exod. xvii. 7.) See also Num. xx. 10; Deut. vi. 16, 17. The refusal to hearken to Jesus, and the questioning his Divine authority, would be a sin and provocation of a similar kind.

⁵ The Hebrew reads, "Forty years long was I grieved," אקוט, or *lothed;* and so also the LXX, " τεσσαράκοντα ἔτη προσώχθισα instead "of Διὸ προσώχθισα."

⁶ 'Αεὶ πλανῶνται, κ.τ.λ. The above quotation differs from the Hebrew, which reads עם תעי לבב הם "a people erring in heart are they"; it also varies slightly from the LXX, besides the important variation already noticed.

Verses 12—15.—Wherefore (see Διὸ of verse 7) take heed, (βλέπετε) brethren,

(continues the writer, with such a terrible example of neglected privilege and unbelief before your eyes in the rejection of your forefathers)

lest there be in any of you an evil heart of unbelief, in ot ·postatising (ἐν τῷ ἀποστῆναι, sc., as some of your number have already done) from the living God. (Their fathers had asked, "Is the Lord among us, or not?" Exod. xvii. 7.) But exhort one another daily (παρακαλεῖτε, so in Mal. iii. 16, "They that feared the Lord spake often, נדברו, one to another"), while it is called "To day" (as in Ps. xcv. 7); lest any of you be hardened by the deceitfulness of sin (*i.e.*, the specious sophisms and plausible reasonings of the unbelieving Jews).—For we have been made partakers of Christ (μέτοχοι γὰρ γεγόναμεν τοῦ Χριστοῦ, *i.e.*, of his rest), if we only hold fast the commencement of our profession (τὴν ἀρχὴν τῆς ὑποστάσεως, *i.q.*, τὴν πρώτην πίστιν, Stuart) stedfast to the end—(I say, exhort one another), in respect to what has been said,[1] "To DAY if ye will hear his voice, harden not your hearts, as in the provocation."

[1] ἐν τῷ λέγεσθαι. Formulam allegationis, ἐν τῷ λέγεσθαι, quod attinet, ea convenit cum Hebræa באמר, *in eo quod ille dicit*, nempe Scriptura, sive Scripturæ auctor, qua formula veteres Hebræorum doctores uti solent, quando sensus loci prima fronte non satis clarus est, sed majori elucidatione indiget. Surenhus. Βιβλ. καταλλ., p. 616.

The writer quotes the first words of the passage again, to make the subject of the mutual exhortations which he enjoins upon them, more clearly understood.

Verses 16—19.—For some,[1] although they did hear, provoked (God). Howbeit not all (ἐν τοῖς πλείοσιν, *the majority*, 1 Cor. x. 5) who came out of Egypt by Moses. But with whom was he grieved forty years?[2] Was it not with those who sinned (trespassed on various occasions and were destroyed), whose carcases fell in the wilderness?[3] And to whom sware he, in his wrath, that they should not enter into his rest, but to those who disbelieved (and, in consequence, refused to obey, ἀπειθήσασι). We see, then, that they could not enter in because of unbelief (δι᾽ ἀπιστίαν).[4]

[1] Professor Stuart, followed by Alford, proposes (with doubtful advantage, I would submit) to translate verse 16, τίνες (not τινὲς) γὰρ ἀκούσαντες, κ.τ.λ., with Griesbach, Dindorff, Tittmann, and others, interrogatively, e.g., "Who now were they, that when they heard, did provoke ? Nay, did "not all (ἀλλ'οὐ πάντες, κ.τ.λ) who came out of Egypt unto Moses ?" and then he says, " He means to intimate by this, that the number who "embrace error cannot sanction it; nor can unanimity in unbelief "render it any more excusable. Consequently, that the great body of "the Jews rejected the Messiah at the time then present, and urged "the Christian converts to do the same, would be no excuse for apostasy. "Πάντες is not to be taken in the strict metaphysical or mathematical "sense here any more than in multitudes of other places......Of the "adults, only Caleb and Joshua among the Israelites are excepted, as "not having taken part in the murmurings against the Lord (Num. "xiv. 30). Of course there could be no scruples in the Apostle's mind "about applying the word πάντες in this case, just as it is applied in a "multitude of others, viz., to designate great multitudes, or the great "majority." The learned Professor, in his above quoted remarks upon πάντες, seems to supply the best reason for rejecting his own interpretation of the passage. Besides, although the sin of Israel in the wilderness, was so widespread as to call for a signal and national punishment, by which all the adults were excluded from Canaan, we have no reason to suppose that all, who shared in their kinsmen's punishment, were guilty of the same offence. The majority were, and with " τοῖς πλείοσιν," St. Paul tells us, "God was not well pleased," and yet the whole nation suffered. Again, " the rest" alluded to, and to which the disobedient did not attain, was God's spiritual rest. They were cut off in their sins; but it is altogether incredible that all the adults, or even a majority of them, were doomed to forfeiture of salvation, upon the occasion of their exclusion from Canaan. The passage of the Epistle to the Hebrews in question, ought to be read by the light of 1 Cor. x. 1—12, where St. Paul specifies some of the occasions upon which prompt excision fell upon the guilty, and tells how they were "overthrown in the wilderness" (κατεστρώθησαν γὰρ ἐν τῇ ἐρήμῳ). The point upon which the writer to the Hebrews here insists is the same as that insisted on by Paul to the Corinthians, viz., that it is possible to commence by enjoying the highest privileges, and yet to fall short. Such privileges were vouchsafed to all who came out of Egypt. Some profited by them, yet others fell deservedly short, because of their faithlessness and perverse rebellion.

[2] Τεσσαράκοντα ἔτη. Surenhusius, with a fanciful elegance, observes that the Apostle specifies the forty years of provocation in

CHAP. IV., 1—3.   41

the wilderness, because a like period had nearly elapsed since the rejection and crucifixion of Christ, and did actually elapse before the destruction of Jerusalem. *Ibid.*, p. 617.

³ Ὧν τὰ κῶλα, κ.τ.λ. Compare Num. xiv. 29, במדבר הזה יפלו פגריכם, ἐν τῇ ἐρήμῳ ταύτῃ πεσεῖται τὰ κῶλα ὑμῶν. LXX. See also verse 32.

⁴ Respicit locum Numer. xiv. 11. עד אנה לא יאמינו בי, *Quo usque non credetis mihi.*—Schoettg. *in loc.*

CHAPTER IV.

ATTENTION has now been drawn to the exact fulfilment by Jesus Christ of his Messianic functions, and of the requirements of the prophetic writings. Like Moses he was faithful to the letter of his Commission. He was greater than Moses, because Moses had only a delegated and ministerial authority. The Rabbies taught with one voice that Messiah would be greater than Moses. (See Note 4, p. 28.) As the Church in the wilderness was Moses's household, so true believers are Christ's. But, as many of the adults who came out of Egypt* perished in their sins, and were not permitted to

* The Talmudical writers interpreted this 11th verse of Ps. xcv., of the fruition of heaven, as appears from the following extract from the Treatise, *Sanhedrin*, col. 274. (*Ugolini Thes.*, vol. xxv.):—

דור המדבר אין להן חלק לעולם הבא ואינן רואין לעתיד לבוא. שאמר במדבר הזה יתמו ושם ימותו. יתמו בעולם הזה. ושם ימותו לעתיד לבוא. וכן הוא אומר אשר נשבעתי באפי אם יבאון אל מנוחתי.

" The generation of the wilderness have no part in the world to come.
" For it is said (Num. xiv. 35), *In this wilderness they shall be consumed,*
" *and there shall they die. They shall be consumed,* in this world : *and*
" *there shall they die,* in the world to come. And this also is meant by
" what is said (Ps. xcv. 11), *To whom I sware in my wrath, if they should*
" *enter into my rest.*"

Rabbi Akiba, nevertheless, following Rabbi Eliezer, qualifies this sentence of excision in favour of those saints who had made a covenant with God by sacrifice. (See Psalm l. 5.) Others, again (*ibid.*, col. 275), argue from Is. xxxv. 10, that God will repent of his oath.

G

enter God's spiritual rest (*i.e.*, the future blessedness of the Redeemed), besides being excluded from Canaan, so also there is a danger now, that through unbelief, and a rebellious rejection of the "words of life" as spoken by Jesus, those who are nominally of his household should apostatize, and fall back into condemnation. The patient forbearance of God is not for ever. Those who do not like to retain Him in their knowledge, but hold the truth in unrighteousness, He gives over to a reprobate mind. The Hebrews are therefore urged to admonish one another, and to remember that all God's offers to the sinner are for "To day." To him who will continue in sin, that grace may abound, there are no promises held out of ultimate amendment. Such as these do provoke the Lord to cut them off. To the believers God will give "his rest," but the persistent cavillers and the unbelieving shall be shut out. We see, therefore, that *unbelief* was the capital sin, which revoked the offer of "rest" in the case of the disobedient and disbelieving Israelites.

Verse 1.—Let us, therefore, fear (iv. 1) lest, although the same offer has been extended to our times, viz., of entering into his rest ($εἰσελθεῖν\ εἰς\ τὴν\ κατάπαυσιν\ αὐτοῦ$), any of you should seem to fail in attaining to it.

The writer shows how a restless and dissatisfied temper, a halting conviction arising out of an undisciplined and disobedient frame of mind, is the natural prelude and parent to apostasy.

Verses 2, 3.—For we have received the glad tidings (of

CHAP. IV., 4—10. 43

spiritual rest, ἐσμεν εὐηγγελισμένοι, i.e., the offer of salvation) as well as they, but the word of hearing (ὁ λόγος τῆς ἀκοῆς,[1] *the matter of hearing*, i.e., the *fact that they heard*) was of no avail, not being conjoined with faith, in the hearers. But we (i.e., all of us, οἱ πιστεύσαντες) who have believed do enter into the rest (τὴν κατάπαυσιν) aforesaid of God (as He has told us, " As I sware in my wrath, that they should not enter into MY REST"), although (καίτοι)[2] the works (of creation) were finished (so long ago as) at the foundation of the world. (Gen. ii. 1—3.)

[1] Philipp. iv. 15, " εἰς λόγον δόσεως καὶ λήψεως."
[2] Prof. Stuart renders, iu his Translation, p. 251, καίτοι, *namely*, "As He says, 'So I sware in my wrath [unbelievers] shall not enter " 'into my rest,' namely, [rest from] the works which had been " performed after the foundation of the world was laid ;" but in his Commentary, p. 339, " The works that were done after the world was " founded." The Vulgate has, " Et quidem operibus ab institutione " mundi perfectis." The object, however, of the writer is plainly as follows :—God's rest commenced after the works of creation were finished, and yet, by the mouth of David, God intimates that it was still possible to enter into that primal REST. It was not the rest which Joshua gave, for, when David wrote, the people were in Canaan ; and yet David specifies a day, TO DAY, plainly intimating that the rest was neither past or present, but future, and heavenly.

In support of his assertion that the rest offered to the believers is that σαββατισμὸς which God instituted for all succeeding time, after the works of creation were finished, the writer quotes two passages. The first (Gen. ii. 2) relates the historical fact of its institution, the second (Ps. xcv. 11) declares that this was the rest, viz., GOD'S REST, from which the rebels in the wilderness were excluded, e.g.

Verses 4—10.—For He hath spoken in a certain place, concerning the seventh day, thus :—AND GOD RESTED ON THE SEVENTH DAY FROM ALL HIS WORKS. And in this place again :—IF THEY SHALL ENTER INTO MY REST. Since, therefore, it remains that some may enter into it, and those to whom the glad offer was formerly (οἱ πρότερον εὐαγγελισθέντες) made did not enter in by reason of unbelief—(again He specifies (ὁρίζει) a particular day; that is, To DAY; saying, by David, after so great an interval of time (nearly 500 years), "*To day*, if ye will "hear his voice, harden not your hearts" : for if Joshua had given them rest, He (*i.e.*, God) would not have spoken of another day afterwards)—it is plain, then, that a Sabbatic rest (σαββατισμὸς) remaineth for the people of God. For the man who enters into His (God's) rest, has rested also from his labours, just as God did from his.[1]

[1] The Talmudical treatise *Berachoth*, fol. 17, col. 1, illustrates in a remarkable manner the nature of the Σαββατισμὸς expected by the ancient Jewish Church :—

מרגליתא בפומיה דרב׳ לא כעולם הזה העולם הבא אין בו לא אכילה ולא שתייה לא
פריות ורבייה לא משא ומתן לא שנאה וקנאה ולא תחרות אלה הצדיקים יושבים ועטרותיהם
בראשיהם ונהגין מזיו השכינה.

"A frequent apothegm (*Margarita*—a pearl, a choice saying) was in "the mouth of a certain Rabbi :—'The world to come is not like this "'world, for in the latter there is neither eating nor drinking, nor "'marriage (lit. *procreation of children*; see Luke xx. 34, 1 Cor. xi. 13), "'nor increasing, nor trafficking, nor hate, nor envy, nor heartburnings, "'but the just shall sit with their crowns on their heads, and enjoy "'the splendour of the Shechinah.'" See J. Rhenferd, *Diss. i.*, *de Seculo Futuro*, p. 1120 (Meuschen).

Verses 11—13.—Let us, therefore, give all diligence (σπουδάσωμεν) to enter into that rest, lest any one fall away after the same example of unbelief; for the Word of God is quick (ζῶν),[1] and mighty in operation (ἐνεργὴς) (see Isaiah xlix. 2, "He hath made my mouth like a sharp "sword," lv. 10, 11; and also Ps. xxix. 4, &c.), and more trenchant[2] than any two-edged sword, and penetrates even to dividing of soul and spirit, and of the joints and marrow, and is a trier (κριτικὸς) of the thoughts and intents of the heart, and there is no creature invisible to his regards. But all things are naked (γυμνὰ), and exposed to the searching scrutiny[3] (τετραχηλισμένα τοῖς ὀφθαλμοῖς) of Him with whom we have to do (*or*, to account, πρὸς ὃν ἡμῖν ὁ λόγος).

CHAP. IV., 11—13. 45

¹ Ἴδε τὸν ἀνθεστῶτα ἐξαναντίας θεοῦ λόγον ἐνωπλισμένον, παρ' ὃν τό, τε εὖ καὶ τὸ μή, συμβέβηκε τελειοῦσθαι. "Behold him that resists the armed "Word of God, by whom what is good, or the contrary, is brought to "pass."—Philo, *De Cherubim*, *ibid.*, Works, Mangey's Edit., vol. i., 145.

² Τομώτερος. Philo uses very similar language (*Quis rerum Divinarum Hœres*, *Works*, Mangey's Edit., vol. i., p. 491) on Gen. xv. 10 :—Εἶτ' ἐπιλέγει, Διεῖλεν αὐτὰ μέσα, τὸ τίς οὐ προσθεὶς, ἵνα τὸν ἀδίδακτον ἐννοῇς θεὸν τέμνοντα, τὰς τε τῶν σωμάτων καὶ πραγμάτων ἑξῆς ἁπάσας ἡρμόσθαι καὶ ἡνῶσθαι δοκούσας φύσεις, τῷ τομεῖ τῶν συμπάντων αὐτοῦ λόγῳ. ὃς εἰς τὴν ὀξυτάτην ἀκονηθεὶς ἀκμὴν, διαιρῶν οὐδέποτε λήγει τὰ αἰσθητὰ πάντα, ἐπειδὰν δὲ μέχρι τῶν ἀτόμων καὶ λεγομένων ἀμερῶν διεξέλθῃ, πάλιν ἀπὸ τούτων, τὰ λόγῳ θεωρητὰ εἰς ἀμυθήτους καὶ ἀπεριγράφους μοίρας ἄρχεται διαιρεῖν οὗτος ὁ τομεὺς, κ.τ.λ. "He says, moreover, *And he divided them through* "*the midst*. He does not add *who* did it, in order that you may under- "stand that it is the undemonstrable God, who cuts asunder the con- "stituent parts of all bodies and objects that appear to be coherent and "united, by his Word, that penetrates all things. Which, being whetted "to the keenest possible edge, never ceases to pierce all things that can "be appreciated by the senses. But because it reaches even to the "minutest particles, even to those that are termed indivisible, the "above mentioned penetrating Word suffices to divide things which "can be appreciated by reason alone, into untold and indescribable "portions, &c. And again, *ibid.*, p. 506, Ὅ, τε γὰρ θεῖος λόγος, τὰ ἐν τῇ "φύσει διεῖλε, καὶ διένειμε πάντα. Ὅ, τε ἡμέτερος νοῦς, ἅττ' ἂν παραλάβῃ "νοητῶς πράγματά τε καὶ σώματα, εἰς ἀπειράκις ἄπειρα διαιρεῖ μέρη, καὶ "τέμνων οὐδέποτε λήγει. Τοῦτο δὲ συμβαίνει, διὰ τὴν πρὸς τὸν ποιητὴν καὶ "πατέρα τῶν ὅλων ἐμφέρειαν. For the Divine Word has pierced and divided "all things in nature. Even our own mind never ceases to divide what "objects or bodies it may have apprehended, into an infinite and un- "appreciable number of particles. But this happens on account of the "resemblance to the Father and Maker of all things."

So, also, Philo declares, in very kindred sentiment to that of the writer to the Hebrews, ὁ θεῖος λόγος ὀξυδέρκεστός ἐστιν, ὡς πάντα ἐφορᾶν εἶναι ἱκανός. "The Divine Word is so sharpsighted, as to be "able to inspect all things."—*SS. Legum Alleg.*, lib. iii., *ibid.*, p. 121.

³ καὶ τετραχ. κ.τ.λ.; *lit.*, with head drawn back and face upturned. J. C. Wolfius writes, *in loco* (*Curæ Phil. et Crit.*, tom. iv., p. 647), "*Et supine exposita oculis ejus*. Ita optime E. Schmidius, vel quod "idem est, *resupinata*, ut J. Perizonius ad Aeliani Var. Hist., xii. 58, "et cum eo Elsnerus, p. 342, reddunt. Atque hic quidem hoc loquendi "genus ab iis ait petitum, quorum capita reclinantur, ne intuentium 'oculos effugiant et lateant. Ita Plinius, *Panegyr.*, cap. 37, de iis qui "hoc habitu ad supplicium ducebantur. *Nihil tamen gratius, nihil* "*seculo dignius, quam quod contingit, desuper intueri delatorum supina*

"*ora retortasque cervices.* Hinc Hesychius :—Τετραχηλισμένα, πεφα-
νερωμένα, et Plutarchus, *de Curiositate,* p. 521. Τραχηλιζομένους
καὶ περιαγομένους curiosos appellat, qui oculos elatos huc illuc con-
vertunt et res circumspiciunt. Eandem sententiam adstruit J. Alberti,
p. 422."

Here, then, the writer terminates his commonitory digression, which extends from chap. iii. 6 to iv. 13. We must bear in mind that it is based upon the proof of the superiority of Christ's authority to that of Moses, and is, in substance, to the following effect :—" If your fathers perished for disobeying "Moses, much greater is *your* danger, if you refuse "obedience to Christ."

Verses 14—16.—Having, therefore, a great High Priest, who has passed into the heavens (in accordance with Ps. cx. 1), Jesus the Son of God (he continues), let us hold fast the profession of our faith (κρατῶμεν τῆς ὁμολογίας, *i.e.,* of Christianity). For we have not an high priest who cannot be touched with the feeling of (sympathise with) our infirmities,[1] but was tempted, in all things, similarly to ourselves, without sin.[2] Let us therefore draw near with boldness (παῤῥησίας, confident assurance) to the throne of his grace (where He sits on the right hand of the Father, Ps. cx. 1), in order that we may receive compassionate pity, and find grace to help in time of need (εἰς εὔκαιρον βοήθειαν, for a *timely succour or assistance*). See Schoettg., tom. i., pp. 645, 646.

[1] Danzius (*De λύτρῳ Redemptionis Humanæ ad* 1 Pet. i. 18, 19, p. 843) observes, "Sic etiam vocatur Messias Servus Dei, Jes. xlii. 1, ubi iterum Chaldæus, הא עברי משיחא *ecce servus meus Messias,* et R. Dav. Kimchi inquit, והו מלך המשיח *hic est Rex Messias.*"— Meuschen, *N. Test. ex Talmude illustr.* This passage of Isaiah (verses 1—4) are referred to our Lord Jesus Christ, in reference to his Divine sympathy with human infirmity, by St. Matthew xii. 15—21.

[2] Χωρὶς ἁμαρτίας. As being sinless, our High Priest has perpetual access to God. He need not wait for the Day of Atonement to come round, before he can draw near to seek relief for his people. He can

always obtain timely succour for us, and by Him, we can always approach the throne of grace; so superior is the Messianic dispensation of substance and reality, over the Levitical one of type and shadow.
" Neque Messias Sacerdos solum est, sed et ipsum quoque sacrificium.
" Tikkune Sohar, c. 18, fol. 28, 1. *Prophetæ reliqui non potuerunt*
" *ascendere ad videndum Regem, nisi horis et diebus notis, quemadmodum*
" *de Aarone constat, qui tamen præcipuus omnium fuit, de quo* Levit.
" xvi. 2. Non omni tempore veniat ad sanctum; *verum* v. 3. בואה,
" cum hoc veniat Aharon ad sanctum: *quanto igitur minus reliqui.*
" *Tu vero, O Pastor fidelis, singulis horis et diebus, quibus voluisti, ad Regem*
" *videndum ascendisti. Ibidem,* c. 20, fol. 47, 2. *Schechina inferior est*
" *suffitus Dei S.B., sacrificium ejus, altare ejus: in illa enim Israelitæ cibos*
" *sacrificiorum,* h.e. *preces ad Deum S.B. instruunt, quippe quæ sunt instar*
" *sacrificiorum matutinorum et vespertinorum, et sicut frusta sacrificiorum,*
" *quæ per totam noctem consumuntur. Ille qui Justus est, est* קרבן מוסף
" *sacrificium intra tempus matutinum, et meridianum, est sacrificium*
" *Sabbathorum et dierum Festorum,* דלית קריבו לעמא קדשא לק״בה נשבח ויום טוב,
" אלא בה: *Non enim accessus est populo sancto ad Deum S.B. nisi per illud.*
" בואה. Per hoc veniet Aaron ad sancta. *Et,* nemo glorietur, nisi
" בואה. Sohar Numer., fol. 103, col. 412. *Quomodo sanatio hominum*
" *comparata est?* Resp. *Ad modum vituli.* (Interpretatio additur,
" nescio a quo profecta: *Intelliguntur passiones, quas Messias pro nobis*
" *sustinet.) Sic enim legitur* Jesa. xxvii. 18. *Ibi pascet* vitulus, *et ibi*
" *cubabit. Priori commate intelligitur Messius filius Josephi, de quo*
" *legitur,* Deuter. xxxiii. 17. Primogenitus bovis ejus gloria est ipsi.
" *Posteriori autem Messias filius Davidis.*" Schoettg. *Hor. Hebr.,*
tom. ii., pp. 645, 646. This fiction of the two Messiahs is found in the Targum on Song of Sol. iv. 5.

CHAPTER V.

Christ's Messiahship has now been proved to be a valid one. He is, agreeably to the prophetic declarations, human as well as Divine. He has a right to be heard as a teacher, and to abrogate the ceremonial appointments of Moses, because he comes in his own hereditary right as a Son to speak of his own things. In Psalm cx., which proclaims his Divinity, his high priesthood is put forward as an equally prominent attribute. Here, then, one of the most formidable Jewish objections against

Christianity is disposed of, viz., You abrogate the Levitic priesthood, you do away with the ancient sacrifices, and give us nothing in their place;—whereas, Moses has expressly declared (Levit. xvii. 11), "It is the blood that maketh an atone-"ment for the soul," and has also enjoined upon us for an "everlasting statute" that the high priest shall bring the blood of the sin-offering within the veil, "to make an atonement for the children of Israel, "for all their sins, once a year." (Levit. xvi. 15, 34.) The answer is plain and conclusive. If Jesus can properly claim to be the Divine Son of David spoken of in Ps. cx., He is also "a priest for ever, after the "order of Melchisedek;" for so, also, it is written in the same Psalm, "Jehovah hath sworn, and will "not repent, Thou art a priest for ever, after the "order of Melchisedek." (על דברתי מלכי־צדק, κατὰ τὴν τάξιν. κ.τ.λ. LXX.) *

* The Rev. G. Phillipps, D.D., in his introductory remarks on Ps. cx., writes as follows :—"By far the greater part of the elder Rabbis "have determined that it (Ps. cx.) treats of the Messiah. Thus the "Midrash Tehillim in Ps. ii., on the words, *I will declare the decree*, "&c., saith, 'מסופרים הם עניני של המשיח וגו', *The affairs of the Messiah are* "*set forth in the Scriptures of the Law, of the Prophets, and of the* "*Hagiographa. In the Law*, Ex. iv. 22 ; *in the Prophets*, Is. lii. 13, "and xlii. 1; *and in the Hagiographa.* Ps. cx., '*The Lord said unto my* "*Lord.*' The Editor of the Venice edition, it must be stated, has, "with a true Jewish spirit, erased the words, עניני של המשיח. Again, "on Ps. xviii. 35, '*Thy right hand shall uphold me*,' the Midrash has "the following note :—'רבי יודן בשם רבי חמא לעתיד לבא וגו', *Rabbi Joden, in* "*the name of R. Kama, said, that in the time to come, i.e.*, in the age of "Messiah, the Holy One (blessed be He !) will make King Messiah to "sit at his right hand, *as it is said*, ' *The Lord said unto my Lord, Sit* "*on my right hand.*' R. Gaon, on Dan. vii. 13, ' *He came with the* "*clouds of heaven*,' saith, *and this is* צדקנו משיח, *Messiah, our Righteous-* "*ness, as it is said*, ' *The Lord said to my Lord*,' &c." The Psalms in Hebrew, with a Commentary, vol. ii., pp. 417, 418.

It being granted, then, that Messiah was to be a High Priest, the next question to be answered is, what had Jesus to offer? To this difficulty the writer adverts in the opening verse of this fifth chapter. The Talmud speaks as follows of the High Priesthood of Messiah (*Tr. Avoth.*, cap. 34): —" Aaron and Messiah are to be understood by " *These are the two anointed ones* (בני היצהר, *sons of* " *oil*) *that stand by the Lord of the whole earth.* " (Zech. iv. 14.) But no one knew which of them " was the dearest. Since, however, it is said (Ps. " cx. 4), *The Lord hath sworn, and will not repent,* " *Thou art a priest for ever*, thou mayest know " that king Messiah is dearer than the priest of " justice." The Rabbinic writers assert that Michael, who is the same as the ANGEL OF THE LORD and the ANGEL OF THE COVENANT, is the High Priest above. In the *Schemoth Rabba*, sect. 2, fol. 104, 3, it is said, " *Wherever Michael appeared,* " הוא כבוד שכינה *it was the glory of the Schechina.*" He is also called " *Metatron.*" Schoettgen, commenting on the Divine appellation הקדוש ברוך הוא, THE HOLY ONE, BLESSED BE HE, remarks that the Jewish writers apply this designation to the Messiah, *e.g., Sohar* Genes., fol. 63, col. 249, ומלכא משיחא דאתקרא בשמא ד"קבה " *And king Messiah, who is called* " *by the name of the Holy One, blessed be He.*" In the same work, fol. 76, col. 301, and 77, col. 305, the words of Genesis iii. 15, " *He shall bruise thy* " *head,*" which are elsewhere interpreted of the Messiah, are there applied to THE HOLY ONE,

BLESSED BE HE. Again, it is written in *Bereshith Rabba*, sect. 5, fol. 63, " *The voice which came to* " *Moses at that time, and said to him* (Deut. xxxii. " 48), Come up to Mount Abarim, *was that of the* " *Holy One, blessed be He, the Metatron,* של ה״קבה מטטרון.*"* And again, " *The voice of the Holy One,* " *blessed be He, the Metatron, came to the waters."* As it is said, Ps. xxix. 3, " The voice of the Lord is " upon the waters." See Schoettg. *Horæ Hebr.*, tom. ii., p. 8; also, pp. 110, 247, 298, 354, 642; also, tom. 1, p. 1218—1220. The *Jalkut Rubeni*, fol. 112, 2, asserts that the High Priest Michael " *stands and offers the souls of the just,* ומקריב " נפשותיהן של צדיקים, *that is the sacrifices, which are* " *offered in the earthly temple, and they are the souls* " *of the beasts that are offered, and are called the* " *souls of the just, because they have taken away their* " *sins."* For further information on this curious and interesting subject, the reader would do well to consult J. A. Danzius' remarkable treatise, *Schechina cum piis habitans*. It is printed at length on pp. 701 —739 of Meuschen, *Nov. Test. ex Talmude illustr.* See also the *Præterita præteritorum* of B. Scheidius, *ibid.*, p. 13.

Verses 1—9.—For every High Priest taken from amongst men[1] is appointed on behalf of men, in reference to their relations to God,[2] for the express purpose (ἵνα) that he may offer gifts (δῶρα, sc., *freewill offerings* *) and sacrifices,

---

* Professor Stuart, I think erroneously, suggests "thankofferings." Expiatory sacrifices are here the topic under consideration. Dr. Gill has, " Freewill-offerings, peace-offerings, burnt-offerings, sin and " trespass-offerings, all kind of sacrifices."

CHAP. V., 1—9.   51

(θυσίας), being in a position to treat with gentle moderation and sympathy (μετριοπαθεῖν δυνάμενος) those who are ignorant and out of the way[3] (i.e., those who have erred unwittingly), inasmuch as he himself is compassed with infirmity. And on account of this (infirmity of his nature, διὰ ταύτην), he must needs offer expiatory sacrifices for himself, as well as for the people. Moreover, no one assumes to himself this honour (intrudes himself into the priesthood), except he be called thereto by God, as was Aaron. (See the case of Nadab and Abihu, Levit. x. 1, of Korah and his sons, Numb. xvi., of King Uzziah, 2 Chron. xxvi. 16—21.) So, also, Christ glorified not himself by assuming the Highpriestly functions, but He who said unto him (Ps. ii. 7), " Thou art my Son : this day have I " begotten thee." As He also says in another place (Ps. cx. 4), " Thou art a priest for ever, after the order of " Melchisedek."[4] Who, in the days of his flesh, after that He had offered up prayers and intercessions, with strong cryings and tears (e.g., at Gethsemane) to Him that was able to save him from death,[5] and was heard on account of his pious submission (ἀπὸ τῆς εὐλαβείας[6]—or perhaps better, with Stuart, *from that which he feared*), although He was SON, learned obedience from the things that He suffered, and, having been made complete[7] (Stuart, *when exalted to glory*, but I think this does violence to the context), became the author (αἴτιος, *originator*) of eternal salvation to all those that obey Him.

[1] Schoettgen asserts that there is an allusion to Levit. xxi. 10, וכהן הגדול מאחיו, "and the High Priest from amongst his brethren ;" a distinction which appears in the LXX., ἀπὸ τῶν ἀδελφῶν: the Vulgate, however, reads, "inter fratres suos"—"der aus den Menschen genom-" men wird."—*Luth.*

[2] ὑπὲρ ἀνθρώπων καθίσταται τὰ πρὸς τὸν Θεόν. Wolfius says, *i.e.*, "*Pro hominibus constituitur in iis, quæ apud Deum sunt agenda*, ut "Beza et Schmidius : h.e., *ut rem divinam faciat, sacra procuret, et* "*populi loco ad Deum accedat*. Ita phrasin recte exponit Elsnerus, et

"huc commode advocat verba Jethronis ad Mosen Exod. xviii. 19,
"γίνου σὺ τῷ λαῷ τὰ πρὸς τὸν Θεὸν, καὶ ἀνοίσεις τοὺς λόγους αὐτῶν πρὸς
"τὸν Θεόν. Sic vero etiam externos scriptores loqui idem aliquot locis
"ostendit. Inter hos est Juliani ille in Fragmento pag. 296. *Sacerdotes*
"*honorandi sunt*, ὡς διακονοῦντες ἡμῖν τὰ πρὸς τοὺς θεοὺς, *utpote qui rem*
"*divinam administrant.*"
³ Μετριοπαθεῖν δυνάμενος, " *Qui possit, quantum satis est, miserari vicem.*
"Ita Schmidius et Beza. Verbi vim ita exposuit Camerarius, ut idem
"esse dicat, atque ὑπὸ ἐπιεικείας τινὶ συμπάσχειν, *alterius malis affici, eo*
"*quod non rigide et severe, sed humaniter et placide de aliis judices, tanquam*
"*si tua ipsius res ageretur, ut qui te putes eadem conditione.* Atque ita
"Hesychius, qui μετριοπαθῆ reddit μικρὰ πάσχοντα, et συγγινώσκοντα
"ἐπιεικῶς. Photius in Lexico M.S. μετριοπαθεῖν, ἐκ μέρους τὰ πάθη
"καταδέχεσθαι, συγγινώσκειν. Stephano in Thesauro non aliud esse
"videtur, quam antecedens iv. 15, συμπαθῆσαι, vel συμπαθῆσαι μετὰ
"μετριοπαθείας. Conf. J. C. Dieterici *Antiq. Bibl.*, vol. ii., p. 20, et Jac.
"Cappelli Observationes, qui vertit : *moderate ferre.* Fortasse per vocem
"μέτριος in verbo hoc composito respicitur eo, ut inferatur, τὸ συμπαθεῖν
"decere sacerdotem. Μέτρια enim Græcis passim dicuntur τὰ πρέποντα,
"et μετρίως λέγειν, apud Platonem et Thucydidem est, *commode* et pro
"rei dignitate dicere. Vide Grævii notas ad Hesiodi *Εργ.* v. 306, p. 33.
"Cappellus l.c. δυνάμενος idem esse putat quod ὀφείλων, ut 2 Cor. xiii. 8.
"Præstat autem in consueto verbi significatu persistere, cum statim
"addatur causa, unde illa facultus ad eum proficiscatur, nempe ex eo
"quod ipse infirmitatem habeat, eamque adeo sentiat." J. C. Wolfius,
in loc. Luther translates the 15th verse, " Denn wir haben nicht einen
"Hohenpriester, der nicht könnte Mitleiden haben mit unserer
"Schwachheit, sondern der versucht ist allenthalben, gleichwie wir,
"doch ohne Sünde."

⁴ Schoettgen, on Matt. xxii. 44, acutely observes that nothing more
clearly demonstrates that Ps. cx. treats of the Messiah than the silence
of the Jews with whom our Lord was disputing, for they might have
replied, " Thou sayest what is false, and seekest to deceive us by thy
"quotation, or the Psalm does not treat of the Messiah, and none of
"our Doctors ever so explained it." Schoettgen might have put his
case more forcibly still, for, from Mark xii. 35, it is plain that our Lord
alleged a known Rabbinic interpretation, " How say the Scribes that
"Christ is the Son of David ? For David himself said, The Lord said
"to my Lord," &c. Dr. Gill, on Ps. cx. 1, remarks :—" The Targum
"is, *The Lord said in his Word.* Galatinus says the true Targum of
"Jonathan has it, *The Lord said to his Word*, and produces an autho-
"rity for it." The ancient Rabbinical doctors agreed with the Chris-

tian interpretation, although the *Vetus Nizzachon* (p. 183) absurdly argues that the Psalm relates to David's persecution by Saul. Saul is the enemy to be put under David's feet, and the invitation addressed by Jehovah to David to sit on his throne is to be read by the light of Ps. cix. 31, " He shall stand at the right hand of the poor ! " A lamer evasion and perversion of the palpable signification of this Scripture can scarcely be imagined. Schoettgen supplies the following examples of early Jewish interpretations in accordance with the Christian rendering of the Psalm ; *Midrasch Tehillim* on Ps. cx. 1 :—" Dixit R. Judan " nomine R. Channa fil. Chanina לעתיד לבא מושיב הק׳׳בה למלך המשיח לימינו "Temporibus N. T. Deus S. B. Messiam (regem) sedere jubebit ad " dextram, et Abrahamum ad sinistram suam. *Bereschith Rabba*, sect. " 85, fol. 83, 4, ad Genes. xxxviii. 18 מטך baculum tuum ; *Intelligitur* " *Rex Messias, quemadmodum de eo dicitur*, Ps. cx. 3. Virgam virtutis " tuæ emittet Dominus ex Sion. In *Sohar* Numer., fol. 99, col. 394, " paullo aliter explicant: Dixit Dominus Domino meo, *i.e.*, דא צדיק לקבליה " משיח בן יוסף *Ille Justus* (Jacobus, de quo ibi sermo est) *dixit ad Messiam* "*filium Joseph:* Sede a dextris meis." *Hor. Hebr.*, tom. i., p. 192. Schoettgen (*ibid.*, p. 949), modestly asserts (on Heb. v. 6) that he has been unable to meet with any passage in Jewish writers that alleges Melchizedek to be a type of the Messiah :—" Quantum nos Judæorum " scripta pervolvimus, nemo eorum unquam cogitavit Melchisedecum " typum Messiæ fuisse. . . . . . Chaldæus qui alias Psalmum cx. de " Davide explicat, hic tamen eleganter sic παραφράζει, דאנת מחמני לרבא " לעלמא דאתי. *Nam tu constitutus es Princeps seculi futuri* (*i.e.*, temporum " N. T.) *idque propter meritum tuum, quia es* מלבא וכי *Rex justus*. Quæ " explicatio, quamvis ad textum originalem non sit satis accurata, in " Messiam tamen nostrum bene quadrat." And yet, on p. 645 of the second volume, Schoettgen writes, " Messiæ Sacerdotis typus fuit Mel- " chisedech," and fortifies his assertion by the following examples :—

" *Bereschith Rabba*, sect. 43, fol. 42, 1, ad verba Genes. xiv. 18. Et " ipse erat sacerdos Dei supremi. *R. Samuel filius Nachman et Rabbini* " *nostri de hoc loco controverterunt. Prior dicit, innui, quod Melchisedecus* " *Abrahamo statuta Sacerdotii summi exposuerit; nam per panem intelligitur* " *panes propositionis, per vinum vero libamina. Sed Rabbini nostri dixerunt,* " *innui, quod legem Abrahamo revelaverit,* q.d. Proverb. ix. 5. Venite, " comedite panem meum, et bibite vinum quod vobis miscui.—Huc " usque Rabboth typis edita. Sed Hadrianus Finus in Flagello Judæ- " orum viii. 20. post recitatam sententiam R. Samuelis hæc addit ; *ut* " *habetur in* Psal. cix. (Hebr. cx.) 4. Juravit Dominus, et non " poenitebit eum, tu es Sacerdos in æternum, secundum ordinem " Melchisedech. *Quis est iste ? Iste est Rex Messias, de quo scriptum*

" *est* Zachar. ix. 9. Ecce Rex tuus venit tibi mansuetus, justus et
" Salvator. *Et sequitur ipse Rabbi dicens: In hoc autem quod dicit:*
" Proferet (*fortasse,* Profert) panem et vinum ; *correspondet ei quod*
" *habetur in* Psalmo lxxii. 16. Erit placentula frumenti sive panis in
" terra in summis montium." It is a matter of notoriety that the
Talmudical writers applied Psalm lxxii. to the Messiah, *e.g.*, "Seven
" things were created before the world—1. The law ; 2. Repentance ;
" 3. The Garden of Eden ; 4. Gehenna; 5. The throne of Glory ;
" 6. The House of the Sanctuary ; and, 7. The name of Messiah ;
" because it is written in Ps. lxxii. 17, His name shall endure for ever,
" before the sun ינון *Jinnun* was his name." (*Pesachim,* f. 45, 1 ;
Nedarim, f. 39, 2 ; and elsewhere.)

The Talmudists render the verb ינון as a proper name of Messiah.
For some excellent remarks on this verse of Ps. lxxii. 17, the reader
may consult *The Psalms in Hebrew, with a Commentary* (vol. ii.,
pp. 145, 146), by the Rev. G. Phillips, D.D. Dr. Phillips observes
(*in loc.*), " The Chaldee translation does not exactly correspond with the
" present Hebrew text. It is as follows :— וקדם כהוי שמשא מזמן הוה שמיה
" *and before the sun was his name was prepared.* The explanation of
" Rosenmüller is, without doubt, the correct one. He observes that
" the Chald. verb וזמן is not unfrequently the rendering of the Hebrew
" כון (see Exod. xix. 15, xxxiv. 2) ; and, consequently, it is by no means
" an improbable conjecture that the interpreter read יכון in his MSS.
" . . . . . " It is proper to mention that De Rossi discovered this
" reading in the MSS. marked by him 879." For the convenience of
readers who desire to inform themselves as to the opinion of the
Talmudists on the subject of the names of the Messiah, *eg., Jinnun,
Shiloh,* &c., &c., I would refer them to p. 30, &c., of B. Scheidii
Præterita præteritorum, printed at length in Meuschen, *Nov. Test. ex
Talmude illustr.*, and also to *Sanhedrin,* col. 969, &c., Ugol. Thes., vol. xxv.

⁵ It is well known that the Rabbies, perplexed by Messianic passages,
in which the sufferings of the Messiah are blended together with the
descriptions of his triumph and glory, invented the figment of two
Messiahs—Messiah ben David, a triumphant Messiah, and Messiah
ben Joseph, a suffering one. The Talmud (*Succah,* f. 52, 1) says,
" Our Rabbies have asserted that Messiah ben David is speedily to be
" revealed in our days, because it is said (Ps. ii. 7), *I will declare the
" decree,* &c. The Holy One, blessed be He, said to him, *Ask of me,
" and I will give thee somewhat,* because it is said, in the fifth verse,
" *Ask of me, and I will give,* &c. But when Messiah the son of Joseph
" saw that he was to be put to death, he said, *Lord of the world, I ask
" nothing of thee but life.* The Lord answered him, *Yea, verily, life ;*

CHAP. V., 1—9.

"*for before thou spakest thy father David foretold concerning thee.* (Ps.
" xxi. 5.) "He asked life of thee, *and thou gavest it to him.*" From
this quotation it will be apparent that the early Jewish Doctors applied
Psalms ii. and xxi. to the Messiah, and that the New Testament writers
introduced no novelty, by their interpreting the former similarly.

The reader may consult, with advantage, Dr. Alexander M'Caul's
Observations (p. 156—163) on Kimchi's Commentary on Zech. (chap.
xii. 19), and also the appendix of interpretation subjoined to Dr.
M'Caul's volume of Warburtonian Lectures, *The Messiahship of Jesus.*
The following passages are commented on in the appendix:—Gen. iii.
14, 15, Gen. xlix. 10; Deut. xviii. 15—19; Psalm ii., xvi., xviii., xxii.
16 (17), xl. 7, 8 (6, 7), lxviii. 19 (18). lxix., lxxii., lxxxix., Ps. xciii.—c.,
cix., cx.; Is. vii. 14, viii. 1, ix. 6, lii. 13—liii. See also Scheidius,
Præterita præteritorum, pp. 11—13, and Schoettg., *Hor. Hebr.*, tom. ii.,
pp. 267, 360, 505, &c. The strong crying and tears of Messiah are
prophetically spoken of in Ps. xxii., and his deliverance especially in
verse 21 (22), הושיעני כפי אריה ומקרני רמים עניתני. (See note 4 on p. 28, and
also Schoettgen, tom. i., pp. 949—950.) In further elucidation of
Ps. xxii. 22 (23), אספרה שמך לאחי, "I will declare thy name unto my
" brethren," I would adduce the Targumic interpretation of Cantic.
viii. 1, "And in that time shall the king Messiah be revealed to the
" congregation of Israel. Then shall the children of Israel say, Come,
" be thou with us for a brother."

⁶ 'Ἀπὸ τῆς εὐλαβείας, "Duplex potissimum vocis εὐλάβεια notio est,
" nempe vel *metus*, vel *reverentiæ*......Priorem tamen a plerisque video
" præferri, quamvis posterior veteribus imprimis se probarit..... Qui
" per *metum* vertunt, illis idem hæc phrasis est, ac si diceretur, *exauditus
" atque adeo liberatus à metu*, sc. mortis; qui per *reverentiam*, illi a
" Patre aiunt exauditum Christum *propter reverentiam* et pietatem,
" in Patrem præstitam. Prætulerim ego *metus* significatum. Hunc
" apud τοὺς LXX. frequentem esse patet ex locis ubi Hebr. ראה, *i.e.*,
" *timorem anxium*, vertunt εὐλάβειαν, v. c. Prov. xii. 25, Jos. xxii. 24,
" Ezech. iv. 16, &c., quemadmodum verbum יגר expounnt per εὐλα-
" βεῖσθαι, nominatim Jes. lvii. 11, et Jerem. xxxviii. 19. Nec profanis
" hæc significatio insueta est. Herodianus, lib. v., p. 112, *latentes* ait,
" et εὐλαβείᾳ ἡσυχάζοντας *metu quiescentes*. Plutarchus de defectu oracu-
" lorum μετὰ εὐλαβείας, *i.e., timide*, Turnebo interprete, dixit. Philo de
" vita Mosis, Mosen τὴν φύσιν εὐλαβῆ, *natura timidiorem*, vocat.......Illis
" addidero, quod Casaubonus ad Aristoph. Equites, vers. 253, observat,
" εὐλαβεῖσθαι eos proprie dici, qui vasa vitrea aut fragilia alia cum
" magna circumspectione tangant. Verbum εὐλαβεῖσθαι, *Actor.* xxiii.
" 10, idem est quod *timere*, *vereri*, qui significatus etiam commode
" admittitur Hebr. xi. 7, ubi Noa εὐλαβηθείς, h.e. timens ab imminente
" Dei judicio, arcam struxisse dicitur."—J. C. Wolfius, *in loc.*

[7] Τελειωθείς. "Rectius agere eos puto, qui de perfecto redemptionis "opere interpretantur, quod ipse servator pronuntiat Joh. xix. 30, "Τετέλεσται."—J. C. Wolfius, *in loc.*

Verses 10—14.—Being saluted[1] by God "a high priest[2] "after the order[3] of Melchisedek." Concerning whom[4] (adds the writer) we have much to say (πολὺς ἡμῖν ὁ λόγος), and difficult to be explained, since ye have become dull in comprehension (ταῖς ἀκοαῖς). For though ye might well be teachers, on the account of the length of time (since your conversion), ye have need again that one should teach you what are the primary elements of the Oracles of God, and have gone back so as to require milk (*i.e.*, rudimentary instruction of the simplest kind), and not solid food (*i.e.*, the more abstruse articles of faith). For whoever partakes of milk is untried[5] (ἄπειρος *unskilled*) in the word of righteousness, for he is an infant. But solid food belongs to fullgrown men, who, by practice, have their perceptive faculties trained so as to discern between good and evil (*i.e.*, what to accept as salubrious, what to reject as unwholesome).

[1] Προσαγορευθείς. This verb occurs here only, in the New Testament. For an example of its use by Philo, see p. 25, line 1.

[2] Δύο γὰρ, ὡς ἔοικεν, ἱερὰ Θεοῦ, ἓν μὲν ὅδε ὁ κόσμος, ἐν ᾧ καὶ ἀρχιερεὺς, ὁ πρωτόγονος αὐτοῦ θεῖος λόγος, ἕτερον δὲ λογικὴ ψυχὴ, ἧς ἱερεὺς ὁ πρὸς ἀλήθειαν ἄνθρωπος. There are two temples, methinks, of God—the one, this universe, in which his firstbegotten and Divine Word is the High Priest; the other the rational soul, of which the truthful man is the priest. Philo, *Works*, vol. i., p. 653, Mangey's Edition.

[3] Κατὰ τὴν τάξιν. This translation of על דברתי agrees with the LXX. Dr. Gill renders the phrase "according to what is said of"; and J. D. Michaelis, who is infatuated with his theory that the Greek Epistle to the Hebrews is only a translation from the Hebrew or Chaldee original, proposes to translate על דברתי by, *over the sanctuary*, assuming as he does, that the Greek translator made the original square with the LXX. The quotations, however, from the Old Testament contained in the Epistle to the Hebrews, as in the other books of the New Testament, are by no means servile reproductions of the LXX. text. Aben Ezra paraphrases על דברתי by כמנהג, *according to the manner or custom of.* So also Surenhusius (βίβλ. Καταλλ., p. 623), "Caeterum "phrasin illam על דברתי etiam venire pro, *ad modum, vel, ad rationem,*

"sive *ad usum*, vel ipsis Judæorum doctoribus fatentibus constabit, ita
"ut litera (ʼ) sit paragogica euphoniæ gratia adjecta, et sic על דברתי idem
"sit quod על דברת id est כּוֹרך, vel כמוֹהג vel בּסְקוּרת, id est *secundum*
"*modum*, vel *ritum*, sive *præfecturam* et *institutionem*."

⁴ Περὶ οὗ. Schoettgen (*in loc.*) applies "concerning whom" to Melchisedek. "Nimirum perstringit h. l. Apostolus Hebræorum negligen-"tiam in excutiendis typis Messiæ, inter quos non exiguo loco est "Melchisedecus. Sed negligentia et inscitia Judæorum ut olim, sic "hodie quoque summa est." I cannot, however, think that the reference is exclusively to Melchisedek, but to the greater and primary subject in hand, viz., Christ, and his eternal priesthood.

⁵ The Jews used to call the disciples of the Rabbies היוֹנקים, *sucklings*, from the verb ינק, "he sucked." So Philo (*De Agricultura*, Works, Mangey's Edition, tom. i., p. 301). Ἐπεὶ δὲ νηπίοις μέν ἐστι γάλα τροφή, τελείοις δὲ τὰ ἐκ πυρῶν πέμματα, καὶ ψυχῆς γαλακτώδεις μὲν ἂν εἶεν τροφαὶ κατὰ τὴν παιδικὴν ἡλικίαν, τὰ τῆς ἐγκυκλίου μουσικῆς προπαιδεύματα. "But "since the food of infants is milk, and that of adults that which is "compounded of corn, the soul also requires its milk diet, in its tender "age," &c. See also *De Congressu quær. erudit. gratia*, ibid., pp. 521, 522. For a multitude of Rabbinical quotations in point, see Schoettgen on 1 Pet. ii. 2, in *Hor. Hebr.*, tom. i, pp. 1036—1038.

CHAPTER VI.

In the preceding chapter the primary essentials of the High Priesthood have been specified, and it has been shown that these are to be found, in consolatory fulness, in our Lord Jesus Christ. He is exactly such a High Priest as the sinner may with confidence resort to. He has a Divine call. He has perpetual access to God. He is able to sympathize with mortal infirmity. Concerning the abstract topic of the mystical correspondence existing between his High Priesthood and that of Melchisedek, the writer reminds his hearers, with an evidently displeasurable tinge in his phraseology, that he might well hesitate to enlarge. To such topics they might once have listened with pleasurable attention; but they had waxed dull of hearing, νωθροὶ ταῖς ἀκοαῖς; the mysteries of the kingdom of God had lost their savour. They lagged behind and halted in their belief. The unsettled frame of mind in which they at present are, indicates a necessity for a recapitulation of the groundwork of their faith. Some of them had already apostatized; others, perchance, were hesitating, in uncertainty whether to go back to the synagogue and the Mosaic ritual, or not. Homely truths, and not the στερεὰ τροφὴ, seemed to be most adapted to their condition. They seemed uncertain what to believe, and what to reject as worthless. The writer decides, however, upon contenting himself with the somewhat caustic reproof contained in the concluding verses. He will hope for the best, and not debar them from the more difficult instruction which he has to impart. And so he commences this sixth chapter with the reassuring invitation,—

Verses 1—3.—Wherefore leaving undiscussed (Διὸ ἀφέντες) the elementary topics of the Christian faith, let us proceed to consider the advanced subjects (τὴν τελειότητα, sc., *suited to full-grown men in Christ*).

What the rudimentary topics are, he now reminds his readers:—

Not laying over again the foundation of repentance from dead works, and faith towards God, nor of the doctrine of baptisms (*sc.*, of John, of Christian, and Jewish[1]), and of laying on of hands,[2] and of resurrection from the dead, and of eternal judgment.[3] And this course we will pursue, if God permit. (*Und thun wir dieses, so Gott es zugibt!*— Ewald.)

¹ Βαπτισμῶν διδαχῆς. Prof. Stuart asks, " What has the apostle here " to do with Jewish rites ?" The answer is plain. *Everything*, when speaking to Jewish converts. We know that the unbelieving Jews took great offence because the disciples neglected the ceremonial ablutions prescribed by the Pharisees. For two very curious treatises on the subject, see J. A. Danzii *Baptismus proselytorum Judaicus ad illustrandum Baptismum Johannis*, and *Antiquitas Baptismi initiationis Israelitarum vindicata*, by the same author. (Meuschen, *N. Test. ex Talmudi illustr.*, p. 233, &c., and p. 287, &c.) Schoettgen understands βαπτ. διδαχ. to include the idea of the Levitic lustrations. Grotius renders it, of the doctrines delivered to newly baptized persons.

² Ἐπιθέσεώς τε χειρῶν. Bp. Bancroft, at the Hampton Court Conference, alleged that Calvin understood this to mean confirmation. Berens, *Hist. of the Prayer-book*, p. 87. J. C. Wolfius exercises a sound discretion when he writes, "Non crediderim cum Rev. Zeltnero " in notis ad Versionem Lutheri Biblicam, respici hic ad impositionem " manuum, quæ victimis afferendis adhiberi solebat."

³ Ἀναστάσεώς τε κ.τ.λ. The Sadducees denied both ; but not only the fact, but the time of these two fundamental truths, were much debated amongst the ancient Jews. For a variety of Talmudical opinions, see Scheidii *Loca Talmudica*, and J. Rhenferdii *Dissertationes* II., *de Seculo Futuro*. (Meuschen, *N. Test. ex Talmudi illustr.*, p. 107, &c., and p. 1116, &c) " Intelligitur articulus de vita æterna, quam Judæi " vocant החיי המתים, cui apponitur κρίμα αἰώνιον, *damnatio æterna*. Vide " ad Joann., iii. 17." Schoettg., *Hor. Hebr.*, tom. i., p. 953.

And now the writer (verses 4—9) gives his reasons for deeming it superfluous to recapitulate the primary elements of the Christian faith. His readers had thoroughly sifted them, prior to embracing Christianity. They knew them by rote, if not by heart. The mere argumentative repetition of these initial doctrines would be of no avail, either to confirm the wavering, or to reclaim the apostates. If the former, in order to escape persecution and obloquy, were no longer willing to bear the reproach of Christ, if his love no longer constrained them to walk worthy of the Gospel, what occasion for further argumentation? In respect to the latter, it could only increase their condemnation. They had made up their minds to choose this present world, sinning against their own convictions, against light and knowledge; and until they renounced their errors, and bewailed their ungrateful apostasy, to talk to them about what they had a "more perfect knowledge" of, would be to "give "that which is holy to the dogs, and to cast pearls "before swine." I feel more and more convinced that no dogmatic assertion, nor theological axiom, is here intended to be laid down, viz., *that the restoration of apostates is impossible.* St. Peter, by his denial of Christ, at the moment of his Divine Master's sorest trial, placed himself in a position precisely analogous to that spoken of in the passage under consideration. He had tasted of the heavenly gift; he had been made partaker of the Holy Ghost; he had confessed that Christ had "the words of "eternal life," declaring, "We believe and are sure "that thou art that Christ, the Son of the living "God" (John vi., 68, 69); he had wielded in his Master's name the supernatural powers τοῦ μέλλοντος αἰῶνος; the very devils had been subject to him; and yet, as soon as the clouds of persecution began seriously to collect themselves, he fell away, and denied that he ever "knew the man." What is apostacy, if Peter's denial of Jesus was not? And yet he was restored, and made one of the twelve pillars of the Church. The grammatical construction of the Greek fully bears out this most reasonable view of the passage. That the apostates were in a position of extremest peril, by their own free

CHAP. VI., 4—6. 61

act, who will deny? But that they *could never repent* who will venture to assert? Every one of us shall give account for himself to God (ἕκαστος ἡμῶν περὶ ἑαυτοῦ λόγον δώσει τῷ Θεῷ. Μηκέτι οὖν ἀλλήλους κρίνωμεν. Rom. xiv. 12, 13). Let us, then, proceed to examine what the writer does actually say.

Verses 4—6.—For it is impossible[1] that those who were[2] once enlightened[3] (φωτισθέντας. See chap. x. 32—34), and have tasted of the heavenly gift (probably *the persuasion of eternal life*, the χάρισμα τοῦ Θεοῦ, Rom. vi. 23), and have been made partakers of the Holy Ghost (sc. *extraordinary gifts*), and have tasted the good word of God (καλὸν ῥῆμα דבר טוב, *i.e., the fulfilment of his promises of blessing through Abraham's seed in the Messiah.* See Ps. cv. 42, " He remembered his holy promise דבר קדשו, and " Abraham his servant "), and the powers of the world to come (δυνάμεις τε μέλλοντος αἰῶνος, the miraculous gifts of the supernatural world[4]), and have [yet] fallen away (παραπεσόντας, *aorist*), to renew them again unto repentance (πάλιν ἀνακαινίζειν εἰς μετάνοιαν).

[1] Ἀδύνατον, γάρ. J. C. Wolfius observes that various writers, following the ancient Latin version, have rendered the above *difficile*.

[2] Ἅπαξ. Vox ἅπαξ hic est *plene, perfecte*, ut Judæ v. 3, 5, et Hebr. ix. 7. Confer M. Christ. Wolle dissert. de vera fictaque particularum emphasi, quæ Ecclesiæ ejus Pharisaicæ et Christianæ subjuncta est p. 306. Ita scholia Thucydidis, lib. i., p. 78. τὸ ἅπαξ per παντελῶς exponunt. J. C. Wolfius, *in loc.* The ordinary signification " once " is the best.

[3] Φωτ. i.e., *brought to a saving knowledge of Christ as the Messiah*. Jesus, in virtue of his office, claimed to fulfil the requirements of Is. xlix. 6, saying (John viii. 12), Ἐγώ εἰμι τὸ φῶς τοῦ κόσμου, ὁ ἀκολουθῶν ἐμοὶ οὐ μὴ περιπατήσει ἐν τῇ σκοτίᾳ ; ἀλλ' ἕξει τὸ φῶς τῆς ζωῆς ; and this witness the " beloved disciple " bears to him (John i. 9), ἦν τὸ φῶς τὸ ἀληθινὸν ὃ φωτίζει πάντα ἄνθρωπον ἐρχόμενον εἰς τὸν κόσμον. R. D. Kimchi admits that the person spoken of by Isaiah, in his forty-ninth chapter, is the Messiah. Compare 2 Cor., iv. 6, " ἔλαμψεν ἐν ταῖς καρδίαις ἡμῶν, πρὸς φωτισμὸν τῆς γνώσεως τῆς δόξης τοῦ Θεοῦ ἐν προσώπῳ Ἰησοῦ Χριστοῦ." In support of my view I would adduce the following very apposite

remarks of J. C. Wolfius:—" Τοὺς φωτισθέντας, Patres Græci et Latini "permulti de *baptisatis* accipiunt. Locos eorum habes apud *Suicerum*, "voce ἀναβάπτισις, *Num.* ii. 1 et verbo ἀνασταυρόω, *Num.* ii. item in "Observatt. Sacris., p. 75, quos et *Fesselius* noster, in *Adversariis* "*Sacris*, tom. ii., p. 108, *sq.* attulit. Uterque tamen eorum rectius censet "*doctrinam veritatis coelestis edoctos*, significari. Hanc Pauli mentem "esse patet, ex loco parallelo *Hebr.* x. 26, ubi φωτίζεσθαι illud dicitur, "λαβεῖν τὴν ἐπίγνωσιν τῆς ἀληθείας, quemadmodum 1 Cor. iv. 4, φωτισμὸς "τοῦ εὐαγγελίου τῆς δόξης τοῦ Χριστοῦ, appellatur. Sic oi LXX. verbum "Hebraicum הורה, i e., *docuit*, Jud. xiii. 8, et 2 Reg. xii. 2, φωτίζειν "reddunt. Qui de *baptismo* acceperunt Patres, illa ætate vixerunt, qua "sacrum hoc lavacrum φωτισμὸς, speciatim appellari coeperat."—*Curæ Philolog. et Crit.*, tom. iv., p. 662.

¹ In further proof that ὁ αἰὼν ὁ μέλλων (העולם הבא) was not understood to denote the present order of things, but of the life to come, and the spiritual, supernatural world, Rhenferd, in the tract before cited, *De Seculo Futuro*, p. 1124, cites R. Chasdai's reconciliation (in Cod. *Schabbat.*) of the two apparently contradictory passages in Isaiah, viz., xxiv. 23 and xxx. 26, in the former of which passages it is said, *the sun shall be ashamed and the moon shall be confounded*, and in the latter, *the light of the moon shall be like the light of the sun*.

The first passage, he says, relates to the days of Messiah, but the second to the world to come (עולם הבא). The passage is as follows:—

רב חסדא רמי כתיב וחפרה הלבנה ובושה החמה וכתיב והיה אור הלבנה כאור החמה
לא קשיא כאן לימות המשיח כאן לעולם הבא:

So also Rabbi Eliezer (*ibid.*, p. 1123):—

ואמרו לשון אחר אמר להם ר' אליעזר אף לימות המשיח אינן בטלין אבל בטלין הן לעולם הבא

"They say that R. Eliezer gave a different opinion, and said that they "(arms) shall not cease in the days of Messiah, but in the world to "come."

Verse 6.—Crucifying, as they do, the Son of God over again, and putting Him to (exposing Him to) a public reproach¹ (ἀνασταυροῦντας, παραδειγματίζοντας, *i.e.*, whilst they continue to do so, and persevere in so scandalous a course of blaspheming opposition. *Während sie, für sich selbst, den Sohn Gottes neu kreuzigen und verhönen.*—Ewald).

The key to the writer's meaning is contained in the change from the aorist to the present participle.*

* Ewald, whose work, *Das Sendschreiben an die Hebräer*, Göttingen, 1870, 8vo., has only come into my hands after the above was in type, takes a similar view of the passage, pp. 80, 81.

CHAP. VI., 7, 8. 63

¹ A primary condition of return to the synagogue was the public and contumelious abjuration of the name of Jesus; and it is to this that St. Paul alludes when he says, Acts xxvi. 11, "And I punished them " oft in every synagogue, and compelled them to blaspheme; and being " exceedingly mad against them, I persecuted them even unto strange " cities." Of the rancorous hatred and spiteful contempt in which the name of Jesus is held amongst Rabbinic Jews, the ordinary Christian reader can form no conception. If the student desires to follow this subject further, he can consult the scurrilous tractate entitled, ספר תולדות ישו *The book of the Generations of Jesus*, and the other treatises contained in Wagenseil's *Tela ignea Satanæ*.

Verses 7, 8.—For the earth which drinketh in the rain that cometh oft upon it, and bringeth forth herbs (βοτάνην) meet for those by whom it is dressed (γεωργεῖται), partakes of God's (primal) blessing (μεταλαμβάνει εὐλογίας ἀπὸ τοῦ Θεοῦ, *shares in the implied promise of fertility given* Gen. i. 11, "Let the earth bring forth grass," &c. Βλαστησάτω ἡ γῆ βοτάνην, κ.τ.λ. LXX.). But that which beareth thorns and thistles, is good for nothing, and nigh to the condition of cursing (as spoken, Gen. iii. 17, 18, "Cursed "is the ground for thy sake... Thorns and thistles it "shall bring forth to thee." Ἐπικατάρατος ἡ γῆ ἐν τοῖς ἔργοις σου... ἀκάνθας καὶ τριβόλους ἀνατελεῖ σοι. LXX.), whose end is for burning (ἧς τὸ τέλος εἰς καῦσιν, *i.e.*, which is only available to make fuel from. See O. Strauss, *Nahumi de Nino vaticinium*, pp. 31, 32. Berolini, 1853, 8vo.)

Having thus illustrated the futility of rehearsing the elements of the Gospel in such unworthy and listless hearing, the writer now, with delicate tact, changes the severity of his tone, and assures those for whom the Epistle is designed, that he is persuaded better things of them, even things that accompany salvation, "although we thus speak." They have already proved themselves like the fertile soil; they have not drunk in the gracious rain for naught, but have brought forth the fruits of righteousness.

Verses 9—14.—But we are persuaded better things (the better alternative, τὰ κρείττονα) concerning you, Beloved, even things that accompany salvation, although we thus speak. For God is not unjust to have forgotten your work and the labour (κόπου) of love which ye have exhibited towards his name (εἰς τὸ ὄνομα αὐτοῦ), seeing that ye have ministered, and yet minister, to the saints. But we are anxious that every one of you should exhibit the same unflagging zeal (σπουδὴν) with respect to the full realisation (πληροφορίαν) of your (heavenly) hope unto the end. So that you may not lag behind (νωθροί, *remiss*, see Stuart, v. 12), but be imitators of those who through faith and longsuffering (μακροθυμίας, ארך רוח *slow of spirit,* patient, Eccl. vii. 8) inherited (κληρονομούντων, *realised*) the promises. For when God gave Abraham the promise, since he had no greater to swear by, he sware by Himself[1] (Gen. xxii. 16, בי נשבעתי), saying (Gen. xxii. 17), "Surely blessing I will bless thee, and multiplying I will multiply thee.[2]

---

[1] ὤμοσε καθ' ἑαυτοῦ. The Talmudical treatise *Berachoth,* fol. 32, 1, has the following on Exod. xxxii. 13, " *Remember Abraham, Isaac, and Israel, thy servants, to whom thou swarest* (בי) *by thine own self.*" "What does בי denote? R. Eliezer answered: Moses spake thus to the "Holy One, Blessed be He; Lord of the World, if thou hadst sworn by "the very heavens and the earth, then I should have said: As the heavens "and the earth shall perish, so also thy oath. But now Thou hast "sworn to them by thy great name, which lives and endures for ever, "so also shall thy oath endure for ever and ever more."

[2] Ἦ μὴν εὐλογῶν εὐλογήσω σε, καὶ πληθύνων πληθυνῶ σε, a nearly literal and Hebraistic translation of the original, כי ברך אברכך והרבה ארבה את זרעך. Professor Stuart, by a singular oversight, says that " in this passage "(Gen. xxii. 17) the Hebrew runs ארבה את זרעך והרבה, *I will greatly* "*multiply thy seed,* but in Gen. xvii. 2 it is ארבה אותך במאד מאד, *I will* "*multiply thee.* The Apostle appears to unite both expressions in the

"quotation before us." The real translation of the latter verse, which reads וארבה את זרעך במאר מאר, is, *And I will multiply thee very exceedingly*, whilst Gen. xxii. 17 concludes with the words, "As the stars of heaven "and as the sand which is on the sea shore, and thy seed shall possess "the gate of his enemies."

Verses 15—20.—And so having patiently waited, he obtained the promise.¹ Now men are in the habit of appealing by oath to Him that is greater (κατὰ τοῦ μείζονος, or *to a thing that is greater*, e.g., the temple, the altar), and the oath (adduced) in confirmation (εἰς βεβαίωσιν) is to them an end of all gainsaying (ἀντιλογίας, i.e., *what is affirmed is thenceforward taken for granted as true*²). On which account (ἐν ᾧ) God, being desirous to demonstrate more abundantly to those that should inherit the promise, the immutability of his purpose, interposed by an oath³ (ἐμεσίτευσεν ὅρκῳ, i.e., *put an oath between Himself and the believers*). In order that by two immutable things (God's word⁴ and God's oath⁵) in which it was impossible for God to prove false (ψεύσασθαι), we, who have fled⁶ to lay hold upon the hope set before us, might have a strong (ἰσχυρὰν) consolation, which (hope) we have as an anchor⁷ of the soul, sure (ἀσφαλῆ, *which slips not its hold*) and stedfast, and which enters into that which is within the veil (i.e., the very presence of God), whither, as a forerunner, on our behalf, Jesus has gone in, being made a high priest for ever after the order of Melchisedek.

¹ Again, oddly enough, Professor Stuart says, "In our text the Apostle "refers to the promised blessing of a Son, which after long waiting "Abraham obtained." I have shown (note 1, p. 64) that the above is a literal quotation from Gen. xxii. 17. The mention of the oath (verse 16) sets the matter at rest, because this circumstance is not found in Gen. xvii., although the renewal of the covenant and the institution of circumcision are therein contained. As, therefore, the writer to the Hebrews plainly cites from Gen. xxii., the ἐπαγγελία received cannot mean the birth of Isaac. It was in consequence of Abraham's readiness to obey the Divine command, and to offer up Isaac his only son, that God renewed the promise of blessing, and multiplication of his

seed, together with the crowning blessing, "in thy seed shall all the "nations of the earth account themselves blessed (והתברכו), because thou "hast obeyed my voice." What, then, was the blessing which Abraham μακροθυμήσας ἐπέτυχε? Undoubtedly the blessing to himself and all his seed by faith, viz., redemption through the Messiah, even Christ. That this is the true meaning of the writer we see from verses 17, 18. God gave the double assurance of his word and his oath, "to demonstrate "(τοῖς κληρονόμοις τῆς ἐπαγγελίας τὸ ἀμετάθετον τῆς βουλῆς αὐτοῦ) to those "who should inherit the promise, the unchangeableness of his purpose, in "order that by two immutable things, in which it was impossible that "God should lie, we who have fled to lay hold upon the hope set before "us, might have a strong consolation." It was a hope, then, which was to be handed on, still in suspense at the death of Abraham, a hope of blessedness and salvation which he then himself personally realised, and also in his lifetime, by the eye of faith. In respect to the personal and individual fulfilment of the promise to ourselves, we still "walk by faith not by sight." To the persecuted Hebrews this allusion to Abraham's hope and reward was full of consolatory meaning. He had forsaken all for this hope, and lived as a stranger and pilgrim upon earth. But he had gained the best of all rewards. The Jewish expression, "Abraham's bosom," denoted the rest of the righteous in the better world (Luke xvi. 22), in which they wait for the "Resurrection of the Just."

² Philo says, "Doubtful things are decided by an oath, things uncon-"firmed are, by it, made sure, and incredible things receive credibility."
Τὰ ἐνδοιαζόμενα τῶν πραγμάτων ὅρκῳ διακρίνεται, καὶ τὰ ἀβέβαια βεβαιοῦται, καὶ τὰ ἄπιστα λαμβάνει πίστιν. *Quod a Deo mittantur Somnia*, Works. *Mangey's Edit.*, vol. i., p. 622.

³ 'Εμεσίτευσεν. A similar use of the word is found in Josephus (Antiq. xvi. 4, 3, near the end of the section): διόπερ ἐπὶ τῷ πάντων δεσπότῃ Καίσαρι μεσιτεύοντι τὸν παρόντα καιρὸν συντιθέμεθα ταύτην τὴν συνθήκην. "Wherefore we will make this agreement, before Cæsar the "Lord of all, who is now a mediator between us."

⁴ The Targums of Onkelos and Jonathan both translate בי נשבעתי, by "*By my Word have I sworn.*"

⁵ Philo (*S. S. Legum Allegoriarum, lib. iii.*) observes (on Gen. xxii. 16) that God alone can swear by Himself, because no created being can speak definitely or certainly concerning his nature and essence, or of his works. They are, therefore, to be accounted impious who declare that they swear by God. To do this is His prerogative alone. "Suffi-"cient is it for us if we are able to know somewhat respecting the "nature of his Name ; that is to say, of his interpreting Word. (Τοῦ

"ἑρμηνέως λόγου.) For he is the God of us imperfect mortals, being the first of all wise and perfect things. Moreover, Moses admiring the excellency of the Unbegotten (τὴν ὑπερβολὴν θαυμάσας τοῦ ἀγεννήτου), says (Deut. vi. 13), *Ye shall also swear by his Name*, not, *by* (God) *Himself*. For it is sufficient to pledge ourselves by his Son, and to obtain the testimony of the Divine Word. (Ἱκανὸν γὰρ τῷ γεννητῷ πιστοῦσθαι, καὶ μαρτυρεῖσθαι λόγῳ θείῳ.)"—*Works*, Mangey's Edit., vol. i., p. 128.

And again, Φησὶ γάρ, κατ' ἐμαυτοῦ ὤμοσα, παρ' ᾧ ὁ λόγος ὅρκος ἐστί, ἕνεκα τοῦ τὴν διάνοιαν ἀκλινῶς καὶ παγίως ἔτι μᾶλλον ἢ πρότερον ἐρηρεῖσθαι.

"He whose word is equivalent to an oath, declares, *by myself have I sworn*, to the intent that his mind might be even more immoveably and firmly fixed in its persuasion than before."—*Ibid.*, De Abrahamo, vol. ii., p. 39.

⁶ They had made shipwreck of all their earthly prospects. The hope of redemption, the "rest of God," is the harbour of refuge into which they had fled for shelter, until life's storms should be overpast. Their aggravated and harassing persecutions are again alluded to, with touching tenderness and sympathy, in chap. x. 32—34.

⁷ Ὡς ἄγκυραν. Dassovius understands ἄγκυραν to mean the hook to which the veil was suspended ; but it is the *hope*, not the anchor, which enters within the veil. An anchor "sure and stedfast" is an apt illustration of the Christian's hope.

CHAPTER VII.

WITH admirable dexterity, the writer has now worked round to the topic originally in hand, viz., the difficult parallelism between the High Priesthood of Christ and the high priesthood of Melchisedek, and he presents it to his readers in the most endearing and engaging aspect. Their sympathies cannot fail to go with their understandings. The tender chord of personal experience has been touched by the delicate allusion to the real hardships which at that moment pressed upon the Hebrew converts on every side. Jesus, in his most beautiful aspect, a "comforter of those that are cast down," a refuge¹ for the afflicted, has been held up to their view. He is not a high priest who cannot be touched with the feeling of their infirmities. His own stedfastness was sorely tried, He is therefore able to succour those that are tempted. Thus having attuned their minds to give heed to the things spoken, the writer proceeds to draw out the correspondence between Christ and Melchisedek, and to show how the greater High Priesthood was evermore designed, ultimately to supersede the Aaronic.

Verses 1, 2.—Now this Melchisedek, King of Salem,² a priest of the Most High God, he, namely, who met Abraham returning from the slaughter of the kings (Gen. xiv. 18), and blessed him; to whom also Abraham divided a tenth of all (the spoils).³

---

¹ Thus had the King Messiah been described in Isaiah xxxii. 1, 2, "Behold, a king shall reign in righteousness, and princes shall rule in "judgment. And a man shall be as an hiding place from the wind, and "a covert from the tempest; as rivers of water in a dry place, as the "shadow of a great rock in a weary land." So also in Isaiah xlii. 1—4, which the Targum thus paraphrases, "Behold my servant the Messiah," הא עברי משיחא &c.

² Βασιλεὺς Σαλήμ. The LXX. version of Gen. xiv. 18 agrees exactly with the Hebrew, καὶ Μελχισεδὲκ βασιλεὺς Σαλὴμ ἐξήνεγκεν ἄρτους καὶ οἶνον, ἦν δὲ ἱερεὺς τοῦ Θεοῦ τοῦ ὑψίστου. "And Melchizedek, King of "Salem, brought forth bread and wine, but he was priest of the Most "High God." The Hebrew reads, ומלכי צדק מלך שלם הוציא לחם ויין והוא כהן לאל עליון. From this it will be seen that the LXX. translators, in common with their Hebrew-speaking brethren, regarded Salem as the name of a locality. From Psalm lxxvi. 2 (3) it is evident that Salem was a designation of Jerusalem, ויהי בשלם סכו ומעונתו בציון, unless perchance the Psalmist refers back to the Salem of which Melchizedek was king,

CHAP. VII., 1, 2.   69

and supposing that Salem was not identical with the holy city. The LXX. here render ויהי בשלם סכו by ἐγενήθη ἐν εἰρήνῃ ὁ τόπος αὐτοῦ, and the Vulgate, "Et factus est in pace locus ejus." Luther translates, "Zu Salem ist sein Gezelt." The Targum and the Syriac version understand Jerusalem to be designated. In Genesis xxxiii. 18 another Salem, or Shalem, is mentioned, ויבא יעקב שלם עיר שכם, καὶ ἦλθεν Ἰακὼβ εἰς Σαλὴμ, πόλιν Σηκίμων, and the Samaritans lay claim to the meeting of Abraham with Melchizedek, for Mount Gerizim. The Targum of Onkelos thus paraphrases Gen. xiv. 8, "And Malki-zedek, King of Yerushelem, "brought forth bread and wine (*chemar*), and he was minister (*mesha-*"*mesh*) before El Illaah (and he was Kohen of the Most Mighty, "*Sam. Vers.*); and he blessed him, and said,

"'Blessed be Abram before El Illaah,
Whose possession is heaven and earth;
And blessed be El Illaah,
Who hath delivered thine enemies into thine hand.'

"And he gave him one in ten of the whole. And the King of Sedom "said," &c.

The Targum of Palestine has, "And Malka Zadika, who was Shem "bar Noah, the King of Yerushalem, came forth to meet Abram, and "brought forth to him bread and wine; and in that time he ministered "before Eloha Ilaha (JERUSALEM Targ., 'And Malki Zedek, King of "'Yerushalem, who was Shem, who was the great priest of the Most "'High'). And he blessed him, and said, Blessed be Abram of the "Lord God Most High, who for the righteous possesseth the heavens "and the earth. And blessed be Eloha Ilaha, who hath made thine "enemies as a shield which receiveth a blow. And he gave him one of "ten, of all which he brought back. And the King of Sedom said," &c.—Etheridge's *Targums*, in loc. From the above it is plain that the Targums give no sanction to Mr. Grove's assertion in his article *Salem*, in Smith's Dictionary of the Bible:—" Indeed, it is not certain that "there is any connexion of time or place between Abram's encounter "with the King of Sodom and the appearance of Melchizedek"! Surely Mr. Grove did not wilfully set aside, as valueless, the words of the canonical writer to the Hebrews, ὁ συναντήσας Ἀβραὰμ ὑποστέφοντι ἀπὸ τῆς κοπῆς τῶν βασιλέων. In Gen. xiv. 17 precisely similar language is held respecting the King of Sodom, who was certainly present at the meeting. With this latter opinion Dr. Delitzsch (see p. 71) coincides, *e.g.*, "Der König Sodoms der dabei gegenwärtig zu denken ist."—*Die Genesis*, p. 267. In verse 17 it is said,

ויצא מלך סדם לקראתו אחרי שובו מהכות את כדרלעמר ואת המלכים. Ἐξῆλθε δέ βασιλεὺς Σοδόμων εἰς συνάντησιν αὐτῷ, μετὰ τὸ ὑποστρέψαι αὐτὸν ἀπὸ τῆς

κοπῆς τοῦ Χοδολλογομόρ, καὶ τῶν βασιλέων κ.τ.λ. Then follows, in verses 18—20, the incident of Melchizedek's meeting with, and blessing Abraham ; and then verse 21 resumes, סדם מלך ויאמר, Εἶπε δὲ βασιλεὺς Σοδόμων κ.τ.λ. The inference from the above is plain. Melchizedek did meet Abraham on his return from the slaughter of the kings. The King of Sodom, who had previously arrived, was present at the meeting. The blessing of Melchizedek is in special reference to the victory which Abraham had just gained (19, 20); and, lastly, the neighbourhood of Sodom makes it very probable indeed that Salem was Jerusalem, if, indeed, the epithet is not to be understood, as the סרום הישנה does, of the "Jerusalem above." Josephus, Antiq., i. 10, 2, arranges the events in a similar order:—'Ἀπήντησε δὲ αὐτῷ ὁ τῶν Σοδομιτῶν βασιλεὺς εἰς τόπον τινὰ ὃν καλοῦσι Πεδίον βασιλικόν· ἔνθα ὁ τῆς Σολύμα πόλεως ὑποδέχεται βασιλεὺς αὐτὸν Μελχισεδέκης· σημαίνει δὲ τοῦτο βασιλεὺς δίκαιος· καὶ ἦν δὲ τοιοῦτος ὁμολογουμένως, ὡς διὰ ταύτην αὐτὸν τὴν αἰτίαν καὶ ἱερέα γενέσθαι τοῦ θεοῦ· τὴν μέντοι Σόλυμα ὕστερον ἐκάλεσαν Ἱεροσόλυμα· ἐχορήγησε δὲ οὗτος ὁ Μελχισεδέκης τῷ Ἀβράμου στρατῷ ξένια καὶ πολλὴν ἀφθονίαν τῶν ἐπιτηδείων παρέσχε, καὶ παρὰ τὴν εὐωχίαν αὐτόν τε ἐπαινεῖν ἤρξατο καὶ τὸν θεὸν εὐλογεῖν ὑποχειρίους αὐτῷ ποιήσαντα τοὺς ἐχθρούς. Ἀβράμου δὲ διδόντος καὶ τὴν δεκάτην τῆς λείας αὐτῷ, προσδέχεται τὴν δόσιν· ὁ δὲ τῶν Σοδομιτῶν βασιλεὺς τὴν μὲν λείαν ἔχειν Ἀβραμον παρεκάλει, κ.τ.λ. "Now the King of Sodom met him at a certain place
"which they called the King's Dale, where Melchisedek, King of the
"city Salem, received him. That name signifies the *Righteous King;*
"and such he was without dispute, insomuch that, on this account,
"he was made the priest of God : however, they afterwards called Salem
"*Jerusalem.* Now this Melchisedek supplied Abram's army in an
"hospitable manner, and gave them provisions in abundance ; and as
"they were feasting he began to praise him, and to bless God for
"subduing his enemies under him. And when Abram gave him a
"tenth of his prey, he accepted of the gift ; but the King of Sodom
"desired Abram to take the prey."

Josephus (*De Bell. Judaico,* vi. 10) again refers to Melchizedek as follows :—Ὁ δὲ πρῶτος κτίσας ἦν Χαναναίων δυνάστης, ὁ τῇ πατρίᾳ γλώσσῃ κληθεὶς βασιλεὺς δίκαιος· ἦν γὰρ δὴ τοιοῦτος. διὰ τοῦτο ἱεράσατό τε τῷ θεῷ πρῶτος, καὶ τὸ ἱερὸν πρῶτος δειμάμενος Ἱεροσόλυμα τὴν πόλιν προσηγόρευσε, Σόλυμα καλουμένην πρότερον. "But he who first built it (Jerusalem)
"was a potent man among the Canaanites, and is in our tongue called
"the Righteous King, for such he really was ; on which account he
"was (there) the first priest of God, and first built a temple (there), and
"called the city Jerusalem, which was formerly called Salem." On this passage Whiston, whose translation I have followed, observes :—

"Why the great Bochart should say (*De Phoenic. Colon.*, b. ii., c. iv.)
"that there are in this clause of Josephus '*as many mistakes as words,*'
"I do by no means understand. Josephus thought Melchizedek first
"built, or rather rebuilt and adorned this city, and that it was then
"called Salem, as Psal. lxxvi. 2; that it afterwards came to be called
"Jerusalem; and that Melchizedek, being a priest as well as king,
"built to the true God therein a temple, or place for public divine
"worship and sacrifice; all which things may be very true for aught
"we know to the contrary; and for the word ίερον, or Temple, as if it
"must needs belong to the great temple built by Solomon long after-
"ward, Josephus himself uses ναος, for the small tabernacle of Moses,
"*Antiq.* iii., 6, 4. See also *Antiq.* iii., 6, 1, as he here presently uses
"ίερον for a large and splendid synagogue of the Jews at Antioch only,
"vii., 3, 3." (Note on *Wars of the Jews*, vi. 10.)

Dr. Gill (on Heb. vii. 1) says, "Aben Ezra says his name signifies
"what he was, *the king of a righteous place.* Salem, of which he was
"king, was not Shalem, a city of Shechem, in the land of Canaan,
"Gen. xxxiii. 18, afterwards called Salim, near to which John was bap-
"tizing, John iii. 23, where is shown the palace of Melchizedek in its
"ruins, which cannot be, since that city was laid to the ground and
"sowed with salt by Abimelech, Judges ix. 15, but Jerusalem is the
"place; which is the constant opinion of the Jews (Targ. Onk., Jon.,
"and Jerus., Levi ben Gersom, Aben Ezra, and Ben Melec in Gen.
"xiv. 18, Tosaphot T. Bab. Taanith, fol. 16, 1), and is called Salem in
"Ps. lxxvi. 2. The interpretation of this word is given in the next
"verse; some of the Jewish writers referred to, say that it was usual
"for the kings of Jerusalem to be called *Melchisedec* and *Adoni-
"zedek*, as in Josh. x. 3, just as the kings of Egypt were called
"Pharaoh."

Dr. Delitzsch (*Die Genesis*, pp. 266, 267) writes as follows:—"Der
"König Sodoms zog dem rückkehrenden Sieger entgegen nach שוה עמק
"d.i. dem später sogenannten Königsthal; auch Malchizedek, der
"König Salems fand sich da ein. Da wir über das Königsthal sonst
"weiter nichts wissen, als dass Absalom sich dort ein Denkmal
"errichtete, 2 Sam. xviii. 18, und aus 2 Sam. xiii. 23, nicht mit
"Sicherheit geschlossen werden kann, das es in oder bei Efraim zu
"suchen sei, so ist es zweifelhaft, ob Malkizedek, wie אדני צדק Jos. x. 1,
"König Jerusalems ist, welches auch Ps. lxxvi. 3, שלם heisst, oder ob
"Salem, seine Königsstadt, das Salem der Jordansaue, Joh. iii. 23,
"Judith iv. 4, ist, das 8 römische Meilen südlich von Scythopolis
"gelegene Salumias, wo man zu Hieronymus' Zeit, Ruinen des
"angeblichen Palastes Malkizedeks zeigte. Im ersteren Falle ist

"Abram, wie schon Eupolemus bei Eusebius, *Præp.* 9, 17, annimmt, durch Samarien auf dem Heimwege nach Hebron begriffen, indem er gelegenen Orts die Gefangenen mit der Beute nach ihrer südöstlichen Heimath zu entlassen gedenkt, im letzteren Falle folgt er dem Jordanthale nach Sodom um Gefangene und Beute selber zurück zu bringen." Those who desire to pursue the subject further may consult Wolfius, *Cur. Phil.*, tom. iv., p. 670, &c. ; Dr. Gill's Commentary on Gen. xiv. 18, and Hebr. vii., Bp. Wordsworth ; and the articles *Salem* and *Melchizedek*, in Smith's Dict. of the Bible.

[a] Δεκάτην ἀπὸ πάντων. Dr. Gill remarks (*in loc.*), "Philo the Jew "(*De Congressu*, p. 438) renders the Hebrew phrase מעשר מכל (Gen. xiv. " 20) just as the Apostle does δεκάτην ἀπὸ πάντων, a tenth part of all, or "out of all ; not of all that he brought back, as Lot's goods, or the "King of Sodom's, or any others ; only of the spoils of the enemy." See verse 4, δεκάτην Ἀβραὰμ ἔδωκεν ἐκ τῶν ἀκροθινίων.

Verses 2—5.—First being interpreted[1] King of Righteousness, and then also King of Salem, which is King of Peace ;[2] without father, without mother, without pedigree,[3] having neither beginning of days nor end of life, but exactly resembling the Son of God,[4] remaineth a priest in perpetuity (εἰς τὸ διηνεκές).[5] But observe how great[6] this personage[7] must have been, to whom Abraham, the patriarch, gave a tenth of the spoils. But those from amongst the sons of Levi who receive the priestly office are expressly directed,[8] according to the law, to exact tithes from the people, their own brethren, although they came forth from the loins of Abraham.[9]

[1] Βασιλεὺς δικαιοσύνης. Schoettgen (*in loc.*) observes, "Sic in Bre-"schith Rabba, sect. 43, fol. 42, 1, מלכי צדק exponitur, מצדיק את יושביו, "*Justificans habitatores suos.* Addunt tamen aliam interpretationem "sed more suo satis detortam. Quia enim Malki Zedek et Adoni Zedek "reges Hierosolymæ fuerunt, concludunt exinde, nomen urbis Hieroso-"lymitanæ fuisse צדק, *justitia*, et huc trahunt verba Jesa. i. 21, "צדק ילין בה, *Justitia habitabit in ea.*" For Josephus' interpretation, which I have given at length, see note on p. 70. Philo (S. S. Legum Alleg., lib. iii., *Works*, *Mang.*, tom. i., p. 103) writes, Καλεῖται γὰρ "βασιλεὺς δίκαιος, κ.τ.λ., " He is called a *Righteous King*," &c.

CHAP. VII., 2—5.

² Βασ. Σαλ. ὅ ἐστι βασ. εἰρήνης.

From note 2, p. 68, it will have been apparent that the writer to the Hebrews assigns a definite locality, whether terrestrial or celestial, to Melchizedek as the seat of his regal jurisdiction, viz., Salem. It is in the first instance the proper name of a city. Now, however, the writer proceeds to explain the symbolical meaning of מלך שלם, as he has already done with the proper name of its king, מלכי צדק. As his interpretation of the latter agrees with that given by Josephus (*Ant.* i. 10, 2, *De Bell. Jud.* vi. 10), so does his interpretation of *King of Salem* agree with that of Philo (*SS. Leg. Alleg.*, lib. iii., *Works*, tom. i., pp. 102, 103), who calls Melchizedek βασιλέα τῆς εἰρήνης, and ἡγεμόνα εἰρήνης. Respecting the Messiah, Isaiah, ix. 6 (5), declared that one of his names should be called שר שלום, *Prince of Peace*, and to the Messiah the Targum applies the prophecy; "Said the prophet to "the house of David: For to us a Son is born, to us a Son is given; "and He shall receive the Law upon Him to keep it; and His name is "called from of old, Wonderful, Counsellor, Eloha the Mighty, Abiding "to Eternity, the Messiah, because peace shall be multiplied upon us "in his days." See also Ewald, *Das Sendschr. a.d. Hebr.*, p. 89.

Schoettgen (tom. ii., p. 18) cites from the Prologue to the *Midrasch Echa*, a passage quoted by Raymond Martin, in his *Pugio Fidei*, ii. 9, 21, and also by Hadrian Finus, in his *Flagellum Judæorum*, ii. 7, iii. 18, which also applies Is. ix 6 (5) to the Messiah:—"*R. Joshua the Galilean* "*said, The name of Messiah is Peace, as it is written in* Is. ix. 5, Father "of the World to come (Eternity), Prince of Peace." Schoettgen, however, declares that he could not find the passage in the printed copies to which he had access. He further (tom. i., p. 958) gives the *Bereschith Rabba* as the authority for the ridiculous Jewish conceit that Melchizedek was called מלך שלם, *Perfect King*, because he was born circumcised, שמול כהול. Circumcised people the Rabbinists call "*perfect*," and justify their doing so from Gen. xvii. 1, where it is said, והיה תמים, "and be thou perfect," which means (say they) "be circumcised."

³ Ἀπάτωρ, ἀμήτωρ, κ.τ.λ. This passage plainly indicates Melchizedek's Divine origin. A solution has been sought in the assertion, that the Jewish High Priests were obliged to be descended from the stock of Aaron both on the father's and the mother's side. To such a genealogy neither Christ nor Melchisedek laid any claim; and could it be shown that the Jews made use of similar phraseology to designate a priest, whose genealogical title to the High Priesthood was defective on the side of either parent, the explanation might have some weight. The words would contain a very intelligible reply to the cavils of the unbelieving Jews

L

against the High Priesthood of Christ, who objected to Jesus, that he was not in any way descended from Aaron, and therefore was no priest at all. The answer would be as follows:—"Melchizedek was, as you say, "'Ἀπάτωρ, ἀμήτωρ, ἀγενεαλόγητος, but it is written in Ps. cx. 4 of "Messiah, *The Lord hath sworn, and will not repent, thou art a priest "for ever after the order of Melchizedek*.—Therefore, Messiah is a true "priest, 'after the order of Melchisedek,' and a greater High Priest "than Aaron, for Abraham your father gave Melchizedek tithes." I have already shown (pp. 53, 54) that the most ancient Jews regarded Melchizedek as a type of the Messiah, if not identical with him. The מדרש הנצלם asserts on Gen. xiv. 18, *Melchisedek the King of Salem*, זו ירושלים של מעלה, *This is the Jerusalem above*. Schoett., tom. i., p. 1210. But unfortunately the information is missing which would enable us to interpret Ἀπάτωρ, κ.τ.λ., certainly, according to Jewish tradition. Schoettgen, indeed, following Suidas, believes that Melchizedek was of the cursed race of Canaan, and endeavours to show that being a Gentile he would be termed in Jewish phraseology ἀπάτωρ. But I would venture to submit that the *premises* upon which this theory is built are, to say the least, doubtful and hazardous, and the example which he adduces from the *Bereschith Rabba*, sect. 18, fol. 18, 2, is not strictly in point. The passage relates to the words, "Wherefore a man shall leave his "father and his mother," and is as follows:—"A proselyte, who has "passed over to the Jewish religion, and has married his sister, whether "she be of the same father, or the same mother, he must put her away : "so says R. Meir. But our wise men say, If she be of the same mother, "he must put her away ; but if she be of the same father, he may keep "her ; שאין אב לגוי, for a Gentile has no father ;" that is, his father is of no account in the genealogies of the Jews. Even granting that ἀπάτωρ is explained by the above, the difficulty concerning ἀμήτωρ is, if anything, increased. Indeed, Schoettgen seems to feel the weakness of his own theory, for he adds :—" Quod in gentilibus usu venit, idem "de reliquis statuendum, quamvis exempla de singulis adferre non "possumus. Canon enim philosophicus est ; Qui in uno tertio con- "veniunt, de illis eadem prædicari solent." Now, granting for the sake of Schoettgen's proposition, that Melchizedek was a Canaanite, our Lord Jesus Christ was of Jewish parents, and two genealogies of his parentage exist. How, then, can He be said to be ἀπάτωρ in this technical sense ? Much more, how can He be said to be ἀμήτωρ and ἀγενεαλόγητος ? In Ezra ii. 61, 62, Neh. vii. 63, 64, we find an example of priests who were disqualified from following the priestly office, in consequence of a defect in the genealogical proofs of the purity of their descent. But the real question at issue, in respect to the word ἀμήτωρ,

CHAP. VII., 2—5.

is this, Did the Mosaic law prohibit the High Priest from marrying any virgin except one of his own immediate family connexions; or, was he permitted to marry any Israelitish maiden under the restrictions mentioned in Levit. xxi. 7, 13, 14 ? The entire dispute turns upon the meaning of the expression, בתולה מעמיו יקח אשה, *he shall take a virgin of his own people to wife*. And again, ולא יחלל זרעו בעמיו, *Neither shall he profane his seed among his people*. The Vulgate renders " puellam de populo suo" and " Ne commisceat stirpem generis sui vulgo gentis sui" as Selden observes (*De Success. in Pontif. Ebræor.*, p. 407, *Lugd. Bat.*, 1638, 12mo.), " Subindicans proculdubio non solum Virginem pontifici " ducendam sed etiam ex genere seligendam sacerdotali, quod per *popu-* " *lum suum*, autor Versionis innui existimavit. Neque ille solus. " Nam sic etiam disserte Philo, Judæus Alexandrinus, lib. ii., *de* " *Monarchia.*"—The words of Philo are, ἀλλὰ καὶ ἱέρειαν ἐξ ἱερέων, ἵνα ἐκ μιᾶς οἰκίας καὶ τρόπον τινὰ τοῦ αὐτοῦ αἵματος ὦσιν νυμφιός τε καὶ νύμφη. " But also a priestess from amongst the priests, in order that the bride- " groom and bride may be of one and the same house, and in a manner " of one and the same blood." Selden, however, declares that he cannot find the least trace of such an interpretation, either in the Talmud or in Josephus. They both understand מעמיו, *of his own people*, of the people of Israel in general. "Et Aben Ezra ad dictum locum, *Ratio est*, " inquit, *in adjectione verborum illorum*, de populis suis, כי הבתולה השבויה, " לו אסורה והמתיהדת *quoniam virgo capta* (è gentilibus) *et Judæa facta, seu* " *proselyta, ei interdicitur.* Quam etiam nomine *Zona*, seu Scorti, ut " mox patebit, comprehendunt. (See note on νόθοι, Heb. xii. 8.) " Ex singulari vero vocabuli Uxoris in sacra de Pontificis nuptiis lege " receptior est sententia polygamiam ei negatam esse." (*Ibid.*, p. 408.) Cunæus (*De Rep. Hebr.*, lib. iii., *Lugd. Bat.*, 1632, 12mo.) devotes an entire chapter to the subject of Melchizedek, which is well argued out. He believes (p. 371), as Ewald does, and I do, that Melchizedek was the second person in the Ever Blessed Trinity, the Divine *angel of the Lord*, who continually appeared to the fathers under the Old Testament dis- pensation. " Ego sic existimo, Melchisedecum, non hominem utique ex " hominibus genitum, sed divinioris naturæ fuisse, majoremque homine " ...... qui tanto benedixit patriarchæ." And again on p. 379, " Neque " alio pertinere mihi videtur, quod scriptum a Joanne est, *Abram gestiit* " *videre diem meum, et vidit et gavisus est*. Id enim uni Abramo contigit, " et singulare quiddam fuit : cum de cæteris illud dicatur, *Multi pro-* " *phetæ et justi cupiverunt videre quæ videtis, et non viderunt.* Sed neque " hoc sententiæ nostræ repugnat, quod *Justitiæ* ille *Pacisque Rex* " ἀπάτωρ καὶ ἀμήτωρ, *sine patre ac sine matre* fuisse dicitur. Non enim " profecto Divus Paulus mysterium illud duplicis naturæ spectavit, "quod ejusmodi est, uti Messiæ quidem divinitas Patrem, mortalitas "vero matrem, ac seorsim neutra utrumque parentem agnoscat. Per- "tinere illud ad ea tempora non potuit, cum nondum hominem induisset "humani generis Servator. Sed hoc utique sensit potius Apostolus, "non esse cum communi lege ex patre atque matre, neque ex libidine "aut conjunctione viri feminæque satum, sed æternum eum esse, et "(quod Esaias vates in cap. liii. 8, ait) *nihil posse dici de generatione ejus* "(τὴν γενεὰν αὐτοῦ τίς διηγήσεται)." For further opinions as to the person and dignity of Melchizedek the reader should consult the indexes to Schoettgen's Hor. Hebr., J. C. Wolfii Curæ Phil., tom. iv. (*in loc.*), and the erudite article, *Melchizedek*, by the Rev. W. T. Bullock, in Smith's Dictionary of the Bible : although, in spite of the dicta of Suidas and Schoettgen and others, I beg emphatically to dissent from Mr. Bullock's altogether unwarrantable assertion, that the opinion "is now generally received" (!) that "Melchizedek was of "one blood with the children of Ham, among whom he lived, chief "(like the King of Sodom) of a settled Canaanitish tribe." How it was possible for one of that accursed race to be endowed with an inherent dignity greater than that of Abraham and of Aaron, and to be, as the canonical writer to the Hebrews describes it, ἀφωμοιωμένος τῷ υἱῷ τοῦ Θεοῦ, I must leave to a "higher criticism" than my own to decide. Ewald's opinion will be given, at length, on a succeeding page.

⁴ 'Αφωμοιωμένος δὲ τῷ υἱῷ τοῦ Θεοῦ. *After the exact pattern, made exactly like to :* ἀφομοίωμα signifies a copy or facsimile. This is doubt- less an allusion to the before cited Psalm ii. 7 : " I will declare the "decree, the Lord hath said unto me, Thou art my Son, this day have "I begotten thee ;" and also to Ps. xlv. 6, 7, " Thy throne, O God, "is for ever and ever; the sceptre of thy kingdom is a right sceptre. "Thou lovest righteousness, and hatest wickedness : therefore God, "thy God, hath anointed thee with the oil of gladness above thy "fellows." Of the inherent and hereditary Divine glory of the eternal Son the writer has already spoken (chaps. i. and ii.). The great importance of the subject may render a little more detailed examination of these passages acceptable. The authorship of Psalm ii. has been with one consent ascribed to David himself. Dr. M'Caul remarks (*The Messiahship of Jesus*, pp. 150, 151), " It is certainly a Psalm of " David. Acts iv. 25 ('who by the mouth of thy servant David hast " 'said, Why did the heathen rage,' &c.) will satisfy on this point any " one who believes the New Testament. Rashi and Kimchi ascribe it " to David himself ; Aben Ezra to the time of David. Even modern " criticism does not make it later than Solomon. Ewald says, ' This " 'beautiful Psalm must necessarily have proceeded from the most

"'glorious period of the monarchy,......confined to the time of David,
"'and the beginning of Solomon's reign.' Venema gives three reasons
"for ascribing it to David......This Psalm proclaims, therefore, the
"hope of the devout Israelite a thousand years before the coming of
"Christ." It is worthy of further notice that St. Paul (Acts xiii. 33)
describes the Psalm as being "the *second* Psalm," *e.g.*, "as it is also
"written in the second Psalm, Thou art my Son, this day have I
"begotten thee." The numerical order of the Psalm was, therefore,
the same in the apostolic days that it is in our own. The Rev. G.
Phillips, D.D., in his very useful commentary on the Psalms, observes
(vol. i., p. 9), "We may remark that the high priest seems to make
"allusion to the Psalm when in Matt. xxvi. 63 he asks Jesus whether
"he were the Christ, the Son of God; and Nathanael also apparently
"does the same when in John i. 49 he addresses this ejaculation to
"Christ, 'Thou art the Son of God; thou art the King of Israel.' Again
"there is ample evidence to prove that the ancient Jews regarded this
"Psalm as predicting the Messiah; for it is quoted and so interpreted
"in nearly all their writings which bear in any degree the stamp of
"antiquity. The Jew in Justin Martyr thus understood the Psalm:
"The Talmud, in the treatise *Succah*, contains a passage in which it is
"stated to be a tradition of the Rabbis, that the 8th verse speaks of
"Messiah, the Son of David. In the *Zohar* there is found an observa-
"tion of the same import on the expression, *Kiss the Son.* In the middle
"ages we find Kimchi admitting that the ancient doctors of his nation
"assigned a Messianic sense to the 2d Psalm. Rashi makes the same
"statement, but he adds to it a remark which, however candid it may
"be thought, shows the sad state of the author's mind. His words are—
"רבותינו דרשו את הענין על מלך המשיח ולפי משמעו ולתשובת המינים נכון לפותרו על דוד עצמו
"*Our Rabbis have explained this Psalm with respect to King Messiah;*
"*but for the sake of a literal sense, and for an answer to the Christians*
"*(Heretics), it is expedient to interpret it with respect to David himself.*
"It is true that the words לתשובת המינים are not found in many editions;
"but Pocock, who searched some MSS. for the purpose of investigating
"the question, has come to the conclusion that the passage as above
"quoted is genuine. Aben Ezra also confesses that the application of
"it to the Messiah is preferable to any other. He says ואם על המשיח,
"הדבר יותר ברור *but if it be interpreted of the Messiah the matter is clearer.*
"The Jews of modern times do not acknowledge that Christ was
"intended to be represented in this Psalm, and agree in applying it
"entirely to David; but in so doing they oppose themselves to the
"universal voice of antiquity, and have no better reason to offer than
"that which is assigned by Rashi." J. A. Danzius, in his treatise

Inauguratio Christi (p. 386, note e), printed at length in Meuschen, agrees with Luther's explanation of היום, *to-day*, in this Psalm. Luther writes :—" Si ut res est loqui velimus, hodie, quotidie, et semper nascitur " et natus est Filius Dei. Nam in æterno nec præt. nec fut. est, sed " perpetuum hodie. Et *hodie* hic accipiendum pro tempore Dei non " nostro. Non enim nobiscum loquitur Deus ; sed cum illo qui est extra " tempus apud Deum." Danzius, in the passage above mentioned, writes " אני היום ילדתיך, notanter cum articulo ; qui in infinitis Scripturæ " locis *distributive* sumitur, ad *universalitatem* inferendam, juxta Inter- " pret. sect. 49, vi., cujus intuitu verteres, *ego* QUOLIBET DIE *te genui*, ut " Ps. xcv. 7, היום QUOLIBET DIE, *i.e.*, *quotiescunque audiveritis vocem ejus*, " *ne obduretis cor vestrum*. Jud. xi. 27. Dominus judicans היום *quolibet* " *die, i.e., quotidie :* quo sensu et יומם sumi Jes. xxi. 8, non tantum תמיד " adjectum indicat ; sed et oppositum הלילות, quod vocem כל additam " habet. Ut enim hoc *noctes quascunque* denotat ; ita illud vi opposi- " torum, *dies quoscunque*. Conf. etiam Gen. xxii. 14, xxxi. 48, non " tamen neglecto Jes. xliii. 13. Isto certe modo expetita omnibus " æternitatis significatio, quam multi magno molimine non potuerunt " eruere, sua sponte se aperit. Ex eadem voce היום Deut. iv. 4, extante, " aliter æternitatem eruit Philo *de Profugis*, p.m. 458 (*Mangey's Edit.*, " tom. i., p. 554) in fine inquiens, σήμερον ἐστὶν ἀπέρατος καὶ ἀδιεξίτητος " αἰών. μηνῶν γὰρ καὶ ἐνιαυτῶν καὶ συνόλως χρόνων περίοδοι, δόγματα " ἀνθρώπων ἐστὶν ἀριθμὸν ἐκτετιμηκότων· τὸ δ' ἀψευδὲς ὄνομα αἰῶνος, ἡ " σήμερον, *i.e.*, Hodie est infinitum et impervium ævum. Mensium enim, " annorum, et in universum temporum circuitus ; dogmata sunt homi- " num magni facientium numeros : verum autem nomen ævi est HODIE." Phillips, however (*ibid.*, p. 24), considers that deriving the important doctrine of the eternal generation of the Son, from היום in this verse, is rather forced criticism. The Talmud, treatise *Succah*, fol. 52, applies this verse of the 2d Psalm to the Messiah.

ה"ר מטיח בן דוד שעתיד להגלות במהרה בימינו אומר לו הק"בה שאל ממני דבר ואתן
לך שנ' אספרה אל חק וגומר אני היום ילדתיך שאל ממני ואתן גוים נחלתך :

" Our Rabbies have taught that Messiah ben David, who is to be " revealed speedily in our days, the Holy One, Blessed be He, said to " him, Ask something of me, and I will give to thee. As it is said, " I will declare as to the decree, &c. I this day have begotten thee. " Ask of me, and I will give the heathen as thine inheritance." As to the interpretation of the words נשקו בר *Kiss the Son*, Dr. M'Caul (*The Messiahship of Jesus*, p. 151) observes that they " are rendered by the " LXX. δράξασθε παιδείας ; by the Chaldee, in the same sense, קבילו " אולפנא, and by the Vulgate, ' Apprehendite disciplinam.' Ewald gives " a similar version, ' Nehmt Rath an ' (*Receive advice*). Of this it is

"sufficient to say that it is a commentary, but not a translation; and
"that learned men are not even agreed as to how this explanation could
"have arisen from the words. The verb נשק to kiss, is not employed
"metaphorically in the sense of embracing, laying hold of. בר does not
"ever signify learning. The rendering is, therefore, false. Some
"modern Jews, anxious to get rid of this command to do homage to
"the Son of God, render the words 'Arm yourselves with purity,' but
"the incorrectness of this is easily proved—1st, the verb נשק, in Piel,
"as it is here, means only to kiss. (See Gen. xxix. 13, xxxi. 28, xxxii. 1,
"xlv. 15.) Gesenius, in his *Thesaurus*, shows that even in Kal it does
"not mean to 'arm.' 2dly, בר does not mean 'purity.' If it be an
"adjective, then it is 'kiss the pure one.' 3dly, The overwhelming
"weight of authority, Jewish and Gentile, is in favour of our English
"version, 'Kiss the Son.' Of ancients, the Syriac version, and the
"Midrash (which interprets 'Kiss the Son' of appeasing the Son.
"נשיקו בן—Jalkut Shimoni, *in loc.*) Aben Ezra (who refers to Prov.
"xxxi. 2), Mendelssohn, Zunz, Dr. Solomon of Hamburg, Gesenius,
"De Wette, all interpret it of doing homage to the Son. The Son,
"the Anointed, is mentioned before as the Being against whom the
"king and nations rebel. Here they are warned against the conse-
"quences. The word בר is used instead of בן, because of פן immedi-
"ately following," *i.e.*, for euphony's sake, and to prevent two words
of nearly the same sound coming together. The reader will find a
number of early Jewish authorities, in favour of the Messianic and
Christian interpretation, quoted by Schoettgen, *Hor. Hebr.*, tom. ii.,
pp. 227, 230. And now with respect to the Messianic application of
Ps. xlv. Dr. Gill observes that "the Targum in the King of Spain's
"Bible begins the 7th verse thus, '*But thou, O King Messiah, because
"'thou lovest.*'" Schoettgen, tom. ii., pp. 234, 235, adduces nearly
twenty passages from the Targum—the Sohar Chadash, the Bereshith
Rabba, the Jalkut Shimoni, R. Joseph Ben Moshe, Aben Ezra, all of
which apply the Psalm to the Messiah. Dr. Phillips has collected a
goodly number of similar testimonies on p. 340, vol. i., of his Commentary. "The Chaldee Interpreter has given the following paraphrase of
"verses 3, 7, 8. Thy beauty, O King Messiah, is more excellent than
"that of the sons of men; the spirit of prophecy is given into Thy lips;
"therefore Jehovah hath blessed thee for ever. 7, The throne of Thy
"glory, O Jehovah, standeth for ever and ever, a righteous sceptre is
"the sceptre of Thy kingdom. 8, Because that Thou hast loved righte-
"ousness, and hated wickedness: therefore Jehovah, Thy God, hath
"anointed Thee with the oil of gladness more abundantly than thy
"fellows. In וזהר הרש (*Sohar Chadash*), fol. 12, 2, on the words *sceptre*

"*of righteousness*, it is remarked that this is spoken of King Messiah, דא מלכא משיחא. Joseph ben Moses, in כתר תורה fol. 36, 4, observes on "the 7th and 8th verses, that they speak concerning the King Messiah, "הפסוקים אלה מדברים נגד מלך המשיח. So, also, the later Jewish commen-"tators have understood the Psalm. Thus Kimchi, at the commence-"ment of his Commentary, states that 'this Psalm is said of the King "Messiah.' Again, Aben Ezra, on verse 2, remarks that 'this Psalm "treats of David, or rather of his Son Messiah.' Even Mendelssohn "heads his edition of it with this observation,—'This Psalm speaks of "the exaltation and greatness of the King Messiah.'" It ought to be remembered that several of the above cited Jewish opinions represent the mind of the Hebrew Church, in the age immediately succeeding that of the Apostles. It will be then apparent that the New Testament writers, in their application of the Old Testament Scriptures, employed a canon of interpretation which was current amongst their unbaptized brethren. They brought in no forced and strained adaptation of the prophetical writings, but spoke the words of "truth and soberness." How grotesque, also, do considerations such as the foregoing make the impudent figment of a modern "Higher Criticism" appear, viz., that the Apostles and their followers learned their reverence for any of the Old Testament writings from the Apocryphal Book of Enoch! Before quitting the subject it may not be out of place to call attention to the LXX. version of the words of Daniel iii. 25. They render ורוה די, רביעיא רמה לבר אלהין by καὶ ὅρασις τοῦ τετάρτου ὁμοία υἱῷ Θεοῦ.

⁵ Μήτε ἀρχ. ἡμερ., μήτε ζωῆς τέλος ἔχων. This is a reference back to Psalm cii. 25—27, which the writer has already adduced (chap. i. 10—12) to prove the eternity of the Son of God, one of whose names is given in Is. ix. 6 as אבי עד, *Father*, *i.e.*, Possessor, *of Eternity*. See Dr. M'Caul, *The Messiahship of Jesus*, pp. 183—185. Schoettgen (*Hor. Hebr.*, tom. ii., p. 240), commenting on Ps. lxxii. 17, *His name shall endure for ever*, &c., writes:—"Pirke R. Eliezer, c. 3, et Bereschith Rabba, sect. 1, "fol. 3, 3. *Sex res* (in Pesachim, fol. 54, 1 ; Nedarim, fol. 39, 2 ; "Midrasch Tehillim, fol. 35, 4 ; et Midrasch Mischle, fol. 53, 3, "numerantur *septem*) *fuerunt ante mundum conditum*; et inter eas *nomen* "*Messiæ*, q.d. Ante solem Jinnon est nomen ejus." (See note 4, pp. 52—54.) Now if Melchizedek was "without beginning of days or end of life," but "abideth a priest continually," how can it be believed of him that he was a mere mortal? Τίνι ὡμοιώσατε Κύριον ; καὶ τίνι ὁμοιώματι ὡμοιώσατε αὐτόν ; Is. xl. 18; see also li. 12. Wolfius' assertion seems to me utterly unsatisfactory:—"Melchisedecus perpetuus hic dicitur "Sacerdos, eo quod nec mortis, nec successoris ejus in sacris literis "mentio est." Melchisedek, as the Divine *Logos*, existed from eternity.

CHAP. VII., 2—5.

⁶ Θεωρεῖτε δὲ πηλίκος οὗτος. Spencer (*De Legibus Hebr. Rit.*, tom. ii., p. 100; *Hag. Com.*, 1686, 4to.) asserts that the heathen nations before the time of Moses were in the habit of paying tithes to their kings in virtue of a regal right or claim, and he cites the example of Abraham in support of his statement :—" Moris autem hujusce fidem haud "obscuram facit exemplum Abrahami, qui Melchisedechum *Salemi* "regem decimâ donavit, in subjectionis, inferioris certe conditionis et "dignitatis argumentum : hoc e verbis Apostoli luculenter intelligen- "dum (Heb. vii. 4). *Spectate vero quantus hic fuerit, ᾧ καὶ δεκάτην* "'Ἀβραὰμ ἔδωκεν, *cui vel decimam spoliorum dedit Abrahamus ille patri-* "*archa.* Sic textum reddo, quòd Apostolus, non hic tantum, sed et versu "secundo, hunc ipsum ordinem loquendi servet, et ᾧ καὶ δεκάτην Ἀβραάμ, "non ᾧ καὶ Ἀβραὰμ δεκάτην, habeat : ut scilicet innueret, ipsam doni "qualitatem, non minus quam donantis conditionem, Melchisedechum "loci regii virum et Abrahamo superiorem indicâsse. Interpretes "itaque, qui sic locum reddere solent, *cui Abrahamus etiam patriarcha* "*decimam dedit* (prout et Anglicani nostri, qui sic vertunt, *unto whom* "*the patriarch Abraham gave the tenth*) ; vim et aculeum argumenti "Apostolici non satis percepisse videantur. Huic argumento simul et "assertioni meæ momenti nonnihil accedat è modo citatis prophetæ "verbis, 1 Sam. viii. 15—17. Nam ibi de rege loquens Israeli præfici- "endo ; *Segetes* (inquit) *vestras, et vinearum reditus addecimabit, ut det* "*eunuchis et servis ejus. Greges quoque addecimabit.*"

⁷ The following eloquent passage from Prof. Delitzsch (*Die Genesis*, p. 267, 268) will prove no unwelcome addition to what has been already adduced upon the subject of Melchizedek's meeting with Abraham :—

"Abram hat mit nur 318 Mann vier Könige besiegt und fünf Könige "gerettet—darin ist er ein Vorbild der in der Kraft des Glaubens die "Welt überwindenden alttestamentlichen Volks und neutestamentlichen "Geistesgemeinde. Er weist jeden Antheil an der Beute zurück, denn "er bedarf der Welt nicht, der er in aufopfernder Liebe dient ; reich "durch Jehova braucht und mag er sich nicht auf Kosten Anderer "bereichern von denen nicht zu nehmen, sondern denen zu geben er "berufen ist. Da tritt die wunderbare Gestalt Malkizedeks so unver- "mittelt aus verborgenem Hintergrunde hervor wie sie wieder in den- "selben verschwindet—ein König der nicht blos als König, wie der "Hausvater als Hausvater den priesterlichen Dienst verrichtet (in "welchem Sinne auch Abram Fürst, נשיא, und Priester zugleich ist), "sondern der in Einer Person mit der Würde des Königs das Amt "eines Priesters vereinigt und deshalb (wie Abram nie) ausdrücklich "כהן genannt wird. Von diesem Priesterkönig, der ausserhalb der "Linie und des Kreises der Verheissung steht, lässt Abram sich segnen,

M

"der Gesegnete Jehova's, der zum Segensmittler aller Völker der Erde
"gesetzt ist. Von diesem Priesterkönig, der keine Berechtigung durch
"Abstammung und Gesetz aufzuweisen hat, lässt sich segnen der
"Ahnherr Israels, der Ahnherr Levi's und Ahrons, der Stammvater
"des Volkes wie des Priesterthums des Gesetzes. Und nicht allein
"das : Abram, in welchem das Priestergeschlecht, welches den Zehnten
"zu empfangen hat, beschlossen ist, giebt diesem Priesterkönig den
"Zehnten der ganzen Beute. Es giebt ein aussergesetzliches königliches
"Priesterthum und priesterliches Königthum—das weissagt diese
"typische Geschichte—dem auch Abram und sein Same sich beugen,
"dem auch das levitische Priesterthum huldigen muss, denn gerade da,
"wo Abram in unvergleichlich erhabener Vorbildlichkeit dasteht, tritt
"Malkisedek neben ihn und ragt über ihn hinaus. Malkizedek ist wie
"die untergehende Sonne der Uroffenbarung die mit ihren letzten
"Strahlen den Patriarchen anscheint, von dem aus das wahre Licht der
"Welt im Kommen begriffen ist. Diese Sonne geht unter um wenn
"die vorbereitende Zeit Israels vorüber sein wird, in Jesu Christo
"gegenbildlich wieder aufzugehen."

⁸ Καὶ οἱ μὲν ἐκ τῶν υἱῶν Λευὶ ἱερατ. λαμβ. (Numb. xviii. 22, 23.) "I have
"given the children of Levi all the tenth in Israel for an inheritance,
"for their service......of the tabernacle of the congregation. Neither
"must the children of Israel henceforth come nigh the tabernacle of the
"congregation, lest they bear sin and die. (לשאת חטא למות *bear mortal*
"*sin*, λαβεῖν ἁμαρτίαν θανατηφόρον. LXX.) But the Levites shall do
"the service of the tabernacle of the congregation, and they shall bear
"their iniquity: it shall be a statute for ever throughout your genera-
"tions," &c. (והם ישאו עונם חקת עולם לדרתיכם, καὶ αὐτοὶ λήψονται τὰ ἁμαρ-
τήματα αὐτῶν, καὶ νόμιμον αἰώνιον εἰς τὰς γενεὰς αὐτῶν. LXX.) J. A.
Danzius acutely observes upon this passage, that Jewish tradition alone
might have taught the Jews that the Levitic ritual was not intended to
be enduring, *e.g.*, תנא דבי אליהו ששת אלפים שנה הוי עלמא שני אלפים תוהו שני
אלפים תורה שני אלפים ימות המשיח.

Tradition of the school of Elijah:—*The world is to stand six thousand
years. Two thousand, confusion; two thousand, the law; two thousand,
the days of Messiah.* (Talmud, *Sanhedr.*, fol. 97, col. 1. See also Dr.
M'Caul's essay, *The Birth of Messiah*, in "The Old Paths.")

⁹ "But here," observes Dr. Gill, "a difficulty arises how the Levites
"that were priests, can be said to receive tithes from the people, when
"they received the tenth part of the tithes, or the tithe of tithes, from
"the Levites (Numb. xviii. 26; Neh. x. 38); but it should be observed
"that it was not necessary that the Levites should give these tithes to
"the priests themselves; an Israelite might do it, and so give the

" Levites the less ; on which account the priests may be said to receive
" from the people ; besides, Ezra in his time ordered that the first tithe
" should not be given to the Levites, but to the priests, because they
" would not go up with him to Jerusalem. T. Bab. Yebamot., fol. 86,
" 2, and Becorot, fol. 4, 1." Reland writes (*Antiq. Hebr.*, p. 380, 381),
" Quæri hoc loco potest de sensu verborum Pauli, *Hebr.* vii. 5, οἱ ἐκ τῶν
" υἱῶν Λευὶ τὴν ἱερατείαν λαμβάνοντες, *mandatum habent accipiendarum*
" *decimarum a populo*. Ubi non Levitis sed sacerdotibus decimæ
" videntur tribui. Dici posset respici hic ad decimas, quas Levitæ
" dabant Sacerdotibus, ita ut populus Sacerdotibus per Levitas decimas
" solveret, quemadmodum Deus ipse primitias accipere dicitur, quæ
" Sacerdotibus dabantur, in *Gem. Sanhedrin*, 39, 1. At videtur potius
" hic agi de Levitis ipsis, sic ut illi qui *Jerem.* xxxiii. 21, appellantur
" הלוים הכהנים, hic nuncupentur *illi qui ex filiis Levi sunt*, id est Levitæ,
" *quorum tribui jura Sacerdotii concessa sunt*, sive τὴν ἱερατ. λαμβ. illi jus
" habent ad decimas. Nam commate 14, tribui Leviticæ Sacerdotium a
" Mose tributum memorat, et commate 9, *Levi*, scribit, *decimas acci-
" perc*. Ita in *Turg. Hieros.*, Gen. xxv. 31, legitur Pontificatum
" Maximum datum tribui Levi, איתיהיבת כהונתא רבתא לשיבתא לוי, et *Jos.*
" viii. 7, Sacerdotium esse hæreditatem Levitarum. Nec dubium esse
" potest, quin Levitæ illi fuerint, quibus Deus mandaverit decimas a
" populo accipere, non sacerdotes : etiamsi, ut Judæi tradunt in *Gem.*
" *Ketuvoth*. 26, 1, stante templo ii., decimas Levitis aliquando non
" dederint, vetante hoc Ezra, sed Sacerdotibus. Hic autem agit Paulus
" non de consuetudine, sed de mandato Dei, quo certe Levitæ ad deci-
" mas jus acceperunt."

Verses 6—14.—But he (Melchisedek), who was not of
their genealogy, took tithes of Abraham, and blessed
him who had received (τὸν ἔχοντα, was holder of) the
promises.[1] But, beyond all dispute, the less is blessed of
the greater[2] (*i.e.*, Abraham, the founder of the race, and
the holder of the promises, was greater than Levi, but
Abraham was blessed of Melchisedek ; therefore, *à fortiori*,
Melchisedek was greater than Levi, or any of the Aaronic
priesthood).—Furthermore (there is one self-evident attribute of the inherent superiority in the inheritor of Melchisedek's office and dignity, which requires only to be stated
to receive assent, viz.,) here on earth dying men receive
tithes (*i.e.*, the sons of Aaron are mortal), but there (ἐκεῖ,

Gen. xiv.), a person, who is testified of, that he is alive.³ Levi also (so to speak), who is the recipient of tithes, was tithed (vicariously) by the act (διὰ) of Abraham, for he was yet in his ancestral father's loins when Melchisedek met him. Besides, if perfection⁴ (τελείωσις, either *perfect expiation*, or *the completion of the Divine purposes and plan*) had been brought in by the Levitical priesthood (for the people [of Israel] received their constitution as based upon it—ἐπ' αὐτῇ νενομοθέτητο), what further need that any other priest should arise, and be distinctively specified (λέγεσθαι) as "after the order of Melchisedek," and not after the order of Aaron? For if the priesthood be set aside, the law is, of necessity, set aside also. But He (Jesus), in reference to whom these things are spoken, belonged to (μετέσχηκεν) a different tribe, of which no man gave attendance at the altar;⁵ because it is a matter of notoriety that the Lord sprung from the tribe of Judah,⁶ to which tribe Moses spake⁷ nothing concerning the priesthood.

¹ Τὸν ἔχοντα τὰς ἐπαγγελίας, *i.e.*, he who held the promises of blessing and blessedness, received additional blessing from Melchizedek. It is worthy of note that, in Gen. xxii. 18, and xxvi. 4, the Hithpael conjugation is used, signifying "*to account oneself blessed*," and not the Niphal, or passive, as in Gen. xii. 3, xviii. 18, xxviii. 14. The Hithpael also occurs in Ps. lxxii. 17, "And men shall be blessed (or *account themselves blessed*) in Him." See also Is. lxv. 16, and Jer. iv. 2. In Gen. xii. 2 it was promised that Abraham should "be a blessing," ברכה, as well as (verse 3) that all families of the earth should be blessed in Him. This was the first form of the promise, which accompanied the call, "Get thee out of thy country," &c.

² Τὸ ἔλαττον ὑπὸ τοῦ κρείττ. εὐλογ. *The less thing is blessed by the greater.* Josephus says that, during the feast, Melchizedek began "to "praise Abraham, and to bless God," αὐτόν τε ἐπαινεῖν καὶ τὸν θεὸν εὐλογεῖν.

³ Καὶ ὧδε μὲν δεκάτ. ἀποθνήσκ, ἄνθρ. λαμβ. ἐκεῖ δέ, μαρτυρούμενος ὅτι ζῇ, *i.e.*, "Melchizedek received tithes, who is testified of (Ps. cx.), that "he is yet alive." Very lame, again, is the explanation offered by Wolfius, in common with others, viz., that we know that the Levitical high priests died off in the natural course of events, but that the

Scripture says nothing of Melchizedek's death, but speaks only of his life. Wolfius is prudently silent upon the interpretation of the latter clause of verse 16, Ὅς οὐ κατὰ νόμον ἐντολῆς σαρκικῆς γέγονεν, ἀλλὰ κατὰ δύναμιν ζωῆς ἀκαταλύτου. It is a moot point whether ὅς refers primarily to Melchizedek or to Christ. In either case the difficulty remains the same, unless we take the words in their literal signification, as I, with Cunæus and Ewald, feel compelled to do. (See note, p. 75, and note 7, p. 93.)

⁴ Εἰ μὲν οὖν τελείωσις. Schoettgen pithily remarks (in loc.), "Si aliud "quoddam sacerdotium ab Aaronitico diversum promittitur, sequitur, "posterius non fuisse sufficiens. Atqui vero Deus sacerdotium æternum "secundum ord. Melch. promittit, quod clarissimum est. Sequitur "ergo, Sacerdotium Christi sec. ord. Melch. longe præstantius esse "Aaronitico. Nemo enim vestem novam abjicit, ut veterem induat, "sed potius vice versa."

⁵ Οὐδεὶς προσέσχηκε τῷ θυσιαστηρίῳ. "De qua nullus altari præsto "fuit."—*Vulg.* "Aus welchem nie Keiner des Altars gepfleget hat."— *Luth.* "None of whom served at the altar."—*Stuart.* "Ex quâ nemo "altari operam dedit."—*Wolfius.* Προσέχω is translated *to give heed to* in the Auth. Vers., Acts viii. 6, 10. See also 11, and xvi. 14 ; 1 Tim. i. 4 ; iv. 1. See also verse 13 ; Tit. i. 14; Heb. ii. 1 ; 2 Pet. i. 19.

⁶ Ὅτι ἐξ Ἰούδα ἀνατέταλκεν ὁ Κύριος ἡμῶν. The late Dr. M'Caul (*Old Paths.* London, 1846. 8vo., pp. 542, 543) says, "The ancient Rabbies "do not leave us to reason upon their words ; on the contrary, they "tell us expressly that Messiah was born about the time that the temple "was destroyed. In the Jerusalem Talmud, R. Judan tells us a story "of a Jew who actually went and saw Him :—

עובדא הוה בחד יהודאי דהוה קאים רדי געא תורתיה קומי עבר חד ערבי ושמע קלה
א״ל בר יודאי בר יודאי שרי תורך ושרי קנקניך דהא חריב בית מוקדש׳ געת וזמן תנינות׳
א״ל בר יודאי יודאי קטור הוריך וקטור קנקניך דהא יליד מלכא משיחא׳ א״ל מה שמה מנחם
א״ל ומה שם דאבוי א״ל חזקיה׳ אמ׳ ליה מן הן הוא׳ א״ל מן בירת מלכא דבית
לחם יהודה :

"*It happened once to a certain Jew, who was standing ploughing, that "his cow lowed before him. A certain Arab was passing, and heard its "voice. He said, O Jew, O Jew! unyoke thine ox, and loose thy plow-"share, for the temple has been laid waste. It lowed a second time, and "he said, O Jew, O Jew! yoke thine oxen, and bind on thy plowshares, "for King Messiah is born. The Jew said, What is his name? Menu-"chem. He asked further, What is the name of his father? The other "replied, Hezekiah. He asked again, Whence is he? The other said, "from the Royal residence of Bethlehem of Judah.* (Berachoth, fol. 5, "col. 1.)—The story then goes on to tell us how he went and saw the "child ; but when he called the second time, the mother told him that

"the winds had carried the child away. We are quite willing to grant
"that this story is a fable. We quote it.........to show that the more
"ancient Jews were so fully persuaded that the right time of Messiah's
"advent was past, that they readily believed also that He was actually
"born. The Babylonian Talmud, also, evidently takes for granted
"that Messiah is born, as appears from the following legend :—

ר' יהושע בן לוי אשכחיה לאליהו דהוי קיימי אפיתחא דמערתא דרבי שמעון בן יוחי א"ל
אתינא לעלמא דאתי א"ל אם ירצה ארון הוה אמר ר' יהושע בן לוי שנים ראיתי וקול ג'
שמעתי א"ל אימת אתי משיח א"ל ויל שייליה לדידיה והיכא יתיב אפיתחא דרומי ומאי
סימניה יתיב בני עניי סובלי חלאים וכולן שרו ואסירי בחד ומנא איהו שרי חד ואסיר חד
אמר דילמא מבעינא דלא איעכב אול לגביה אמר ליה שלום עליך רבי ומורי אמר ליה שלום
עליך בר ליואי א"ל לאימת אתי מר אמר ליה היום :

"R. Joshua, the son of Levi, found Elijah standing at the door of the
"cave of R. Simeon ben Jochai, and said to him, Shall I arrive at the
"world to come? He replied, If this Lord will. R. Joshua, the son of
"Levi, said, I see two, but I hear the voice of three. He also asked,
"When will Messiah come? Elijah replied, Go, and ask himself. R.
"Joshua then said, Where does he sit? At the gate of Rome. And how
"is he to be known? He is sitting amongst the poor and sick; and they
"open their wounds and bind them up again all at once; but he opens
"only one, and then he opens another; for he thinks, perhaps I may be
"wanted, and then I must not be delayed. R. Joshua went to him, and
"said, Peace be upon thee, my master and my Lord. He replied, Peace
"be upon thee, son of Levi. The Rabbi then asked him, When will my
"Lord come? He replied, TO-DAY (alluding to the words of the Psalm,
"To-day, if he will hear his voice)." Dr. M'Caul goes on to observe,
"This is evidently a fiction, and a proof how little those doctors re-
"garded the truth; but it shows that he who invented it, and those
"who received it, all equally believed that Messiah was born, and
"ready waiting to come forth for the redemption of Israel." (*Sanhedrin*, fol. 98, col. 1.) See also Matt. ii. 1—6. So, also, the Rabinnic
libellous legend, entitled TOLDOTH JESCHU, *The Generations of Jesus* (p. 3),
bears similar testimony as to the Saviour's birthplace. Having stated
that Joseph was of the tribe of Judah, it proceeds to give the following
particulars as to his place of residence, and that of Mary, his espoused
wife :—

שובן בבית לחם יהודא וקרוב לביתו היתה שוכנת אלמנה אחת ולה בת ושמה מרים והיא
מרים מגדלה נשייא הנזכרת בתלמוד

"He resided at Bethlehem-Judah. And a certain widow lived near
"his house, and she had a daughter named Mary, and this Mary was an
"adorner of female hair; of whom mention is made in the Talmud."
The tract is printed at length in Wagenseil's *Tela Ignea Satanæ*.

CHAP. VII., 15—19.   87

J. C. Wolfius (*in loc.*) writes, "Alludi hic ad משה, Jes. xi. 1, post "alios monuit Vitringa in Commentar, ad h.l., p. 308, ubi etiam con- "tendit, Mariam ex tribu Levitica nonnullis ortam falsò videri, cum " alioquin Apostolus h. l. forte non neglexisset, ortum Christi ex utraque " tribu, Judæ respectu patris, et Levi ratione matris, in usus suos vertere, "quando e contra *Christum* totum tribui Judæ vindicat." The present Bishop of Bath and Wells, Lord A. C. Hervey, has treated on the genealogy of our Lord in a separate work, and also in his Lordship's excellent article, *Genealogy of Jesus Christ*, in Smith's Dictionary of the Bible.

[7] Εἰς ἣν φυλὴν οὐδὲν περὶ ἱερωσύνης Μωσῆς ἐλάλησε. " In qua tribu "nihil de sacerdotibus Moyses locutus est."—*Vulg.* " Zu welchem " Geschlecht Moses nichts geredet hat vom Priesterthum."—*Luther.*

Verses 15—19.—And the matter becomes much more clearly apparent still, if another priest arises in the likeness (κατὰ τὴν ὁμοιότητα, *resembling in every particular*) of Melchisedek, who was constituted not according to the law of a carnal prescription, but in virtue of (κατὰ δύναμιν) a life of undying perpetuity (ζωῆς ἀκαταλύτου).[1] For this is the testimony[2] (concerning Messiah), " Thou art a priest " FOR EVER after the order of Melchisedek." Thus (we see that) there is a setting aside of the foregoing prescriptive commandment (προαγούσης ἐντολῆς, viz., that limited the priesthood to the family of Levi) ; inasmuch as it was devoid of real virtue, and inefficacious (ἀσθενὲς καὶ ἀνωφελές).[3] Because the law made nothing perfect, but it was the introduction (or initiation, ἐπεισαγωγὴ) of a better hope,[4] by which we draw nigh to God. (See note 8, p. 82, on Num. xviii. 22, "Neither must the children of "Israel henceforth come nigh the tabernacle of the con- " gregation," &c.)

[1] Stuart renders the above passage (verse 16) thus, " *Who was not* " *made* (a priest) *by an ordinance of temporary obligation, but by an* " *authority of endless duration.*" He seems to me, by such an interpretation, to miss somewhat of the real purport intended, viz., that the mortal frailty of the Levitic priesthood was a preliminary source of dissatisfaction, and that therefore Christ's Divine priesthood, as ever-

more abiding, was substituted in its place. Philo remarks as follows upon the uncertain duration of the lives of the Jewish high priests:—

Μακροβιώτατοι γὰρ, οἱ δὲ ὀλιγοχρονιώτατοι τῶν ἀρχιερέων εἰσί· καὶ οἱ μὲν νέοι, οἱ δὲ πρεσβύται καθίστανται.

"For some of the high priests are very long lived, whilst others, on "the contrary, are very short lived. Some of them are appointed "when young, and others advanced in life." (*De Profugis*, Works, *Mangey's Edit.*, tom. i., p. 562.)

² Μαρτυρεῖ γὰρ, " Scil. כהן, γραφὴ, *Scriptura,*" Wolfius *in loc.*

³ Spencer, *De Legibus Hebr. Rit.*, tom. ii., p. 13, has some very good remarks upon the subject. See also *ibid.*, tom. i., p. 6.

⁴ Stuart understands the writer to say that "the introduction of a "better hope did make men perfect." The sentiment is true, viz., that the fathers obtained salvation by faith in a promised and coming Redeemer, but I question whether this is the writer's meaning on the present occasion. See Gal. iii. 23, "But before faith (*i.e.*, the Gospel "dispensation) came, we were kept under the law, shut up unto the "faith, which should afterwards be revealed. Wherefore the law "became our schoolmaster (παιδαγωγὸς ἡμῶν γέγονεν εἰς Χριστὸν) with "reference to Christ, *i.e.*, to direct us to Christ."

Verses 20—25.—And from the fact (καθ' ὅσον) that (in the case of Christ) an oath is not wanting, by this very circumstance (κατὰ τοσοῦτον) Jesus has been made the surety¹ of a better covenant. For the other priests had no oath in confirmation of their commission, but Jesus had an oath, received from Him who said unto him (διὰ τοῦ λέγοντος πρὸς αὐτὸν), "Jehovah hath sworn, and will "not repent, Thou art a priest for ever after the order of Melchisedek" (*i.e.*, the Levitic commission was not irrevocably permanent and enduring, but Christ's is. The FOR EVER of eternal perpetuity is the distinguishing feature of Melchizedek's priesthood, and this is the "order" of priesthood which Christ can claim as his own). Besides, the Aaronic priests have been numerous, because death prevented their remaining. But Jesus, from the fact that he continues FOR EVER, holds (ἔχει) the (*not* a) priesthood which does not pass to another (ἀπαράβατον ἔχει τὴν ἱερωσύνην). On which account (ὅθεν) He is also able to save to the uttermost those who come to God through him, as He evermore liveth to make intercession² for them.

¹ Ἔγγυος, *a surety or bail;* a word only occurring once in the New Testament and three times in the Apocr. See Sirach xxix. 15, Χάριτας ἐγγύου μὴ ἐπιλάθῃ, ἔδωκε γὰρ τὴν ψυχὴν αὐτοῦ ὑπὲρ σοῦ. 16, Ἀγαθὰ ἐγγύου ἀνατρέψει ἁμαρτωλός. 2 Macc. x. 28, where it has the sense of a *token* or *pledge,* οἱ μὲν ἔγγυον ἔχοντες εὐημερίας καὶ νίκης. The rainbow was the token of the covenant of Noah. (Gen. ix. 12—17.) Circumcision (Gen. xvii. 11—14) of the covenant with Abraham; the blood of sprinkling (Exod. xxiv. 8) was the token of the covenant of Moses. Jesus the Messiah, by his atoning death, is the token of the New Covenant of Grace, and so it is promised that he should be (Is. xlii. 6, xlix. 8), in both of which passages it is said that he should be given "for a covenant of the people" (ואתנך לברית עם).

² The character of intercessor was one of the distinguishing attributes of Messiah. And the prophecy of Is. lix. 16, "He wondered that there "was no intercessor," וישתומם כי אין מפגיע, is referred to Messiah by R. Jochanan in the Talmud (*Schabbath,* fol. 139), whilst very many Rabbinical writings, including the book of *Zohar* (concerning which the late Dr. M'Caul writes, "If not a testimony from the first century of "Christianity, it is, to say the least, an authority of great weight amongst "the Rabbinical Jews, both in the East and in the West"), distinctly applies Isaiah liii. to Messiah, and there it is written concerning him, ולפשעים הפגיע, "And he made intercession for the transgressors." The following most remarkable passage from Philo demonstrates the belief of the ancient Græco-Jewish Church upon the subject of a Divine Mediator and Intercessor between God and man:—"But to the "Archangel and eldest Word (πρεσβυτάτῳ λόγῳ), the Father who begat "all things, has given the especial gift (δωρεὰν ἐξαίρετον) that standing "in the midst (μεθόριος) he might judge the act of the doer of it. He "evermore intercedes (ἱκέτης μέν ἐστι) with the Immortal on behalf of the "mortal who is in a state of anxious suspense (τοῦ θνητοῦ κηραίνοντος); "and is the ambassador (πρεσβευτής) of the king to his subjects. He "rejoices, moreover, in his office, and magnifies its dignity, saying "(Numb. xvi. 48), 'I also stood between you and the Lord.' He is "not unbegotten like God, nor begotten like ourselves, but midway "between each extreme, acting as a hostage or go-between (ἀλλὰ μέσος "τῶν ἄκρων ἀμφοτέροις ὁμηρεύων) to both."—Philo, *Quis Rerum Div. Hæres* (Works, vol. i., Edit. Mangey, pp. 501, 502).

CHAP. VII., 26—28.

Verses 26—28.—For such an high priest became us (ἔπρεπεν, *was suitable, or eminently adapted to our condition*), viz., holy, harmless, undefiled,[1] separated from sinners,[2] and exalted above the heavens;[3] and who has no daily[4] necessity (ὅς οὐκ ἔχει καθ' ἡμέραν ἀνάγκην), first for his own sins,[5] and then for the people's, to offer up sacrifices; for this he did once for all (ἐφάπαξ), when he offered himself. For the law constitutes men high priests who have infirmity, but the word of the oath, which was subsequent to the law (Ps. cx. 4) (constitutes as high priest), the Son perfected[6] for evermore (εἰς τὸν αἰῶνα τετελειωμένον, *consecrated*, Authorized Vers.).[7]

---

[1] Ὅσιος, ἄκακος, ἀμίαντος. The Messiah is described as God's *Holy One*, חסיד, *thy Holy One*, in Ps. xvi. 10, τὸν ὅσιόν σου, LXX., and applied by St. Peter, Acts ii. 27, to our Lord Jesus Christ. For a very satisfactory vindication of the reading חסיד, instead of חסידי, see Phillips on the Psalms, vol. i., p. 98. In Deut. xxxiii. 8 the term חסד is applied to Aaron in his pontifical capacity, and in immediate connexion with the Urim and Thummim, לאיש חסידך, τῷ ἀνδρὶ τῷ ὁσίῳ, LXX., and so it is explained in the Targums of Onkelos, Palestine, and Jerusalem. In Ps. xvi., the Messiah speaks (verses 4. 5) in his capacity as a priest. (See J. D. Michaelis and Gill.) Dr. M'Caul, on p. 154— 156 of his *Messiahship of Jesus*, gives a brief exposition of the Psalm, and writes on verse 10,—"חסידך, singular, *Thy Holy One*, as the great "majority of Jews and Christians, ancient and modern, testify. De Rossi "says, 'Lectio ipsa communis puncta habet singularis numeri, multique "'codd. et edd., cum Hooghtiana, notant ad marg. *redundat jod*; alii "'vero complures, sive MSS., sive edd. habent Keri חסידך, *lege sanctum* "'*tuum*; paucissimi codices sistunt puncta lectionis pluralis.' See "Roger's beautiful and most instructive edition of the Psalms." In elucidation of the meaning of ἄκακος, the reader may, with advantage, consult Selden, *de Success. in Pont. Ebræor.* In chap. vi. of part 2 he treats at length *de vitiis animi, quæ tam functioni sacerdotali quam success. in Pontificat. obstarent.* Schoettgen, erroneously I think, explains the expression ἀμίαντος, as if it were the equivalent of ἄμωμος of Heb. ix. 14; comp. 1 Pet. i. 19. Ἀμίαντος means here *unsullied* in soul, of which mental purity the legal precautions against ceremonial defilement were the type, whilst ἄμωμος signifies without "blemish" (מים, μῶμος, LXX.,

Lev. xxi. 17, *et passim in V. T.*), which disqualified sacrifice as well as priest, from the service of God. See Selden, *ibid.*, pp. 449–470.

² Κεχωρισμένος ἀπὸ τῶν ἁμαρτωλῶν. The tract *Joma* says (c. 1), Seven days before the day of Atonement they used to shut up or separate the High Priest from his own house (מפרישין כהן גדול מביתו ללשכת פרהדרין) in the chamber *Parhedrin*). Mishna Surenh., tom. ii., p. 206. Reland (p. 100) adds, " Ipsique adsederint membra quædam Synedrii וזקני בית דין, "ut eum ritus festi secuturi docerent, hinc apte nomen *Paredrin* ei "datum fuit." Another separation of the High Priest took place when the Elders (וזקני בית דין) brought the High Priest into the temple, and took an oath of him before leaving that he would make no alteration in the things which they had taught him. והוא פרש ובוכה, "Then he sepa-"rates himself and weeps," והן פורשין ובוכין "And they separate them-"selves and weep." (*Joma*, p. 209.) The whole tribe of Levi was separated unto the Lord, "instead of all the firstborn among the "children of Israel," in commemoration of the Passover. So also it is written concerning Aaron, that he "was separated (ויבדל) that he should "sanctify the most holy things, he and his sons for ever, to burn incense "before the Lord, to minister unto him, and to bless in his name for "ever." (1 Chron. xxiii. 13.) Whilst in Lev. xxii. 2 it is said, "Speak "unto Aaron and to his sons, that they separate themselves (וינזרו) from "the holy things of the children of Israel, and that they profane not "my holy name *in those things* which they hallow unto me." The preeminent sanctity attaching to the high priestly office, in contradistinction to the priestly, is apparent from the minute instructions given, Lev. xxi. 10, &c. Aaron is there called כהן הגדול מאחיו, ὁ ἱερεὺς ὁ μέγας ἀπὸ των ἀδελφῶν αὐτοῦ, LXX. He was forbidden to incur ceremonial pollution from contact with a dead body, "or defile himself for his "father or his mother." Josephus says that Moses "did not think it "proper for the high priest to marry even a widow of one that was "dead, though he allowed that to the priests ; but he permitted him "only to marry a virgin, and to retain her. Whence it is, that the "high priest is not to come near to one that is dead, although the rest "are not prohibited from coming near to their brethren, or parents, or "children, when they are dead ; but they are to be unblemished in all "respects."—Antiq. iii. 12, 2. But not only were the high priests to be "separated from sinners," but it was also their especial function (Lev. x. 10) to "put difference between holy and unholy, and between clean and "unclean," להבדיל בין הקדש ובין החל בין הטמא ובין הטהור, Διαστεῖλαι ἀναμέσον τῶν ἁγίων καὶ τῶν βεβήλων, καὶ ἀναμέσον τῶν ἀκαθάρτων καὶ τῶν καθαρῶν, LXX. "Auf das ihr könnet unterscheiden, was heilig und unheilig, "was unrein und rein ist."—*Luther*.

³ See Isaiah liii. 12 (and note 4 on p. 28).

⁴ I suspect that the meaning here is, *no necessity for expiatory sacrifice, which was daily experienced,* but was only alleviated, once a year, on the great Day of Atonement. Prof. Stuart (*in loco*) writes, "Who has not, " like the high priests, any daily necessity of offering sacrifices, first for " his own sins, and then for those of the people." Many doubts have been raised by critics about the meaning of καθ' ἡμέραν here because they have supposed that the high priest officiated in person only on the great day of atonement. But that these doubts are without any ground may be seen by consulting Lev. vi. 19—22, Num. xxviii. 3, 4. Philo, who was contemporary with the Apostles, says, "ἀρχιερεὺς, κατὰ "τοὺς νόμους, εὐχὰς δὲ καὶ θυσίας τελῶν καθ' ἑκάστην ἡμέραν, *the high priest,* " agreeably to the laws, makes daily supplications and sacrifices." On the other hand, Josephus (Wars, v. 5, 7) says, "The high priest did " also go up with them (the priests), not always, indeed, but on the " seventh days and new moons, and if any festival belonging to our " nation, which we celebrate every year, happened." From Lev. vi. 22 it would appear that the high priest on ordinary occasions was represented by one of his sons. I confess that I have failed to discover how Num. xxviii. 3, 4, applies to the high priest at all. It is true that a daily meat offering of flour, &c., "of Aaron and his sons" (Lev. vi. 20) was offered, morning and evening, by the high priest, or *in his name.* (See Reland *Antiq. Sacr. Vet. Hebr.,* p. 152, Traject. Bat., 1712, 8vo.) But the priest who was to slay the lamb for the daily sacrifice was selected by lot (see Reland, *ibid.,* p. 193) from amongst his brethren. The writer to the Hebrews is evidently speaking of the high priest *par excellence,* and not of his family.

⁵ Philo, in allegorising the death of the high priest, after which it should be lawful for the manslayer to return, writes,—λέγομεν γὰρ, τὸν ἀρχιερέα οὐκ ἄνθρωπον, ἀλλὰ λόγον θεῖον εἶναι, πάντων οὐχ ἑκουσίων μόνον, ἀλλὰ καὶ ἀκουσίων ἀδικημάτων ἀμέτοχον, κ.τ.λ. "My opinion is, " that the high priest is no (mere) man, but the Divine Word, who " partakes not of sins, either voluntary or involuntary."—*De Profugis,* Works, *Mangey's Edit.,* vol. i., p. 562.

And again, Δύο γὰρ, ὡς ἔοικεν, ἱερὰ θεοῦ, ἐν μὲν ὅδε ὁ κόσμος, ἐν ᾧ καὶ ἀρχιερεὺς, ὁ πρωτόγονος αὐτοῦ θεῖος λόγος, κ.τ.λ. "There are, methinks, " two temples of God. The one is this universe, whose high priest is " his firstbegotten Divine Word," &c.—*Quod a Deo Mittantur Somnia, ibid.,* vol. i., p. 653.

⁶ Stuart translates τετελειωμένον "exalted to glory," whilst the authorized English version, following the LXX. of Lev. xxi. 10, translates "consecrated," *e.g.,* "and he that is consecrated to put on

CHAP. VII., 26—28.   93

" the garments," τετελειωμένον ἐνδύσασθαι τὰ ἱμάτια. And so also the Vulgate, *cujus manus in sacerdotio consecratæ sunt;* whereas Luther translates ומלא את ידו (lit., *and his hand filled*) as if connected with the preceding words, *sc.*, " filled with the consecrating oil." Gesenius, however, says (*in Lex.* מלא) " *implevit Manum* alic., *i.e.*, sacerdotium " ei in manus tradidit. Exod. xxviii. 41, xxix. 9, Lev. xxi. 10." The Septuagint has again in Exod. xxix. 9, τελειώσεις, whilst in Exod. xxviii. 41 it reads καὶ ἐμπλήσεις αὐτῶν τὰς χεῖρας. Luther, " *ihre Hände füllen* " and " *die Hände fullen.*" I cannot but think that if Prof. Stuart had observed the above coincidence he would have modified his opinion, as regards the present passage at least. There seems to be, again, an allusion to Ps. cx., and also to the words of Psalm xlv., already quoted in Heb. i. 8, 9 ; a Psalm which the Chaldee Paraphrast, Joseph Ben Moses, Kimchi, Aben Ezra, and Mendelssohn all refer to " King Messiah." See "The Psalms in Hebrew, with a Commentary," by the Rev. G. Phillips, D.D., vol. i., 340, 341, and also my note on p. 20.

⁷ Dr. Ewald's remarks upon the person and identity of Melchisedek are so weighty, and of such paramount importance, as proceeding from one of the most colossal geniuses and illustrious scholars that Theological Germany ever produced, that I have taken the liberty of extracting them here, in their integrity, from pp. 86—90, of *Das Sendschr. a. die Hebr.* (Göttingen, 1870, 8vo.) :—" Und nun erst, nachdem die Rede " durch ihre höchst geschickte Leitung unter dem Steuerruder des " Redners zu Malkhissedeq zurückgekehrt ist, kann sich durch eine " nähere Vergleichung der drei Persönlichkeiten auf welche es hier " ankommt, 1) des Malkhissedeq, 2) Abraham's, seines Nachkommens " Levi, und des Levitischen Hohepriesterthumes, und 3), Christus' in " aller Ruhe und Bestimmtheit beweisen wer Christus als Hohepriester " näher betrachtet wirklich sei. So beweist sie denn dass wenn schon " Malkhissedeq verglichen mit Abraham, Levi und dem Levitischen " Priesterthume, ein ganz anderer Hohepriester war als alle die Leviti-" schen, unvergleichlich ewiger, erhabener, geheimnissvoller, und auch " dadurch göttlicher, dann sein mit ihm auch nach anderen hier wich-" tigen Seiten zu vergleichendes Urbild Christus als Hohepriester noch " unaussprechlich höher stehen müsse. Diese ganze Beweisführung " geht von vorne an nur von den hohen und so geheimnissvoll klingen-" den Psalmenworten über Malkhissedeq, aus welche der Redner zuerst " v. 6, erwähnt hatte, und welche er eben vi. 20, die Rede so absichtlich " zurückleitete, und die, nachdem alles aus ihnen zu schöpfende hier " erläutert ist zum guten Schlusse davon vii. 17, mit derselben Gewand-" theit als die Worte wiederholt werden welche hier den weiter zu " erläuternden h. Text bilden. Allein wohl fühlt der Redner dass er

" um seinen Zweck leichter zu erreichen in das Gewebe der Wortfügung
" jener Psalmenstelle auch noch alles das verflechten müsse was Gen. xiv.
" 18—20, von Malkhissedeq erzählt wird : diese kurze Erzählung über
" den unter Abraham lebenden, und mit ihm in eine engere Berührung
" kommenden Priesterkönig klingt nun schon wie sie dort gegeben wird
" nach ihrem einfachen Wortsinne vielfach ungewöhnlich und seltsam.
" [Note 1, p. 87, Woher dies komme, kann mann rein geschichtlich nach
" alle dem richtig schäzen was in der *Gesch. d. v. Isr.* Bd. 1, über den
" Ursprung des ganzen Stückes Gen. c. 14, erläutert ist.] Aber schon
" lange vor unserm Redner hatte der seltzam klingende Inhalt dieser
" so überaus abgerissenen kurzen Erzählung auch schon die Aufmerk-
" samkeit, den Scharfsinn und die Dichtungssucht vieler Schriftgelehrten
" beschäftigt. [Note 2, p. 87, Est ist für diese Sache sehr zu beklagen
" dass gerade die Stelle des *B. der Jubiläen*, welche uns hier aller
" Wahrscheinlichkeit nach, die wichtigsten Aufschlüsse geben könnte,
" in der Aethiopischen Übersezung verloren ist ; nach Dillmann's
" Ausgabe, s. 54, 19), fehlt sie jezt in allen Handschriften, und fehlte
" wol schon als das Buch in's Aethiopische übersetzt ward ; aber sie
" erscheint hier auch nicht etwa absichtlich und für sich allein ausge-
" stossen, da schon von dem ihr voraufgehenden einiges fehlt. Auch
" in den Bruchstücken der *Genesis Parva*, welche Ceriani im ersten
" Hefte der *Monumenta sacra et profana* veröffentlichte, findet sich
" diese Stelle mit ihrer weiteren Umgebung nicht.] Wie es damals
" viele gab welche mit der äussersten Neugierde und Sorgfalt alle die
" so einzeln, und an sich etwas unverständlich dastehenden Namen
" der Männer und Weiber der Genesis untersuchten, deren Ankunft
" und Verwandschaft erforschten und was dort zu fehlen schien durch
" allerlei Mittel ergänzten [Note 3, p. 87, Wie wir am deutlichsten
" aus dem B. Henokh und dem Buche der Jubiläen ersehen], so war es
" vielen aufgefallen dass dieser Priesterkönig dort so ganz vereinzelt
" und unvermittelt erscheint, ohne dass man auch nur erfährt wessen
" Sohn, oder wessen Stammes und Geschlechtes, oder Volkes er war ;
" und eine Menge, oft sehr ausschweifender und höchst willkührlicher
" Vermuthungen waren darüber ausgesprochen, und sezten sich auch
" in Schriften fest. [Note 4, pp. 87, 88, Wie dass Malkhissedeq einerlei
" mit Sem Noah's Sohne, oder gar mit Henokh sei, was man auch
" dadurch beweisen wollte dass ja nach den Zahlen Gen. xi. und v.
" jener, oder gar dieser noch gelebt haben könne. Und doch sind die
" Bestrebungen jener Mittelalterigen Gelehrten noch sehr unschuldig
" gegen die sovieler neuesten, mitten in unserer heutigen Deutschen
" Wissenschaft, welche die ebenso bodenlosesten, als abscheulichsten
" Dinge in Gen. c. 14, hineinlegen, und dabei absichtlich das schon

"sicher genug erläuterte gewisseste und beste übersehen.—*And yet,*
"*the efforts of those mediæval scholars are guiltless indeed, in comparison*
"*with those of the multitude of the latest (scholars) of our modern German*
"*science, who foist the most groundless and revolting matters into the*
"*14th chapter of Genesis, and at the same time wilfully overlook all that*
"*has been already sufficiently cleared up, and all that is most palpably cer-*
"*tain and excellent*] Unser Verfasser weist alle solche ganz willkührlich
"erfundene und festgehaltene Vermuthungen über ihn ab (*our author*
"*rejects all such gratuitous guesses*), hält sich streng nur an eine Verglei-
"chung und in einander Verarbeitung der Worte Ps. cx. 4 und Gen.
"xiv. 18, 20, hält aber aus den Worten jener Psalmenstelle desto
"strenger fest dass jener uralte, seltsame, und so geheimnissvoll
"abgerissen dort stehende Priesterkönig in der engsten Beziehung
"mit Christus stehen müsse, und leitet übrigens nach der gelehrt-
"en Sitte vieler seiner Zeitgenossen aus einer engen Zusammen-
"stellung jener beiden Bibelstellen und Ausbeutung des möglichen
"Sinnes ihrer einzelnen Worte solche Folgerungen ab, welche ihm
"hieher zu gehören scheinen, um den hochwichtigen Beweis welchen
"er geben wollte, auch auf diesem Wege zu vollenden Wie Paulus
"nun die höhere Nothwendigkeit und Wahrheit des Christenthumes zu
"beweisen bis über Mose hinaus in das Zeitalter Abraham's und die
"Erzählungen der Bibel über jene Urzeiten zurückgehen musste,
"ebenso kommt unserm Redner beim neugeschärften Blicke in jene
"Zeiten gerade von der seite Malkhissedeq's aus vieles entgegen was für
"diesen dienen konnte ; und vorzüglich auf drei Einzelheiten lenkt er
"hier auf die Aufmerksamkeit. *Zuerst* vii. 1—4, darauf wie man doch den
"gesammten Inhalt jener Erzählung mit der Psalmenstelle zusammen-
"haltend, jenen Priesterkönig nicht für einen der gewöhnlichen Männer
"der alten Geschichte halten könne, sondern ihm unwillkürlich eine
"ewige Dauer und ähnliche Erhabenheiten geheimnissvollen göttlichen
"Sinnes zuschreiben müsse, wie man schon früher wenigstens in einem
"entfernter ähnlichen Sinne dem Henôkh eine geheimnissvolle Unster-
"blichkeit zugeschrieben hatte. Und hier besonders zeigt sich die
"Sitte der damaligen Schriftgelehrten aus dem engen zusammenhalten,
"und in einander verarbeiten zweier an sich weit von einander liegender
"Schriftstellen den Beweis für etwas neues, bis dahin nicht beachtetes,
"und oft sehr überraschendes zu ziehen. Den der Redner beginnt
"zwar einfach mit den Worten *Denn dieser M.*, wie er Gen. xiv. 18,
"kurz bezeichnet wird *König Salem's, Priester des höchsten Gottes, der*
"*dem* nach der ganzen Erzählung von Gen. xiv. *von der Niederlage der*
"*Könige zurückkehrenden Abraham*, freundlich und theilnehmend *entge-*
"*genging und ihn segnete, dem* gegen alle damalige menschliche Erwart-

" ung, *sogar einen Zehnten von allem* was er in diesem Kriege erbeutet
" hatte *zutheilte*, kein geringerer als *Abraham*, weiter *der* wenn man
" auf die Bedeutung seiner beiden Namen in der altheiligen geheimniss-
" vollen Hebräischen Sprache, und auf deren Folge unter einander
" sieht *zuerst zwar* (wenn dieser Name Malkhissedeq *verdollmetscht* wird)
" *Gerechtigkeitskönig, dann aber auch König Salem's, das ist Friedens-*
" *könig, ist* als wäre jeder dieser beiden Königsnamen eben im König-
" lichen d.i. Messianischen Sinne so denkwürdig, so offenbar anspielend
" auf den Messias welcher zuerst Gerechtigkeit in der ganzen Welt,
" dann aber eben dadurch Frieden herstellen muss, [Note 1, p. 89.
" Diese Hinweisung soll hier offenbar in den Worten liegen. Aber
" ähnlich sucht auch Philon in der Übersetzung und Ausdeutung von
" Eigennamen des Pentateuches Geheimnisse, vgl. die *Geschichte des*
" V. Isr. vi., s. 272], welcher sieht man sich, wie er in der Bibel erscheint
" noch weiter um, *vaterlos, mutterlos*, versteht sich ohne menschliche
" Aeltern, *stammbaumlos*, ohne dass er auch nur auf ein bestimmtes
" menschiches Geschlecht oder Volk zurückgeführt wird, *weder* einen
" *zeitlichen Anfang noch ein Lebensende habend*, ist weil weder von
" diesem noch von jenem in der Bibel etwas erzählt wird, *der aber*
" vermöge jener Psalmenstelle unverkennbar *dem Sohne Gottes verähn-*
" *licht wird*, sodass man vor allem hieraus jedoch in Übereinstimmung
" mit den vorigen Merkmalen sehr wohl schliessen kann wer er denn
" wirklich seyn musste, *bleibt Priester ohne Unterlass* wiederum Kraft
" jener Psalmenstelle und der übrigen Merkmale, als wäre er Christus
" oder vielmehr der Logos selbst, der sich nur damals in dieser Gestalt
" den Menschen sichtbar machte (*as if he were Christ, or rather the Logos*
" *himself, who for that time only, manifested himself to men in this likeness*),
" aber auch für jenen Augenblick schon einmahl als Priester wie zur
" Vorbedeutung dessen was er jetzt noch in ganz anderer Weise als ewiger
" Hohepriester für die Seinigen ist. [Note 2, p. 89. Das ist nämlich
" deutlich genug der lezte Sinn aller dieser Worte, der freilich bloss
" angedeutet wird. Aber inderthat konnte ihm unser Redner weder mit
" einem Engel noch mit einem einstigen Menschen wie Henokh wirklich
" zusammenstellen, so dass nichts weiter übrigbleibt, als ihn für eine
" schon in jenes frühe Alterthum hineingefallene augenblickliche
" geheimnissvoll leibliche Offenbarung des Logos zu halten.—*This,*
" *indeed, is plainly enough the real signification of all these words, a*
" *signification, however, which is only hinted at. But truly the speaker*
" *could not compare him with an angel, nor with any mortal man that ever*
" *lived like Enoch. Hence we have no alternative but to regard him as a*
" *momentary and mysterious revelation of the Logos in bodily shape, that*
" *was thus vouchsafed in those earliest ages of antiquity.*]"—Schoettgen

(*Hor. Hebr.*, tom. ii., p. 104) has the following, which is a curious illustration of ἀπάτωρ of Hebr. vii. 3 :—" Breschith Rabba ad Genes. xxxvii.
" 22, cit. Raymundo, part iii., distinct. iii., 8, 5, et Hieron, a S. Fide I. 5,
" *R. Berachias dixit, Deum S.B. dixisse ad Israëlitas: Vos dicitis ad me.*
" Thren. v. 3, אב אין יתומים היינו. Etiam *Goël* (Redeemer), *quem ex vobis*
" *excitabo*, אין לו אב *non habebit patrem*, q.d. Zachar. vi. 12. Ecce vir,
" Zemach nomen ejus, צמח ומתחתיו, et de sub se germinabit. *Sic quoque*
" Jesa. liii. 3, Et ascendit ut virgultum coram eo. *De eodem Davides*
" Ps. cx. 3. Ex utero auroræ tibi ros juventutis tuæ. *Et alibi* Ps. ii. 7,
" Dominus dixit ad me : Filius meus es tu."

CHAPTER VIII.

Verses 1—5.—Now the sum (κεφάλαιον, *the result, the gist*) of the things spoken is as follows. We have such (τοιοῦτον, i.e., *not a whit inferior to the prophetic portraiture*) an High Priest, who has sat down on the right hand of the Majesty in the heavens (Ps. cx. 1),[1] a minister of the most holy things[2] (τῶν ἁγίων λειτουργὸς.[3] The article is emphatic. See note 2 on p. 91; 1 Chron. xxiii. 13 ; and Levit. xxii. 2. The exact correspondence between Jesus and the Aaronic high priests who were "separated to " bless the most holy things," &c., is here drawn out) and of the true tabernacle,[4] which the Lord pitched, and not man. Every high priest, moreover, is appointed for the express purpose of offering gifts and sacrifices. Jesus, therefore, must needs have somewhat to offer. For if He were upon earth[5] (*a mere mortal*, or *denizen of earth*) He could not be a priest, because there are priests who offer gifts in conformity to the law ; who discharge their ministry (λατρεύουσι, perform their sacrificial and ministerial functions) in a copy and shadow of the heavenly things. Even as Moses was oracularly admonished, when he was about to make the tabernacle (ἐπιτελεῖν, *to complete in detail*), for "See," saith He (Exod. xxv. 40), "that

o

"thou make all things according to the pattern (τύπον, "תבנית, *an architectural projection*) shewed to thee "(Exod. xxv. 9) in the mount."[6]

[1] Schoettgen (*Hor. Hebr.*, tom. ii., p. 566) adduces the following curious Rabbinical legend, respecting the exaltation of Messiah, from the *Pesikta Rabbathi in Jalkut Simeoni* :—" Rabbini nostri tradunt : "עתידין אבות העולם לעמוד בניסן, Patriarchæ futuro tempore stabunt mense "Nisan, et dicent : O Messia, *Justitia nostra*, quamvis nos patres tui "sumus, tu tamen melior es nobis, quia peccata filiorum nostrorum "portasti, et decreta satis dura et mala in te transierunt, qualia neque "ante, neque post te quisquam sustinuit. Fuisti gentilibus derisui, et "subsannationi propter Israel, sedisti in tenebris et caligine, oculi tui "non viderunt lucem, et lux tua tibi soli ahæsit (*i.e.*, others were not "able to see thy Divine Majesty). Corpus tuus exaruit sicut lignum, "oculi tui præ jejunio obscurati sunt, robur tuum exaruit sicut testa, "et hæc omnia propter peccata filiorum nostrorum. An igitur voluntas "tua est, ut filii nostri fruantur illo bono, quod Deus S. B. Israelitis "splendide exhibuit ?—Respondit ipsis Messias : O Patriarchæ, quæ- "cunque feci, non nisi vestri et filiorum vestrorum caussa feci, ut illo "bono fruantur, quo Deus S. B. illos illustravit. Dixerunt Patriarchæ : "O Messia, Justitia nostra, Placatus esto nobis, שהתנחת דעת קינך ודעתנו, "quia Conditorem tuum et nos reconciliasti. R. Simeon filius Passi "dixit : Eo ipso tempore Deus S. B. Messiam super coelos coelorum "exaltavit, et splendorem gloriæ suæ super ipsum expandit, ne gentiles "et Persæ ipsi nocere queant. Dixerunt ipsi Patriarchæ : O Messia, "Justitia nostra, judex esto in eos, et fac ipsis quodcunque voles." So also the *Sohar Chadash*, fol. 41, 3, on Ps. cxxxiii. 2, "*It is like the "precious Ointment upon the head, that ran down upon the beard, even "Aaron's beard*," explains, דא כהנא רבא לעילא, " it is the High Priest "above," ימינא דמלכא, "at the right hand of the King," כהן לעולם, " a priest "for ever ;" again, *ibid.*, fol. 42, 1, on Ps. xlv. 2 (3), לעולם, *for ever*, by עולם is here understood "the right hand on high," ימינא לעילא, as it is written (Ps. cx. 4), "*Thou art a priest for ever,*" *ibid.*, fol. 63, 3, on Ps. lxiii. 1 (2). By אתה is understood דליצילא ימינא, He who is at the right hand above, as (in Ps. cx.) "*Thou art a priest for ever.*"

[2] Stuart renders, in accordance with the Authorized Version, "a "minister of the sanctuary."

[3] Λειτουργὸς, *a public functionary*, one who discharged some special, and usually obligatory service, in the Athenian State. Demosthenes divides the λειτουργίαι into domestic and political. Εἰσὶ γὰρ δήπου παρ᾽ ἡμῖν αἵ τε τῶν μετοίκων λειτουργίαι, καὶ οἱ πολιτικαί. (Dem. *in Leptinem*,

curavit J. H. Bremius, § 15, pp. 104-6. *Turici*, 1831. 8vo.) The most important of the regular ἐγκύκλιοι λειτουργίαι were the *choregia*, viz., the furnishing the requisites for dramatic representations, &c. ; the *gymnasiarchia*, or making suitable provision for the celebration of the public games ; and the *hestiasis*, or catering for the public entertainment of the tribes. This species of service occurred but seldom. Amongst the extraordinary ones were the *trierarchia, i.e.*, furnishing ships of war to the State ; the *cisphora*, a property tax in time of war ; &c. From signifying the sacred and patriotic service of the State, the word passed over to signify religious worship and the public services of God.

⁴ Probably an allusion to the words of Amos ix. 11, "In that day I "will raise up the tabernacle of David that is fallen" (סכת דויד הנפלה, called in Is. xvi. 5 אהל דוד). As a rule, the Mosaic tabernacle is exclusively designated by the word אהל. Respecting the various changes of abode which the Ark underwent, see Reland, *Ant. Sacr. Hebr.* Traject. Bat., 1712, 8vo., pp. 18—21. God's true tabernacle is the Church of Christ ; although the σκ. ἀληθ. may also denote the celestial pattern and original which God showed Moses in the mount.

The above prophecy of Amos ix. 11 is applied by Jewish commentators to Messiah. "R. Nachman said to R. Isaac, What do you under-"stand by the phrase, 'When בר נפלי *Bar Nephele*, that is, *the son of* "'*lapses*' (*falls*, or *the abortion*)? Who is this *Bar Nephele?* The "other answered, Messias. R. Nachman.—That can't be so: surely "you don't call Messiah the son of lapses? R. Isaac.—Yes, assuredly, "because it is written (Amos ix. 11), *In that day, I will raise up the* "*tabernacle of David* (הנפלה) *that is fallen*."—*Sanhedr.*, f. 96, 2, in Ugol. Thes., tom. xxv., col. 953.

⁵ Εἰ μὲν γὰρ ἦν ἐπὶ γῆς, οὐδ' ἂν ἦν ἱερεύς ; if He had asserted to himself a priesthood on earth, He could not have established his claim, being genealogically disqualified by his descent from Judah, instead of from Levi ; but now his priesthood as well as his kingdom are not of this world ; both are heavenly and spiritual, and more excellent than the earthly and transitory. "For the things which are seen are temporal, "but the things which are not seen are eternal."

⁶ The Rabbies, as will be seen from the following quotation from the Talmudical treatise *Menachoth*, held that there exist in heaven the exact counterparts of the tabernacle in the temple, with all its sacred furniture:—

רבי יוסי ברבי יהודה אומר ארון של אש ושלחן של אש ומנורה של אש ירדו מן השמים
וראה משה ועשה כמוהן שנאמר וראה ועשה בתבניתם אשר אתה מראה בהר אלא מהתה
והקמת את המשכן כמשפטו אשר הראית בהר הכי נמי הכא כתב כמשפטו התם כתב
כתבניתם . אמר רבי חייא בר אבא אמר רבי יוחנן גבריאל חגור כמין פסקיא היה והראה
לו למשה מעשה מנורה דכתב וזה מעשה המנרה:

"Rabbi Jose, son of Rabbi Judah, said: A fiery ark, and a fiery "table, and a fiery candlestick descended from heaven. And Moses "saw them, and made according to their similitude. According as it is "said, *See now that thou makest them according to the pattern which thou* "*sawest in the mount.* And also, *Thou shalt erect the tabernacle, according* "*to the pattern which thou sawest in the mount.* In this latter passage it "is written *according to its pattern*, whilst in the former, *according to* "*the similitude.*" Rabbi Chijan bar Aba says : Rabbi Jochanan says, "Gabriel, girt, as it were, with breeches, it was who showed to Moses "the workmanship of the candlestick ; for it is written, *And this is the* "*workmanship of the candlestick.*"—*Menachoth*, col. 862, 863. (Ugol. Thes., vol. 19.)

Schoettgen, in his Dissertation *de Hierosolyma Coelesti,* writes:—
"Hoc vero ante omnia tenendum est, Judæos Hierosolymam, et quæ in "eadem erant, tanto honore et amore coluisse, ut eadem in cœlo exstare "sibi persuaderunt. *Sohar*, Genes., fol. 91, col. 362, כל מה די בארעא הכי "נמי בעילא. *Quodcunque in terra est, id etiam in cœlo est, et nulla res tam* "*exigua est in mundo, quæ non ab alia simili, quæ in cœlo est, dependeat.* "Id quod quidem non tum crasse semper accipiendum est, quasi cre- "diderint, necesse esse, ut ex in cœlo exstarent." *Hor. Heb.*, tom. i., p 1206.

Bishop Wordsworth (on Exod. xxv. 9) observes, " Whether Moses "saw a real heavenly temple, of which the tabernacle was to be a copy, "or whether God showed him a plan, a design, a sketch which he was "to follow and embody in the structure of the tabernacle, is not stated. "The former is maintained by the Rabbis and Delitzsch on Heb. viii. 5, "the latter by Keil, and this seems to be confirmed by the use of the "pattern of the temple in 1 Chron. xxviii. 19." The words of 1 Chron. xxviii. 19 are, according to the Hebrew, הכל בכתב מיד יהוה עלי השכיל כל מלאכות התבנית, "*everything in writing, from the hand of the Lord upon me,* "*He caused me to understand, all the works of this pattern.*" But the LXX. reads, Πάντα ἐν γραφῇ χειρὸς Κυρίου ἔδωκε Δαυὶδ Σαλαμών, κατὰ τὴν περιγενηθεῖσαν αὐτῷ σύνεσιν τῆς κατεργασίας τοῦ παραδείγματος. On the whole, the only certainty at which we can arrive is, that God showed a *pattern*, or *plan* to Moses and to Solomon. The other interpretation is conjectural and hazardous, and to my mind ill in accordance with the dignity and spirituality of the subject. To this latter view Stuart inclines, *Excursus*, xv.

Verses 6—13.—But now He (Jesus) has obtained a more excellent ministry, just as (ὅσῳ) He is also a mediator of a better covenant, which has been constituted (νενομοθέτηται) upon better promises. For if that first one had been faultless, no place for a second would have been sought. But finding fault (μεμφόμενος, *i.e.*, in disparagement of it), He speaks[1] thus (Jer. xxxi. 31—34. Comp. xvi. 14, 15, xxiii. 5—8) to them (the children of Israel) :—Behold the days come,[2] saith the Lord, and I will conclude (συντελέσω)[3] a new covenant with the house of Israel and with the house of Judah. Not according to the covenant that I made with their fathers in the day when I took them by the hand to lead them out of the land of Egypt, because they (αὐτοὶ) continued not in my covenant, and I disregarded[4] (ἠμέλησα) them, saith the Lord (ואנכי בעלתי בם נאם יהוה). For this is the covenant that I will make with the house of Israel, after those days, saith the Lord. I will put my laws into their minds (διάνοιαν, *understanding*) and write them upon their hearts, and I will be to them a God, and they shall be to me a people : and they shall not teach every one his neighbour, and every one his brother, saying, Know the Lord ; for all shall know me, from the least to the greatest.[5] For I will be merciful to their unrighteousness (ἵλεως ἔσομαι ταῖς ἀδικίαις, אסלח, *I will condone, be lenient to*), and their sins and their iniquities will I remember no more. By saying the word " new "[6] (ἐν τῷ λέγειν καινὴν), He has antiquated (πεπαλαίωκε) the first (covenant, because what is *new* is antithetic to what preceded it. The moment one can speak of a successor, whatever went before it is, so to speak, and by comparison, made old). But that which is antiquated, and growing out of date, must shortly disappear (τὸ δὲ παλαιούμενον καὶ γηράσκον, ἐγγὺς ἀφανισμοῦ).

[1] The Talmudical writers assign the period here mentioned, to the days of Messiah, THE LORD OUR RIGHTEOUSNESS, spoken of in the parallel passage of the same prophet, Jer. xxiii. 6, in reference to which R. Alshech says, ומשיח ה' צדקנו *Messiah is called the Lord our Righteousness.* Compare Kimchi's Commentary on Zech., translated by the late Dr. M'Caul, p. 175—177.

[2] Ἡμέραι ἔρχονται. Schoettgen (tom i., p. 968) observes that Grotius

remarks rightly " באו, *sono est præsens, sensu sæpe futurum.*" Singularly enough, the word is not באו, but באים, in Jer. xxxi. 31. He quotes the following from the *Jalkut Simeoni*, pt. 1, fol. 78, 3, to prove that the ancient Jews interpreted this passage of Jeremiah, of the days of Messiah :—" Ad verba Exod. xix. 1, ביום הזה, illo die venerunt in de- " sertum Sinai ; *Non dicitur* ביום ההוא (*in that day*), sed ביום הזה (*in this* " *day*), h.e., הזה בעולם, *in hoc mundo* (tempore scilicet veteris Testamenti) " *dedi vobis legem et singuli in illa studebitis.* *Verum*, לעתיד לבא, *tempore* "*futuro* (Novi Testamenti) *ego illam docebo omnes Israelitas, ipsique eam* " *addiscent et nunquam oblivioni tradent*, q.d., Jerem. xxxi. 33. Hoc " erit foedus," &c. Schoettgen is right in his intimation that some of the Jews applied the prophecy to the " world to come ;" but surely he has forgotten the quotation which he gives (tom. ii., p. 619) from the *Midrasch in Jalkut Simeoni*, ii., fol. 46, 1 :—" Deus S. B. sedebit in " paradiso et docebit : et omnes justi sedebunt coram ipso, omnis autem " familia coelestis in pedibus suis stabunt : Sol et Planetæ ad dextram, " Luna autem cum stellis ad sinistram ejus. Ipse autem Deus S. B.

"יושב ודורש תורה חדשה שעתיד ליתן על ידי משיח"

" sedebit, et proponet legem novem, quam daturus est per manus " Messiæ." The scene of the giving of the new law by the hands of Messiah, is here laid in the spiritual region of the Garden of Eden, and not, as Schoettgen would render, לעתיד לבא, *tempore futuro* (Novi Testa- menti). Jac. Rhenferdius has, as I have before noticed, conclusively proved, in his Dissertation *De Seculo Futuro*, that the days of Messiah are included in העולם הזה *this world* :—" Illa autem pars extrema erit " אחרית הימים, *finis dierum*, vel *ultima dies* hujus mundi, quemadmodum " quidem ipsi Judæi phrasin illam explicant כי לדברי הכל באחרית הימים ימות " המשיח הם, *Nam extremum dierum consensu omnium Doctorum sunt* " *Dies Messiæ*" (p. 1122). The Talmudic writers held that in the *world to come* (לעתיד לבא) there would be no death, and wars would cease, but that in the days of Messiah both would still exist. Rhenferd's disserta- tion will repay perusal, and is to be found at length in Meuschen. He most satisfactorily demonstrates that, in its stricter usage, הבא העולם does not mean *Messiah's days*, but the supernatural, and spiritual *world to come*. (See also J. Rhenf., Diss. II., *ibid.*, p. 1138.)

³ LXX. διαθήσομαι, וכרתי, " *I will cut.*" The Hebrew expression, כרת ברית, i.e., *to cut a covenant* (a mactatione et dissectione hostiarum in foederibus pangendis consueta), is more literally rendered by συντελέσω than by διαθήσομαι. The ἐποίησα of verse 9 is again כרתי in the Hebrew, and διεθέμην in the LXX. Λέγει Κύριος of verse 8, 9, is φησὶ Κύριος in the LXX. Διδοὺς νόμους is διδοὺς δώσω in the LXX., the former agreeing with the reading of the Hebrew נתתי. Again, the LXX. has καὶ τῶν

CHAP. VIII., 6—13. 103

ἁμαρτιῶν αὐτῶν οὐ μὴ μνησθῶ ἔτι, in place of καὶ τῶν ἁμαρτιῶν αὐτῶν καὶ τῶν ἀνομιῶν κ.τ.λ., which latter corresponds with the Hebrew לעונם ולחטאתם. It is a great mistake to suppose that the New Testament writers are servile followers of the LXX. version in their quotations.

⁴ 'Ημέλησα, אנכי בעלתי בם. Lud. Cappellus (*Crit Sacr.*, p. 61 and 266) asserts, without reserve, that the LXX. translators read געלתי, *fastidivi*, instead of בעלתי, *dominatus sum*. Such an alteration of the text, however, is unnecessary. Pococke has shown that בעל has the signification of *disdaining*, derived from the Arabic ; and Kimchi asserts that whenever it is used in construction with ב, it is to be taken in an ill part, and is here equivalent to בחלתי, *I have lothed*. Compare Zech. xi. 8, וגם נפשם בחלה בי. The original signification of the verb בעל is, *to be lord over, to possess, to own*, and, hence, *to marry, be a husband to*, and in the first sense it is used in Isaiah xxvi. 13, בעלונו אדנים זולתך, " Other Lords have " had dominion over us besides Thee." Another meaning, as has just been shown, is *to disdain, to treat with scorn, to reject*. The sense is fixed, *in this particular case*, for the Christian student, by the above authoritative rendering of the writer to the Hebrews. 'Ημέλησα is the inspired interpretation, of what might otherwise be regarded as an open question. We do not adopt it on the authority of the LXX. version, but as the explanation of the Holy Ghost concerning his own declaration contained in Jer. xxxi. 32. In Jer. iii. 14, כי אנכי בעלתי בכם, according to the authorized Engl. vers., " for I am married to you," is διότι ἐγὼ κατακυριεύσω ὑμῶν in the LXX. Gesenius renders this passage, "*nam ego vos rejeci*," as he does xxxi. 32, "*egoque eos rejicerem.*" Whereas, in Is. lxii. 4, בעולה, *married*, and תבעל, *shall be married*, the LXX. vers. has οἰκουμένη and συνοικηθήσεται ; and in verse 5, כי יבעל בחור בתולה יבעלוך בניך, " as a young man marrieth a virgin shall thy sons marry " thee," is translated, καὶ ὡς συνοικῶν νεανίσκος παρθένῳ, οὕτω κατοικήσουσιν κ.τ.λ.

⁵ למקטנם ועד גדולם, "*from the youngest to the oldest*," probably of age, and not of station.

⁶ " En parlant d'une alliance nouvelle, il déclare vielle la première ; " or ce qui est devenu ancien et vieux, est près d'être aboli."—*French Translat.*

The Rabbies themselves looked forward to the law ultimately falling into abeyance. R. Bechai says, " This passage of Scripture (Deut. " xxxi. 21) appears to me, by this passage, to denote that a time will " come in which the law will be forgotten (שיבא זמן שתשהכח התורה), " which is the time of abolishing the ' *evil imagination* ' (יצר הרע). See " Gen. vi. 5, viii. 21). That is the time of the resurrection, because the " Law will be abolished at that time, except the feast of Purim. And

"this is what is said (Deut. xxxi. 21) :—'*For the Law shall not be
"'forgotten out of the mouth of his seed, for* (כי) *I know their imagination*,'
"i.e., '*as long as I know their imagination.*' From this it follows, by
"inference, that when the evil imagination shall be taken away, the
"law also shall be forgotten (or consigned to oblivion). And so, of old
"time, our Rabbies of blessed memory have spoken. The Law shall
"be forgotten by Israel ; that is, in the time of the Resurrection, but
"not in the days of Messiah, &c. For our Rabbies have said that there
"is no difference between this present world (העולם הזה) and the days of
"Messiah, excepting the servitude of the nations. But the Law will
"continue as a possession to us and to our posterity, for ever, all the
"time of this present world, in which this present corporeal order of
"things shall continue. But at the resurrection of the dead there shall
"be a change for the better, and things will proceed in a different
"manner, and then, say they (our Rabbies), the law will be forgotten
"by Israel." (Rhenferdius, *De Seculo Futuro*, p. 1158, Menschen.)
Maimonides, however (see Dr. M'Caul's " Old Paths," Feast of Purim),
says, " All the books of the prophets, and all the Hagiographa, except
"the roll of Esther, will cease in the days of Messiah. But it is
"perpetual as the five books of the written law, and the constitutions
"of the oral law, which shall never cease." (*Hilchoth Megillah.*)

CHAPTER IX.

THE writer now has conclusively shown that Jesus is an Eternal High Priest, a Minister of the Most Holy things, and of the True Tabernacle. He has, moreover (viii. 3), asserted the self-evident fact that if He be a priest at all, he must have somewhat to offer. The engrossing, cardinal idea of the priestly office is the offering of sacrifices. Had our Lord Jesus Christ belonged to the tribe of Levi, He would have offered according to the Mosaic ritual. But his priesthood is no earthly one, not ἐπὶ γῆς, He is not of the tribe of Levi but of Judah, and therefore no Aaronic priest. What, then, did Jesus offer? The writer has not yet told us, nor does he until chap. ix. 11. But he *has* said that the entire apparatus of the Levitic ceremonial was the copy and shadow of the heavenly (viii. 5). Such being the case, Jesus has obtained a more excellent ministry. Why? Because his priesthood passes not away. It is not one of parabolic promise, but one of abiding and substantial efficacy. He is a priest FOR EVER, after the order of Melchisedek. With such a priesthood as this no fault could be found. It is not open to the objection of typicality (if I may coin the word) and transitoriness. It is the substance, of which the Mosaic was the shadow. Moreover, Jeremiah (xxxi. 31, &c.) had distinctly foretold the abrogation of the first covenant, with its attendant rites and ceremonies and priesthood. The first covenant was so wrapped up and interwoven with the religious worship of the tabernacle and the temple, that to invalidate a part was to abrogate the whole. Jeremiah speaks of a " new " covenant, and by mention of the word *new* he has decisively antiquated the former. Having now concluded the necessary digression (viii. 4—15), wherein the writer has shown that it is possible for a new and extra Levitic priesthood to arise, and one based upon and in connexion with a new covenant, he proceeds to enumerate the leading features of the worship and ritual of the tabernacle, which were temporal and symbolical, or parabolic, and to contrast them with the " good things to come," of which Christ is the high priest. The antithesis to chap. ix. 1 is verse 11, "but Christ being come," &c.; the intermediate verses contain only parenthetic details and elucidations. In verse 11, et seq., the writer shows what it is that Christ does offer in his capacity of high priest, viz., HIS OWN BLOOD, and dilates upon its supereminent expiatory efficacy. So excellent is it, that having once been offered, the repetition of the offering is for ever superfluous, supererogatory, and impossible.

The writer thus resumes, ix. 1, Εἶχε μὲν οὖν καὶ ἡ πρώτη σκηνή, to which the antithetic Χριστὸς δὲ . . . διὰ τῆς μείζονος καὶ τελειοτέρας σκηνῆς, οὐ χειροποιήτου, τουτέστιν, οὐ ταύτης τῆς κτίσεως, is found in the eleventh verse.

Verses 1—5.—The first tabernacle,[1] therefore, that is to say, the terrestrial sanctuary,[2] had also ordinances[3] of worship. For the tabernacle was arranged (κατεσκευάσθη) as follows. The first (or outer apartment), in which were the candlestick, and the table, and the shewbread (ἡ πρόθεσις τῶν ἄρτων), which is called HOLY (the Holy Place). But (secondly) behind the second veil,[4] the apartment called the HOLY OF HOLIES, which contained the golden censer,[5] and the ark of the covenant (τὴν κιβωτὸν τῆς διαθήκης) entirely overlaid with gold. In which were[6] the golden vase containing the manna, and the rod of Aaron that budded (Num. xvii. 8, Heb. 23), and the tables of the covenant. And above it (ὑπεράνω δὲ αὐτῆς) the Cherubim of glory,[7] overshadowing the Mercy-seat[8] (τὸ ἱλαστήριον, כפרת, *propitiatorium*, Vulg.); concerning which it is not now my purpose to speak in detail.

[1] Εἶχε μὲν οὖν καὶ ἡ πρώτη σκηνή. Prof. Stuart, Dindorff, and others, including the Authorized English Version, adopt the reading διαθήκη,

CHAP. IX., 1—5.

instead of σκηνή, but by it the strong comparison and contrast is spoiled. The introduction of the covenant, viii. 6—13, is only parenthetical and explanatory. The real subject is the first old tabernacle as contrasted with the new. Πρώτη is here, doubtless, *first* in point of time, and not of arrangement as in verse 2. Wolfius, *in loco*, writes,—" σκηνὴν Codices " varii et Versiones quoque omittunt : nec habet Chrysostomus : qui " potius post ἡ πρώτη, in commentario subintelligi vult διαθήκη. Hinc ' Millius non dubitat σκηνὴν ex sequentibus irrepsisse tum ad loc. tum " in prolegomenis sec. 886, quæ et Braunii ad h.l. est sententia. Recte " vero illi contriaratur Whitbius in Examine, p. 35, observans, exstare " σκηνὴν etiam apud Chrysostomum, *de Die Natali Domini*, tom. v., " edit. Morellian. p. 472, nec minus apud Theodoretum et Oecumenium. " Idem quoque in Annotationibus ad h.l. Anglice editis rem amplius " urget......B. Gothofredus Olearius *in Analysi* ita : *Bene se habet* " σκηνή : *nimirum λειτουργίαν prioris σκηνῆς excellentissimam fuisse in* '· *præcedente capite fuit monstratum ; jam igitur cum ea specialius com-* " *parat τὴν λειτουργίαν, vel, ut hic vocat,* λατρείαν σκηνῆς κοσμικῆς. *Quid* " *quod ut mox videbimus, in sequentibus per* partes σκηνὴν *dilineet.* " Sanctum *primum, et deinde* Sanctum Sanctorum *ob oculos ponens :* '· *totam itaque antea nominari par erat.* Addidero his, quod infra vers. 8, " itidem σκηνὴ ἡ πρώτη diserte commemoretur, quemadmodum h.l. '· ἡ πρώτη ideo dicitur, ut opponatur τῇ σκηνῇ τῇ ἀληθινῇ, de quâ cap. " viii 2, quæque ita imposterum exhibenda erat vere, quemadmodum " prior illa tempore, instar typi antecessit. Tenenda igitur hæc lectio " est, quæ subintelligenda ex vers. 2 fuerat, etiamsi non diserte ex-" pressa fuisset. Sic non desunt editiones vetustæ, in quibus ἡ πρώτη " simpliciter legitur. Inter eas sunt Erasmi tres et Basileensis. Eas, " vel potius Vulg. qui itidem non habet, secutus est Lutherus in ver-" sione. Omisit etiam Beza, et ex nostratibus Erasmus Schmidius," &c.

² Τὸ τε ἅγιον κοσμικόν. Olearius rightly suggests that these words should be taken in apposition to ἡ πρώτη σκηνή. The entire passage would then read thus :—" But the first tabernacle, that is to say, the " terrestrial sanctuary, had ordinances of worship." This affords an intelligible translation of what is otherwise, to my mind, one of the most difficult passages in the whole Epistle. J. A. Danzius (*Functio Pontif. M. in Adyto Anniversaria*, p. 942, Meuschen) remarks that the court of the Gentiles was never called "holy," and that St. Paul (whom he believes to be the writer of the Epistle to the Hebrews) is speaking exclusively of the Mosaic Tabernacle. Danzius understands τὸ τε ἅγιον κοσμικόν in the same sense as Olearius, *e.g.*, " Apostolus de tabernaculo " stricte sumto loquitur, quod in duas tantummodo partes erat divisum :

" et sic quoque duo modo vela habuit. Atrii nullam facit mentionem,
" ut hinc ejus posses connumerare Velum. Atrium gentium nullibi
" vocatur ἅγιον, sed, eo ipso quod gentibus patuit, חל dicabatur, sive
" profanum. Ex voce κοσμικὸν nihil aliud inferri potest, quam quod
" illud ἅγιον sit terrenum et caducum, utpote ex materia terrena con-
" structum ; in oppositione coelestis et æterni." The translators of the
London Jews' Society's edition of the Hebrew New Testament render
τὸ τε ἅγιον κοσμικόν by הוא מקדש ארצי. They also rightly supply משכן
(σκηνή) instead of ברית (διαθήκη) in the first clause of the verse. Wolfius
writes, *in loc.* :—" Hombergius ἅγ. κοσμ. interpretatur *Sanctum ornatum*,
" vel quod in ornatu consistebat, instrumentis scilicet ad tabernaculi
" cultum spectantibus. Recte autem monuit Lamb. Bos., p. 246,
" κοσμικὸς significare *mundanum*, a κόσμος *mundus*, et κόσμιος *elegantem*
" a κόσμος *ornatus*, quemadmodum λογικὸς est *rationalis* a λόγος, *ratio*,
" λόγιος autem *disertus* a λόγος, *oratio*. Idem vero *mundanum* ait vocari,
" tanquam oppositum τῇ ἐπουρανίῳ, *coelesti*, quæ et plerorumque est
" sententia. Patres fere eo referunt, quod omnibus in aditum in illud
" patuerit."

³ Δικαιώματα λατρείας. The following is extracted from Wolfius, *in
loc.* :—" Constitutos ritus cultuum, ut Erasmus Schmidius, vel, *constitutos*
" *religionis ritus*, ut Beza ; vel, *constitutiones ad cultum pertinentes*, ut
" Jac. Capellus. Sic et B. Lutherus, Rechte des Gottes-Dienstes.
" Respondet vox δικαιώματα Hebraicis חוקים, מצווה, vel משפטים, quas
" scilicet oἱ LXX., per δικαιώματα reddere consueverunt. Olearii judicio
" in Analysi, p. 27, ita accipi potest phrasis, ac si diceretur λατρεία
" δικαία, quomodo μωρία κηρύγματος, περισσεία τῆς χάριτος explicari
" soleat, ita ut λατρεία δικαία sit cultus, cui sua sit integritas et perfectio,
" qua se probare hominibus possit, tanquam divinitus constitutus, et
" gloria sua conspicuus." Wolfius sagaciously observes, " Non dubito
" ego, præstare priorem expositionem. Hoc enim sensu vox δικαίωμα
" τοῦ Θεοῦ, ii. 26, et. viii. 4, τὰ δικαιώματα τοῦ νόμου, nec non infra v. 10,
" δικαιώμασι σαρκός. In harum phrasium nullâ δικαίωμα pro adjectivo
" haberi potest. Non prolem etiam, qui δικαιώματα et λατρείας tanquam
" duas voces distinctas, et in accusandi casu positas considerari cupiunt.
" Nusquam video vocem illam sine genitivo positam, et ipsa phrasis
" δικαιώμασι σαρκός, ix. 20, exponit, quæ illa δικαιώματα λατρείας fuerint,
" nempe σαρκικά." It is worthy of remark, as affording a curious
example of the technical use of the word, that the LXX. translate
משפטים of Ezek. xx. 25 by δικαιώματα, *e.g.*, προστάγματα οὐ καλὰ, καὶ
δικαιώματα ἐν οἷς οὐ ζήσονται ἐν αὐτοῖς.

⁴ Μετὰ δὲ τὸ δεύτ. καταπέτασμα. It must be borne in mind that the
writer is speaking strictly in reference to the Tabernacle, and not,

except by implication, of the first or second temple. In the Tosaphta to Joma (*Gemar. Hierosol*, chap. ii. 10, col. 174) the following is found :—
"The High Priest walked on through the temple until he arrived
" between the two veils, which separated between the Holy Place and
" the Holy of Holies ; and there was a cubit space between them. Here
" was the place of the Oracle which Solomon made."

מהלך בהיכל עד שמגיע לבין שתי הפרכות המבדילות בין הקדש ובין קודש הקדשים וביניהן
אמה זה מקום הדבור שעשה שלמה :

The same passage occurs, with the exception of the last clause, in the Mishna, *Joma*, cap. v. 1. (Mishn. Surenh., tom. ii., p. 231.) The Tosaphta and the tract *Joma* are printed at length in vol. xviii. of Ugolini *Thes.* Professor Stuart writes, *in loc.*:—"As the inner veil is here
" called δεύτερον, the necessary implication is that there was a πρῶτον
" also, and accordingly we find it described in Exod. xxvi. 36, 37,
" xxxvi. 37, 38." The learned Professor proceeds to say that the
" outer veil served as a door for the Tabernacle." If the Talmudical statement given above be a correct one as regards the Tabernacle (but this is doubtful), then the "Second Veil" was the inner one of the two, which enclosed a space of a cubit's breadth, as a sort of lobby between the Holy Place and the Holy of Holies. Reland, *Antiq. Sacr. Vet. Hæbr.*, p. 119, writes of the second temple, "Hoc (*sc.* Sacrum) nec
" murus nec ostium a Sancto Sanctorum dividebat, sed duo vela, cubiti
" intermedii spatio sejuncta, inter quæ Pontifex M. Sanctum Sanctorum
" intraturus ab Austro versus Septentrionem incedebat, quæ putamus
" fuisse illud καταπέτασμα quod, moriente Christo, ruptum tradit Mat-
" thæus xxvii. 51, nulli quippe usui futurum, postquam Christi mors
" peccata vere expiasset." This space of a cubit's breadth is called
טרקסין, *Tarkesin*, the meaning of which is held by some to be equivalent to τάραξις, because the builders of the temple were in "confusion" or uncertainty whether the space belonged to the Holy Place or the Holy of Holies. Reland prefers to give it a Persian derivation, בר *Porta* and קסן *electa*. He says, in conclusion :—" Quod autem R. Jona
" Bostrensis in *Gem. Hier. Kilaim.* 31, 3, et in Gem. Hier. Joma 42, 2,
" tradit hanc vocem significare מבהוץ כבפנים, *intus* et *extra*, verum est de
" voce priore *Tar* vel בר, aptissima ad hujus historiæ memoriam con-
" servandum. Quod si quis Græcam vocis originem mavult, videat an
" non a Θρίγκωσις vel θριγκός, quod est περίφραγμα, μικρὸν τείχειον
" Hesychio duci debeat."—*Ibid.*, p. 120. Wolfius, *in loc.*, unhesitatingly adopts the idea that, as in the temple so in the tabernacle, there was a twofold veil at the entrance to each apartment ; "utrumque aulæum
" tabernaculi duobus velis munitum." He gives, however, no authority for his assertion. J. A. Danzius (*Functio Pontif. M. in adyto anni-*

versaria, ad Hebr. iv. 4 pp. 935, 936, Meuschen) rejects the notion that there were two veils at the entrance to the Holy of Holies, either in the tabernacle or in the first temple. He says :—" Καταπέτασμα, quod
" h.l. adhibetur, in N. T., Syriacide, ac Maccabæorum libris, tantum de
" velo Sanctissimi usurpatur : quod nec in tabernaculo, nec templo a
" Salomone ædificato, erat geminum ; sed in solo templo secundo post
' exilium exstructo. Ita de hoc Maimonides (*Hilc. Beth habbechira*,
" cap. iv. sec. 2) e Cod. Joma :—

בבית ראשון היה כותל מבדיל בין הקדש ובין קדש הקדשים עביו אמה ובונן שבנו הבית
שני מסתפק להם אם עובי הכותל היה ממדת הקדש או ממדת קדש הקדשים לפיכך עשו
קדש הקדשים עביו עשרים אמה תמימו, ועשו הקדש ארבעים אמה תמיתי, והניחו אמה
יחידה בין הקדש ובין קדש הקדשים ולא בנו כותל בבית שני אלא עשו שתי פרכות אחד מצד
קדש הקדשים ואחד מצד הקדש וביניהן אמה כנגד עובי הכותל שהיה בראשון אבל במקדש
ראשון לא היתה שם אלא פרכת אחת בלבד שנאמר והבדילה לכם וגו'

" *In templo primo paries erat intergerinus inter Sanctum ac Sanctissi-*
' *mum, cujus densitas erat unius cubiti. Cum vero templum secundum*
' *exstruentibus dubium foret, utrum crassities istius parietis ad Sanctum*
' *pertineat, an vero ad mensuram Sanctissimi : ideo confecerunt Sanctum*
' *Sanctorum viginti cubitorum completorum ; Sanctum quoque cubitorum*
" *quadraginta integrorum, cubito uno inter Sanctum et Sanctissimum*
" *vacuo relicto. Non enim exstruxerunt in templo secundo parietem*
" *intergerinum : sed confecerunt duo Vela, quorum alterum a parte*
" *Sanctissimi, alterum vero a parte Sancti : inter quæ cubitus erat vacuus*
" *correspondens crassitiei parietis istius, qui fuit in templo primo. Quippe*
" *in Sanctuario primo non fuit nisi unum tantummodo velum, quia*
" *dicitur* (Exod. xxvi. 33), Et separet velum illud vobis inter Sanc-
" tum et Sanctissimum.—Cum itaque talis Sanctissimi h.l. recordetur
" Apostolus, quod μετὰ τὸ δεύτερον καταπέτασμα, v. 3, plurimi vel hac
" sola ratione ducti sunt, ut statuerent de templo secundo h.l. sermonem
" fore ; non de ullo alio. Quod si vero καταπέτασμα de aliis quoque
" Velis usurpari dicas, quam quæ Sanctissimum dirimunt a Sancto,
" prouti in V. T. apud LXX. interpretes adhiberi certum est (*vid.* Exod.
" xxvi. 37, xxxv. 11, xxxviii. 18, xl. 5, 8, 20) ; dicendum tunc potius
" Apostolo fuisset : *post tertium velum*, quam *post secundum.* Cum et
" atrium tabernaculi Mosaici velo aliquo in introitu fuerit instructum.
" Exod. xxvii. 16." Philo, *De Sacrificantibus*, uses the expression ἐν ἀδύτῳ εἴσω τοῦ προτέρου καταπετάσματος, as designating the position of the golden altar within the Holy Place, in opposition to the altar of stones in the court of the temple, clearly referring, in this instance, to the first veil that hung at the entrance of the Holy Place.—Works, *Mangey*, tom. ii , pp. 253, 254.—In Exod. xxvi. 36, 37, xxxvi. 37, the veil is called מסך. The LXX. give ἐπίσπαστρον in Exod. xxvi. 36, and

καταπέτασμα in verse 37, whilst in chap. xxxvii. 3, 5 (the Hebrew and Greek texts do not correspond) καταπέτασμα occurs in both verses. The veil of the Holy of Holies in Exod. xxvi. 31, 33, and elsewhere, is פרכת from פרך *separavit*.

⁵ Χρυσοῦν ἔχουσα θυμιατήριον; certainly not the altar of incense which was in the holy place, but a golden censer, which was exclusively devoted to the use of the Holy of Holies, on the day of Atonement. Ewald renders the words "einen goldenen Rauchaltar," but the translators of the London Society's Hebrew New Testament have more correctly adopted אשר לו מחתת הזהב in their version. I cannot help thinking that there was a permanent golden censer before the mercy-seat, in which the high priest deposited the smaller censer full of burning coals, which he brought in with him in his hand on the Day of Atonement. " And he shall take a censer full of burning coals of fire from off " the altar before the Lord, and his hands full of sweet incense beaten " small, and bring it within the veil. And he shall put the incense upon " the fire before the Lord, that the cloud of incense may cover the mercy " seat that is upon the testimony, that he die not." Levit. xvi. 12, 13. This latter censer, then, must be placed, with its burning contents, in some safe receptacle, in front of the mercy seat, whilst the priest returned for the blood of sprinkling, or else sprinkled it from another vessel, brought in at the same time. The object of placing burning incense before the mercy seat was to screen the Divine Glory or Schechinah from the priest's gaze. The Mishna, *Joma*, cap. 5, 2, says that, in the second temple, the censer was placed upon a stone called the Stone of Foundation.

מטניטל הארון אבן היתה שם מימות נביאים ראשונים ושהייה נקראת גבוהה מן הארץ שלש אצבעות ועליה כותן:

" Ex quo abducta est arca, lapis ibi erat à diebus priorum prophet-" arum, et lapis fundationis fuit vocatus, altus è terra tribus digitis, et " super ipsum thuribulum collocabat." *Mishna Surenhus.*, tom. ii., p. 233. In the same treatise, cap. 4, 4, the censer is particularly described which the high priest specially employed to carry the coals into the Holy of Holies on the day of atonement:—

בכל יום היה חותה בשל כסף ומצרה בתוך של זהב והיום חותה בשל זהב ובה היה
מכניס בכל יום חותה בשל ארבע קבין ומטיח בתוך של שלשי קבין והיו' חותה בשל שלשה
קבין ובה היה מכניס ר' יוסי אומר בכל יום חותה בשל סאה ומצרה בתוך של שלשה קבין
והיום חותה בשל שלשה קבין ובה היה מכניס בכל יום היה כבדה והיום קלה בכל יום היתה
ידה קצרה והיום ארוכה בכל יום היה והנה ירוק והיום אדום וגו׳/

" In omni die deprompsit thuribulo argenteo, et in aureum infunde-" bat; hodie deprompsit aureo, et intrabat cum eo. In omni die " deprompsit thuribulo quod quatuor cabos continebat, et in alterum

"infundebat quod tres cabos capiebat...............R. Jose ait: In omni
"die deprompsit thuribulo, quod Satum continebat, et in alterum
"infundebat, quod tres cabos continebat; hodie deprompsit thuribulo,
"quod tres cabos continebat, et intrabat cum eo. In omni die grave,
"hodie leve ;........ in omni die aurum ejus viride erat, hodie rufum."
(*Ibid.*, p. 229.)—In respect to this particular censer, which was employed
only once a year on the day of atonement, Reland writes (*Antiq.
Sacr. Vet. Hebr.*, p. 54; *Traject. Batav.*, 1712, 8vo.), " Θυμιατήριον
"quoque aureum in Sancto Sanctorum fuisse legitur, *Hebr.* ix. 4, quo
"nomine non altare aureum suffitus, sed acerra thuris, quæ quotannis
"in S. Sanctorum solemni die expiationis inferrebatur, et respectu usus
"vas huic loco proprium dici potest, videtur debere intellegi, quum et
"Josephus, lib. 1, 5, *de Bell.* Θυμιατήρια ολόχρυσα istius modi memoret,
"et Pollux, l. 1, 28, et 10, 28. Hesychius aliique acerras vocent θυμια-
"τήρια." So also T. Goodwin (*Moses et Aaron*, Franc. ad Moen, 1710,
8vo., p. 326), " Die expiationis solenni Pontifex Thuribulum aureum
"huic actui appropriatum loco sacerrimo inferebat, atque per aliquot
"horas in illo relinquebat tr. יומא, c. iii. 4, v. 1, vii. 4. Hoc est Pauli
"Θυμιατήριον, Hebr. ix. 4." So also J. A. Danzius (*Functio Pontif. M.
in adyto anniversaria*, p. 952; Meuschen), "Sic quidem Talmudici (*Joma*,
"cap. 7, 4; Babyl., fol. 70, &c.) docent, postquam circa initium functi-
"onum, in primordio diei, in Sanctissimum semel Pontifex introduxerat
"hoc *Thuribulum*, suffitu accenso, id ibi relinquebat, ac alios interea
"perficiebat cultus omnes, non tantum huic diei proprios, sed ipsum
"etiam sacrificium *vespertinum juge*; et sic circa vesperam demum,
"Sanctissimum denuo ingrediens, id ex illo efferebat."

ולפי שאין ראוי שיוציא משם הכף והסחתה כדם השלם הציבול לקטרת ולאש אשר
במסחתה והיה זה ממה שלא יתאמת שישלם בכמו זה העת הנה יצטרך להמתין לסלק הכף
והסחתה עד הערב וראוי שיהיה זה כעת שיצטרך לבא אל אהל מועד להקטיר קטרת הסמים
ולהזלות את הנרות קודם שיקטיר קטרת הסמים ויעלה את הנרות כדי שלא יהוה ענן הקטרת
לפנים מאהל מועד ולפני לפנים יחד כי התורה בו באלו השני מקומות קרובה להיות אחת
כמו שנבאר ולוה אין ראוי שהתיה בשני המקומות ובכלל הנה אן ישלם בלי ספק הציבול
לאש ולקטרת ואין ראוי שיכנס שם הכהן אם לא אחר שיתברר לו שישלם זה כדי שלא יכנס
שם שלא לצורך ויתחייב מיתה בידי שמים וגו'

" *Quandoquidem*, ut R. Levi f. Gerson (Comm. ad Lex. xvi., fol. 165,
" col. 3, l. 1, sqq.) loquitur, *inconveniens erat, ut efferat exinde acerram
" atque thuribulum, antequam suffitus ac ignis in thuribulo totaliter fuerint
" consumti: et vero certum tempus intra quod consumerentur, stabiliri non
" poterat, ideo necesse habuit, ut, ad acerram ac thuribulum auferendum,
" ad vesperam expectaret usque. Atque optime conveniebat, ut fieret id eo
" tempore, quo opus habebat ingredi in tentorium conventus, ad adolendum
" suffitum aromatum, ac accendendas Lucernas, antequam hæc duo efficiat;*

"*ut ne nubes sit suffimenti in tentorio pariter conventus, atque ejus intimo
"*simul. Nam quæ ex hoc doctrina elicitur, de duobus istis locis tam vicina
"*sibi invicem, est, ut haberi queat pro unica, sicut interpretabimur. Atque
"*ideo minime erat conveniens, ut fiat in locis istis duobus. Et quanquam
"*valde probabile sit, quod tunc absque dubio ignis ac suffimentum sit
"*consumtum: non tamen licitum est, ut ingrediatur illuc Pontifex, nisi
"*postquam clarè ipsi constiterit, omnia ista esse consummata. Ne extra
"*urgentem causam illuc se ingerens, reus fiat mortis per Deum inferendæ.
"*Quæ si vera sunt, prouti communi ore Ebræi statuunt: quamdiu esse
"*hujus Thuribuli operativum, sive usus ipsius durat, ad quem unice erat
"*destinatum, nulla alia templi pars id habuit, quam ipsum Sanctum
"*Sanctorum. Atque sic neque in hoc aliquid continet hæc epistola,
"*quod auctoritatem ejus canonicam infringeret.*" From the above it
will be evident that, if there were no more massive and stationary
censer in the Holy of Holies, as I believe there was, devoted to receive
the incense which the priest brought in with him on the Day of Atonement, there was at least a censer exclusively reserved for the service of
the Most Holy Place, on this great annual solemnity, and that the
Writer to the Hebrews well knew what he was writing about, when he
draws the attention of his coreligionists to the χρυσοῦν θυμιατήριον.

⁵ 'Ἐν ᾗ. It is expressly stated in 1 Kings viii. 9, אין בארון רק שני לחות
אבנים אשר הנח שם משה בחרב, lit., "There was not in the ark, only the
"two tables of stone, which Moses deposited there in Horeb." The
same statement is repeated, with a few verbal differences, in 2 Chron.
v. 10. Danzius (like many others) proposes to get over the difficulty by
translating ἐν ᾗ, una cum, together with, and refers to ἐν αἵματι ἀλλοτρίῳ in verse 25 in support of his suggestion, as well as to Luke xiv. 31,
"'Ἐν δέκα χιλιάσιν,*" and a variety of other passages. Now I think that
the statement of 1 Kings viii. 9, and 2 Chron. v. 10, may fairly be
limited to the particular occasion of which they speak, viz., to the
moment when the ark was carried into the temple. The word στάμνος
implies a tall standing jar or vase, which would be liable to be shaken
down by the act of removal. The venerable rod of Aaron might also
suffer damage from the tables of stone. Why may we not suppose the
pot of manna and the rod to have been laid up in the ark, but taken
out on this occasion? Indeed Dr. Gill writes (*in loc.*) that "What Levi
"ben Gerson (so also others, in Laniado, *Celi Yekar*) writes on 1 Kings
"viii. 9 is so express, as if it was designed to vindicate our Apostle.
"His remark is this:—The intention is not to deny that there were not
"the things mentioned in the law, for these were מניחים בו, *left in it*, as
"Aaron's rod, and the pot of manna; only to deny, hereby, that there
"was not anything of the Law, save the Decalogue." Had an express

command been at first given upon the subject, which there was not, that nothing but the tables should be deposited in the ark, even then there would be no insurmountable difficulty in the statement of the writer to the Hebrews. The usual course of the sacrifices was interrupted in the wilderness, as also the rite of circumcision (Amos v. 25; Josh. v. 1—9. See my tract, *Bishop Colenso's Criticism Criticised*, 3d edit., pp. 27—34); the Sabbatic laws were also relaxed upon cases of pressing need; and, furthermore, we know (1 Sam. xxi. 1—6; Matt. xii. 4) that Ahimelech the priest felt himself at liberty to feed David and his hungry followers with the shewbread. The high priest, moreover, in all occasions of difficulty, could have recourse to the oracle of the Urim and Thumim, and so obtain a Divine sanction for any needful alterations in the ceremonial precepts. The material of which the pot for containing the manna was made is not mentioned in the Hebrew of Exod. xvi. 33. It is there simply called צִנְצֶנֶת, a word that only occurs once in the Old Testament. Gesenius derives it from צֵן, *acutus fuit*, from whence is derived צֵן, *a thorn*. May it not have resembled one of those tapering or pointed antique alabaster and earthen vessels or jars for containing wine or ointment, of which there are many specimens in the British Museum? The LXX. of Exodus xvi. 33 calls it στάμνον χρυσοῦν. The Palestine Targum calls it an "earthen vase."

J. D. Michaelis, in pursuit of his pet theory that the Epistle was originally written in Hebrew, and that the "inaccuracies" which he professes to discover in some of its statements are due to the incompetency of the Greek translator, indulges in the following extraordinary piece of criticism:—"With respect to the last instance in particular "(ix. 4), the passage, as worded in the Greek, implies that the golden "pot of manna, and Aaron's rod, were kept in the ark of the covenant, "which directly contradicts what is related in the books of Moses and "of the Kings (!) Now a mistake of this kind could hardly have been "committed by the author of so excellent an Epistle as that to the "Hebrews; but it might have been made by a translator who was less "acquainted with Jewish customs, and it took its rise, perhaps, in the "following manner. In the place where ἐν ᾗ is used in the Greek, "אֲשֶׁר בּוֹ was probably used in the Hebrew Original, which may be "construed either with Holy of Holies (in Hebrew, קֹדֶשׁ הַקֳּדָשִׁים), verse "3, or with *ark of the covenant* (in Hebrew אָרוֹן), verse 4. The author "of the Epistle to the Hebrews intended to refer to the former (!), for "the golden pot of incense, and the rod of Aaron, were really kept in "the Holy of Holies, but not in the ark of the covenant. The trans"lator, therefore, should have rendered the Hebrew relative by ἐν οἷς, "in reference to ἅγια ἁγίων; instead of which he falsely referred it to

CHAP. IX., 1—5.

" the ark of the covenant, which being in Greek κιβωτος, he translated " it by ἐν ᾗ." (*Introd. to New Testament*, translated by Marsh, vol. iv., " pp. 224, 225.) Now, as I have already shown, 1 Kings viii. 9 and 2 Chronicles v. 10 do not assert that nothing " was ever *kept* " in the ark, except the tables of stone, but that nothing *was in* the ark besides the tables of stone, at the time of its removal. These are two very different matters. Secondly, the subject nominative of verse 3 is not ἅγια ἁγίων, but, σκηνὴ ἡ λεγομένη ἅγια ἁγίων. The difficulty of dealing with ἐν ᾗ of verse 3, in connexion with ὑπεράνω δὲ αὐτῆς Χερουβὶμ κ τ.λ. of verse 5, remains untouched by the proposed " original " reading of Michaelis. If we dared to refer ἐν ᾗ to σκηνή of verse 3, then all difficulty in the passage would be at an end; but even so venturesome a critic as Michaelis might well hesitate upon so hazardous a proposal. The eminent confraternity of Christian and Hebrew-Christian scholars, who translated the New Testament into Hebrew for the London Society for Promoting Christianity amongst the Jews, have thus rendered the entire passage:—

אולם גם למשכן הראשון היו הקי הצבודה הוא מקדש ארצי: כי נעשה משכן החיצון אשר בו המנורה והשולחן ולחם הפנים הנקרא קדש: ומאחרי הפרכת משכן הנקרא קדש הקדשים: אשר לו מזבח הזהב וארון הברית מצפה זהב סביב.* ובו צנצנת זהב אשר בו המן ומטה אהרן אשר פרח לוחת הברית: ומלמעלה כרובי הכבוד סוככים על הכפרה וגו'

Michaelis' suggestion that ἐν ᾗ should be ἐν οἷς, would necessitate the omission of the words σκηνὴ ἡ λεγομένη, and the insertion of τὰ, in verse 3 of the Greek. Such a wholesale mutilation of a passage is not often to be met with, even in practised " emendators." Nor can I perceive, with a competent Hebrew translation of the passage as the above before me, how it could be possible, by any known rules of construction, to refer back the relative words אשר בו (ἐν ᾗ of verse 4, ובו, *vid. supr.**), as proposed by Michaelis, to קדש הקדשים, instead of construing them in reference to ארון, the nearest, and only natural antecedent. Ewald (*Das Sendschreiben an die Hebräer*, Göttingen, 1870. 8vo., p. 40) translates as follows:—" Nach dem zweiten " Vorhange aber, das Zelt genannt, 'Allerheiligster,' enthaltend einen " goldenen Rauchaltar, und die Bundeslade rings mit Gold bedeckt, " worin ein goldener Krug das Manna enthaltend, und Ahron's Stab " welcher sprosste, und die Bundesplatten; über ihr aber, die Cherûbim " von Herrlichkeit den Sühnedeckel beschattend."

The Jerusalem Gemara (*Shekalim*, col. 117; *Ugol. Thes.*, vol. 18), after computing the space which the tables of stone would occupy in the ark, asserts that there were two hand-breadths left, לספר תורה, "*for* " *the Book of the Law.*" The same treatise (col. 113) says :—

משנגנז הארון נגנז עמו צנצנת המן וצלוחית שמן המשחה ומקלו של אהרן ופרחיו
ושקידיו . וארגז שהשיבו פלשתים אשם לאלהי ישראל . מי גנזו . יאשיהו גנזו .

"After the ark was hidden, they hid with it the pot of manna, and
"the vase of the oil of unction, and the rod of Aaron, with its blos-
"soms and almonds, and the chest which the Philistines sent as a
"trespass offering to the God of Israel. Who hid it (the ark)? Josiah
"hid it." The Rabbies, therefore, connected the disappearance of the
pot of manna, and Aaron's rod that budded, with the disappearance of
the ark. The "Book of the Covenant" (Exod. xxiv. 7) which Moses
wrote (verse 4), containing, as it did, only chapters xx. to xxiii. of the
book of Exodus, would not have been of too great bulk to be contained
in the ark, but it is somewhat doubtful whether so large a roll as that
of the Pentateuch, when completed, could have found room in a chest
of such moderate dimensions. Nevertheless the compilers of the
Jerusalem Talmud, as cited above, and who were doubtless not altogether simpletons, held a different opinion. To assert offhand that the
Epistle to the Hebrews (as we have it, and which is, at least, the
oldest form in which it has come down to us,) contains mistakes in its
statements, is very near akin to presumption of a somewhat offensive
description.

Dr. Prideaux (*The Old and New Testament Connected*, London, 1845.
8vo. Vol. i., p. 138, &c.) says:—"The ark of the covenant was a
"small chest (Exod. xxv. 10—27) or coffer, three feet nine inches in
"length, and two feet three inches in breadth, and two feet three inches
"in height, in which were put the two tables of the law, as well the
"broken ones (say the Rabbins) as the whole. For proof of this they
"bring the second verse of the tenth chap. of Deut., which they read
"thus:—'And I will write on the tables the words that were in the
"'first tables, which thou brakedest, and hast put into the ark';
"and it is true the word is ושמתם, *i.e.*, 'thou hast put,' in the
"preter tense; but it being with a vau (ו) before it, that turns the
"preter tense into a future, and therefore it must be read, 'thou shalt
"'put them,' as in our translation, and not 'thou hast put them,' as
"the fautors of this opinion would have it. And that there was nothing
"else in it, when it was brought into Solomon's temple, is said in two
"places of Scriptures (1 Kings viii. 9; 2 Chron. v. 10); but the
"Rabbins raise a controversy concerning Aaron's rod (Numb. xvii. 10;
"in the Heb. xvii. 25) and the pot of manna (Exod. xvi. 33), and the
"original volume of the law written by Moses' own hand, whether they
"were not also in the ark. It is said of Aaron's rod and the pot of
"manna that they were laid up before the testimony; and it being
"agreed on all hands that by '*the testimony*' is meant the two tables,

"those who interpret these words *before the testimony* (לפני העדוה) in the
"strictest sense, will have the said rod and pot of manna to have been
"laid up immediately before the tables, within the ark; but others
"who do not understand the words in so strict a sense, say that they
"were laid up in the Holy of Holies without the ark, in a place just
"before it, thinking that in this position, without the ark, they may
"be well said to be laid up before the testimony or tables of the law,
"as if they had been placed immediately before them within the ark.
"But the holy Apostle St. Paul decides this controversy, for he posi-
"tively tells us 'that within the ark were the golden pot that had
"'manna,' &c. (Heb. ix. 4); and hereto agree Abarbanel on 1 Kings,
"viii. 9, and R. Levi Ben Gersom, &c."

Danzius, however (*Functio Pontif. M.*, &c.), cites from R. Levi Ben
Gersom the following opposite, or at least indecisive opinion :—
לפני העדות והוא בקרש הקדשים, "before the testimony, which was in the
"Holy of Holies"; whilst from Abarbanel he adduces the following :—

לפני העדות שהוא ארון ברית יהוה והיתה הצנצנת מנוחה לפני לפנים במקום המקדש.

"The expression '*before the testimony*' means the ark of the covenant
"of the Lord, and the pot of manna was deposited in the most sacred
"place of all."

Prideaux, who speaks so decisively in favour of the literal reading of
Heb. ix. 4, observes, further, "The ark was not of capacity enough to
"hold the volume of the whole law of Moses, with the other things
"placed therein." (*Ibid.*, p. 139.)

[7] Χερ. δόξης, erroneously translated by Prof. Stuart "*splendid
"cherubim.*" The Targum of Jonathan renders Levit. xvi. 2, "The
"cloud of the glory of my Shechina is revealed over the place of the
"mercyseat"; and so here Δόξης might, with advantage, be rendered
"*of the Shechina.*" (See J. A. Danzii, *Shechina*, Meuschen, N. Test.
ex Talm. illustr., p. 701.) The writer to the Hebrews is here making
a skilful appeal to the consciousness of his readers, that all these
majestic, and once essential, accompaniments of the tabernacle and
temple worship had long since passed away. It contained an unanswerable demonstration that the Mosaic ceremonial comprised, in itself, no
inherent and sempiternal perpetuity. If these things were not indispensable, why should not the entire structure, based originally upon
Divine appointments, be ultimately dissolved, and give place to a new
and better order of things? Nearly all of the things above specified
in this chapter were absent in the second temple, and yet the prophet
Haggai was bidden to tell the elders, who wept over these departed
excellencies, "I will fill this house with glory, saith the Lord of Hosts
"………The glory of this latter house shall be greater than that of the

"former, saith the Lord of Hosts." (Hag. ii. 7—9.) R. Akiba expressly refers this passage to the days of Messiah. (See Balth. Scheidii, *Præterita præteritorum*, p. 20, Menschen.) The Rabbinical writers made no secret of these palpable deficiencies. R. Samuel bar Inja (in *Joma*) says :—

אלו חמשה דברים שהיו בין מקדש ראשון למקדש שני אלו הן ארון וכפורת וכרובים אש
ושכינה ורוח הקודש ואורים ותומים :

"The following five particulars constituted the difference between "the first sanctuary and the second, to wit, the ark, the mercyseat, and "the cherubim, the [holy] fire, and the Shechinah, and the Holy Spirit "[of prophecy], and the Urim and Thummim." The same passage is found in the Jerus. Gemara, *Taanith*, cap. 2, 1, col. 711 (Ugol. Thes., vol. 18), on which Abarbanel remarks (Comment. ad Hag. 1, fol. 278, col. 1) :—

אף אמנם ראוי לדעת שלא לבד אלה הדברים חסרו שמה כי גם המנורה והשלחן וכל כלי
המשכן ויריעותיו וקרשיו ושאר הדברים שעשה משה במדבר וצנצנת המן ומקלו של אהרן
ושמן המשחה כולם נגנו ולא שבו בבית שני :

"But it is certainly proper to notice that these were not the only "things wanting there. For besides these, the candlesticks, and the "table, and all the vessels of the tabernacles, and its curtains, and "boards, and the rest of the things which Moses made in the wilder- "ness, and the pot of manna, and Aaron's rod, and the oil of anointing, "were all of them hidden, and did not return, during the second "temple." (See Danzii *Functio Pont. M.*, p. 941.)

ⁿ Ἱλαστήριον, כפרת, from כפר, *to make expiation;* in its primary signification, *to cover*. It is first mentioned in Exod. xxv. 17, and is there called, in the LXX., ἱλαστήριον ἐπίθεμα. It was directed to be made of pure gold, and was placed upon the ark, the top of which it exactly equalled in size, viz., 2½ cubits in length, and a cubit and a half in breadth. The Targum of Jonathan (or Palestine) adds that "its depth "shall be a handbreadth" (*pusheka*). It was surrounded by the cherubims, and Jehovah promised (Exod. xxv. 22), "There I will meet with "thee, and I will commune with thee from above the mercyseat, from "between the two cherubims, which *are* upon the ark of the testimony, "of all *things* which I will give thee in commandment unto the children "of Israel"; which passage Onkelos thus paraphrases :—"And I will "appoint my Word (*Memra*) with thee there," &c. "Here it was," says Prideaux, "where the *Shechinah*, or Divine presence, rested, both "in the tabernacle and temple, and was visibly seen in the appearance "of a cloud over it; and from hence the Divine oracles were given out "by an audible voice (Exod. xxv. 22, and Num. vii. 89) as often as God "was consulted in the behalf of his people. And hence it is that God

CHAP. IX., 6—7.   119

" is so often said to dwell between the cherubims, that is, between the
" cherubims on the mercyseat, because there was the seat or throne of
" the visible appearance of his glory among them; and for this reason
" the high priest appeared before the mercyseat once every year, on the
" great day of expiation, when he was to make his nearest approach to
" the Divine presence to mediate and make atonement for the whole
" people of Israel. And all else of that nation who served God
" according to the Levitical law, made it the centre of their worship ;
" and not only in the temple when they came up thither to worship, but
" everywhere else in their dispersion through the whole world, when-
" ever they prayed, they turned their faces towards the place where the
" ark stood, and directed all their devotions that way. And, therefore,
" the author of the book *Cozri* (part 2, s. 28) justly saith, that the ark,
" with the mercyseat and cherubims, were the foundation, root, heart,
" and marrow, of the whole temple, and all the Levitical worship therein
" performed." (*Connexion of the Old and New Testament*, vol. 1, p. 140.)

Verse 6.—Such being the arrangement of the objects above
specified (Τούτων δὲ οὕτω κατεσκευασμένων), the priests
go in and out of the first tabernacle (or apartment) continually in the performance of their ministerial functions.¹

¹ Abarbanel, defining the particular functions of the ordinary priests,
as contradistinguished from those of the Levites, says, in reference to
the words לכל דבר המזבח ולמבית לפרכת, *in every matter concerning the altar
and within the veil.* (Numb. xviii. 7.) הם יקריבו הקרבנות על מזבח העולה והם
ישרתו בהדלקת הנרות ובקטורת, " They ought to offer sacrifices upon the altar
" of whole burnt-offering, and minister in lighting the lamps, and in
" the offering of incense." J. A. Danzius (in *Funct. Pontif. Max. in
Adyt. anniversaria*, Meuschen, p. 915) observes that none of the priests
with the exception of the Sagan (deputy high priest), and that only in
case of urgent necessity, could discharge the duties of the high priest
(כהן גדול) on the day of atonement. כל עבודת יום הכפורים אינה כשרה אלא בו,
" *No ministration of the day of atonement is in order, or lawful, except it
" be performed by him.*" (Gemar. Babyl. *Horajoth*, cap. 3, fol. 12.)
Maimonides says that the high priest might offer whenever and whatever he pleased, like an ordinary priest. On the word *Sagan*, see
Reland, *Ant. Sacr.*, p. 170.

Verse 7.—But into the second (once in the year, ἅπαξ τοῦ
ἐνιαυτοῦ, viz., *the Day of Atonement*)¹ the high priest [goes
in] alone (μόνος), not without blood,² which he offered on

his own behalf (ὑπὲρ ἑαυτοῦ),² as well as for the sins (ἀγνοημάτων) ¹ of the people.

¹ Ἅπαξ τοῦ ἐνιαυτοῦ, אחת בשנה, Levit. xvi. 24, *i.e.*, on one stated day in the year, viz., tenth day of Tisri, the first month of the civil year (Sept., Oct.). Maimonides (*Moreh Nevochim*, pt. iii., c. 45, fol. 164, edit. Sabionet.), after observing that the high priest alone might enter the Holy of Holies, and only on the day of atonement, whilst the ordinary priests might enter the holy place daily, *provided always that it was at the appointed hour of service*, goes on to ask how many times the high priest might enter the Holy of Holies (but only at service time) on the Day of Atonement? He answers, "Four times; but if he enters "a fifth time, he incurs the penalty of death at the hands of God." What these four times are, we learn from the same writer (*Hilch. jom hakkippurim*, c. 4, § 1) :—1, with the incense ; 2, with the blood of the bullock ; 3, with the blood of the goat ; 4, when he goes in to fetch out the spoon and the censer (see note, p. 112) ; and yet, in exact accordance with the form of speech used by the writer to the Hebrews, Maimonides elsewhere says, בא שם פעם אחת בשנה, "He goes in there "but once in the year."

The following extract from the Gemara (*Tract. Rosh. Hashshanah*, chap. 1) will serve to show the legendary sanctity attaching to the month Tizri :—

ר״ אליעזר אומר בתשרי נברא העולם בתשרי נולדו אבות בתשרי מתו אבות בפסח נולד יצחק בראש השנה נפקדה שרה רחל וחנה בראש השנה יוסף יצא מבית האסורים בראש השנה בטלה עבדה מאבותינו במצרים בניסן נגאלו ובתשרי עתידין ליגאל :

"R. Eliezer says, the world was created in Tizri, in Tizri the "Patriarchs were born, and in Tizri they also died. On the Passover "Isaac was born ; on the first month of the year Sarah, Rachel, and "Hannah were visited. In the first month of the year Joseph went "forth from the prison house ; in the first month of the year the "servitude of our fathers ceased in Egypt, although in Nisan they were "released." According to the same Rabbi, in Tisri the Jews are also to be delivered by the Messiah. R. Joshua, however, places the consummation of Messiah's redemption, like the release from Egyptian bondage, in the month Nisan. (See J. A. Danzius, *ibid.*, pp. 956, 959, 961, where the whole subject is discussed at length.)

The above traditional coincidences serve to illustrate the Messianic and typical characteristics attributed by the ancient Jewish teachers to the Day of Atonement.

² From the following extract from Maimonides (*Hilc. avod. jom hakkip.*, cap. iv., sec. 1) it will be seen that it is not improbable that

the High Priest did not bring in the blood on the first occasion of his entering the Holy of Holies.

מקבל את דמו של פר וניתנו למי שהוא מנדנדו שלא יקרש על הרובד הרביעי של היכל
כנהוין ונוטל את המחתה שהיתה בה אש מעל מזבח.המובח מן הסמוך למערב שני מעל המזבח
מלפני י׳ ויורד ומניחה על הרובד שבעזרה׳ ומיציאין לו את הכף וכלי מלא קטרת דקה מן
הדק והופן ממנה מלא הפניו לא מחוקית ולא גדושית אלא בטפופות הגדיל לפי נדולו והקן
לפי קוטנו וניתן להוך הכף מפני כובד המחתה וחוד שהוא המה אינו יכול לסובל בשמאלו
עד הארון לפיכך נוטל המחתה בימינו וכף הקטורת בשמאלו ומהלך בהיכל עד שהוא מניע
לקדש הקדשים, כצא הפרוכת פרושה נכנס לקדש הקדשים עד שהוא מניע לארון, הגיע לארון
נותן המחתה בין שני הבדים ובבית שני שלא היה ארון היה מניחה על אבן השתייה

"Sanguinem Juvenci recipit [*in cratere aureo*] ac tradit cuidam, qui
"extus in quarto Templi scamno agitet, ne coaguletur. Ipse vero
"accipit Thuribulum [*allatum sibi ab aliis*], ac depromit eo ignem ab
"Altari [*exteriori*] ea parte, quæ occidenti erat vicinior ; quia dicitur :
"'*desuper Altari coram Domino*.' Descendens autem, collocat illud
"super scamnum, quod in atrio. Præterea producunt quoque ad ipsum
"Acerram aliquam, et vas plenum suffimenti semel utrumque contusi :
"e quo plenos caput pugillos suos, non rasos, nec accumulatos, sed
"planos, quilibet pro capacitate staturæ suæ, eosque acerræ isti indit.
"Ob gravitatem Thuribuli, ejusque calorem, non potest id portare in
"sinistra sua ad Arcam usque : ideo accipit Thuribulum dextera sua,
"et Acerram suffimenti sinistra, atque progreditur per templum, donec
"pervenerit ad Sanctum Sanctorum. In quod, Velo allevato, ingreditur
"ad Arcam usque, quo si accesserit, ponit Thuribulum inter duos ejus
"vectes ; in templo secundo vero, ubi non extitit Arca, id posuit super
"Lapidem istum Fundationis." (J. A. Danzii *Funct. Pontif.*, pp. 993,
994, Meuschen.)

[3] From Lev. xvi. 6, 11, compared with verse 24, we see that ὑπὲρ ἑαυτοῦ (בעדו ובעד ביתו) included his family, and so the Targums of Palestine and Onkelos render *for himself and the men of his house*. Maimonides (Hilc. *Jom Hakkip.*, chap. ii., sec. 6, &c.) gives the formula of confession employed by the High Priest on his own account as follows :—

אנה השם חטאתי עויתי ופשעתי לפניך אני י׳ כפר נא לחטאים ולעוונות ולפשעים
שחטאתי ושעויתי ושפשעתי

"And now, O Lord, I have sinned, and done iniquity, and trespassed
"before Thee. I pray therefore, O Lord, cover (or expiate) *my sins,*
"*and iniquities, and trespasses*, which I have sinned, done wrongly, and
"trespassed against Thee." The confession to be used for the sins of the people was couched in words exactly similar. (See Danzius, *ibid.*, pp. 1000 and 1010.) The same writer explains the meaning of this threefold enumeration of faults. He understands them not as being accumulative, but particularising and specificatory. His words are—

כי צינות הם הענות שאדם עושה במזור וחטאים הם הנעשים בשוגג ופשעים הם מיני
הכפירה והמרד בהשם וכו׳

"By iniquities are understood those things which a man does de-
"signedly wrong. Sins signify things which a man is betrayed into
"unawares, and transgressions come under the head of dissimulation
"and rebellion against God."—Danzius, *ibid.*, p. 1010.

⁴ Dr. Alford, as will be apparent from the above note as well as from
the following, erroneously renders ἀγνοήματα by *sins of ignorance*.
Danzius (*ibid.*, pp. 1008, 1009) sagaciously remarks:—" Peccata quæ
"expianda sunt, vocantur hic ἀγνοήματα, quæ Socinianis haud alia sunt,
"quam *quæ vel ex ignorantia sive oblivione juris alicujus divini, vel ex
"ignorantia facti et circumstantiarum, vel etiam ex humanâ quadam
"imbecillitate proficiscuntur.* Equidem concedendum omnino est, ἀγνοή-
"ματα hinc inde in scriptis sacris ac profanis pro hujus generis exstare
"peccatis. Quod autem et *voluntaria* ac *graviora* haud raro denotet,
"satis superque docent dicta Psal. xxv. 7, ubi פשע (quod quam magnum
"designet peccatum, mox dicturi sumus) LXX. rediderunt per ἀγνοίαν.
"Hoseæ iv. 15, spiritualis Israelitarum scortatio per verbum ἀγνοέω, pro
"Hebraico זנה positum, exprimitur. Quæ sane leve, ac ex ignorantia
"commissum peccatum non fuit ; prouti ex toto hoc capite clare apparet.
"Etiam Jud. v. 19, 20, pro quibusvis delictis idem vocabulum ponitur.
"Hinc et *Syrus* interpres h l. pro ἀγνοήμασι Apostoli posuit ܡܒ̈ܨܠܬܗ
"quâ voce quævis designantur peccata, etiam illud ab Adamo perpe-
"tratam, quod certe nec leve fuit, nec ex ignorantiâ commissum. Imo
"ex collatione loci Lev. xvi., sole lucidius patet, hic sub voce τῶν
"ἀγνοημάτων, omnis generis contineri peccata. Siquidem ibi a satis
"perspicuis docetur, *omnia* peccata, in anniversario isto Sacrificio
"expiari. Et quidem omnia *illa*, quæ supra vocibus עון, פשע ac חטאה
"erunt expressa atque sub se continent quiquid omnino venit sub
"*peccati* nomine. Vox enim עין (quæ formatur ab עוה *curvus, pravus,
"perversus fuit, iniquus fuit, inique ac perverse egit,* cum contra Deum,
"tum proximum), denotat vitiositatem non modo naturæ, seu peccatum
"innatum, iniquitatem, perversitatem, sed graviora peccata, quæ inde
"oriuntur, ut *abnegationem Dei, Idololatriam, adulterium* ac quævis alia.
"Et quidem non ex errore, sed ex malitia, seu destinato proposito
"commissa, cum sc. mens quidem quid rectum quid æquum sit videt
"et agnoscit : deteriora tamen sequuntur. פשע (cujus origo est verbum
"פשע *transgressus est*, voluntatem scil. ad mandatum ejus cui quis ad
"obediendum est obstrictus, *defecit, seditiosus, rebellis fuit*), designat
"transgressionem *defectionem* ac *rebellionem* malitiosam : ut ex citatis
"perspicuum evadit. חטא (a verbo חטא *erravit, aberravit a via, vel
"scopo,* metaphorice *peccavit,* siquidem peccando a lege divina aberra-

" mus), significat peccatum, prouti aberratio seu digressio a recta via
" est. At vox hæc tam late patet ut non tantum notet peccatum
" originale, ac actualia illa quæ per errorem sunt commissa, sed et
" quævis alia graviora," &c. The same writer goes on to remark how
in Exod. xxxiv. 7 and other passages, all these words are found in
juxtaposition, as including every kind of sin that can be possibly committed, e.g., והחטאה פשע ועין נשא לאלפים חסד נצר, " *Keeping mercy for*
" *thousands, forgiving iniquity, and transgression, and sin,*" &c.

Verses 8, 9.—The Holy Ghost making it clearly understood (*hoc significante Spiritu Sancto*, Vulg.) that the way
(τὴν τῶν ἁγίων ὁδὸν, i.e., the right of entering) into the
holy places had not yet been indicated (μήπω πεφανερῶσθαι,
i.e., *was straitly forbidden*), whilst the first tabernacle was
still in existence. (These words must be limited to the
actual restrictions which excluded any but the High Priest
from going into, and allowed him only once a year to
enter, the Holy of Holies.) Which (tabernacle, ἥτις) is
a parabolic representation referring to the present time
(παραβολὴ εἰς τὸν καιρὸν τὸν ἐνεστηκότα).

In other words, the condition of those who obsti-
nately hold by the Temple as it now is, with its
figurative and ceremonial observances and ritual
(based upon the ancient model of the Tabernacle),
is not a whit nearer the reality, the things signified
and hoped for, than that of the Israelites under
Moses. What was then indicated by the Holy Ghost
holds good for all time, as long as the Mosaic ritual
is kept up. The worshippers are yet in the region
of shadow and type. They cannot and dare not
penetrate within the veil. And what is worse,
they are content with their condition. They will
not understand the lesson inculcated by the Holy
Spirit Himself. The parable or figurative lesson

is a sealed book to them. They look at the outside, and are content to remain excluded and "afar off," even at the present time.

Verses 9, 10.—In which (*sc.* καιρὸν) gifts and sacrifices are offered, which cannot make the worshipper perfect in respect to his conscience, being imposed (ἐπικείμενα, Stuart, *enjoined*) until the time of reformation (διορθώσεως, *rectification, placing things on a better footing*), simply in respect to meats and drinks, and various washings, and carnal ordinances (δικαιώμασι σαρκὸς).[1]

[1] Alford, with Scholz, Lachmann, and Griesbach, read δικαιώματα. (See note 3, p. 108.) Spencer (De Legibus. Heb. *Rit.*, tom. ii., p. 161, *Hag.* Com., 4to.) writes :—" Vix ulla tot baptismorum Judæorum ratio " assignari potest, nisi eorum originem a seculi moribus, non facile cito- " que dediscendis, arcessamus. Haud ex nihilo est, quod asserit Apos- " tolus, Judæorum cultum stetisse (Heb. ix. 10) μόνον ἐπὶ βρώμασι, καὶ " πόμασι, καὶ διαφέροις βαπτισμοῖς ; alia enim erat Pontificis et sacer- " dotum lotio, Exod. xxix. 4, alia Levitarum, Num. viii. 7, Israelitarum " alia : eáque, vel ob officii alicujus sacri reverentiam et solemnitatem, " Exod. xix. 10, 11, vel immunditiem contractam, e tactu seminiflui, " Lev. xv. 8, reptilis, Levit. xxii. 5, cadaveris, cap. xvii. 5, aliis que " causis. Quid autem Deus (qui cordis non cutis, munditiem spectare " solet) tot frigidos et omni virtute cassos corporis baptismos in cultum " suum recipere dignaretur, nisi ut Illius instituta ad ruditatem " Hebræorum, jam diu (Gal. iv. 3) ὑπὸ τὰ στοιχεῖα τοῦ κόσμου δεδουλω- " μένων, aliquatenus accomodaret."

The writer having now enumerated the leading characteristics of the first Tabernacle and the Mosaic ritual as yet carried out in his own days, as far as its departed glories and essential ornaments would permit, in the Temple, and having also pointed out some leading defects, now proceeds in the 11th and following verses to bring out the superior excellences and superlative completeness of the High Priesthood of Jesus.

Verses 11—14.—But Christ (Messiah) being come, a High Priest of the good things to come (τῶν μελλόντων ἀγαθῶν, i.e., *the spiritual and heavenly;*—see note 2 on p. 37) through (per amplius et perfectius.—*Vulg.*) the (*not* a) greater and more perfect tabernacle, which is not made with hands, that is, not of this creation (ταύτης τῆς κτίσεως, *visible, material creation*, Stuart); not in virtue (διὰ, *with*) of the blood of goats and calves (פר a bullock), but in virtue (διὰ δὲ) of his own blood (see verse 7, οὐ χωρὶς αἵματος ὃ προσφέρει, κ.τ.λ.), he entered once for all (ἐφάπαξ) into the Holy places (τὰ ἅγια, i.e., *the heavenly*), having found an eternal redemption for us (*i.e.,* a *redemption whose efficacy evermore abides, and is ever fresh and enduring*). For if the blood of bulls and of goats, and the ashes of a heifer sprinkling [1] the unclean (κεκοινωμένους *ceremonially defiled*), sanctifieth to the purifying of the flesh, how much rather shall the blood of Christ, who through the Eternal Spirit [2] offered himself (Ps. xl. 6, 7) without spot (ἄμωμον) to God, cleanse your consciences from dead works,[3] so that you may serve the living [4] God? (εἰς τὸ λατρεύειν κ.τ.λ.)

---

[1] Σποδὸς δαμάλεως ῥαντίζουσα κ.τ.λ. (Num. xix. 11—19.) The ashes of the heifer were employed in the composition of the water of separation (מי הנדה) wherewith any person or vessel which had contracted ceremonial defilement in connexion with a dead body or a bone of a dead person, &c., &c., were to be purified. Hence the allusion to "dead" works," from which Christ, by the Spirit of Sanctification, shall much more cleanse the conscience.

[2] Διὰ πνεύματος αἰωνίου (compare Ps. cx. 4, Σὺ ἱερεὺς εἰς τὸν αἰῶνα). This very peculiar expression is nowhere else found in the New Testament. Stuart renders it "by an eternal Spirit," and "in an eternal "spiritual nature." I cannot help thinking that there is a Messianic allusion to the anointing of the Holy Ghost, viz., to that "oil of glad-" ness," typified by the Aaronic holy oil, wherewith Christ was anointed above his fellows, and which accompanied his designation to the High-priesthood. (Ps. xlv. 7.) Concerning this Psalm, the late Dr. M'Caul

writes (*Lectures on the Prophecies.* London, 1846. 8vo., p. 59), "The "Targum, David Kimchi, and even R. Isaac in the CHIZZUK EMUNAH, "interpret it positively of the Messiah." The latter says also of Is. lxi., "The whole chapter refers to the future, and speaks of the "gathering of the captivities of Israel, and the coming of the true "Messiah, which we expect in the last days." Whilst Rabbi David Kimchi says plainly, that "it is the Messiah whose name is mentioned "in all generations, and whom the Gentiles shall praise." Christians are apt to forget that the word *Christ* means *Anointed one*, and that the priestly unction of Christ is the Holy Ghost. (See Is. xi. 2 ; xlviii. 16 ; lxi. 1. Comp. Luke iv. 18.) So also the Targum of Jonathan on Is. xlii. 1 :—"Behold my servant the Messiah......I will put the Spirit "of Holiness upon Him." (הא עבדי משיחא.)

Now it is expressly foretold by Isaiah, iv. 4, that in the days of the "Branch," an epithet universally applied by the Rabbies and by the Targums to the Messiah, "Jehovah will have washed away the filth of "the daughters of Zion, and shall have purged the blood of Jerusalem "by the *Spirit of Judgment and by the Spirit of burning*" (ברוח משפט וברוח בער), and this is in exact accordance with the declaration of John Baptist (Matt. iii. 11), "He shall baptize you with the Holy Ghost "and with fire." J. A. Danzius, in his very able *Programma de Spiritu Ardente,* Meuschen, p. 790, observes how "R. Samuel Laniado רוח "המשפט Spiritum judicii, exposuit quidem, דין יסורין *judicium castigati-* "*onum ;* רוח בער *Spiritum ardentem* vero explicavit omnino רוח קדש מאת השם "שיבער הכל עד תומו *Spiritum sanctificationis ex Deo, qui tollet stercus, donec* "*defecerit,*" and then proceeds, "Paraphrastes Chald. רוח per מימרא "*Verbum* transtulit, quæ vox æque ac משיחא, de *divina persona* ab ipso "sumi putatur, eaque ut plurimum *secunda,* quam Joannes λόγον cog-"nominavit." Here, then, we see that the Spirit of Messiah, or the "*Spirit of burning*," is THE SPIRIT OF SANCTIFICATION, πνεῦμα ἁγιωσύνης, Rom. i. 4 ; and although Danzius does not allude to this fourteenth verse of Heb. ix. in the passage quoted, I feel that very considerable help is, by his remarks, afforded to its proper understanding.

It is quite true that, in Matt. xii. 28, "If I cast out devils by the "Spirit of God," the Divine power and energy of Christ is intended, as will be seen by comparing the parallel passage in Luke xi. 20 :— "But if I by the finger of God cast out devils, no doubt the kingdom "of God is come unto you." The expressions "Spirit of God" and "finger of God" are here convertible terms. The "sin against the "Holy Ghost" of which the Pharisees were guilty was a malicious and wilful denial of the proper Deity of Jesus. They blasphemously compared his real miracles to the charms and exorcisms of which the

CHAP. IX., 15.   127

Rabbinical writings are full, and by which their children pretended to cast out devils. The form of speech "the finger of God" is taken from Exod. viii. 19 (Heb. 15), where the magicians say to Pharaoh, in reference to the plague of lice, "*This is the finger of God*" (אצבע אלהים הוא), and in this sense, Dean Alford seems to understand διά πν. αἰων. κ.τ.λ., "It is not the Spirit of the Father dwelling in Christ, nor is it the Holy "Spirit given without measure to Christ, but it is the Divine Spirit of "the Godhead which Christ himself had, and was his inner personality." This indeed is an explanation, but it is not a solution of the present difficulty. In a case like the present it is always safer, if possible, to seek the key to the difficulty in the immediate context and the subject in hand, and not to run away from them to discover a palliative, so to speak, in the statement of some general and unquestionable truism, which has only an adapted bearing upon the point at issue. We may be quite sure that the writer to the Hebrews knew, and enunciated precisely, what he intended to convey; and, also, it cannot be questioned that the subject of which he is treating, and so closely handling, is a minute comparison and contrast between the temporal highpriesthood of Aaron, and the eternal highpriesthood of Christ.

³ It had been distinctly foretold by the prophet Zechariah (xiii. 1) that in Messiah's days such a spiritual fountain should be provided :— "In that day there shall be a fountain opened to the house of David "and to the inhabitants of Jerusalem for sin and for uncleanness." (הלנדה--"נדה, *abominatio, impuritas*, a נדר *removit, abjecit,* מי הנדה *aqua impuritatis* h.e. *aqua, qua impuri purgantur, aqua lustratoria.*" Gesen.) In reference to this passage of Zech., R. Alshech on Jer. xxiii. 6, as quoted in Dr. M'Caul's *Kimchi on Zech.*, pp. 175, 176, says, "Messiah is called "The Lord our Righteousness; that is to say, through the super- "abundance of his righteousness and purity, righteousness will be "communicated to Israel from heaven. Messiah will be like a reservoir "into which it is poured, and from whence it is spread among the "people; and this is the meaning of *The Lord our Righteousness*. That "is to say, that as the Lord sends forth righteousness to him that comes "to be cleansed, and still more to the clean, so also the Messiah "shall be like the blessed God, and his name shall be called *The Lord* "*our Righteousness*, for from Thee our righteousness shall be derived as "from the Lord."

⁴ Θεῷ ζῶντι, *i.e.*, the true and living God [אלהים חיים Deut. v. 23 (25)], whose voice our Fathers heard, and from whom we are falsely accused of departing.

Verse 15.—And in consequence of this (διὰ τοῦτο) He is a

Mediator of[1] a new covenant (or Testament), so that his death having really taken place (nachdem ein Tod .... vollendet war.—*Ewald*) for the redemption of the transgressions under the first covenant, those who have been called might receive the promise of the eternal inheritance.

[1] Διαθήκης καινῆς μεσίτης, i.e., "*the Messenger of the Covenant,*" מלאך הברית, of Mal. iii. 1, ὁ ἄγγελος τῆς διαθήκης ὃν ὑμεῖς θέλετε LXX., "Angelus testamenti quem vos vultis," *Vulg.* This Divine person is elsewhere called מלאך יהוה (correctly translated "*The Angel of the Lord,*" in the authorized version), and in the Targums, מימרא די "The word of the Lord," "commonly used," as Etheridge says, "in the Targums to denote the Divine Being in self-manifestation, "and identified with the Shechinah;" *e.g.*, Onkelos paraphrases Gen. xvi. 13, 14, thus,—" And she prayed in the name of the Lord who had "spoken with her, and she said, Thou art Eloha, seeing all, for she "said, I also have begun to see after that He hath been revealed to me. "Therefore she called the name of the well, *The well at which appeared* "*the Angel of the Covenant.*" Whilst the Targum of Jonathan has, "And she gave thanks before the Lord whose Word spake to her, and "thus said, Thou art He who livest and art eternal; who seest, but art "not seen. For she said, for behold here is revealed the glory of the "Shechinah of the Lord after a vision. Wherefore she called the well, "*The well at which the Living and Eternal One was revealed.*" The Jerusalem Targum reads, "And Hagar gave thanks, and prayed in the "name of the Word of the Lord, who had been manifested to her, "saying, Blessed be Thou, Eloha, the Living One of all ages, who hast "looked upon my affliction." So also the Targum of Jonathan in Mal. iii. 1 identifies the מלאך הברית *the angel of the covenant,* with the מימרא די or *Word of the Lord.* The Rabbies, as also the Targum of Jonathan, make the מלאך פניו *the angel of his presence,* which redeemed them, of Is. lxiii. 9 (המלאך הגאל) "the redeeming angel" of Gen. xlviii. 16) to be one and the same with God, Jehovah, the Shechinah, and the Word of the Lord, or *Memra.* He is also called Michael (מיכאל i.e., *who is as God*), as will appear from the following Talmudical passages:— "When three men walk along a road together, the principal personage "walks in the middle, the most honourable of the two remaining ones "on the right hand, and the other on the left. And this we find to be "the case in respect to the three ministering angels who came to "Abraham. Michael walked in the middle, Gabriel on his right, and "Raphael on his left." *Joma,* 37. a, line 28, &c. Edit. Amst. And again, "Who, then, were those three men who tarried with Abraham ?

"Michael, Gabriel, and Raphael. Michael came to bring the good news
"to Sarah, Raphael to heal Abraham, who was not yet recovered of his
"circumcision, Gabriel went away to overthrow Sodom." *Bava Metzia*,
fol. 86 b, line 41, &c. And further, "The three angels who came to our
"father Abraham were Gabriel, Michael, and Raphael.........Whilst
"Abraham was looking upon these angels, and the Schechina (Michael)
"came over to him and stood opposite to him, Abraham said to the
"others, My Lords, wait ye here while I go with the Shechina, for He
"is greater than you," &c. *Derech Erez*, chap. iii., fol. 19, col. 2.
Again, in the treatise *Shabbath*, Bab., fol. 127 a, line 37, &c., "It is
"written concerning the Holy One, Blessed be He, *and Abraham said*,
"*O Lord* (אדני Adonai)! *if now I have found grace, wait until I have
"brought in those travellers*, to wit, Gabriel and Raphael." On which
J. A. Danzius remarks in his most erudite treatise *Schechina cum
piis cohabitans* (Meuschen, *N. T. ex Talmude illustr.*, p. 719), " A quibus
"suam mutuatus est Glossam *Raschi*, qua contendit quod Angelum
"istum medium vocarit ADONAI, sc. Dominum, Abrahamus : ' cum hoc
"ordine ante ipsum venerint, ut Michael in medio procederet, Gabriel
"ab ejus dextera, et Raphael a sinistra. Et quod Sanctum Bendicen-
"dum allocutus sit: quia in præcedentibus scriptum, quod appa-
"ruerit ipsi (sc. Abrahamo) Jehova ; et deinceps ecce tres viri.
"Dixerit itaque Sancto isti Benedicendo *ne quæso! transeas a vicinitate
"servi tui; expecta me hic donec introducerim viatores istos.'*" And again,
p. 721, "Quem ipsum eundem dicunt cum *Angelo* isto, *in cujus medio
"esse dicitur nomen Dei*, h.e. *Deus ipse*, juxta communem linguæ Ebreæ
"indolem : cui usitatissime nomen מיטטרון seu METATORIS (quo sensu
"castrorum *metator* et urbis, apud Ciceronem occurrit), tribuunt: qui,
"ut et nominibus proxime præcedentibus memoratus, idem sit ac
"SCHECHINA. In quo acquieverit Moses verbis (Exod. xxxiv. 9):
"*si nunc inveni gratiam* in oculis tuis, O ADONAI, *incedat quæso!
"*ADONAI in medio nostro.* Quam vocem SCHECHINÆ æquipollentem
"jam supra monuimus," &c. The Targum of Jonathan on Exod.
xxiv. 1, instead of "And He (God) said unto Moses, come up unto the
"Lord," has, "And Michael, the Prince of Wisdom, said," &c. The
late Dr. M'Caul, in his Observations on מלאך יהוה *The Angel or Messenger of the Lord (R. D. Kimchi's Comment. on Zech. translated*, p. 25),
says, " R. Bechai testifies unreservedly to the fact that the angel here
"(Exod. iii. 6) calls himself the God of Abraham, Isaac, and Jacob.
"' Ask not,' he says, ' how Moses could hide his face before the angel,
"' for the angel mentioned here is the angel, the Redeemer of whom it
"' is written, *I am the God of Bethel*, and in like manner it is said here,
"' *I am the God of thy father, the God of Abraham, the God of Isaac,*

s

"'*and the God of Jacob*, and He it is of whom it is said, *My name is in him.*' (Comment. in loco.) R. Moses ben Nachmann goes a step further; he not only confirms the fact, but rejects the explanation that the angel was speaking in the name of him that sent him. His words are, 'The explanation, that in the words, *I am the God of thy father*, the messenger spoke in the language of Him that sent him, is not correct, for Moses's degree in prophecy was too high for him to hide his face before the angel. Our Rabbies have said in Bereshith Rabba, *This angel is Michael. As in the case of R. Jose the Patient, wherever he was seen, they said, there is our holy Rabbi, so wherever Michael is seen, there is the glory of the Shechinah.* They meant to say that at first Michael appeared to him, and that the glory of the Shechinah was there, but he did not see the glory, for he did not apply his mind to the prophetic vision; but when he applied his mind and turned aside to see, then the appearance of the Shechina was revealed unto him, and God called unto him out of the midst of the bush. And in the way of truth, this angel was the Angel the Redeemer, for it is said, *My Name is in him.* He it is who said to Jacob, *I am the God of Bethel*, and of him it is said, *and God called to him.* But he is called מלאך *angel*, with reference to the government of the world; and thus it is written (in one place), *And the Lord brought us out of Egypt* (Deut. vi. 21), and (in another) it is written, *And he sent an angel, and hath brought us forth out of Egypt* (Num. xx. 16). Again it is said, *the Angel of his Presence saved them*, that is to say, *the Angel who is his Presence.* (Is. lxiii. 9.) For it is written, *My Presence shall go, and I will give thee rest* (Exod. xxxiii. 14); and this is what is said, *The Lord whom ye seek shall suddenly come to his temple, even the* MESSENGER OF THE COVENANT *whom ye delight in, behold He shall come*' (Mal. iii. 1)." Those who desire to pursue this subject further may with advantage consult Dr. M'Caul's Kimchi's Zech., pp. 9—27, Danzius's very learned treatise *Schechina* above mentioned, and the introduction to Etheridge's Targums. On διαθήκη, see note on p. 131.

The writer does not mean to say, that the mediator, or introducer of a Testament must himself die, but that, unless the death of the testator can be proved, the testament is a dead letter and of no legal value. But Christ entered into the Heavenly Sanctuary, after his resurrection, bearing his own blood in token that He had truly died; that He had given

CHAP. IX., 16—19.   131

his life a ransom for many; for "the blood is the "life;" and thus the terms of the testament of our redemption immediately came into force, and took formal effect. We have now a right to speak of the Testament as an instrument of recognized validity.

Verses 16—19.—For (says the writer) where a testament (is produced) it is absolutely needful (*before it can be acted upon*, or properly be called a "Testament") that the death of the testator shall be established (φέρεσθαι).[1] For a testament is valid (ἐπὶ νεκροῖς βεβαία) in reference to the dead (*in the case of the dead*, Alford. *Auf Todte gültig*, Ewald; *i.e.*, no one can claim the discharge of any bequest or stipulation of a will, until after the testator's death), since it is of no validity at all during the testator's lifetime. Wherefore it came to pass, that the former was not inaugurated (ἐγκεκαίνισται *initiated*) without blood. (It was a type of the better covenant, and had its typical representation of the testator's death in the blood of the sacrifices.) For after every Commandment according to the Law (κατὰ νόμον) had been rehearsed by Moses to all the people, he took the blood of the calves and goats, with water, and scarlet wool, and hyssop, and sprinkled both the book itself,[2]

---

[1] Ὅπου γὰρ διαθήκη, θάνατον ἀνάγκη φέρεσθαι τοῦ διαθεμένου. The word διαθήκη is adopted both in the Mishna and the Talmud, *e.g.*, דייתיקי, and signifies both a covenant, and also the last will and testament of a dying man, *e.g.*, Mishna, *Moed Katon*, cap. 3, 3, ואלו כותבין במועד קידושי נשים וגיטין /וגו ושוברין דייתיקי, *Et hæc scribunt in diebus festi intermediis, sponsalia mulierum, divortia, apocham, contractum*, &c. Mishna, Surenh., tom. ii., p. 409. Again, *Bava Metzia*, cap. i., 7, מצא גיטי נשים ושחרורי עבדים דייתיקי וגו׳, *Si quis invenerit libellos repudii mulierum, et servorum manumissorum*, διαθήκης, &c. *Ibid.*, tom. iv., p. 110. Again, *Bava Bathra*, cap. viii. 3, מי שמת ונמצאת דייתיקי קשורה על ירכו וגו׳, *Si quis mortuus fuerit et testamentum ipsius foemori alligatum fuerit*, &c. *Ibid.*, pp. 192, 193. J. D. Michaelis (*Introd. to the New Testament*, tr. by Marsh, vol. iv, pp. 227, 228) writes:—"The word διαθήκη was adopted both by the Syrians and "the Rabbins. In Syriac it was......used both in the sense of *Covenant*

"and that of *Testament*, as Castell and Schaaf have clearly shown,
"from many passages of the Syriac version." The Talmudic writers
could not have adopted the word from the New Testament writers. It
is therefore evident that the writer to the Hebrews was employing a
well-known Rabbinical formula when he uses διαθήκη in the sense of a
Testament. Buxtorf gives the following article on דייתיקי, in his Chaldee
and Rabbinical Lexicon, col. 534 : — "דייתיקי, διαθήκη, *Testamentum*,
" *Tabulæ extremæ voluntatis de hæreditate*. Glossa Talmudica explicat,
"שטר צואת שכיב מרע. Literæ præceptionis sive mandati, scil. ultimi,
"quibus homo præcipit. quid post mortem suam de bonis relictis fieri
"velit, ex locutione, צו לביתך, *Præcipe domui tuæ*, 2 Reg. xx. 1, vide et
"2 Sam. xvii. 23. Apud Talmudicos, דייתיקי מתנה, Testamentum donati-
"onis, Moed Katon, fol. 18, 2, in Mischna, Metzia, fol. 13, 1, et 18, 1.
"איזהו דייתיקי, Quare dicitur דייתיקי? Quasi דא תהי קיים. Hoc (quod scil.
"hic scriptum est) erit ratum et firmum ab hoc tempore, et post mortem
"meam, Metzia, fol. 19, 1. Bathra, fol. 135, 2, משה עשה דייתיקי, Moses
"fecit testamentum : דייתיקי מבטלה דייתיקי, Testamentum (posterius) irritum
"reddit Testamentum (prius), Bathra, fol. 152, 2, et 135. 2. *Plural*,
"אידי ואידי דייתקאות, Utrumque est testamentum, Metzia, fol. 19, 2."
R. Obad. de Bartenora says the word means "The testament, or last
"wish of a sick person," and is compounded of the words דא תהא למיקם,
hoc esto ad confirmandum. Maimonides gives the same derivation (!), and
includes the meaning of a *contract* in its signification. See Mishna
Surenhusii (*Bara Metzia*), tom. iv., p. 110, note on sect. 7. The LXX.
translate ברית by διαθήκη throughout the Old Testament, hence the twofold use of the Hebraised word διαθήκη, in the Epistle to the Hebrews,
would be readily understood by those to whom the latter was addressed.
If St. Paul was the author, we must remember that he was a Rabbinical
Jew, a Pharisee of the Pharisees, writing in their own phraseology, to
those who, from their infancy, lived in the atmosphere of "the Tradition
"of the Elders."

² Αὐτό τε τὸ βιβλίον. The Writer here supplies details, as in the case
of the golden censer, and of the material of the vase which contained the
manna, which are not contained in the narrative of Moses. (Exod.
xxiv. 5—8.) It is there simply related that he sent "young men of
"the children of Israel which offered burnt offerings and sacrificed
"peace offerings of oxen unto the Lord ;" וישלח את נערי בני ישראל ויעלו
עלת ויזבחו זבחים שלמים ליהוה פרים. Under the term עלת, *holocausts*, the
goats are doubtless included. The Targums of Onkelos and Jonathan
inform us that the "young men" above mentioned were firstborn sons,
whilst the latter adds, "for until that hour had the firstborn had the
"worship, the tabernacle of ordinance not being made, nor the priest-

"hood given unto Aaron." Again Moses mentions neither the water, nor the scarlet wool and hyssop, nor yet the sprinkling of the book. But these were, doubtless, ordinarily employed in purificatory aspersions, and Professor Stuart judiciously observes:—"That water was "used as well as blood, in order to sprinkle various things, is clearly "implied in Lev. xiv. 4—7, compared with Lev. xiv. 49—52, Num. xix. "18, Ps. li. 17, Ezek. xxxvi. 25." The scarlet wool (שני תולעת) probably tied the bunch of hyssop to a cedar wood handle (see Lev. xiv. 4, 6, 49, 51, 52, Num. xix. 6), and being the ordinary mode of applying the water and the blood, did not call for special mention in Exod. xxiv. Nor yet is it related by Moses that he sprinkled the book of the covenant (ספר הברית). Dr. Gill has erroneously remarked, "the book of the law "was sprinkled, not because of any impurity in it, but to show the "imperfection of it and its insufficiency to justify men." According to the writer to the Hebrews the object of the sprinkling the book of the covenant with blood, was to give it the validity of a Testamentary document. Its contents are comprised in Exodus xx., xxiii. The "Angel of the Covenant" (referred to in Mal. iii. 1) is here promised (xxiii. 20—23), and is probably so called, because he is mentioned in this "Book of the Covenant." (See note 1 on pp. 128—130.)

Verses 19—21.—And all the people,[1] saying, "This is the "blood of the covenant, which God enjoined[2] upon you." He sprinkled (at a later period, Exod. xl.) the tabernacle[3] and all the vessels of the service also, with blood in like manner. Almost all things, moreover, are purified with blood,[4] according to the law, and without shedding of blood remission is not effected (οὐ γίνεται ἄφεσις).

[1] Πάντα τὸν λαόν. This expression must not be pressed too closely. Moses probably sprinkled those who stood immediately around him. In the Hebrew of Exod. xxiv. 8, ויקח משה את הדם ויזרק על העם "And "Moses took the blood, and sprinkled upon the people." Half the blood was sprinkled upon the altar (v. 6), whilst the other half was reserved in basons for the sprinkling of the people and the book, &c. Respecting the true signification of the word all, as used by the Sacred Hebrew writers, see my tract, Bishop Colenso's Criticism Criticised. Third Edition, pp. 21—27, and pp. 55—59.

[2] Τοῦτο τὸ αἷμα τῆς διαθήκης ἧς ἐνετείλατο κ.τ.λ. These words are a paraphrase of the Hebrew:—הנה דם הברית אשר כרת יהוה עמכם על כל הדברים האלה (The LXX. has, ἰδοὺ τὸ αἷμα τῆς διαθήκης, ἧς διέθετο κύριος κ.τ.λ.) Behold

the blood of the covenant, which the Lord hath made (cut) with you concerning all these words (or things). Surenhusius (in his Βίβλ. καταλλ, p. 635) observes on this passage :—" Hebraicum הזה, et Chaldaicum הא " promiscue veniunt pro Græco τοῦτο, et ἰδού. Denique notandum est, " quod Apostolus כרת אשר *quod scidit*, dixerit elliptice, ἧς ἐνετείλατο *quod* "*præcepit*, nempe, יהוה, perinde ac si scriptum esset, אשר צוה לכרת, *quod* " *præcepit ad feriendum* sive *pangendum*, vel dici etiam potest, quod כרת " et ἐντέλλομαι sint synonima, eundem sensum varie exprimentia, ut " doceret Apostolus illud foederis pactum ex mandato divino factum, " quandoquidem enim ipse ritus pangendi jam notus erat Hebræis non " opus erat, ut Apostolus formali verbo כרת uteretur, verum eo quod rem " notam leviter attingeret......Deinde pro יהוה, κύριος, recte dicit אלהים, " Θεὸς, quandoquidem hicce Domini stylus passim est apud Prophetas ut " foedera sua observantibus pro mittat. ואהיה לכם לאלהים ואתם תהיו לי לעם. " *Et ero vobis in Deum, vos autem mihi eritis in populum.*"

³ In Exod. xl. we are only told that " the tabernacle and all that was therein," as well as Aaron and his son, were anointed with the holy oil, yet Philo assures us (*De Mose*, lib. 3, *Works*, Mangey's Edition, vol. ii., p 157) that not only were the High Priest and his garments and the altar and all the sacred vessels anointed with the holy oil, but the priests were anointed with the blood of a ram on the head, the hands, and the feet. Again on p. 158, Πάλαι μὲν οὖν ἱερείου ἑνὸς, ὃ προσηγορεύετο τελειώσεως, ἀκράτῳ αἵματι τὰ λεχθέντα τρία μέρη κατέχριε τῶν ἱερέων. αὖθις δ'ἐκ τοῦ παρὰ τῷ βωμῷ λαβὼν ὅπερ ἐξ ἁπάντων ἦν, τῶν τε θυομένων καὶ τοῦ λεχθέντος χρίσματος, ὃ μυρεψοὶ κατεσκεύασαν, ἀναμίξας τὸ ἔλαιον τῷ αἵματι τοῦ κράματος, τοῖς ἱερεῦσι καὶ ταῖς ἐσθήσεσιν αὐτῶν ἐπέρραινε. " On the former occasion he anointed the three specified " parts of the priests with the unmixed blood of the one sacrifice, which " was called that of *perfection*. But afterwards he took of the " blood of all the victims that had been offered, from off the altar. He ' then took some of the chosen chrism, or anointing oil, compounded " by the apothecaries, and mingled the said oil with the mixed blood, " and with it sprinkled the priests and their garments." Josephus also, *ntiq. iii 8, 6,—" And when Moses had sprinkled Aaron's vestments, xxi. *elf and his sons, with the blood of the beasts that were slain, and " the ͨᵘ ˙fied them with spring water and ointment, they became God's " peace oft. he same he did to the tabernacle and the vessels thereto שלמים ליהוה פרים . with oil first incensed, as I said, and with the blood goats are doubtles. ," &c.
inform us that the " yͧ Lev. xvii. 11,—" For the life of the flesh is in whilst the latter adds, " ˙ren it to you upon the altar to make an " worship, the tabernacle of ͧ-ͭ is the blood that maketh an atone-

"ment for the soul." The antithesis here is between *purification* and *remission*. In certain cases simple washing (*e.g.*, of clothes, Lev. xvi. 26, 28) or the passing of metal vessels through the fire (Num. xxxi. 23) were permitted to remove the ceremonial taint. But expiation, and atonement for sin could only be obtained by the shedding of blood (for "the blood is the life"), which was offered in vicarious symbolism, representing at once the life of the sinner forfeited by disobedience, and the life of the Perfect Sacrifice once for all offered, when the fulness of the time came, for the sins of the whole world. The familiar proverbial saying of the Rabbies אין כפרה אלא בדם, *There is no expiation, except by blood alone*, is illustrated by the following Talmudical comment on Lev. i. 4 ("And he shall put his hand upon the head of the burnt-"offering, and it shall be accepted for him to make atonement for him." (וסמך ידו על ראש העלה ונרצה לו לכפר עליו) "What then! Does the laying "on of the hands make expiation? Certainly not. Expiation is made "by nothing else than blood, because it is said, Lev. xvii. 11, 'For it is "'the blood that maketh an atonement for the soul.'" *Zevachim*, col. 105. וסמך ונרצה וכי סמיכה מכפרת והלא אין כפרה אלה בדם שנאמר כי הדם הוא בנפש יכפר. (Ugolini, *Thes.*, vol. xix.) A very similar passage is found in tract *Menachoth*, ibid., col. 1179. See also *Zerachim*, in Mischna Surenhus., tom. v., p. 43, sec. 2. The Mishna (tract *Joma*) says:—

הבמאת ואשם ודאי מכפרין מיתה ויום הכפורים מכפרין עם התשובה התשובה מכפרת על עבירות קלות על עשה ועל לא תעשה ועל החמורות היא תולה עד שיבא יום הכפורים ויכפר

"A sin-offering and a victim make expiation for certain sins and "faults. Death and the Day of Atonement make expiation with "repentance. Repentance makes expiation for lighter sins, both "against affirmative as well as negative precepts. It also suspends the "graver ones until the Day of Atonement arrives and expiates them." *Mischna Sur.*, tom. ii., p. 257.

Verses 23—26.—It was needful, therefore, that the copies (ὑποδείγματα) of the celestial things should be purified with the things above enumerated. But the heavenly things themselves (see note 6, p. 99) with more excellent sacrifices than these. For Christ (the Messiah) has not entered into Holy places made with hands, which latter were made in imitation (ἀντίτυπα, *copies*) of the true, but [he has gone] into heaven itself, now to appear before the face of God (*i.e.*, God's unveiled presence [1]) on our behalf. Not, indeed, that he may frequently (πολλάκις) offer himself, in like manner as the high priest enters yearly into the Holy places, with blood that is not his own (ἐν αἵματι ἀλλοτρίῳ). For if such were the case, He must needs have frequently suffered since the foundation of the world (ἐπεὶ ἔδει αὐτὸν πολλάκις παθεῖν ἀπὸ καταβολῆς κόσμου).

That is, Christ's death is retrospective[2] in its expiatory virtue. Otherwise he must have repeated the sacrifice of himself, in every year, since the Fall. The blood vicariously shed, and which the High Priest brought in, and, in fact, in virtue of which he was permitted to enter the Holy of Holies, spoke of his own imperfection. He dared not to enter in his own right. He must bring the blood of his own atonement in his hand. But Jesus has entered into the Heavenly Sanctuary for us, with, and in virtue of, his own blood. It testifies to the sinless perfection of his offering, and as such it requires not to be repeated. It was the substance, of which all the others were the shadow and prophetical types. He is the Lamb of God that taketh away the sins of the world.

[1] Νῦν ἐμφανισθῆναι τῷ προσώπῳ τοῦ Θεοῦ ὑπὲρ ἡμῶν. The phrase "before the face of God" is a translation of the Hebrew לפני אלהים. Christ appears before the Father, as the High Priest appeared on the typical day of Atonement, before the Shechinah.

[2] The Targum of Jonathan (on Gen. iii. 15) implies the consolatory doctrine expressed above :—"And I will put enmity between thee and "the woman, and between the seed of thy son and the seed of her sons, "and it shall be when the sons of the woman keep the commandments "of the law, they will be prepared to smite thee upon thy head, but "when they forsake the commandments of the law, thou wilt be ready "to wound them in their heel. Nevertheless, for them there shall be a "medicine, but for thee there will be no medicine ; and they shall make "a remedy for (or make a bruise with) the heel in the days of the King "Meshiha." Etheridge's Targums, vol. i., p. 166.

CHAP. IX., 26.   137

Verse 26.—But now, once (continues the writer), at the consummation of the ages[1] (i.e., *at the appointed close of the Jewish dispensation, the time specified by Daniel, and predicted by all the Holy Prophets since the world began,*) he has been manifested (πεφανέρωται, *revealed*), for the putting away of sin *by means* of the sacrifice of himself.[2]

---

[1] Ἐπὶ συντελείᾳ τῶν αἰώνων. " Et revera Christus venit, et se ipsum
" immolavit ἐπὶ συντελείᾳ τῶν αἰώνων, *circa consummationem seculorum.*
" Heb. ix. 26, h.e. fine temporis prioris. Restare enim debebant αἰῶνες
" ἐπερχόμενοι, *supervenientia secula,* quibus ostenderet Deus τὸν ὑπερ-
" βάλλοντα πλοῦτον τῆς χάριτος αὐτοῦ, Eph. ii. 7. Potuisset ita in fine
" dierum Christum mittere, ut statim sequeretur resurrectio mortuorum.
" Sed voluit annum gratiæ, a Christi missione cœptum, Jes. lxi. 2, per
" multa secula producere, ut amplitudinem divitiarum beneficientiæ
" suæ tam longi temporis duratione illustrius mundo patefaceret."
(H. Witsii *Diss. de seculo hoc et futuro,* p. 1181, Meuschen.) Schoettgen
(*in loc.*) explains the passage in a manner which, to my mind, is altogether inadmissible :—" Particula ἐπὶ cum Dativo denotat, cujus
" rei caussa, qua conditione Christus venerit, nimirum, ut mundus
" expiaretur. Συντέλεια est a τελέω, *purgo, initio, lustro,* quod hac
" notione aliquoties hac epistola occurrit." Ewald translates, " Nun
" aber ist er einmahl, am Schlussende der Weltzeiten, zur Sünden-
" vernichtung durch sein Selbstopfer, erschienen." The word συντέλεια occurs in Matt. xiii. 39, 40, 49, xxiv. 3, xxviii. 20, but always in reference to the " end of the world," and never in the signification which Schoettgen would assign to it. Wolfius observes that, in this 26th verse of Heb. ix., ἐπὶ συντελείᾳ τῶν αἰώνων, is antithetic to ἀπὸ καταβολῆς κόσμου. He utterly rejects the explanation which Schoettgen gives, as being contrary to the usage, not only of the New Testament, but also of the LXX. writers. The translators of the London Society's Hebrew New Testament have באחרית העולמים.

[2] I cannot help believing that a direct citation from Dan. ix. 24, 25, is here intended. The prophet there describes the righteousness which shall be brought in, in the days of " Messiah the Prince," as צדק עלמים, lit., *the righteousness of ages,* or as the LXX. has it, δικαιοσύνην αἰώνιον. And in exact accordance with Is liii, Daniel also declares that " *Messiah* " *shall be cut off, but not for himself,*" ואין לו יכרת משיח, ἐξολοθρευθήσεται χρίσμα, καὶ κρίμα οὐκ ἔστιν ἐν αὐτῷ, LXX. The object of his appearing is " to finish transgression (לכלא הפשע) and to make an end of sins " (ולחתם חטאות, lit., *to seal up sins*), and to make reconciliation for iniquity

T

(ולכפר עון lit., *to expiate iniquity.*—See Schoettgen, tom. ii., pp. 98, 246, 655.) Τοῦ συντελεσθῆναι ἁμαρτίαν, καὶ τοῦ σφραγίσαι ἁμαρτίας, καὶ ἀπαλεῖψαι τὰς ἀδικίας, καὶ τοῦ ἐξιλάσασθαι ἀδικίας, LXX. It must be ever borne in mind that the Epistle is written to Jews and by a Jew. His phraseology is, so to speak, saturated with the spirit and language of the Old Testament writings, which his readers knew by heart, regarding these Scriptures, not only as the repository of their spiritual hopes, but as the charter and digest of their national expectations and political history. A passing allusion, which would fall unnoticed upon a Gentile ear, would strike with living and intelligent significance upon the attuned chords of the Jewish patriot's soul. The Scriptural element was the very atmosphere in which he lived. It comprised the entire sum of his most cherished hopes for this world as well as for the world to come. (*N.B.* The above quotations from the LXX. are taken from the Edition of Amsterdam, 1683. 8vo.)

Verses 27, 28.—And just as it is appointed (καθ' ὅσον ἀπόκειται) to men once to die, and after this the judgment, so also Christ having been once offered for the special object of bearing (εἰς τὸ ἀνενεγκεῖν) the sins of many (Is. liii. 11), shall appear (ὀφθήσεται) the second time to those who wait for Him (τοῖς αὐτὸν ἀπεκδεχομένοις, expect him back again), without sin (χωρὶς ἁμαρτίας), to announce to them their salvation (εἰς σωτηρίαν).[1]

[1] The writer here alludes to the anxious expectation of the people for the safe return of the high priest from the Holy of Holies on the Day of Atonement. It was an awful moment of suspense, and the congregation looked eagerly for the high priest's reappearance. And so the Mishna informs us, that after he had deposited the incense before the ark, and the Holy of Holies was filled with the fumes, he came back into the outer house, and offered up a short prayer, making it very short, in order that the congregation might not be unduly apprehensive on his account.

יצא ובא לו בדרך בית כניסתו ומתפלל תפילה קצרה בבית החיצון ולא היה מאריך בתפילתו שלא להבעית את ישראל:

Joma, cap. iv. 7, *Mishna Surenh.*, vol. ii., p. 231. It will be remembered that it was strictly forbidden (Levit. xvi. 17) for any one to be in the tabernacle at the time. "And there shall be no man in the tabernacle "of the congregation, when he goeth in to make an atonement in the "holy *place*, until he come out, and have made an atonement for him- "self, and for his household, and for all the congregation of Israel."

Then he would appear to them, χωρὶς ἁμαρτίας, having left their sins behind and cancelled by the blood of expiation, and assure them that the atonement had been accepted. Maimonides (*Ibid.*, p. 232, note) observes on the above quoted passage of the Mishna, " For if he (the " high priest) tarried long, the Israelites feared that he might have been " overtaken by death, for many high priests died in the Holy of Holies, " in consequence of their want of skill, or of making alterations in the " mode of offering incense; for so the Holy One, blessed be He, inti-" mated to Aaron, Levit. xvi. 2, 13."

So, also, we learn on the authority of the Mishna (*ibid.*, p. 248), that after the whole of the solemnities had been completed, the high priest divested himself of his pontifical robes, and put on his ordinary attire, which his attendants brought him. They then accompanied him home, and he gave a banquet to his friends in honour of his having come forth in safety from the sanctuary.

ומלוין אותו עד ביתו ויום טוב היה עושה לאוהביו בשעה שיצא בשלום מן הקדש Sheringham remarks on the words "בשעה שיצא בשלום", i.e., *safe and* " *sound.* For at that season of the year, in which the cold began to be " somewhat felt, he might easily be taken ill." "Id est salvus et in-" columis, eâ enim tempestate quâ frigus aliquantulum rigere incepisset, " facile poterat ægrotare," &c. (*Ibid.*, note 3.)

Christ has in like manner gone into the Most Holy Place. His people anxiously expect his return. When He comes forth again, it will be χωρὶς ἁμαρτίας, without a sin-offering. They will have ocular demonstration that the atonement has been accepted, in the completion of their salvation. And so it is predicted in Isaiah xxv. 7—9 :—" And " he will destroy in this mountain the face of the covering (פני הלוט) cast " over all people, and the veil (המסכה) that is spread over all nations. " He will swallow up death in victory, and the Lord God will wipe " away tears from off all faces, and the rebuke of his people shall He " take away from off all the earth. For the Lord hath spoken it. And " it shall be said in that day, Lo, this is our God; we have waited " (קוינו) for Him, and He will save us: this is the Lord, we have " waited (קוינו) for him, we will be glad and rejoice in his salvation."

The translators of the London Society's Hebrew New Testament render the entire passage thus :—

וכאשר נגזר על בני האדם למות פעם אחת ואחרי כן המשפט ׃ כן גם המשיח הצלה פעם אחת לשאת חטאות רבים ׃ ולמיחלים לו יראה שנית בלי חטאת (*without a sin-offering*) לישועה ׃ (For this use of חטאת, see Exod. xxix. 14, 36, and *passim*, in the Old Testament.)

CHAPTER X.

THE writer now proceeds to illustrate and apply his beautiful and delicately-worded figure of the shadow and the substance.

Verses 1—4.—For the law, as having (ἔχων *comprising*) the shadow of the good things to come, and not the exact resemblance[1] of the things as they really are (οὐκ αὐτὴν τὴν εἰκόνα τῶν πραγμάτων), never can make those who come to it perfect, with the same sacrifices which they offer perpetually (εἰς τὸ διηνεκὲς) from year to year. For then would they not have ceased being offered (*i.e.*, on behalf of each individual sinner, because in the expiation of every several Day of Atonement, every soul of the congregation, as well as the high priest, was included in the expiatory offering, no matter how many times previously they had participated in its purifying solemnities), because the worshippers (τοὺς λατρεύοντας), when once cleansed, would no longer retain any consciousness of sins. But, on the contrary, in the aforesaid (sacrifices, ἀλλ' ἐν αὐταῖς) there is a repeated calling into remembrance of sins (ἀνάμνησις ἁμαρτιῶν) from year to year. For it is impossible that the blood of bulls and of goats should take away sins.[2]

[1] The shadow of anything is never the exact resemblance, although it is a certain proof that the substance which casts the shadow has a real and substantial existence. It is exaggerated and distorted. Sometimes it is larger in unsubstantial bulk, sometimes it is dwarfed and smaller than the reality. So, also, the Mosaic ritual, with its cumbrous paraphernalia, although it was the very shadow cast before it by God's own plan of atonement, could only afford a conjectural criterion of the tangible benefits which the Lord's Messiah should introduce. In this respect the ancient Patriarchal and Mosaic Church were in a position, in regard to Christ's first coming, precisely analogous to that of the

CHAP. X., 1—4. 141

Christian Church in reference to his second appearing. We now see, as in a metal mirror, enigmatically (Βλέπομεν γὰρ ἄρτι δἰ ἐσόπτρου ἐν αἰνίγματι, τότε δὲ πρόσωπον πρὸς πρόσωπον), but then, face to face (1 Cor. xiii. 12). We now know partially, but then shall we know even as we are known (ἄρτι γιγνώσκω ἐκ μέρους, τότε δὲ ἐπιγνώσομαι καθὼς καὶ ἐπεγνώσθην). This partial knowledge did not hinder the ancient Church from entertaining a very positive assurance that the Saviour should come, nor yet does it, at present, interfere with the certainty of our belief as to the consummation of our redemption. God will have his children in all ages to "walk by faith and not by sight." There has been always a unity of Hope, as well as of Faith, in this particular. Εἰκών means *the likeness, similitude, resemblance* of anything ; and, in this, the law is the ἐπεισαγωγή κρείττονος ἐλπίδος (Heb. vii. 19). The realization of this hope will find place in our completed redemption, at Christ's second appearing.

² The writer here states no unknown doctrine to the Hebrews. He is simply applying one, of which the more intelligent were already deeply conscious. It therefore comes home with the irresistible force of conviction. This statement is abundantly confirmed by the following remarkable statement of Philo :—'Ιερουργίαι γεμὴν καὶ ἡ περὶ τὰς θυσίας πίστις, βλάστημα κάλλιστον, ἀλλὰ παραναπέφυκεν αὐτῷ κακὸν, δεισιδαιμονία· ἣν πρὶν χλοῆσαι, λυσιτελὲς ἐκτεμεῖν. Ἔνιοι γὰρ ᾠήθησαν τὸ βουθυτεῖν εὐσέβειαν εἶναι, καὶ ἐξ ὧν ἂν κλέψωσιν, ἢ ἀρνήσωνται, ἢ χρεωκοπήσωσιν, ἢ ἁρπάσωσιν, ἢ λεηλατήσωσι, μοίρας ἀπονέμουσι τοῖς βωμοῖς, οἱ δυσκάθαρτοι, τὸ μὴ δοῦναι δίκην ἐφ' οἷς ἐξήμαρτον, ὤνιον εἶναι νομίζοντες. Ἀλλὰ γὰρ εἴποιμ' ἂν αὐτοῖς, ἀδέκαστόν ἐστιν, ὦ οὗτοι, τὸ θεοῦ δικαστήριον, ὡς τοὺς μὲν γνώμῃ κεχρημένους ὑπαιτίῳ, κἂν ἅπασαν ἡμέραν ἑκατὸν βόας ἀνάγωσιν, ἀποστρέφεσθαι· τοὺς δ' ἀνυπαιτίους, κἂν μηδὲν θύωσι τὸ παράπαν, ἀποδέχεσθαι. Βωμοῖς γὰρ ἀπύροις, περὶ οὓς ἀρεταί χορεύουσι, γέγηθεν ὁ θεὸς, ἀλλ' οὐ πολλῷ πυρὶ φλέγουσιν, ὅπερ αἱ τῶν ἀνιέρων ἄθυτοι θυσίαι συνανέφλεξαν, ὑπομιμνήσκουσαι τὰς ἑκάστων ἀγνοίας τε καί διαμαρτίας. Καὶ γὰρ εἶπέ που Μωϋσῆς, θυσίαν ἀναμιμνήσκουσαν ἁμαρτίαν.

"Assuredly religious rites, and the belief in sacrifices, are a most
" admirable growth, but a noxious one has sprung up alongside of it ;
" to wit, superstition. This ought to be rooted out before it vegetate
" further. For some have supposed that to sacrifice oxen is piety, who
" lay upon the altars a portion of their thefts, of that which they have
" fraudulently withholden, of that which they have cheated, or taken
" by violence, or purloined ; e.g., men who will hardly find any atone-
" ment, and who suppose that they can thus purchase immunity from
" paying the penalty due to their deeds. To such as these I would say,
" The Tribunal of God is not to be thus bribed, but revolts from all those

"who have an evil conscience, although they should daily offer a
"hundred oxen. But He accepts the guiltless, although they never
"bring a single sacrifice. For God delights in fireless shrines, which
"the virtues encircle, not in those that blaze with extensive fires, which
"the profane unaccepted sacrifices of impious offerings light up, and
"which only call to mind their transgressions (ἀγνοίας. See note 4, page
"122) and sins. For Moses himself has somewhere (Numb. v. 15) said,
"'*that sacrifice calls sin to remembrance.*'" (*De Plantatione Noe*,
Works, Mangey's edit., vol. 1, p. 345.)

See also *ibid.*, vol. ii., p. 151, *De Mose*, and p. 254, *De Sacrificantibus*.
The same doctrine is also unequivocally propounded in the Mishna,
Joma, cap. viii. sec. 9 :—

האומר אחטא ואשוב אחטא ואשוב אין מספיקין בידו לעשות תשובה אחטא ויום הכפרים
מכפר אין יום הכפורים מכפר עבירות שבין אדם למקום יום הכפורים מכפר עבירות שבין אדם
לחבירו אין יום הכפורים מכפר עד שירצה חבירו את זו דרש רבי אלעזר בן עזריה מכל חטאתיכם
לפני ה' תטהרו עבירות שבין אדם למקום יום הכפורים מכפר עבירות שבין אדם לחבירו אין
יוה"כ מכפר עד שירצה את חבירו אמר רבי עקיבא אשריכם ישראל לפני מי מיטהרין אתם
מי מטהר אתכם אביכם שבשמים שנאמר וזרקתי עליכם מים טהורים וטהרתם ואומר מקוה
ישראל ה' מה מקוה מטהר את הטמאים אף הקדוש ברוך הוא מטהר את ישראל :

"He who says, *I will sin and repent, I will sin and repent;* the means
"of repentance are not ready to his hand. (If he says) *I will sin, and*
"*the Day of Atonement shall make expiation;* the Day of Atonement
"does not make expiation. Transgressions which are between man
"and God the Day of Atonement expiates. Transgressions which are
"between man and his neighbour, the Day of Atonement does not
"expiate, until he has reconciled his neighbour. Rabbi Eleazar, the
"son of Azariah, thus explains the words, *Ye shall be clean from all*
"*your sins before the Lord.* The transgressions which a man commits
"against God the Day of Atonement expiates. The transgressions
"which a man commits against his neighbour the Day of Atonement
"does not expiate, unless he has first given his neighbour satisfaction.
"Rabbi Akiba says, Blessed are ye, O Israel, before Him, before whom
"ye purify yourselves! Who is He that purgeth you? It is your Father
"in heaven, because it is said, *I will sprinkle upon you clean water, and*
"*ye shall be clean.* The Lord also says, *the fountain of Israel.* What
"fountain is it that purifies the defiled? Even the Holy One, Blessed
"be He, it is that purifies Israel." *Mishna Surenh.*, vol. ii. 2, pp. 257,
258.

Verse 5.—Wherefore He (the Messiah) on his entering
(εἰσερχόμενος) into the world says (Ps. xl. 6—10), Sacrifice and offering [1] thou wouldest not,[2] a body hast thou
prepared for me.

CHAP. X., 5. 143

¹ Θυσίαν καὶ προσφορὰν οὐκ ἠθέλησας, זבח ומנחה לא חפצת, ובגו, i.e, *slain beast, and bloodless oblation thou hadst no pleasure in.*—Gesen.
² Σῶμα δὲ κατηρτίσω μοι. The Greek of the New Testament and the LXX. differ in sound, but not in reality, from the Hebrew. Where they have σῶμα δὲ κατηρτίσω μοι, the Hebrew has אזנים כרית *mine ears hast thou pierced.* The verb כרה (see also Ps. xxii. 16 [17]) is here used for רצע of Exod. xxi. 6, *And his master shall bore* (ורצע) *his ear through with an awl* (במרצע), *and he shall serve him for ever.* This was to be done in the case of a Hebrew servant, who refused, out of devotion to his master, to go out free at the end of the sixth year of servitude. The clue to the Greek paraphrase, I cannot help feeling justly certain, is to be found in Rev. xviii. 13, καὶ σωμάτων, "and slaves," *et mancipiorum,* Vulg. The Greek, I take it, is a paraphrase of the Hebrew, and is equivalent to "Thou hast made me thy servant" (remembering always that the piercing of the ears indicated a spontaneously chosen servitude), although, with a subtle play upon the word σῶμα, the writer includes the idea of Christ's humanity. This is in strict accordance with the Jewish habit of thought. St. Paul in his Epistles not unfrequently indulges in this assimilation of sound with sense. The above rendering of this most difficult passage obviates entirely any tampering with the Hebrew text. The verb ברה *barah* is never used in the Hebrew Bible in the sense of *he prepared,* although Surenhusius (Βίβλος καταλλ., p. 636) apparently confounds it with ברא *bara, he created, e.g.,* he speaks of the Apostle as "pro כרית effodisti legens ברית *parasti."* And again, *ibid.* :—" Verbum ברא (*not* ברה) notare *disponere, aptare, parare,* docet Paraphrastes Chaldæus, quando id "vertit per הקן, Jos. xvii. 15. Conferantur Ezek. xxi. 19, et cap. "xxiii. 47, ubi eadem verbi significatio occurrit." As the question is not concerning בראה, but כרית, the learned critic's remarks, I would submit, are somewhat beside the mark. But כרית is not the only difficulty which the emendator of the Hebrew text has to deal with. To torture the reading אזנים *ears* into גיה or גופה, *body,* or גוף, as Surenhusius has it, is a miracle of emendation, commendable more for its ingenuity than for its soundness or probability. Wettstein, on Rev. xviii. 13 (although he makes very little indeed of the Passage of the Hebrews under consideration), adduces a variety of authorities in which σῶμα is made to stand for δοῦλος, *a slave,* e.g., " Pollux iii. 71, " σώματα ἁπλῶς οὐκ ἂν εἴποις, ἀλλὰ σώματα δοῦλα.—Phrynichus, p. 166, " Σώματα ἐπὶ τῶν ὠνίων ἀνδραπόδων εἴωθε καλεῖν.—*Aristoteles* in narrat. " mirand., ἀντὶ ἑνὸς σώματος θηλικοῦ διδόναι τοῖς ἐμπόροις τέσσαρα ἢ πέντε " σώματα ἄρρενα.—*Libanius* D. xvii., p. 472, C. τοῦτ' οὖν λογίζεσθαι, " ποῦ πιπράσκεται ; τίς ὁ ὠνούμενος, τὸν ἔμπορον τοῦ σώματος.—*Eustathius*

"in Od. a., pp. 34, 51, ἀνδραποδοκάπηλος, ὁ καὶ σωματέμπορος καὶ μετα-
"βολεὺς ἀνδραπόδων.—Strabo xiv., p. 985, B. σώματ' ἐμπορεῖν.—Tob.
"x. 11.—Anthol i. 12, 10, σώματα πολλὰ τρέφειν.—*Demosthenes*, Phil. iii.,
"καὶ σωμάτων πλῆθος, ἢ χρημάτων πρόσοδοι.—Aristoteles Rhet. 1,
"εὐσθένεια κτημάτων καὶ σωμάτων.—πλῆθος χρημάτων καὶ ἰσχὺς σωμάτων."
Prof. Stuart (in loco) somewhat hastily, I think, asserts "that רצע
"and כרה indicate very distinct actions is sufficiently plain, for to
"*bore through* anything, and *to dig* or *hollow out* a pit, grave, or well,
"are surely very different actions, indicated in Hebrew by verbs as
"different as the English *dig* and *bore through*." The learned Professor
is surely strangely forgetful of the twofold signification of *fodio* and
ὀρύσσω, and also of the LXX. rendering of that vexed passage of
Ps. xxii. 16, ὤρυξαν χεῖράς μου καὶ πόδας, which the Vulgate also (in
accordance with the reading כארו or כרו from כאר or כור) translates
"*foderunt manus meas*," &c. The verb רצע occurs in Exod. xxi. 6 only.
The parallel passage of Deut. xv. 17 reads ונתתה באזנו את המרצע ולקחת.
Even Pr. Stuart would admit that נתן has a very different signification
from רצע, and yet here it does duty for it, and the meaning is perfectly
intelligible. The Syriac also adopts the same reading, "they pierced."
Schoettgen (*Hor. Heb.*, tom. i., p. 978) says,—"In Hebræo est:
"אונים כרית לי, *aures perforasti mihi*: h.e. servum me tibi perpetuum
"fecisti; ex more Hebræorum, qui Exod. xxi. 6, describitur." There
is, therefore, at least respectable authority, I would submit, for understanding כרה as a synonyme of רצע of Exod. xxi. 6. The reason for the
latter verb being employed in this last-cited passage is obvious enough.
Moses specifies the instrument with which the ear is to be pierced,
viz., מרצע *an awl*. It is unquestionably more convenient, as well as
more elegant, to employ the very verb רצע from which the name of the
instrument is derived, than to substitute a synonyme in its stead. And
in this sense *of piercing*, R. Isaac (in the *Chizzuk Emunah*, p. 369) takes
the verb כרה in Ps. xl., and observes how grossly the writer to the
Hebrews (x. 8) had corrupted the passage,—an accusation as utterly
unfounded as unfair,—as a glance at the LXX. version of the Psalm
would have demonstrated. The writer to the Hebrews does no more
than ratify the interpretation of the ancient Greek-speaking Jewish
Church. The writer of the *Nizzachon Vetus* (pp. 162, 163), referring to
Ps. xxii. 7, combats the interpretation "they pierced" (פירינש, *foderunt*)
on the ground that the Jews had no custom of piercing the hands or
feet of those that were condemned to be stoned or hanged; a silly
quibble, of which, in another form, Hengstenberg has demonstrated
the futility. But it is downright dishonesty in this Jewish Controversialist to insinuate that the Christians altered the passage to suit their

views. (See Gill, *in loc.*) J. C. Wolfius writes (tom iv., p. 723, *in loco*), "Altera (sententia) est eorum qui verbum כרה *perforandi* sensu acci-"piunt, et ad ritum in servis, perpetuæ servituti addicendis, illisque "perfossione auris ab hero initiandis, receptum (de quo Deuteronom. "xv. 17, et Exod. xxi. 6), a τοῖς LXX. respectum, *corpus* vero, tanquam "totum, pro *auribus*, instar partis, positum esse, existimant. Ita cum "Coccejo et Altingio plerique, et novissime Cl. Elsnerus, cujus ex "pag. 362, hæc habe verba: *Sensus Hebraici textus est:* Servum me "perpetuum, per omnem vitam constituisti. *Igitur verissime et feliciter* "*sensum expresserunt* LXX., σῶμα κατηρτίσω μοι, corpus mihi formasti. "*Corporis enim* indutio *Christum* reddebat servum, hoc ὁμοίωμα et "σχῆμα ἀνθρώπων, *est* μορφὴ δούλου, Philipp. ii. 7, 8, filius hominis venit, "*scilicet in mundum assumto corpore*, ut serviret, Matt. xx. 28, et Jes. "xlix. 5, *Unde hic notanter dicitur;* εἰσερχόμενος εἰς τὸν κόσμον, cum in "mundum veniret, *scilicet per incarnationem; tunc dixit,* σῶμα κατηρτίσω "μοι, corpus, atque adeo servi personam imposuisti mihi. Idem porro "monet, σώματα dici *mancipia*, tum apud LXX. Genes. xxxiv. 29, "tum apud Scriptores," &c. Lud. Cappellus (*Criticæ Sacræ,* Paris, 1650, fol., p. 67) remarks on Heb. x. 5,—"Σῶμα δὲ κατηρτίσω μοι, in "Hebræo autem est, *aures perforasti mihi,* hoc est, mancipasti me tibi "in perpetuum, nempe juxta legem quæ est Exod. xxi. 6. Videntur "autem LXX. scripsisse, σῶμα δὲ μὲ κατηρτίσω σοι, h.e. *mancipasti* me "tibi; nam σῶμα Græcis interdum *mancipium* significat, unde illud "σώματα πολλὰ τρέφειν καὶ δώματα πολλὰ ἐγείρειν." It is a matter of surprise that Cappellus, when suggesting an emendation in the text, did not propose to read σῶμα δὲ κατηρτίσω σοι, instead of μοι, which would have involved the alteration of one letter only, and would have rendered the passage perfectly clear of all difficulties. Dr. Samuel Davidson (*Introd. to the New Testament,* vol. iii., p. 281) writes as follows:—"Here we must proceed on the assumption, that the Hebrew "text (Ps. xl. 7) was as it now stands when the Greek translator "rendered it into another tongue. The Hebrew signifies, *mine ears* "*hast thou opened;* the Greek, *a body hast thou prepared for me.* The "meaning of the former is, *thou hast made me attentive or obedient to* "*thy will;* that of the latter, *thou hast provided me a body in which* "*that obedience may be exemplified.* The argument turns on the sen-"tence, *thou desiredst not sacrifices but the fulfilment of thy will.* The "ancient sacrifices are declared to be of no avail, and doing the will of "God is substituted for them. In the clause σῶμα δὲ κατηρτίσω μοι, *the* "manner of doing the will of God perfectly is *incidentally* noticed, "though not essential to the argument, since it is *the thing itself* which "is contrasted with the Jewish sacrifices, viz., *willing obedience to God,*

"or *the doing of his will*. Here no essential part of the argument is
"built on the clause under consideration, and the futility of Hug's
"assertion appears : 'If the Epistle had been written in Hebrew,
"'the deduction from the quotation as to the offering of a body, and
"'all which is further said of the single offering that made every
"'other superfluous, could have had no foundation.' The Septuagint
"rendering of the clause gives *the sense* of the Hebrew, and the
"quotation is taken from the Septuagint as more *palpably* apposite
"to the writer's purpose in the context." The late Dr. M'Caul (*The
Messiaship of Jesus*, London, 1852. 8vo., pp. 161—163) gives the
following interpretation of Ps. xl. 7, 8 :—" In these verses there is an
"apparent difficulty arising from the citation of certain words in the
"Epistle to the Hebrews. The original text has אזנים כרית לי, which
"our translators have rendered 'mine ears hast thou opened.' The
"LXX. and Epistle to the Hebrews, σῶμα δὲ κατηρτίσω μοι, 'A body
"'hast thou prepared for me,' a rendering which sounds very different.
"The only fair way to compare them is to ascertain first the sense of
"each. 1. Then, with regard to the Hebrew, the literal sense of the
"words is, 'Ears hast thou digged or perforated for me.' Now, what
"would a Hebrew understand by digging, or perforating the ears ? To
"answer this question we have, first, similar expressions in the Bible.
"In Isaiah l. 5, 'The Lord hath opened the ear for me,' פתח לי אזן,
"'and I was not rebellious,' from which it appears that *to open the ears*
"is *to make obedient ;* and, again, another passage of the same prophet,
"xlviii. 8, where *the ear not being opened* is connected with *disobedience*.
"'Yea, thou heardest not ; yea, thou knewest not ; yea, of old thy ear
"'was not opened : truly I knew thou didst deal very treacherously :
"'even transgressor wast thou called, from the womb.' 2. We have
"the interpretation of the Jews. The Chaldee says, 'My ears, in order
"'to listen to thy salvation, thou hast perforated for me.' Rashi says,
"'*Mine* ears hast thou perforated, saying, Hear ye my voice. *Perforated*
"'means, ye have made holes that ye might hear.' Kimchi says,
"'Ears hast thou opened for me, that I might hear thy voice'; and so
"R. Isaac explains, by reference to Exod. xix. 5, Jer. vii. 22, and
"1 Sam. xv. 22, that the opening of the ears signifies obedience.
"According, then, to Bible usage, and the interpretation of learned
"Jews speaking and writing Hebrew, the meaning of the words, 'Mine
"'ears hast thou digged, or opened,' is, 'Thou hast rendered me
"'obedient.' 3. To confirm this interpretation, we have the parallel-
"isms.—

"'Sacrifice and offering thou didst not desire.'
"'Mine ears hast thou opened.'

"'Burnt-offering and sin-offering thou didst not require.'
"'Then I said, Lo I come... ......to do thy will, O my God, I did
"'desire.'
"The antithesis to *burnt-offering* and *sin-offering*, in the latter
"clause, is *obedience*. The antiparallel to sacrifice and offering must be
"synonymous—i.e., *perforating* the ears must mean *obedience*. II. Now,
"then, let us examine what the Greek translators intended by σῶμα
"κατηρτίσω μοι, 'A body hast thou prepared me,' or 'My body hast
"'thou prepared.' It is clear that they did not mean it as a literal
"translation of the Hebrew words. The idiomatic meaning of 'digging
"'or perforating the ears' was peculiarly Hebrew. They therefore
"gave what they considered as an equivalent, 'The preparation of the
"'body,' as more pleasing to God than sacrifice and offering. That by
"the *preparation* of *the body* they meant *obedience* is to be gathered
"from the context, and from the fact that they understood the Hebrew
"phrase (*to dig* or *perforate*), as appears from the parallel passage, Is. l. 5,
"where they have ἡ παιδεία Κυρίου Κυρίου ἀνοίγει μου τὰ ὦτα, ἐγὼ δὲ οὐκ
"ἀπειθῶ. That the words conveyed this meaning to a person accustomed
"to speak and write Greek is seen from the commentary of Theodorit,
"who says, on the place, 'To these words agrees the apostolic admoni-
"'tion, *I beseech you, therefore, brethren, by the mercies of God, that ye
"'present your bodies a living sacrifice, holy, acceptable unto God, which
"'is your reasonable service;* for instead of the sacrifices of the Law,
"'God has commanded us to consecrate our bodies.' He understood
"the words to signify *obedience*. The sense, therefore, of the Hebrew
"and of the Greek words is substantially the same. They both signify
"*to render obedient*."

Verses 6, 7.—Holocaust and sin-offering thou hadst no
pleasure in (οὐκ εὐδόκησας, לֹא שָׁאַלְתָּ, *thou didst not
demand*). Then I said, Lo, I am come (ἥκω, בָאתִי) to do
thy will, O God, in the volume [1] of the book (ἐν κεφαλίδι
βιβλίου, בִּמְגִלַּת סֵפֶר, *in der Buchrolle*, Ewald) it is written
concerning me (περὶ ἐμοῦ, עָלַי) to do thy will, O God.[2]

[1] Let it be observed that the words ἐν κεφαλίδι agree with the Jewish
interpretation of the LXX., where they are employed as the equivalent
to במגלת ספר. They are no mere Christian adaptation of the Hebrew,
although, inasmuch as they are found in a canonical book of the New
Testament, the Christian student has no alternative but to accept them
as expressing *the correct sense* of the original Scriptures. The only
question to be solved is, are these words a paraphrase, or are they a

literal translation of the Hebrew? *i.e.*, is κεφαλίς ever used as a synonyme for a roll, מגלה? Stuart asserts that as "the Hebrew ספר, "βιβλίον, was a manuscript rolled upon a cylinder of light wood, at "the extremity of which were *heads* or *knobs*," therefore, "the *knob* or "*head*, κεφαλίς, is here taken as a *part*, which is descriptive or emblem- "atic of the whole. Κεφαλὶς βιβλίου means, therefore, a βιβλίον, or "ספר, with a κεφαλίς, *i.e.*, a manuscript roll.........It coincides, then, "with regard to signification, very exactly with the Hebrew מגלת ספר, "of which it is a translation." For my own part, although not prepared to contradict Prof. Stuart, as the writer to the Hebrews gives a paraphrastic citation, and not a verbal quotation, I see no necessity to find a literal conformity. The next question to be solved is this :— If David wrote Psalm xl., what are we to understand by "the roll of the "Book"? In other words, to what portion of the Scriptures had he access? Does he refer to the Book of Jasher, or to some other of the now extinct writings of the time? or does he allude to God's book, mentioned in Ps. cxxxix. 16, which the Targum renders "in the book of "thy memory"? or does the Psalmist allude to the Messianic passages of the Pentateuch, to the book of Job, or to any of his own previously written Psalms? If I may hazard a conjecture, I would suggest that the citation is referable to 1 Sam. xv. 22 :—"And Samuel said, Hath "the Lord *as great* delight in burnt-offerings and sacrifices, as in "obeying the voice of the Lord? Behold, to obey is better than "sacrifice, and to hearken than the fat of rams." The expression עלי, περὶ ἐμοῦ, does not necessarily imply that the passage cited was a Messianic one, but that it was Messianic in its doctrinal application. Much, however, may be said, especially on the perusal of the Targumic explanations of the Messianic passages, as to the probable reference made to the Pentateuch.

Surenhusius (βίβλ. καταλλ., pp. 637, 638) writes:—"Jam vero "Christum aliquando venturum esse, ut Patris sui voluntatem faceret, "jam prædictum fuisse במגלת ספר *in volumine libri*, tradit Psaltes, quam "phrasin ellypticam esse scribit ille Hebræorum Doctor Raschi, pro "במגלת ספר תורת משה *in volumine libri legis Mosis*, sive Pentateuchi, "quoniam libri Vet. Test. in membrana conscripti, ad columnam "ligneam in forma cylindri convolvi solent, et cum liber Geneseos sit "primus inter quinque libros Mosis, hinc nos non multum errasse puta- "mus, si dixerimus Apostolum vel ad primam promissionem de Semine "mulieris serpentis caput contrituro respexisse (see note 2. p. 136), etsi "passim in Pentateucho et aliis libris sacris prædictus sit Messiæ adven- "tus, et illius Sacrificii efficacia, Legisque Mosaicæ imbecillitas, et abro- "gatio ; hanc enim sententiam Apostolus juvare videtur, quando vertit,

CHAP. X., 8—10.   149

"ἐν κεφαλίδι βιβλίου in frontispicio libri, etenim per vocem כס אׁ, sim-
"pliciter positam, indigitari libros sacros, abunde patet, ex cod. Misnico
"*Megilla*, cap. 3. (The passage of the *Mishna* here referred to is found
"vol. ii., p. 394, of *Surenhusius'* edition, at the foot of the page.)
"Quare omnino explodendi sunt isti auctores, qui statuunt, epistolam
"Pauli inter libros canonicos non esse referendam, eo quod in illa male
"allegationes fiant; quod falsissimum est, quoniam inter במלת כסר et
"ἐν κεφαλίδι βιβλίου nullum est discrimen." 'Ανώτερον κ.τ.λ. Ewald translates, " Weiter oben sagend, *Opfer und Darbringungen und Sündopfer*
"*wolltest du nicht, noch hattest sie gerne*, die doch nach Gesetz dargebracht
"werden, hat er dann gesagt, *Siehe ich komme zu thun deinen Willen?*
"Er hebt das erste auf um das zweite zu bejahren."

² The Hebrew words are, לעשות רצונך אלהי חפצתי, ותורתך בתוך מעי, *To do
thy will (or good pleasure), O my God, I have delighted, and thy law is
in the midst of my inward parts.* And viewed in reference to this prophetic declaration of Ps. xl. 8, what a depth of meaning attaches to the
testimony vouchsafed to Jesus at his baptism:—"And lo a voice from
"heaven, saying, This is my beloved Son, in whom I am well pleased"
(Matt. iii. 17), compared with Is. xlii. 1, "Behold my servant, whom
"I uphold, mine elect *in whom* my soul delighteth; I have put my
"spirit upon him," &c. The Targum here reads הא עבדי משיחא, *behold
my servant Messiah;* and R. David Kimchi says explicitly וזהי מלך המשיח,
This is King Messiah. Thus approved, Christ the second Adam was
sent forth into the wilderness, to reconquer, on the battle-field of temptation, that which the first Adam in Paradise, through temptation, had
lost.

Verses 8—10.—Having first said (ἀνώτερον λέγων) "Sacri-
"fice and offering and holocaust and sin-offering thou
"wouldest not, nor tookest pleasure in them" which are
offered (*i.e.*, albeit they are offered) in accordance with the
law; then he said (τότε εἴρηκεν, *he said immediately after*),
Behold I am come to do thy will, O God.¹ He taketh
away the former order of things (τὸ πρῶτον, viz., the
ceremonial law with its sacrifices) in order that he may
establish (στήσῃ) the latter (τὸ δεύτερον, viz., *God's will*).
(And now the writer explains what is the will of God,
which Christ has wrought, concerning us (1 Thess. iv. 3),
even our sanctification.) By the which will we have been

sanctified, through the offering of the body of Jesus Christ once for all.

¹ There is no real difficulty in the Messiah's thus speaking in the present (future) tense. Isaiah (vii. 14) describes his prophetic vision as he saw it, so to speak, accomplished. "Behold a virgin with child, "and bearing a son!" (הנה עלמה הרה וילדת בן). The author of the *Nizzachon Vetus* (p. 185), with a true Rabbinic contempt for women, remarks, that "the first Adam was possessed of a far higher dignity "than Jesus, because God made him come forth from pure and holy "earth, and that he had neither father nor mother, nor did he incur "the taint and soil of a mother's womb." הארם הראשון היה גדול הימנו שהוציאו הק"בה מארמה בהורה וקדושה ולא היה לו אב ואם ולא סרח מבטן אשה. Our controversialist forgets that the promise of redemption was through the seed of the woman, and not of Adam (בין זרעך ובין זרעה הוא וגו', "I will put enmity between thy seed and her seed, he shall bruise," &c.). And to this vantage ground of the woman St. Paul appears to allude (1 Tim. ii. 15) where he says, Σωθήσεται δὲ διὰ τῆς τεκνογονίας, *i.e.*, by giving birth to the Messiah, who should repair the consequences of her fall. For the interpretation of Is. vii. 14, see Dr. M'Caul's *Messiaship of Jesus*, pp. 175—182.

Dr. Gill writes, on Ps. xl. 7, "*In the volume of the book it is written of* "*me;* either in the book of divine predestination, in the purposes and "decrees of God, Ps. cxxxix. 16, or in the book of the Scriptures ; "either in general, John v. 39, Luke xxiv. 27—44, or particularly in "the Book of the Psalms, Ps. i. 1, 2, and ii. 2, 6, 7, or rather in the "book of the law, the five books of Moses, since these were the only "books or volumes that were composed at the writing of this Psalm ; "and it has respect not to Deut. xviii. 15, nor ch. xvii. 18, nor Exod. "xxi. 6, but rather Gen. iii. 15." Ewald (*Das Sendschreiben an die Hebräer*, pp. 114, 115) thus concludes his remarks upon chap. x. 7:—
"Wenn aber unser Redner, in seiner Erklärung und Anwendung der "Psalmenworte, das mittlere Glied, *in der Buchrolle ist über mich* "*geschrieben*, v. 7, als ein dort bloss eingeschaltetes, nicht weiter "berücksichtigt, so folgt doch daraus nicht dass es für ihn keine weitere "Bedeutung hatte : vielmehr fand er auch, in diesen Worten, ein "Merkmal dass der Logos so geredet haben könne, sofern er es ist, auf "welchen, schon in der Buchrolle, d. i. im Pentateuche, hingewiesen "werde."

Verses 11—18.—Moreover every priest stands daily ministering, and offers the same sacrifices repeatedly, which can never remove (the guilt of) sins (περιελεῖν ἁμαρτίας). But He (Jesus), when He had offered one sacrifice on behalf of sins, sat down for ever on the right hand of God. (Ps. cx. 1.) Thenceforward waiting until his enemies be made the footstool under his feet. (Why?) Because by one offering He has perfected FOR EVER those who have been sanctified (τοὺς ἁγιαζομένους, *those who have been made holy, by his expiatory blood*). Moreover the Holy Ghost is our witness on this point. For after having first (Jer. xxxi. 33) said, *This is the covenant which I will make with them:*—The Lord saith (Jer. xxxi. 33, 34), *after those days*[1] (אחרי הימים) *I will put my laws into their hearts, and upon their understandings will I write them, and their sins and their iniquities I will remember no more* (οὐ μὴ μνησθῶ ἔτι, לא אזכר עוד). Now where remission (ἄφεσις) of these is, sacrifice (προσφορά) for sin is no longer (requisite.)

[1] On the meaning of אחרי הימים, see note 3, p. 9.

Because, as Daniel had foretold (ix. 24), the time has arrived " to finish the transgression, and to make an end of sins, and to make reconciliation for iniquity, and to bring in everlasting righteousness." The day of type and shadow is now over; the high priest needs no more to go, as the people's representative, once a year to make symbolical atonement for them in the Holy of Holies. They require no longer a fallible representative. The sentence of exclusion is revoked. The whole congregation is holy, and can go in boldly, in their own imparted right. The day of the Mosaic priesthood is past. Their occupation is gone. Nothing remains for them to do. Christ has done perfectly, and once for all, what they were evermore setting forth in prophetic parable. The vail is rent, and the mercy seat lies FOR EVER open, to those who draw near in reliance upon the all-atoning blood of Jesus.

Verses 19—21.—As we have (ἔχοντες οὖν) therefore (continues the writer, in the triumphant application of his unanswerable logic), as we have therefore unrestrained access[1] to the Holiest, by (ἐν, *in virtue of*) the blood of Jesus, to wit, that new (πρόσφατον)[2] and living way which He has consecrated (ἐνεκαίνισεν) for us, leading through (διὰ) the veil; that is to say, his flesh; as well as a High Priest[3] (to preside) over the house of God (ἐπὶ τὸν οἶκον τοῦ Θεοῦ).

[1] Παῤῥησίαν εἰς τὴν εἴσοδον τῶν ἁγίων ἐν τῷ αἵματι Ἰησοῦ. The following extract from the Mishna (*Joma*, cap. 8, sect. 8) excellently illustrates the unsatisfactory position of the Jewish penitent, who felt himself without any ready or certain access at all times to the forgiving presence of a reconciled God :—

הביאת ואשם ודאי מכפרין כיתה ויום הכפורים מכפרין עם התשובה תשובה מכפרת על
עבירות קלות על עשה ועל לא תעשה ועל החמורות היא תולה עד שיבא יום הכפורים ויכפר

"Victima pro peccatis, et victima pro delictis certis expiant:
"Mors et Dies Expiationis expiant cum poenitentia; et poeni-
"tentia expiat peccata levia, tam contra præcepta affirmativa quam
"negativa; et gravia suspendit, donec veniat Dies Expiationis et
"expiet." Mishn. Surenh., tom. ii., 257. How different is the invitation of the writer to the Hebrews (iv. 16):—Προσερχώμεθα οὖν μετὰ παῤῥησίας τῷ θρόνῳ τῆς χάριτος, ἵνα λάβωμεν ἔλεον, καὶ χάριν εὕρωμεν εἰς εὔκαιρον βοήθειαν. Ewald renders verses 19—23 as follows :—" Da wir
"also, ihr Brüder, Freimuth zum Eintritte des Heiligen mit Jesu's
"Blute (welchen er uns als einen frischen und lebendigen Weg durch
"den Vorhang einweihete das ist durch seinen Leib), und einen grossen
"Priester über das Haus Gottes haben : so lasset uns mit wahrhaftem
"Herzen herantreten im Vollstrome von Glauben, geläutert die Herzen
"vom bösen Bewusstseyn, und gewaschen den Leib mit reinem Wasser,
"lasset uns das Bekenntniss der Hoffnung ungebeugt festhalten, den
"treu ist der verhiess."

[2] Πρόσφατον, literally, *newly slain*; then, *fresh, recent, new.* It probably here signifies *ever fresh.* Wettstein, with a strange misapprehension of the easy transition from the sublime to the irreverent, heads

CHAP. X., 22.   153

(*in loco*) a very elaborate collection of authorities upon the meaning of this word with the following quotation from Florus, 1, 15, 3 :—" Alter " [Decius Mus] quasi monitu deorum, capite velato primam ante aciem " diis manibus se devoverit, ut in confertissima se hostium tela jacu- " latus, novum ad victoriam iter sanguinis sui semita aperiret."

² I think that Prof. Stuart rightly understands ἱερέα μέγαν as equivalent to כהן גדול, which is the ordinary Hebrew for high priest. The writer has proved how groundless were the cavils and objections of the unbelieving Jews, who asserted that the converts had surrendered all their national and covenanted privileges at their baptism. He has step by step, turned the tables upon the objectors, and demonstrated that they are clinging to the discarded, worn-out types and shadows, whilst the believers in Jesus have chosen the good part, which cannot be taken from them. He here uses ἱερέα μέγαν, in preference to ἀρχιερέα, as having a more technical and Jewish sound. He selects, so to speak, weapons of their own armoury, and beats them out of the field.

Verse 22.—Let us draw near with a sincere heart (ἀληθινῆς καρδίας, *frank sincerity of purpose*), having our hearts sprinkled from an evil conscience (ἀπὸ συνειδήσεως πονηρᾶς, *from a guilty reserve?*), and our bodies washed with pure water.¹

¹ A parallelism may be here intended between the water of baptism and the injunction given to Aaron (Levit. xvi. 4) that before he put on the highpriestly garments, which were symbolical of the beautiful attire of Christ's imputed righteousness, he should "wash his flesh in " water, and so shall he put them on." But I think rather that there is allusion made to the fulfilment of such prophecies as Ezek. xxxvi. 25. The Mishna closes its treatise Joma (*On the Day of Atonement*) with the following explanation of the mystical efficacy of this annual expiatory ceremonial :—

אמר רבי עקינא אשריכם ישראל לפני מי מיטהרין אתם מי מטהר אתכם אביכם שנבמים
שנאמר וזרקתי עליכם מים טהורים וטהרתם ואומר מקוה ישראל ה'' מה מקוה מטהר את
הטמאים אף הקדוש ברוך הוא מטהר את ישראל:

" Rabbi Akiba said, Blessed are ye, O Israel, before Him in whose " presence ye purify yourselves! Who cleanses you? Your Father " which is in heaven, even as it is said, *I will sprinkle clean water upon* " *you* (Ezek. xxxvi. 25), *and ye shall be clean*. The Lord speaks also of " the *Fountain of Israel* (Jer. xiv. 8 ; xvii. 13). What is the fountain " that cleanses the impure? The Holy One, blessed be He, cleanses " Israel." (*Mishna Surenh.*, tom. ii., p. 258.)

x

Schoettgen gives (*Hor. Hebr.*, tom ii., pp. 206, 207) the following early Rabbinical and Talmudical interpretations of Ezek. xxxvi. 25 :—
"*Et spargam in vos aquas mundas, et mundi eritis.* Targum : *Et remittam*
"*peccata vestra, tanquam si mundati essetis aquis puris et cinere vaccæ,*
"*quæ sacrificium est pro peccato.*—Sohar Exod., fol. 107, col. 435.
"*Beata est portio Israelitarum, quos Deus S.B. purificat aquis mundis*
"*supernis q.d.* Et Spargam.—Sohar Levit., fol. 20, col. 80, ad verba
"Numer. viii. 7, Et sic facies ad mundandum eos. *Quid sibi volunt hæc*
"*verba:* וכה, et sic? Resp. לגוונא דלעילא, *Ad modum supernum* (h.e.
"*spiritualem*). Insperge ipsis aquas sacrificii pro peccato, *quæ sunt*
"*reliquiæ roris bdellii ex Paradiso* לומא דאתי, *ad tempus futurum, q.d.*
"Et Spargam.—Sohar Levit., fol. 29, col. 113. *R. Jehuda dixit:*
"*Beati sunt Israelitæ in quibus Deus S.B. beneplacitum habet, illosque*
"*mundare cupit, ne peccatum in illis inveniatur, ut in palatio illius*
"*habitent. Et de* וזמנא דאתי, *tempore futuro scriptum est:* Et spargam
"vos.—Sohar Numer., fol. 75, col. 299. *Beata est portio Israelitarum,*
"*quibus Deus S.B. consilium dedit omnis sanationis, ut digni habeantur*
"*vita mundi futuri, et inveniantur mundi in hoc seculo. Sancti vero*
"לעלמא דאתי. *De his scriptum est:* Et spargam in vos.—Pesikta, fol.
"25, 4, et in Jalkut Simeoni 1, fol. 235, 1. *In hoc mundo Israelitæ*
"*mundi et immundi pronunciati sunt per ministerium Sacerdotis: verum*
"לעתיד לבא, *Deus S.B. ipse purificabit eos* q.d. et spargam.—Tanchuma,
"fol. 44, 2. *Deus immisit mala per ministerium Angeli: verum* לעתיד לבא,
"*Deus bona exhibebit per semet ipsum, q.d. Et spargam.* Ibidem, fol.
"51, 1. *Dixit Deus S.B. ad Israëlem: In hoc mundo vos equidem*
"*mundastis, sed rursum vos polluistis: verum* רצתיד לבא *ego purificabo vos,*
"טהרת עולמית, *purificatione æterna, ut non pollui debeatis,* q.d. Et
"spargam.—Schir haschirim rabba, fol. 5, 1. *Dixerunt Israelitæ ad*
"*Mosen: Utinam Deus se adhuc semel nobis revelaret, utinam osculuretur*
"*nos osculo oris sui. Respondit ipsis Moses: Hoc nunc fieri non potest:*
"*verum* לעתיד לבא, *fiet, q.d.* Et auferam cor lapideum ex carne vestra.
"—Kidduschin, fol. 72, 2. *Tradunt Rabbini nostri: Spurii et Nethinæi*
"*mundi erunt* לעתיד לבא: *ita statuit R. Jose. R. Meir vero dixit, non esse*
"*mundos. Sed R. Jose objecit: Annon jamdudum scriptum est; Et*
"Spargam."

The Mishna (*Joma*, cap. iii. 3) says, in reference to the washing of the priests,—

אין אד' נכנס לעזרה לעבודה אפי' טהור עד שיטבול חמש טבילות ועשרה קדושין טובל
כהן גדו' ומקדש בו ביום וכולן בקדש על בית הפרוה' חוץ מזו בלבד

"No one entered into the hall [of the priests] to perform any minis-
"tration, however clean he might be, until he had washed. The high
"priest made use of five washings, and ten sanctificatory washings on

" the day of atonement, and all of them were performed in the House
" of *Happarveh*, in the holy place, the first washing alone excepted," *i.e.*,
the one before he came into the hall, which took place in the common
place above the water-gate. *Mishna Surenh.*, vol. ii., p. 218.

" Domus Happarvœ locus erat in atrio, quo pelles victimarum
" saliebant......In tecto ejus erat domus lotionis pro Sacerdote magno
" in die expiationis."—Sheringham (*ibid.*). The authority for this
statement is to be found in the Mishna (*Middoth*, cap. 5, 2) :—

לשכת הפרוה שם היו מולחין עורות קדשים ועל גגה היה בית ט:בילה לכהן גדול ביום
הכפורים

" In the Chamber Happarveh they used to salt the hides of the
" sacrifices, and upon the roof thereof there was a lavatory for the
" high priest on the day of atonement." *Mishnah*, Surenh., tom. v.,
p. 376.

Verses 23—29.—Let us hold fast the confession of our
hope without wavering (*i.e.*, let us be outspoken and unhesitating in our profession of hope in Christ, unmoved by
the sophistries and jeers and persecutions of the unbelieving
Jews), and let us consider one another (κατανοῶμεν, *study
one another*) for the purpose of inciting one another to love
and to good works. Not forsaking (ἐγκαταλείποντες,
intermitting, leaving off) the assembling of ourselves together (doubtless for the purpose of worship and Christian fellowship), as is the custom of some[1] (probably " for
" fear of the Jews," who would set spies[2] to watch, and to
report against them), but rather comforting (παρακαλ-
οῦντες, and *exhorting*.—See Mal. iii. 16) one another, and
so much the more, as ye see the day (foretold by Christ in
reference to the destruction of Jerusalem, and also previously
by Daniel ix. 26, 27, as to follow closely upon the times of
Messiah's earthly ministrations and death—) approaching.
For when we sin (ἁμαρτανόντων, *i.e.*, apostatize) deliberately (ἑκουσίως, *of free choice, voluntarily*) after we have
received the knowledge of (μετὰ τὸ λαβεῖν τὴν ἐπίγνωσιν,
after having accepted and acknowledged) the truth, there is
no further sacrifice for sin in reserve, but (on the contrary)
a certain terrible anticipation of judgment (κρίσεως, *con-*

demnation) and fiery indignation (πυρὸς ζῆλος),[2] which shall presently consume (ἐσθίειν μέλλοντος) the adversaries. (Mal. iv. 1—3.)[4] Whosoever set at naught (ἀθετήσας, *infringed, violated; i.e.,* the presumptuous rebel) the law of Moses, is doomed to death (ἀποθνήσκει), without mercy, upon the testimony of two or three witnesses. (Numb. xv. 30, 31, xxxv. 30; Deut. xvii. 6.) Of how much sorer punishment, think ye, shall he be thought worthy, who has trodden under foot[5] (Matt. vii. 6) the Son of God, and accounted the blood of the covenant, wherewith He was sanctified, a common (κοινὸν, *profane, unclean*) thing, and has outraged (ἐνυβρίσας) the Spirit of Grace? (See note 2, pp. 125—127.)

[1] Μὴ ἐγκαταλείποντες τὴν ἐπισυναγωγὴν ἑαυτῶν, Ewald (*Das Sendschreiben an die Hebr.*, p. 118) writes on these words:—"Insbesondere *nicht* "*unterlassend das*, den Heiden gegenüber, *eigne Zusammentreten* mit "einander in den sontäglichen Fristen und übrigen christliche Feierta- "gen, *wie einige pflegen* (was nun ganz nahe auf die in jener besondern "Gemeinde gemachten Erfahrungen anspielt) *sondern* dieses christliche "mit einander Zusammentreten *aufmunternd* mit allen guten Mitteln "der Rede und Ermahnung fördernd. Damit wird deutlich genug auf "die Lässigkeit in allem christlichen Eifer angespielt, welcher gerade "zu Anfange dieses ganzen Abschnittes, v. 11, schon sehr empfindlich "kurz bezeichnet war, und unten weiter zu bezeichnen seyn wird; das "lässige besuchen der gemeinsamen Erbauung war der schlimmste "Anfang davon." Schoettgen (*Hor. Hebr.*, tom. i., pp. 982, 983) gives amongst others, the following illustrations from the Jewish writers:— "Sohar Exod., fol. 14, col. 56, "Non necesse habet homo אתרשא מכללא, "דסניאין *ut se separet a congregatione multorum, quia solus non observatur,* "*et Satanas talem facile in coelo accusat.*"—Berachoth, fol. 8, 1, *R. Levi* "*dixit: Quicunque habet Synagogam in urbe sua, et illam non ingreditur* "*ad orandum, ille vocatur incola malus q.d.* Jerem. xii. 14. Sic dicit "Dominus ad omnes incolas malos, tangentes hæreditatem, quam dedi "populo meo Israel: ecce ego evellam illos ex terra sua. *Neque hoc* "*tantum sed etiam caussa exilii est sibi et filiis suis*—Pirke Aboth, "c. ii., 4, *Hillel dixit:* אל תפרוש עצמך מן הציבור, *Ne separes te a congre-* "*gatione.*—Taanith, fol. 11, 1, *Tradiderunt Rabbini nostri: quando-* "*cunque Israelitæ* in afflictione versantur, וסירש אחר מהן, et unus eorum "se abstrahit, duo Angeli ad ipsum veniunt, manusque capiti ipsius

CHAP. X., 30, 31. 157

"imponunt, dicentes : Hic homo, שטים כן הציבור, qui se separat a coetu
"non videbit consolationem, quæ Ecclesiæ tanget."
² When my father, the late Dr. M'Caul, was Rector of St. James's,
Duke's Place, which is in the heart of the Jewish quarter in London,
we heard that Jewish watchers were placed at the avenues leading to
the church, to exercise oversight over any Jew that might be tempted
to enter the place, and to report on his conduct.
³ This is a Hebraism equivalent to אש קנאה, *fire of Jealousy*, Ps. lxxix.
5, Ezek. xxxvi. 5 (comp. xxxviii. 19), Zeph. i. 18, iii. 8, comp. Deut.
xxix. 19 (20).
⁴ There is no doubt that the Writer refers to the predicted and
awful woes that were coming upon Jerusalem and Judæa at the hands
of the Romans. Even then the Judge was before the doors.
⁵ An allusion to the blasphemous abjuration of an apostate to
Judaism. (See note 1, p. 63.)

Verses 30, 31.—For we know who it is that hath said,
"Vengeance is mine, I will repay" (Deut. xxxii. 35),¹
saith the Lord, and again, "The Lord will judge his
people." (Deut. xxxii. 36.) "It is a fearful thing² to
fall into the hands of the living God" (*i.e.*, such a fate,
so terrible a doom is impending over the impenitent, God
is ready to judge them. Will you forsake your own
mercies, whereby you have clean escaped the judgment
of the wicked and the adversaries? God himself will
presently interpose on behalf of his people—*See note
below*—Why should you participate in the condemnation
of the wicked ?).

¹ Οἴδαμεν γὰρ τὸν εἰπόντα· ἐμοὶ ἐκδίκησις κ.τ.λ. לי נקם ושלם *to me
belongeth avenging and recompensing.* LXX., ἐν ἡμέρᾳ ἐκδικήσεως
ἀνταποδώσω. The Targum of Onkelos thus paraphrases these words
in the preceding and following verses :—"Are not all their works
"manifest before Me, laid up in my treasures against the day of
"Judgment? *Their punishment is before me, and I will repay* in the
"time of their dispersion from their land ; for the day of their ruin
"draweth near, and that which is prepared for them maketh haste."
The Targum of Jonathan reads, " Vengeance lies before me, and I will
"recompense them at the time when their foot shall move to the cap-
"tivity, for the day of their destruction is coming near, and the evil

"which is prepared for them maketh haste." Now if these Targums correctly represent the current traditional interpretation of the ancient Jewish Church, as there is no reason to doubt they do, it will be seen that the above quotation from Deut. xxxii. 35 was, by it, regarded as a prophetic indication of *national* punishments coming upon the Jewish people. The verse quoted follows upon a terrible catalogue of woes denounced by Moses upon the Jews, as yet to come upon them for their, yet future, departure from God. The reason why the Writer to the Hebrews employed it upon the present occasion, becomes very apparent. He warns the converts from again, by apostacy, casting in their lot with that evil generation of men upon whom God's wrath was speedily about to come to the uttermost. Whereas, the words quoted from Deut. xxxii. 36, "*The Lord will judge his people*," are words of reassurance to the same converts under their persecutions. The entire verse (the first two clauses of which are repeated verbatim in Ps. cxxxv. 14) reads,—"For the Lord shall judge his people, and repent himself for "his servants, when he seeth that their power (Heb., *hand*) is gone, "and that there is none shut up and left (עצור ועזוב, *i.e.*, 'bond or free,' "*clausus et manumissus*, i.e., *mancipium et liber*, sc. *omnes homines*, "Gesen)" The Targum of Onkelos has on this latter verse, "For the "Lord shall decide the judgment of his people, and the avengement of "his righteous servants shall be avenged, for it is seen before Him, "that in the time when the stroke of their enemies would prevail "against them they will be wavering, (as those who) are forsaken." The Targums of Jonathan and Jerusalem, in like manner, both understand the words, "He shall judge his people," in a consolatory sense, and as equivalent to "He shall judge the cause of his people." (See Etheridge's *Targums*, in loc.) Ewald (in loc., p. 119) remarks upon this 30th verse :—" Und um alles zu schliessen wird v. 30 f. noch hinzuge-"fügt : *Denn wir wissen*, aus den bekannten Worten welche in dem "Messianischen Liede Deut. 32, 31 f. nahe genug bei einander stehen, "was diese Gericht zu bedeuten habe, und wie *furchtbar es sei in die* "*Hände*, nicht etwa menschlicher Richter, welche höchstens den Leib "vernichten können, sondern *des lebendigen Gottes* selbst *hineinzufallen*, "sin Saz welcher für einen Christen aus Christus' worten selbst Matt. "10, 18, deutlich genug ist, und hier schon nach dem ganzen Zusam-"menhange der Rede, auch nach der grossen Veränderung der Zeiten, "eine ganz andere Bedeutung hat, als dort 2 Sam. 24. 14, vgl. Jer. 22, 25, "1 Chr. 21, 13." Michaelis (*Introd. to New Testament, vol. iv., tr. by Marsh,* p. 256), basing his statement, doubtless, upon the fact that the words λέγει κύριος are not found in the Hebrew text, but which are palpably supplied by the writer in explanation of οἴδαμεν κ.τ.λ, asserts

that the passage "differs both from the Hebrew text and the Septua-
"gint, and this passage is again quoted in the very same words in
"Rom. xii. 19." With regard to the LXX. Michaelis is right, but
with regard to the Hebrew, לי נקם ושלם. he is guilty, to say the least, of
a misrepresentation. The fact is, the Writer here, as also in Romans
xii. 19, translates literally from the Hebrew, quite independently of the
LXX. This coincidence, *in translation*, in both passages seems to
point to a common authorship of both epistles, and not, as Michaelis
continues, " This agreement in a reading, which has hitherto been dis-
"covered in no other place (!), might form a presumptive argument
"that both quotations were made by the same person. and consequently
"that the Epistle to the Hebrews was written by St. Paul. But the
"argument is not decisive ; for it is very possible that in the first
"century there were manuscripts of the LXX. with this reading in
"Deut. xxxii. 35, from which St. Paul might have copied (!) in Rom.
"xii. 19, and the translator of this Epistle in Heb x. 30." Such were
the commencements of that miserable style of forced criticism to bolster
up some favourite theory, with which Scriptural philology has been
afflicted ever since.

² φοβερὸν τὸ ἐμπεσεῖν κ.τ.λ. " Sohar Exod., fol. 23, col. 92,
ווי לאינון קדישא דמלכא קדישא יחצר עלייהו קרבא Væ illis, quibus Rex Sanctus
" bellum indicit, q.d. Exod. xiv. 3. Deus est vir belli." (Schoettg.
Hor. Heb., tom. i., p. 983.)

And now the Writer appeals to the early experience of his readers. When first they embraced
Christianity they had made up their minds to suffer
for the Gospel's sake. They did, moreover, suffer
loss of all things. He appeals to them, and asks,
What reason do you now see for altering your mind,
and repining at persecutions and distresses, which
you then bore with unflinching fortitude and
equanimity? And so he continues:—

Verses 32—34.—But remember the former days, viz.,
those in which after ye were first enlightened (see note 3,
p. 61), ye endured (ὑπεμείνατε, *ye bore up stedfastly
and patiently*) against a great fight (πολλὴν ἄθλησιν, a

mighty struggle, see pp. 2, 3) of sufferings. Being on the one hand, made a public spectacle[1] by insulting outrages (ὀνειδισμοῖς) and afflictions (θλίψεσι, *vexatious and harassing troubles*), and on the other, having become the companions (κοινωνοὶ, *the associates*) of those who were thus treated.[2] Ye also sympathised with my own bonds,[3]

i.e., in those days you had compassion to spare for me also. A beautiful and touching allusion, adroitly introduced, and which could not fail to make them ashamed of repining, when they remembered the Writer's heroic constancy, and the admirable manner in which he supported his heavy chain. This, to my mind, stamps the Epistle as St. Paul's. The master-hand betrays itself.

[1] Θεατριζόμενοι. So St. Paul writes of himself and the other Apostles. 1 Cor. iv. 9, θέατρον ἐγενήθημεν τῷ κόσμῳ, καὶ ἀγγέλοις καὶ ἀνθρώποις. There is no need to take θεατριζόμενοι in a literal sense as Alford does, much less can any argument be founded upon the expression as to the Greek style of the writer. The word θέατρον, תיאטרון, was early adopted into the Rabbinical phraseology, and is found in the Targum of Jonathan, Deut. xxviii. 19, *e.g.*, "Accursed shall you be in your going into the "houses of your theatres (לבתי תיאטרוניכין במיכלכון אתון ליטין), and the places "of your public shows, to make void the words of the Law." For further examples see Buxtof. *Lex. Chald.* Art. האב, col. 2549 and 2550. Ewald, in pursuance of his theory that the community to which the epistle was addressed was not resident in Palestine, says :— "Aus " diesen geschichtlichen Anspielungen erhellet dass hier nur eine jener " aus der AG. bekannten städtischen Unruhen gemeint ist, welche bei, " oder nicht lange nach, der Gründung dieser Gemeinde ausgebrochen " war, wobei einzelne hervorragende Mitglieder derselben, von einer " wüthenden Gassenmenge aufs frechste verhönt, ausgeplündert und " misshandelt, auch durch die hinzutretende Obrigkeit, ins Gefängniss " geworfen wurden, aber von allen übrigen Mitchristen die thätigste " Theilnahme und Hülfe fanden. Das war gewiss ein furchtbarer " Aufruhr gewesen : aber dass dabei doch kein Blut geflossen war, " folgt nicht bloss aus unseren Worten, sondern auch aus der Andeutung " unten xii. 4."

² A generous spirit will revolt at cruelty or injustice perpetrated upon others, which he will bear himself in silence. No small portion of the fiery trial which came upon the early martyrs and confessors to endure must have been the witnessing the indignities and brutal treatment of their unresisting and defenceless friends and relatives.

³ Τοῖς δεσμοῖς μου συνεπαθήσατε. Compare chap. xiii. 3, μιμνήσκεσθε τῶν δεσμίων, ὡς συνδεδεμένοι; and Col. iv. 18, μνημονεύετέ μου τῶν δεσμῶν. Dr. S. Davidson (*Introd. to the New Testament*, vol. iii., p. 203) writes:— "An argument that Paul was the author has also been founded on "Heb. x. 34, in the received reading of the passage. Euthalius argued "long ago from καὶ γὰρ τοῖς δεσμοῖς μου συνεπαθήσατε in this manner. "But the received reading has been abandoned by the best critics. "Griesbach, Knapp, Lachmann, Tischendorf, and even Scholz, have "adopted τοῖς δεσμίοις, *ye sympathised with the prisoners.* The evidence "in favour of this latter reading is *decided.*" (!) Dean Alford, though he adopts in his text τοῖς δεσμίοις, does not speak, in his note, with the same emphatic assurance as Dr. Davidson. Michaelis is not prepared to determine absolutely in favour of either reading, until the question of the Pauline authorship has been decided. The Coptic, Syriac, and Vulgate versions read in accordance with τοῖς δεσμίοις. Origen reads δεσμοῖς without μου, whilst Chrysostom and Theophylact, Estius, Grotius, Mill, Wall, Ewald, &c., adopt the later reading. Luther, Carpzov, Wolfius, Matthæi, Rink, and others adhere to the received reading. Ewald (*Das Sendschr. a.d. Hebr.*, p. 169) makes the following admission :—" 10, 34, hat zwar auch (*Cod.*) *Sin.* δεσμοῖς μου : allein "wieviele schwere Fehler sich auch in solch alte Urkunden schon "einschleichen konnten, zeigt derselbe *Sin.* sogleich hier in aller Nähe "wieder, indem er v. 32, ἁμαρτίας ὑμῶν für ἡμέρας gibt. Dagegen hat er "eben hier v. 34 richtig ἑαυτοὺς für ἑαυτοῖς." Believing that τοῖς δεσμοῖς μου was originally rejected as being a forcible testimony to the Pauline Authorship of the Epistle, I would commend to my readers the following excellent remarks of J. C. Wolfius (*in loc. Cur. Phil. et Crit.*, tom. iv., p. 734):—" Recte tenetur lectio communior. Apostolus enim v. 33, "jam laudaverat Hebræos in universum, quod in societatem eorum, "qui varia, atque adeo etiam vincula perpessi essent, venerint, nempe "vices eorum miserantes, et opem, qualem poterant, ferentes. Atque "hoc ipsum vers. 34, suo comprobat exemplo. Ita omnino accipienda "sunt verba, nisi idem repetita vice dixisse videri debeat. Ex adhor- "tatione Paulina, cap. xiii. 3, μιμνήσκεσθε τῶν δεσμίων non magis confici "potest, legendum h.l esse δεσμίων, quam dissentientes admiserint, legi "debere δεσμῶν quia Coloss. iv. 18, legitur μνημονεύετε τῶν δεσμῶν μου. "Quod porro nostra lectio δεσμῶν μου ab illis derivatur qui Pauli hanc

Y

"epistolam esse crediderint, id eadem veri specie torqueri in contrariæ
"sententiæ patronos potest. Quis enim præstiterit, eos, qui negabant,
"esse Pauli, atque hæc verba sibi efficaciter opponi posse sentiebant,
"non libentissime vel lectionem alteram, casu forte expressam, admis-
"isse, vel destinata opera invexisse ? Taceo, fraude ejusmodi recte
"sentientibus opus non fuisse, cum validiora sententiæ suæ argumenta
"in promptu haberent, quibus inniti possent. Et si talia non exsta-
"rent, sola vinculorum Apostoli mentio rem non erat confectura, cum
"plures ex Apostolis vincti fuerint, ut ab alio vel sic exarata credi
"potuisset. Obsignabo hæc Jacobi Cappelli verbis :—Et *hæc certe*
"*lectio,* inquit, *probabilior est, ut quæ melius conveniat tum Hellenismo,*
"*tum Pauli stilo, sua vincula passim in epistolis suis commemorantis, non*
"*inani jactantia, sed ut catenis ac stigmatis suis, quasi totidem sigillis,*
"*uteretur ad veritatis Evangelicæ confirmationem.* Quod ad Hellenis-
"mum attinet, Cappellus procul dubio id voluit, quod Paulus alias
"cap. iv. 15, συμπαθῆσαι ταῖς ἀσθενείαις dicit, quemadmodum συγκοινωνή-
"σαντες τῇ θλίψει, Philipp. iv. 14, appellat." Wolfius's remark that in
chap. xiii. 3 the writer enjoins upon his readers the duty of remembering "them that are in bonds," seems to me to be of great force in
deciding the real reading of the passage in favour of the *textus receptus.*
To praise them in the verse before us for their consideration to prisoners,
and then to admonish them in xiii. 3 of their duty in this very particular, seems altogether contrary to common sense. Some very excellent illustrations of the general value of Alford's Greek Testament as a
critical authority are to be found in *The Lord's Prayer, with various
readings and critical notes, showing the entire genuineness of the received
Text of the Prayer, both in St. Matthew and in St. Luke ;* by the Rev.
J. Forshall, M.A., F.R.S , *formerly Keeper of the MSS. in the British
Museum*, Oxford, 4to., and also in the Preface to the *Gospel of St. Mark*,
London, 1862, 8vo., by the same very learned and much to be lamented
scholar. It is greatly to be regretted that Mr. Forshall was removed
by death before he had completed his proposed work, " *The Holy
Gospels in the received Text of the original Greek, with various readings......
and maintaining the general integrity of Scripture as read in the Church of
England.*" In conclusion, it is worthy of remark that St. Paul, in his
acknowledged Epistles, speaks of himself as a prisoner, δέσμιος, five
times, viz., Eph. iii. 1, iv. 1, 2 Tim. i. 8, Philemon 1, 9, and alludes to
his bonds no fewer than eight times, viz., Philipp. i. 7, 13, 14, 16, Col.
iv. 18, 2 Tim. ii. 9, Philem. 10, 13. The translators of the London
Jews' Society's Hebrew New Testament have, כי בכל מסרותי צר להם, in
Heb. x. 34.

CHAP. X., 34—39. 163

Verses 34—39.—And ye also acquiesced with joy in the despoiling[1] of your goods (as a Jewish convert to Christianity is, at the present time, immediately disinherited; and, if it be possible, if he be a married man, his wife is persuaded to demand a divorce from him), knowing that you have in yourselves (ἐν ἑαυτοῖς) a more excellent inheritance *above* (ἐν οὐρανοῖς, *i.e.*, the inward assurance of salvation[2]), and that an enduring one. Cast not away, therefore, your frank and bold avowal of your faith (in Christ, τὴν παρρησίαν ὑμῶν), which has a great recompense of reward (μισθαποδοσίαν).[3] For ye have need of patience (ὑπομονῆς, *long-suffering endurance and capacity for waiting*) in order that, after having done God's will, ye may receive the promise. For yet a *very little*[4] while (ἔτι γὰρ μικρὸν ὅσον ὅσον), and He who cometh will come,[5] and will not put you off (χρονιεῖ, *tarry, disappoint by unseasonable delays*). But, [as you know it is written, Hab. ii. 3] "The just shall " live by faith;"[6] and "if *any man* hold back[7] (ὑποστείληται, shrink back. See Luke ix. 62. Vulg., *incredulus est*), my soul has no pleasure (οὐκ εὐδοκεῖ) in him." But we are not of those who shrink back to perdition (ὑποστολῆς εἰς ἀπώλειαν), but "of faith," so as to save (εἰς περιποίησιν) the soul (*zur Seelengewinnung*.—Ewald).

[1] Καὶ τὴν ἁρπαγὴν κ.τ.λ. " Polybius, p. 397, similiter ἁρπαγὰς ὑπαρ-
" χόντων, *direptiones facultatum* appellat. Epictetus ad Deum ita fatur;
" *πένης ἐγενόμην σοῦ θέλοντος, ἀλλὰ χαίρων.* De re ipsa lege apud Gata-
"kerum ad M. Antoninum, p. 205." J. C. Wolfius, *Cur. Phil.*, tom.
iv., p. 735.
[2] Οὗτός ἐστιν ὁ πολὺν ἄκρατον σπάσας τῆς εὐεργέτιδος τοῦ Θεοῦ δυνάμεως,
καὶ λόγων ἱερῶν καὶ δογμάτων ἑστιαθείς. Οὗτος, ᾧ φησιν ὁ προφήτης τὸν
Θεὸν ἐμπεριπατεῖν, οἷα βασιλείῳ, καὶ γάρ ἐστι τῷ ὄντι βασίλειον καὶ οἶκος
Θεοῦ, σοφοῦ διάνοια. " Such an one as this has drunk deep of the wine
" of God's benevolent power, and feasted upon sacred words and doc-
" trines. Of such sort is he, concerning whom the prophet declares
" that God *walks in them*, as in a palace; for in very truth the mind of
" a wise man is a palace and house of God." (Philo, *De Præmiis et
Pœnis*, Works, *Mangey's Edition*, tom. i., p. 428.)

CHAP. X., 34—39.

³ Οἷς μὲν γὰρ ἀληθινὸς πλοῦτος ἐν οὐρανῷ κατάκειται. *Ibid.*, p. 425. "But those for whom the true riches in heaven are reserved," &c. See Matth. v. 10—12, x. 32, 33; Luke xii. 8—9.

⁴ Ἔτι γὰρ μικρὸν κ.τ.λ. The same expression is found in the LXX. version of Is. xxvi. 20. Βάδιζε λαός μου, εἴσελθε εἰς τὰ ταμεῖά σου, ἀπόκλεισον τὴν θύραν σου, ἀποκρύβηθι μικρὸν ὅσον ὅσον, ἕως ἂν παρέλθῃ ἡ ὀργὴ Κυρίου. It is here equivalent to the Hebrew כמעט רגע, which Gesenius translates by, *per exiguum momentum*, as he does רגע by *nutus* sc. oculi, *Augenblick*, *i.e.*, the twinkling of an eye, an instant, or moment. J. C. Wolfius (*Curæ Phil. et Crit.*, tom. iv., p. 736, *in loco*) observes:—"Ita *Aristophanes* in Vespis: τί οὐχ ἀπεκοιμήθημεν ὅσον ὅσον "στίλην. *Quidni minutum quantum quantum obdormiscamus.* Ibi "Scholiastes observat ὅσον ὅσον στίλην significare τὸ ἐλάχιστον." Ewald translates ἔτι γὰρ κ.τ.λ., "Est ist doch noch eine kleine, kleine Weile."

⁵ "Wie sicher diese Verheissung aber in Erfüllung gehen, und *der* "*Kommende* d.i. Christus in seinèr Herrlichkeit dessen Kommen zum "Gerichte auch alle die alten Propheten stets verhiessen, wirklich "Kommen werde, wird v. 37, f. zwar absichtlich mit solchen Bibel- "stellen erhärtet, welche von Glauben reden, und welche hier in einer "freieren Zusammenstellung der Worte Jes. 10, 25, 29, 17 auch 26, 20, "mit Hab. 2, 3, f. gegeben werden: aber sie werden doch nur angeführt "um die Anwendung, welche hierher gehörkurz und schlagend zu "ziehen: *wir aber*, als Christen, *sind nicht*, wie ich hoffe Leute von "dem in jenem Prophetenworte als möglich vorausgesetzten *Klein- "muthe* was nur *zum Verderben* führen Könnte, sondern *von Glauben* "*zur Gewinnung von Seele*, und ewigem Leben." Ewald, *Das Sendshr. an d. Hebr.*, p. 122. The deletion of the Jewish polity is the leading idea.

⁶ Ὁ δὲ δίκαιος ἐκ πίστεως ζήσεται. This passage of Hab. ii. 4, וצדיק באמונתו יחיה, is quoted by St. Paul in Rom. i. 17, καθὼς γέγραπται· ὁ δὲ δίκαιος ἐκ πίστεως ζήσεται; and also in Gal. iii. 11, ὅτι ὁ δίκαιος ἐκ πίστεως ζήσεται. The LXX. of Hab. ii. 4 is, Ἐὰν ὑποστείληται, οὐκ εὐδοκεῖ ἡ ψυχή μου ἐν αὐτῷ· ὁ δὲ δίκαιος ἐκ πιστεώς μου ζήσεται. The LXX. translators apparently, read באמונתי, instead of באמונתו. See further on the passage, in Lud. Cappelli *Crit. Sacr.*, p. 62 and p. 537.

⁷ Καὶ ἐὰν ὑποστείληται κ.τ.λ. The real difficulty in this passage is that it agrees in the main with the LXX. of Hab. ii. 4. The correctness of the LXX. rendering of the *sense* of the Hebrew words is therefore, in this particular instance, guaranteed by the canonical author of the Epistle to the Hebrews. The Christian student has, in consequence, no alternative but to accept ἐὰν ὑποστείληται, οὐκ εὐδοκεῖ ἡ ψυχή μου ἐν αὐτῷ as accurately representing the sense, *if not the exact translation*, of הנה עפלה לא ישרה נפשו בו, "Behold [if] lifted up, his (*i.e.*, that man's)

"soul is not upright in him." The only legitimate clue to this riddle of exposition is to be found by a comparison of the circumstances under which both passages were originally written. That they have some *striking similarity* of adaptation, is apparent from the New Testament quotation on the present occasion. Let us then inquire what object the writer to the Hebrews proposes to himself in his present exhortation. It is to dissuade the converts from apostacy, on account of the severity of the persecutions to which they were subjected at the hands of their unbelieving brethren. They were subjected to hardships and outrages as unjust as they were cruel. Some of them had actually gone back to Judaism ; others were wavering. From chap. xii. 5 we find that they were inclined to repine against the justice of their being thus dealt with. They had forgotten the exhortation which was addressed to them (Prov. iii. 11, 12) by Solomon, *My son, despise not the chastening of the Lord, neither be weary of his correction* (בתוכחתו). They chafed under their miseries, and were inclined to question the goodness of God, forgetting that chastening was a proof of love, and not an exercise of His arbitrary power and severity. They began to sit in judgment upon the Almighty, and to impugn the equity of His dispensations. Their "souls were "lifted up ;" they were ready to apostatize, in offended pride, from the living God. Now let us examine the occasion upon which the words of the original prophecy were vouchsafed to Habakkuk. The occasion was one exactly and marvellously similar. In Habak. i. 2—4 the prophet complains of the inequality of the sentence that dooms Israel to punishment by the more wicked Chaldeans :—" O Lord, how long shall I cry, " and thou wilt not hear! *even* cry out unto thee *of* violence, and " thou wilt not save ! Why dost thou show me iniquity, and cause *me* " to behold grievance ? for spoiling and violence *are* before me, and " there are *that* raise up contention. Wherefore the law is slacked, " and judgment shall never go forth, for the wicked doth compass about " the righteous ; therefore wrong judgment proceedeth." And again, in verses 12, 13 :—" O Lord, thou hast ordained them (the Chaldeans) " for judgment! And O mighty God, thou hast established them for " correction ! *Thou art* of purer eyes than to behold evil, and canst " not look on iniquity. Wherefore lookest thou upon them that deal " treacherously, *and* holdest thy tongue when the wicked devoureth " *the man that is* more righteous than he ? and makest men as the fishes " of the sea, as the creeping things *that have* no ruler over them ?" Here, then, we see that Habakkuk was ready to fall into the very same mistake as that which the writer to the Hebrews indicates that his readers had actually fallen into. But how were Habakkuk's eyes opened to behold his sinful presumption ? He resolved to look within, and to seek a solution of his difficulty, by a recollection of God's personal dealings with his own soul. "I will watch to see what He will say unto "me (גי *in me*, in my own personal case), and what I shall answer when "I am corrected" (על הוכחתי *concerning my correction*, the very word used in Prov. iii. 11). And then he received as an answer, first that God would certainly bring his judgments to pass as threatened, and secondly, that this rebellious questioning of God's goodness was a grievous sin. It indicated no meritorious frame of mind. God views all alike, as guilty sinners deserving of punishment. The prophet's comparative estimate of guilt is a false standard of measurement, "*Behold* (if it be) *lifted up, his (i.e.*, that man's) *soul is not upright in him*, "*but the just shall live by his faith*" (וצדיק באמונתו יהיה). The reassuring, consolatory effect of this declaration is vividly depicted in chap. iii. 1, 2, 17—19. We see, moreover, that the idea of revolting and rebellious apostacy is contained in both נפשו עֻפְּלָה, and ἐὰν ὑποστείληται, and that the Hebrew readers of the Epistle (to whom the words of the prophet Habakkuk were perfectly familiar, as relating to a well-known episode in their national history,) must at once have caught the coincidence between their own position and that of Habakkuk. The words of the LXX. are therefore a paraphrase, but such an one as embodies, with marvellous fidelity, the entire scope of the Divine instruction which the Hebrew oracle was intended to teach. It seizes at once upon the pith and kernel of the lesson, and reproduces in it a form beautifully concise, and universally applicable to all similar occasions of faithless mistrust of God's providential albeit afflictive appointments. Professor Stuart writes :—" The LXX., who have rendered the Hebrew text in "exact accordance with the words of our Epistle, must have read נפשו "*my soul* here, as they did באמונתי, *in my faith*, in the clause preceding. "This is the more probable reading, but it cannot now be critically "defended." For the best of all possible reasons.—This proposed emendation would entirely alter the construction of both עֻפְּלָה and יֹשֶׁר, which are both feminine in connexion with נפשו, which is a feminine substantive in the present instance, although of the common gender. Such a wholesale and audacious alteration of the Hebrew text would be as unscientific, as it is unsupported by MS. authority. Some MSS. insert μου after δίκαιος, a reading which Alford adopts ; and so also the Vulgate reads, "justus autem meus" in this 38th verse of Heb. x. "Recte renitente," as J. C. Wolfius remarks, "*Whitbio* in Examine, pag. 76, his verbis : *Sed*, "*cum Apostolus citet hæc ipsa verba absque* μου, Rom. i. 17, Galat. iii. 11, "*cur sententiam suam hic variarit, causa nulla est, præsertim cum lectionem* "*in textu firment omnia Græca scholia.*" The Vulgate of Hab. ii. 4 reads, "justus autem in fide sua vivet." See Dr. S. Davidson (*in loc.*)

ou p. 283 of vol. iii. of his *Introduction to the New Testament.* Ewald says (*Das Sendschr. a d. Hebr.*, p. 169), " Will man nicht annehmen der " Redner führe die Worte x. 37, f. só an, wie er sie aus der erwähnten " Bibelstellen (see *ibid.*, p. 122) ganz frei zusammengesezt in einer " anderen späteren Schrift vorfand, so muss man annehmen dass er " sie selbst hier bloss nach dem Gedächtnisse so frei wiedergebe. Die " LXX. liegt hier zwar überall zum Grunde : allein sogleich der erste " kleine Saz kann, so wie er hier erscheint, nur aus verschiedenen " Stellen des B. Jesaia zusammengesezt seyn ; im dritten Saze ist " ὁ δίκαιός μου, für das einfache ὁ δίκαιος, aus der Lesart LXX., ἐκ " πίστεώς μου, versezt : und das dieser ganze Saz ὁ δίκαιός μου, dem " folgenden voraus gesezt ist, erklärt sich freilich desto leichter, je " mehr dieser nach der üblen Griechischen Übersezung des ersten " Gliedes von Hab. ii. 4, keinen Sinn gibt, während er nach dieser " Umsezung einen ganz passenden darreichen Kann."

Since writing the above I have read with regretful surprise the report in the "Guardian" newspaper of this day (Feb. 22, 1871, p. 221) of the speech of a Right Reverend Prelate in Convocation on Thursday, Feb. 16. The Bishop is reported to have spoken as follows :—" I said, my Lords, " that even in our comparatively faultless Authorised Version instances " have been found, and instances are to be found, of the three deviations " that I have adverted to. I am sure that at this moment when I allude " to the first,—that of violating the grammatical construction for a " doctrine,—when I name that first class of perverting the sound " principle of translation, your Lordships will at this moment be " remembering the words which are, I think, to be found at the end of " the 10th chapter of the Hebrews, within a verse or two of the end— " ὁ δὲ δίκαιός μου ἐκ πίστεως ζήσεται· καὶ ἐὰν ὑποστείληται, οὐκ εὐδοκεῖ ἡ " ψυχή μου ἐν αὐτῷ. And you may remember very well how we read in " our authorised translation, ' Now the just shall live by faith, but if " ' any man draw back, my soul shall have no pleasure in him.' But " whence, my Lords, come the words, ' any man' ? Is there any particle " in the Greek corresponding to our translation ? Is there any of us " who would not adopt the view of good honest old William Tyndale, " that the words can have no other meaning than ' *But should he, the* " ' *righteous man, fail in his righteousness*' ? I believe that the per- " verted translation first found its place in what is called the first edition " of the Geneva Bible, but there it is, an instance plain and patent."

The above specimen of sacro-forensic criticism affords a signal example that the knowledge of a great deal of Greek in a Biblical revisionist (which his Lordship undoubtedly possesses), without a corresponding decent familiarity with Hebrew, is a dangerous thing. The translators of the Authorised Angl. Version in Heb. x. 38 were doubtless guided in their rendering by the Hebrew of Hab. ii 4. הִנֵּה עֻפְּלָה לֹא יָשְׁרָה נַפְשׁוֹ בּוֹ וְצַדִּיק בֶּאֱמוּנָתוֹ יִחְיֶה.—The first clause of the Hebrew requires such "a particle" as that of which the Bishop speaks in order to render it intelligible and translateable. Moreover the Bishop, as reported in the "Guardian," did not fairly state the case. The translators have put the words "*any man*" into italics, to indicate that they are not to be found in the original text! If the necessity for a new translation of the English Bible be based upon grounds possessing no greater cogency than the above, old-fashioned folks, to whom the present version is dear, may well tremble for what is before them in the way of "improvements." Luther, doubtless misled by his Hebrew scholarship, commits the same enormity in Heb. x. 38 which our translators were guilty of, only without the extenuating circumstance of italics :— "Wer aber weichend wird, an dem wird meine Seele keinen Gefallen haben." The Vulgate, although it has in Heb. x. 38, *Justus autem meus ex fide vivit, quod si subtraxerit se*, &c., yet inserts *qui* in Hab. ii 4, *Ecce qui incredulus est*, &c. Greatly to be lamented it is, that whilst the Revisionists have called in the aid of Socinians, &c., &c., to help them in the work of correction so called, they have neglected to avail themselves of the services, as far as I know, of any of the numerous converted Jewish clergymen in the Holy Orders of our own Church, to whom the Hebrew text and the Rabbinical idiom are as familiar as the alphabet. The attempt to elucidate the writings of Jewish Apostles, without a competent knowledge of the Jewish habit of thought and the Rabbinical formulas of interpretation, is a proceeding about as hopeful as would be the efforts of a converted Jew to annotate Euripides, which lay before him only in a modern translation. His familiarity with the opinions of the Rabbis and the most accurate laws of Hebrew syntax would, I trow, stand him in very little stead in such a case. The painful feebleness of Alford's Greek Testament, in all points requiring real Biblical (*i.e.*, Hebrew and Rabbinical) erudition, is a lamentable case in point. In this respect Dean Alford's work is almost entirely worthless, and affords a sorry specimen of the present state of theological learning in the Church of England. The notion that the Jewish writings of the New Testament are to be explained rigorously in accordance with the requirements of a starched modern Greek philology, is simply childish.

CHAPTER XI.

In the closing verse of the tenth chapter, the writer, with that delicate facility of adaptation to the temper and circumstances of his readers, which is so pre-eminently a characteristic of the speeches and writings of St. Paul, strikes a twofold chord. He appeals to their conscientious convictions. He does not threaten, but, by a passing allusion to the awful consequences of a presumptuous apostacy, he awakens a train of the most heart-searching reflections. A rejection of Christ, a wilful departure from the truth, out of pique, or to avoid persecution, or from any other motive of worldly advantage, must end in perdition. This must be the self-chosen fate, the deliberate choice of the apostates—ἡμεῖς δὲ οὐκ ἐσμὲν ὑποστολῆς εἰς ἀπώλειαν. To deny Christ will be, to be denied by Him before God the Father and his holy angels, when He comes in his kingdom. The second chord vibrates with a thrilling melodiousness, which cannot fail to arouse a glow of holy and patriotic emulation in their susceptible Jewish bosoms. He appeals to the mighty past. He calls to his aid the consecrated reminiscences of the former years. He leads them back, by a glance at the glowing pages of Israel's history, to a hoarier and a more illustrious antiquity. In those words ἀλλὰ πίστεως εἰς περιποίησιν ψυχῆς, he reminds them what spirit they are of, and of the glorious muster-roll of worthies from which they are lineally descended. The Church of God did not date only from Abraham. It included every saved soul, from the death of Abel, to the moment of their reading the epistle. Mankind have evermore been divided into two great subdivisions. Decide, then, to which you will belong! Are you πίστεως εἰς περιποίησιν ψυχῆς, i.e., are you worthy children of the elders who, through faith, obtained a good report? Or do you belong to, and will you choose your portion amongst, the unbelieving, the unthankful, the unholy, who are fitly designated as being ὑποστολῆς εἰς ἀπώλειαν? Upon the painful side of the picture he lingers but for a moment. He casts but a passing regard at a subject so fraught with anguished and apprehensive reminiscences. From the very midst of his readers certain of their companions had fallen away. They had gone back to the enemies of the Cross. They had "blasphemed that Holy Name." It was a topic too agonising and terrible to dilate upon. With loving discrimination, and a masterly appreciation of the Divine superiority of an appeal to the nobler affections, as a *persuasive*, over the most graphic delineations of judgment to come, he passes on to the brighter, more enduring subject of the triumphs of faith. He points, therefore, to the great cloud of witnesses. This, he would say, is the ancestry from which you are descended! Behold your lineage! Let us speak together of the noble acts that your forefathers did; of the temptations and the trials which they sustained; of the difficulties they overcame; of the tribulations through which they passed; of the hope they set before them, and of the crown that they won. First of

CHAP. XI., 1, 2. 171

all the Hebrews are reminded what it is, to be *of faith;* in other words, what faith is.

Verses 1, 2.—But faith (he commences) is a substantial persuasion (ὑπόστασις)¹ of things hoped for; an evidence (ἔλεγχος, *a proof that convinces, carries a satisfying conviction home to the mind*) of things not seen. For by such a faith as this (ἐν ταύτῃ γὰρ) the elders² obtained a good report (ἐμαρτυρήθησαν, *i.e.*, were approved, and obtained the testimony of commendation from God in the Scriptures; or else, *were made witnesses*).³

---

¹ Ὑπόστασις occurs five times in the New Testament. 2 Cor. ix. 4, ἐν τῇ ὑποστάσει ταύτῃ τῆς καυχήσεως, "in this same *confident* boasting." 2 Cor. xi. 17, where the same Greek words are rendered in the authorised version, "in this *confidence* of boasting." Heb. i. 3, χαρακτὴρ τῆς ὑποστάσεως αὐτοῦ, "the express image of his *person;*" iii. 14, τὴν ἀρχὴν τῆς ὑποστάσεως, "the beginning of our *confidence;*" and, fifthly, as above, xi. 1, ἐλπιζομένων ὑπόστασις, "the substance of things hoped "for." In Ps. lxviii. 2 (Heb. lxix. 3) the LXX. translate יְקֹוִי, *standing* (sc. footing), by ὑπ. So, also, in Ruth i. 12, תִּקְוָה, *hope*, or *expectation*. Again, the same word is found in Ezek. xix. 5; whilst, in Lament. iii. 18, תּוֹחַלְתִּי, *hope*, is rendered by ἐλπίς; and, in Ps. xxxviii. 7 (Heb. xxxix. 8), by ὑπόστασις. Philo (*De Abrahamo*, Works, *Mangey's Edit.*, tom. ii., pp. 38, 39) thus describes the efficacy and excellencies of faith :—Μόνον οὖν ἀψευδὲς καὶ βέβαιον ἀγαθόν, πίστις, ἡ πρὸς τὸν θεὸν πίστις, παραγόρημα βίου, πλήρωμα χρηστῶν ἐλπίδων, ἀφορία μὲν κακῶν, ἀγαθῶν δὲ φορά, κακοδαιμονίας ἀπόγνωσις, εὐσεβείας γνῶσις, εὐδαιμονίας κλῆρος, ψυχῆς ἐν ἅπασι βελτίωσις ἐπερηρεισμένης τῷ πάντων αἰτίῳ, καὶ δυναμένῳ μὲν πάντα, βουλομένῳ δὲ τὰ ἄριστα. "The sole good thing that disappoints not, and is "firm, is faith; that is to say, faith in God. It is the consolation of "life, the fulness of beneficial hopes, the dispeller of evils, the bringer "of good things, the renunciation of unhappiness, a confession of "piety, the inheritance of felicity, the advancement, in all things, of "the soul, which leans upon the Author of all things, even upon Him "who has power to do all things, but who wills the things that are "best."

² Οἱ πρεσβύτεροι, זְקֵנִים, *ancients.* See Is. xxiv. 23, where it is foretold of Messiah that "He shall reign before his ancients gloriously."

³ Ἐμαρτυρήθησαν κ.τ.λ. Ewald translates the first and second verses

thus:—"Es ist aber Glaube, Bestand in dem was man hofft, Beweis "für Dinge welche man nicht schauet; denn in diesem wurden die "Aelteren zu Zeugen" (for in this the Elders became, or, were made Witnesses). On which he remarks (pp. 122, 123), "*Wurden doch in* "*diesem*, und in nichts anderem, indem sie ihn hatten, *die Aelteren*, "die allverehrten Vorfahren aller Art, *zu zeugen* fur die göttliche Wahr- "heit." The London Jews' Society's translators have כי בואה הוקנים השיגו עדות.

And now, first of all, before entering upon the enumeration of the splendid muster-roll of worthies who "obtained a good report through faith," in terse and telling phraseology the writer gives a practical illustration of what faith is, and will be, unto the end of time.

Verse 3.—By faith we grasp the idea (νοοῦμεν)[1] that the worlds (universes) were framed by the word of God,[2] so that the things which we see, sprung from things that do not appear (εἰς τὸ μὴ ἐκ φαινομένων τὰ βλεπόμενα γεγονέναι, *ut ex invisibilibus visibilia fierent*.—Vulg. In other words, the conception of God pre-existent to matter, and by his fiat calling it into being, is beyond the domain of reason or demonstration. It is simply acquiesced in by an act of faith).

[1] Πίστει νοοῦμεν κατηρτίσθαι τοὺς αἰῶνας κ.τ.λ. The more literal translation of the Greek is, "by faith we grasp the idea that the worlds "(universes) were made by the word of God, so that the things which "we see, did not spring from things which have been indicated to us." And this agrees exactly with the assertion of Genesis i. 1, which tells us that *in beginning* (בראשית) God created the heavens and the earth. How long ago this event took place we are not told. We are not informed, in any other respect, concerning the primal materials of which the present creation (far less of previous creations) was elaborated. All that we know is, that immediately before the first day of our creation, the globe which we inhabit was in a state of chaos (תהו ובהו), and "darkness was upon the face of the deep, and the Spirit of God "moved upon the face of the waters." Here, then, the solid and fluid materials of our earth are mentioned, but *how* these were originally

called into existence we are not told. It is a matter of faith. We take the whole account upon the authority of God's Word. No written or traditional records survive the wreck of former worlds. The Hebrew word עולם, αἰών, is derived from עלם, *he concealed*, which derivation excellently illustrates the assertion of the writer to the Hebrews. God has entered into no præ-Adamite *details.* But this He has revealed, that creation had been for countless ages in a state of progression. And this is the answer which St. Peter gives to the ignorant and silly *dictum* of those who assert that, "since the fathers fell asleep, all things "continue exactly the same from the beginning of (not *the*) creation " (ἀπ' ἀρχῆς κτίσεως); "for," says he, "this intentionally escapes their "observation, that ages ago (ἦσαν ἔκπαλαι) the heavens existed, and "the earth, by the word of God (τῷ τοῦ Θεοῦ λογῷ), formed out of "water, and by means [*Alford*] of water."

J. C. Wolfius observes (*Curæ Phil. et Crit.*, p. 740, in loco), "Lucianus "in Philopatr., p. 138, edit Genev., ad h.l. merito existimatur allusisse, "quando ait ; ἐκ μὴ ὄντων εἰς τὸ εἶναι παρήγαγε." Again, Wolfius (*ibid.*, p. 741), "R. Elias, in *Adderet Elijahu*, distinguit inter creationem "דבר מן דבר שיהוה, *quâ res existit ex re alia*, et inter creationem, שיהוה "דבר כלא דבר, *quâ res ex alia* [non ?] *producitur*, h.e. quod addit, *ex* "*beneplacito Dei ad robur potentiæ suæ significandum.*" Compare 2 Macc. vii. 28, Ἀξιῶ σε, τέκνον, ἀναβλέψαντα εἰς τὸν οὐρανὸν καὶ τὴν γῆν, καὶ τὰ ἐν αὐτοῖς πάντα ἰδόντα, γνῶναι ὅτι ἐξ οὐκ ὄντων ἐποίησεν αὐτὰ ὁ Θεός, καὶ τὸ τῶν ἀνθρώπων γένος οὕτως γεγένηται. So also Philo (*SS. Legum Alleg.*, lib. i., Works, Mangey's Edit., tom. i , p. 47), writing on the words of Gen. ii. 4, "This is the book of the generations of the heavens and the "earth, when they were created," says :—

Ἵνα δὲ μὴ καθ' ὡρισμένας χρόνων περιόδους ὑπολάβῃς τὸ θεῖόν τι ποιεῖν ἀλλ' ἀειδῆ, ἄδηλα, ἀτέκμαρτα καὶ ἀκατάληπτα τῷ θνητῷ γένει τὰ δημιουργούμενα, ἐπιφέρει τὸ ὅτε ἐγένετο, τὸ πότε κατὰ περιγραφὴν οὐ διορίζων. Ἀπεριγράφως γὰρ γίνεται τὰ γινόμενα ὑπὸ τοῦ αἰτίου· ἀνῄρηται τοίνυν τὸ ἐν ἓξ ἡμέραις γεγενῆσθαι τὸ πᾶν. " In order to prevent you from supposing that the "Divinity does anything in specified periods of time, but that his "creative works are wrought after an unknown manner, unspecified, "undefined, and incomprehensible to the human race, he adds the "phrase ὅτε ἐγένετο, to show that he does not limit the exact period. "For whatever is done by the First Cause is illimitable. And thus it "is denied that *everything* was made in six days." (See note 4, p. 9.)

Ewald (*Das Sendschr. a.d. Hebr.*, p. 123) writes, in terms of forcible eloquence, upon this third verse of chap. xi., "Aber kaum hat der "Redner so den ersten Abschnitt geschlossen, und steht in Begriffe die "lange Reihe der Glaubenszeugen aus der vorchristlichen Zeit vorzu-

"führen, als er fühlt das die Wunderkraft unseres Glaubens, blickt
" man einmal in die Urzeiten, und dringt mit dem suchenden Geiste
" hier soweit als nur möglich im Andenken zurück, sogar noch über
" die bekannten Beispiele geschichtlicher Glaubenshelden hinausreicht.
" Fängt man nun xi. 3, bei der Ubersicht aller alten Geschichte überall
" gerne mit der Schöpfung an, so Können zwar die ersten Menschen
" nicht gerade als Muster des Glaubens dienen, da dieser erst in den
" hohen Verwicklungen der menschlichen Geschichte seine rechte Stelle
" findet: aber achtet man auch nur auf die Wunder der Schöpfung
" selbst wie schon bevor ein Mensch lebte *die Welten*, die himmlischen
" soweit sie geschaffen und vergänglich, sind die irdischen und die unter-
" irdischen, nach Gen. c. 1, in der wunderbarsten Weise vergänglich,
" und doch so wohl eingerichtet geschaffen wurden *sodass nicht aus*
" *erscheinendem* sinnlichem *durch das Wort Gottes das zu sehende* sinnlich
" *geworden ist*, so müssen wir sagen : auch dass jene allerersten über
" alles was man gewöhnlich Geschchite nennt herausgehenden, und in
" vielerlei Hinsicht wunderbarsten Dinge, wirklich einst so wurden,
" haben wir ja nicht sinnlich gesehen, wir *werden* dessen aber *durch*
" *Glauben inne*, weil wir es Gen. c. 1, lesen, und alle weitere Unter-
" suchung uns das dort von einer noch nicht menschlichen, sondern
" rein göttlichen Geschichte gesagte bestatigt. Und gewiss est ist die
" Wunderkraft des Glaubens welche nicht nur die Weissagung und
" Ahnung jeglicher Art, sondern auch alle ächte Wissenschaft trägt.
" Der Redner aber erinnert hier beilaufig umso lieber an *das Wort*
" *Gottes* je näher ihm, nach i. 3, iv. 12, überall auch *der Wort* Gottes
" vor dem Geiste steht."

[2] Ῥήματι Θεοῦ. Are these words a citation from Ps. xxxiii. 6 (LXX. xxxii. 6) ? And, if so, is it not a little remarkable that the writer has translated בדבר יהוה (τῷ λόγῳ τοῦ Κυρίου of the LXX.) by ῥήματι ? Ewald (*Das Sendschr. a d. Hebr.*, p. 10, and elsewhere) seems to imply that Philo's doctrine of the *Logos* largely leavens the Epistle to the Hebrews:
—" Nicht als hätte sich diese damals nicht schon seit vielen Jahrhun-
" derten innerhalb des Volkes der alten wahren Religion ausgebildet."
Now, although Philo and the Writer to the Hebrews frequently exhibit a surprising coincidence of thought and even of phraseology, it is not a little remarkable that our writer, apparently studiously, avoids the term *Logos*, as applied to the Son of God. A glance at the Greek concordance will show that, in Hebr. iv. 12 alone, can the term λόγος (and not necessarily even then) be applied to the Son of God. Such an omission is not a little significant. Philo and the New Testament writers held a great deal of religious truth in common, and especially the doctrine of the Logos, but that the Epistle to the Hebrews is

CHAP. XI., 4. 175

coloured by Philo's phraseology is contrary to fact.—Γεγένηται γὰρ ὁ κόσμος, καὶ πάντως ὑπ' αἰτίου τινὸς γέγονεν. Ὁ δὲ τοῦ ποιοῦντος λόγος αὐτός ἐστιν ἡ σφραγίς, ᾗ τῶν ὄντων ἕκαστον μεμόρφωται· παρ' ὃν καὶ τέλειον τοῖς γενομένοις ἐξ ἀρχῆς παρακολουθεῖ τὸ εἶδος, ἅτε ἐκμαγεῖον καὶ εἰκὼν τελείου λόγου. Τὸ γὰρ γενόμενον ζῶον, ἀτελές μέν ἐστι τῷ ποσῷ, μάρτυρες δ' αἱ καθ' ἡλικίαν ἑκάστην παραυξήσεις, τέλειον δὲ τῷ ποιῷ, μένει γὰρ ἡ αὐτὴ ποιότης, ἅτε ἀπὸ μένοντος ἐκμαχθεῖσα καὶ μηδαμῇ τρεπομένου θείου λόγου. "The world came into being, and it must assuredly have "had some author. But the very Word of the Creator is the seal, "according to which everything in existence was framed. Therefore "the perfect and ancient similitude accompanies every creature ; that "is to say, the impress and likeness of the perfect Word. For a living "being, when called into existence, is imperfect, perchance, in quantity, "as its gradual growth testifies ; but in quality it is perfect. For the "same workmanship it remains, having been modelled by the abiding "and immutable Divine Word."—Philo, *de Profugis*, Works, *Mangey's Edit.*, vol. i., pp. 547, 548. See Coloss. i. 15, and J. Wesselius' *Dissertat. Sacr.*, p. 497, *Lugd. Bat.* 1721. 4to. (See also note 4, p. 9.)

Verse 4.—By faith Abel offered to God a more ample (πλείονα, more excellent)[1] sacrifice than Cain, by which he obtained witness that he was righteous, God himself giving approving testimony to his gifts, and by it (*i.e.*, his faith, that led to his martyrdom) he being dead, yet speaketh.

[1] Πλείονα θυσίαν. See Heb. iii. 3, πλείονος δόξης, πλείονα τιμήν. Matt. v. 20, vi. 25, xii. 41, 42—Mark xii. 33, πλεῖόν ἐστι πάντων τῶν ὁλοκαυτημάτων καὶ τῶν θυσιῶν—Luke xi. 31, 32, xii. 23. Ewald (*Das Sendschr. a.d. Hebr.*, p. 44) translates :—"In Glauben brachte Abel "mehr Opfer als Kain Gotte dar, ihn durch den er das Zeugniss empfing "ein Gerechter zu seyn indem Gott über seinen Gaben dies bezeugte ; "und durch ihn redet er gestorben noch." See also *ibid.*, pp. 124, 125. The translators of the London Jews' Society's Hebrew New Testament have באמונה הקריב הבל לאלהים זבח יקר מקין וגו'. Abel is called δίκαιος, Matt. xxiii. 35. Comp. 1 John iii. 12. In both of these places he is spoken of in the light of a martyr, whilst in the former passage our Lord himself declares that his righteous blood, together with the righteous blood of all the other martyrs, even to that of Zacharias the son of Barachias, should be exacted of that guilty generation, *i.e*, at the destruction of Jerusalem by the Romans. Thus Christ places Abel at the head of the noble army of witnesses to God's truth, and denounces a terrible retribution

upon the Scribes and Pharisees, who should fill up the measure of their fathers' iniquity, by the persecutions and martyrdom of his disciples and followers. Here, I think, we obtain the clue to Abel's being placed by the Writer to the Hebrews at the head of the list. The Gospel of St. Matthew was early accepted, in the original *Syro-Chaldaic*, amongst the Hebrews. They were acquainted with the passage above cited. According to the familiar *usus loquendi* of the Hebrew idiom, he is spoken of there as *Abel the Just*. I cannot but think, then, that the Writer to the Hebrews alludes not only to typical atonement of the blood of the sacrifice of Abel, but also to the blood of Abel's own martyrdom which he simultaneously offered, and by which he also yet spake. It is quite worthy of remark that in Gen. iv. 10 the Hebrew expression is, קול דמי אחיך צעקים, "*a voice of bloods of thy brother crying*" (plur.), &c. (although the same expression is used in 2 Sam. iii. 28, מדמי אבנר, "*from the bloods* of Abner"). The same phrase, דמי אחיך, is repeated in verse 11. Of this peculiarity the Mishna (*Sanhedr.*, cap. iv. 5) takes especial notice. Speaking of the charge delivered to witnesses in case of life and death, viz., that they should be scrupulously conscientious in their statements, it says:—"Know that causes con-"cerning money are of a totally different character from capital causes. "Mistakes in the former may be compromised for a sum of money, but "in the latter the blood of the accused and the blood of his posterity "will be imputed unto the end of the world. We therefore read con-"cerning Cain when he slew his brother (Gen. iv. 10) קול דמי אחיך צעקים "*a voice of bloods of thy brother crying*. He says not דם, *blood*, but "דמי אחיך, *thy brother's bloods*, that is, *his blood, and the blood of his pos-*"*terities*, וזרעיותיו (his seeds). Another interpretation is, that דמי *bloods*, "are spoken of because his blood was sprinkled abroad on the trees and "stones."—*Mishna Sarenh.*, tom. iv., p. 229. Coccelus remarks on the above (*ibid.*, p. 230), "His דם est נפש (*i.e.*, by *blood* they understand "*soul*). Hi sic philosophantur: Animam Abelis non potuisse cœlo "recipi, quia nulla adhuc anima in cœlum intrasset: neque etiam "inferno, quia corpus sepultum nondum fuerit. Nam priusquam "corpus sepeliatur, animæ quietem non contingere.

*Nec ripas datur horrendas nec rauca fluenta
Transportare prius, quam sedibus ossa quierunt.*

"Ideo anima Abelis in sanguine super ligna, lapidesque dissipata est. "Miserum! Præclaram hanc expositionem habes in *Bereschith Rabba*, "cap. 22."

I have called attention to the above Rabbinic gloss, not as indorsing its interpretation, but as showing that the Talmudical writers regarded the expression דמי אחיך as peculiar, and deserving of a special explanation, an explanation which is in exact accordance with the Targum of Onkelos, who writes, "The voice of the blood of generations which "were to come from thy brother, complaineth before Me from the "earth." The Targum of Jonathan, on the other hand, has, "The "voice of the bloods of the murder of thy brother which are swallowed "up in the sod, crieth before me from the earth. And now because "thou hast killed him, thou art cursed from the earth, which hath "opened the mouth, and received the bloods of thy brother from thy "hand." The Jerusalem Targum has, "The voice of the blood of the "multitude of the righteous who were to arise from Habel thy brother," &c. The voice, then, that went forth from the innocent blood of Abel, was a cry for vengeance, even as St. John describes the souls of the martyrs beneath the altar as crying, "How long, O Lord, holy and true, "dost thou not judge, and avenge our blood on them that dwell on the "earth?" And this is probably one portion, and no small portion, of the signification which the Writer to the Hebrews intends to impart to the words of chap. xii. 24, καὶ αἵματι ῥαντισμοῦ, κρείττονα λαλοῦντι παρὰ τὸν Ἄβελ. J. C. Wolfius observes that two Codices have παρὰ τὸ Ἄβελ. But in either case the signification would not be materially different, when read by the light of Gen. iv. 10, 11. The blood of Abel cried for retribution ; the blood of Jesus, the first martyr's great antitype, speaks of Peace and Atonement. But how can it be affirmed that Abel died as a witness to the truth? In Gen. iv. 8 it is abruptly said, ויאמר קין אל הבל אחיו *and Cain said* (not וידבר *spake to his brother Abel*). And then, without mentioning the topic of Cain's address, the verse continues, "And it came to pass when they were in the field that Cain rose up "against Abel his brother and slew him." J. Selden (*de Jure Nat. et Gent.*, col. 1338, 1340, printed in Ugolini *Thes.*, vol. xxvii.) on the word בית דין, observes :—"Quo spectat etiam vetustissima illa Caini et Abelis "altercatio de Judicio coelesti et seculo futuro,

ואמר קין להבל אחוהי לית דין ולית דיין עלם אחרן ולית אגר טב לצדיקיא ולית פורענות לרשיעיא ואמר לקין אחוהי אית דין ואית דיין ואית עלם אחרן אית אגר טב לצדיקיא ואית פורענות לרשיעיא והוא במהויהון בחקלא וקם קין על הבל אחוהי וקטליה ׃

(" And Cain said to Abel his brother, *There is neither Judgment nor a* "*Judge, nor a world to come, nor any good reward for the just, nor punish-* "*ment for the wicked*. But Abel answered Cain his brother, *There is indeed* "*a Judgment, and a Judge, and a world to come. There is, moreover, a* "*good reward for the just and a punishment for the wicked*. And it came "to pass that whilst they were together in the field, Cain rose up against "Abel his brother and killed him.") Selden goes on to say that the above altercation is found in certain editions of the Hebrew Pautateuch, amongst the "additiones sive complementa, quibus, ex veterum tra-

A A

"ditione loca nonnulla insigniora Hebraici codicis Chaldaice expli-
"cantur," and specifies one printed at Constantinople, about 90 years
before, as containing it, where it is expressly פסוק ויאמר קין היספתא של
אל הבל אחיו "additio seu complementum versus, seu commatis. *Et dixit*
"*Cain Abeli fratri suo.*" He adds that in certain editions, which have
been more correctly printed according to the Hebrew MSS., *e.g.*,
Bomberg's, Buxtorf's, &c., the 8th verse of Gen. iv. is given as follows,
so as to show the hiatus, *sic.*,—

   * * * * ויאמר קין אל הבל אחיו
  ויהי בהיותם בשדה ויקם קין על הבל אחיו ויהרגהו

And Cain said to his brother Abel ——
And it came to pass whilst they were in the field that Cain rose
up against Abel his brother and slew him.

The Targum of Jonathan gives the conversation between Cain and
Abel almost exactly as above, prefacing it thus, "And Cain said to
"Abel his brother, Come and let us two go forth into the field. And it
"was that when they two had gone forth into the field, Cain answered
"and said to Abel, I perceive that the world was created in goodness,
"but it is not governed (or conducted) according to the fruit of good
"works, for there is respect to persons in judgment, therefore it is that
"thy offering was accepted, and mine not accepted with goodwill.......
"And because of these words they had contention upon the face of the
"field; and Cain arose against Abel his brother, and drave a stone into
"his forehead and killed him." The Jerusalem Targum is nearly identical
in its paraphrase. It will be seen, therefore, that the ancient Jewish Church
regarded Abel as a martyr to the truth. That the sacrifice which he
brought "of the firstlings of his flocks and of the fat thereof" was offered
in faith, and accepted as a typical atonement made by blood, who will deny?
Meanwhile, it will appear from the above-mentioned reasons that the
Writer to the Hebrews, with a felicitous discrimination, selected Abel's
name to stand foremost upon the muster-roll of worthies who obtained
a good report through faith, as the radiant crown of the bright cloud of
witnesses for the truth of God, as being the first who paid the forfeit
of his life for his faith. Philo (*De Sacrif. Abelis et Caini*) having noticed
(p. 176) how Cain was rejected because he brought his offering, neither
promptly (but "*after certain days,*" "*in process of time*") nor with a
willing mind, says :—"Ἄβελ δὲ ἤνεγκεν οὐ τὰ αὐτά, οὐδὲ τὸν αὐτὸν τρόπον,
ἀλλὰ ἀντὶ ἀψύχων ἔμψυχα, ἀντὶ νεωτέρων καὶ δευτερείων πρεσβύτερα καὶ
πρῶτα, ἀντὶ δὲ ἠσθενηκότων ἐρρωμένα καὶ πιότερα. Ἀπὸ γὰρ τῶν πρωτοτόκων τῶν προβάτων αὐτοῦ καὶ ἀπὸ τῶν στεάτων αὐτῶν φησι τὴν θυσίαν
ποιεῖσθαι κατὰ τὸ ἱερώτατον διάταγμα κ.τ.λ. "But Abel brought not the
"same things nor in the same fashion, but he brought, instead of

"lifeless, living things; instead of younger and secondary things, the "eldest and first; instead of weaker, strong and fat things. For he is "said to have made his sacrifice of the firstborn of his sheep, and of "their fat, in accordance with the most holy commandment." Exod. xiii. 11. (Works, *Mang.*, tom. i., p. 180.) So also on Gen. iv. 8, 10 (*deterius potiori insidiatur*, ibid., pp. 200, 201), he observes:—Ὦσθ' ὁ Ἀβελ, τὸ παραδοξότατον, ἀνῄρηταί τε καὶ ζῇ. Ἀνῄρηται μὲν ἐκ τοῦ ἄφρονος διανοίας, ζῇ δὲ τὴν ἐν θεῷ ζωὴν εὐδαίμονα. Μαρτυρήσει δὲ τὸ χρησθὲν λόγιον, ἐν ᾧ φωνῇ χρώμενος, καὶ βοῶν ἃ πέπονθεν ὑπὸ κακοῦ συνθέτου τηλαυγῶς εὑρίσκεται. Πῶς γὰρ ὁ μηκέτ' ὢν διαλέγεσθαι δυνατός; Ὁ μὲν δὲ σοφὸς τεθνηκέναι δοκῶν τὸν φθαρτὸν βίον, ζῇ τὸν ἄφθαρτον, ὁ δὲ φαῦλος ζῶν τὸν ἐν κακίᾳ, τέθνηκε τὸν εὐδαίμονα.

"So that Abel, most strange to tell, was killed and yet lives. He "was killed, as the simple may suppose; but he lives in God a life "of felicity. The Sacred Oracle will prove this. Where he is found "speaking, and expressly crying of the things which he suffered from "an evil person. But how is he able to discourse when he is no longer "alive? The Wise Man verily, whom men suppose to have died to this "mortal life, lives the immortal one, but the wicked, even whilst he "lives an evil life, has died to the life of felicity." (See 1 Tim. v. 6.) See also *ibid.*, p. 206 and p. 209.—See also Spencer, *De Legibus Hebraeorum Ritualibus*, Lib. iii., pp. 146—152, *Hagae Comitum*, 1696, 4to.—Reland, *Antiq. Sacrae Vet. Hebraeor.*, p. 315, *Ultraject.*, 1712, 8vo.,—also D. Asellius, *Veteris Testamenti Sacrificia*, pp. 18, 19 (*Duisburgi ad Rhen.* 1712, 8vo.), where he writes, "Ex loco Genes. iv. 4, *et respexit Jehovah ad Habelem et* "*ad Munus ejus,* vide vim vocis Num. xvi. 15, Amos v. 22, Ps. cxix. 117, "Ezech. xvi. 4, quod beneplacitum Deus, sine dubio et ex communi "Eruditorum consensu, ἐμπυρισμῷ, coelestique Sacrificii inflammatione "comprobavit, hinc illud ישׁו a Theodotione translatum per ἐνεπύρησε, "*inflammavit*, ut et Jarchi cum R. Salmone ad h.l. scite notat, אש ירדה "וילהב, *descendit ignis et inflammavit ejus victimam;* idem sentit Aben-"ezra......... *Verisimile est*, inquit, *ignem descendisse et Abelis quidam* "*oblationem* דשׁנה *in cinerem redigisse, Caini vero oblationem non item.* "Ex quo Apostolus, Ebr. xi. 4, Abelis in peracta oblatione fidem "concludit, *per quam testimonium nactus est, quod justus esset, testi-*"*monium perhibente super donis illius Deo, et per quam mortuus adhuc* "*loquitur,* sine fide enim est Deo εὐαρεστῆσαι, placere," &c.

Michaelis (*Introd. to New Testament, transl. by Marsh,* pp. 225, 226) says, "If the Epistle to the "Hebrews was written in Greek, and consequently

" the words quoted from the LXX. were quoted by
" the author himself, it is very extraordinary that,
" in the eleventh chapter, when he quotes from the
" Old Testament so many examples of faith, he
" should have omitted to mention, in vers. 4, 5, the
" name of Enosh, of whom it is said, in the LXX.,
" Gen. iv. 26, οὗτος ἤλπισεν ἐπικαλεῖσθαι τὸ ὄνομα Κυρίου
" τοῦ Θεοῦ, words which are so obviously to his
" purpose. Philo (*De Abr.*, Works, *Mang.*, tom. ii.,
" p. 2, and *De Poenis*, ibid., p. 410) has twice made
" use of this passage, in describing the hope which
" we ought to place in the Supreme Being," &c.
First of all, even as the passage is given in the
LXX., the instance is by no means one in point.
Enosh, according to it, affords the example of a
man who ventured upon the public worship of
Jehovah, but nothing is recorded of his career, that
would justify the Writer to the Hebrews in enrolling
his name amongst the noble army of martyrs, who
suffered for their faith, or overcame through it.
Secondly, no one was better aware than Michaelis
himself that the Writer to the Hebrews, and the
other New Testament writers, never copied slavishly
from the LXX. Lastly, the LXX. text is at variance with the Hebrew. In this instance, I do not
believe that the Septuagint translators had a "various
reading" before them, as Lud. Cappellus suggests
they had, in his *Crit. Sacr.*, p. 231. They gave a
paraphrase of what they thought was the intention
of the Sacred Writer, and they gave a wrong one.
The Hebrew of Gen. iv. 26 is, אז הוחל לקרא בשם יהוה,
literally, *then it was begun to call upon the name of*

Jehovah. The Targum of Onkelos paraphrases these words with an exactly opposite meaning:— " Then in his days the sons of men desisted (or " forbore) from praying in the name of the Lord ;" and the Targum of Palestine or Jonathan, " That " was the generation in whose days they began to " err, and to make themselves idols, and surnamed " their idols by the name of the Word of the Lord." Doubtless these latter interpretations arose from the well-known signification of the verb חלל, *to profane*. J. A. Danzius (*Schechina, ad Joh.* xiv. 23, p. 738e) quotes from *Bamidbar Rabba*, " Cum " generatione Enosi succedente, idololatræ fierent, " juxta (Gen. iv. 26) *Tunc profanatio introducta fuit*, " *nomine Jehovæ aliis tributo :* ideo subduxit Sche- " chinam vel cohabitationem (*sc.* Deus) in Expansum " tertium." Nevertheless, although חלל occurs only in Gen. iv. 26, in the *Hophal* conjugation, the *Englishman's Hebrew Concordance* gives more than fifty examples in which it signifies *to begin*, in the Hiphil. J. G. Meuschen, in his *Oratio de Directoribus Scholarum Hebræorum*, p. 1200 (printed in his *Nov. Test. ex Talmude illustr.*), quaintly asserts, " Hoc certum est, piissimi Sethi " optimum filium Henosum scholam, docente scrip- " tura (Gen. iv. 26), erexisse publicam ; et in illa " expossuisse divina oracula." Luther translates, " Zu derselbigen Zeit fing man an zu predigen von " des Herrn Namen " ; whilst the authorized Dutch version agrees with our English translation—" Toen " begon men den naam des Heeren aan te roepen." And so Delitzsch (*Die Genesis*, p. 163), "Damals,

" in der Zeit des Enos, wurde begonnen ה' בשם לקרא
" d.i. den Namen Jehova's anzurufen. . . . . Verg-
" leich man xii. 8, xiii. 4, xxi. 33, xxvi. 35, so
" kann man über den Sinn dieser Worte nicht
" zweifelhaft sein: mit Enos begann die förmliche
" und feierliche Verehrung Jehova's." The Vulgate,
on the other hand, has " Iste coepit invocare nomen
" Domini." It is but justice to Michaelis to add
that he says, " It may be said, however, in answer
" to this argument, that the author of the epistle
" consulted the Hebrew text, and, finding that the
" Greek differed from it, omitted the quotation."
Evidently our Göttingen Professor entertained a
very poor notion of the accurate acquaintance of
the canonical Jewish writers of the New Testament
with their own national records, as contained in the
Hebrew Scriptures. As to the notion of inspired
guidance in their writings, it is not worthy to be
taken into consideration !

Verses 5, 6.—By faith Enoch[1] was translated, so as not to
see death, and he was not found, for God translated him.
For, before his translation, it was testified of him that he
pleased God. But without faith it is impossible to please
Him. For he who cometh to God must believe that He is
(*i.e.*, in his personal and direct agency), and that He
becomes a rewarder of those who seek Him out carefully[2]
(καὶ τοῖς ἐκζητοῦσιν αὐτὸν μισθαποδότης γίνεται).

[1] Πίστει 'Ενὼχ μετετέθη κ.τ.λ. Having now spoken of Abel the first
martyr, the writer proceeds to mention Enoch, who was, to the Ante-
diluvian World, what Elijah was to the Mosaic, and Christ to our own,
viz., a guarantee of the reasonableness of the hope of a glorious immortality, even of that true life which is hid with Christ in God. Enoch
and Elijah doubtless form no exception to the laws of our nature which

CHAP. XI., 5, 6. 183

make it impossible for flesh and blood to see the kingdom of God. They underwent the change which St. Paul assures the Corinthians (1 Cor. xv. 51, 52) shall overtake those who are on earth at Christ's appearing. We shall not all sleep (κοιμηθησόμεθα), but we shall be changed (ἐν ἀτόμῳ, ἐν ῥιπῇ ὀφθαλμοῦ). The dead shall be raised, and "we who remain shall be changed." This putting off corruption was instantaneously effected by the power of God in the two cases abovementioned. Of Christ, the apostle emphatically writes (1 Cor. xv. 20), Νυνὶ δὲ Χριστὸς ἐγήγερται ἐκ νεκρῶν, ἀπαρχὴ τῶν κεκοιμημένων ἐγένετο. It was needful, in order to show forth the exceeding greatness of his power, and the reality of his victory over death and the grave, that He should sleep among the dead. It was by his power, that these his servants, Enoch and Elijah, were translated. Although Philo (*De Abrahamo*, Works, Mangey's edition, vol. ii., pp. 3, 4, and *De Præmiis et Pœnis*, ibid., p. 411, and also *De Nominum Mutatione*, ibid., vol. i., p. 584) allegorises the translation of Enoch, and the fact that he "was "not found," and explains it of "conversion from a worldly life and "carnal pursuits"; yet, in the last mentioned passage, he says, Ἐπειδὴ καὶ μετατεθῆναι λέγεται, τὸ δ' ἐστι, μεταστῆναι καὶ μετοικίαν στείλασθαι τὴν ἀπὸ θνητοῦ βίου πρὸς τὸν ἀθάνατον, "But when he is said to have been "translated, this signifies that he migrated, and proceeded from this "mortal life to the immortal." In like manner Philo speaks of Abraham (*De Sacr. Abelis et Caini*), Καὶ γὰρ Ἀβραὰμ ἐκλιπὼν τὰ θνητὰ προστίθεται τῷ θεοῦ λαῷ, καρπούμενος ἀφθαρσίαν, ἴσος ἀγγέλοις γεγονώς· ἄγγελοι γὰρ στρατός εἰσι θεοῦ, ἀσώματοι καὶ εὐδαίμονες ψυχαί. "Abraham also having "quitted this mortal state, is united to the people of God, being a "partaker of incorruption, and having become equal to the angels; for "the angels are the host of God, incorporeal and happy souls." (Works, *Mang.*, vol. i., p. 164.) Josephus (*Antiq.* i., 3, 4) mentions the translation of Enoch in the following terms :— Οὗτος ζήσας πέντε καὶ ἑξήκοντα πρὸς τοῖς τριακοσίοις, ἀνεχώρησε πρὸς τὸ θεῖον· ὅθεν οὐδὲ τελευτὴν αὐτοῦ ἀναγεγράφασι. "This man having lived 365 years, departed to "the divine estate; and this is why they have not recorded his end." The Rabbies, and especially the Cabbalists, have indulged in a variety of wild theories respecting Enoch, *e.g*, that he was identical with מטטרון, Metatron, a name given to the Angel of the Covenant, or Michael, and which statement is found in the Targum of Jonathan. See Surenhusius, Βιβλ. Καταλλ., pp. 708—712, and J. Rhenferdii, *Observatio ad Judæ epist.*, v. 14, p. 1044 (Meuschen). But what is more important, is the fact that the doctors of the early Jewish Church were not ignorant of the prophetic declaration of Enoch cited by St. Jude (who calls him, after the Jewish fashion, ἕβδομος ἀπὸ 'Ἀδὰμ, שביעי מאדם),

and which declares that Christ shall come with ten thousands of his saints, to execute judgment upon all." Here, then, we have in miniature, the sum of Enoch's faith, by which he pleased God, and also the explanation of the statement that " he that cometh to God, must believe " that He is, and He is a μισθαποδότης of all those who diligently seek " Him." Observe, that St. Jude by no means guarantees the authenticity of the apocryphal book of Enoch. He simply endorses as genuine, a single saying of the prophet's. Enoch's faith, then, consisted in a persuasion that Christ would come ; that He would come to judgment; that He would bring his saints with Him. It was a very definite one (see Ewald, *Das Sendschr. a.d. Hebr.*, p. 128), being, in fact, a Præmessianic Christianity. Surenhusius observes (p. 712), in reference to Jude 14, " Eadem Phraseologia occurrit apud Mosem Deut. xxxiii. 2, " ואתה מרבבות קדש *et veniet* (Dominus) *cum myriadibus sanctitatis*, ubi " D. Raschi notat per simplicem vocem קדש intelligendos esse מלאכי קדש " *angelos sanctos*. Hanc phrasin Apostolus Paulus etiam imitatus est in " 1 Thess. iii. 13, μετὰ πάντων τῶν ἁγίων αὐτοῦ." It is plain, however, from 1 Thess. iv. 14, that not only the angels are intended, for there it is written, " Them also which sleep in Jesus will God bring with him." In conclusion, I would observe that Enoch is cited by the wiiter to the Hebrews, as an example and witness to the consoling truth, that a careful walk with God, in the midst of a crooked and blaspheming generation, cannot fail to meet with the promised recompense of reward in eternal life.

² Πιστεῦσαι γὰρ δεῖ κ.τ.λ. Philo writes as follows (*Quis rerum divin. hæres.*) in commendation of the excellency of an unhesitating faith in God :—Εὖ δὲ τὸ φάναι, λογισθῆναι τὴν πίστιν εἰς δικαιοσύνην αὐτῷ. Δίκαιον γὰρ οὕτως οὐδέν, ὡς ἀκράτῳ καὶ ἀμιγεῖ τῇ πρὸς θεόν μόνον πίστει κεχρῆσθαι. Τὸ δὲ δίκαιον καὶ ἀκόλουθον τοῦτο τῇ φύσει, παράδοξον ἐνομίσθη διὰ τὴν τῶν πολλῶν ἀπιστίαν ἡμῶν, οὓς ἐλέγχων ὁ ἱερὸς λόγος φησίν, ὅτι τὸ ἐπὶ μόνῳ τῷ ὄντι βεβαίως καὶ ἀκλινῶς ὁρμεῖν, θαυμαστὸν μὲν παρ' ἀνθρώποις, οἷς ἀγαθῶν ἀδόλων κτῆσις οὐκ ἔστιν, οὐ θαυμαστὸν δὲ παρ' ἀληθείᾳ βραβευούσῃ, δικαιοσύνης δ' αὐτὸ μόνον ἔργον. " It is well spoken, that faith was reckoned to him " for righteousness ; since there is nothing so just as to have a sincere " and unmixed faith in God alone. But this, although just and agree-" able to nature, has been accounted paradoxical, on account of the " unbelief of many amongst us. In reproof of whom, the Holy Scrip-" ture declares, that to lean fixedly and firmly upon HIM WHO ALONE " Is (Jehovah), although surprising to men who do not possess unalloyed " good things, is nevertheless not so in Truth's award, for it is the very " work of righteousness itself." (Works, *Mangey's Edit.*, vol. i., p. 486.)

And again, *ibid.*, pp. 485, 486 :—

Ἀναγκαίως οὖν ἐπιλέγεται, ἐπίστευσεν Ἀβραὰμ τῷ Θεῷ, πρὸς ἔπαινον τοῦ πεπιστευκότος. Καίτοι τάχα ἄν τις εἴποι, τοῦτ' ἄξιον ἐπαίνου κρίνετε; τίς δὲ οὐκ ἄν τι λέγοντι καὶ ὑπισχνουμένῳ Θεῷ προσέχοι τὸν νοῦν, κἂν εἰ πάντων ἀδικώτατος καὶ ἀσεβέστατος ὢν τυγχάνοι; πρὸς ὅν ἐροῦμεν, μὴ ὦ γενναῖε, ἀνεξετάστως, ἢ τὸν σοφὸν ἀφέλῃ τὰ πρέποντα ἐγκώμια, ἢ τοῖς ἀναξίοις τὴν τελειωτάτην ἀρετῶν πίστιν μαρτυρήσῃς, ἢ τὴν ἡμετέραν περὶ τούτων γνῶσιν αἰτιάσῃ. Βαθυτέραν γὰρ εἰ βουληθείης ἐρευνᾶν καὶ μὴ σφόδρα ἐπιπόλαιον ποιήσασθαι, σαφῶς γνώσῃ ὅτι μόνῳ Θεῷ χωρὶς ἑτέρου προσπαραλήψεως οὐ ῥᾴδιον πιστεῦσαι, διὰ τὴν πρὸς τὸ θνητὸν ᾧ συνεζεύγμεθα, συγγένειαν· ὅπερ ἡμᾶς καὶ χρήμασι, καὶ δόξῃ, καὶ ἀρχῇ καὶ φίλοις, ὑγείᾳ τε καὶ ῥώμῃ σώματος, καὶ ἄλλοις πολλοῖς ἀναπείθει πεπιστευκέναι. Τὸ δὲ ἐκνίψασθαι τούτων ἕκαστον, καὶ ἀπιστῆσαι γενέσει τῇ πάντα ἐξ ἑαυτῆς ἀπίστῳ, μόνῳ δὲ πιστεῦσαι Θεῷ· τῷ καὶ πρὸς ἀλήθειαν μόνῳ πιστῷ, μεγάλης καὶ ὀλυμπίου διανοίας ἔργον ἐστί, πρὸς οὐδενὸς οὐκέτι δελεαζομένης τῶν παρ' ἡμῖν.

"Of necessity therefore it is added, *Abraham believed God*, in praise
"of him who believed. Perchance some one will say, Do you, then,
"think this worthy of praise? What man is there, however depraved
"and irreligious he might be, who would not render credence to God,
"should He speak to him and promise him anything? To such an
"objector we would reply, Beware, good Sir, that you defraud not the
"wise man of the encomiums which he has so well deserved; nor impute
"to unworthy persons faith, that most perfect of virtues; nor impugn
"the opinion which we have expressed above. If you will only be at
"the pains to investigate a little deeper, and not to act in so entirely
"superficial a manner, you will clearly discover that to believe in God
"only, without the aid of any other support, is no easy matter, on
"account of our close affinity with the mortal nature to which we are
"so nearly yoked together. For the latter persuades us to believe in
"money, and glory, and power, and friends, and bodily health and
"strength, and many other objects. But to purge away all these, and
"to renounce entirely any confidence in the creature which is most
"unworthy of credit, and to believe only in God, who is, in very truth,
"alone worthy of belief, this is the achievement of a great and celestial
"mind, uncaptivated by anything such as this world affords us."

From Enoch, the writer passes on to the example of Noah, who believed in God's predictions of coming doom at a time when all things seemed to speak of the permanency of the world that then was, instead of its overthrow. He acted upon the admonition that he had received, and made all needful preparations, and so when the time came for God's vengeance to awake, and to destroy an unbelieving and apostate earth, Noah realised that he had made a wise choice. He entered into the ark with his family, and was saved from the overthrow of the wicked.

Verse 7.—By faith [1] Noah, having been oracularly advertised concerning things of which there was not the smallest visible indication (περὶ τῶν μηδέπω βλεπομένων), took the warning reverently to heart (εὐλαβηθεὶς) and constructed an ark for the preservation of his household, by which he condemned the world (κατέκρινε τὸν κόσμον), (*i.e.*, he demonstrated its fatuous incredulity in refusing to listen to his protracted preaching—the world derided, but he was saved), and (also) became an heir of the righteousness which is by faith (καὶ τῆς κατὰ πίστιν δικαιοσύνης ἐγένετο κληρονομος, *i.e.*, he became an heir expectant).[2]

---

[1] Πίστει χρηματισθεὶς Νῶε κ.τ.λ. Ewald translates the passage thus :—
" In Glauben bereitete Noah, gottgewarnt über das noch nicht zu
" schauende, in ächter scheu einen Kasten zum Heile seines Hauses,
" ihm durch den er die Welt verurtheilte," &c.

[2] We must not, in interpreting these signal victories of faith over temptation and the world, suffer ourselves to wander into vague generalities and diffuse platitudes, but keep closely to the design which the Writer to the Hebrews has in view, in holding them up to the persecuted and wavering converts for imitation. Many true and excellent remarks may be made in respect to the above, but such digressions can only serve to divert our attention from the primary warning and consolation which they are intended to convey. The real point at issue is, *how did these historical events bear upon the subject which occupied the writer's thoughts?* How are the episodes related, in consolatory parallelism with the condition of those to whom, *for a very definite purpose,* they

were recited ? The writer is contrasting the advantages πίστεως, with the perilous drawbacks ὑποστολῆς. He is illustrating and exemplifying the declaration in Habak. ii. 4, "His soul which is lifted up is not upright "in him, but the just shall live by his faith." (See note 7, pp. 164—168) To this idea we must keep close if we would elicit the true meaning of the writer to the Hebrews. The words of Habakkuk are, so to speak, the text upon which the discourse contained in the 11th and 12th chapters of the Hebrews is based. To understand the real drift of the sermon, we must not allow the text to pass out of our recollections. To my mind, then, the resemblance between the position of Noah and the Hebrew Christians consists in the condition of isolation in which, as believers, they found themselves. Noah must have made great sacrifices to accomplish what the world considered a mad scheme. The construction of the ark must have given occasion to many a sneer and witticism. The result proved that he was right and they were wrong. The flood came and destroyed all the infidels. So it was with the converts from Judaism. They had sacrificed their all. They had become the filth and offscouring of the world. Was, then, the loss commensurate with the expected reward ? Yes verily ! It was but ἔτι μικρὸν ὅσον ὅσον, and then the deluge of fire and blood broke loose upon devoted Judæa. The Hebrew Church and nation, the temple, and all else that seemed so fair and substantial (Matt. xxiv. 1, 2,— Mark xiii. 1, 2,—Luke xxi. 5, 6), were swept away. But at Pella the believers had taken refuge ; they had fled from the city, as Christ bid them to do when they should see Jerusalem encompassed with armies, and not one of them perished in the overthrow of the unbelievers. Thus they also "condemned" the world, and afterwards became inheritors of the righteousness which is by faith. I cannot help thinking the expression τῆς κατὰ πίστιν δικαιοσύνης ἐγένετο κληρονόμος means far more than merely that Noah was *put in possession* of justification by faith. It seems to me to indicate that he became a progenitor of the promised Messiah. (Luke iii. 36.) Philo (*De migratione Abrahami*) in commenting on the promise given to Abraham, "In thee shall all "the families of the earth be blessed," adduces Noah as an illustration of the fact that the blessings of good men are transmitted to latest posterity, inasmuch as he became one of the ancestors of Israel : ἐναργέστατον δὲ παράδειγμα Νῶε ὁ δίκαιος, ὃς τῷ μεγάλῳ κατακλυσμῷ τῶν τοσούτων μερῶν τῆς ψυχῆς ἐγκαταποθέντων, ἐρρωμένως ἐπικυματίζων καὶ ἐπινηχόμενος, ὑπεράνω μὲν ἔστη τῶν δεινῶν ἁπάντων, διασωθεὶς δὲ μεγάλας καὶ καλὰς ἀφ' αὑτοῦ ῥίζας ἐβάλλετο, ἐξ ὧν οἷα φυτὸν τὸ σοφίας ἀνεβλάστησε γένος, ὅπερ ἡμεροτόκησαν, τοὺς τοῦ ὁρῶντος Ἰσραὴλ, τρίττους ἤνεγκε καρποὺς, αἰῶνος μέτρα, τὸν Ἀβραὰμ, τὸν Ἰσαὰκ, τὸν Ἰακώβ. " We

"have a bright example in Noah the Just, who at the great flood,
"when so large a portion of human life was drowned, bravely rode out
"the waves and swam aloft, and so escaped all the horrors of the dread
"scene. But after his escape he put forth fair and widespread roots,
"from which, like a plant, the race of Wisdom buddeth forth. This
"plant with genial fecundity bore the three fruits of Israel who yet
"sees it, coæval with eternity, to wit, Abraham, Isaac, and Jacob."
(Works, *Mangey's Edit.*, vol. i., p. 455.) So also the same author writes
again (*De Abrahamo*),— Μόνος δὲ εἶς οἶκος, ὁ τοῦ λεχθέντος ἀνδρὸς δικαίου
καὶ θεοφιλοῦς, διασώζεται, δύο λαβόντος τὰς ἀνωτάτω δωρέας, μίαν μὲν, ἥν
εἶπον, τὸ μὴ πᾶσι τούτοις συναπολέσθαι, ἑτέραν δὲ τὸ πάλιν αὐτὸν ἀρχηγέτην
ὑπάρξαι νέας ἀνθρώπων σπορᾶς· ἠξίωσε γὰρ αὐτὸν ὁ Θεὸς καὶ τέλος ἡμῶν
τοῦ γένους καὶ ἀρχὴν γενέσθαι, τέλος μὲν τῶν πρὸ τοῦ κατακλυσμοῦ, τῶν
δὲ μετὰ τὸν κατακλυσμὸν, ἀρχήν. " But only one household, to wit, that
" of this aforesaid just and God-beloved man, was saved ; and he
" received the two above-mentioned gifts: first, that he should not
" perish with the rest of mankind ; the second, that he should be the
" head and founder of a new generation of men. For God honoured
" him to be, so to speak, the end and the beginning of our race. The
" last of those before the flood, and the first of those that came after
" it." (Works, *Mangey's Edit.*, vol ii., p. 8.)—In Ezek. xiv. 14–20, Noah
is spoken of as being one of the cardinal saints of the Old Testament
dispensation, and Philo (*De Congress. quær. erudit. gratia*, ibid. p. 533)
notices that Noah is the first to be called "just" in the Holy Scriptures,
πρῶτος δ' οὗτος δίκαιος ἐν ταῖς ἱεραῖς ἀνερρήθη γραφαῖς. He alludes to
Gen. vi. 9, vii. 1, where it is said, איש צדיק תמים היה בדרתיו את האלהים
התהלך נח, and, כי אתך ראיתי צדיק לפני בדור הזה. Here, then, we see that
Noah received the same testimony that " *he walked with God,*" as
Enoch did. What Enoch's faith was we have already seen. The
hopes and belief cherished by Noah are apparent from Gen ix. 26, 27,
which the Targum of Onkelos paraphrases thus,—" Blessed be the
" Lord God of Shem, and Canaan shall be servant to them. The Lord
" shall enlarge Japheth, and he shall make his Shekinah to dwell in the
" tabernacles of Shem." The Targum of Jonathan renders the concluding words thus,—" The Lord shall beautify the borders of Japheth,
" and his sons shall be proselyted and dwell in the schools of Shem,"
&c. From this it will be evident that the early Jewish doctors regarded
the prophecy of Noah as predictive of the kingdom of Messiah and the
conversion of the Gentiles. Great importance attaches to these Targumic interpretations of Scripture, inasmuch as there is good ground
for believing that they afford a fair index of current Jewish opinion in
apostolic times. Some even assign to them an earlier date. The

assent of our judgment may not *always* go with them, but in very many instances they are palpably right. Consolatory it is to see that in all ages of the Church there has been but "one faith,"—that God from the very first appointed one and the same method of salvation, viz., faith in the atoning blood of his Blessed Son. The patriarchs and the "Seed of Wisdom" looked for a coming Saviour, whilst we who live in the "latter days" can take up the exulting words of the Beloved Disciple (1 John iv. 14) and say, "We have seen and do testify, that "the Father sent the Son to be the Saviour of the World." For an excellent sketch of the times of Noah, and of the condition of mankind immediately before the flood, the reader may, with profit, consult Dr. Delitzsch's work *Die Genesis*, pp. 172—179.

The examples have now been adduced of Abel the first martyr; of Enoch the Witness to the hope of Immortality and Glory; of Noah the Just, whose faithful walk, and the unshakeable credit which he ascribed to the promises of God, not only carried him safely through the wreck of an apostate world, but also made him the progenitor and heir-expectant of the Messiah. The writer now proceeds to dilate upon the self-abnegation and sacrifices which Abraham made by faith. He was the founder and father of the Hebrew race; the depositary of all the promises, whether to the Jewish people or to the world at large. And yet, illustrious as he was, his career was one of self-denial, of agonising suspense, of renunciation of all family ties and worldly endearments. He was honourable at home, and very rich in cattle, in silver, and in gold (Gen. xiii. 2), yet all these advantages were to be foregone. Had he been so minded, he might have lived in affluence and respect amongst his kindred in his father's house. But instead of this, a life of perpetual pilgrimage and vagrancy was imposed upon him. His rich possessions were to be dependent upon the precarious tenure of the goodwill and forbearance of the lawless inhabitants of Canaan. Living *in* the world, he lived above it. The one object which he placed before him, as the solace of his renunciation of all that was dear and desirable in this life, was the certain fulfilment of the Promise, that *in his seed* all the families of the earth should be blessed. This was the next example set before the repining and persecuted Hebrew converts to take pattern by.

Verses 8, 9.—By faith Abraham when called [1] (Gen. xii. 1—3) obeyed, even to going forth to the place which he was to receive as an heritage (εἰς κληρονομίαν), and he did go forth, having no definite knowledge whither he was bound.[2] (Gen. xii. 5—7.) By faith he migrated to the land of promise, although it was not yet his own (ὡς ἀλλοτρίαν *while it belonged to strangers*.—Stuart), taking up his abode in tents with Isaac and Jacob, and the other joint heirs-expectant (συνκληρονόμων) of the same promise.

[1] Πίστει καλούμενος ᾿Αβραάμ. Ewald renders "he who is to be called Abraham," remarking, " Nicht umsonst wird Abraham sogleich " von vorne v. 8, als *der Abraham zu* nennende vorgeführt, theils weil " er nach Gen. xii. damals erst Abram, noch nicht Abraham hiess, " theils und noch mehr weil dieser Name nach Gen. xvii. 4, f. mit der " Verheissung der zahlreichsten Nachkommenschaft zusammenhängt." (*Das Sendschr. a.d. Hebr.*, p. 127.) And again (*ibid.*, p. 170), " Das " Wörtchen ὁ, vor καλούμενος, findet sich zwar in *Sin.* nicht, ist aber " gewiss ursprünglich. Sollte das Wort bedeuten *berufen*, so müsste " es κληθείς heissen und hinter ᾿Αβραάμ stehen." The translators of the London Jews' Society's New Testament have באמונה שמע אברהם בהקרא.

[2] Μὴ ἐπιστάμενος ποῦ ἔρχεται. This was the first practical demonstration of Abraham's faith. He forsook all that was most dear and desirable, and followed the hope of the promised Messiah. He committed his lifelong prospects to the custody of the promise. It was no

rash and ill-weighed enterprise. He was at the time of his call of the mature age of 75 years, " when he departed out of Haran " (Gen. xii. 4). He had counted the cost, and come to the conclusion that "the suffer-"ings of this present time are not worthy to be compared with the "glory that shall be revealed." He obeyed, therefore, unhesitatingly when God said unto him, "Get thee out of thy country, and from thy "kindred, and from thy father's house, unto a land that I will shew "thee: and I will make of thee a great nation, and I will bless thee, "and make thy name great; and thou shalt be a blessing: and I will "bless them that bless thee, and curse him that curseth thee; and in "thee (ונברכו בך) shall all families of the earth be blessed." (Gen. xii. 1—3). This last clause the Jerusalem Targum renders, "*and in thy* "*righteousness shall all the generations of the earth be blessed.*" The promise was a very wide one; but Abraham was contented to act upon it, and to leave the accomplishment to God. His faith was therefore in the strictest sense ἐλπιζομένων ὑπόστασις, πραγμάτων ἔλεγχος οὐ βλεπομένων. By it he exchanged immediate advantage for future blessedness, good things present for good things to come. " Glauben war es " hier und dort welcher ihn trieb, Glauben an Gott und seinen höheren " Segen welcher zur rechten Zeit schon kommen werde, wie es v. 6, " hiess: sowie hier v. 10 hinzugefügt wird dass es doch inderthat nicht " dieses unruhige Zeltleben seyn konnte in welchem er die Erfüllung " aller Verheissungen zu sehen hatte, dass vielmehr schon Abraham " die nach Ps. lxxxvii. 1, *wohlgegründete Stadt erwartete deren Künstler* " *und Werkmeister* kein geringerer als *Gott ist*, das himmlische oder " Messianische Jerusalem, in dessen Bilde sich zur Zeit unseres Redners " alle Messianische Hoffnung leicht zusammen drängte, und das er hier " umso triffender beiläufig erwähnt, da es ja auch dem oben soviel " besprochenen irdische Heiligthum engegensteht." (Ewald, *Das Sendschr. a.d. Hebr.*, pp. 126, 127.) And so Philo writes,—ἅμα τῷ κελευθῆναι μετανίστατο, καὶ τῇ ψυχῇ πρὸ τοῦ σώματος τὴν ἀποικίαν ἐστέλλετο, τὸν ἐπὶ τοῖς θνητοῖς ἵμερον παρευημεροῦντος ἔρωτος οὐρανίου. Οὐδενὸς οὖν φροντίσας, οὐ φυλετῶν, οὐ δημοτῶν, οὐ συμφοιτητῶν, οἷχ ἑταίρων, οὐ τῶν ἀφ' αἵματος ὅσοι πρὸς πατρὸς ἢ μητρὸς ἦσαν, οὐ πατρίδος οὐκ ἀρχαίων ἐθῶν, οὐ συντροφίας, οὐ συνδιαιτήσεως, ὧν ἕκαστον ἀγωγόν τε καὶ δυσαπόσπαστον, ὁλκὸν ἔχον δύναμιν, ἐλευθέροις καὶ ἀφέτοις ὁρμαῖς ᾗ τάχιστα μετανίσταται, τὸ μὲν πρῶτον ἀπὸ τῆς Χαλδαίων γῆς, εὐδαίμονος χώρας, καὶ κατ' ἐκεῖνον ἀκμαζούσης τὸν χρόνον, εἰς τὴν Χαρραίων γῆν· ἔπειτα οὐ μακρὰν ὕστερον, καὶ ἀπὸ ταύτης εἰς ἕτερον τόπον κ.τ.λ.

" As soon as ever he (Abraham) received the command, he moved " out; but he began his removal from home in spirit before he did so " in person, and subordinated his affection for mortal things to the love "of heavenly things. He set on one side, therefore, the ties of "nationality, of people, of associations, of friends, of paternal and "maternal relationships, of country, of time-honoured habits, inti- "macies, and daily intercourse, each of which has a potent and attractive "influence, which cannot lightly be burst asunder or neutralized ; and, "of his pure and simple free will, he set out as quickly as he could, at "first from the land of the Chaldæans, which was at that period a "well-to-do and flourishing region, to the land of Charran. And no "long period afterwards, he migrated into another place," &c. (*De Abrahamo*, Works, *Mangey's Edit.*, vol. ii., p. 11.)

And again (*De Migratione Abrahami*, ibid., vol. i., p. 442, 443), Παρατετηρημένως δὲ οὐ τὸν ἐνεστῶτα, ἀλλὰ τὸν μέλλοντα τῇ ὑποσχέσει χρόνον προδιωρίσται, εἰπὼν, οὐχ ἣν δείκνυμι, ἀλλ' ἣν σοι δείξω, εἰς μαρτυρίαν πίστεως ἣν ἐπίστευσεν ἡ ψυχὴ Θεῷ, οὐκ ἐκ τῶν ἀποτελεσμάτων ἐπιδεικνυμένη τὸ εὐχάριστον, ἀλλ' ἐκ προσδοκίας τῶν μελλόντων. Ἀρτηθεῖσα γὰρ καὶ ἐκκλεμασθεῖσα ἐλπίδος χρηστῆς, καὶ ἀνενδοίαστα νομίσασα ἤδη παρεῖναι τὰ μὴ παρόντα, διὰ τὴν τοῦ ὑποσχομένου βεβαιοτάτην πίστιν ἀγαθὸν τέλειον, ἆθλον εὕρηται.

"Very guardedly, he defines, in the promise, not the *present*, but "the *future* time ; for he says, not [a land] *which I do tell thee of*, but, "*which I will tell thereof*, in testimony of the faith wherewith his soul "believed in God, and gave thanks, not for completed favours, but "from an expectation of things yet to come. For as it hung and was "suspended from a good hope, and unhesitatingly esteemed things "which were not as yet present to be present, on account of the most "assured fidelity of Him who promised, it received a perfect good "thing as its reward."

The same writer (*De Abrahamo*, ibid., vol. ii., p. 38) refers to Abraham's faith in the following terms :—Ἔστι δὲ καὶ ἀνάγραπτος ἔπαινος αὐτοῦ, χρησμοῖς μαρτυρηθεὶς, οὓς Μωϋσῆς ἐθεσπίσθη, δι' οὗ μηνύεται ὅτι ἐπίστευσε τῷ Θεῷ. Ὅπερ λεχθῆναι μέν βραχύτατόν ἐστιν, ἔργῳ δὲ βεβαιωθῆναι μέγιστον. "But his eulogy exists in writing, witnessed to by the "sacred oracles which Moses, by Divine inspiration, indited. By him "(Moses) it is intimated that *he believed God*. This is a thing very "easily said, but very difficult to be carried into practice."

Verse 10.—For he expected (ἐξεδέχετο, i.e., *waited, kept his hopes and desires in reserve for*) the city which hath the foundations, whose architect and founder is God.¹

¹ It had been distinctly revealed to Abraham (Gen. xv. 7, 13—21) that the promise and grant of Canaan was for a remote period, and

would not be ratified until after his death. "And He said, I am the
"Lord that brought thee out of Ur of the Chaldees to give thee this
"land to inherit it. And he said, Lord God, whereby shall I know
"that I shall inherit it.........And He said unto Abraham, Know of a
"surety that thy seed shall be a stranger in a land that is not theirs,
"and shall serve them, and they shall afflict them four hundred years.
"And also that nation whom they shall serve, will I judge ; and after-
"ward shall they come out with great substance. And thou shalt go to
"thy fathers in peace; thou shalt be buried in a good old age. But in
"the fourth generation they shall come hither again : for the iniquity
"of the Amorites is not yet full.........In the same day the Lord made
"a covenant with Abraham, saying, Unto thy SEED have I given this
"land, from the River of Egypt, unto the Great River, the river
"Euphrates." This promise for Abraham's seed, and not for himself,
was given to him immediately after the assurance that God himself
would be his "shield and exceeding great reward." The Patriarch,
upon receiving this personal promise, had complained, "Behold to me
"thou hast given no seed, and lo one born in my house is my heir."
"And behold the word of the Lord came unto him, saying, This shall
"not be thine heir (viz.. Eliezer of Damascus), but he that shall come
"forth out of thine own bowels shall be thine heir. And he brought
"him forth abroad, and said, Look now toward heaven, and tell the
"stars, if thou be able to number them ; and He said, So shall thy seed
"be. And he believed in the Lord; and He counted it to him for
"righteousness." Here, then, Abraham was left in no doubt whatever,
that he should not participate in the possession of Canaan, at the same
time that he was told, that his own reward should be a Divine one. He
was contented to dwell in tents, to fulfil the appointed days of his
sojourning, because he expected *the city above that hath foundations,
whose builder and maker is God.*—Ewald (*Das Sendschr. a.d. Hebr.* p.
128) observes, *in loc.*, "Und jedenfalls erhellt.........das die Religion
"der Erzväter schon eine verhältnissmässig sehr geistige von ewig
"nachwirkender Bedeutung war." Abundant mention is made of the
heavenly city of God, in the Old Testament Scriptures. It signified the
eternal rest and peace, which God has provided in heaven, for all his
believing servants. It is truly "the mother of us all." (Gal. iv. 26.)
And thus the Rabbies have referred, Is. xxvi. 1—2, to the world to
come. (See Balth. Scheidii, *Loca Talmudica, in Matt.* xix. 14, Meuschen,
Nov. Test. ex Talmudi illustr., p. 99.) J. Wesselius writes in his
Fasciculus Dissertationum (*Groningæ*, 1756, 4to., p. 465), "Rabbini
"frequenter loquuntur de ירושלים של מעלה, *Hierosolyma superiori*, seu
"*coelesti*.........Videntur per *Jerusalem Coelestem* intelligere omne illud

"gloriosum delectabile et sanctum, quod in Coelo est." The very learned dissertations of this author on Heb xii. 18—24 may be consulted with great advantage, and will be found on pp. 409—519 of the above-mentioned volume. This is that "strong city" which the אמונים, *faithful*, shall inhabit (Ps. xxxi. 23.—See Wesselius, *ibid.*, p. 464), and into which Isaiah xxvi. 3 declares גוי צדיק שמר אמנים, (*the righteous nation that keepeth truth*,) shall enter. Of this heavenly city Philo in several places makes allegorical mention. Speaking of the "cities of refuge," he says, Τῷ μὲν γὰρ ἑαυτοῦ λόγῳ ὁ Θεὸς πατρίδα οἰκεῖν τὴν ἐπιστήμην ἑαυτοῦ, ὡς ἂν αὐτόχθονι δεδώρηται, τῷ δ' ἐν ἀκουσίοις γενομένῳ σφάλμασι, καταφυγὴν, ὡς ὀθνείῳ ξένην, οὐχ ὡς πατρίδα ἀστῷ. "God has "given to His own Word the knowledge of Himself to inhabit as his "native fatherland, but to him who sins unwittingly, as a refuge offering "hospitality to a stranger, not as a fatherland to a citizen." (*De Profugis*, Works, *Mangey's Editn.*, vol. i., p. 557.) And again, *ibid.*, 'Αλλ' οὐ ζωὴ μέν ἐστιν αἰώνιος ἡ πρὸς τὸ ὂν καταφυγή, θάνατος δ' ὁ ἀπὸ τούτου δρασμός ; "But "is not eternal life an escaping to the Selfexistent, and death fleeing "from Him ?" And again, Μήποτ' οὖν ἡ μὲν πρεσβυτάτη καὶ ὀχυρωτάτη καὶ ἀρίστη μητρόπολις, οὐκ αὐτὸ μόνον πόλις, ὁ θεῖός ἐστι λόγος, ἐφ' ὃν πρῶτον καταφεύγειν ὠφελιμώτατον ; "Is not, then, the Divine Word the oldest "and strongest and best metropolis, (for it is not a city only) and to "flee to it, the most profitable of all ?" (*Ibid.*, p. 560.)—Πάγκαλοι δὲ καὶ εὐερκέστατα πόλεις, ἀξίων σώζεσθαι ψυχῶν τὸν αἰῶνα ἄρισταί γε καταφυγαί, χρηστὴ δὲ καὶ φιλάνθρωπος ἡ διάταξις, ἀλεῖψαι καὶ ῥῶσαι πρὸς εὐελπιστίαν. "There are, then, passing fair and most secure cities, "excellent places of refuge to boot, for souls that are worthy of eternal "salvation. It is verily a kind and humane institution, and well "calculated to brace a man up and strengthen him to entertain a good "hope." (*Ibid.*)—Προτρέπει δὲ οὖν τὸν μὲν ὠκυδρομεῖν ἱκανὸν συντείνειν ἀπλευστὶ πρὸς τὸν ἀνωτάτω λόγον θεῖον, ὅς σοφίας ἐστὶ πηγὴ, ἵνα ἀρυσάμενος τοῦ νάματος, ἀντὶ θανάτου ζωὴν ἀΐδιον ἆθλον εὕρηται. "He intimates, there-"fore, that he who is able to run fast, should betake himself with "straight course to the Divine Word above, who is the fountain of "wisdom, in order that, having drawn from that river, he may find "eternal life instead of death, as his reward." (*Ibid.*)—The same writer (*Quod a Deo mittantur Somnia, lib. ii.*, ibid., p. 691) declares that the "River of God" (Ps. lxv. 9) is the Divine Word, who is replete with a fountain of wisdom; and again (*ibid.*), in reference to Ps. xlvi. 5, "There is a river whose streams make glad the city of God," he observes that this cannot be the literal Jerusalem, because it stands remote from the sea and rivers; it must therefore signify the "influence "of the Divine Word, which is shed everywhere abroad, and cheers all

" things. The city spoken of, is either the universe, or the sanctified soul
" which drinks of the Divine Word." It will be almost superfluous to
remark, how wonderfully the above-cited sentiments of Philo correspond
with the teaching of St. Paul, and of St. John in the Apocalypse, as
well as with the statements of the Writer to the Hebrews respecting
the hopes of the Fathers, and their expectation of an eternal and
abiding city above.

Verses 11—13.—By faith,[1] Sarah herself received power
to conceive[2] (δύναμιν εἰς καταβολὴν σπέρματος ἔλαβε,
virtutem in conceptionem seminis accepit. Vulg.—Empfing
auch Sara Kraft, das sie schwanger ward.—*Luth.*), and
gave birth after the ordinary time of life, because she
believed[3] Him who had promised to be faithful (πιστὸν,
as good as his word. Treu.—*Luth.*). Wherefore there
sprung from one, and him as good as dead (*zwar einen
abgelebten*. Ewald.), like the stars of heaven in multitude, and as the sand which is along the seashore and
cannot be numbered (ἡ παρὰ τὸ χεῖλος τῆς θαλάσσης—
על שפת הים, upon the lip of the sea— ἡ ἀναρίθμητος.
See Gen. xxii. 17). All these died[4] in faith (κατὰ πίστιν),
not having received possession (μὴ λαβόντες) of the
promises: but having seen them from a distance (πόρρω-
θεν), and having been persuaded of them, and having
embraced (ἀσπασάμενοι) them (joyfully), and confessed
(Gen. xxiii. 4) that they were strangers and sojourners
(ὅτι ξένοι καὶ παρεπίδημοί εἰσιν) upon the earth.[5]

[1] In Gen. xvii. 17 we learn that the promise of a son by Sarah had
been given to Abraham a whole year before Isaac was born, and also
some months before the promise was repeated in Sarah's hearing.
[Comp. Gen. xvii. 15—19 with Gen. xviii. 10 and xxi. 5.] On this first
occasion Abraham laughed, as Sarah did upon the second. He had
apparently considered that the promise, " He that shall come forth out
" of thine own bowels, shall be thine heir," (Gen. xv. 4) should be
fulfilled in Ishmael ; and, therefore, when his name was changed from
Abram to Abraham, in token that he should be a father of many
nations (Gen. xvii. 5—18), and also when he was assured that Sarah
herself should have a son, we find him saying unto God, " O that

"Ishmael might live before thee!" For he "said in his heart, Shall a "child be born unto him that is an hundred years old? and shall Sarah "that is ninety years old bear?" The real fact of the case seems to be explained by St. Paul, Rom. iv. 19, when he writes μή ἀσθενήσας τῇ πίστει [Gen. xv. 6], οὐ κατενόησε τὸ ἑαυτοῦ σῶμα ἤδη νενεκρωμένον ἑκατονταέτης που ὑπάρχων, καὶ τὴν νέκρωσιν τῆς μήτρας Σάῤῥας. Εἰς δὲ τὴν ἐπαγγελίαν τοῦ Θεοῦ οὐ διεκρίθη τῇ ἀπιστίᾳ, ἀλλ᾿ ἐνεδυναμώθη τῇ πίστει, δοὺς δόξαν τῷ Θεῷ. It was a momentary shock that both Abraham and Sarah experienced at an announcement so unexpected, and so contrary to the ordinary course of nature. But as soon as ever they realised the fact that such was God's promise, doubt and hesitation were for ever dismissed. They were made strong in their faith. Not only did they assent to the possibility of the thing, but they firmly believed that God would keep his word. The Bible never represents flesh and blood as endowed with transcendental virtues, such as we know by experience we do not by nature inherit. God's grace is evermore magnified, in its triumph over mortal frailty and infirmity. Instead of depicting these "elders who obtained a good report through faith" as paragons of virtue, they are represented with truthful fidelity, as subject to like weaknesses with ourselves. Thus, through patience, and comfort of the Scriptures, we have hope. We learn what we are by nature, and what we may become by grace. We look to the great cloud of witnesses, and are encouraged to trust in the same Captain of our Salvation by whom they prevailed.

² Although the above translation is in accordance with a commonly accepted rendering of δύναμιν εἰς κατ. κ.τ.λ., I cannot help feeling it to be of great weight that this is the only instance out of the eleven in which καταβολή occurs in the New Testament, where it seems to be used out of the ordinary signification of *foundation*. (See Matt. xiii. 35, xxv. 34, Luke xi. 50, John xvii. 24, Eph. i. 4, Heb. iv. 3, ix. 26, Rev. xiii. 8, xvii. 8.) A translation more consonant to these latter passages would be, "*By faith, Sarah had strength imparted to her, in order that a* "*posterity might be founded.*" And this rendering is in harmony with the repeated use of the word זרע, σπέρμα, in the Old Testament in reference to the posterity of Abraham, not only as regards the Hebrew nation, but as applied to the true Seed, even Christ. I cordially agree with what Professor Stuart says respecting the physiological torturing of these words, "to the disgust of every delicate reader, by some of the critics." J. C. Wolfius (*in loco*), although he indulges pretty freely in comments of the nature so properly reprehended by Professor Stuart, yet candidly mentions the other opinion, saying, "In "alia abiit Gassetius in Commentariis L. Hebr., p. 234, *rad*. זרע, *lit*. B,

"qui phrasin hanc cum illa καταβολὴ κόσμου, comparat et per *fundati-*
"*onem sobolis* interpretatur, sicut p. 846, *rad.* שות, *lit.* C, σπέρμα h.l. de
"posteritate, non autem humore genitali accipit."

[3] Οὐ μόνον αὐτὸς, ἀλλὰ καὶ ἡ γυνὴ γελᾷ. Λέγεται γὰρ αὖθις, ἐγέλασε δὲ Σάῤῥα ἐν ἑαυτῇ, λέγουσα, οὔπω μέν μοι γέγονεν ἕως τοῦ νῦν ἄνευ μελέτης ἀπαντοματίζον ἀγαθόν· ὁ δ' ὑποσχόμενος κύριός μου καὶ πρεσβύτερος πάσης γενέσεώς ἐστιν, ᾧ πιστεύειν ἀναγκαῖον. "Not only he (Abraham) laughed,
"but his wife laughed also. For it is said presently, *And Sarah laughed
"within herself,* saying, There never yet up to the present time happened
"to me any spontaneous good thing without care on my part. But He
"who promises is my Lord, and more ancient than the whole creation.
"I must needs therefore believe Him."—Philo, *De nominum Mutatione,*
Works, *Mangey's Edit.,* vol. i., p. 603. See also *De migratione Abrahami,*
ibid., p. 455:—Ἀκούσασαν γοῦν ἐν ἀρχῇ τὴν γυναῖκα φασὶ γελάσαι, καὶ μετὰ ταῦτ' εἰπόντων, Μὴ ἀδυνατεῖ παρὰ τῷ Θεῷ ῥῆμα, καταιδεσθεῖσαν ἀρνήσασθαι τὸν γέλωτα· πάντα γὰρ ᾔδει Θεῷ δυνατὰ, σχεδὸν ἐξέτι σπαργάνων τουτὶ τὸ δόγμα προμαθοῦσα. Τότε μοι δοκεῖ πρῶτον οὐκ ἐθ' ὁμοίαν τῶν ὁρωμένων λαβεῖν φαντασίαν, ἀλλὰ σεμνοτέραν, ἢ προφητῶν τινων ἢ ἀγγέλων μεταβαλλόντων ἀπὸ πνευματικῆς καὶ ψυχοειδοῦς οὐσίας εἰς ἀνθρωπόμορφον ἰδέαν. "They relate that his wife also laughed, and yet after they had
"said, *Is anything too hard for God?* she was ashamed, and denied
"that she laughed. For she knew that with God all things are possible,
"for she had learned this doctrine almost from her swaddling clothes.
"From that moment she seems to me to have formed quite a new idea
"of the men she saw before her, viz., a much more respectful one, *i.e.,*
"that they were prophets or angels, who had exchanged their spiritual
"and incorporeal natures into the form and fashion of men." (*De
Abrahamo,* ibid., vol. ii., p. 17.)

[4] In Gen. xv. 15 it had been promised to Abraham that he should "go
"to his fathers in peace, and be buried in a good old age." In Gen. xxv. 8
we are told that he was "gathered to his people." The same is said
respecting Isaac, Gen. xxxv. 29, and Jacob, Gen. xlix. 33, on which Philo
remarks (*de Sacr. Abelis et Caini,* ibid., vol. i., p. 164), Ἀβραὰμ ἐκλιπὼν τὰ θνητὰ, προστίθεται τῷ θεοῦ λαῷ, καρπούμενος ἀφθαρσίαν, ἴσος ἀγγέλοις γεγονὼς, ἄγγελοι γὰρ στρατός εἰσι θεοῦ, ἀσώματοι καὶ εὐδαίμονες ψυχαί.
"Abraham, leaving mortality behind, was added to the people of God,
"entering upon the fruition of immortality, and was made equal to the
"angels. Now the angels are God's host, being incorporeal and happy
"souls." He elsewhere remarks that "to go to his fathers" could not
signify a return to his relatives in Chaldæa. (*Quis rerum Div. Hæres.,*
ibid., p. 513.) The expression, doubtless, signifies to be gathered to his
ancestors, who had preceded him to their eternal rest above. With

such repeated declarations respecting the immortality of the soul, how can we possibly deny that the doctrine was familiar to the Hebrews under Moses? Philo writes as follows respecting the death and burial of Sarah:—Μαρτυρίαι δὲ τούτων ἐν ταῖς ἱεραῖς βίβλοις κατάκεινται, ἃς οὐ θέμις ψευδομαρτυριῶν ἁλῶναι· αἱ μηνύουσιν ὅτι βραχέα τῷ σώματι ἐπιδακρύσας, θᾶττον ἀπανέστη τοῦ νεκροῦ· τὸ πενθεῖν ἐπὶ πλέον, ὡς ἔοικεν, ἀλλότριον ἡγησάμενος σοφίας, ὑφ' ἧς ἀνεδιδάχθη, τὸν θάνατον νομίζειν μὴ σβέσιν ψυχῆς, ἀλλὰ χωρισμὸν καὶ διάζευξιν ἀπὸ σώματος, ὅθεν ἦλθεν ἀπιούσης, ἦλθε δὲ, ὡς ἐν τῇ κοσμοποιίᾳ δεδήλωται, παρὰ Θεοῦ. "The evidences of these things "are contained in the sacred books, which it were impiety to accuse of "false witness; and they inform us, that having wept for a short time "over the corpse, he quickly rose up from the dead, accounting it to be "alien from wisdom to mourn too much, for by it he was taught to "esteem death, not as extinction of the soul, but a separation and dis-"junction from the body, and that it went to the place whence it had "come forth. But it came, as we learn in the history of the creation, "from God." (De Abrahamo, ibid., p. 137.)

⁵ In Gen. xxiii. 3, 4 we read, "And Abraham stood up from before "his dead and spake unto the sons of Heth, saying, I am a stranger "and a sojourner with you," &c. Philo remarks that by Moses all the wise men are called sojourners, παροικοῦντες, and adds, αἱ γὰρ τούτων ψυχαὶ στέλλονται μὲν ἀποικίαν δή ποτε τὴν ἐξ οὐρανοῦ ... Ἐπειδὰν οὖν ἐνδιατρίψασαι σώμασι τὰ αἰσθητὰ καὶ θνητὰ δι' αὐτῶν πάντα κατίδωσιν, ἐπανέρχονται ἐκεῖσε πάλιν, ὅθεν ὡρμήθησαν τὸ πρῶτον, πατρίδα μὲν τὸν οὐράνιον χῶρον ἐν ᾧ πολιτεύονται, ξένον δὲ τὸν περίγειον ἐν ᾧ παρῴκησαν, νομίζουσαι· τοῖς μὲν γὰρ ἀποικίαν στειλαμένοις ἀντὶ τῆς μητροπόλεως ἡ ὑποδεξαμένη δή που πατρίς, ἡ δ' ἐκπέμψασα μένει τοῖς ἀποδεδημηκόσιν, εἰς ἣν καὶ ποθοῦσιν ἐπανέρχεσθαι. Τοιγαροῦν εἰκότως Ἀβραὰμ ἐρεῖ τοῖς νεκροφύλαξι καὶ ταμίαις τῶν θνητῶν, ἀναστὰς ἀπὸ τοῦ νεκροῦ βίου καὶ τάφου, Πάροικος καὶ παρεπίδημός εἰμι ἐγὼ μεθ' ὑμῶν. "For their souls "are sent down from heaven to sojourn for a while. But after they "have tarried awhile in their bodies, and inspected all things perceptible "to the senses and mortal, they ascend again to the same place whence "they originally came, esteeming the heavenly place, where their "citizenship is as their country, but the terrestrial one, wherein they "sojourn, as a foreign land. Colonists usually esteem the land of their "adoption as taking the place of their native country. But with the "above-mentioned, the country that sent them forth always remains "the same, and to it they long to return. Abraham, therefore, properly "said to the custodians of the dead and the stewards of mortality, "having himself risen from the dead life and the tomb, *As for me, I* "*am a sojourner and a stranger* amongst you." (De Confusione Linguarum,

Works, *Mangey's Edit.*, vol. i., pp. 416, 417.) See also *De Cherubim,* ibid., pp. 161, 162.

Verses 14, 15.—For they who speak after this fashion (τοιαῦτα λέγοντες) show plainly (ἐμφανίζουσιν) that they are (yet) seeking a country (ὅτι πατρίδα ἐπιζητοῦσι, das sie ein Vaterland suchen, *Luth.*)[1]; and if indeed they had been mindful of that one from which they came out, they would have had opportunity (καιρὸν) to return back again.[2]

---

[1] Παροικεῖν, οὐ κατοικεῖν ἤλθομεν. Τῷ γὰρ ὄντι πᾶσα μὲν ψυχὴ σοφοῦ πατρίδα μὲν οὐρανόν, ξένην δὲ γῆν ἔλαχε κ.τ.λ. " We come hither to sojourn " and not to make our home. For in reality every wise man's soul has " obtained heaven as his fatherland, but earth is a foreign place to " him." (Philo, *De Agricultura,* Works, vol. i., p. 310.) And so David confesses, Ps. xxxix. 12 (13), " For I am a stranger with thee, and a " sojourner, as all my fathers were" (כי גר אנכי עמך תושב ככל אבותי); and again, 1 Chron. xxix. 15, " For we are strangers before Thee, and " sojourners, as were all our fathers." (כי גרים אנחנו לפניך ותושבים ככל אבותינו)

[2] Philo often refers to the hardships and inconveniences which Abraham underwent during the days of his earthly pilgrimage,—Καίτοι τίς ἕτερος οὐκ ἂν ἠχθέσθη, οὐ μόνον τῆς οἰκείας ἀπανιστάμενος, ἀλλὰ καὶ ἐξ ἁπάσης πόλεως ἐλαυνόμενος εἰς δυσβάτους καὶ δυσπορεύτας ἀνοδίας; τίς δ' οὐκ ἂν μετατρεπόμενος ἐπαλινδρόμησεν οἴκαδε, βραχέα μὲν φροντίσας τῶν μελλουσῶν ἐλπίδων, τὴν δὲ παροῦσαν ἀπορίαν σπεύδων ἐκφυγεῖν, εὐήθειαν ὑπολαβὼν ἀδήλων χάριν ἀγαθῶν ὁμολογούμενα αἱρεῖσθαι κακά; Μόνος δ' οὗτος τοὐναντίον πεπονθέναι φαίνεται κ.τ.λ. " But who else would not have " repined at being separated not only from his own native city but " from every other city alike, and driven forth into rugged and in- " accessible bye paths? Who else would not have turned round and " hastened home again, making little account of future hopes, and " eager to escape from present pressure of necessities, esteeming it the " part of a simpleton to choose palpable inconveniences for the sake of " uncertain good? But this man (Abraham) alone seems to have enter- " tained a contrary opinion," &c. (*De Abrahamo,* Works, vol. ii., p. 14.)

Verses 16—18.—But now their aim is (ὀρέγονται) a better one, that is to say a heavenly. Wherefore God is not ashamed of them, to be called their God,[1] for he hath prepared a city for them. (See note 1 on pp. 192—195. Consult also Schoettgen, *De Hierosolyma cælesti*, in his Horæ Hebr. et Talm. tom. i., p. 1205.) By faith[2] Abraham offered up Isaac, when he was tried (πειραζόμενος, *tempted, put to the test*), even he who had waited for the promises (ὁ τὰς ἐπαγγελίας ἀναδεξάμενος), and did offer up his only begotten son, with respect to whom it had been said (Gen. xxi. 12), *For in Isaac shall thy seed be called.* (ὅτι ἐν Ἰσαὰκ κληθήσεταί σοι σπέρμα, כי ביצחק יקרא לך זרע—*Soll der eine Same genannt werden.*—Ewald.)[3]

[1] Διὸ οὐκ ἐπαισχύνεται αὐτοὺς ὁ Θεὸς κ.τ.λ. We must here again bear in mind that the writer is addressing Jews. He refers to the distinctive and perpetual designation by which it had pleased God to reveal himself as the God of their nation, as we read in Exod. iii. 13—16:—"And "Moses said unto God, Behold, when I come unto the children of "Israel, and shall say unto them, The God of your fathers hath sent "me unto you, and they shall say unto me, What is his name? What "shall I say unto them? And God said unto Moses, I AM THAT I AM "(אהיה אשר אהיה, ἐγώ εἰμι ὁ "Ων, LXX.); and he said, Thus shalt thou "say unto the children of Israel, I am (אהיה, ὁ "Ων) hath sent me unto "you. And God said moreover unto Moses, Thus shalt thou say unto "the children of Israel, Jehovah, God of your fathers (יהוה אלהי אבתיכם) "THE GOD OF ABRAHAM, THE GOD OF ISAAC, AND THE GOD OF JACOB, 'hath sent me unto you: this is my name for ever, and this is my "memorial unto all generations. (זה שמי לעלם וזה זכרי לדר דר, τοῦτό μου "ἐστὶν ὄνομα αἰώνιον, καὶ μνημόσυνον γενεῶν γενεαῖς, LXX.)." Here, then, we have an incidental application of the argument employed by our Saviour against the Sadducees to prove the resurrection of the dead (Matt. xxii. 31, 32), "But as touching the resurrection of the dead, "have ye not read that which was spoken unto you by God, saying, I "am the God of Abraham, and the God of Isaac, and the God of Jacob? "God is not the God of the dead, but of the living;" or as Mark xii. 26, 27 has it, "And as touching the dead, that they rise, have ye not "read in the book of Moses, how in the bush God spake unto him, "saying," &c., and Luke xx. 37, "Now that the dead are raised Moses "shewed at the bush, when he called the Lord the God of Abraham," &c. B. Ugolinus (*Trihæresium, sive Diss. de tribus sectis Judæorum*, Thes., vol. xxii. col. 72) gives the following Rabbinical illustrations of the above interesting subject:—"*Tanchum*, fol. 13, 3. Dicit R. Simeon "ben Jochai; Deus Sanctus Benedictus nomen suum justis non adjungit,

CHAP. XI., 16—18.

" sicut dicitur, *Sanctis qui in terra sunt*, Psal. xvi. 3. Quandonam sunt
" sancti ? Cum in terra reponuntur ; nam dum vivunt nomen suum
" Deus non adjungit ; eo quod de iis non certum habeat, malum affectum
" eos non abducturum ; at cum mortui sunt, nomen suum adjungit.
" Ast invenimus Deum nomen suum adjunxisse Isaaco dum viveret :
" Genes xxviii. 13, *Ego sum Deus Abraham et Deus Isaac*. Respondent
" sapientes, Pulverem ejus respexit ac si collectum super altare. R.
" Berachiah dixit. Ex quo caecus factus est, fuit sicut mortuus. *Vide*
" etiam R. Menahem in legem, fol. 621.—Gemara Hierosolymitana
" *Berachot.*, fol. 5, 4. Justi etiam in morte dicuntur vivere, atque
" impii etiam in vita dicuntur mortui. (See similar words of Philo,
" note, p. 179.) Ex eo quod dicitur, במות המה אחפוץ לא, *Non delectatus*
" *sum morte mortui*. Num ille qui dicitur מת jam est mortuus ? Atque
" unde probatur, quod justi etiam in morte sua dicantur vivi ? Ex eo
" quod scribitur. *Haec est terra de quâ juravi Abrahamo, Isaaco, et*
" *Jacobo*, לאמר. Quid sibi vult vox לאמר ? Dicit ei : Abi et die patribus
" quodcunque promisi vobis praestiti filiis vestris."

² Πίστει προσενήνοχεν 'Αβρ. κ.τ.λ. Here, then, as in James ii. 21—23,
we have the inspired answer to the modern resuscitators of a very
ancient blasphemy, who dare to ascribe this heroic act of Abraham's
faith to an incontrollable impulse of Moloch worship ! This crude
calumny is on a par with the revolting profanities which have recently
been propounded as specimens of Christian interpretation, viz., that
Isaac was the adulterous offspring of Eleazar and Sarah, palmed off
upon unsuspecting Abraham as his own child (see Balth. Scheidij
Praeterita praeteritorum, pp. 61, 62. Meuschen, *Nov. Test. ex Talmude*
illustr., where a similar insinuation, viz., that Isaac was an adopted
foundling, is illustrated in a quotation from the *Bava Metzia*, f. 87, 1) ;
and that St. Peter assassinated Ananias and Sapphira in order to strike
terror into the multitude ! The very learned Spencer in his treatise,
De lege cultum Molechi prohibente (De legibus Hebraeor. ritualibus,
lib. ii., p. 290, *Hagae-Comitum*, 1686, 4to.), writes :—" Probè novi,
" quamplurimos alia omnia de ritûs hujus nefarij fonte sentire, quasi
" ex Abrahami, filium suum offerentis, historiâ, corruptâ et depravatâ,
" profluxisset. Huic autem sententiae fidem adhibere nescio, cum historia
" illa, nisi plane mutilata, magna praebeat contra morem illum inhu-
" manum argumenta ; et verisimile sit multas gentes, liberos suos
" immolare solitas, de Abrahami exemplo nè vel faudo quicquam
" audivisse." Rabbi D. Kimchi, on Jer. xvi. 31, represents God as
saying, " ' I have not commanded them to offer their sons as holocausts,
" ' nor did I ever say any such thing to any of my prophets ; and when
" ' I spake to Abraham concerning the sacrifice of his son, it never

"'came into my heart that he should actually sacrifice him, but that his righteousness might be manifested.'" Porphyry suggested that Abraham was Saturn, and that he put to death the son which he had by Anobret. See Goodwin, *Moses et Aaron* (*Ugolini. Thes.*, vol. ii, col. 310), Danielis Dietzschii *Dissertatio de Cultu Molochi* (*ibid.*, vol. xxiii, col. 874), and C. S. Ziegra, *Dissert. prima*, on the same subject (*ibid.*, vol. xxiii., col. 891). The latter writer, whilst utterly repudiating the idea that Abraham was in any way influenced by any motive but the express command of God, is not unwilling to admit that heathen nations perverted his example to Moloch worship. He also imagines that Jephtha actually put his daughter to death in fulfilment of his vow. (See my note on ver. 32.) See also *ibid.*, vol. i., col. 780, where it is shown that others, before Abraham, offered their sons as holocausts. The same is very conclusively proved by Whiston in his learned Dissertation, *Concerning God's Command to Abraham to offer up Isaac*, where he asserts that the human sacrifices which had existed long before Abraham's time at Heliopolis in Egypt, were abolished by Amosis about the time of Abraham's sacrifice. The above Essay is printed at the end of Whiston's *Josephus*, pp. 673—678 (Halifax, 1859, 8vo.), and will repay perusal. The accusation above alluded to is older than Philo. Well worthy of study is the indignant defence which he makes (*De Abrahamo*) against the assailants of the sacred narrative and the traducers of the founder of the Hebrew race. The passage is too long for transcription here, but will be found on pp. 26—29 of vol. ii. of Mangey's Edition of his works. Josephus also alludes, by implication, to the audacious calumny in the first book of his Antiquities, chap. xiii. 4,—"The deed had been done if God had not opposed it, for he "called loudly to Abraham by his name, and forbade him to slay his "son, and said, It was not out of a desire of human blood that he was "commanded to slay his son,......but to try the temper of his mind, "whether he would be obedient to such a command." That so gross an outrage upon God's Word should be offered to it by a Sadducee, or by a Pagan antagonist of Judaism, might perhaps be capable of explanation, if not of palliation ; but for a so-called Christian Theologian, with the consciousness upon his mind that the sacrifice of Isaac is the cardinal type of the voluntary sacrifice of Christ's death, thus to suffer himself to descend to the exploded scurrilities of the heathen atheist, is indeed a phenomenon of advanced and shameless impiety, from which, the warning words addressed by the Saviour to his Pharisaic blasphemers (Matt. xii. 31), might well induce the thoughtful mind to recoil with no superstitious dread. Voltaire (*Dictionnaire Philosophique*, Art. *Abraham*, and *Jephté*) makes similar insinuations.

CHAP. XI., 16—18.

I cannot forbear extracting at length the following from the late Dr. M'Caul's "*Canon Stanley's Lectures on the History of the Jewish Church Reviewed,*" &c., pp. 16—24 (London, 1863, 8vo):—"The most "flagrant exhibition of contempt for Scripture is found in the Pro- "fessor's new version of Gen. xxii. Dr. Rowland Williams excited a "thrill of horror in all English Christendom by those memorable words, "'When the fierce ritual of Syria, with the awe of a Divine voice, bade "'Abraham slay his son, he did not reflect that he had no theory of the "'absolute to justify him in departing from traditional revelation, but "'trusted that the Father, whose voice from heaven he heard at heart, "'was better pleased with mercy than with sacrifice; and this trust was "'his righteousness.' And yet this is the view now put forward by "the Professor of Ecclesiastical History in Oxford; it would almost "seem as a sort of compensation to Dr. Williams for the wounds in- "flicted by the Edinburgh Reviewer, on account of 'his direct breach "of' that 'compact,' which is now, in theology, as famous as the "Lichfield-house compact in politics. Dr. Stanley's statement is long, "and guarded, and tedious, and, that no injustice may be done, must "be quoted at length. In the Second Lecture he says, 'Lastly, the "'history of the world and of the Church requires us to notice the act "'of faith which takes us back into the innermost life of Abraham "'himself, and marks at least one critical stage in the progress of the "'true religion. There have been in almost all ancient forms of religion, "'in most modern also, strong tendencies, each in itself springing from "'the best and purest feelings of humanity, yet each, if carried into "'the extremes suggested by passion or by logic, incompatible with the "'other, and with its own highest purpose. One is the craving to "'please, or to propitiate, or to communicate with the powers above, "'by surrendering some object near and dear to ourselves. This is the "'source of all sacrifice. The other is the profound moral instinct "'that the Creator of the world cannot be pleased, or propitiated, or "'approached by other means than a pure life and good deeds. On "'the exaggeration, on the contact, on the collision, of these two ten- "'dencies, have turned some of the chief corruptions, and some of the "'chief difficulties, of Ecclesiastical history. The earliest of these we "'are about to witness in the life of Abraham. There came, we are "'told, the Divine intimation, "Take now thy son, thine only son "'Isaac, whom thou lovest .....and offer him for a burnt-offering on "'one of the mountains which I will tell thee of." It was in its spirit "'the exact expression of the feeling of self-devotion, without which "'religion cannot exist, and of which the whole life of the Patriarch "'had been the great example. But the form taken by this Divine

"'trial or temptation was that which a stern logical consequence of
"'the ancient view of sacrifice did actually assume, if not then, yet
"'certainly in after ages, among the surrounding tribes, and which
"'cannot, therefore, be left out of sight in considering the whole
"'historical aspect of the narrative. Deep in the heart of the
"'Canaanitish nations was laid the practice of human sacrifice; the
"'very offering here described of "children passing through the fire,"
"'" of their sons and daughters," "of the first-born for their trans-
"'gressions, the fruit of their body for the sin of their soul." On the
"'altars of Moab, and of Phœnicia, and of the distant Canaanite
"'settlements in Carthage and in Spain,—nay even, at times, in the
"'confines of the chosen people itself, in the wild vow of Jephtha,
"'in the sacrifice of Saul's sons at Gibeah, in the dark sacrifices of the
"'valley of Hinnom, under the very walls of Jerusalem—this almost
"'irrepressible tendency of the burning zeal of a primitive race found its
"'terrible expression. Such was the trial which presented itself to
"'Abraham. From the tents of Beersheba he set forth at the rising
"'of the sun, and went unto the place of which God had told him. It
"'was not the place which Jewish tradition has selected on Mount
"'Moriah at Jerusalem, still less that which Christian tradition shows,
"'even to the thicket in which the ram was caught, hard by the
"'Church of the Holy Sepulchre; still less that which Mussulman
"'tradition indicates on Mount Arafat at Mecca. Rather we must
"'look to that ancient sanctuary of which I have already spoken, the
"'natural altar on the summit of Mount Gerizim. On that spot, at
"'that time the holiest in Palestine, the crisis was to take place. One,
"'two, three days' journey from Beersheba—in the distance the high
"'crest of the mountain appears. And "Abraham lifted up his eyes,
"'and saw the place afar off." The sacrifice, the resignation of the
"'will in the father and son, was accepted; the literal sacrifice of the
"'act was repelled. On the one hand, the great principle was pro-
"'claimed that mercy is better than sacrifice—that the sacrifice of self
"'is the highest and holiest offering that God can receive. On the
"'other hand, the inhuman superstitions towards which the ancient
"'ceremonial of sacrifice was perpetually tending, were condemned and
"'cast out of the true worship of the Church for ever. There are,
"'doubtless, many difficulties which may be raised on the offering of
"'Isaac; but there are few, if any, which will not vanish away before
"'the simple pathos and lofty spirit of the narrative itself, provided we
"'take it, as in fairness it must be taken, as a whole; its close not
"'parted from its commencement, nor its commencement from its
"'close—the subordinate parts of the transaction not raised above its

"'essential primary intention. And there is no difficulty which will
"'not be amply compensated by reflecting on the near approach, and
"'yet the complete repulse, of the danger which might have threatened
"'the early Church. Nothing is so remarkable a proof of a Divine and
"'watchful interposition as the deliverance from the infirmity, the
"'exaggeration, the excess, whatever it is, to which the noblest minds
"'and the noblest forms of religion are subject.' (Pp. 47—50.) In
"this long and prosy disquisition, the bold, nervous language of Dr.
"Williams is diluted by the outpourings of a mawkish sentimentalism,
"which represents the cruel and unnatural sacrifices of the Phœnicians
"'as springing from the best and purest feelings of humanity,' 'the
"'infirmity, the exaggeration, the excess, whatever it is, to which the
"'noblest minds and the noblest forms of religion are subject.' But
"the offence against the Scripture and the Christian faith is essentially
"the same. However that want of moral courage, which is charac-
"teristic of the whole school to which he (Professor Stanley) belongs,
"may prevent him from saying so distinctly, he does in fact reject
"the whole Bible history of this transaction, from beginning to end,
"and construct a new narrative of what he, following the Baron von
"Bunsen, thinks was the true history. The Bible says distinctly, 'God
"'did tempt Abraham, and said unto him, Abraham ; and he said,
"'Behold, here I am. And he said, Take now thy son, thine only son
"'Isaac, whom thou lovest, and get thee into the land of Moriah ; and
"'offer him there for a burnt-offering upon one of the mountains which
"'I shall tell thee of.' In every particular Professor Stanley contradicts
"these words of Scripture. First, he says plainly that not Moriah, but
"Gerizim was the place where the sacrifice was to be offered ; and
"therefore, in his citation of these verses, leaves out the words, 'Get
"'thee into the land of Moriah.' In the next place, he says, that the
"journey to offer up Isaac was not in obedience to a Divine command,
"but that 'craving to please, or to propitiate, or to communicate with,
"'the power above us, by surrendering some object near and dear to
"'ourselves,' which led the Canaanites to offer their children to
"Moloch ; 'the infirmity, the exaggeration, the excess, whatever it is,
"'to which the noblest minds and the noblest forms of religion are
"'subject.' Professor Stanley tries to justify his new narrative by
"saying, in a note,—' That this temptation or trial, through whatever
"' means it was suggested, should in the sacred narrative be ascribed to
"'the overruling voice of God, is in exact accordance with the general
"' tenour of the Hebrew Scriptures.' This is one of those big general
"assertions regarding the Hebrew Scriptures to which men have
"recourse when they are in extreme difficulty, and have no particular

"proofs to give for what they assert, which, therefore, the reader may
"always reject, as being without foundation. There is not one passage
"in the Old Testament where the sins or errors of men are fathered
"upon God. He is said to harden the hearts or blind the eyes of the
"obstinate sinner, but that is as a punishment of their own previous
"wickedness, and rejection of His chastisements as well as His mercies.
"But their own voluntary wickedness or mistakes are never ascribed to
"God. It is a libel upon the Hebrew Scriptures and their Divine
"Author. The Professor himself has only one apparent example to
"offer in order to justify the sweeping assertion about the general
"tenour of the Hebrew Scriptures. 'A still more striking instance,'
"he says, 'is contained in the history of David, where the same
"'temptation, which in one book is ascribed to God, is in another
"'ascribed to Satan.' 'The Lord moved David to say, Go, number
"'Israel.' (2 Sam. xxiv. 1.) 'Satan provoked David to number
"'Israel.' (1 Chron. xxi. 1.) Very good. But does any other book
"of the Bible ascribe to Abraham's infirmity that which Gen. xxii.
"ascribes to God's trial of his faith? If so, then we are ready to
"submit to the decision of Scripture. But if not, then we think it
"something not far removed from presumption, for any man to ascribe
"to man's infirmity and superstition that which Scripture especially
"ascribes to God's wisdom and love, to reject the plain narrative of
"Scripture and substitute another of his own. Besides, the two asser-
"tions that God moved David, and that Satan moved David, may both
"be true. Satan may have been the unconscious or the permitted
"instrument. The cause was one—the anger of the Lord. But the
"narrative in the Bible and Professor Stanley's narrative of the sacrifice
"of Isaac cannot both be true. Gen. xxii. describes the sacrifice of
"Isaac, Abraham's willingness to kill him, as a good deed, deserving
"the highest commendation. 'By myself have I sworn, saith the
"'Lord, for because thou hast done this thing, and hast not withheld
"'thy son, thine only son, that in blessing I will bless thee, and in
"'multiplying I will multiply thy seed as the stars of heaven.' Pro-
"fessor Stanley, on the contrary, describes the idea of killing Isaac as
"a bad deed, the offspring of superstition, and his final unwillingness
"to execute his intention, as that which is good. The two narratives
"are therefore hopelessly irreconcileable, and the learned Professor has
"no warrant whatever in Hebrew usage for his rejection of the plain
"meaning of the words of Gen. xxii. and substituting a story of his
"own, or of Baron Bunsen's composition. Indeed, the Professor's
"criticisms are the weakest part of these Lectures. There is an osten-
"tatious display of Hebrew lore, but it is not of a kind to increase the

"reputation of Oxford, or of the English Church among foreign
"scholars. The explanation of Sarai, as ' = my princess' and Eleph
"(אלף) in Judges xv. 16, as 'an ox-load of men,' will cause a sensation
"on the continent by no means desirable.

"But to return to the matter in hand. The Scripture represents the
"whole as a trial sent immediately from God to Abraham, and, on his
"obedience, an equally immediate interposition to prevent the sacrifice;
"a transaction between God and Abraham, which could never result in
"any injury to the true religion of the Church of God. Professor
"Stanley describes it as a temptation arising from the infirmity of a
"noble mind, which, if followed to its intended end, would have left
"in the Church the abomination of human sacrifice. He therefore
"repudiates the whole of the sacred narrative, and presents to the
"candidates for holy orders a new history, teaching them by his example
"to treat the Bible with scorn, and leading them either to avoid holy
"orders, because they cannot say that they unfeignedly believe what
"he has taught them to regard as a fiction, or what is far more
"appalling, to tell a deliberate falsehood on the most solemn occasion
"of their lives. But in thus rejecting the narrative in Genesis, Pro-
"fessor Stanley also shakes the authority of the New Testament. The
"Epistle to the Hebrews says, 'By faith Abraham, when he was tried,
"'offered up his only begotten son.' Professor Stanley says, It was not
"by faith,—on the contrary, that Abraham's attempt to offer his son
"was the mistaken suggestion of his own mind, similar to the abominable
"superstition of the Phœnicians in burning their children. St. James
"says, 'Abraham was justified by works, having offered Isaac upon
"'the altar.' Professor Stanley, on the contrary, teaches that Abraham
"was to be condemned for having laid him on the altar, and that so far
"from being a proof of his obedience, it was a proof of his infirmity,
"and erroneous ideas of sacrifice. But apostles are as little regarded
"by the Professor's school as prophets. Their inspiration does not
"protect them from error, and whenever their interpretation of the
"Old Testament differs from that of the 'free' and easy 'handlers' of
"Scripture it must give way. Such is the principle acted upon in this
"explanation of the offering of Isaac. But who can expect apostles
"and prophets to be treated with respect, when their Lord and Master
"is by Professor Jowett convicted of error and ignorance in his prophecy
"concerning his second coming?

"Here we conclude our remarks upon Professor Stanley's picture of
"Abraham. It suggests many reflections. It throws a blaze of light
"on the question now agitated with so much anxiety, 'Why is it that
"'there are not so many and so well qualified candidates for holy

"'orders?' These Lectures suggest one answer. The Church of
"England requires unfeigned belief in all the canonical Scriptures.
"But their University training teaches them to disbelieve all canonical
"Scripture, and the youthful mind cannot receive the casuistry of
"the day, nor receive the judgment of Dr. Lushington in opposition
"to the judgment of their own consciences. They therefore stay
"away."
Excellently does Professor Franz Delitzsch (*Die Genesis*, Leipzig,
1852, 8vo., pp. 300—303) expose the gnostic and dualistic fallacies of
Schelling, who asserts that the command to sacrifice Isaac was given by
אלהים *God*, and that the prohibition to complete the sacrificial tragedy
came from מלאך יהוה *the Angel of Jehovah*. The learned Professor closes
his remarks upon the subject in the following admirable sentences
(p. 303) :—" Was Gott von Abraham verlangt, das ist ja, wie sich zeigt,
" nur zu dem Zwecke der Glaubensprüfung verlangt, es stellt sich
" heraus, dass Gott nicht das Opfer Isaaks in seinem äusserlichen
" Vollzuge, sondern nur in seinem innerlichen geistlichen wollte, nicht
" die Opferung Isaaks mit dem Schlachtmesser, sondern die heiligende
" Hingabe desselben an Jehovah. Zugleich aber wird das äusserliche
" Menschenopfer durch Gott selbst gerichtet. 'Die höchste Glaubens-
" prüfung ist mit dem Gewinne einer neuen erhabenen Wahrheit
" verbunden, nämlich der dass Jehovah das Menschenopfer nicht wolle.'
" Ein Widder tritt an die Stelle Isaaks, das Thieropfer ist so sanctionirt
" und zwar auf demselben Berge, wo durch die ganze alttestamentliche
" Zeit das vorbildliche Thieropferblut fliessen sollte, und Isaak, der
" nur ἐν παραβολῇ geopfert wird, ist nur die bleibende Parabel des
" Menschensohns, der sein Kreutzholz trägt und auf dem Kreuzesholze
" in Wirklichkeit geopfert wird. Die That Abrahams is nur ein Bild
" der unendlich grössern Liebesthat Gottes, die sich vollzieht durch eine
" Verlängnung seiner ewigen Liebe die alles menschliche Bewusstsein
" unendlich übersteigt. Was Abraham thut, that im Gegenbilde der
" Vater Jesu Christi Röm. viii. 32 ; was Isaak erleidet, erlitt im
" Gegenbilde der Sohn Gottes, 1 Pet. ii. 24, der Vorgang auf Morija
" ist das Vorspiel des welterlösenden Vorgangs in Jerusalem."
Dr. Ewald translates verse 19, "Bedenkend dass auch aus Todten
"Gott zu erwecken vermag, von wo er ihn auch vergleichsweise
"davontrug." His remarks on the sacrifice of Isaac (*Das Sendschr.
a.d. Hebr.*, p. 129) are replete with forcible and devout eloquence.

[3] The writer quotes the words exactly as they stand in Gen. xxi. 12.
They are there assigned as the reason why Abraham should not
hesitate to send away Ishmael at the demand of Sarah. Doubtless he

intends to call attention to the previous trial of Abraham's faith and obedience which he had already undergone. Ishmael had been sent away, and now Isaac was required as a sacrifice!

Verse 19.—Accounting that God was able to raise even from the dead (καὶ ἐκ νεκρῶν ἐγείρειν), from whence also He received him back figuratively (ἐν παραβολῇ ἐκομίσατο, *in a figure*).[1]

[1] Λογισάμενος κ.τ.λ. Luther translates the above verse, which the perverse ingenuity of critics has rendered difficult, " Und dachte, Gott " kann auch wohl von den Todten erwecken, daher er auch ihn zum " Vorbilde wieder nahm," i.e., *And thought, God can assuredly raise from the dead also, wherefore He received him back as a type*, sc., *of the Resurrection*.—This rendering of Luther's is consonant with the Vulgate: —" Arbitrans quia et a mortuis suscitare potens est Deus: unde cum et " in parabolam accepit." These two renderings are paraphrastic, rather than grammatically literal. I cannot help feeling that Philo has unconsciously expressed the true meaning of the Writer to the Hebrews when he says, Τῷ δ' ἡ πρᾶξις εἰ καὶ μὴ τὸ τέλος ἐπηκολούθησεν, ὁλόκληρος καὶ παντελὴς, οὐ μόνον ἐν ταῖς ἱεραῖς βίβλοις, ἀλλὰ καὶ ἐν ταῖς τῶν ἀναγινωσκόντων διανοίαις ἀνάγραπτος ἐστηλίτευται. " But as far " as he was concerned, the deed, although it was not carried into " actual effect, is inscribed legibly not only in the Sacred Books, " but also in the minds of the readers, as complete and accomplished." (*De Abrahamo*, Works, *Mangey's Edit.*, vol. ii., p. 26.)—Abraham had braced himself up to the ordeal. He had prepared to slay his son, feeling convinced that death itself could not interfere with the ratification of the promise, " In Isaac shall thy seed be called." God *would* raise Isaac from the dead; and so, he had so completely made up his mind to do the deed, that unless the Angel of the Lord had interposed, when the knife was outstretched, Isaac would have died. Similar in sentiment is the Vulgate translation of Job xiii. 15: *Etiam si occiderit me, in ipso sperabo*, הן יקטלני לא (לו) איחל. And such is the confidence expressed by St. Paul to the Romans, viii. 38—39:—" For I am per- " suaded that neither death, nor life,............nor any other creature " shall be able to separate us from the love of God which is in Christ " Jesus our Lord." And to this faith of Abraham, viz., that God would raise Isaac from the dead, St. Paul alludes, Rom. iv. 16—17, where Abraham is said to be " the father of us all, in the sight of " that God (κατέναντι οὗ ἐπίστευσε Θεοῦ κ.τ.λ.) whom he believed, who " raises the dead, and accounts things that are not, as if they were."

And *thus* it was that Abraham figuratively received his son from the dead. He was dead as far as Abraham was concerned, until his hand was stayed from heaven. By the same God who imposed the trial, was Abraham released from his obedience to the command. But to no inferior summons would he have rendered like obedience. Dr. Alford, in discussing the meaning of ἐκομίσατο, observes well that "Josephus (Antiq. i. "13, 4) uses the word of Abraham and Isaac on the very occasion in "question—οἱ δὲ παρ' ἐλπίδας ἑαυτοὺς κεκομισμένοι." I cannot, however, congratulate the Very Reverend Dean upon the lucidity of the argument by which he proves, to his own satisfaction, that the "true identification "of the παραβολή is to be found in the figure under which Isaac was "sacrificed, viz., the ram, as already hinted by St. Chrysostom." The ram was the instrument of no *figurative* recovery of Isaac, but of a real one from impending death. The restoration of Isaac to his father was symbolical of the resurrection. Abraham figuratively received him ἐκ νεκρῶν, when he dismounted from the altar and returned to his father's arms. The ram could not have been at once the symbol of Isaac's deliverance, and his actual and vicarious substitute in death. Besides, what was the object of, and instruction to be conveyed in, the parable of the ram, when a far more obvious and intelligible parable had been enacted by Isaac himself? As far as Isaac was concerned, the parable was over as soon as he was safely restored to his father's bosom. He was delivered from death *actually*, but was raised from the dead ἐν παραβολῇ. Equally untenable is Prof. Stuart's proposed rendering of the entire verse, "Abraham believed that God could raise Isaac from "the dead, because he had as it were obtained him from the dead, *i.e.*, "he was born of those who (κατὰ ταῦτα νεκροὶ ἦσαν).........Abraham "believed God could raise his son from the dead. Why? He had "good reason to conclude so, for God had already done *what was* "*equivalent to this, or like this;* He had done this ἐν παραβολῇ, *in a* "*comparative manner*, i.e., in a manner that would compare with rising "from the dead, when he brought about his birth from those who were "dead as to the power of procreation. Παραβολή means *comparison*, "*similitude; ἐν παραβολῇ, comparatively, in like manner, with similitude,* "*as it were.*" Equally objectionable is Hombergius' proposal to render ἐν παραβολῇ *in præsentissimo periculo*, i.e., in the most extreme peril of his life. The reader will find these latter suggestions ably and amply discussed in J. C. Wolfii, *Curæ Philologicæ et Criticæ*, tom. iv., pp. 760—762.

The author of the *Nizzachon Vetus*, whose remarks upon the subject are singularly like Philo's, observes, "It may be asked, *Was it then so* "*great a matter that Abraham was willing to slay his son at the command*

"*of God? Verily there does not exist a man so wicked in the world, who
"if God, in his glory and personally* (בכבודו ובעצמו) *said to him*, Slay thy
"son, would not have done it. Answ.—Nevertheless it was a great
"matter, because he was his only son, and was born in the time of
"their old age (שבן) יהיד הוא ילוד וקנותם), and yet he did not shrink, nor
"make objections. It may be asked further, *Could not Abraham
"perceive that it was for the sake of trying him that he was tempted,
"seeing that God had made him trust that* 'in Isaac shall thy seed be
"'called'; *and how could He annul the former promises?* Quite true;
"but learn from this that Abraham did not hesitate in the smallest
"degree. And also, it may fairly be said, that he thought in himself,
"*The Holy One, blessed be He, will bring him to life again, for He
"quickens the dead*" (ועוד י״ל שהוא חשב [נ]ינו הקב״ה יהיהו, כי הוא מחיה
מתים).—*Nizz. Vet.*, p. 22; printed at length in Wagenseil's *Tela Ignea
Satanæ.* (For Philo's words, see p. 185.)

Wettstein (*in loco*) quotes from the *Pirke Eliezer*, 31, "R. J. dixit:
"cum appropinquaret gladius collo ejus, fugit et exiit anima Isaaci:
"cum autem audiret vocem inter duos Cherubinos: *noli immittere manum
"tuam puero*, rediit anima in corpus suum. Et solvit eum, stetit que
"super pedes suos, et novit Isaacus resurrectionem mortuorum ex Lege,
"quia omnes mortui resurgent: ea hora dixit, *Benedictus tu, Domine,
"qui vivificas mortuos.*" In illustration of the above, Wettstein refers
to Rom. iv. 19. See also his note on Rom. iv. 17.

Verses 20, 21.—By faith Isaac[1] blessed Jacob and Esau concerning things to come (περὶ μελλόντων, see verse 1). By faith Jacob when dying (ἀποθνήσκων, *moriturus*) blessed each[2] of the sons of Joseph separately (ἕκαστον τῶν υἱῶν Ἰωσὴφ) and worshipped [*leaning*] upon the top of his staff (καὶ προσεκύνησεν ἐπὶ τὸ ἄκρον τοῦ ῥάβδου αὐτοῦ, und neigte sich gegen seines Scepters Spitze.— *Luth.*).[3]

[1] Isaac's blessing is a bright illustration of the definition of faith in the first verse of this chapter. Abraham had been gathered to his fathers, and rested as a stranger in a strange land. Isaac was expecting to lay his ashes far from his ancestral home in Chaldæa, and without the remotest human probability that his descendants would ever possess the land of Canaan, and yet he leaves them a legacy of prophetic blessing. His partiality for his eldest son is defeated by Jacob's stratagem. But yet the promise to Abraham is the one engrossing idea that occu-

pies his thoughts. It is the blessing promised to Abraham (Gen. xii. 3) which he proposes to transmit. As soon, however, as his eyes are opened by Esau's return, he acquiesces in God's overruling appointment. He gives his secondary benediction to Esau. How literally fulfilled it was is apparent from 2 Sam. viii. 14 and 2 Kings viii. 20. (See Smith's Dict. Articles, *Esau, Edom.*)

² Commentators have been so eager to display their ingenuity upon the closing words of this verse, that they have reserved but little space to discuss the illustration of faith which Jacob's particular blessing of Ephraim and Manasseh affords. Why does the writer to the Hebrews select this example of Jacob's faith, in preference to that afforded by his wondrous prediction respecting the destinies of his own children? The true explanation lies in the word ἕκαστον (*i.e.*, individually). Jacob did not content himself with a general blessing upon Joseph. He did not bestow a collective blessing upon Joseph and his sons, but he wittingly crossed his hands, as Manasseh and Ephraim knelt before him, and laid his right hand on Ephraim the youngest. What more improbable that the posterity of young Egyptian princes, for such they were, and also, by the mother's side, of the priestly family (Gen. xli. 45), would ever forsake Egypt their native land, and migrate into Canaan? What more improbable that they should become each of them a separate clan or tribe, much more that the elder should be subordinated in importance to the younger, and that Ephraim's seed should become "a fulness of the nations" (מלא הגוים)? Gen. xlviii. 19. Jacob's recapitulation of the original promise renewed to himself of the grant of Canaan, his formal adoption of Ephraim and Manasseh, separating them from any children that should hereafter be born to Joseph in Egypt (Gen. xlviii. 3—6), the terms, moreover, of Jacob's blessing as recorded in the 15th and 16th verses, all show that his object was to transmit the promise made to Abraham and Isaac to Joseph's posterity through Ephraim, the representative of the kingdom of Israel: "And " he blessed Joseph, and said, God before whom my fathers Abraham " and Isaac did walk, the God which fed me all my life long unto this " day. The Angel which redeemed me (המלאך הגאל אתי, see J. Wesselii " *Dissert. Sacr. Leidens*, pp. 311—313, Lugd. Bat., 1721, 4to., and " Schoettgen, *Horæ Hebr.*, tom. ii., pp. 15, 125, 144, 333, 375, 450) from " all evil, bless the lads; and let my name (observe it is said in verse 14, " '*And Israel* stretched out his hands,' &c.) be named on them, and " the name of my fathers Abraham and Isaac; and let them grow into " a multitude in the midst of the earth." The closing words of the blessing (Gen. xlviii. 21, 22) abundantly exhibit the firmness of Jacob's faith in the promise of Canaan, so that he even assigns one particular

locality (viz., Shechem, Josh. xxiv. 32) to the family of Joseph ; and Jacob said unto Joseph, "Behold, I die ; but God shall be with you, " and bring you again unto the land of your fathers. Moreover, I have " given to thee one portion above thy brethren, which I took out of the " hand of the Amorite with my sword and my bow." Here, then, is a signal specimen of that faith which is the ἐλπιζομένων ὑπόστασις, πραγμάτων ἔλεγχος οὐ βλεπομένων. And all these superlative tokens of Jacob's implicit confidence in the promises of God amply justify the Writer to the Hebrews in holding them up to the persecuted and wavering converts for imitation.

³ Καὶ προσεκύνησεν ἐπὶ τὸ ἄκρον κ.τ.λ. The occasion here referred to was not the one recorded in Gen. xlvii. 31, where it is said, according to the Masoretic punctuation, "And Israel bowed himself upon the "bed's head" (וישתחו ישראל על ראש הַמִּטָּה), but "upon the top of his staff," according to the LXX, but the Vulgate has *adoravit Israel Deum, conversus ad lectuli caput*. (For an account of the *Masorites* and the *Masorah* see Prideaux's connexion of the Old and New Testament, vol. i. pp., 334—348. London, 1845, 8vo.) There is no such passage in Gen. xlviii., where the blessing of the sons of Joseph is related. Had the words there occurred, we should have the true reading of the word מטה decided for us, upon inspired authority. As it is, we have no certain data to go upon, but can conjecture with every degree of probability that the punctuation of הַמִּטָּה hammittah, *the bed*, in Gen. xlvii. 31, should have been הַמַּטֶּה, hammatteh, *staff*. One fact, however, is decided for us upon the authority of Heb. xi. 21, *i.e.*, when Jacob blessed the sons of Joseph, he *leaned upon the top of his staff, and worshipped*. Jacob, when his end was approaching, was told, Gen. xlviii. 2, " Behold, thy son Joseph cometh unto thee ; and Israel " strengthened himself, and sat upon the bed." (עַל הַמִּטָּה.—For the figure of an Egyptian bedstead see Smith's Dict., Article *Bed*.) That the patriarch's feet rested upon the ground when he sat up to make this final effort, we may gather from the fact that Manasseh and Ephraim stood " between his knees " to receive his embrace (verse 12). Most probably, then, Jacob leant upon his staff, as he conversed with Joseph, and gave his benediction to him and his children, and also to his own sons, whom he sent for (Gen. xlix. 1) to receive his parting charge ; and then, spent with the effort, we read, Gen. xlix. 33, " When " Jacob had made an end of commanding his sons, he gathered up his " feet into the bed (ויאסף רגליו אל המטה) and yielded up the ghost, and " was gathered unto his people." It is plain, therefore, that the inspired Epistle to the Hebrews furnishes an incidental detail, which is wanting in Gen. xlviii. and xlix. Surenhusius observes that the

New Testament writers not unfrequently supply omissions in the sacred narrative of the Old, and remarks that David in Ps. cv. mentions the iron fetters which Joseph wore in his prison-house, but which are not alluded to in the book of Genesis. (Βίβλος καταλλ., p. 645.) The learned writer gives other specimens of similar omissions in his 27th Thesis on pp. 106, 107 of the same work. By a curious oversight Surenhusius writes, *ibid.*, p. 647:—"Denique notandum est quod "Apostolus pro verbo חלה *ægrotans*, quod Gen. xlviii. 1, occurrit "dixerit ἀποθνήσκων, *moriturus*, quia eventus docuit, Jacobum in illa "ægritudine mortuum fuisse." Such a supposition is rendered entirely unnecessary by Jacob's own words as recorded in verse 21 of this same chapter, הני אנכי מת, *behold, I am dying*. Surenhusius rightly regards Gen. xlviii. and xlix. as describing one continuous event, which makes his assertion above quoted the more untenable.—Why, then, is mention made of Jacob's leaning upon his staff? Probably the writer intended to contrast, as strikingly as possible, the Patriarch's indomitable faith with his bodily prostration. His life was fast ebbing away. His earthly tabernacle was about to be taken down, his frame was bent, and his eyes dim with the gathering mists of dissolution, but his faith was erect and invincible, the eyes of his soul penetrated into the far-off ages of futurity, and saw the promise realized, and the covenanted blessings vouchsafed. *Be ye*, the writer would say to his discouraged readers, *in like manner faithful unto death, and He will give you the crown of life!* The act of leaning, indicating the dying Saint's extreme infirmity, and not the staff itself, is the point to which attention is directed. The word used in Gen. xxxii. 10 (11), of Jacob's staff, is מקל and not מטה. I cannot think that any allusion is here intended to this staff of Jacob's, far less to the Rabbinical fables respecting the Rod of Moses, which it is affirmed was created of a sapphire stone on the evening of the Sabbath day, and delivered to Adam in Paradise, and passed on through Enoch, Noah, Shem, Abraham, Isaac, and Jacob, to Joseph in Egypt, where it ultimately came into the possession of Moses. Dr. Alford (*in loco*) well observes,—"An incalculable quantity of "idolatrous nonsense has been written on these words by Roman "Catholic Commentators, taking as their starting-point the rendering "of the Vulgate, *et adoravit fastigium virgæ ejus*, and thence deriving "an argument for the worship of images, assuming that there was an "image or symbol of power upon Joseph's staff, to which they apply "the words. But first it must be Jacob's, and not Joseph's staff which "is intended, ' *virgæ suæ*,' not *ejus*," &c. For a further and very copious discussion of the subject the reader may with advantage consult J. C. Wolfius, in loco, *Curæ Philol. et Crit.*, tom. iv., pp. 762—766, as well as Surenhusius, as above indicated.

Verse 22.—By faith Joseph[1] when dying made mention of the exodus of the children of Israel, and gave injunctions (ἐνετείλατο) concerning his own bones.

[1] The writer passes over all Joseph's early self-denials and sufferings, and brings out into strongest relief the object and end of his whole life, viz., his unwavering devotion to the hope of the Patriarchs. He and his fathers considered themselves only as instruments to accomplish the one great end, viz., the ratification of the blessings promised to and in Abraham. By faith they lived, and in the faith they died, passing away with the certain assurance that the Divine plan had been one step advanced to its accomplishment, that another link had been added to the golden chain which should at last bind together into one all the children of God that are scattered abroad. He had been very great in Egypt, but he asked no memorial of colossal proportions, such as the Egyptians were wont to raise, to be erected to his memory. He rather charged his posterity to carry forth his bones to the land of Promise, to which by anticipation they already belonged. There he would have them to rest in hope. In Egypt he was but a stranger and a pilgrim. He knew that at the end of the 400 years God would be as good as his word, and so, τελευτῶν, περὶ τοῦ Ἐξόδου τῶν υἱῶν Ἰσραὴλ ἐμνημόνευσε, καὶ περὶ τῶν ὀστέων αὐτοῦ ἐνετείλατο. The circumstance above alluded to is narrated in Gen. l. 24, 25,—" And Joseph said unto " his brethren, I die : and God will surely visit you, and bring you out " of this land unto the land which he sware to Abraham, to Isaac, and " to Jacob. And Joseph took an oath of the children of Israel, saying, " God will surely visit you, and ye shall carry up my bones from hence. " So Joseph died, being an hundred and ten years old, and they em-" balmed him, and he was put in a coffin in Egypt." In Exod. xiii. 19 we read that " Moses took the bones of Joseph with him," &c. In Josh. xxiv. 32 it is written, " And the bones of Joseph, which the " children of Israel brought up out of Egypt, buried they in Shechem... " and it became the inheritance of the children of Joseph." Compare Jacob's bequest to Joseph, Gen. xlviii. 22. Philo, when speaking of Joseph's dying injunction to his brethren, writes :—Τὰ δ' ἀξιομνημόνευτα ταῦτα ἦν. Τὸ πιστεῦσαι ὅτι ἐπισκέψεται ὁ Θεὸς τὸ ὁρατικὸν γένος, καὶ οὐ παραδώσει μέχρι παντὸς αὐτὸ ἀμαθίᾳ, τυφλῇ δεσποίνῃ· τὸ διακρῖναι τά τε θνητὰ τῆς ψυχῆς καὶ τὰ ἄφθαρτα· καὶ τὰ μὲν ὅσα περὶ τὰς σώματος ἡδονὰς καὶ τὰς ἄλλας παθῶν ἀμετρίας, θνητὰ ὄντα, Αἰγύπτῳ καταλιπεῖν. Περὶ δὲ τῶν ἀφθάρτων σπουδὴν ποιήσασθαι, ὅπως μετὰ τῶν ἀναβαινόντων εἰς τὰς ἀρετῆς πόλεις διακομισθῇ, καὶ ὅρκῳ τὴν σπουδὴν ἐμπεδώσασθαι. " The things " worthy to be noted are as follows : that he believed that God would

"visit the Israelitish race, and would not give them over perpetually to
"ignorance as to a blind mistress. Also that he distinguished between
"the mortal parts of the soul and those that are immortal. And
"that he left in Egypt those that were mortal, viz., bodily enjoyments
"and immoderate affections. That he also made a covenant concerning
"the imperishable things that they should take along with them (the
"Israelites) when they went up to the cities of virtue, and made this
"covenant obligatory by an oath." (*De Migratione Abrahami*, Works,
Mangey's Edit., vol. i., p. 439.)

Verses 23—25.—By faith Moses, when he was born, was hid for three months by his parents (τῶν πατέρων αὐτοῦ) because they saw that the child was goodly[1] (ἀστεῖον, טוב, Exod. ii. 2), and they did not fear (οὐκ ἐφοβήθησαν, *paid no respect to*) the king's injunction.[2] By faith Moses when he had grown up[3] (μέγας γενόμενος, *grandis factus*, Vulg. *Da er gross ward*, Luth.) declined (ἠρνήσατο, *objected, refused*) to be called the son of Pharaoh's daughter. Electing rather to endure hardship with the people of God, than to have a temporary enjoyment[4] (πρόσκαιρον ἀπόλαυσιν, i.e., *shortlived, evanescent, transitory*) of sin.

[1] Γεννηθεὶς οὖν ὁ παῖς εὐθὺς ὄψιν ἐνέφηνεν ἀστειοτέραν ἢ κατ' ἰδιώτην, ὡς καὶ τῶν τοῦ τυράννου κηρυγμάτων, ἐφ' ὅσον οἷόν τε ἦν, τοὺς γονεῖς ἀλογῆσαι. "At his birth the child immediately displayed an appearance fairer "than an ordinary person's, so that his parents disregarded, as far as "they could, the edicts of the king."—*Philo de Mose*, Works, *Mangey's Edit.*, vol. ii., p. 82.

[2] Πίστει Μωσῆς γεννηθεὶς ἐκρύβη κ.τ.λ. How is this an example of faith, and to what object was this faith directed? The writer points to two actions, in illustration of his meaning. First, Moses' concealment for three months by his parents. Secondly, his parents' courageous disregard of the king's edict. How, then, do these two examples of faith bear directly upon the circumstances of the Hebrews for whose consolation and encouragement they are called to remembrance? The time of Moses' birth was one of bitter persecution. The life of Israel's greatest lawgiver hung in suspense for the first three months of his existence. His parents, undismayed by the risk they ran in disobeying the tyrant's orders, hid him away (affectionately yearning over their

beautiful babe, respecting whom St. Stephen, by a well-known Hebraism [see Gen. x. 9, respecting Nimrod], says, Acts vii. 20, ἦν ἀστεῖος τῷ Θεῷ), and firmly believing that God, who had promised to Abraham that his posterity should be as the stars and the sea-shore sand innumerable, would never acquiesce in Pharaoh's scheme for their extirpation. Upon this promise Jacob, when dying, took his stand (Gen. xlviii. 4); and so (*ibid.*, 16) he prays that Joseph's sons may "grow into a multi-"tude (וידגו לרב, i.e., *multiply like fishes*) in the midst of the earth." Now, it was in consequence of the visible and growing fulfilment of this prophecy that Pharaoh and his people had taken alarm, and resolved to frustrate its further accomplishment. In Exod. i. 7 we read, " And the children of Israel were fruitful, and increased abund-"antly (וישרצו, *swarmed*, as Gesenius observes, ' Passim locus [terra vel "'mare] dicitur *reptare* reptilibus, *i.e.*, iis *scatere* [von etwas wimmeln], "'sq. acc., velut mare bestiis aquatilibus. Gen. i. 20, 21 ; Aegyptus "'ranis, Ex. vii. 28 ; Ps. cv. 30'), and multiplied, and waxed exceeding "mighty, and the land was filled with them." No secret was made of the object of the inhumanities inflicted upon the Hebrews. The avowed purpose was the extinction of the people. The King directed the Hebrew midwives (ויאמר מלך מצרים למילדת העבריה) to destroy all the male infants. (Exod. i. 15) It has been attempted to be shown, upon very inadequate grounds, that Shiphra and Puah were Egyptians, and not Jewesses, but the Hebrew text (if the construction of Exod. i. 20 be followed), the Targums, and the Jewish writers lend no sanction whatever to such a theory. The Targum of Palestine or Jonathan, and the Targum of Jerusalem, both declare that Shiphra was Jochebed, and Puah was Miriam. The Targum of Jonathan, moreover, relates that it was in consequence of a dream of Pharaoh's, in which the birth of Moses was announced, and which was interpreted by Jannes and Jambres, that the order to kill the children was issued to the midwives. This is not unlike the narrative of Josephus. Was it probable that Egyptians, to whom it was an abomination to eat with the Hebrews (Gen. xliii. 32), and to whom shepherds were also an abomination (Gen. xlvi. 34), would have undertaken the office of midwives to the Hebrews ? Or how can we explain the religious scruples of Shiphra and Puah, if they were mere heathens ? We read, Exod. i. 17, " But "the midwives feared God, and did not as the King of Egypt com-"manded them, but saved the men children alive." It was no mere excuse that the midwives alleged in explanation of their disobedience. The miraculous multiplication of the Israelites was of God ; and in consequence of their humane conduct, God himself rewarded the midwives. (*Ibid.*, 20, 21.) We see, therefore, that the period of Moses' birth was a period of palpable conflict between the powers of darkness and the power of God. The parents of Moses (and doubtless some few others, like the midwives) held fast to the promises made to the fathers. They had implicit faith in their ultimate accomplishment, and so they concealed their infant until further secresy became impossible, and then, in the ark of bulrushes, they committed him, not to the safe keeping of chance or fortune, but to the plighted love of a covenanted God. By their example, the afflicted Hebrews of the apostolic ages, whose lives were also made bitter to them, might take comfort. The Church of God was again passing through a crisis of persecution, and the furnace of affliction, but faith should ultimately triumph, and the promised redemption should be accomplished.

[3] Μέγας γενόμενος, Alford rightly translates "when grown up"; but he is mistaken when he asserts, in reference to Schulz's and Bretschneider's proposed rendering "become great," viz., in dignity as a "citizen," that the usage is the other way. The Hebrew expression ויגדל, in Exod. ii. 10, 11, doubtless signifies an increase in stature and years, but the verb גדל is very frequently employed to denote accession of dignity and importance; *e.g.*, Gen. xxvi. 13, 2 Sam. vii. 22, Ps. civ. 1, Eccl. ii. 9, Jer. v. 27, Esth. iii. 1, v. 11, x. 2, and *passim* in the Old Testament. The words, as used by the Writer to the Hebrews, are equivalent to the expression employed by St. Stephen, Acts. vii. 23, ὡς δὲ ἐπληροῦτο αὐτῷ τεσσαρακονταετὴς χρόνος.

[4] Ἠρνήσατο λέγεσθαι κ.τ.λ. Philo suggests (*De Mose*, Works, *Mangey's Edit.*, vol. ii., p. 86) that Moses was the heir apparent (by adoption) to the crown of Egypt, and adds, in the very sentiment of the Writer to the Hebrews, Τὴν συγγενικὴν καὶ προγονικὴν ἐζήλωσε παιδείαν, τὰ μὲν τῶν εἰσποιησαμένων ἀγαθὰ, καὶ εἰ λαμπρότερα καιροῖς, νόθα εἶναι ὑπολαβών, τὰ δὲ τῶν φύσει γονέων, εἰ καὶ πρὸς ὀλίγον ἀφανέστερα, οἰκεῖα γοῦν καὶ γνήσια. "He emulated the training of his kindred and ancestors, esteeming the "good things of those who had adopted him, although more splendid "for a season, to be in reality spurious, but those of his natural "parents, although they might be for a while less appreciable, to be "true and genuine." Why should this latter statement of Philo's, so exactly in harmony with the inspired statements of the New Testament, be sneered at as "inflated"? That Moses was in a position to be well acquainted with the hope of the patriarchs is shown by Rawlinson (*Bampton Lectures*. Second Edition, 1860. 8vo., p. 39), when he observes, "Adam, according to the Hebrew original, was for 243 years "contemporary with Methusaleh, who conversed for 100 years with "Shem. Shem was for 50 years contemporary with Jacob, who "probably saw Jochebed, Moses' mother. Thus Moses might, by mere

"oral tradition, have obtained the history of Abraham, and even of the "Deluge, at third hand, and that of the temptation and the fall at "fifth hand." The mere fact of the degraded condition of the great bulk of the Israelites in their Egyptian servitude, does not militate against the probability of the preservation of the true faith amongst a select few, any more than the well-known circumstance that there are hundreds of thousands of so-called Christians in England at this moment who never heard of Christ, would supply a safe argument to some antichristian writer centuries hence for asserting that, in 1871, the religion of Jesus was extinct in Great Britain. Elijah supposed (1 Kings xix.) that he was the last worshipper of the true God left in Israel, and yet, undiscernible to the eye of sense. God had reserved to Himself seven thousand devoted followers. Schoettgen, *in loco*, remarks, " Nam Moses tanquam filius filiæ Pharaonis educatus erat. " Exod. ii. 10 ; Actor. vii. 20 ; Tanchuma, fol. 48, 4. *Moses educatus* " *est in domo Pharaonis*, היה סבור שהיה בן ביתו, *et existimibatur, quasi in* " *domo ipsius* natus esset."

Verses 26—28.—Esteeming the reproach of Christ (τὸν ὀνειδισμὸν τοῦ Χριστοῦ, i.e., *the obloquy, and derisive ill-will, on account of his faith in the Messiah*)[1] greater riches than the treasures of Egypt, for he looked away to the recompense of reward (ἀπέβλεπε γὰρ εἰς τὴν μισθαποδοσίαν). By faith, he relinquished (κατέλιπεν, *abandoned, quitted*) Egypt, after having braved (μὴ φοβηθεὶς τὸν θυμὸν) the exasperation of the King.[2] For he persevered as if he saw the Invisible. By faith he celebrated *or* prepared (πεποίηκε, *the sacrificial rite*) the passover, and the sprinkling of the blood, in order that He who destroyed the firstborn might not touch them.[3]

[1] These words are very explicit, and must on no account be explained away, but ought to be read by the light of 1 Cor. x. 3, 4, Καὶ πάντες τὸ αὐτὸ βρῶμα πνευματικὸν ἔφαγον. Καὶ πάντες τὸ αὐτὸ πόμα πνευματικὸν ἔπιον, ἔπινον γὰρ ἐκ πνευματικῆς ἀκολουθούσης πέτρας, ἡ δὲ πέτρα ἦν ὁ Χριστός. The faith of Moses was that of the Patriarchs. Abraham rejoiced to see Christ's day. Enoch prophesied concerning the consummation of all things in and by Him. The Gentile self-esteem that would limit all true perception of "good things to come" to the so-called Christian dispensation, would be grotesquely ridiculous, were it

not too pernicious in its consequences to be smiled at. God's revelation in every age was sufficient to *save* sinners. The Divinely appointed medium of salvation to the Patriarchal and Mosaic dispensations was faith in a coming Messiah. Of Himself our Lord Jesus testified that Moses spake. His mediatorial office is clearly set forth in Deut. xviii. 15—19. The spiritual nature of the believer's life is described in Deut. viii. 3. The ingathering of the Gentiles is hailed with holy rapture (according to St. Paul's interpretation, Rom. xv. 10) in Deut. xxxii. 43. The Resurrection is established, by the very same argument that St. Peter (2 iii. 8) employs to demonstrate the certainty of Christ's return, in Ps. xc. 3, 4; and in this latter Psalm (put into the mouth of a generation, all the adults of which were to perish within the forty years' wandering in the wilderness) the Israelites are taught to pray, "So "teach us to number our days, that we may apply our hearts unto "wisdom." Bishop Warburton's theory, copied by Davidson (*Discourses on Prophecy*, p. 124, &c. 3d Edit., 1834, 8vo.) and others, that the Israelites under Moses knew nothing of the life after death, is palpably contrary to fact. If Moses was the writer of the Book of Genesis, the history of "The tree of life," the translation of Enoch, the gathering of Abraham, Isaac, and Jacob to their fathers, &c., &c., were familiar topics to his people. Even Balaam, the heathen prophet, desired "to die the death of the righteous," and that his "last end "might be like his." The pertinacious devotion of the Israelites to necromancy and witchcraft is decisive as to the popular belief entertained by them respecting the life after death. See Deut. xviii. 11, where the expression דרש אל המתים, *a seeker of, or enquirer after, the dead*, is rendered by the Authorized Version "necromancer." Moreover, had not the immortality of the soul been a dogma (as with Job) of their ancestral faith amongst the Israelites, they might have learned it in Egypt, where it was an article of the popular creed, and upon whose very walls the judgment-scene is depicted. (See Sharpe's *Egypt*, vol. i., p. 56—59 and 66; see also Gesenius, *Lexicon Manuale*, p. 20, article אוב.) The recompense of reward, moreover, which Moses looked to, was doubtless that promised to Abraham (Gen. xv. 1), viz., the fruition of eternal life with God, although he was to die (15) in a good old age, without having received the temporal promise. The "reproach of Christ," therefore, which Moses elected in preference to the treasures of Egypt, was assuredly the obloquy to which he exposed himself in setting aside the religious tenets of his protectors, and his preferring to commit his fortunes to the custody of the Divine promises, rather than to settle down in the arms of dignity and affluence which lay open before him. In this respect, his self-denial and unhesitating faith afforded a bright and a consolatory example to the persecuted readers of the Epistle to the Hebrews to copy from. The ever-increasing results of Moses' self-denial God's judgment-day alone will reveal. Incalculably and immeasurably great is the μισθαποδοσία which he shall daily receive as long as the world shall last. In Moses, as in Abraham, all the families of the earth can yet account themselves blessed. With Elias he appeared to the apostles in the "Holy Mount," as a partaker of Christ's transfiguration glory. Ewald (*Das Sendschr. a.d. Hebr.*, pp. 130, 131) speaks decisively as to the faith which Moses entertained in Christ, and to which he gave expression, in the Messianic prophecies contained in the Pentateuch, of which latter he was the author. Remarking on the words τὸν ὀνειδισμὸν τοῦ Χριστοῦ, *die Schmach Christus*, he says, " Und hier drängt sich mit diesem kleinen Worte, " dem Redner plözlich wieder ein Gedanke und eine Redensart ein, " welche die Leser mitten in ihre eigene nächste Gegenwart versezt, die " aber vor allem aus seiner eigensten tiefsten Empfindung floss, und " die er trozdem dass sie beinahe 2000 Jahre überspringt, dennoch " wagen Konnte, weil ihm nach 1, 1—4, und den anderen oben " bemerkten Zeichen der Gedanke an den Logos, und daher an den " unzerreissbaren festen Zusammenhang aller Bestrebungen und aller " Leiden der Kinder Gottes, aufs lebendigste vorschwebte ; wozu " kommt dass auch schon der Pentateuch Messianische Weissagungen " enthält, und dieses mit Recht, gerade bei Mose als dessen Verfasser, " so geheimnissvoll denkwürdig schien."

[2] Πίστει κατέλιπεν Αἴγυπτον μὴ φοβηθεὶς κ.τ.λ. This, doubtless, partly refers to the indignation which Moses' avowed sympathy with his suffering kinsmen excited at the court of Egypt. He was regarded as an ingrate and a traitor thwarting the scheme for ridding Egypt of a troublesome incubus, if not as a renegade. We have no reason to decide that the occasion upon which he slew the Egyptian was the first time on which he had endeavoured to mitigate the rigours of their condition. Moreover, his steady adherence to the true faith must have brought him into collision with the idolatrous court. This is probably one aspect in which we may legitimately understand the ὀνειδισμὸν τοῦ Χριστοῦ. He incurred ill-will, hostility, dislike, and ridicule by his steadfastness, and yet he persevered, as if he saw the Invisible. Willing to live godly, he had to suffer persecution. He had been trained in all the wisdom and learning of the Egyptians, and yet all this pagan lore went for nothing. Like Daniel, he stood upright and immoveable, though surrounded by every inducement to forego his ancient faith. I would then propose to understand the passage thus. By faith, Moses at last took the final step that necessitated his

abandoning Egypt with all his prospects, having first braved the displeasure of the King. He remained steadfast (ἐκαρτέρησε), proof alike against blandishments and threats, as if he saw the Invisible God. Some would desire to explain these words, of Moses' heroic and inflexible firmness in his demands upon Pharaoh to let the people go. This, however, would take the subject out of its chronological order. It seems more in harmony with the lesson of suffering faith and self-denial for the kingdom of heaven's sake, which the writer is inculcating upon his readers, to refer the passage to Moses' early life and renunciation of all that is usually desirable in the eyes of men. His decision was justified ultimately by a reward more than commensurate with the sacrifice required of him. He stood not only amongst earthly princes, but he spake face to face with Jehovah himself, as the Mediator of his Covenant, and the type of Christ. The above notice of the persecutions which Moses endured accords with the traditions preserved by Josephus and Philo. Before dismissing the subject of Moses' abandonment of Egypt, I would make one remark upon Dean Stanley's unscholarly and unwarranted insinuation that Moses, when he smote the Egyptian, was guilty of nothing less than a deliberate and cowardly murder. The Dean writes, "All that remains of these traditions is "the simple and natural incident that, seeing an Israelite suffering the "bastinado (!) from an Egyptian, and thinking that they were alone, "he slew the Egyptian (the later tradition, preserved by Clement of "Alexandria, said 'with a word of his mouth'), and buried the corpse "in the sand," &c. (*Smith's Dict.*; Article, MOSES.) Now, the Hebrew word which Dr. Stanley ventures to paraphrase "suffering the bastinado," he ought to have known is מַכֶּה. A cursory reference to a Hebrew Concordance would have shown him that the verb נכה, the Hiphil participle of which is used in Exod. ii. 11, is ordinarily employed in the sense of *smiting so as to inflict mortal injury*, i.e., *to kill, to smite and extirpate in battle;* and, even of inanimate things, *to destroy*, as of the standing crops, Exod. ix. 31, 32. The Englishman's Hebrew and Chaldee Concordance gives more than six columns of references under נכה, and, in the great majority of instances, the word includes the signification of killing. It is quite true that, in Exod. v. 14—16, יֻכּוּ and מַכִּים must be understood of *corporal punishment*. But a reference to the LXX. and Vulgate versions would have shown the Dean that a distinction was to be made between Exod. ii. 11 and Exod. v. 14, 16. The LXX. has τύπτοντα in Exod. ii. 11, and the Vulgate *percutientem*, whilst in Exod. v. 14—16 the LXX. version has ἐμαστιγώθησαν and μεμαστίγωνται, and the Vulgate *flagellati sunt*, and *flagellis caedimur*, respectively. St. Stephen, indeed, speaks of the outraged Hebrew,

Acts vii. 24, simply as ἀδικούμενον, but to this it may be answered that πατάξας does not necessarily or primarily mean *to wound mortally*, and yet we know by the sequel that Moses did kill (ויך) the Egyptian. Again, the Hebrew words ויפן כה וכה וירא כי אין איש, "and he looked this way "and that way, and saw that there was no man," express nothing whatever as to the motive of his looking. In Isaiah lix. 16 the same expression, probably in symbolical allusion to this very passage, is used, but in the signification of "looking for help or assistance," before going forth to judgment and vengeance:—

וירא כי אין איש וישתומם כי אין מפגיע ותושע לו זרעו צדקתו היא סמכתהו

"And he saw that there was no man, and wondered that there was no "intercessor; therefore his arm brought salvation unto him, and his "righteousness it sustained him." Why, then, should we put the most atrocious construction upon what was really an action humane in itself, and undoubtedly necessitated by the dire exigency of the occasion? Moses' subsequent alarm at what had occurred, considering the ill-savour in which he already was, and the barbarous resolution of the Egyptians to extirpate their bondmen, and the utter impossibility of obtaining a fair hearing, is natural enough; but it leaves the morality, as well as the necessity of putting the Egyptian to death exactly where it was. A reverent mind would adopt any alternative, before deliberately imputing connivance at, and approval of assassination, to the inspired writers of the Old and New Testament, in both of which Moses' deed is spoken of in terms of tacit approval, if not of commendation. Adroit insinuations like the above, against the morality of God's Word, are marvellously in the style of Voltaire, but when they come to be subjected to closer examination, they are not a whit more trustworthy than the sneering falsities of that pitiful "inventor of evil things." One thing is quite certain, viz., that the Writer to the Hebrews distinctly affirms that Moses' abandonment of Egypt was an act of faith, compulsory, doubtless, at the last, in consequence of the exemplary vengeance inflicted upon the would-be murderer of his poor kinsman, whose life Moses saved at the peril of his own. Nor was it only *an act*, but *the crowning act* of his steadfast self-denials in Egypt, the treasures of which he had relinquished, in resolution, long before he escaped for his life from the vengeance of the King.

³ The preparation of the Passover was, of its kind, an act of faith, similar to that of Noah's preparation of the ark. Pharaoh and the Egyptians remained as obdurate as ever; in fact, the tyrant had threatened Moses with death, if he again molested him with the demand for the liberation of the Israelites. (Exod. x. 28, 29.) It was therefore a crisis in which even God's judgments had apparently failed to bring

about the desired effect. The successive plagues had left the Hebrews only in more evil case. For Moses, with the consciousness of his ill-success, to go to the Israelites and bid them to choose a lamb on the tenth day of the month, to be slain on the fourteenth, as the next step in the drama of deliverance, must have carried with it a consciousness of inadequacy, if not of absurdity, that required a strong faith indeed to propound it to his exasperated countrymen. Hitherto his efforts had only availed to set oppressor and bondman more completely by the ears. The rigour of the oppressors had been increased instead of diminished, and now Pharaoh had refused ever to see Moses again. To convince his people, therefore, of the peremptory necessity of complying with the command to be in readiness to celebrate the Passover, was doubtless a very difficult task, but faith overcame, and the Passover was got ready, and the Exodus was accomplished. (For much interesting matter upon this subject, see the late Dr. M'Caul's *Examination of Bishop Colenso's Difficulties*, 1863. 8vo., pp. 56—65.) So, also, with regard to the sprinkling of the blood. Doubtless many of the Hebrews were inclined to laugh at the proposal as a silly superstition. No ordinary pertinacity would be required to see the order carried out, and yet Moses' belief in what he enjoined was so transparent and convincing, that the thing was done, and "he that destroyed the firstborn "did not touch them."—Here, then, was an argument for making a bold avowal of Christ, in spite of all risks entailed by the public profession of Christianity. It was a plain command, and God would take care of the results. The duty was plain; the consequences in the hands of God himself.

The timorous convert might ask, *Cannot I be saved? Cannot I serve Christ equally well without incurring the odium of baptism, and the reproach of the Cross?* The allusion to the blood of sprinkling supplied the answer. It was the badge of distinction between the saved and the lost; the token of salvation, the mark of God's covenanted favour and acceptance. Surenhusius writes (Βίβλος καταλλ., p. 654), "Per ποίησιν "τοῦ πάσχατος, *Hebraice* עשית הפסח, intelliguntur omnia illa præcepta quæ "asservationem agni a decimo die mensis ad decimum quartum, et "deinde mactationem et sanguinis exceptionem spectant; per πρόσχυσιν "τοῦ αἵματος, intelligitur sanguinis aspersio ad postes et superliminaria; "per ὀλοθρευθήν, sive ὀλοθρεύων, intelligitur משחית *destructor*, de quo "Exod. xii. 13 et 23," &c.

Verses 29—31.—By faith,[1] they (the Israelites) passed through the Red Sea (סוּף יָם *sea of weeds*, Exod. xv. 4;

ἐν ἐρυθρᾷ θαλάσσῃ, LXX. *ibid.*), which the Egyptians assayed to do, and were drowned. By faith, the walls of Jericho fell, after they had been compassed (κυκλωθέντα, *encircled*) about for seven days.² By faith, Rahab the harlot did not perish with the unbelievers (τοῖς ἀπειθήσασι, *the contumacious*), having received the spies (Josh. ii.) with peace (μετ' εἰρήνης, *in a friendly manner.* Stuart.)³

---

¹ The Israelites *proved* their faith by doing as they were bidden. At first a panic seized them, shut in by precipices as they were on either hand, with the armies of Egypt behind them, and with the swelling billows of the Red Sea before them. Moses' heroic belief infused confidence into their desponding souls. At his word they went forward and accomplished the miraculous passage. To the persecuted and wavering Hebrews of apostolic times this allusion would be full of consolatory significance. They carried their lives in their hands. They seemed hedged in unto destruction, and, like their forefathers, were ready to exclaim, "Because there were no graves in Egypt, hast thou "taken us away to die in the wilderness? Wherefore hast thou dealt "thus with us, to carry us forth out of Egypt? *Is* not this the word "that we did tell thee in Egypt, saying, Let us alone, that we may "serve the Egyptians? For it *had been* better for us to serve the "Egyptians than that we should die in the wilderness." Exod. xiv. 11, 12. Here, then, we see that the Israelites expected that they would be slaughtered by the Egyptians. The last thing thought of was to look to the sea as a means of escape. Similar was the case of their descendants; but God himself, with the temptation, would make the way of escape, in order that they might be able to bear it. As St. Paul writes, 1 Cor. x. 13, Ἀλλὰ ποιήσει σὺν τῷ πειρασμῷ καὶ τὴν ἔκβασιν, τοῦ δύνασθαι ὑμᾶς ὑπενεγκεῖν. The Egyptians showed foolhardiness, and not faith. They were not in the path of duty, but flying in the face of God's palpable resistance, and they perished in the waters.

² Josh. vi. Upon the above 30th verse Dean Alford somewhat pointlessly observes, "A second example of the strength of faith in "Israel generally." The real point at issue is, how did the Writer to the Hebrews intend the converts to apply it to their present critical position? I cannot but think it is designed as an encouragement to perseverance in personal steadfastness in the use of the appointed means of grace, and also in fervent entreaty to God that He would soften the hearts of their unbelieving brethren and persecutors. The

ark of God was carried seven times round the walls of Jericho, and at last they fell at the blast of the trumpets. Why, then, should not the strong prejudices of the gainsayers be overcome by a gospel acted in the life, as well as preached by word of mouth? The writer, out of a multitude of examples ready to hand, contents himself with a few appropriately selected instances of faith, such as he would have his readers to follow. He does not deal in vague generalities, but in well-chosen and pertinent illustrations.

³ Rahab exhibited her faith by her reception of the spies. It was a practical faith. She showed that she believed her own statements by the way she treated her guests. Betrayal would have been an easy matter, but she acted as if she believed that the Israelites would take possession of the land, and stipulated for the safety of herself and her relatives. Josh. ii. 12, 13. And this is what is meant in Josh. vi. 25, " And Joshua saved Rahab the harlot alive, and her father's household, " and all that she had ; and she dwelleth in Israel even unto this day ; " because she hid the messengers, which Joshua sent to spy out Jericho." St. James (ii. 25) adduces her as an instance of practical faith. Her deeds answered to her professions, when she said to the spies, " I know " that the Lord hath given you the land......For the Lord your God, he " is God in heaven above and in the earth beneath." Josh. ii. 9—11. But why is the example of Rahab adduced on the present occasion ? I think the reason lies in the fact that to harbour inquirers and converts was a charity not unattended with danger and obloquy. The writer has already skilfully touched upon the subject (x. 33) when he reminds his readers that formerly they were associates of those who were similarly treated with themselves. The position of a Jewish inquirer into Christianity was in those days one of peculiar difficulty and distress. By his own relatives he was abhorred, and treated as a criminal who was worthy of a hundred deaths. His heathen neighbours despised and looked down upon him because he was a Jew, an outcast, and in disgrace with his own people. If, then, his converted brethren were too timid to offer him an asylum, and shut the doors in his face, whither was he to look for countenance and support? Such is the position of the Hebrew convert at the present day; much more in the former times when Christians were few, and Christian sympathy was circumscribed. And this, I take it, is why the writer admonishes the Hebrews (xiii. 1, 2), ἡ φιλαδελφία μενέτω· τῆς φιλοξενίας μὴ ἐπιλανθάνεσθε, διὰ ταύτης γὰρ ἔλαθόν τινες ξενίσαντες ἀγγέλους. The example of Rahab was therefore pregnant with instruction. She a poor heathen had acted like a true believer. What a scandal, then, if believers in Jesus should be outdone and put to shame by her faith and

ready hospitality! In reference to Rahab's former conversation the writer, as also does St. James, calls her ἡ πόρνη. Here we have the inspired interpretation of the Hebrew words, אשה זונה, *a woman a harlot*, Josh. ii. 1. (γυναικὸς πόρνης. LXX.) Josephus (Antiq. v. 1, 2, 7) suppresses the fact of Rahab's vocation, and merely speaks of her as keeping an inn, and Whiston in his note (*in loco*) writes:—" Observe, " that I still call this woman Rahab, an *innkeeper*, not a *harlot;* the " whole history, both in our copies and especially in Josephus, implying " no more. It was indeed so frequent a thing, that women who were " innkeepers were also harlots, or maintainers of harlots, that the word " commonly used for real harlots was usually given them." The probable reason of this euphemistic designation of Rahab by Josephus lies in the fact that she married Salmon, a prince of the house of Judah, as related in Matt. i. 5. The Targum calls her פונדקיתא, *Pundakitha*, πανδοκεύτρια, which Buxtorf, in his *Lexicon Chaldaicum*, thus explains: " *Caupona, Hospita, esculenta vendens, et quoslibet hospitio* excipiens " *Et ingressi sunt in domum mulieris cujusdam* ויעלו לבית אתתא פונדקיתא ; " *cauponæ*. Hebr. בית אשה זונה, Jos. ii. 1. *Et vidit* והוא חמן אתתא פונדקיתא " *illic mulierem cauponam*, apud quam scilicet Schimschon divertit, " hospitandi et pernoctandi causâ, cujus amore captus, et ab ea admissus " fuit, Jud. xvi. 1, והוא בר אתתא פונדקיתא. *Et ipse* (Jephtha) *erat filius* " *mulieris cauponæ*, Jud. ii. 1. Hanc concubinam, non cauponam " publicam, aut scortum fuisse Hebræi tradunt; unde R. Davidis in " Comment. ad hunc locum, tale monitum. *Ista olim in Israel con-* " *suetudo fuit ne devolveretur hæreditas ab una tribu ad aliam, ideo non* " *licebat cuiquam ducere uxorem, quæ non esset ex sua tribu. Unde si* " *forte quis amasset quandam ex tribu alia, exibat illa absque hæreditate,* " *et vulgo appellata fuit* פונדקיתא (ein Wirtin, ein Köchinne, non *Uxor*) " *Hospita, curatrix, aut cibatrix, et talis fuit mater Jephtæ.* Hæc ille— " *Plurale*, בכן אתאה תרתין נשין פונדקן. *Tunc venerunt duæ mulieres cauponæ,* " Hebraicè, נשים זונות, 1 Reg. iii. 16. Rabbi David ad locum Josuæ " scribit mentem Jonathanis esse, quod honestâ appellatione mulieris " cauponariæ intelligat etiam meretricem, quod meretrix sit instar " cauponæ, se cuilibet prostituens, ut caupona omnibus cibum minis- " trans." The following extract from the Babyl. Gemara (treatise *Zevachim*, printed at length in Ugolini's Thes., vol. xix.) is decisive as to the Talmudical opinion respecting Rahab's early career. The passage is found in col. 605:—

ואף רחב הזונה אמרה לשלוחי יהושע כי שמענו את אשר הוביש יהוה את מי ים סוף.
מאי שנא ההם דאמר ליה ולא היה עוד רוח ומאי שנא הכא דקאמר ולא קמה עוד רוח
באיש דאפילו אקשויי נמי לא מקשו וכמנא ידעה דאמר מר אין לך כל שר ונגיד שלא בא
על רחב הזונה. אמרו בת עשר שנים היה כשיצאו ישראל ממצרים וזנתה ארבעים שנה שהיו
ישראל במדבר אחר חמשים שנה נתגיירה אמרה יהא מחל לי בשכר הבל חלון ופשתים :

"Similiter Rachab meretrix dixit legatis Josuæ : *Audivimus, quod
"siccaverit Dominus aquas maris Suph.* Quid ibi repetit dicendo : *et
"non fuit in nobis spiritus?* Et cur hic repetit dicendo : *Et non fuit in
"iis amplius spiritus?* Licet indurescerct, tamen non indurescebat. Et
"Unde cognovit? Dicit Mor : Nullus est tibi princeps, et dux, qui non
"sit congressus cum Rachab meretrice. Dixerunt : Decimum et secun-
"dum annum agebat, quando egressi sunt Israelitæ de Aegypto, et
"scortata est quadraginta annos, in quibus fuerunt Israelitæ in deserto,
"post quinquaginta annos facta est proselyta. Dicit : Ignoscatur mihi
"propter mercedem funiculi lini in fenestra." B. Scheidius, in his
Præterita præteritorum, gives a considerably broader translation of
the above passage, and adds, " *Glossa :* Traditur ita eam dixisse :
"Domine mundi, per tria peccavi, per tria fit condonatio. Per funem
"et linum et fenestram. Nam adulteri ascendebant ad eam funibus,
"viâ fenestræ, et descendebant, et quoque abscondebat eos in linis ligni,
"et per ea ipsa tria, merita est, liberando legatos." (Meuschen, *Nov.
Test. ex Talmude illustr.,* p. 40.) Scheidius quotes at length also a
somewhat celebrated passage from the treatise *Megilla,* f. 14, 2, where
it is asserted that Joshua married Rahab, by whom he had daughters
but no sons, and in which also the following ridiculous statement
occurs :—" Tradiderunt *Rabbini,* Rachab, nomine suo audito, ad forni-
"cationem irritavit. *Glossa :* Siquis commemoret nomen ejus, trahitur
"libidine scortationis ; Jaël voce sua ; Abigail, memoria sui ; Michael
"aspectu sui," &c. (*Ibid.,* pp. 40, 41.) See also Smith's Dict., Article
Rahab, and Surenhusius' Conciliationes de Genealogia Jesu Christi.
(Βίβλος καταλλ., pp. 121—123.)

Verse 32.—And what shall I say more? (καὶ τί ἔτι λέγω;
or perhaps, *Why should I yet run on?*) For the time
would fail me (when) discoursing, in detail, concerning
Gideon,[1] and Barak, and Samson, and Jephtha.[2]

[1] The writer, kindling to his subject with a glow of holy enthusiasm,
surveys the mighty cloud of witnesses grouped around, as it were, in
illustrious conclave. He loses himself in the contemplation of their
achievements, and as his eye flashes from one end to the other of the
glorious assemblage, he forgets the orderly sequence of their acts. He
sees them, not singly as they severally fought and conquered upon life's
laborious arena, but with the triumphant glance of patriotic rapture he
penetrates into the shining courts above, where in radiant fellowship they
stand clustered, so to speak, suspensefully watching the issue of the conflict
yet carried forward, by their brethren in arms who yet remain behind. In
this sublime and vehement outburst of pathetic and fiery eloquence we

must not limit the writer's allusions to any particular age or crisis in the Church's history. He culls at random a posy of historic examples of well-known and familiar deeds, and presents it to his readers in the exulting consciousness that each name that he utters, and every incident that he lightly touches, will awaken responsive echoes in their faltering hearts. As a Jew he speaks to Jews. He reminds them of what their forefathers have done, and by the acts of sacred prowess that endear the memories of the mighty dead to the Hebrew soul, he exhorts them to lay aside all puling fears, to be strong, and play the man. To show themselves worthy descendants of such distinguished ancestry and such heroic sires, to endure unto the end, and so, faithful unto death, to win the fadeless palm and the crown of life. Now in imagination he re-awakens the battle cry of *The Sword of the Lord and Gideon!* He conjures back the fierce onset of the forlorn hope of Israel's three hundred men, the wild dismay and rout of Midian's outlandish chivalry, the shrill clangour of the trumpets and the fiery tongues of the lamps illumining the midnight sky with their vengeful glare; anon he passes on to Barak, nerved into heroic resolution by the inspired appeals of Deborah, going forth to the overthrow of Jabin's hosts with their nine hundred chariots of iron, and afterwards celebrating the subjugation of Sisera in Deborah's immortal *Te Deum*. (Jud. v.) Now Jephthah's impetuous valour rises to his lips, and his sublime self-abnegation in devoting his only child, his darling daughter, to the service of the sanctuary and a perpetual virginity, as a thank-offering to God for his country's deliverance. Then again he sees blind Samson in Dagon's house feeling for the pillars, pouring forth his mighty soul in prayer to the God of Israel, and then bowing himself with recovered strength until the roof collapses, burying idol and revellers, his country's tormentors and himself, in the ruins of the temple. And now Samuel, the restorer of his country's ruined estate, the repairer of the breaches of many generations, the inflexible judge, the blameless prophet; and now David, the friendless shepherd lad—the vanquisher of the Giant of Gath, the founder of Judah's sovereign house, the royal ancestor of Messiah, the sweet singer of Israel; and, lastly, the goodly fellowship of the prophets claim to themselves their several meed of honourable mention and reverential respect. To these foremost paladins in the noble army of martyrs he points with triumphant exultation, contenting himself with the bare mention of the deeds and sufferings of others, equally great, whose memories are embalmed in their fellow-citizens' love—whose epitaphs are engraved upon the hearts of their admiring children. Let it not be forgotten that every allusion recalled some sainted name, some act of superhuman endurance, some successful resistance to the oppressors of Israel, some victory over sin and idolatrous might for the sake of Israel's good or the hope of the Fathers, and then we shall, at least partially, realise the nature of the writer's appeal to the passionately devoted patriotism of his Hebrew brethren. Those who know by experience and personal intercourse with devout Jews, their unbounded devotion to their country and its consecrated memories, will feel no difficulty in assenting to the masterly appropriateness of this closing address, directed as it is to the holiest sentiments of an enthusiastic race. The despairing pertinacity displayed in the defence of Jerusalem, as related by Josephus, will serve to illustrate the patriotic self-devotion of the Jewish people, a sentiment which still survives in many a Hebrew breast. No other nation under heaven has such glorious reminiscences, hoary with the most venerable antiquity, and luminous with the splendours of Divine interpositions on its behalf, to cherish and to hug to their desolate bosoms, as the children of the Patriarchs and the Prophets. They still in the lands of their dispersion style themselves בני מלכים, *sons of kings*.

² The Rev. W. T. Bullock, in Smith's Dictionary (Article *Jephtha*), writes "that the daughter of Jephtha was really offered up to God in "sacrifice, slain by the hand of her father, and then burned, is a "horrible conclusion, but one which it seems impossible to avoid. "This was understood to be the meaning of the text by Jonathan the "Paraphrast and Rashi, by Josephus, *Ant.* v. 7, 10, and by perhaps "all the early Christian fathers......For the first eleven centuries of "the Christian era this was the current, perhaps the universal, opinion "of Jews and Christians." The Rev. Author of the article mentions a considerable list of distinguished writers who are of the contrary opinion. To that list ought to be added the illustrious names of Reland, Selden, and Whiston. I would venture to suggest that Mr. Bullock arrives at his conclusions from faulty premises and a misinterpretation of Judg. xi. 29, which he finds it necessary to explain away in order to establish his theory. There it is written ותהי על יפתח רוח יהוה, "*And the Spirit "of Jehovah came upon Jephtha.*" On this passage he writes:—"Then "the Spirit of the Lord (*i.e.*, force of mind, for great undertakings, and "bodily strength, *Tanchum:* comp. Judg. iii. 10, vi. 34, ix. 29, xiv. 6, "xv. 14) came upon Jephtha. He collected warriors throughout Gilead "and Manasseh," &c. As a preparation for this Rabbinical gloss Mr. Bullock refers the words of verse 11, (וידבר יפתח את כל דבריו לפני יהוה במצפה), "*And Jephtha uttered all his words before Jehovah in Mispeh,*") simply to the occasion of his accompanying the elders of Gilead, when he consented to be elected as their chief. Luther, indeed, renders—"Und

"Jephtha redete solches Alles vor dem Herrn zu Mizpa," but this is not the strict meaning of the Hebrew words, which the Vulgate correctly translates *Locutusque est Jephte omnes sermones suos coram Domino in Maspha.* The idea of Jephtha's acting under the Divine influences of God's Holy Spirit militates no doubt against Mr. Bullock's suggestions, that he was at the time of his call at the head of a "company of freebooters," and that " a Gileadite born in a lawless age, living as a " freebooter (!) in the midst of rude and idolatrous people who prac- " tised such sacrifices, was not likely to be unusually acquainted with, " or to pay unusual respect to, the pure and humane laws of Israel." Now the assertion that Jephtha "lived as a freebooter" is a pure invention of the fancy. The Hebrew text simply informs us that Jephtha fled from the persecutions of his brethren, "and dwelt in the " land of Tob, and vain persons gathered themselves to Jephtha, and " they went out with him." The picturesque allusion to the habits of a " Scottish border chieftain in the middle ages," in other words, that Jephtha lived by murder and plunder, is equally unsupported by the Word of God. The allusion to David's manner of life at Ziklag is equally unhappy, as far as tending to show that Jephtha was a godless bandit. Surely Mr. Bullock forgets that at this period some of David's most affecting Psalms were written. The real vocation of David at this period is evident from 1 Sam. xxv. 14—16, where it appears that he and his men acted as protectors to their countrymen against the incursions of foreign marauders. But the actual question at issue is, whether the gloss of *Tanchum* is admissible or not. Does the phrase in Jud. xi. 11 invariably signify "force of mind for great undertakings and bodily " strength"? On the contrary, it invariably signifies an extraordinary and particular Divine *afflatus,* frequently accompanied with the gift of Prophecy, and discontinued as soon as the particular emergency had passed away, *e.g.,* in the case of Eldad and Medad, Num. xi. 25 ; of Balaam, Num. xxiv. 2 ; of Saul, 1 Sam. x. 6—11 ; of David at his anointing, 1 Sam. xvi. 13, where it is also said (verse 14) ורוח יהוה סרה מעם שאול ובעתתו רוח רעה מאת יהוה *and the Spirit of Jehovah departed from with Saul, and an evil spirit from Jehovah troubled* (or tempted) *him,* 2 Chron. xv. 1 ; of Azariah,—2 Chron. xxiv. 20, where it is said, "The " Spirit of God clothed לבשה as in Judg. vi. 34) Zechariah the son of " Jehoiadah the priest, who stood above the people, and said unto them, " Thus saith God," &c. See also Ezek. ii. 2, iii. 12, 14, 24, viii. 3, xi. 1, 5, 24, in all of which passages *Tanchum's* interpretation is utterly inadmissible. In the next place Mr. Bullock admits that he does not exactly know where to fix the precise locality of Jephtha's settlement. He calls it "a debateable land, probably belonging to Ammon, 2 Sam.

"x. 6." Possibly his conjecture may be correct, but until the point is decisively settled it is rather premature, I would submit, to assert that the inhabitants of this *terra incognita* (see Wells' Geography, vol. i., 360, ii., 49) were addicted to the practice of human sacrifices. Such slipshod conjecture is not critical certainty. In 2 Kings iii. 27 we are told, indeed, that the King of Moab, when beleaguered in Kirhareseth, offered his eldest son as a burnt offering upon the city wall. But the terms of Jephtha's twofold message to the King of Ammon (Judges xi. 14—27) affords the best index, not only to his character for humanity and justice, but also to his religious belief. He was certainly not the ignorant and reckless desperado that he is represented in Smith's Dictionary. On the contrary, any one who will carefully read Judges x. will perceive that it was God's providential guidance which directed the men of Gilead in the choice of a leader. The expression of a persistent sentiment of reverential alliance in the revelation of the ways of God to man in times of old, will doubtless awaken a derisive smile in these days of haphazard experimentalising upon God's Word. It is, however, assuredly a more consolatory basis of trust to rest one's faith upon the inspired assertions of the Old and New Testaments, than to drift wittingly away from the ancient landmarks, and to commit oneself as "a waif and a stray" upon the sea of conjecture, to the safe keeping of admitted guesses against the veracity, the common sense, nay, the ordinary sagacity of the sacred penman. According to the modern school of interpretation the holy men of old were either dupes, or fools, or knaves, or all three together. Jephtha's rash vow, spoken in the enthusiasm of his indignation against the Ammonites who had twice rejected his offers for an amicable settlement of the disputed territory, affords a memorable illustration of weakness, even in the most heroic characters. But in the Bible, God's saints are never represented as perfect. An ideal portrait of perfection would bear upon the face of it the justification for rejecting it as untrue. Here it is told of Jephtha, like Moses, that he spake "unadvisedly with his lips"; and yet he is held up by the Writer to the Hebrews as an example of the faith that overcame. His vow was made according to zeal, but not according to knowledge. But that he was a true servant of, and believer in, Jehovah, is certain from the 11th and 12th chapters of the book of Judges. He acted under strong religious impressions and with a holy ardour for the vindication of Jehovah's honour. That he would offer, and God would accept, or rather would not reprobate by one word of indignant disapproval, Jephtha's immolation of his child, is a theory altogether incredible. The literal translation of the Hebrew words in Judges xi. 39, 40 by no means necessitates the inference which the surreptitious introduction of the words *according to*, apparently sanctions in the English version. It is there said ויעש לה את נדרו אשר נדר, the exact sense of which is given by the LXX., καὶ ἐποίησεν ἐν αὐτῇ τὴν εὐχὴν αὐτοῦ ἣν ηὔξατο. And then it is added by way of explanation והיא לא ידעה איש *and she knew no husband*, i.e., she remained for ever single. This explanation would be meaningless and unnecessary if her father had sacrificed her immediately on her return, after her two months' sojourn in the mountains. She had left him a virgin, probably already betrothed to a husband, and being the only child of Jephtha, all hope of posterity was abandoned, and she was devoted by her own consent to perpetual maidenhood. Surely the advocates of the immolation theory would not insinuate that it was needful to intimate that Jephtha's daughter suffered no violence at the executioner's hands before she suffered death for her father's sins. Jephtha, moreover, who "uttered "all his words before Jehovah in Mizpeh," would have ample opportunity for ascertaining the will of the Lord during the two months of his daughter's absence. The assertion contained in Mr. Grove's article *Mizpah*, in Smith's Dictionary, that "we can hardly doubt that "on the altar of that Sanctuary" (previously described in the same article as *a Sanctuary of Jehovah*) "the father's terrible vow was con-"summated," is simply revolting to every pious mind. For further discussion of this topic see Whiston's Essay on the Sacrifice of Isaac before alluded to, on page 202; Selden's treatise, *De Success. in Pontif. Heb.*, lib. i., col. 234, and in the 12mo. edition of Leyden, 1638, pp. 228—230. The treatise is printed at length in vol. xii. of *Ugolin. Thes.*, see also Selden, *De jure Natur. et Gent.* (of which chapter ix., book iv., is devoted to the discussion of Jephtha's vow. The treatise is found in vol. xxvii. of *Ugol. Thes.*).—Car. Sigonius, *De Rep. Hebræor.*, ibid., vol. iv., col. 490, note 5, and Reland, *Antiquitates sacræ veterum Hebr.*, pp. 387—390. (*Trajecti Bat.*, 1712, 8vo.) The latter writer proposes to translate the words of Jephtha's vow והיה ליהוה והעליתיהו לעולה, *erit illud Deo sacrum*, AUT *in holocaustum id offeram*, i.e., *it shall be for the Lord*, OR *I will offer it as a burnt-offering*. He cites Exod. xxi. 15 in support of his theory, although Gesenius, *Lexicon Manuale*, p. 262, hh., stoutly denies that ו ever has the signification of *aut*, or, and refers to Exod. xxi. 15—17 in support of his assertion. Nevertheless, R. David Kimchi supplies the very same interpretation, based upon Exod. xxi. 15, and tells us that it was his father's, R. Joseph Kimchi's, view of the subject, and accords his unqualified approval to this view of the subject. R. Levi Ben Gerson is strongly in favour of the same opinion. See Selden, *De Jure Nat. et Gent.* (ibid., col. 1048, 1049). That virgins were sometimes offered, *i.e.*, set apart, to the Lord for the service of the Tabernacle, Reland implies from Num. xxxi. 35. He alludes to God's utter detestation of human sacrifices as expressed in Is. lxvi. 3; and, lastly, he shrewdly remarks that the daughters of Israel are not related to have bewailed the maiden's death, but *her condition of virginity*. The reader may also with great advantage consult the famous Abbé Guénée's inimitable rejoinder to M. de Voltaire's assertions that the Jewish law authorised and commanded human sacrifices in reference to the sacrifice of Isaac, Jephtha's vow, and the dedication of the Midianitish women, &c., &c. *Lettres de quelques Juifs Portugais, Allemands et Polonais à M. de Voltaire, par M. l'Abbé Guénée.* Tom. ii., Lettre iii. (*Si les Juifs immolaient des hommes à la Divinité, et si leur loi autorisait ces sacrifices*), pp. 39—61. (Paris, 3 Tom. 8vo.) From the last-mentioned writer it will be seen that the attempt to foist the sacrifice of a human being upon the altar of Jehovah, is only an insipid warming up of the ill-savoured impieties of the so-called "Philosopher" of Verney. The audacity of pretending originality for these exploded impieties will be obvious to every moderately well-read student. Most of the objections of the modern school of "*Higher Biblical Criticism*" are to be found, in some shape or other, in the writings of the French and English Atheists and Deists of the last century. Many of these silly impieties are admirably disposed of in Bishop Watson's *Apology*.

Verses 32, 33.—And David and Samuel and the prophets. Who, through faith, subdued kingdoms[1] (κατηγωνίσαντο, *entered into successful conflict with the resources of kings and kingdoms?*), wrought righteousness[2] (εἰργασάντο δικαιοσύνην), obtained (ἐπέτυχον, *realised*) promises,[3] stopped the mouths of lions.[4]

[1] Dr. Gill refers the subduing of kingdoms to the conquests especially of David, who subjugated Syria, Moab, Ammon, Amalek, Edom, and the Philistines, 2 Sam. viii. 12, 14; but I cannot help thinking that reference is here made to the heroic stand and protest which the prophets, from Samuel and Elijah onwards, made against Royal and national apostacy, and departure from God. They strove and wrestled mightily against the encroachments of Royal libertinism upon the altar and the constitution, fearlessly pleading the cause of a Naboth against an Ahab and a Jezebel; of the forlorn and oppressed people, as Micaiah did against Ahab, and Jeremiah did against Jehoiakim; and this in spite of the persecution and neglect and despiteful treatment

which they suffered at the hands of their ungrateful countrymen. For an excellent treatise on the subject of Elijah, see J. Wesselii, *Dissertatio de Epistola Eliæ Prophetæ, ad* 2 Chron. xxi. 12 (Dissertationes Sacræ Leidenses, *Lugd. Bat.*, 1721. 4to.). Ewald translates the passage thus :—" Welche unter Glauben Königreiche niederkämpften, Gerech-" tigkeit vollführten, Verheissungen erlangten, Löwenrachen verstopften," &c.

[2] Dr. Gill paraphrases the expression " wrought righteousness " by " exercised vindictive justice, in taking vengeance on the enemies of " God," &c. It probably signifies " asserted the right," " foretold " God's retributive justice," and were instruments in its accomplishment. So Elijah destroyed the Baal prophets and priests, and denounced vengeance on Ahab and his posterity. So the man of God that came from Judah prophesied against the altar, and gave a sign which, many long years after, was fulfilled by Josiah. So, also, " the Lord spake by " his servants the prophets" (2 Kings xxi. 10—16) against Manasseh, because of the " very much innocent blood that he shed." Such was the commission which Jeremiah received :—" See, I have set thee over " the nations and over the kingdoms, to root out, and to pull down, and " to destroy, and to throw down, to build and to plant." (Jer. i. 10.)

[3] Such were Joshua and Caleb, Gideon (Judges vi. 13), Manoah (*ibid.*, xiii. 24); such was David, who waited God's time until the kingdom was given to him, without raising his finger to hasten on the crisis. Such was Hezekiah, who obtained the promised deliverance from the Assyrian invaders ; and Ezra and Nehemiah, whose faith was rewarded in beholding the return from captivity. Ewald considers the Writer to refer to the Messianic promises successively received by the prophets, and which were confirmatory of and supplementary to the Promise made to Abraham. He writes :—" *Erlangten Verheissungen,* " wie David 2 Sam. vii., und soviele Propheten, neue Verheissungen, " und doch nur zu den noch im Anfange des vorigen Abschnittes, v. 17, " erwähnten alten Messianischen hinzukommende, und ihre Gewissheit " mehrende, aber deswegen auch hier nicht vergessene."

[4] Samson (Judges xiv. 5), David (1 Sam. xvii. 34), Daniel (vi. 22, 23), ἔφραξαν, shut up. The LXX. has, in Dan. vi. 22, ἀνέφραξε τὰ στόματα κ.τ.λ. ; and, in verse 18, ἔκλεισεν ὁ Θεὸς τὰ στόματα τῶν λεόντων, καὶ οὐ παρηνώχλησαν τῷ Δανιήλ, which passage is not in the Chaldee.

Verse 34.—Quenched the violence ($δύναμιν$) of fire,[1] escaped the edge of the sword[2] ($ἔφυγον\ στόματα\ μαχαίρας$, פי חרב), out of weakness[3] were made strong ($ἐνεδυναμώθησαν\ ἀπὸ\ ἀσθηνείας$), were made valiant in war, put to

CHAP. XI., 35.

flight the armies of the aliens (παρεμβολὰς ἔκλιναν ἀλλοτρίων).⁴

¹ Shadrach, Meshach, and Abednego in the burning fiery furnace. A direct allusion to Dan. iii. 27. נורא בנשמחין שלם לא, οὐκ ἐκυρίευσε τὸ πῦρ τοῦ σώματος αὐτῶν. LXX.
² Rahab, David, Elijah (1 Kings xvii. 3, xix. 3, 2 Kings i. 9—16); Elisha (2 Kings xiv. 13—20); the prophets hidden away by Obadiah (1 Kings xviii. 4); Jeremiah (Jer. xxxvi. 26); Baruch (ibid.); Ebedmelech (Jer. xxxix. 16—18).
³ David, as may be seen from many of his Psalms; Hezekiah (2 Kings xx.; Isaiah xxxviii.) after his sickness. But I think that the writer has chiefly in his mind spiritual feebleness and depression such as Moses exhibited at his call (Exod. iv. 1—13); also at the ill-success of his mission (Exod. v. 22, 23); the men of Israel for fear before the Philistines, when Jonathan smote the garrison (1 Sam. xiii. 6; comp. with xiv. 1—23); again, before David slew Goliath (1 Sam. xvii.); Obadiah (1 Kings xviii. 9—16); Elijah himself (1 Kings xix. 3, 4, 8); Hezekiah, for fear of Sennacherib (2 Kings xix. 6—21; Isaiah xxxvii. 1); Isaiah at the vision of Jehovah (vi. 5—8); Jeremiah at his call. "Then said I, Ah, Lord God! behold, I cannot speak; for I am a "child," &c. (Jer. i. 6—10); Ezekiel at the vision preceding his commission (Ezek. i. 28, ii. 1, 2, iii. 14, 23, 24); Nehemiah (iv. 4, 5, 9, 14); Mordecai (Esther iv. 1, viii. 15, &c.). For the use of the word ἐνδυναμόω (always in a spiritual sense), see Acts ix. 22, Rom. iv. 20, Eph. vi. 10. Philipp. iv. 13, 1 Tim. i. 12, 2 Tim. ii. 1, iv. 17.
⁴ See Joshua and Judges, as well as the other historical books, *passim*. The exploits of Abraham (Gen. xiv. 15), of Shamgar (Jud. iii. 31), of Samson (xv. 15), of Jonathan with his armourbearer (1 Sam. xiv.), and David singlehanded against Goliath, are prominent instances of the discomfiture of the armies of the aliens. Παρεμβολή occurs ten times in the New Testament. In Acts xxi. 34, 37, xxii. 24, xxiii. 10, 16, 32, it is translated, in the Authorized Version, "castle." In Heb. xiii. 11, 13, and Rev. xx. 9, it is rendered by "camp." Possibly allusion is here made to the Maccabæan exploits, but I confess that I doubt it.

Verse 35.—Women received their dead to life again¹ (ἐξ ἀναστάσεως, *von der Auferstehung.*—Luth.), but others were cudgeled² to death (ἐτυμπανίσθησαν, *zerschlagen.*—Luth.), not accepting the proffered release (i.e., *on the*

CHAP. XI., 36—40. 237

condition of apostatizing), in order that they might attain to (τύχωσιν) a resurrection that was preferable (κρείττονος, i.e., *to be chosen before a release from torment purchased by a denial of the faith*).[3]

[1] Resuscitation is, in this case, a rendering more consonant with the sense than *resurrection*. Two of the examples recorded in the Old Testament of restoration to life are found 1 Kings xvii. 17, of the son of the widow of Sarephath, and of the Shunammite (2 Kings iv. 17). The first was restored to life by the prayer of Elijah, the other by the intercession of Elisha. The third instance is recorded 2 Kings xiii. 21, where the occurrence seems to have been entirely unforeseen and unexpected. The effective cause, at least in the case of the widow of Sarephath, was the faith, not of the mother, but of the prophet. See 1 Kings xvii. 18.

[2] Ἐτυμπανίσθησαν. Probably under the persecutions of Jezebel and Manasseh. The τύμπανον seems to have been an instrument in the shape of a drum or wheel, and is mentioned 2 Macc. vi. 19—28; although, as the verb not unusually signifies *to beat to death*, there is no absolute necessity for deciding that the above-mentioned instrument of torture is here alluded to. For a vast number of authorities upon the subject, see Wettstein, *in loco*, and also J. C. Wolfii, *Curæ Philologicæ*, &c., tom. iv., p. 768. The last-mentioned writer (*ibid.*, p. 769) speaks with a very qualified certainty, as to the allusion having any reference to the case of the Maccabees. Κρείττονος should be referred to ἀπολύτρωσιν, and not to the resurrection mentioned in the commencement of the verse, nor yet to the resurrection of the just, *as opposed to that of the ungodly* (Dan. xii. 2). The proposal to refer it to Daniel's prophecy is far-fetched.

[3] Josephus writes:—"Every good man hath his own conscience "bearing witness to himself; and, by virtue of our legislators' pro-"phetic spirit, and of the firm security which God affords to such an "one, he believes that God hath made this grant to those that observe "these laws, even though they be obliged readily to die for them, that "they shall come into being again, and, at a certain revolution of "things, receive a better life than they enjoyed before." (*Jos. against Apion*, ii. 31. Whiston.)

Verses 36—40.—And others were put to the test of (πεῖραν ἔλαβον; or else, *experienced*) mockings[1] and scourgings,[2] as well as of bonds and imprisonment.[3] They were stoned,[4] they were sawn asunder,[5] they were tempted (ἐπειράσθησαν),⁶ they were butchered by the sword⁷ (ἐν φόνῳ μαχαίρας ἀπέθανον, *they were beheaded?*), they went about in sheepskins and goatskins,⁸ destitute,⁹ afflicted (θλιβόμενοι, *chafed, cruelly harassed*), evil entreated (κακουχούμενοι), of whom the world was not worthy,¹⁰ wandering up and down (πλανώμενοι) in desert places and mountains, and caves, and dens (ὀπαῖς, *holes, cavernous retreats*) of the earth.¹¹ And all these aforesaid, although they obtained a good report through the faith (καὶ οὗτοι πάντες μαρτυρηθέντες διὰ τῆς πίστεως), did not receive (οὐκ ἐκομίσαντο) THE PROMISE; God having predestined (προβλεψαμένου, *looked forward to*) some far more excellent thing concerning us (*i.e.*, his whole Church and people) : so that without us (*that remain, and shall remain unto the coming of Christ*, ἵνα μὴ χωρὶς ἡμῶν) they might not attain to their final perfection (τελειωθῶσι).¹²

---

¹ Samson (Judges xvi. 25); David by Shimei (2 Sam. xvi. 5—13. See also *passim* in the Psalms); Micaiah (1 Kings xxii. 24); Jeremiah smitten and put into the stocks by Pashur (Jer. xx. 1, 2); Jeremiah complains, "I am in derision daily, every one mocketh me" (*ibid.*, 7); the Jews when rebuilding Jerusalem by Sanballat and Tobiah (Neh. iv. 1—4); the Prophets of God by the Jews (2 Chron. xxxvi. 16), where it is said, "They mocked the messengers of God, and despised his words, and "misused his prophets," &c. Καὶ ἦσαν μυκτηρίζοντες τοὺς ἀγγέλους αὐτοῦ, καὶ ἐξουθενοῦντες τοὺς λόγους αὐτοῦ, καὶ ἐμπαίζοντες ἐν τοῖς προφήταις αὐτοῦ.—LXX. The Hebrew מתעתעים is probably better rendered by ἐμπαίζοντες than by "misused." See the parable of the vineyard, Matt. xxi. 33, &c., Mark xii. 1, &c., Luke xx. 9, and also the Saviour's lament over Jerusalem, Matt. xxiii. 34—37.

² This is in exact accordance with the account given by Josephus, *Antiq.* xii. 5, 4, of the outrages and cruelties practised by Antiochus:— "And when the King had built an idol-altar upon God's altar, he slew "swine upon it, and so offered a sacrifice neither according to the law, nor "the Jewish religious worship in that country. He also compelled them "to forsake the worship which they paid their own God, and to adore "those whom he took to be gods, and made them build temples, and "raise idol-altars, in every city and village, and offer swine upon them "every day. He also commanded them not to circumcise their sons,

"and threatened to punish any that should be found to have trans-
"gressed his injunction. He also appointed overseers, who should
"compel them to do what he commanded. And, indeed, many Jews
"there were who complied with the King's commands, either volun-
"tarily, or out of fear of the penalty that was denounced; but the
"best men, and those of the noblest souls, did not regard him, but did
"pay a greater respect to the customs of their country than concern as
"to the punishment which he threatened to the disobedient; on which
"account they every day underwent great miseries and bitter torments,
"for they were whipped with rods, and their bodies were torn to
"pieces, and were crucified while they were still alive and breathed:
"they also strangled those women, and their sons whom they had
"circumcised, as the King had appointed, hanging their sons about
"their necks as they were upon the crosses. And if there were any
"sacred book of the Law found, it was destroyed, and those with
"whom they were found miserably perished also." (*Whiston's Josephus*.)
That the establishment of idolatry in the kingdoms of Israel and Judah
was accomplished without persecution is very improbable. Under
Jezebel's bloody tyranny the outward worship of Jehovah was, for a
time at least, extinct. We know from 2 Chron. xi. 14—16 that Jero-
boam stripped the Levites of their possessions and property, and prohibited them from executing their functions. They emigrated in a body
to Judah, "and after them out of all the tribes of Israel, such as
"set their hearts to seek the Lord God of Israel, came to Jerusalem,
"to sacrifice unto the Lord God of their fathers." A further and
numerous exodus "out of Ephraim, and Manasseh, and of Simeon"
is mentioned 2 Chron. xv. 9, in the reign of Asa; whilst in 2 Chron.
xxx. 10 we learn how the messengers of Hezekiah were received with
scorn and mocking when they invited the Israelites to participate in the
Passover at Jerusalem, although "divers of Asher and Manasseh and
"of Zebulum humbled themselves, and came to Jerusalem." Under
Ahaz and Manasseh, as well as under Jehoiakim, idolatrous intolerance
and persecuting malevolence made themselves severely felt. The writer
of the article *Manasseh*, in Smith's Dictionary, justly observes (although
there are some of his other suggestions which are open, to say the least,
to grave objections), "The struggle of opposing worships must have
"been as fierce under Manasseh, as it was under Antiochus, or Decius,
"or Diocletian, or Mary. Men must have suffered and died in that
"struggle, of whom the world was not worthy."

[a] Joseph (Psalm cv. 18); Micaiah (1 Kings xxii. 26); Hannani the Seer, by Asa (2 Chron. xvi. 10); Jeremiah (Jer. xxxii. 2, xxxvi. 5, xxxviii. 6).

' Naboth the Jezreelite was truly a martyr to his allegiance to the law of his God (1 Kings xxi). By Leviticus xxv. 23, 24, he was expressly forbidden to alienate his inheritance for ever. " The land shall not be " sold (והארץ לא תמכר לצמתת), *lit.* to extinction), for the land is mine, for " ye are strangers and sojourners with me. And in all the land of your " possession ye shall grant a redemption (גאלה תתנו) for the land." And therefore he declined the King's offer with the words, "Jehovah forbid " it me, that I should give the inheritance of my fathers unto thee." Let it be observed it was a total alienation that Ahab aimed at ; for he offered to give him " a better vineyard than it," or the " worth of it in " money" (כסף מחיר לה). Dean Stanley (*Smith's Dictionary;* Article, *Naboth*), with his usual temptation to say something striking and flippant, writes, "Naboth, in the independent spirit of a Jewish " landholder, refused. Perhaps the turn of his expression implies that " his objection was mingled with a religious scruple at forwarding the " acquisitions of a half-heathen king (!). ' Jehovah forbid it to me that " ' I should give the inheritance of my fathers unto thee.' " The truth is that Dean Stanley feels not unwilling to explain away Naboth's reply, inasmuch as it affords incontrovertible testimony to the fact that the Mosaic system of jurisprudence was in full force in the days of Ahab, and that the theocratic settlement of landed estates was so rigidly and sacredly adhered to, that even Ahab did not feel himself strong enough to encroach upon a right so ancient, and so universally acknowledged as the basis of the social system. The Dean proceeds to say, " Naboth " was set on high in the public place of Samaria." These words, " in " the public place of Samaria" are an ornamental addition not found in the text, but calculated to divert the attention from the fact that Jezebel herself felt compelled to observe the Mosaic constitution, at least outwardly, in her scheme to destroy Naboth, and therefore directed that he should be tried, *according to the law,* for blasphemy. The charge of high treason was added, according to all the best Rabbinical and philological authorities, in order that the goods of Naboth might legally revert to the crown. (See Selden, *De Successionibus ad leges Hebræorum in Bona defunctorum* [cap. 25, *De successione Fisci, seu hæredibus morte damnatorum*], pp. 173—187.) A striking example of this law is afforded in the generous restitution by David of Saul's property, which had been forfeited by the treason of Ishbosheth, to Mephibosheth, 2 Sam. ix. 7. Dean Stanley mentions that Naboth's sons suffered with their father, correctly enough, for it is implied in Jehu's speech (2 Kings ix. 26). He forgets, however, to remark that this extirpation of Naboth's family was according to the precedent of Achan (Josh. vii. 25), who suffered for high treason against God when he appropriated the idolatrous spoils. The "public place," then, was the gate of the city, where the court was held. According to the Mosaic Law, Jezebel commits the case of Naboth to the "elders" and nobles of the city; in other words, to the lesser Council or Sanhedrin (בית דין) of twenty-three members, who had power of life and death. (See Selden, *ibid.*; Cunæus, *de Rep. Hebr.*, p. 106, *Lugd. Bat.*, 1632, 12mo.; Gemara Jerus., tract *Sanhedrin*, col. 3, &c.; Ugolin. Thes., vol. xxv.; Mishna, Surenhusius' edition, tom. iv., p. 212, § 4— דיני נפשות בעשרים ושלשה, "Causes of life and death [are tried] by the "three-and-twenty," &c.; also, p. 207, § 1, p. 214, § 6, and p. 232, § 5; A. Pfeiffer, *Antiquitates Selectæ*, cap. ii., *De Poenis Judæorum forensibus*, in Ugolin. Thes., vol. iv., col. 1083.) The punishment of stoning, itself, was constitutionally according to the law of Moses, and one which a king had no power to inflict. Execution by the sword was the only form of death which he could legally impose, as Maimonides asserts, *Hilc. Sanhedr.*, chap. xiv. (See Coccius' note, Mishna, *Sanhedr.*, ibid., p. 237, § 7.) The chattels of a criminal who was convicted of blasphemy or idolatry, or any graver offence against the majesty of Jehovah, did not revert to his heirs. The city was destroyed, and was not to be rebuilt (Deut. xiii. 16, 17); and so Maimonides writes, כמונם נשרפה ואינו ליורשיהם כאשר הרוגי בית דין, *Their goods are to be burnt, and are not to belong to their heirs, as they do belong in the case of those who suffer death by a decree of the Council.* On the other hand, the Babyl. Gemara (*Sanhedrin*, col. 637; Ugolin. Thes., vol. xxv.) asserts as follows :—הרגי מלכות נכסיהן למלך הרוגי בית דין נכסיהן ליורשין, *When any one suffers capital punishment on account of the kingdom, his goods belong to the King; if by the decree of the Council, they belong to his heirs.* R. Levi Ben Gerson observes, למדנו מזה שהרוגי מלכות נכסיהן למלכות. "We learn from this passage that those condemned to death for "high treason forfeited their goods to the King." Selden justly concludes that Naboth having been arraigned under the twofold indictment, ברכת אלהים ומלך, *thou hast blasphemed God and the king*, was visited by confiscation of his vineyard for his high treason, although he underwent the formality of trial by the local magistracy or בית דין. The Jerusalem Gemara, *Sanhedrin*, fol. 20, col. 2, asserts that anyone who cursed the Royal family of David, מלכות בית דוד, was capitally punished. The reviling of the magistracy was, however, an offence against the Mosaic Statute-book (Exod. xxii. 27) לא תקלל ונשיא בעמך לא תאר. See Ugolini Thes., vol. xxv. (*Gemara Sanhedr.*, col. 173, &c.) The letter of Jezebel itself was as consonant with the exact letter of the Mosaic law as the indictment against Naboth, and the punishment to be inflicted for his pretended offences was in accordance with its enactments. She wrote that after the sentence had been established upon the testimony of "two witnesses" (Num. xxxv. 30, Deut. xvii. 6, 7, xix. 15) he was to be carried out of the city to the place of execution. This was in accordance with Levit. xxiv. 14, and therefore the Mishna says:— "When the trial is over, they lead forth the condemned to be stoned. "The place of stoning was outside the place of trial, for it is said "הוצא את המקלל, *carry forth the blasphemer* (lit. *cause to go forth*). An "official stands at the door of the court holding a handkerchief, another "on horseback places himself some distance off, so that he can keep "the other in view. Then, if any witness presents himself who can "testify to the innocence of the criminal, he waves the handkerchief, "and the mounted man gallops off and fetches the culprit back. Even "if he himself alleges proof of his own innocence he may be brought "back four or five times, provided that what he says appears to have "some solid foundation," &c. (*Sanhedrin*, p. 233, *Mishna Surenh.*, vol. iv.) It is also related (p. 234, *ibid.*) how, when arrived within 10 cubits of the fatal spot, the criminal was urged to confess with a view to expiate his crime. We see, therefore, that there was a humane principle involved, at least in the minds of the Talmudical writers, in the fact of the place of execution being remote from the place of trial. It afforded opportunity of reprieve and confession. See also the Jerusalem Gemara, *Sanhedrin Ugolini Thes.*, vol. xxv., col. 129—131. Respecting the law of Blasphemy, see *ibid.*, col. 174—182 ; also *Gemara Babyl.*, ibid., col. 596, &c. The Rabbies held that every one who was stoned was afterwards hung upon a cross until the evening (*ibid.*, col. 698, &c.). This was the opinion of R. Eliezer, but others asserted that none but blasphemers and idolaters were thus treated. (Mishna Surenhus., *Sanhedrin*, tom. iv., 235.) With all the above quoted helps to the right understanding of the passage, the following note appended by Dean Stanley to his article *Naboth*, above cited, becomes all the more extraordinary ; either the Very Reverend writer does himself great injustice, or it was a piece of inconceivable rashness for him to undertake to write an article upon a subject, of which the execution of his task appears to justify his confession of entire ignorance. The Dean writes :—" The Hebrew word which is rendered here only "'on high,' is more accurately 'at the head of,' 'or in the chiefest place "among.' (1 Sam. ix. 22.) The passage is obscured by our ignorance (!) "of the nature of the ceremonial in which Naboth was made to take "part ; but in default of this knowledge we may accept the explanation "of Josephus, that an assembly (ἐκκλησία) was convened, at the head of "which Naboth, in virtue of his position, was placed, in order that the "charge of blasphemy might be more telling." The translation of the words בראש העם "on high amongst the people" is, after all, no such abstruse mystery. A glance at the Englishman's Hebrew Concordance, article ראש, *head*, will afford almost numberless examples, which will justify the rendering—times without number it is applied to the top of a mountain, &c., &c., and would there signify an exalted position— *i.e.*, that Naboth was set up in a conspicuous place in the midst of the Council. Or else if the Dean prefers to stand by Josephus' version, viz., that when the Council of Elders was called together, Naboth was treacherously placed in the chief seat in order to make him a readier mark for his traducers' false accusations, I would venture to submit for his approval the following extract from *S. F. Bucheri Synedrium Magnum* (printed at length, Ugol. Thes., vol. xxiii., col. 1167), "Summus hujus Curiæ præses proprio nomine appellatur Nasi נשיא, "*princeps, ad dignitatem summum evectus aut elevatus*, quâ notione radix "Hebræa נשא sumitur. Supremus Dux κατ' ἐξοχὴν ראש הישבה, *Caput*, "*seu primarius* Consessus, &c." The exact words of 1 Kings xxi. 9 are, והשיבו את נבות בראש העם, *and cause Naboth to sit in the head of the people*. The common-sense view of the passage is that given by our version, and also by Luther, *und setzet Nabot oben an im Volk*. Probably the position in which he was placed was on the top of the gate itself, where he would be conspicuous to all, and would be above the heads of the people. The proclamation of the fast seems to be explained by the statement of the Mishna and Gemara that criminals guilty of heresy were executed on days of solemnity (בגדל), in order "that all the people "might hear and fear." Deut. xvii. 13 ; Mishna Sanedh. (*Sanhedrin*), vol. iv., p. 258; Gemara (*Sanhedrin*), Ugol. Thes., vol. 25, cols. 285, 286. Be this as it may, it is quite plain from the multitude of incidental allusions to the enactments of the Mosaic Statute-book contained in this 21st chapter of 1 Kings, that Dr. Stanley's conjecture as given above, respecting Naboth's refusal to sell his vineyard, is gratuitous and untenable. *Naboth died a martyr to his constancy to God's written law*, and not owing to some confused notion that it was improper to sell a piece of land to a "half-heathen king!" This view of the subject is at least as trustworthy as the information which Dr. Stanley unhesitatingly imports into his article from the Septuagint, that Naboth and his sons were eaten by swine as well as dogs, and that the pool or tank into which their blood ran "was the common bathing-place of the prostitutes of the city." It is also far more trustworthy than the Dean's attempt to show that the LXX. account of the scene of the transaction is at variance with that of the Hebrew. He writes :—"He "(Naboth) was a Jezreelite and the owner of a small portion of ground, "2 Kings ix. 25, 26, that lay on the eastern slope of the hill of Jezreel.

" He had also a vineyard, of which the situation is not quite certain.
" According to the Hebrew text, 1 Kings xxi. 1, it was in Jezreel, but
" the LXX. render the whole clause differently, omitting the words
" *which were in Jezreel*, and reading instead of the *palace, the threshing-*
" *floor* of Ahab king of Samaria. This points to the view, certainly
" most consistent with the subsequent narrative, that Naboth's vine-
" yard was on the hill of Samaria, close to the threshing-floor (the
" word translated in the Authorized Version, 'void place'), which
" undoubtedly existed there, hard by the gate of the city, 1 Kings xxiv. (?)
" The Royal palace of Ahab was close upon the city wall at Jezreel."
The assumption that Ahab's palace was on the city wall, may be taken
for what it is worth. Josephus, Antiq. ix. 6, 4, in referring to 2 Kings
ix. 30—33, speaks of "a tower," and not " the palace." But the large
assertion that " the LXX. render the whole clause differently," is simply
contrary to historic truthfulness, as a comparison of the three texts
will show :—

1 Kings xxi. 1.	Authorized Version.	LXX.
ויהי אחר הדברים האלה כרם היה לנבות היזרעאלי אשר ביזרעאל אצל היכל אחב מלך שמרון:	And it came to pass after these things, that Naboth the Jezreelite had a vineyard, which *was* in Jezreel, hard by the palace of Ahab king of Samaria.	1 Kings xx. 1. Καὶ ἀμπελὼν εἷς ἦν τῷ Ναβουθαὶ τῷ Ἰεζραλίτῃ παρὰ τῇ ἅλῳ Ἀχαὰβ βασιλέως Σαμαρείας.

Now I fearlessly appeal to the candour of critics of any shade whatever to say whether there is any *contradiction* whatever expressed or implied in these three statements.

To argue from mere coincidence that the LXX. speaks of Ahab's
" threshing-floor," and the word גרן is used in 1 Kings xxii. 10 of the
" void place " where the two kings sat in state, that Samaria must be
intended in xx. 1 instead of Jezreel, is inconceivably childish. To
answer Dr. Stanley in the spirit of his own reasoning, I might reply,
that in xxii. 10 it is not said *in Ahab's threshing-floor*, but *a threshing-*
floor; therefore the King's threshing-floor cannot be intended ! The
statement of the Hebrew text is quite reconcilable with that of the
LXX. Both are probably according to fact. The threshing-floor was
doubtless on the Royal premises, and adjoined the vineyard of Naboth.

Further, the only colour for asserting that Naboth had two pieces of
ground, which are mentioned in the narrative, is contained in the
Auth. Version of verse 18, where it is said, " Arise, go down to meet
" Ahab, King of Israel, which *is* in Samaria. Behold *he is* in the
" vineyard of Naboth, whither he is gone down to possess it." The

marginal references to 1 Kings xiii. 32, 2 Chron. xxii. 9, might have saved the Dean from this blunder, and would have shown him that "which *is in* Samaria" refers to Ahab's territorial title, and not to Naboth's vineyard. (See also verse 1 of this chapter.) But the LXX. version speaks decisively in the notes, Ἀχαὰβ βασιλέως Ἰσραὴλ τοῦ ἐν Σαμαρείᾳ. The Vulgate is stronger still:—"Achab regis Israel qui est "in Samaria; ecce ad Vineam Naboth descendit ut possideat eam." Of course, if once this discrepancy can be established, the fulfilment of Elijah's prophecy respecting Jezebel, recorded by Jehu (2 Kings ix. 36, 37, with minuter particulars, not contained in 1 Kings xxi. 23) as spoken in his hearing, would seem to have failed in its literal and minute accomplishment. But the assertion that Naboth's vineyard was close to the city of Samaria is based upon a careless and inexcusable blunder, as shown above, whilst any description of its shape or extent, such as the Dean propounds, is purely an imaginary one. Naboth was a Jezreelite. He was tried according to the Law of Moses by the elders and nobles of his own city. After his condemnation, again *according to the strict letter of the law*, he was led forth from the city to the place of execution. This place of execution for state criminals, for he was tried on the double charge of blasphemy and high treason, may have been outside the city of Samaria, for we read of Ahab, 1 Kings xxii. 38, "And *one* washed the chariot in the pool of Samaria; and the "dogs licked up his blood. And they washed his armour, according "unto the word of the Lord which he spake." Or else a tank or piece of standing water, near Jezreel, went by the name of *the Pool of Samaria*, for Josephus distinctly asserts, "They took the dead body to "Samaria, and buried it there; but when they had washed his chariot "in the fountain of Jezreel, which was bloody with the dead body of "the King, they acknowledged that the prophecy of Elijah was true." There is, however, no reason for pressing this suggestion respecting the nomenclature of the Pool of Jezreel, as there is nothing in the Hebrew to show that the chariot was not twice washed, or that the armour was not washed at Jezreel and the chariot at Samaria. Indeed, 1 Kings xxii. 38 seems to imply that they were washed at different times.

Dr. Stanley's note on the word "cursed," whereby he renders "*blasphemed*" of the Authorised Version of 1 Kings xxi. 10, 13, affords so novel and startling a specimen of criticism, that when I first read it I almost thought it was intended as a joke. The learned Dean writes, "By the LXX. this is given ἐυλόγησε, *blessed;* possibly merely for the "sake of euphemism." Surely Dr. Stanley cannot be ignorant that it is a literal rendering of the Hebrew ברן, *he blessed;* or, in the sense of blasphemy against God, *he cursed.* Job i. 5, 11, ii. 5—9; Ps. x. 3

(*Gesen.*). See Selden, *De Jure Nat. et Gent.;* Ugolini Thes., vol. xxvii., col. 740—748; Buxtorf, *Lexicon Chald.*, Article ברכא. The LXX. translators here, as in Job i. 11, ii. 5, have retained the equivalent to בְּרֵךְ, as being most reverently appropriate. On the subject of what constituted blasphemy, see Mishna Surenhus., *Sanhedrin*, vol. iv., p. 242; and on the subject of the mode of legal procedure amongst the Hebrews, see *ibid.*, p. 205—268 *passim*.

Zechariah, the son of Jehoiada the priest, was stoned in the court of the house of the Lord (2 Chron. xxiv. 20—22), at the command of Joash, because he remonstrated with King and people on account of their departure from God. This is he to whom, some have asserted, our Lord referred as "Zacharias" in Luke xi. 51, and "Zacharias the "son of Barachias," Matt. xxiii. 35. It has been suggested that the words *Son of Barachias* may have crept into the text of St. Matthew from a marginal gloss, inasmuch as in the Gospel which the Nazarenes used "the son of Jehoiada" was substituted in place of the above. Whiston, however, understands our Lord to allude to Zechariah the prophet's death, viz., the writer of the prophetical book, whose name it bears:—"Since Zechariah was really *the son of Barachiah*, and "grandson of Iddo (Zech. i. 1), and how he died, we have no other "account than that before us in St. Matthew." (See Whiston's *Josephus*, Wars of the Jews, iv. 5, 4, *note*.) Dean Alford (Hebrews xi. 37) says positively, "Zechariah, son of Jehoiada" (2 Chron. xxiv. 20—22), is "referred to by our Lord" (Luke xi. 51; Matt. xxiii. 35); and in his note on the last passage writes:—"Υἱοῦ Βαραχίου does not occur in "Luke xi. 51, and perhaps was not uttered by the Lord himself, but "may have been inserted by mistake, as Zacharias was the son of "Barachiah (see Zech. i. 1); a circumstance suppressed by Dr. Words- "worth in his elaborate account of the mystical reason of the patro- "nymic being used here." Dr. Alford's accusation of "suppression" might perchance have come with a better grace if he had in any way referred to Whiston's opinion as above cited, that there is really no mistake at all in the text of St. Matthew, but that our Lord has there informed us of the manner of that distinguished prophet's martyrdom. The Gemara, *Sanhedrin*, cols. 951, 952, relates, respecting Zechariah the son of Jehoiada, that, when Nebuchadnezzar destroyed the temple, Nebuzaradan beheld with astonishment the martyr's blood trickling from the ground. Having ascertained the cause of the phenomenon, he resolved to pacify his manes. When he had slaughtered 940,000 (!) of the chief men of the Jews, he addressed the spirit thus:— זכריה וזריה טובים שבהן איברהם ניחי לך דאיקטלינהו לכולהו, *Zechariah, Zechariah, I have destroyed the goodliest of them! Is it your pleasure that I should slay them all?* Upon this, the Gemara says, the blood ceased to flow, and Nebuzaradan was struck with remorse, and became a proselyte. (Ugol. Thes., tom. xxv.)—The supposition that our Lord prophetically referred to the Zacharias the son of Baruch, who was put to the sword by the zealots in the temple, about thirty-four years after Christ's death, is justly rejected by Whiston. Nor is the obscure tradition, that the father of John the Baptist is pointed to, worthy of serious attention. Tradition makes Jeremiah to have been stoned in Egypt. Dr. Gill well observes, "The character of Jerusalem is, that she stoned "the prophets that were sent unto her." Matt. xxiii. 37.

⁵ Ἐπρίσθησαν, Dr. Gill writes, "to which there seems to be allusion "in Matt. xxiv. 51 ('and shall cut him asunder,' καὶ διχοτομήσει αὐτὸν). "There is no instance of any good men being so used in Scripture: "perhaps reference is had to some that suffered thus in the time of "Antiochus. The Jews have a tradition that the prophet Isaiah was "sawn asunder in the times of Manasseh, and by his order," &c. The tradition thus alluded to by Dr. Gill is found in the Jerusalem Gemara, *Sanhedrin* (the tract is printed at length in Ugol. Thes., vol. 25), where it is said that Isaiah fled from the pursuit of Manasseh, and took refuge in a cedar tree, whereupon the cedar swallowed him up. The fringes of his garment, however, were visible. Whereupon they went and told Manasseh, and he commanded the cedar tree to be sawn asunder. Upon obeying the King's orders, the prophet's blood gushed forth. The passage is as follows:—

כד דקם מנשה הוה פרי הורי ישעי׳ בעי מיקטלוניה והיא עיק מן קדמי עדק לארוא ובלעיה ארוא . חסר ציציתה דגולתיה אתון ואבריו קרמוי, אמר לון אולון ונסרון ארוא לטלוח . ולא אבה י״י ולא אבה י״י לסלוח . ונסרו לארוא ואיתחזי דמא נגד . "Quando concitatus est "Manasse, cucurrit post Isaiam, quærens eum occidere, et aufugit ab "ejus conspectu, aufugit in cedrum, et eum absorpsit cedrus; vide- "bantur fimbriæ pallii sui; abeuntes dixerunt coram eo; et ille iis "dixit. Ite dissecate cedrum, et visus est ejus sanguis ex adverso. "*Et ob hanc rem noluit Dominus propitiari.* 2 Reg. xxiv. 4." (*Ibid.*, col. 255–256.)

Schoettgen writes on the same subject, as follows:—"Communis "Judæorum, et post hos patrum Christianorum traditio est, Jesaiam "Prophetam jussu Manassis Regis Israëlitici serrâ dissectum esse. "Quæ si non probabilis ex hoc loco redditur, certe constat, hoc supplicii "genere quosdam olim Hebræorum adfectos fuisse. *Jevamoth,* fol. "49, 2. *Manasses interemit Jesaiam..........Præcepit quippe, ut ligno* "*cedrino interficeretur,* אהיה לאריא ונכריהו, *quo facto adduxerunt cedrum,* "*ut ipsum dissecarent. Quum ad os ejus pervenirent, animam efflavit.* "Ex patribus unum tantum proferimus Gregentium Tephrensem, "disput. cum Herbano Judæo, p. 19, qui Judæis, inter alia, hoc "objicit, τὸν 'Ησαίαν ἐπρίσατε," &c. Schoettg., Horæ Hebr., tom. i., p. 987. J. C. Wolfius, Curæ Philog. et Crit., tom. iv., writes:— "Receptum hoc supplicii genus olim fuisse, ostendit Gatakerus (Advers., "cap. xlv.) quem Elsnerus hic affert, Cassaubonus ad Sueton. Calig., "cap. 27, et ad Aristoph., Equites v. 767. Confer P. C. Kragelund, "Disp. de serra martyrii instrumento, Hafniæ, 1700." He remarks further, that Whiston suspects that the fact and circumstances of Isaiah's and Jeremiah's martyrdom were wilfully suppressed by the Jews.

⁶ 'Επειράσθησαν. A multitude of readings have been suggested in place of this word. It is wanting in the Syriac and Ethiopic versions, and is omitted, according to J. C. Wolfius, in two codices, as well as by some of the Fathers. Luther translates it "zerstochen" (ἐπάρθησαν), thrust through, whilst Alford inclines to ἐπρήσθησαν, were burned. I cannot help feeling that Prof. Stuart is right when he says it must mean "temptations presented by persecutors to the victims of their "torture, in order to induce them to forsake their religion, and worship "the gods of idolaters. Such was a common practice among the "heathen persecutors of Christians. Not only life, but wealth and "honour, were frequently proffered in the midst of torture the most "agonising to the human frame, in order to tempt the martyrs to "forsake their religion." Thus did Pashur seek to silence Jeremiah, when he put him in the stocks, and of which Jeremiah bitterly complains (Jer. xx. 1, 2, 7, 14, &c.), cursing the very day of his birth. Similar was his condition when he was thrust into the dungeon, and sank "into the mire" (Jer. xxxviii. 6). What cruelties were practised by Jezebel, and Ahaz, and Manasseh, God's judgment-day alone will reveal. In the apostolic times, we read how Saul "compelled" the believers "to blaspheme." The unbelieving Jews indulged a ferocious and rancorous hatred against the converts, and left no means untried to reclaim them to Judaism. The inquisitorial phrase, "to put to the "question," i.e., to examine by torture, affords a parallel to this signification of πειράζω. The seeming "mildness of the word" probably conveyed a deep and sinister significance to the persecuted Hebrews. What more terrible trial to constancy than to witness the agonies of beloved relatives, or to withstand the entreaties of wife, husband, parents, and children ? This was indeed to "take up the cross and "follow Christ."

⁷ The Talmudical tradition, that execution by the sword was the only punishment which the Hebrew Sovereigns could constitutionally inflict, has been already noticed. From the Jerusalem Gemara, Sanhedr.

(Ugol. Thes., vol. 25, cols. 156—158), it will be seen that the Rabbies understood the expression "to slay with the sword" as equivalent to beheading. See also *ibid.*, cols. 147—148, § 3. From the Mishna, *Sanhedrin* (Suren. Edit., vol. iv., p. 238), we learn that beheading with an axe was included in the form of execution :—

מצית הנהרגין; היו מתיזין את ראשו בסייף כדרך שהמלכות עושה ר׳ יהודה אומר
ניוול הוא זה אלא מניחין את ראשו על הסדן וקוצץ בקופיץ

"The prescription respecting those slain with the sword; they cut "off his head with a sword, according to the manner of the kingdom "(*i.e.*, as in executions by the king's orders). R. Judah said that this was "a disgraceful manner, but that they rested the criminal's head on a "block, and struck it off with an axe." This explanation throws light upon Rev. xx. 4, "The souls *of them that were beheaded* (τῶν πεπελεκισ-"μένων) for the testimony of Jesus and for the word of God." It includes all the martyrs who had been unjustly sentenced to die by the sword, in mockery of justice and humanity, by the Jewish tribunals, from Ahab's time to the days of the Apocalypse. The Writer to the Hebrews probably takes a broader view of the subject, although he seems to give the equivalent of the technical Hebrew term הרג, by ἐν φόνῳ μαχαίρας. (See Mishna Suren. *Sanhedr.*, p. 237, sec. 7.) The word הרג, however, as Coccejus (*ibid.*) observes, has a wider signification, and is applied even to stoning, as it is to the manner of Abel's death. Of Jezebel it is said (1 Kings xviii. 4) that she "cut off" the prophets of the Lord (בהכרית, *in causing to cut off*). The manner of their death is stated in verse 13, בהרג, and also xix. 10, 14, הרגו בהרב, *they have slain with the sword*. Thus perished also Abimelech and his brethren (1 Sam. xxii.) at the command of Saul, by the hand of Doeg the Edomite. In verse 18 it is said וימת, *and he put to death*, but in verse 21 הרג. So died also, doubtless, many in the persecution of Manasseh. See also Neh. ix. 26; Ps. xliv. 22 (23). Somewhat hazardous is Dr. Alford's decisive assertion (*in loco*), "One prophet "only perished by the sword in the kingdom of Judah, viz., Urijah, "Jer. xxvi. 23." Of him it is said, "and they smote him with the "sword" (ויכהו בהרב). So also John the Baptist by Herod Antipas, Matt. xiv. 10, Mark vi. 16, 27 (28), Luke ix. 9, where the verb ἀποκεφαλίζω is employed; and James the brother of John, by Herod Agrippa, Acts xii. 2 (ἀνεῖλε μαχαίρᾳ).

⁸ Ἐν μηλωταῖς, ἐν αἰγείοις δέρμασιν. L. Küsterus suggests that μηλ. signifies the skin of any quadruped, and that therefore the words that follow are a gloss to designate that goat skins are meant. J. Hasæus justly repudiates this very unnecessary proposition, calling attention to the fact that Elijah's mantle is called μηλωτή by the LXX., 1 Kings

xix. 13, 19. The Hebrew word אדרת means a capacious mantle or cloak, and must not be confounded with the אזור עור the girdle of leather, or hide, either with the fur on or without, which was girt about his loins. Probably the אדרת is alluded to under the word שער, δασύς, *hairy*, for we find אדרת שער, *i.e.*, a hairy, or rough garment, or mantle, in both (LXX. ὡσεὶ δορὰ, δασύς) Gen. xxv. 25, and Zech. xiii. 4 (LXX. δέρριν τριχίνην), "Neither shall they wear a garment of hair to "deceive," on which Kimchi, *in loco*, says, "This was the custom of "the false prophets to wear sackcloth, or a garment of hair;" in imitation, doubtless, of the self-denial of Elijah and Elisha and the other prophets of God. John the Baptist wore a garment (ἔνδυμα) of camel's hair and a leathern girdle (ζώνην δερματίνην) about his loins. And to this rugged austerity our Lord alluded when he asked, "What "went ye out for to see? A man clothed in soft raiment? Behold, "they that wear soft *clothing* are in kings' houses." Matt. xi. 8, Luke vii. 25. F. A. Lampius suggests that μηλωτὰς signify garments made of skin, whilst δέρμ. αἰγ. designate raw hides, "pelles crudas," leaving a great part of the body uncovered. See J. C. Wolfius, *Curæ Philol.*, tom. iv., pp. 770 and 771.

⁹ ὑστερούμενοι, David, Elijah, &c.

¹⁰ Ὧν οὐκ ἦν ἄξιος ὁ κόσμος. Professor Stuart writes:—"This is a "proverbial expression, and plainly to be included in a parenthesis, as "it is an ejaculation of the writer, interrupting the regular series of "the discourse." The passage upon which the Professor's assertion, doubtless, is based is found in the Babyl. Gemara, *Sanhedrin*, col. 385, 386, Ugol. *Thes.*, vol. xxv. It is here given, for what it is worth, as follows:—

תר״ו משמתו נביאים האחרונים הגי זכריה מלאכי נסתלקה רוח קדש מישראל ואף ע״פ כן היו משתמשין בבת קול פעם אחד היו מסובין בעלית בית גוריה ביריחו ונהנה עליהם בת קול מן השמים יש כאן אחד שראוי שתשרה עליו שכינה כמשה רבינו אלא שאין דורו זכאי. לכך נתנו חכמים את עיניהם בהלל הזקן. וכשמת אמרו עליו הי חסיד הי עניו הי תלמידו של עזרא. שוב פעם אחת היו מסובין בעליה בינבה. ונהנה עליהם בת קול מן השמים. יש כאן אחד שתשרה עליו שכינה אלא שאין דורו זכאי. לכך נתנו חכמים את עיניהם בשמואל הקטן וכשמת אמרו עליו הי חסיד הי עניו תלמידו של הילל. אף הוא אמר בשעת מיתתו שמעון וישמעאל לחרבא וחברוהי לקטלא ושאר עמא לביזא ועקן סגיאן עתידן למיתי על עלמא. ועל יהודה בן בבא בקשו לומר בו אלא שנטרפה שעה:

"Our Rabbies say that after the later prophets died, viz., Haggai, "Zechariah, and Malachi, the Holy Spirit was withdrawn from Israel. "Nevertheless, they made use of the 'daughter of a voice' (*i.e.*, an "oracular utterance from heaven, see Buxtorf. Lex. Chald. *in loco*, "col. 320, 321, and John xii. 27—30). Once upon a time a company "were gathered together in the guest chamber of the house of Goriah

"in Jericho, and the 'daughter of a voice' was sent to them from
"heaven. 'Is there not one here worthy that the Shechinah should
"'rest upon him, as upon Moses our Lord? But this generation
"'is not worthy of him.' Then the wise men cast their eyes
"upon Hillel the Elder. But when he died they said of him, 'He was
"'pious, he was humble as a disciple of Ezra.' It came to pass again
"that there was an assemblage in a guest chamber at Javneh, and
"there was sent to them 'a daughter of a voice' from heaven. 'Is
"'there not one here worthy that the Shechinah should rest upon
"'him? But this generation is not worthy of him.' Then the wise
"men cast their eyes on Samuel the less, and when he died they
"said, 'He was pious, and humble as a disciple of Hillel.' He also
"himself said, 'When Simeon and Samuel shall have died by the
"'sword, and his companions shall have been slain, and the remnant
"'of the people given over for a prey to the spoiler, great calamities
"'are destined to come upon the world.' They sought to speak in like
"manner concerning Judah ben Bava, but the time was gone by."

[11] David, Elijah; the prophets hidden by Obadiah, John the Baptist. See also 2 Macc. x. 6. Καὶ μετ' εὐφροσύνης ἦγον ἡμέρας ὀκτὼ σκηνωμάτων τρόπον, μνημονεύοντες ὡς πρὸ μικροῦ χρόνου τὴν τῶν σκηνῶν ἑορτὴν ἐν τοῖς ὄρεσι καὶ ἐν τοῖς σπηλαίοις θηρίων τρόπον ἦσαν νεμόμενοι. Josephus, *Antiq.* xii. 6, 2, gives a terrible account how nearly 1,000 men, with their wives and children, were smothered by fire, in the caves to which they betook themselves, rather than fight on the Sabbath-day, in the revolt of Mattathias.

[12] These concluding words must be read by the light of chapter x. 36, ὑπομονῆς γὰρ ἔχετε χρείαν ἵνα τὸ θέλημα τοῦ θεοῦ ποιήσαντες κομίσησθε τὴν ἐπαγγελίαν. The writer has now shown how the Elders, who obtained a good report through faith, were one and all in a position precisely similar to that of the persecuted Hebrew converts, as regards the attainment of their ultimate and final reward. They were one after another gathered to their rest in the hope of a better resurrection. They looked beyond this vale of tears for their recompense. Their life below was one of harass and conflict, of persecution and perpetual self-denial. It was the faith which is ἐλπιζομένων ὑπόστασις, πραγμάτων ἔλεγχος οὐ βλεπομένων, which supported them through life and deserted them not at the place of execution, at the scaffold and at the stake. The treatment which they met with, the hardships which they underwent, awakened no surprise and no repining dissatisfaction. They looked heavenward for their recompense, and felt no disappointment at their hard lot, as if they had lived in vain. They knew that as yet all things were not put under Christ's feet, his enemies had not been made

his footstool, Death was not swallowed up in victory. This could only occur at his second appearing, εἰς σωτηρίαν, when sin and suffering shall be abolished, when Satan's head shall be finally bruised, and death swallowed up in victory. As long as the grave retains one single trophy of the devil's victory, the consummation of the believer's hopes cannot be completed. On the resurrection morning, when Christ shall come "to be glorified in his saints, and to be admired in all them that "believe," 2 Thes. i. 10, then shall that κρεῖττόν τι which God has provided for us all be manifested. For "since the beginning of the world " *men* have not heard, nor perceived by the ear, neither hath the eye seen, " O God, beside thee, *what* He hath prepared for him that waiteth for " Him." Is. lxiv. 4. Sufficient for the Hebrews to whom the Epistle was addressed, if with the Elders (who renouncing the world "died in " the faith, not having received the promises, but having seen them " afar off, and were persuaded of *them*, and embraced *them*, and con- " fessed that they were strangers and pilgrims upon earth") they could only have faith and patience also "to wait for his Son from heaven, " whom he raised from the dead, *even* Jesus, which delivered us from " the wrath to come." 1 Thess. i. 10. On the one hand, God has determined that they without us shall not be made perfect, and on the other, "if we believe that Jesus died and rose again, even so them also " which sleep in Jesus will God bring with Him. For this (says St. Paul) " we say unto you by the Word of the Lord, that we which are alive, *and* " remain unto the coming of the Lord, shall not prevent them which " are asleep. For the Lord himself shall descend from heaven with a " shout, with the voice of the archangel, and with the trump of God, " and the dead in Christ shall rise first. Then we which are alive and " remain shall be caught up together with them in the clouds, to meet " the Lord in the air, and so shall we ever be with the Lord." This restoration to God's presence must have been the hope of Adam and his children, consoling them for the loss of Eden by the certainty of its recovery. Enoch prophesied concerning it. The Elders in every age have longed for it.—The Church of God is even now redeemed, but it is not yet triumphant. God's suffering saints on earth, together with the souls beneath the altar above, yet cry out, "How long, O Lord, " holy and true?"—" White robes," indeed, says St. John, Rev. vi. 10, 11, "were given to every one of them ; and it was said unto them, " that they should rest for a little season, until their fellow-servants " also and their brethren, that should be killed as they *were*, should be " fulfilled (πληρωθῶσι)." But when this season of rest and expectation is completed, there shall "be heard a great voice out of heaven saying, " Behold, the tabernacle of God is with men, and He will dwell with "them, and they shall be his people, and God Himself shall be with them, *and be* their God. And God shall wipe away all tears from their eyes; and there shall be no more death, neither sorrow, nor crying (κραυγὴ), neither shall there be any more pain: for the former things are passed away." (Rev. xxi. 3, 4.) How consonant with the best aspirations of the pious Jew such sentiments as these were, is evident from the following remarkable declaration of Philo:—Ὁ μὲν οὖν ἡγεμὼν τῆς θεοφιλοῦς δόξης, ὁ πρῶτος ἐκ τύφου μεθαρμοσάμενος πρὸς ἀλήθειαν, διδακτικῇ χρησάμενος ἀρετῇ πρὸς τελείωσιν, ἆθλον αἱρεῖται τὴν πρὸς τὸν Θεὸν πίστιν. Τῷ δὲ κατ' εὐμοιρίαν φύσεως αὐτήκοον καὶ αὐτομαθῆ καὶ αὐτοδίδακτον κτησαμένῳ τὴν ἀρετὴν βραβεῖον ἀναδίδοται χαρά. Τοῦ δ' ἀσκητοῦ καὶ πόνοις ἀτρύτοις καὶ ἀκαμπέσι περιποιησαμένου τὸ καλὸν, ὁ στέφανός ἐστιν ὅρασις Θεοῦ. Τοῦ δὲ πιστεύειν Θεῷ καὶ διὰ παντὸς τοῦ βίου χαίρειν καὶ ὁρᾶν τὸ ὄν, τί ἂν ὠφελιμώτερον ἢ σεμνότερον ἐπινοήσειέ τις;

"But (Abraham) the author of the sentiment so well pleasing to God, who was the first to devote himself heart and soul, from vanity to truth, having employed the virtue which had been taught to him with a view to perfection, receives as his prize faith in God. To the man, indeed, who puts to the best use the virtue which good fortune has placed in his reach, enabling him to acquire it spontaneously, self-taught and self-acquired, the satisfaction which accompanies it is given as his reward. But the vision of God is the crown of the man, who attains to excellence by self-discipline and unflagging and unwearied toils. For what more desirable and more worthy conception could a man entertain, than to believe in God, and all his life long continually to rejoice, and to see the Self-existent?"—*De Præmiis et Poenis*, Works, *Mangey's Edition*, vol. ii., p. 412.

CHAPTER XII.

The writer has now illustrated his exhortation to patient endurance (ὑπομονὴ), by the stirring rehearsal of the deeds of the Elders who obtained a good report through faith. These are they whom the Church has accounted Saints, even as St. James writes (v. 11) to Hebrew Christians also, Ἰδοὺ μακαρίζομεν τοὺς ὑπομένοντας (" Siehe, wir preisen " selig, die erduldet haben," *Luther*), after having encouraged them in the preceding verse, ὑπόδειγμα λάβετε τῆς κακοπαθείας, ἀδελφοί μου, καὶ τῆς μακροθυμίας, τοὺς προφήτας οἳ ἐλάλησαν τῷ ὀνόματι Κυρίου. The greatness of the Prophets, the Apostles and martyrs, consisted not in the earthly honours which they received, but in the patient fortitude, the unflinching perseverance, the unfaltering faith with which they held on to the last, looking to God as their exceeding great reward, to heaven as their rest and home, and to the resurrection of the just as the consummation of the promise of redemption, which was the one master idea of their lives. An affectionate reproof, a rebuke to impatience and faithless repining at their hard lot, is intended by the writer to accompany the encouragement conveyed by the examples of the Elders. Had these Saints of olden time refused to endure, and had they relinquished their steadfastness, when the fires of persecution waxed hot, they could never have been cited as witnesses to the reasonableness of the hope set before us, and the power of God's grace made perfect in human infirmities. But now they afford a testimony which nothing can gainsay or controvert, that the promise hereafter to be realised, is worth living for, and worth dying for. Men " of " whom the world was not worthy," from the very beginning, have set to their seal that God is true, that for God's promise they were willing to sacrifice everything that renders existence desirable, yea, even life itself. And all for what? For that which the unbelievers and the worldling would deride as the vague and indefinite day-dreams of a morbid enthusiasm! The Elders, therefore, are witnesses to the certainty of our expectations; to the truth of the promises made to the fathers; to the nothingness of worldly advantages and temporal sufferings in comparison with the glory that shall be revealed in us. They prove to us that no self-abnegation, no self-denial, is too costly when God in the way of his afflictive providence, in seasons of persecution and fiery trial, calls upon us to forsake all and to follow Christ. It is true of the disciple as of the Master, "*No Cross, no Crown.*"

In these days when the form of godliness carries with it respectability, and when an outward compliance with the ordinances of public worship and the Churches' formularies is needful even to pass muster in the world, we can scarcely realise to ourselves the forlorn and abject condition of the Jewish believer of those days. His nationality was against him. His foes were those of his own household. The wife of his bosom, his children, were among the first to rise up and betray him. The love of parents was estranged. His dearest friends and acquaintances assailed him with reproaches, and shut their doors in his face. Well might he at times, in the extremity of his anguished regrets at seeing every familiar countenance averted, and the commonest offices of humanity denied to him, ask himself, "Is the object set before me com-
" mensurate with the cost? May I not by a little

"dissimulation contrive to keep my friends and
"my convictions at once? Can a merciful God
"take pleasure in the wretchedness and daily
"torture which I suffer?" But when the material arguments of stripes and imprisonments, of cruel mockings and scourgings, of the stake and the gibbet, of the execrations of the howling mob that thirsted for his blood, were superadded to the moral dissuasives from stedfastness, then indeed it required no ordinary share of constancy and pious fortitude to resist unto blood, striving against sin. The days in which the Epistle to the Hebrews were written were pre-eminently days of perplexity and distress. They were critical times of panic and alarm. Satan and unbelief were girding themselves for that decisive conflict with the religion of Jesus, in which truth was to prevail, but only after innumerable lives had been sacrificed, and the foundations of the Church cemented with the blood of the martyrs. Well might St. Paul declare to the Corinthians in unanswerable testimony to the certainty of the resurrection, "If in this life only "we have hope in Christ, then are we of all men "most miserable, εἰ ἐν τῇ ζωῇ ταύτῃ ἠλπικότες ἐσμὲν ἐν "Χριστῷ μόνον, ἐλεεινότεροι πάντων ἀνθρώπων ἐσμέν." (1 Cor. xv. 19.) These considerations seem to limit, in a great measure, the meaning of the νέφος μαρτύρων of Heb. xii. 1 to its primary signification of *attesting witnesses*. The Elders are not represented *simply* as a concourse of spectators, as Alford, in approval of Schlichting, would have it, surveying the conflict from the abodes of rest and peace with

wrapt attention and liveliest sympathy. This picturesque and encouraging aspect is doubtless to be included in the writer's meaning. But we must not forget that they were circumstances of fearful earnestness and urgency which occasioned the Epistle to be written. Apostacy was rife. The love of many had grown cold. Many were hesitating as to which course to pursue. Whether to dissemble and relinquish τὴν ὁμολογίαν τῆς ἐλπίδος, *i.e.*, the bold avowal of their hope in Christ as the Messiah, or to go back to the Synagogue from the love of this present world and the hope of material gain. A tone of depression and despondency seems to have pervaded the entire community. The Writer has for his object, to recall the waverers to their allegiance, to alarm the deserters as to the danger, as well as the treachery, of their defection, to encourage the weak, to build up the strong in their most holy faith. It is, therefore, no mere dulcet strain of poetic fancy in which he indulges. There is a nervous earnestness, a masculine sobriety, as well as a sympathetic sweetness in the arguments he adduces. He blows a trumpet-call suited to the prevailing frequency of war's alarms. He points to what the Elders have done by patience and faith. *Patience and faith!* This is his rallying war-cry. He shows that in the example of their fervid stedfastness, of their invincible faith in the soundness of their cause, of their patient endurance to the end, his readers have the best warranty for holding fast their profession with unshakeable tenacity and perseverance. And therefore, in terse and telling phraseology, he thus sums up the lesson to be derived from the examples of victorious faith which he has just detailed.

Verse 1.—Inasmuch, therefore, as we have so great a cloud of witnesses [1] (νέφος μαρτύρων) encompassing us (περικείμενον ἡμῖν), let us lay aside every weight [2] (ὄγκον ἀποθέμενοι πάντα) and the sin that so easily besets us, and run by dint of PATIENCE (δι' ὑπομονῆς) [3] the race that is set before us (τὸν προκείμενον ἡμῖν ἀγῶνα).

[1] This expression is perchance borrowed from Is. lx. 8, מי אלה כעב התעופינה. Τίνες οἶδε, ὡς νεφέλαι πέτανται, LXX. See also Joel ii. 2. Somewhat forced and objectionable is the suggestion of Lampius, that by the *cloud of witnesses* an allusion is intended to the statues of the victors, wherewith the course and the arena were adorned.

[2] Although there is ample authority for understanding ὄγκον as *superfluous encumbrance*, by which the combatant might be impeded in his contest for the mastery, I cannot help feeling that the signification of haughtiness, self-conceit, offended self-respect, also underlies its meaning in this passage. (See note 7, pp. 164—168, on ὑποστολή.) The transition to "the sin that so easily besets us" is otherwise abrupt and forced, unless we take the latter to be the explanation of the former, as Luther does, "Lasset uns ablegen die Sünde, "so uns immer anklebt und träge macht," i.e., *let us lay aside the sin that evermore cleaves to us, and makes us slothful*. It is very improbable that any general allusion to "original sin," as some ingenious critics assert, is intended. Elsner suggests that εὐπερίστατον ἁμαρτίαν is here equivalent to φρόνημα τῆς σαρκὸς. The Writer probably intends nothing more than to intimate that a proneness to sinful indulgences is the real cause of the apostacies, the unsanctified murmuring, and lukewarmness of which he has spoken. On the word εὐπερίστατον, see J. C. Wolfius, *Curæ Philol.*, tom. iv., pp. 776—778, and Wettstein, *in loco*.

[3] In chap. x. 36, the writer reminds his readers that they lacked patient endurance ὑπομονῆς γὰρ ἔχετε χρείαν. In chap. xi. he shows them how by it the Elders conquered. Here he urges his readers to follow in their footsteps.

Verse 2.—Looking unto Jesus [1] (ἀφορῶντες, *fixing your regards upon*) the author and finisher of the faith (τῆς πίστεως ἀρχηγὸν καὶ τελειωτὴν),² who for the joy³ set before Him (ἀντὶ τῆς προκειμένης αὐτῷ χαρᾶς) stedfastly endured (ὑπέμεινε)⁴ the cross,⁵ despising the shame (αἰσχύνης καταφρονήσας), and is set down (κεκάθικεν, Alford, rec. ἐκάθισεν) at the right hand of God.⁶

¹ Ἀαρών......ὀνήσκει τοῦ πλήθους εἰς αὐτὸν ἀφορῶντος, Jos. Ant. iv. 4, 7, εἰς τὸν θεὸν ἀφορῶντας ἐν παντὶ μικρῷ καὶ μεγάλῳ Arrian. Epict. ii. 19. Luther translates ἀφορ. κ.τ.λ., " Und aufsehen auf Jesum, den Anfänger "und Vollender des Glaubens," i.e., *looking attentively to Jesus*, &c. Aspicientes in Jesum, *Vulg*. The Hebrews are invited to look to Jesus, and see whether He has not exhibited exactly the same characteristics of stedfast constancy and endurance as did all the prophets and elders. The inference is, that they must not give way to impatience, nor repine, if they are not greater than their Lord.

² The signification of ἀρχηγ. κ.τ.λ. is determined by τῆς πίστεως, i.e., *the faith* in which all the fathers trusted from the very beginning. The promise of the "Seed of the woman" was the first and original basis upon which the eye of faith has rested. It is the golden thread of prophetic redemption, which shall run through all time until the consummation of the Church's object of existence, viz., the completed salvation of sinners. The "bruising of the serpent's head" denotes Christ's final victory over the Devil, and the annihilation of his power. If, then, Jesus be the true Messiah, he is fitly designated as "the "Author and the Finisher of the faith." The writer keeps closely to the subject of which he has been all along speaking, and does not extravagate into generalities. Christ's salvation is the "All in all" of our hopes. In Him they commence, and with Him they shall attain their final consummation. In this sense of the *original author* or *source* Philo speaks of Abraham, as ἡγεμὼν τῆς θεοφιλοῦς δόξης, *the author of the sentiment so well pleasing to God*. (*De præm. et pænis*, Works, vol. ii., p. 412.) Ἀρχηγὸν might here with advantage be translated *the originator*, or *inaugurator*, den Anfänger, *Luth.*, and τελιωτὴν, *consummator*. This is apparently the view that Wettstein takes of ἀρχηγὸν, but Alford, in disregard of the context and of the subject in hand, translates it *the Leader*.

³ The joy set before Christ was the certain assurance that He should accomplish man's redemption, and so it was promised, Isaiah liii. 11, "He shall see of the travail of his soul and be satisfied." So also Is. xlii. 4, "He shall not fail nor be discouraged (יִרוֹץ *be broken*, θραυσθήσε- "ται, LXX.) till he have set judgment in the earth ; and the isles shall

"wait for his law." Gen. xlix. 10; Ps. ii. 8. Alford justly rejects the reading of the Syr., Nazianz. in Oec., Beza, and others, "instead of the joy which he had before his incarnation." Luther has, "da er wohl hätte mögen Freude haben, erduldete er das Kreuz und achtete der Schande nicht," *i.e.*, although he might assuredly have had joy, &c., viz., *he might have lived a life of pleasure upon earth*. The word προκειμένης seems, however, fatal to this latter theory.

⁴ ὑπέμεινε is emphatic. It points out the particular aspect under which the writer would have his readers to contemplate Christ's earthly career of redeeming self-abnegation. This appears more fully from the 3d verse.

⁵ The Rev. Dr. Margoliouth, in the second edition of his able and ingenious work, *The Penitential Hymn of Judah and Israel after the Spirit: an Exposition of Isaiah liii.*, Lecture iv., pp. 72, 73, writes:—
"There are, indeed, few passages in the ancient writings of the Hebrews "which show plainly that their writers had an idea of an eternal com-
"pact between the Father and the Son respecting our redemption.
"Those passages are certainly now mixed up with fables, still they
"evidence that the Scriptural doctrine of the economy of redemption
"is not altogether obliterated from the pages of Jewish books. The
"following remarkable passage occurs as a quotation from one of the
"most ancient writers in the *Yalkut Shimoni*..... It is part of an Exposi-
"tion on Isaiah lx. After stating that the *Light* is the Messiah, and
"that Satan trembled at his very sight (see James ii. 19), and that God
"announced to Satan his final overthrow by the Messiah, the passage
"continues to run thus: *The Holy One, Blessed be He, began to stipulate
"with Him* (the Messiah). He said to Him, The sins of those who are
"treasured up beside thee, will bring thee under a yoke of iron, and
"make thee like this calf, whose eyes are dim, and will torment thy
"spirit with unrighteousness, and because of transgression thy tongue
"will cleave to the roof of thy mouth. (Ps. cxxxvii. 6.) Dost thou
"accede to this? *Messiah rejoined before the Holy One, Blessed be He*,
"'Lord of the universe, perhaps this trouble is for many years.' *The
"Holy One, Blessed be He, said*, 'By thy life and the life of thy head,
"'a week have I decreed upon thee. (Dan. ix. 27.) If it grieve thy
"'soul, I will expel, or afflict thee now.' *He replied before Him*, 'Lord
"'of the universe, with heartfelt gladness and with heartfelt joy, I
"'take this upon myself, on condition that not one of Israel shall
"'perish: and that not only those that are alive shall be saved in my
"'days, but also those that are hid in the dust.' And not only the
"dead shall be saved in my days, but also those dead, who died from
"the time of the first man until now, and not these only......but also

"all that is in thy mind to create, and have not been yet created; thus
"I consent, and on these terms I take this office upon myself."

התחיל הק״בה מתנה עמו א״ל הללו שגנוזים אצלך עונותיהם עתידים להכניסך בעול ברזל
ועש״ איזהך כברזל הזה שכהו עיניו ומשתקין את רוחך בעול ובגזנותיהם של אלו עתיד לשינך
להרבץ נחכך רצונך בכך אמר משיח לפני הק״בה רבונו של עולם שמא אותו צער שנות
רבות הם א״ל הק״בה חייך וחי׳ ראשך שנוע גזרה עליך אם בנפשך יצבגה אני מורדן
מיכשיו אמר לפניו רבונו של עולם בגילת לבי ובשמחה לבי אני מקבל עלי ע״מ שלא יאבד אחד
מישראל ולא היים בלבד יושעו בימי אלא אף אותם שגנוזים בעפר ולא מתים בלבד יושעי
בימי אלא אף אותם מיתים שמתו מימות אדם הראשון עד עכשו ולא אלו בלבר [אלא אף
נפלים יושעו בימי ולא נפלים בלבד] אלא אף למי צלחה על דעתך להבראות ולא נבראו כך
אני רוצה בכך אני מקבל.

The words between brackets, which the learned Doctor has left
untranslated, refer to those untimely born (τῷ ἐκτρώματι, 1 Cor. xv. 8).
The passage is also given at further length, with an English translation,
in the late Dr. M'Caul's *Doctrine and Interpretation of Is. liii.*, pp.
37—39.

⁸ The writer refers back to the prophetic invitation of Psalm cx. 1:
—" Jehovah saith unto my Lord, Sit thou on my right hand until I
" make thine enemies thy footstool." Christ has fulfilled the conditions
of humiliation imposed in the last verse of the Psalm. He has drunk
of the wayside stream of affliction and distress. And so God the
Father has ratified His share in the compact also. He has exalted Him
to be head over all principality and power. See note 4, pp. 28—30; also,
J. Jac. Schudt's " Commentarius Philologico-Theologicus in Psal. cx.,"
Frankfort-on-the-Maine, 1718. 8vo. Schudt was Rector of the University in Frankfort, and his work is a masterpiece of Rabbinical as
well as Biblical erudition. He summarises as follows the contents of
the 7th verse of the Psalm under consideration :—" I. *Emphatica
"passionis descriptio.* II. *Triumphans capitis exaltatio.*" The fifth
dissertation, pp. 179—217, *De gloriosa Regis Messiae ex Passione emersione*, is devoted entirely to the discussion of this subject, in which he
adduces a multitude of Jewish and Christian authorities in support of
the interpretation above given. See also J. Wesselii *Dissert. decimatertia de Messia ex torrente in via bibituro.* (Dissertationes Academicæ
ad selecta quædam loca Vet. et Nov. Test. *Lugd. Bat.*, 1734, 4to., pp.
352—379.) The Babylonian Gemara applies the parallel prediction of
Isaiah liii. to the Messiah. In *Sanhedrin* (Ugol. Thes., vol. xxv., col.
969) a variety of Rabbinical opinions are brought together respecting
the name of the Messiah. Some say that it is *Shiloh*, citing Gen. xlix.
10, as their authority; others, *Yinon* (Ps. lxxii. 17); others, *Chaninah*
(Jer. xvi. 13); others, *Menachem* (Lam. i. 16); whilst others, again,
say that He shall be called *A leper of the house of Rabbi* (" *Leprosus de
" domo Rabbi.*" *Buxt. Lex. Chald.*; Art. חיור, col. 724), because it is

written, "Surely He hath borne our griefs and carried our sorrows, yet "did we esteem him stricken, smitten of God, and afflicted":—

ורבנן אמרי חיוורא דבי רבי שמו . שני' אכן חליינו הוא נשא ומכאובינו סבלם , ואנחנו חשבנוהו נגוע , מוכה אלהים , ומענה .

A variety of other important Rabbinical interpretations respecting the Messiah are to be found in the immediate vicinity of the above cited passage of the Gemara.

Verses 3—6.—For consider (ἀναλογίσασθε,[1] *recogitate*, Vulg.) Him who patiently endured (ὑπομεμενηκότα) such contradiction (Widersprechen, *Luth.*) of sinners against himself (ὑπὸ τῶν ἁμαρτωλῶν εἰς αὐτὸν ἀντιλογίαν; Alford, ἑαυτὸν); lest ye grow weary (ἵνα μὴ κάμητε, or, *that ye be not discouraged*), waxing fainthearted in your souls (ἐκλυόμενοι, *disheartened*). Ye have not yet resisted unto (μέχρις) blood, striving against[2] (ἀνταγωνιζόμενοι) sin; and have forgotten (ἐκλέλησθε, *completely forgotten*, Alford) the exhortation (τῆς παρακλήσεως, *consolationis*, Vulg.) which reasons with (διαλέγεται, *discourses with*, Alford) you as with sons (Prov. iii. 11, 12); My son, undervalue not (μὴ ὀλιγώρει) the chastening of the Lord, neither faint when reproved by Him. For whom the Lord loveth,[3] He chasteneth (παιδεύει; LXX., ἐλέγχει), and scourgeth every son whom He receiveth.[4]

[1] The idea of contrast and comparison is here intended. The Hebrews are invited to draw an analogy between their own fancied unexampled troubles and persecutions and the contradictions and unutterable insults which Christ endured at the hands of sinners. I think the writer here intends specially to emphasise the ἀντιλογία; because it is plain, from verse 4, that hitherto the persecutions, at which the Hebrews were at present so sorely discouraged, had not yet taken the shape of the forfeiture of their lives. To be counted the "filth of the earth, the "offscouring of all things" (περικαθάρματα τοῦ κόσμου, πάντων περίψημα, 1 Cor. iv. 13) was hard enough. It was unjust as it was cruel; but what was it all in comparison of the ignominy, the brutal affronts, the misconstruction of his every word and motive to which Christ was subjected! When He condescended to eat with publicans and sinners, He was pointed at as a winebibber and a glutton. When He cast out devils, it was by Beelzebub that He cast them out. When He sat at

meat with the Pharisees, they treated Him with studied neglect and indecent rudeness. (Luke vii. 44—46; xi. 53.) Before Herod, the chief priests and scribes "vehemently accused Him" (Luke xxiii. 10); before the Council, many false witnesses laid things to his charge that He had never known, and yet no burning retort, no words of indignant self-justification burst from his lips. Even under the charge of blasphemy against his Divine Father, He entered upon no personal vindication. Upon the cross, the revilings and unmanly scoffs of his murderers called forth nothing but a prayer for their forgiveness. For thus it had been written by the Evangelic Prophet concerning Him:— "He was led as a lamb to the slaughter, and as a sheep before her "shearers is dumb, so He opened not his mouth." (Is. liii. 7.) See Dr. M'Caul's *Doctrine and Interpretation of Is. liii.*, passim; and Dr. Margoliouth's volume, *The Penitential Hymn of Israel and Judah: an Exposition of Is. liii.* Second Edition, pp. 74—87; and also the Appendix, *ibid.*, p. 161, &c.—The following remarkable account of the insults and outrages to which our Lord Jesus Christ was subjected before his crucifixion is given in the *Sepher Toldoth Jesu*, and is all the more noteworthy, as it is contained in a book which is one of the most indecent libels upon our blessed Redeemer's origin and parentage that was ever published. After relating the treacherous plan of Judas for the Saviour's betrayal, and how the elders of the Jews danced for joy at the prospect of his capture, it goes on to tell how an armed multitude came upon Jesus and his company unawares, took Him captive, and bound Him, with many of his followers; the rest either being slain or compelled to flee for their lives to the mountains. It then proceeds :—

ויקחו וקני ירושלים את ישו ויביאוהי העירה ויקשרוהו בעמוד של שיש אשר בעיר ויבוהו בשוטים ויאמרו לו איה כל נפלאותיך אשר עשית ויקחו קוצים וישו מהם כתר וישימו על ראשו ויצמא הממזר ויאמר להם תנו לי מעט מים ויתנו לו חומץ חזק וכאשר שתה צעק בקול גדול לאבי עלי ניבא דוד וקיימי ויתנו בברותי ראש ולצמאי ישקוני חומץ ויאמרו לו אם אלהים אתה למה לא הגדת קורם שתהיתה שהוא חומץ ויאמרו לו ועתה אתה עומד כל פתח קצרך ואין אתה תיור בתשובה וישא ישו את קולו וינך . ואמר אלי אלי למה עזבתני . ויאמרו לו אם בן אלהים אתה למה לא העלה את נפשך מידינו . ויאמר ישו דמי יכפר על באי עולם שכן ניבא ישעיהו ובחבורתו נרפא לנו .

"But the elders of Jerusalem took Jesus, and brought him into the "city, and bound him to a marble column which was in the city, and "they chastened him with whips, and said to him, Where are now all "thy miracles which thou hast wrought? [*the miracles of Jesus are "admitted, but ascribed to magical arts.*] Then they took sharp thorns, "and made a crown of them, and placed it on his head. And the "illegitimate one [*a term of derision*] waxed thirsty, and said, Give me "a little water to drink. And they gave him strong vinegar. But

"when he had drunk, he cried with a loud voice, *Concerning me my
"ancestor David prophesied,* 'They gave me also gall for my meat, and
"'in my thirst they gave me vinegar to drink.' (Ps. lxix. 21; Heb. 22.)
"And they said to him, If thou art God, why didst thou not tell us,
"before drinking it, that it was vinegar? And now thou standest in
"the door of thy grave, and yet thou turnest not to repentance. And
"Jesus lifted up his voice and wept, and said, *My God! my God! why
"hast thou forsaken me?* And the elders said to him, If thou art the
"Son of God, why hast thou not delivered thy soul from our hands?
"And Jesus said, *My blood shall make expiation on behalf of those who
"come into the world, for so Isaiah prophesied.* And by his stripes we
"are healed," &c. (*Sepher Toldoth Jesu,* pp. 16, 17, printed at length
in *Wagenseil's Tela Ignea Satanæ Altdorfii Noricorum,* 1681. 4to. It is
the sixth tract in the volume.)

² Οὔπω μέχρις αἵματος κ.τ.λ. Alford, with Bengel, and other far older
critics, is inclined to adopt the idea that this phrase is borrowed from
the pugilistic prize-ring. The meaning of the words is very obvious,
without any such forced adaptation.—J. C. Wolfius, *Curæ Philog. et
Crit.,* tom. iv. p. 780, writes, *in loc.,* "Ita M. Antoninus i. 16, ἕως
"ἱδρῶτος. Vide ibi Gatakerum, p. 41, et p. 195 Adversariorum.
"Josephum Philo, p. 414,' ait μέχρι θανάτου διωχθῆναι. Cl. Roman.
"Epist., § 4, ἄχρι νίκης οὐ μέχρι θανάτου. Sext. Empiricus xi., § 99,
"διαγωνίζεται μέχρι θανάτου, de gallis dimicantibus, iterumque § 102,
"sicut 101, μέχρι τῆς ὑστάτης ἀναπνοῆς διαγωνίζεσθα; and, § 107, μέχρι
"τελευτῆς ἀριστεύοντες. *Vide* Fabricii notas, p. 709. Pugiles et pan-
"cratiastas ad sanguinem et mortem usque decertasse ostendit C. Adami
"in Obs., p. 454. Ex Athleticis quoque Olearius in Analysi, p. 38
"explicat, ut sensus sit, eos quasi ad *ruborem* tantum pugnasse, *sudor-
"emque* ad summum, non vero ad *sanguinem:* quemadmodum de
"Diogene Cynico Laertius Diogenes dicat, exercuisse eum Xeniadæ,
"domini sui, liberos οὐκ ἀθλητικῶς, ἀλλ' ἐρυθήματος καὶ εὐεξίας χάριν."
With far greater probability and propriety, allusion is here made to
Messiah's dread conflict, as described by Isaiah ix. 5:—"For every
"battle of the warrior is with confused noise, and garments rolled in
"blood, but *this* shall be with burning *and* fuel of fire." (This translation agrees in the main with the Vulgate, but the LXX. rendering is
altogether different, and is perchance based upon a different reading of
the Hebrew.) Or else it is not improbable that the reference is to
Isaiah lxiii. 1—3, where Messiah is depicted as "coming from Edom,
"with dyed garments from Bozrah," and where he declares, "I have
"trodden the winepress alone, and of the people *there was* none with
"me," as in declaration of the unapproachable severity and magnitude

of his sufferings. To Messiah the passage is applied in the *Pirke Rabbi Eliezer*. See Schoettgen, *Horæ. Hebr. et Talm.*, tom. ii., pp. 503, 504. So also in the *Sohar* (see *ibid.*, pp. 555, 556).

³ For a variety of Rabbinical apopthegms in consonance with the above consolatory assurance, see Balth. Scheidii *Præterita præteritorum, Loca Talmudica*, printed in Meuschen, *Nov. Test. ex Talmude illustr.*, pp. 217, 218, and Schoettgen's *Horæ Hebraicæ*, tom. i., pp. 988, 989.

Philo, writing on this same passage, declares:—

'Ενθέν δέ μοι δοκεῖ τις τῶν φοιτητῶν Μωσέως ὄνομα εἰρηνικὸς, ὃς πατρίῳ γλώσσῃ Σαλομὼν καλεῖται, φάναι, Παιδείας θεοῦ υἱέ μὴ ὀλιγώρει, καὶ μὴ ἐκλύου ὑπ' αὐτοῦ ἐλεγχόμενος. Ὃν γὰρ ἀγαπᾷ κύριος ἐλέγχει. Μαστιγοῖ δὲ πάντα υἱὸν ὃν παραδέχεται. Οὕτως ἄρα ἡ ἐπίπληξις καὶ νουθεσία καλὸν νενόμισται, ὥστε δι' αὐτῆς ἡ πρὸς θεὸν ὁμολογία [καὶ] συγγένεια γίνεται. Τί γὰρ οἰκειότερον υἱῷ πατρὸς, ἢ υἱοῦ πατρί;

"For this reason, methinks, one of the disciples of Moses, *Pacific* "by name, who is called in his native language Solomon, said, 'Son, "'despise not the chastening of God, neither faint when reproved by "'Him, for whom the Lord loveth, He reproveth; and scourgeth every "'son whom He receiveth.' So excellent a thing, therefore, is chastise- "ment and admonition esteemed, that confidence and relationship "spring therefrom. For what can be more familiarly intimate than a "father with his son, or a son with a father?"—*De Congr. Quær. Erudit. Gratia*, Works, Mangey's Edit., vol. i., pp. 544, 545.

Also, in commenting upon Deut. viii. 3, he observes:—

Ἡ κάκωσις αὕτη ἱλασμός ἐστι......ὅταν γὰρ τὰ ἡδέα περισυλᾶται, δοκοῦμεν κακοῦσθαι. Τό δ' ἐστι πρὸς ἀλήθειαν ἵλεω τὸν θεὸν ἔχειν.

"Affliction is of itself a propitiation. For when we are despoiled of "enjoyments, we seem to suffer affliction, whilst it is, in truth, to have "God reconciled [or propitiated] to us."—Philo, *SS. Leg. Alleg.*, lib. iii., Works, vol. i., p. 121.

⁴ It will be observed that the above quotation differs slightly from the LXX., and considerably from the Masoretic reading of Prov. iii. 11, 12.

CHAP. XII., 3—6.

Prov. iii. 11, 12. Hebrew, Masoretic Reading.	Auth. Version.	Vulgate.	LXX Bagster's Text.	Heb. xii. 5, 6.
מוּסַר יְהֹוָה בְּנִי אַל תִּמְאָס וְאַל תָּקֹץ בְּתוֹכַחְתּוֹ׃ כִּי אֶת אֲשֶׁר יֶאֱהַב יְהֹוָה יוֹכִיחַ וּכְאָב אֶת בֵּן יִרְצֶה׃	My son, despise not the chastening of the Lord, neither be weary of his correction: For whom the Lord loveth he correcteth: EVEN AS A FATHER (וּכְאָב) the son in whom he delighteth.	Disciplinam Domini, fili mi, ne abjicias, nec deficias cum ab eo corriperis. Quem enim diligit Dominus corripit: ET QUASI PATER IN filio complacet sibi.	Υἱέ μὴ ὀλιγώρει παιδείας κυρίου, μηδὲ ἐκλύου ὑπ' αὐτοῦ ἐλεγχόμενος. "Ον γὰρ ἀγαπᾷ κύριος, ἐλέγχει, μαστιγοῖ (וּכְאָב) δὲ πάντα υἱὸν ὃν παραδέχεται.	Υἱέ μου, μὴ ὀλιγώρει παιδείας κυρίου, μηδὲ ἐκλύου ὑπ' αὐτοῦ ἐλεγχόμενος. "Ον γὰρ ἀγαπᾷ κύριος παιδεύει, μαστιγοῖ δὲ (וּכְאָב) πάντα υἱὸν ὃν παραδέχεται.

From the above it will be seen that the variation hinges simply upon the correct punctuation of וכאב. The right rendering is settled for Christian readers by the canonical decision of the Writer to the Hebrews. The question is not whether the LXX. translators have given a preferable interpretation, but, Which interpretation is adopted, and thereby authoritatively sanctioned as the true meaning of the Word of God? Surenhusius, whose punctuation (וּכְאָב *Partic.* Kal) has been adopted above, observes how the sense and antithesis gains by the reading of וכאב, as a verb with conjunction, rather than as a substantive with conjunction and adverb. "Etenim textus Hebræus obscurus et "hiulcus est, si ei nihil addatur, vel is alio modo non legatur, nam "verbo tenus ita dicitur ובאב את בן ירצה *et sicut pater filio bene volet,* si "verbum ירצה divellatur a præcedentibus, vel si hoc cum illis con- "jungatur, hoc sensu erit vertendum, et *sicut pater bene vult* sive "*benevolus est filio,* quibus verbis necessario aliquid addendum est ex "præcedentibus, ut oratio melius fluat." (Βίβλος καταλλαγῆς. pp. 656, 657.) Surenhusius, however, is so in love with his theory, *de modis allegandi Scripturas Sacras,* that he seems to imply that the Writer to the Hebrews has adopted וּכְאָב rather as a matter of convenience and elegance, and to avoid tautological repetition, than as expressing the mind of the Holy Spirit of Truth. Be it observed that the *dictum* of an *inspired* writer of the New Testament respecting a difficult passage is a very different matter from the presumptuous and farfetched experiments at emendation which modern criticism proposes, often in direct opposition to conclusive and final decisions, similar to the one instanced above. Scarcely less offensive to a sense of piety and reverent feeling is the patronising and qualified approval which it, now and then, condescends to bestow upon Apostles and Evangelists, should they happen to countenance in any measure a favourite theory, or, in other words, "to fall in with its views!" Surely concerning such speakers of "great swelling words of vanity" it is written beforehand, "He that "sitteth in the heavens shall laugh, the Lord shall have them in "derision." For the various passages in the Hebrew Bible in which the *verb* נָאַב occurs, see Job xiv. 22, "shall have pain;" Prov. xiv. 13, "is sorrowful;" Gen. xxxiv. 25, "sore;" Ps. lxix. 29 (Heb. 30), "sorrowful;" Ezek. xiii. 22, "made sad;" 2 Kings iii. 19, "mar," *Marg.* "grieve;" Job v. 18, "maketh sore;" Ezek. xxviii. 24, "grieving" thorn. The substantive מַכְאֹב is translated μάστιγες by the LXX., Ps. xxxii. 10, and in Ps. xxxviii. 17 (Heb 18), ἀλγηδών in connexion with μάστιγας of the preceding clause. See also in Ps. lxix. 26 (Heb. 27), ἄλγος, of the pain inflicted by striking. In Isaiah liii. 3, the Messiah is described as "a man of sorrows," איש מכאבות, ἄνθρωπος ἐν πληγῇ ὤν, LXX., see also verse 4 in LXX. See Fuerst's Hebrew and Chaldee Conc., article נאב. Lud. Cappellus, *Critica Sacra*, p. 61, writes:—"Heb. xii. 6, *Quem Deus diligit, corripit*, μαστιγοῖ δὲ πάντα υἱὸν ὃν παραδέχεται, ex Proverb iii. 12, ubi in Hebraeo est יְהוָה אֶת בֶּן יֶאֱהַב, "*et sicut pater, castigat scilicet, filium quem diligit*. At LXX pro כְּאַב, "legerunt נאב, hoc est, *dolore afficit*, flagris nempe caedendo à radice "נאב, *dolor*. Apoc. ii. 27, xii. 5, xix. 15, de Christo dicitur, et de quovis "fideli, ποιμανεῖ αὐτοὺς ἐν ῥάβδῳ σιδηρᾷ, *pascet eos* in virgâ ferreâ, ex "Psal. ii. 9, ubi in Hebraeo est תְּרֹעֵם, hoc est, *confringes eos*, at LXX. "legerunt תִּרְעֵם, hoc est, *pasces eos*, sed prior lectio magis quadrat sequen- "tibus, *instar vasis figuli comminues eos*."

Verses 7—10.—If, therefore, ye endure (παιδείαν ὑπομένετε)¹ the discipline of chastening, God dealeth with you (προσφέρεται) as with sons.² For what son is there whom a father chastens not? But if ye be without the discipline of chastening (παιδείας) of which all³ have been made partakers (μέτοχοι γεγόνασι), then are ye bastards (νόθοι),⁴ and not sons. Moreover (εἶτα, *besides, furthermore*), we used to have the fathers of our flesh (τῆς σαρκὸς ἡμῶν, i.e., *of the same nature as ourselves, earthly parents*) as correctors (παιδευτὰς, *chasteners*, i.e., *who were accustomed to punish us*), and we reverenced them (ἐνετρεπόμεθα). Shall we not, then, much rather be in subjection (ὑποταγησόμεθα, i.e., *reverently submit ourselves*) to the Father of the Spirits, and live?⁵ Besides, the former used to chasten (ἐπαίδευον, i.e., *in the way of disciplinary training*) with a view to a few days (πρὸς ὀλίγας ἡμέρας, i.e., *to fit us for the short span of our earthly career*) according as they pleased (κατὰ τὸ δοκοῦν αὐτοῖς, i.e., *according to the plan and method which seemed best to their finite and fallible judgments. They could only act for the best and by the uncertain criterion of their own experience*), but the latter, [God corrects us] with a view to that which is really profitable (ἐπὶ τὸ συμφέρον, i.e., *without any possibility of mistake, either in the object or the severity of the discipline*), in order that we might be partakers of his holiness. (Εἰς τὸ μεταλαβεῖν τῆς ἁγιότητος αὐτοῦ.)

The writer has already intimated (verse 1), by his allusion to " the sin that so easily besets," that amendment of life was necessary. Castigation is designed to correct a fault. He would have his converts consider their ways and alter them. Affliction is sent in mercy, but yet it has a very definite object. They were evidently inclined to refuse correction, and to rebel, instead of humbly setting themselves to cure what was amiss. Impurity of life seems to be one especial sin against which they are warned. (See verses 15, 16, and xiii. 4.) In a similar strain St. Paul writes to the Corinthians, 1 Cor. xi. 30—32. Διὰ τοῦτο ἐν ὑμῖν πολλοὶ ἀσθενεῖς καὶ ἄῤῥωστοι καὶ κοιμῶνται ἱκανοί. Εἰ γὰρ ἑαυτοὺς διεκρίνομεν, οὐκ ἂν ἐκρινόμεθα. Κρινόμενοι δὲ ὑπὸ τοῦ Κυρίου παιδευόμεθα, ἵνα μὴ σὺν τῷ κόσμῳ κατακριθῶμεν. There was evidently a departure from holiness, to which the present troubles were designed to recall them. And therefore he dwells upon the painful nature of all real punishment, which has a corrective object in view, adding,

Verse 11.—And every correction whilst it lasts (πρὸς μὲν τὸ παρὸν) seems not to be a matter of joy but of grief, but afterwards it yields the peaceable fruit of righteousness to those who have been exercised thereby (τοῖς δι' αὐτῆς γεγυμνασμένοις, i.e., to those who have accepted it in the spirit in which it was designed, supporting it with resignation and fortitude, admitting its justice and necessity, but not to those who draw back in offended pride (x. 30—39), and refuse to kiss the rod, and acknowledge Him who has appointed it. See Micah vi. 9, Jer. v. 3.)

---

[1] " 'Υπομένετε has the use here of *enduring, undergoing, suffering;* "and not that of *supporting, bearing up* under, persevering."—*Stuart.* In other words, it refers to the condition and process of discipline, not to the effort by which it is cheerfully undergone. Alford, upon ample MS. authority, adopts εἰς παιδείαν ὑπομένετε, i.e., the sufferings that you endure have a disciplinary object in view, instead of εἰ παιδ. ὑπομ. J. C. Wolfius, however, strongly objects to this emendation, "Codices "aliquot habent εἰς παιδείαν, prave omnino, cum sequens ἀπόδοσις "ostendat, πρότασιν hic per εἰ afferri. Confer Millium."

[2] Philo, commenting upon Deut. viii. 2, "Remember all the way "which the Lord God led thee in the wilderness, how He afflicted "thee," &c., says:—

Τίς οὖν οὕτως ἀνίσιώς ἐστιν, ὡς ὑπολαβεῖν κακωτὴν τὸν θεὸν, καὶ λιμὸν οἴκτιστον ὄλεθρον ἐπάγοντα τοῖς ἄνευ τροφῆς ζῆν μὴ δυναμένοις ; Ἀγαθὸς γὰρ καὶ ἀγαθῶν αἴτιος, εὐεργέτης, σωτήρ, τροφεύς, πλουτοφόρος, μεγαλόδωρος, κακίαν ὅρων ἱερῶν ἀπεληλακώς. Οὕτω γὰρ τὰ τῆς γῆς ἄχθη, τόν τε Ἀδὰμ καὶ Κάϊν ἐφυγάδευσεν ἐκ τοῦ παραδείσου. Μὴ παραγώμεθα οὖν ταῖς φωναῖς, ἀλλὰ τὰ δι' ὑπονοιῶν σημαινόμενα σκεπῶμεν, καὶ λέγωμεν, ὅτι τὸ μὲν, ἐκακώσε, ἴσον ἐστὶ τῷ ἐπαίδευσε καὶ ἐνουθέτησε καὶ ἐσωφρόνισε, κ τ.λ.

"Who is there, therefore, so impious as to insinuate that God inflicts "wrong, and brings famine, most miserable of deaths, upon men who "cannot live without food? For he is good, and the Author of good (see " James i. 17), a Benefactor, a Saviour, a Pastor, a Dispenser of wealth, "a liberal Giver, and has driven malignity far away from the sacred "boundaries. So did He banish Adam and Cain, those two troublers "of the earth, from Paradise. We must not, therefore, allow ourselves

" to be misled by mere words, but pay attention to the hidden meaning
" that underlies them, and so explain *He afflicted*, as equivalent to *He
" corrected, He admonished, He brought to a better mind.*" Philo, *De Congr.
Quær. Erudit. Gratia.*, Works, vol. i., p. 544. The entire passage is
singularly worth reading, viz., pp. 542 – 545.

³ Even Christ Himself has been made a partaker of chastisement,
Heb iv. 15, Is liii. 4 – 10. The word πάντες is doubtless inclusive and
emphatic. It appeals to the murmurers and desponding, upon the
very highest and most persuasive grounds. They are reminded how
they are made partakers of the sufferings of their Lord.

⁴ "Ἄρα νόθοι ἐστὲ καὶ οὐχ υἱοί. There are many difficulties surrounding
this passage arising from the variety of significations in which the
Hebrew word ממזר *Mamzer*, a bastard, is used. Dean Alford contents
himself with quoting from *Phavorinus*, "νόθος, ὁ μὴ γνήσιος υἱός, ἀλλ᾽ ἐκ
" παλλακίδος," and setting over against it a quotation from Philo. which
would imply a totally different meaning. " So Philo *de confus.* Ling 28,
" vol. i., p. 426, speaking of the υἱοὶ τῶν ἀνθρώπων who built Babel, says
" that they were τῶν ἐκ πόρνης ἀποκυηθέντων οὐδὲν διαφέροντες, οὓς ὁ νόμος
" ἐκκλησίας ἀπελήλακε θείας," and then Dr. Alford winds up with a somewhat diffuse explanation from Chrysostom, which leaves the real perplexity unsolved.—There is a very wide distinction between the son of a
concubine (who might be a Hebrew woman, or a purchased slave, or a free
Gentile, although such connexions with heathen women were forbidden,
or at least strongly discouraged by the law) and one sprung ἐκ πόρνης.
J. Selden (*De successionibus ad leges Ebræorum*) in the 3d chapter (p. 17),
which is headed, " *De Liberis Naturalibus e Concubina, Ancilla, Extranea
" genitis. De Mamzeribus ac liberis ex incestu susceptis*, et de Jephthe e
" *patrimonio a fratribus ejecto*," shows how the natural offspring of a
Hebrew concubine, and even those born " *ex Incestu damnato*, צרוה, *seu
" turpitudinis nomine*," were eligible to succeed to the inheritance as if
they were legitimate sons, and he quotes in support of his opinion the
saying of Maimonides, *Halach Nechaloth*, cap. i. : —

כל הקרובין בעבירה יורשין בכשרים כיצד כגון שהיה לו בן ממזר או אח ממזר הרי אלו
כאשר בנים וכאשר אחין לנחלה :

" Every next of kin, although born of transgression, succeeds, as if
" he were legitimate. How ? If any man has a son or a brother a
" bastard (ממזר), they will succeed to the inheritance, just like other
" sons and brothers." Such as these would of course be born of Hebrew
parents If, then, we are to understand that Jephtha's mother was a
Hebrew woman, although she were אשה זונה (*meretrix*), his brethren
unjustly defrauded him of his share in the inheritance ; but if the
words כי בן אשה אחרת אתה, *quia filius es ex foemina alia* (Jud. xi 2), are

to be understood that his mother was a Gentile foreigner, then he had no legal claim upon the property. (See *ibid.*, pp. 29, 30.) Selden sagaciously observes that there is nothing in the Hebrew text answering to the *non poteris* ("thou canst not be heir," &c.) of the Vulgate. The words are simply לא הנחל, *thou shalt not inherit.* He, therefore, is inclined to believe that Jephtha was unfairly deprived of his rights. Here, then, we see that there was nothing to preclude (in the ordinary way) a base-born son from participating in the home, institutions, and discipline of a Hebrew household, provided that his mother was a Jewess. The son of a foreign concubine, however, were she a bondservant or a free harlot, could not be heir with the sons of the Hebrew *woman*, were she wife or concubine (Gal. iv. 30), as is illustrated by the Rabbinic aphorism, מי שיש לו בן מכל מקום, בנו הוא לכל דבר, חוץ מי שיש לו מן השפחה ומן הנכרית, *He who has a son from any source, he is a son in every respect, excepting only he be born from a bondmaid or a foreign woman.* Bondservants and bondmaids had no right to use the endearing epithets of *Father* (Abba) and *Mother* to the heads of the family, as is asserted in the Bab. Gemara (tract *Berachoth*), c. ii., fol. 16 :— העברים והשפחות אי קורינן אותם לאו אבא פלוני ולא אימא פלונית, *Bondmen and bondwomen do not make use of the expression* Father (Abba) *so and so, or* Mother *so and so.* Here, then, I think we have the clue to the meaning of the word νόθοι, as used by the Writer to the Hebrews. He refers to children born of foreign mothers, who could lay no claim to the "Adoption of Sons," and were not regarded as members of the inner family circle. They would not receive the same discipline with the other children. They would be exempted, as inferiors, from the training and educational advantages of the more happily born. To refuse God's corrective chastening would be voluntarily to assume the position of *bastards.* The Rabbinical writers derive the word כמזר from מים זר, *macula extranea, i.e., one who wears the stigma of foreign extraction.* And the Targum of Jonathan paraphrases the words of Deut. xxiii. 2, "A bastard (ממזר); *Kein Hurenkind*, Luther; *Geen Bastaard*, authorized "Dutch transl.) shall not enter into the congregation of the Lord: even "to his tenth generation shall he not enter into the congregation of the "Lord," by "He who is born of fornication, or who hath upon him "the evil mark which is set upon the unclean Gentiles, is not fit to take "an upright wife from the congregation of the people of the Lord, nor "unto the tenth generation shall it be fit for him to enter into the "congregation of the Lord." (Etheridge's *Targums*, vol. ii., p. 625.) The LXX. have here translated ממזר by ἐκ πόρνης, and it is from this source that the expression in Philo, cited by Dr. Alford, is borrowed (see *in loco*). But in Zech. ix. 6, ממזר is rendered by ἀλλογενεῖς. The word occurs only in these two passages in the Hebrew text. In its stricter Rabbinical application, the word ממזר is confined to those who were born of incestuous commerce, or of adultery, whose parents, if discovered and convicted, were by the Mosaic Law punishable with death, after trial before the Council of twenty-three elders, and at the express command of God. And so the Mishna defines a bastard :—

איזהו ממזר כל שאר בשר שהוא נלא ינא דברי רבי עקיבא שמעון התימני אימר
כל שחיינן עליו כרת בידי שמים והלכה כדבריו רבי יהושע אומר כל שחיינן עליו מיתת
בית דין

"Who is a bastard? Every one who is begotten in contravention of "the command, לא ינא, 'He shall not come,' according to R. Akiva. "Simeon the Temanite says: 'Every one on account of whom [his "'parents] are guilty of death at the hands of Heaven.' And his "opinion is the received one. R. Joshua says: 'Every one on account "'of whom [his parents] are guilty of death at the hands of the "'Council." (Surenhusius' Mishna, *Jeramoth*, tom. iii., p. 17. See also Selden *de Success.*, p. 24.) R. O. Bartenora excludes from this definition of bastardy one begotten " *ex fœminâ meretrice.*" For further curious exemplification of the prohibition of a Jewess to marry a bastard, see the Mishna, *Tract, Jeramoth*, Surenhus. Edit., tom. iii. See also Selden, *De Jure Nat. et Gent.*, lib. v., chap. xii. (*De Matrimonio et Coitu, qua sive vetitus, sive permissus inter Judæos et Servos ac Ancillas exteræ originis*, &c.); *ibid.*, chap. xvi.; *De Originariorum aliquot conjugiis, Proselytis, Justis, et Libertinis, etiam et Ancillis, permissis, quæ interim Originariis ceteris vetita sunt, scilicet Mamzerum, et Eunuchorum*. (Selden's entire treatise is reprinted in Ugolini. Thes., vol. 27.) See also Buxtorf, *Lex'con Chald.* (Art. ממזיר), col. 1184; and Gesen., *Lex Manuale* (Art. ממזיר). Be it observed, in conclusion, that the prohibition of Deut. xxiii. 2 for a *Mamser* to enter into the congregation of the Lord, is interpreted by the Targum and the Rabbies to mean intermarriage with people of pure Hebrew descent. Intermarriage with proselytes was not forbidden. See Selden, *ut supr.*, and also *Table Talk*, art. *Bastard*. Respecting the heathen captive taken in war, whom a Jew might make his wife, see Selden, *De Jure Nat. et Gent.*, lib. v., chap. 13.

⁵ Τῷ πατρὶ τῶν πνευμάτων. There is considerable difficulty in this expression, which the Rev. J. C. Reichardt and his fellow-translators of the Hebrew New Testament have rendered אבי הרחות. It is intended to be in strong contrast and antithesis to the τοὺς τῆς σαρκὸς ἡμῶν πατέρας of the preceding clause. The Father of the Spirits, when He corrects us, does so positively and certainly for our good. His chastening is as salutary as it is infallibly just. He can make no mistakes. Con-

tented and cheerful resignation, therefore, and a submissive acquiescence in his disciplinary decrees, are our bounden duty and privilege. The context furnishes the key to the signification of the designation. He who has created the soul; to whose penetrating discrimination its subtle constitution and inmost requirements are transparently familiar; evermore adapts his dispensations to its highest and everlasting benefit. He who endures God's chastening can comfort himself with the consciousness that he is in the master-hand of his Creator. Man's discipline is, to a great extent, at haphazard; it is guesswork. Probably it may turn out well, but the very opposite effect may be produced. It is often prompted by mere impatient caprice. Often it is mistaken in its judgment: but from the wisdom and the love of God there can be no appeal. It is in this sense, as the allseeing and impartial Searcher of the hearts, as well as the Divine Father and Upholder of all the souls that He has created, that Moses and Aaron intercede with Jehovah on behalf of the congregation (Numb. xvi. 22) :—" O God, the God of the spirits of "all flesh, shall one man sin, and wilt thou be wroth with all the "congregation ?" (אל אלהי הרוחת לכל בשר, &c.) So, also, Moses appeals (Num. xxvii. 16, 17) to the Lord as the supreme Shepherd and Guardian of his people :—" Let the Lord, the God of the spirits of all flesh, set "a man over the congregation, which may go out before them, and "which may go in before them, and which may lead them out, and "which may bring them in; that the congregation of the Lord be not "as sheep which have no shepherd." (יפקד יהוה אלהי הרוחות לכל בשר, &c.) The Targum of Jonathan renders Num. xvi. 22 by " El Elhoa, who hast "put the spirit of life in the bodies of the children of men, and from "whom is given the spirit of all flesh;" and the Jerusalem Targum by " O God, who rulest over the spirit of all flesh " (*Etheridge's Targ.*, vol. ii., pp. 393, 394); whilst in Numb. xxvii. 16, the Targum of Jon. reads, "The Word of the Lord, who ruleth over the souls of men, and " by whom hath been given the inspiration of all flesh;" and the Jerus. Targ., "The Word of the Lord, the God who ruleth over the spirit of " all flesh " (*ibid.*, p. 441). There is a slight variation from the Hebrew in the reading of the LXX, in both the above cited passages of the book of Numbers, viz., Τῶν πνευμάτων, καὶ πάσης σαρκὸς, *of the spirits, and of all flesh*, which makes a considerable difference in the signification, and, if adopted, would obviously greatly increase the difficulty of the interpretation of the τῶν πνευμάτων of Hebrews xii. 9, inasmuch as any allusion to God's paternity in respect to the angelic host is apparently foreign to the writer's purpose, whilst an allusion to the guardian angels, or ministering spirits (Heb. i. 7—14), seems forced, and too indefinitely expressed to be accepted. Philo, although he describes Moses as invoking the auditory of men and ministering angels, at the commencement of his closing hymn (*De Humanitate*, Works, vol. ii., p. 387), yet seems to restrict the sense of τῶν πνευμάτων, in Numb. xxvii. 16, to the spirits and nature of men. (*Ibid.*, pp. 384, 385.) Speaking of Moses' intimate and personal acquaintance with the qualifications of Joshua to be his successor, he writes:—'Αλλὰ καίτοι βάσανον ἀκριβῆ λαβὼν ἐκ μακρῶν χρόνων, τῆς ἔν τε λόγοις αὐτοῦ καὶ ἔργοις καλοκαγαθίας, καὶ τὸ ἀναγκαιότατον, εὐνοίας τῆς πρὸς τὸ ἔθνος, οὐδὲ τοῦτον ᾠήθη χρῆναι καταλιπεῖν διάδοχον. Δεδιὼς μὴ ψευδοδοξῇ, νομίζων ἀγαθὸν τὸν οὐκ ὄντα πρὸς ἀλήθειαν, ἐπειδὴ τὰ κριτήρια τῆς ἀνθρωπίνης γνώμης ἀμυδρὰ καὶ ἀβέβαιά πως εἶναι πέφυκεν. Ὅθεν οὐ προπιστεύων ἑαυτῷ, ποτνιᾶται καὶ καθικετεύει τὸν ἀοράτου ψυχῆς ἔφορον Θεὸν μόνον, ὃς διάνοιαν ἀκριβῶς θεωρεῖ, ἀριστίνδην ἑλέσθαι τὸν ἐπιτηδειότατον εἰς ἡγεμονίαν, ὃς οἷα πατὴρ ἐπιμελήσεται τῶν ὑπηκόων. Καὶ τὰς καθαρὰς, καὶ, ὡς ἂν εἴποι τις τροπικώτερον παρθένους, χεῖρας εἰς οὐρανὸν ἀνατείνας. Ἐπισκεψάσθω δὴ, φησὶ, Κύριος ὁ Θεὸς τῶν πνευμάτων καὶ πάσης σαρκὸς, ἄνθρωπον ἐπὶ τῆς πληθύος κ.τ.λ. "Although "he (Moses) had tested him (Joshua) accurately, during a long course "of years, as to his excellent qualifications both of word and deed, and "also in what was most important of all, viz., his devotion to the "people, he did not even so venture to leave him as his successor, "fearing lest he might after all be mistaken in his judgment, and "suppose him to be a good man when he was not so in reality, inasmuch "as the criterions employed by human opinion frequently prove short- "sighted and unreliable. He placed, therefore, no reliance in himself, "but invoked and implored God, who alone regards the invisible soul, "and who accurately discerns the intents of the heart, that He would "select the person fittest from his intrinsic worth for the chieftainship, "who, as a father, should take charge of his subjects. And so, "stretching forth pure, or as I might more figuratively express myself, "virgin hands, to heaven, *Let the Lord*, says he, *the God of the spirits*, "*and of all flesh, look out a man over this multitude*," &c. See also Philo, *De Posteritate Caini*, ibid., vol. i., 238, and *De Agricultura*, p. 307.—R. Jochanan, in reference to Isaiah xxi. 11. "The Burden of "Dumah. He calleth to me out of Seir, Watchman, what of the "night? Watchman, what of the night?" asserts that the angel who has charge of the spirits of the departed is called Dumah, and that it is they who ask, "when the day of redemption will dawn," saying, "*Watchman! what of the night? Watchman! what of the night?*" See Gemara Babyl. *Sanhedr.*, f. 94, 1. The passage is quoted in Latin, with the glosses, by B. Scheidius, *Praeterita Praeteritorum* (Meuschen, p. 36), and is found on col. 927 of Ugolino's reprint of the Treatise *Sanhedrin* (in Thes., vol. 25). It runs as follows:—

אמר רבי יוחנן אותו מלאך הממונה על הרוחות דומה שמו . נתקבצו כל הרוחות אצל
דומה . אמרו לו , שמר מה מלילה , שמר מה מליל . אמר שמר , אתא בקר &c.
See also Buxtorf, *Lex. Chald.*, art. דומא, col. 510.—Schoettgen, *Horæ Hebr.*, tom. i., p. 989, and Wettstein (*in loco*), adduce various passages from the Rabbinical writers, in which God is spoken of as "the God of "the spirits of all flesh," *i.e.*, as Creator of the soul, and Supreme Discerner of the thoughts, &c.

The encouragements to perseverance and patient submission have thus been set before the desponding Hebrews. The Writer now proceeds to give them homely advice as to the impediments which they themselves may have originated and perpetuated in "running the race that is set before" them. He has already glanced at this subject in the first verse of this twelfth chapter. The object of God's fatherly correction is to lead them to amend what is amiss. It must eventuate in good, provided that they do not provoke Him to extremities, by rebelliously refusing his chastisement, or by continuing in the wilful indulgence of sin. Instead, therefore, of giving way to despondency, and bemoaning themselves as if they were hardly used, they are bidden to bestir themselves to a radical reformation. When the necessity of the infliction is over, then, in God's good time, it will be removed. Meanwhile it behoves them to look well to their ways, and see how far, by their sinful conduct, by their resentful impatience, or by any other hurtful cause, they are giving the adversaries a handle, or calling for severer punishment than has, as yet, come upon them.

Verses 12, 13.—Wherefore (Διὸ) lift up (ἀνορθώσατε, erigite, *Vulg.*; richtet wieder auf, *Luth.*; strengthen,

Stuart) the hands that hang down (παρειμένας) and the enfeebled knees [1] (παραλελυμένα, *faltering?*), and make straight paths for your feet, in order that that which halts (τὸ χωλὸν)[2] may not to be turned aside, but rather may be healed.

---

[1] We have here, probably, another example of St. Paul's custom of quoting the first four words of a passage of the Old Testament, and trusting to his readers' memory to supply the remainder. The quotation is from Is. xxxv. 3, &c. The entire passage, according to the Authorized Version, runs thus :—" Strengthen ye the weak hands, and " confirm the feeble knees. Say to them *that are* of a fearful heart, Be " strong, fear not: behold, your God will come *with* vengeance, *even* " God *with* a recompence ; he will come and save you. Then the eyes " of the blind shall be opened, and the ears of the deaf shall be un-" stopped. Then shall the lame *man* leap as an hart, and the tongue " of the dumb shall sing : for in the wilderness shall waters break out, " and streams in the desert. And the parched ground shall become a " pool, and the thirsty land springs of water: in the habitation of " dragons, where each lay, *shall be* grass with reeds and rushes. And " an highway shall be there, and a way, and it shall be called The way " of holiness ; the unclean shall not pass over it ; but it shall be for " those (למו יהוא) : the wayfaring men, though fools, shall not err *therein*. " No lion shall be there ;......but the redeemed shall walk *there :* and the " ransomed of the Lord shall return, and come to Zion (see Heb. xii. 22) " with songs and everlasting joy upon their heads : they shall obtain " joy and gladness, and sorrow and sighing shall flee away." The third verse, which is in the Hebrew חזקו ידים רפות וברכים כשלות אמצו, is in the LXX. Ἰσχύσατε χεῖρες ἀνειμέναι, καὶ γόνατα παραλελυμένα. Most probably an allusion is also intended to the words of Is. xl. 1—4. Surenhusius (Βίβλος καταλλαγῆς, pp. 656, 657) writes :—" Verba Apostoli sine ulla " allegationis formula, adducta, ut a veteribus Hebræorum Doctoribus " interdum fieri solebat (times without number in the Gemara and " Mishna), sicuti docet thesis nostra 36 *De formulis allegandi Scripturas* " *Sacras*, petita sunt ex Jesaiæ xxxv. 3, ubi in textu Hebræo,

חזקו ידים רפות וברכים כשלות אמצו

" *Confirmate manus remissus, et genua labantia corroborate*, ad quæ verba " cum Apostoli verbis concilianda, notandum est quod propheta, com-" mutatis verbis et sententiis, more oratorio loquens, singulis subjectis " aliquod verbum jungat, et sic rem exornet, Apostolus brevitatem " amans, et lectorem Hebræum, cui locus erat notus, ex duobus unum

"conficit, et duas speciales significationes ad unum generalem revocat,
" quæ basis est utriusque, quando dicit ἀνορθώσατε, *emendate, corrigite,*
" cum enim verba אמן et רהב fere synonyma sint, ille commode ad unam
" generalem significationem revocari possunt, videsis thesin nostram
" 19 et 20, *De Modis interpretandi Scripturas Sacras,* cui 4, *De Modis*
" *allegandi,* est jungenda, ubi dicitur quod cum sensus brevior sit
" verbis, verba sint contrahenda. Tandem Apostolus textui allegato
" quædam verba adjungit, et sic sensum amplificat ad majorem exhor-
" tationem, quando dixit, καὶ τροχιὰς ὀρθὰς ποιήσατε τοῖς ποσὶν ὑμῶν,
" *atque orbitas rectas facite pedibus vestris,* quæ verba, non in textu
" allegato, sed aliis in locis occurrunt, ut Prov. ii. 15, iv. 11, item v. 6,
" 21, 22, 23, vel etiam Jes. xl. 3, ubi eadem fere phrasis occurrit."
The omission of the second verb, however, may be accounted for by presuming that the writer had quoted quite sufficient of the passage to recall it, in its integrity, to the minds of his readers, and deemed it, therefore, unnecessary to draw out a familiar theme of which the keynote had been distinctly struck. Very similar to the words of the Writer to the Hebrews are the expressions used by Philo when speaking of the trials and hardships which the Israelites underwent in the wilderness. Commenting on Exod. xv. 23, in reference to the bitter waters of Marah, he says :— Οἱ μὲν γὰρ προκαμόντες ἀνέπεσον, βαρὺν ἀντίπαλον ἡγησάμενοι τὸν πόνον, καὶ τὰς χεῖρας ὑπ' ἀσθενείας, ὥσπερ ἀπειρηκότες ἀθληταὶ, καθῆκαν, παλινδρομεῖν εἰς Αἴγυπτον ἐπὶ τὴν ἀπόλαυσιν τοῦ πάθους ἐγνωκότες. Οἱ δὲ τὰ φοβερὰ καὶ δεινὰ τῆς ἐρημίας πάνυ τλητικῶς καὶ ἐρρωμένως ἀναδεχόμενοι, τὸν ἀγῶνα τοῦ βίου διήθλησαν ἀδιάφθορον καὶ ἀήττητον φυλάξαντες, καὶ τῶν τῆς φύσεως ἀναγκαίων κατεξαναστάντες, ὡς πεῖναν, δίψος, ῥῖγος, κρύος, θάλπος, ὅσα τοὺς ἄλλους εἴωθε δουλοῦσθαι, κατὰ πολλὴν ἰσχύος περιουσίαν ὑπάγεσθαι.

" Not a few, indeed, early succumbed, accounting the toil to be a
" conflict too grievous to bear up against, and hung down their hands
" in helpless feebleness like discouraged athletes, and made up their
" minds to return back again to Egypt, in order to enjoy their sensual
" appetites. But others bearing up manfully and courageously against
" terrors and hardships of the desert, maintained the battle of life with
" invincible and unflagging constancy, and held out against the pressing
" necessities of nature, viz., hunger, thirst, cold, exposure to the incle-
" mency of the weather, heat, by which men usually are overcome, but
" may be surmounted by a superabundance of resolution." Philo, *De Cong. quær. erudit. gratia,* Works, vol. i., p. 543.

² The exhortation to make "straight paths," &c., doubtless signifies to remove every stone of stumbling, and rock of offence out of the way, which by incaution, or negligence, or wilful departure from God's law,

they may have placed, either before themselves, or before others. The τὸ χωλὸν evidently refers to the waverers who are halting, in a state of discouragement and indecision, whether to go back to the synagogue or not. Such as these would naturally be greatly swayed by the pervading tone, and aspect of their stronger, and elder brethren in the faith. To these latter the writer appeals, on behalf of the irresolute, and the weak. They should try to heal, instead of to aggravate their distress, and to increase their timorousness and fears.

Verses 14, 15.—Pursue (διώκετε) peace with all men,[1] and the sanctification (τὸν ἁγιασμὸν) without which no man shall see the Lord.[2] Giving diligent oversight (ἐπισκοποῦντες), lest any one falling short of the grace of God, lest any root of bitterness[3] springing up, trouble you (ἐνοχλῇ), and by it the many be polluted (μιανθῶσιν οἱ πολλοί).[4]

[1] This partakes strongly of the nature of Christ's exhortation to his disciples (Luke xxi. 12—19) when after setting before them the aggravated severity of the persecutions which, for his sake, they should endure, He concludes, "In your patience possess ye your souls," ἐν τῇ ὑπομονῇ ὑμῶν κτήσασθε τὰς ψυχὰς ὑμῶν. Forbearance and gentleness, with a manifest desire for peace, were to be the weapons wherewith they should counteract, and if possible disarm, the bitterness of their enemies.

[2] "The sanctification without which no man shall see the Lord," is in evident allusion to the sanctification of the children of Israel preliminary to their going forth out of the camp "to meet with God" at Sinai when the law was given. Exod. xix. 6—15. (Compare Ps. xxiv. 3, 4, "Who shall ascend to the Mount of Jehovah," &c.) The correctness of this view is established by the οὐ γὰρ προσεληλύθατε κ.τ.λ. of verse 18, &c. The Israelites were commanded to sanctify themselves, when they were about to go up to the material Mount of God, which was indeed an occasion of solemnity sufficiently terrible in its every sight and sound. We, however, are called upon to prepare ourselves for an ordeal more heart-searching and awe-inspiring still. We are bidden to draw nigh to the spiritual realities, of which the Mount that might be touched was but the passing symbol and typical foreshadowment. According to Talmudical tradition the entire congregation of Israel was delivered from the taint of "original sin" when they stood

upon Mount Sinai. The late Dr. M'Caul (*Old Paths*, 1846, 8vo., p. 216) quotes from the tract *Shabbath*, fol. 145, col. 2, as follows:—

מפני מה גוים מזוהמין שלא עמדו על הר סיני שבשעה שבא הנחש על חוה הטיל בה
זוהמא ישראל שעמדו על הר סיני פסקה זוהמתן גוים שלא עמדו על הר סיני לא פסקה
זוהמתן אמר ליה רב אחא בריה דרבא לרב אשי גרים מאי אמר ליה אע"ג דאינהו לא הוו
מזליהו הוה דכתיב את אשר ישנו פה עמנו עומד היום ה' אלקינו ואת אשר איננו פה וגי':

"Why are the Gentiles defiled? Because they did not stand upon "Mount Sinai, for in the hour that the serpent came to Eve, he com-"municated a defilement, which was taken away from Israel when they "stood on Mount Sinai......Rav Acha, the son of Rabba, said to Rav "Ashai, How then does it fare with the proselytes? He replied, "Although they went not there, their good fortune (or star) was there "as it is written, *With him that standeth here with us this day, before* "*the Lord our God and also with him that is not here with us this day*" (Deut. xxix. 15). Dr. M'Caul continues, "The Commentary on this "passage quotes still further particulars from Shipri, and says:—

כל שעמדו על הר סיני נתקדשו ונגהרו ונתרפאו מכל מום ואף סורים ופסחים שהיו
בישראל כדתניא בסיפרי:

"All that stood on Mount Sinai were sanctified and purified, and were "healed from every blemish, even the blind and the lame that then "happened to be in Israel, as is taught in Shipri." It is evident, therefore, that the idea of sanctification and purification occupied a very prominent position in the Jewish mind, in connexion with the giving of the law on Mount Sinai. The allusion of the Writer to the Hebrews would be easily intelligible to the Hebrew reader. And this, perhaps, gives us the clue to the meaning of the word πόρνος, *fornicator*, of verse 16, and furnishes us with the explanation of verse 4 in chapter xiii. In Exod. xix. 15, Moses enjoins upon the people היו נכנים לשלשת ימים אל תגשו אל אשה. According to Authorized English Version, "Be ready against the third day; come not at *your* wives." The LXX, however, renders literally μὴ προσέλθητε γυναικί, *come not near a woman*. So also the Targum of Onkelos. Luther does not follow *uxoribus vestris* of the Vulgate, but has "zum Weibe," and the Authorized Dutch translation has "tot de vrouw." The Mishna (*Shabbat*. Surenh., tom. ii., p. 36), commenting on Exod. xix. 15 by the light of verses 10, 11, understands this prohibition to refer to the Marriage-bed. So also Bartenora and Maimonides, the Targums of Palestine and Jerusalem, and also Josephus. It must be remembered, however, that the ceremonial law had not yet been promulgated. Whilst the words אל תגשו אל אשה might well be paraphrased by the μή τις πόρνος of the Writer to the Hebrews as prohibiting all illicit connexion and impurity. Lest, however, he should appear to give colour of authority to any Essene figment respecting the unlawfulness of marriage, or to any Rabbinic commandment respecting ceremonial defilements, he writes, xiii. 4, "Marriage is honourable in all, and the bed undefiled, "but whoremongers (πόρνους) and adulterers God will judge." What he would say is this : " Moses forbid the Israelites to present themselves " with any sexual impurity upon them, when the Lord came down *in the* " *sight of all the people upon Mount Sinai.*" (Exod. xix. 11.) You are called to stand before the true Mount Zion. " Cleanse yourselves, therefore, " from all filthiness of flesh and spirit, and put on that true *sanctification* " *without which no man shall see the Lord.*" The word πόρνος does not primarily, if at all, refer to Esau, whose character, as estimated by the Jewish writers, is expressed exactly by the word βέβηλος. Let it be observed that verses 15—17 are a parenthetic, and *explanatory* illustration of the ἁγιασμὸν of verse 14. As Moses forbid the impure, and the profane, or unsanctified, from coming near to the mount of God, to witness the descent of Jehovah in the presence of his people, on the day when the Law was given upon Sinai, much more are professing Christians prohibited from drawing near to the spiritual mount of God, where the God of the spirits of all flesh reveals Himself to the eye of faith, and speaks to us by Jesus the Mediator of the new covenant, in the midst of the congregation of his saints.

³ The writer is warning his readers against the sin and infectious example of apostasy, and he illustrates his meaning from a similar warning of Moses, Deut. xxix. 18 :—" Lest there should be among you " man, or woman, or family, or tribe, whose heart turneth away this " day from the Lord our God, to go and serve the gods of these nations ; " lest there should be among you a root that beareth gall and worm- " wood." It is plain, from verses 22—28, that Moses intimates that the guilt, as well as the punishment of such a departure from God, would be contagious, and that by it " the many" would be polluted ; for he intimates that the entire land would be visited by the direst curses. It is very noteworthy that the quotations, made by the New Testament writers from the Old, are not pressed into their service on account of a mere similarity of sound, but will, if examined, in the context, be generally found to refer to circumstances exactly in point, and immediately bearing upon and illustrative of the subject under consideration. Such a root of bitterness and troubles of Israel we have in Achan. Josh. vii. 25. Comp. with Josh. vi. 18, where the verb עכר is the exact equivalent of ἐνοχλέω, although the LXX. have ἐκτρίψητε in Josh. vi. 18, and ὠλόθρευσας, ἐξολοθρεῦσαι in Josh. vii. 25. The Hebrew text according to the Masoretic reading of Deut. xxix. 18 (Heb. 17) is יֶשׁ בָּכֶם שֹׁרֶשׁ פֹּרֶה רֹאשׁ וְלַעֲנָה, μή τις ἐστὶν ἐν ὑμῖν ῥίζα ἄνω

φύουσα ἐν χολῇ καὶ πικρίᾳ, LXX.; whilst the words of the Writer to the Hebrews are a citation, and not a verbatim quotation of the words of Moses, e.g., μή τις ῥίζα πικρίας ἄνω φύουσα ἐνοχλῇ κ.τ.λ. He includes the idea of both לִעֲנָה and ראשׁ in the ῥίζα πικρίας. Both these Hebrew words are understood to designate bitter and poisonous herbs. לִעֲנָה is rendered *hemlock* in Amos vi. 12 by the English translators, whilst in Amos v. 7, and the other six passages in which it occurs, it is *wormwood*. ראשׁ on the other hand, is *hemlock* in Hos. x. 4; *venom*, Deut. xxxii. 33; *poison*, Job xx. 16; and *gall* in the other eight passages in which it occurs. A comparison of the Hebrew with the LXX., as above, will obviate any excuse for adopting the fanciful suggestion of Surenhusius, " Cum " itaque ראשׁ et לִעֲנָה ambo sint synonyma amarorem significantia, suffici- " ebat Apostolo לִעֲנָה meminisse sub voce πικρίας, et ראשׁ, quod tam " *caput*, et *summitatem rei*, quam *fel* significat, vertere maluit per " לְמַעְלָה ἄνω, ut illud ἄνω φύουσα sit Hebraeum פֹּרֶה ראשׁ *sursum germinans*." (Βίβλος καταλλαγῆς, p. 660.) Equally untenable is Spencer's explanation (*De Legibus Hebr. Ritualibus*, lib. ii., cap. 3, sec. 1), who, with a strange misapprehension of the Writer's meaning, understands ῥίζα πικρίας, as well here, as in the LXX. of Deut. xxix. 18 (where, by the way, the expression does not occur) to signify some heathenish festival orgie. The only shadow for such an interpretation would be a supposed allusion to the lascivious excesses that celebrated the erection of the golden calf (Exod. xxxii. 6—17, 19—25; 1 Cor. x. 7), whilst Moses was absent in the Mount, and whereby " many were defiled." The passage of Spencer is found on pp. 449, 450 of the Hague Edition of 1686, and on p. 714 of the Leipsic Edition. For a variety of other proposed emendations of the Hebrew text, see J. C. Wolfii, *Curæ Philologicæ*, &c., vol. iv., pp. 784—787, which Wolfius himself, however, rejects as untenable, believing that St. Paul cited in general terms from Deut., but did not quote from it. Dr. Alford exercises a prudent discretion in declining to adopt the alteration, advocated by Delitzsch, of ἐνοχλῇ into ἐν χολῇ (Alford, *in loco*). See also Wettstein, *in loco*.

* The article οἱ is omitted from the received text, but is inserted by Alford, on the authority of the Codex Alexandr. and Codex Sinaiticus.

Verse 16.—Lest there be any fornicator (πόρνος),[1] or profane person (βέβηλος), as Esau,[2] who, in exchange for one morsel of meat (ἀντὶ βρώσεως μιᾶς, *one meal*, Alford; *unam escam*, Vulg.; *um einer Speise*, Luth.), surrendered (ἀπέδοτο, *sold*) his own birthright (τὰ πρωτοτόκια αὐτοῦ).

[1] See note 2, on pp. 278—281.

² The profanity of Esau's act consisted in parting with his privilege as the head of Abraham's posterity (and, as a matter of consequence, the distinguished honour of being the direct ancestor of the Messiah), and, not only so, but with the priesthood also, which in those days, and until the institution of the Levitic hierarchy, belonged to the eldest son. And so J. Saubert, in his Commentary *De Sacerdotibus et Sacris Ebræorum personis* (printed at length in Ugolin. Thes., vol. xii.), writes, "Esau, qui propter unicam escam vendidit sacrum illud primo-"geniti jus, vocatur βέβηλος profanus h.e. ad Sacerdotium ineptus." *Ibid.*, col. 2. See also J. Selden, *De Success. in Pontif. Ebr.*, cap. 1. I cannot help feeling, however, that the writer includes, more especially, the signification of an *unhallowed* and *unsanctified* person, in the word βέβηλος, in allusion to the sanctification, before alluded to, enjoined upon the Israelites by Moses, Exod. xix., before presenting themselves at the holy Mount. The unholy liver, as well as the profane despiser of sacred privileges, shall "not see God." The Hebrew converts have been first warned against the contamination of lustful indulgences; secondly, they are admonished not to sell their Christian birthright, under any apparent necessity or pressure of bodily necessity, as profane Esau did, who, to appease his appetite when he was hungry, said, הנה אנכי הולך למות ולמה זה לי בכרה, "Behold, I am going to die, and what "use now to me is a birthright?" If, in consequence of the poverty and distress from which they were then suffering, and to escape from the persecutions and privations attendant upon their profession of Christ, or from a base desire to better their position, they should renounce their baptismal privileges, this would be to act like Esau, who for a mess of pottage sold his birthright, and forfeited the blessing. His profanity consisted in setting a passing and temporal necessity over against the enduring promises, and eternal blessings of God. He chose the good things of this life, as possessing an immediate and definite value, before the future, distant, deferred promises of God, for the sake of which Abraham, Isaac, and Jacob were content to forsake all, and to live as strangers and pilgrims upon earth, looking to heaven as their home, and to the life to come as their reward. Spencer strongly asserts, that the Writer to the Hebrews does not so much apply the term βέβηλος to Esau, as to the Christian who, in consideration of any worldly advantage, should lapse to heathenism :—"Addi potest, quod "in verbis illis Apostoli, *profani* nota non tam Esavo, quam Christiano, "voluptatis alicujus mundanæ causâ ad Gentilismum deficienti, inuri "videatur." *De legibus Hebr. Ritualibus*, lib. i., cap. 6, sect. 2 (*Hagæ Com.*, 1686. 4to.), p. 116. Had the learned, but eccentric writer substituted the words *Jewish Convert* for Christian, and *Judaism* for

heathenism, his remark would have been far nearer the truth of the case. J. A. Danzius, in his remarkable essay, *Antiquitas Baptismi initiatonis Israelitarum vindicata*, p. 302 (printed at length in J. G. Meuschen's *Nov. Test. ex Talmude illustr.*), cites the Rabbinic figment that Esau, in the fury of his vexation at being deprived of the birthright, obliterated the traces of his circumcision:—"Esavum ob jus "primogeniturae sibi subductum, in tantum effervisse dicunt, ut "notam circumcisionis in se deleverit, praeputio arte maligna reducto." I have referred to this Rabbinical tradition, as illustrative of the estimation in which Esau is held by the earlier Jewish Commentators, viz., as one who had "denied the faith." The following extract, however, from the Targum of Palestine on Gen. xxv. speaks more explicitly still, although it introduces an abundance of legendary details which are unknown to the sacred text:—"Esau was a man of idleness to "catch birds and beasts, a man going forth into the field to kill lives, as "Nimrod had killed, and Hanok his son. But Jakob was a man peace-"ful in his works, a minister of the instruction-house of Eber, seeking "instruction before the Lord. And Izhak loved Esau, for words of "deceit were in his mouth; but Rivekah loved Jakob. On the day "that Abraham died, Jakob dressed pottage of lentiles, and was going "to comfort his father. And Esau came from the wilderness, exhausted; "for in that day he had committed five transgressions: he had wor-"shipped with strange worship, he had shed innocent blood, he had "gone in unto a betrothed damsel, he had denied the life of the world "to come, and had despised the birthright. And Esau said to Jakob, "Let me now taste the red pottage, for I am faint; therefore he called "his name Edom (*Red*). And Jakob said, Sell to-day, as (on this very) "day, what thou wouldst hereafter appropriate, thy birthright, unto "me. And Esau said, Behold, I am going to die, and in another "world I shall have no life; and what then to me is the birthright, or "the portion in the world of which thou speakest? And Jakob said, "Swear to me to-day that so it shall be. And he sware to him, and "sold his birthright to Jakob. And Jakob gave to Esau bread and "pottage of lentiles. And he ate and drank and arose and went, and "Esau scorned the birthright, and the portion of the world that "cometh." *Etheridge's Targums*, vol. i., p. 241. So also the Jerusalem Targum:—"And he arose and went. And Esau despised the birthright, "and vilified the portion in the world that cometh, and denied the "resurrection of the dead." *Ibid.*, p. 242. Again, the Targum of Palestine on Gen. xxvii. absurdly represents Esau as killing a dog, and endeavouring to palm it off upon his father instead of venison (p. 248). And again, p. 250:—"And Esau kept hatred in his heart against Jakob "his brother, on account of the order of blessing with which his father "had blessed him. And Esau said in his heart, I will not do as Kain "did, who slew Habel in the life (time) of his father, for which his "father begat Sheth, but will wait for the death of my father to come, "and then will I kill Jakob my brother, and will be found the killer and "the heir." The Rabbinical writers apply the term *Edom, Edomites* to Christians generally, and more particularly to the Church of Rome. See Caroli Sigonii, *lib. vii. de Rep. Hebræor.* (lib. i., cap. i., note.), printed at length in Ugol. Thes., vol. iv. (col. 158—160). See also Buxtorf. Lexicon Chald., &c., col. 29—32, article אדום. The Cabbalists blasphemously assert that the soul of Edom migrated into Jesus, which calumny is repeated by Abarbanel in his Commentary on Isaiah xxxiv. — Dr. Gill observes, *in loco,* "The Jewish writers speak of this bargain "and sale much in the same language as the apostle here does. They "say (*Tzeror Hammor,* fol. 26, 4, and 27, 1) of him (Esau), this is the "man that sold his birthright בעד ככר לחם, *for a morsel of bread;* and "apply to him the passage in Prov. xxviii. 21, *For a piece of bread that* "*man will transgress.*"

The example, then, of Esau's flippant irreverence in disposing of his birthright for a meal, is adduced as the example of that profanity against which the Hebrew converts are warned. They are not left in doubt as to the precise and definite meaning of the admonition which the writer intends to impress upon them. There was a great danger lest they should follow his example, and so exclude themselves from the blessings of their Christian birthright.

Verse 17.—For ye know that afterwards, when he even (καὶ)[1] wished to inherit the blessing, he was rejected (ἀπεδοκιμάσθη), for he found no opportunity to change his mind (μετανοίας γὰρ τόπον οὐχ εὗρε), although he sought it carefully with tears.

[1] Dr. Alford unnecessarily proposes to translate καὶ, *on his part.* Isaac had promised to bless Esau, and unwittingly bestowed the blessing intended for the firstborn, upon the younger son. Esau had made up his mind that the forfeited primogeniture would, by his father's voluntary act, be restored to him. And, as far as his father's intentions went, it was actually given to him. Isaac believed that he was blessing Esau, when he blessed Jacob. It was not until Isaac discovered the stratagem by which he had been duped, that he refused to rescind his solemn benediction. Vainly did Esau seek to move him, even by tears,

to alter his decision. The birthright and the blessing had irrevocably been conveyed to Jacob. The μετανοία here spoken of does not refer to repentance for sin. So far from feeling contrition for his wicked act, by which he had bartered away his privileges, we know that Esau harboured intentions of fratricidal vengeance against Jacob, perhaps intending thus, by putting his brother out of the way, to regain what he had lost. Had Esau truly sought repentance, he would have assuredly found it. Schoettgen apparently understands μετανοίας γὰρ κ.τ.λ. to refer to Esau's inability to alter Isaac's determination to adhere to what he had done ; "The change of mind" being Isaac's, not Esau's. "Verte : *non potuit efficere, quamvis multas lacrymas effunderet, ut* "*patrem consilii et benedictionis suæ poeniteret.*" It is not, however, of Isaac, but of Esau, of whom the writer speaks, and Dr. Alford wisely rejects so farfetched and unsatisfactory an interpretation, albeit it is supported by many distinguished commentators both ancient and modern. As to Esau's ultimate repentance, respecting which the Scriptures are silent, the Rabbinical writers are divided. Dr. Gill reminds us that the Targum on Job asserts, " All the days of Esau " the ungodly, they expected that he would have repented, but he " repented not," whereas the *Yalkut Chadash* (see Car. Sigonius *de Rep. Hebræor.*, col. 158, 159, Ugol. Thes., vol. iv.) seems to imply that upon his shedding tears he obtained mercy.

Verse 18.—For[1] ye are not come near to the palpable Mount (ψηλαφωμένῳ ὄρει, or better, "that was groped after"),[2] and which burned with fire,[3] and to blackness and darkness, and tempest.[4]

[1] Here, then, the parenthesis of verses 15—17 ends. The writer now assigns the reason why holiness was even more indispensably necessary, under the Christian dispensation, than under the Mosaic. The sense would run on from verse 14, " and the holiness (*sanctification*, καὶ τὸν " ἁγιασμὸν, *und die Heiligung*, Ewald. See Ps. xxiv. 3, 4, Matt. v. 8) " without which no man shall see the Lord......For ye are not come to the " Mount that might be touched," *i.e.*, to Sinai.—The Israelites were commanded to purge themselves from all fleshly impurities, before presenting themselves, in solemn conclave, before the material Mount of God, to hear the Mosaic covenant promulgated. The Hebrews, to whom the Epistle is addressed, were privileged to be summoned to the spiritual Mount of God—God's Holy hill of Zion. How needful was it, therefore, that they should present themselves *with consciences purged from dead works to serve the living God!*

² Ψηλαφωμένῳ ὄρει, "the Mount that might be touched," *Angl. Vers.*—"Ad tractabilem montem," *Vulg.*—"Den man anrühren konnte," *Luth.*—"Contrectabili monti," *Beza.*—"Zu einem betastbaren Berge," *Ewald.* The verb ψηλαφάω occurs four times in the New Testament, viz., Luke xxiv. 39, "handle me and see;" Acts xvii. 27, "might feel after Him;" 1 John i. 1, "our hands have handled," and in the above passage of this Epistle. Wesselius considers it as here describing the earthquake which accompanied the descent of Jehovah, Exod. xix. 18, "the whole "mountain quaked greatly." But this is not in accordance with the proper meaning of the word ψηλαφάω, which signifies "*to feel for*," to "*grope, as a blind man, or in the dark.*" It may suitably be referred to the smoke, "the blackness and the darkness," which obscured the mountain, as it is written, "And Mount Sinai was altogether on a "smoke (עשן כלו), because the Lord descended upon it in fire, and the "smoke thereof ascended as the smoke of a furnace." (*Ibid.*) Ψηλαφωμένῳ ὄρει may therefore be fitly rendered, "the mountain that had to "be groped after." We are distinctly informed in Exod. xix. 16 that there was "a thick cloud upon the mount." (*Heb.* ענן כבד, "a heavy cloud.") Doubtless this obscured the view, so as to make access difficult even to Moses. To apply ψηλαφωμένῳ to the contact of the Deity, in reference to Ps. civ. 32 and cxliv. 5, is altogether unsuitable. Professor Stuart wisely observes,—"The idea of *de coelo tactus, thunder-struck*, "is here assigned by some respectable expositors......but without any "good philological support." We are told (Exod. xxiv. 16) that later, the cloud covered the mount during six days, and on the seventh day God called to Moses "from the midst of the cloud" (מתוך הענן); and again, verse 18, "And Moses went up into the midst of the cloud." (ויבא משה בתוך הענן.) It is worthy of remark that the words of the Authorized Version in Exod. x. 21, "darkness which may be felt" (וימש חשך), are rendered in the LXX. by ψηλαφητὸν σκότος. The passage runs thus,—Καὶ γενηθήτω σκότος ἐπὶ γῆς Αἰγύπτου, ψηλαφητὸν σκότος. Ἐξέτεινε δὲ Μωυσῆς τὴν χεῖρα εἰς τὸν οὐρανόν, καὶ ἐγένετο σκότος γνόφος, θύελλα ἐπὶ πᾶσαν γῆν κ.τ.λ. So also in Gen. xxvii. 21, 22, "And Isaac "said unto Jacob, Come near......that I may feel thee (καὶ ψηλαφήσω "σε)...... and he felt him" (καὶ ἐψηλάφησεν αὐτόν). Schoettgen writes (*in loc.*, Hor. Hebr. tom. i., p. 991):—"Vulgo vertunt ψηλαφητῷ, qui "*tangi potest*, h.e. materiali: sed non observaverunt Hebraismum, "qua Deus montes tangere dicitur, ut fumum emittant. Ps. civ. 32, "יגע ההרים ויעשנו, *Attinget montes, et fumabunt*. Ps. cxliv. 5, גע ההרים "ויעשנו, *Attinge montes, et fumabunt*. Antecedens ergo, nempe tactus "Dei, h.l. ponitur pro consequenti, h.e. fumo: ut ὄρος ψηλαφώμενον "sit *mons fumans.*"

³ Κεκαυμένῳ πυρί. The construction of these words seems to be decided, in accordance with the Angl. Version, by the LXX. Vers. of Deut. iv. 11, v. 23, ix. 15, καὶ τὸ ὄρος ἐκαίετο πυρί, בֹּעֵר בָּאֵשׁ, and not as Stuart, Wesselius, and others have suggested, that it may be taken to signify "flaming fire," "*ad ardentem ignem.*" In Exod. xxiv. 17 it is said, "And the sight of the glory of the Lord was like devouring fire "(כְּאֵשׁ אֹכֶלֶת, πῦρ φλέγον, LXX.) on the top of the mount, in the eyes "of the children of Israel. And Moses went into the midst of the "cloud (εἰς τὸ μέσον τῆς νεφέλης)." So also in Deut. v. 22—25 the terrors of the darkness, and of the fire are especially enlarged upon :—
" And it came to pass, when ye heard the voice out of the midst of the "darkness (for the mountain did burn with fire), that ye came near "unto me, *even* all the heads of your tribes, and your elders : and ye "said, Behold, the Lord our God hath shewed us his glory and his "greatness, and we have heard his voice out of the midst of the fire : "we have seen this day that God doth talk with man, and he liveth. "Now, therefore, why should we die ? for this great fire will consume "us : if we hear the voice of the Lord our God any more, then we "shall die. For who is there of all flesh that hath heard the voice of "the living God, speaking out of the midst of the fire, as we *have*, and "lived ?" For a variety of Jewish legends on the subject of the giving of the law, see Dr. M'Caul's *Old Paths*, pp. 199—230. *London*, 1846. 8vo.

⁴ Καὶ γνόφῳ, καὶ σκότῳ, καὶ θυέλλῃ. The first of these words corresponds, in the LXX. of Exod. xx. 21, to עֲרָפֶל of the Hebrew. In Deut. iv. 11, חֹשֶׁךְ עָנָן וַעֲרָפֶל are rendered by σκότος, γνοφός, θύελλα. The same words occur again in the LXX. of Deut. v. 22, where, in the Hebrew (verse 19), they are represented by the two words הֶעָנָן וְהָעֲרָפֶל, "cloud and thick darkness." Gesenius translates עֲרָפֶל *caligo nubium*, *nubes densæ*, and says, Conflatum esse videtur ex trilitteris עָרִיף *nubes*, et אֵל *caliginosus fuit*. Congruit gr. ὀρφνός *obscurus, caliginosus*, ὄρφνη *caligo*, max. *noctis*. With respect to the tempest that occurred at the giving of the law, it is described in Exod. xix. 16, קֹלֹת וּבְרָקִים, thunders (lit. *voices*, φωναί, LXX.) and lightnings. See also in Exod. xx. 18 :— "And all the people saw the thunderings (הַקּוֹלֹת) and the lightnings. (וְאֶת הַלַּפִּידִם) ;" καὶ πᾶς ὁ λαὸς ἑώρα τὴν φωνὴν, καὶ τὰς λαμπάδας, LXX. See Rev. iv. 5, viii. 5, x. 3, 4, xi. 15—19, xvi. 18.

Verse 19.—And to the sound of a trumpet,¹ and to a voice of words,² which (voice) they that heard, entreated ³ that a word should not be added to them.⁴

¹ Καὶ σαλπίγγος ἤχῳ. In Exod. xix. 16, 19, xx. 18, the word שׁוֹפָר is used; whilst in xix. 13, יֹבֵל is employed; the latter word signifies rather the clangour of the trumpet than the instrument itself. Here the LXX. has αἱ σάλπιγγες; whilst in the other passages σάλπιγξ is in the singular. For references to the last trumpet of doom, see Matt. xxiv. 31; 1 Cor. xv. 52; 1 Thess. iv. 16.

² Καὶ φωνῇ ῥημάτων. "Alterum *sonus inarticulatus*, nempe tubæ "sonitus... ..alterum erat *sonus articulatus*, καὶ φωνῇ ῥημάτων, &c. *Et ad vocem verborum:* intelligit Paulus *vocem* illam Dei qua præcepta Decalogi pronunciavit coram Populo, per tubæ sonitum convocato." Wesselii *Fasc. Diss.*, p. 420. Prof. Stuart misses this antithesis altogether, and says, "Καὶ σάλπιγγος ἤχῳ, *and to the sound of the trumpet.* See Exod. "xix. 16—19. Probably the meaning is, *a voice like that of a trumpet*, "i.e., very loud. In Deut. v. 22 it is called *a great voice:* in ch. iv. 12 "it is called *the voice of words*, i.e., articulate sounds; and, in verse 33, "*the voice of God.* From comparing all these passages together it "seems evident that the meaning is, 'an articulate voice, loud, like "'that of a trumpet.'" The learned Professor seems to have overlooked Exod. xix. 19, where it is said, "And when the voice of the trumpet "sounded long, and waxed louder and louder, Moses spake, and God "answered him by a voice." This distinction is observed in the LXX. Ἐγίνοντο δὲ αἱ φωναὶ τῆς σαλπίγγος προβαίνουσαι ἰσχυρότεραι σφόδρα. Μωυσῆς ἐλάλησεν, ὁ δὲ Θεὸς ἀπεκρίνατο αὐτῷ φωνῇ. Curiously enough, Moses does not specify the trumpet at all in Deut., but only speaks of the "voice" (Deut. iv. 33, 36). There were then, two sounds of awe to which the people listened—the first, the inarticulate sound of the trumpet which was to summon them "to come up unto the mount" (Exod. xix. 13); the other, the articulate "voice of God speaking out "of the midst of the fire" (Deut. iv. 33). Professor Stuart seems to have had Rev. i. 10, iv. 1, before his mind when he wrote the above passage. Be it observed that in Exod. xx. 18, where the Authorized Version has "the *noise* of the trumpet," the Hebrew word is קוֹל, which is elsewhere rightly translated voice, *e.g.*, Exod. xix. 16—19. The exact passage from which the Writer to the Hebrews appears to quote is Deut. iv. 12. קוֹל דברים, φωνὴν ῥημάτων, LXX. The whole passage runs thus:—Καὶ προσήλθετε καὶ ἔστητε ὑπὸ τὸ ὄρος, καὶ τὸ ὄρος ἐκαίετο πυρὶ ἕως τοῦ οὐρανοῦ· σκότος, γνόφος, θύελλα. Καὶ ἐλάλησε Κύριος πρὸς ὑμᾶς ἐκ μέσου τοῦ πυρός φωνὴν ῥημάτων, ἣν ὑμεῖς ἠκούσατε, καὶ ὁμοίωμα οὐκ εἴδετε, ἀλλ' ἢ φωνήν. The Ten Commandments are described as the "Ten Words."

What, then, was the "voice of words" to which the children of Israel listened? עשרת הדברים, τοὺς δέκα λόγους, LXX.; Exod. xxxiv.

28; Deut. x. 4; and not τὰ δέκα ῥήματα, as Professor Plumptre asserts in his article TEN COMMANDMENTS in Smith's Dict. This latter translation of עשרת הדברים: occurs in the LXX. of Deut. iv. 13. It seems plain, from Exod. xix. 19, that God spake with Moses in their hearing, *before* He commanded him to come up into the mount. This voice came to Moses from heaven, apparently before God " came down on Mount " Sinai, on the top of the mount"; and this is also why it is said, in Deut. iv. 36, " Out of heaven He made thee to hear his voice..........and " upon earth He shewed thee his great fire : and thou heardest his " words out of the midst of the fire." This is a striking instance of the extreme accuracy of the Deuteronomist. After this, the Lord called Moses up to the top of the mount; and then, because the priests and people were evidently giving way to an unhallowed curiosity (Exod. xix. 21—25), Moses was sent down to warn them of their danger in so doing. *Then*, doubtless, before Moses returned into the mount, the Ten Commandments were uttered in the hearing of the people. (Exod. xx. 1.) After this they entreated Moses to be the medium of communication between God and themselves :—" Speak thou with us, and we " will hear; but let not God speak with us, lest we die..........And the " people stood afar off, and Moses drew near unto the thick darkness " where God was" (19, 20). The book of Deut. (v. 22) expressly limits the words spoken in the ears of the people to the above occasion : —" These words the Lord spake unto all your assembly..........And He " added no more," ולא יסף. (Heb., verse 19.) See following note.— Some writers have asserted that the first and second commandments only were spoken by God himself, and the remainder were " given by " the disposition of angels." They observe that the speaker employs the third, not the first person, in the third and succeeding commandments. And so Wesselius remarks, "Deum quædam saltem verba " Decalogi, voce immediate à se formata pronunciasse, certum est ; tum " ex phrasi illa, *facie ad faciem locutus* est Jehova vobiscum ; tum ex " ipsis verbis in *prima* persona prolatis, in exordio decalogi, et in primo " atque secundo præcepto. Nulla enim creatura id sibi sumeret, ut " sine ulla præfatione præmissa, *sic dicit Jehova*, diceret, *Ego sum* " *Jehova Deus tuus, &c*.......Quod tamen reliqua præcepta decalogi, " inde a *tertio*, ubi est mutatio personæ primæ in tertiam, mediate per " Angelos pronunciata sint, haud improbabiliter asseritur à nonnullis " ob loca Act vii. 53, Gal. iii. 19, et potissimum ob Heb. ii. 2. Etenim " si per Angelos dictus sermo fuit firmus," &c. (Fasc. Diss., pp. 420, 421.) The reader may also consult with advantage the first dissertation by the same author, entitled, "*De Angelo Jehoræ ab Hagara viso*," § 11—17, in his *Diss. sacr. Leidenses*, Lugd. Bat., 1721, 4to. It was the opinion of the Talmudists that angels did assist at the solemnities of Sinai, *e.g.*,

בשעה שהקדימו ישראל נעשה לנשמע באו ששים ריבוא של מלאכי השרת לכל אחד ואחד
מישראל קשרו לו שני כתרים אהד כנגד נעשה ואחד כנגד נשמע וכיון שחטאו ישראל ירדו
מאה ועשרים ריבוא מלאכי חבלה ופירקו' שנ' ויתנצלו בני ישראל את עדים מהר חורב:

(*Shabbath*, fol. 88, 1.)

"In the hour when Israel caused '*We will do*' to precede '*We will hearken*,' there came six hundred thousand ministering angels, one to each Israelite, and invested him with two crowns, one answering to '*We will do*,' and the second answering to '*We will hearken*.' But when Israel sinned, there descended twelve hundred thousand evil angels, and took them away: as it is said, 'The children of Israel stripped themselves (or were stripped) of their ornaments by Mount Horeb.'" Again in *Shabbath*, fol. 88, 2,—

אמר ריב"ל כל דיבור ודיבור שיצא מפי הקב"ה חזרו ישראל לאחוריהן י"ב מיל והיו מלאכי
השרת מדדין אותן שנא' מלאכי צבאות ידודון ידודון אל תקרי ידודון אלא ידדון:

"Rabbi Joshua, the son of Levi, says as each commandment proceeded from the mouth of the Holy One, Blessed be He, Israel went back twelve miles, and the ministering angels led them back, as it is said the angels of the host did flee apace," &c. (For Dr. M'Caul's remarks upon the above, &c., see *Old Paths*, pp. 202–205.) J. A. Danzius, in his marvellously learned treatise, *Inauguratio Christi ad docendum haud obscurior Mosaica*, p. 335, observes:—"Quod adeo certum credebatur antiquis Ebræorum, ut verba Cantici I. 2, *Osculetur me osculo oris sui*, haud illepide ad promulgationem applicent Decalogi in *Medrasch Rabba*, f. 4, col. 4. Quasi singula Præceptorum *verba* a Deo pronunciata, vel immediate, vel ope angeli cujusdam unicuique Israelitarum fuerint instillata: sensu ac valore cujusque expresso, cum blandissimis his illicebris, *an me recipis in te? num quid meam agnoscis divinitatem?* Quo affirmante, ilico osculum infixerunt ori cujusque recipientis." Whilst on the pages immediately preceding, Danzius adduces the testimony of R. Moses Alschech and others to show that a fundamental article of the faith is, that each individual Israelite received the commandments directly from the mouth of Jehovah Himself. R. Tanchuma, f. 26, c. 3, l. 35, repeats the same legendary traditions respecting the intervention of angels. Whilst R. Joseph Albo, *Ikkarim*, lib. iii., c. 11, p. 73, b. l. 1, &c., asserts that the highest grade of the prophetical status was the speaking with God face to face. To this grade Moses attained, and not only Moses, but the entire congregation of Israel at Mount Sinai.

CHAP. XII., 19.

והוא מבואר כי שש מאות אלף רגלי שיצאו ממצרים מורגלים בצנורים קטה בחומר
ובלבנים לא היו ראויים למדרגה גדולה כזו' ואעפ"כ כן הגיעו אליה באמצעות מרע"ה אמר
ה"ית הנה אנכי בא אליך בעב הענן בעבור ישמע העם בדברי עמך כלומר אני רוצה לבוא
אליך ולהגלות לך במדרגה גדולה שהיא מדרגת פנים פנים :

"But this is manifest, that the six hundred thousand footmen which
"went out of Egypt who had been downtrodden with hard service in the
"bricks and the mortar, did not deserve (had no expectations of?) a
"degree so great as this. Notwithstanding, they did attain to it by the
"mediation of Moses our Master. For God said (Exod. xix. 9), Behold,
"I am coming to thee in the darkness of the cloud, in order that the
"people may hear when I speak with thee; that is to say, I am pleased
"to come to thee and to be revealed to thee in this great degree, namely,
"face to face," &c. The above, in reference to the dignity of Moses'
prophetical grade, is in strict accordance with the opinion of Maimonides, who writes, *Moreh Nevochim*, Pt. II., ch. xlv., f. 122, Edit.
Sabionet:—

יסודנו שכל נביא ישמע הדבור באמצעות מלאך אלא מרע"ה אשר נאמר בו פה אל פה
אדבר בו :

"Our proposition is, that every prophet heard the speech (*or com-*
"*munication*) by the mediation of an angel, excepting Moses, concern-
"ing whom it was said (Num. xii. 8), *I will speak with him face to face*."
Maimonides, however, strenuously combats the notion that the people
shared the honour with Moses of hearing an articulate voice; and he
bases his opinion upon the fact that in the Decalogue the Almighty
addresses the Ten Commandments to Moses in the second person
singular, and not to the people in the plural. He says that the Israelites heard the "voice of words," but not the "words" themselves, and
draws attention to the fact that the words of Deut. iv. 12 give colour to
this distinction, *e.g.*,

ואמר קול דברים אתם שומעים ולא אמר דברים אתם שמעים :

"He (Moses) says, *ye heard the voice of words*, but he does not say,
"*ye heard words*." Nachmanides is emphatically of the same opinion.
Maimonides further asserts that many authorities believed that the
sound even, of the eight concluding Commandments, was not heard by
the people at all, but by Moses only. Others, *e.g.*, Raschi, Tanchuma,
R. Bechai, &c., supposed that God uttered the whole of the Ten Commandments, with one voice or single utterance. Nachmanides, Tanchuma, and others assert that "the voice" was divided into seven
voices (the Gemara says *five*), and then multiplied into seventy languages. R. Joseph Albo (Serm. ii. c. 28, p. 54), in common with others,
from the words of Exod. xxiv. 1, "And he said, come up unto the
"Lord" (comp. vers. 12), deduces the fact that a mediator spoke on

this later occasion to Moses. This mediator, however, he declares to have been none other than the *Metatron*, and not such an angel as mediatised between the other prophets. ההוא היה מטטרון ששמו כשם רבו והוא שר הפנים "This was the *Metatron*, whose name was the same as "that of his Lord, and he is the Prince of faces." Danzius observes that this discourse (Exod. xxiv. 1), addressed to Moses, is ascribed in the *Sohar* to the Shechina: "Unde sequitur, *Schechinam* et Mediatorem "unum fore. Quod ingenue fatetur *Jalkut Rubeni*, f. 24, c. 3, l. 30." Danz., p. 383. See also his Essay, "*Schechina cum piis cohabitans*," in the same volume, p. 701, &c. The Targum of Onkelos (Exod. xix., xx.) reads. "And Mosheh went down to the people and spake with them. "And the Lord spake all these words, saying," &c. And again, "And "all the people saw the thunders, and the flames, and the voice of the "trumpet, and the mountain smoking; and the people saw, and "trembled, and stood afar off. And they said to Mosheh, Speak thou "with us, and we will hearken; but let it not be spoken to us from "the Lord, lest we die......And the Lord said to Mosheh, thus shalt "thou speak to the children of Israel; you have seen that I have spoken "to you from the heavens," &c. And again the Targum of Onkelos on Deut v., "Word with word hath the Lord spoken with you, at the "mountain, from the midst of the fire (I stood between the Word of the "Lord and you, to announce to you at that time the Word of the Lord)... "These words spake the Lord with all your congregation at the mount "from the midst of the fire......with a great voice, and hath not ceased "(Pesch Syriac, 'a great voice which hath no limit,' Hebr. ולא יסף, and "he added not). And he wrote them upon two tables of stone, and gave "them to me. But it was when you heard the voice from the midst of "the fire.........you said, Behold.........we have heard the voice of his "Word out of the midst of the fire; this day have we seen that the "Lord speaketh with a man, and he liveth." (*Etheridge's Targums,* in loco.) From the above extracts it will be seen (though R. Bechai claims the Targum of Onkelos as favouring the idea that the Israelites only heard the "voice of words," and not the words themselves. ישראל שומעין קול דברים ומשה שומע הדברים, "Israel heard the voice of words, but Moses "heard the words") that the Targum leaves the matter very doubtful. The Targum of Palestine or Jonathan, on Exod. xix., xx, contains a variety of legendary amplifications:—"And Mosheh went down from "the mountain to the people, and said unto them, Draw nigh and "receive the Ten Words. And the Lord spake all these Words, saying: "The first word, as it came forth from the mouth of the Holy One, "whose Name be blessed, was like storms and lightnings and flames of "fire, with a burning light on his right hand and on his left. It

"winged its way through the air of the heavens, and was made
"manifest unto the camp of Israel, and returned, and was engraven on
"the tables of the covenant that were given by the hand of Mosheh,
"and were turned in them from side to side : and then called He, and
"said, Sons of Israel, my people, I am the Lord your God," &c. This
Targum here makes each of the commandments to be addressed to the
Israelites collectively, as it does also in Deut. v. :—" Word to word did
"the Lord speak with you at the mountain, from the midst of the fire.
"I stood between the Word of the Lord and you at that time, to
"declare to you the Word of the Lord, because you were afraid before
"the voice of the Word of the Lord, which you heard from the midst of
"the fire; neither did you go up to the mountain whilst He said, Sons
"of Israel, my people," &c. And again (*ibid*):—" These words spake
"the Lord with all your congregation at the mount, from the midst of
"the fiery cloud and tempest, with a great voice which was not limited:
"and the voice of the Word was written upon two tables of marble,
"and He gave them unto me. But when you had heard the voice of
"the Word.........your sages drew nigh unto me. and said, Behold the
"Word of the Lord our God hath showed us his glorious Shekinah and
"the greatness of his excellency (*tushbachteih*, his magnificence), and
"the voice of his Word have we heard out of the midst of the fire.
"This day have we seen that the Lord speaketh with a man in whom is
"the Holy Spirit, and he remaineth alive," &c. (Etheridge's Targums,
in loco.)—Josephus (*Antiq.* iii. 4, Whiston's transl.) emphatically asserts
the opinion that the congregation heard every word of the Ten Commandments :—

"When he (Moses) had said this, he brought the people, with their
"wives and children, so near to the mountain, that they might hear
"God himself speaking to them about the precepts which they were to
"practise, that the energy of what should be spoken might not be
"hurt by its utterance by that tongue of a man which could but
"imperfectly deliver it to their understanding. And they all heard a
"voice that came to all of them from above, insomuch that no one of
"these words escaped them, which Moses wrote on two tables ; which
"it is not lawful for us to set down directly, but their import we will
"declare." Though elsewhere he says, Ἡμῶν τὰ κάλλιστα τῶν δογμάτων,
καὶ τὰ ὁσιώτατα τῶν ἐν τοῖς νόμοις δι' ἀγγέλων παρὰ τοῦ Θεοῦ μαθόντων,
"As we have learned the most excellent and holiest of our dogmas
"which are in the laws, from God, by angels." Ant. xv. 5, 3. Philo
(*De decem Oraculis*) thinks that God miraculously created a voice, which
was visible in the air, and turned to flaming fire, with a sound similar
to that of a trumpet. (Works, *Mangey's Edit.*, tom. ii., p. 185.) On

the whole, it is decidedly preferable to refer φωνῇ ῥημάτων to the words of the Decalogue, as intelligibly pronounced by God himself.

* Παρῃτήσαντο. Though I have retained the authorized English version, I cannot help thinking, looking at verse 25, that there is an idea of petulance and impatience underlying the expression. The awful restraints imposed upon the people, both before and during the enacting of this terrible legislative drama, were doubtless irksome to them. From Exod. xix. 20—25 we see that, though Moses believed that he had sufficiently interdicted all access to the Mount, yet God sent him down again to add further and more imperative warnings, over and above those already given :—" And the Lord came down upon " Mount Sinai, on the top of the Mount, and the Lord called Moses up " to the top of the Mount : and Moses went up. And the Lord said " unto Moses, Go down, charge (העד, protest) the people, lest they " break through (יהרסו, ἐγγίσωσι, LXX.) unto the Lord to gaze, and " many of them perish. And let the priests also, which come near to " the Lord, sanctify themselves, lest the Lord break forth upon them. " And Moses said unto the Lord, The people cannot come up to Mount " Sinai; for thou chargedest us, saying, Set bounds about the Mount, " and sanctify it. And the Lord said, Away, get thee down (לך רד), " and thou shalt come up, thou and Aaron with thee, but let not the " priests and the people break through (יהרסו, βιαζέσθωσαν, LXX.), to " come up unto the Lord, lest He break forth upon them. So Moses " went down unto the people and spake unto them." And, moreover, though God was pleased to accede to the people's request that He should thenceforward address himself to Moses instead of to themselves, and also to say, "They have well spoken all that they have spoken," היטיבו כל אשר דברו (Deut. v. 25), yet He adds, with Omniscient intuition of the deceitfulness of their hearts, and instability of their professions, " Oh that there were such an heart in them (מי יתן והיה לבבם זה להם), that " they would fear me, and keep my commandments always," &c. (See note 1 opposite.)

⁴ Μὴ προστεθῆναι αὐτοῖς λόγον. Professor Stuart proposes to understand αὐτοῖς as referring to ῥήμασι. This, however, is not in accordance with the Vulgate, " excusaverunt se, ne eis fieret verbum," nor with Luther's translation, " Welcher sich weigerten, die sie hörten, dass " ihnen das Wort ja nicht gesagt würde." It seems far preferable to apply the αὐτοῖς to the Israelites. It was not only the voice, but the terrible fire, and the other dread accompaniments of the occasion, that actuated the Israelites to prefer their request. (Comp. Exod. xx. 18— 21 with Deut. v. 25—27.) The phraseology seems to be borrowed from the LXX. of Deut. v. 22, Καὶ οὐ προσέθηκε, " and He added no more" ;

CHAP. XII., 20.

Heb., ולוא יסף ; and also of verse 25, Ἐὰν προσθώμεθα ἡμεῖς ἀκοῦσαι τὴν φωνὴν Κυρίου τοῦ Θεοῦ ἡμῶν ἔτι. The Hebrew words of Deut. v. 22, ולוא יסף, *and He added not*, have given rise to a multitude of conjectural interpretations on the part of the Rabbinical writers, although it is sufficiently plain that, in this verse, Moses states the historical fact, of which he gives the reason, viz., the entreaty of the Israelites, in the 23rd and following verses. The writers of the *Shemoth Rabba* (sect. xxviii. and xxix) gravely assert that ולוא יסף means that there was *no echo*, or reverberation (*Bath. Kol.*) to the voice, שלא היה לו בת קול. The Targums of Onkelos and Jonathan have respectively "and hath not "ceased," and " which was not limited." Rashi suggests as an improvement upon the Chaldee paraphrase, לא הוסיף להראות באותו פומבי, "He did "not appear any more in the same pomp." R. Sol. Ben Meir suggests, " No voice as great as this will ever be repeated whilst the world lasts." Aben Ezra reads יסף as the future tense, and says, לא יסף כי זה היה פעם אחת, "He will not add (or *repeat*), for this was the only occasion." The Arabic version has " with a voice never to be repeated." Abarbanel is very much of the opinion of S. Ben Meir. The context, however, naturally suggests that the LXX. version, with which the English agrees, is the right one. The Vulgate reads, in like manner, "nihil "addens amplius." (See also Danzius, *Inaug. Christi.*, p. 336, &c., and 381.)

Verse 20.—For they could not endure (or, rather, took impatiently, submitted with impatience to)[1] that which was enjoined;[2] "And if even a beast touch the mountain,[3] it shall be stoned, or shot down with a dart."

[1] Οὐκ ἔφερον γάρ. The verb φέρω is, in one other passage only of the New Testament, translated "to endure," in our Authorized Version, viz., Rom. ix. 22, " endured with much longsuffering." As the passage here is ordinarily understood, I confess that it seems to me one of the most obscure in the entire Epistle to the Hebrews. But the sense becomes at once apparent, if we explain it as expressive of impatience and fretful murmuring at the extreme severity and irksomeness of the restraint which kept the people in a state of terror, vigilant alarm, and supernatural dread, for so many days, and which extended even to the very beasts. "And thou shalt set bounds unto the people round about, " saying, Take heed to yourselves that ye go not up into the mount, or " touch (θίγειν, LXX.) the border of it: whosoever toucheth (ἁψάμενος) " the mount shall be surely put to death. There shall not a hand touch " (ἅψεται) the mount, but he shall be surely stoned, or shot through

" (יִיָּרֶה יָרֹה אוֹ יִסָּקֵל סָקוֹל, λίθοις λιθοβοληθήσεται, ἢ βολίδι κατατοξευθήσεται);
" whether it be beast or man, it shall not live." Exod. xix. 12, 13.
(Compare 20–25, and note 3 on p. 294.) In chap. xxxiv. 1–3 we read
that when Moses was commanded to hew and bring up the second
tables of stone, instead of the two which God himself had at first provided, it was forbidden for "any man to be seen throughout all the
"mount, neither let the flocks nor herds feed before that mount."

[2] Τὸ διαστελλόμενον. Doubtless all the prohibitions and restraints
already alluded to, whose rigid severity culminated in the example here
adduced, "And if even a beast," &c. On these words Wesselius
observes, "Id est ; quod hinc inde emittebatur a monte, ut erant
" fulgura, tonitrua, sonus tubæ, et imprimis, *Vox illa magna* Dei
" legem promulgantis ; vel, uti Beza, *quod interdicebatur ;* vel ut alii,
" *quod dicebatur*, ut Vulg. Vel denique, *quod tam graviter edicebatur*
" *et mandabatur*." *Fasc. Diss.*, p. 424, &c.

[3] Κἂν θηρίον θίγῃ τοῦ ὄρους λιθοβοληθήσεται, ἢ βολίδι κατατοξευθήσεται.
The LXX. of Exod. xix. 12, 13, reads, Προσέχετε ἑαυτοῖς τοῦ ἀναβῆναι
εἰς τὸ ὄρος, καὶ θίγειν τι αὐτοῦ· πᾶς ὁ ἁψάμενος τοῦ ὄρους, θανάτῳ τελευτήσει.
Οὐχ ἅψεται αὐτοῦ χείρ· ἐν γὰρ λίθοις λιθοβοληθήσεται, ἢ βολίδι κατατοξευθήσεται ἐάν τε κτῆνος ἐάν τε ἄνθρωπος, οὐ ζήσεται. Professor Stuart writes :
—"The Vulgate edition of the New Testament adds to this clause,
" ἢ βολίδι κατατοξευθήσεται ; but no MS. of any authority exhibits this
" phrase, nor any ancient version, nor any of the ecclesiastical Greek
" writers, Œcumenius excepted. It is, beyond all doubt, an addition
" of later time, taken from the LXX. of Exod. xix. 13." Dr. Gill,
however, would retain it :—"The last clause, 'or thrust through with
"'a dart,' is wanting in the Alexandrian and Beza's Claromontare
" copies, in the Vulgate Latin, and all the Oriental versions ; and yet
" it is necessary to be retained, being in the original text, in Exod.
" xix. 12, 13."

Verse 21.—And so terrible was the spectacle enacted [1]
[that] Moses said, I am terrified, and quake. [2]

[1] Τὸ φανταζόμενον. This word occurs in this passage of the New
Testament only. Φαντασία is translated "pomp" in Acts xxv. 23, where
it also alone is found. Luther has, "Und also erschrecklich war das
" Gesicht ;" and Ewald, "So furchtbar war das sich hell offenbarende."

[2] This passage (see Matt. ii. 23, Ὅπως πληρωθῇ τὸ ῥηθὲν διὰ τῶν προφητῶν, ὅτι Ναζωραῖος κληθήσεται ; and Acts xx. 35, Μνημονεύειν τε τῶν
λόγων τοῦ Κυρίου Ἰησοῦ, ὅτι αὐτὸς εἶπε, Μακάριόν ἐστι διδόναι μᾶλλον ἢ
λαμβάνειν) occurs nowhere in the narrative of the publication of the

Decalogue in Exodus, nor yet in Deut. J. A. Fabricius supposes that St. Paul took it from Deut. ix. 19, Καὶ ἔκφοβός εἰμι διὰ τὸν θυμὸν καὶ τὴν ὀργήν, κ.τ.λ. The probability of this latter conjecture appears to me more than doubtful. "These words," writes Dr. Gill, " are nowhere "recorded in Scripture; wherefore the Apostle had them either by "Divine revelation, or from tradition confirmed by the former; for the "Jews have a notion that Moses did quake and tremble when upon the "mount, and that he expressed his fear and dread. Moses said before "Him, 'Lord of the world (אנא מתירא), I am afraid lest they (the angels) "should burn (or consume) me with the breath of their mouths.'" "(*T. Bab. Sabbat*, fol. 88, 2.) Compare this last clause with 2 Thess. "ii. 8, and elsewhere (*T. Bab. Yoma*, fol. 4, 2), those words being "cited, '*He called unto Moses*' (Exod. xxiv. 16), it is observed, 'The "' Scripture comes not but (לאיים עליו) to terrify him, that so the law "' might be given with fear, fervour, and trembling; as it is said, "' Ps. ii. 11.' Once more (*Zohar* in Exod., fol. 24, 4), 'At the time the "' Holy Blessed God said to Moses, *Go, get thee down, for thy people* "' *have corrupted themselves* (Exod. xxxii. 7, אזדעזע משה), *Moses trembled,* "' and he could not speak.' And again it is said (*Midrash Kohelet*, fol. "69, 4) that when Moses was on Mount Sinai, supplicating for the "people of Israel, five destroying angels appeared, and immediately "(נתירא משה), *Moses was afraid.*" J. C. Wolfius pertinently remarks on Deut. ix. 19, in connexion with the present passage, "Nihil vero "sensui, sed tantum ad emphasin vocis ירה magis declarandam, voca- "bulum synonymum ἔντρομος Paulus addidit."— Wesselius (*Fasc. Diss.*, p. 427) observes, "Habuit hoc Paulus non ex libro aliquo canonico "deperdito, sed vel ex *Traditione* antiqua Judæorum, de qua aliquid "adnotavit Lud. Cappellus in locum, vel ex sola Revelatione Dei "immediata, vel potius ex traditione simul et revelatione, confirmante "traditionem. Ex quo utroque fonte quoque haussisse videtur nomina "Magorum Ægypti *Jannes* et *Jambres* (2 Tim. iii. 8), et dictum Domini in "vita terrestri sua prolatum Act. xx. 35, et quædam forte ex illis quæ "commemoravit in hac epistola, cap. ix. 19, *coll.* Exod. xxiv. 6, 7, 8," &c. It ought not to be overlooked, however, that in Exod. xix. 16 it is said that "all the people" in the camp "trembled." This expression, doubtless, included Moses himself.

The writer having thus recapitulated some of the leading, but transient, circumstances of awe under which the forefathers of his readers drew near to listen to the giving of the Law on Mount Sinai, now proceeds to set over against them the not less real, and more majestic and abiding accompaniments of the Believer's approach to God, under the Gospel Dispensation. If the most scrupulous ceremonial sanctification was required of the Israelites at Sinai, how much greater need has the Christian, of that " holiness without which no man shall see the Lord."

Verse 22.—But ye have come unto Mount Zion, and to the city of the living God, the heavenly Jerusalem.[1]

---

[1] Dr. Gill remarks, "The Alexandrian copy reads, as in verse 18, "*for ye are not come*, which may seem to favour that interpretation of " this passage which refers it to the heavenly state, to which saints, in " this present life, are not as yet come ; but by *Mount Sion*, and the " other names here given, is meant the Church of God under the Gospel " dispensation, to which the believing Hebrews were come, in distinc-" tion from the legal dispensation, signified by Mount Sinai, from which " they were delivered : and this is called *Mount Sion*, because, like that, " it is beloved of God ; chosen by Him ; and it is the place of his " habitation. Here his worship is, and his word and ordinances are " administered ; here He communes with his people, and distributes " his blessings ; and this, as Mount Sion, is a perfection of beauty, " the joy of the whole earth ; is strongly fortified by Divine power, and " is immovable, and is comparable to that mountain for its height and " holiness : and *to come to Sion* is, to become a member of a Gospel-" Church, and partake of the ordinances, enjoy the privileges, and " perform the duties belonging to it." See a curious passage in the Jerusalem Gemara, *Megillah*, col. 911—913 (*Ugol. Thes.*, tom 18) :—

אית תני הני מניחה וו שילה . נחלה וו ירושלם . אית תני תני מניחה וו ירושלם
נחלה וו שילה . מאן דאמר מניחה וו שילה כי לא באתם עד עתה אל המנוחה . נחלה
וו ירושלם . העיב צבית נהלתי לי . מאן דאמר נחלה וו שילה היתה לי נחלתי כאריה
ביער . מניחה וו ירושלם . ואת מניחתי עדי עד וגומר .

"Est qui docet : *Quies:* Hæc est Siloh : *Possessio* est Hierusalem :
" Est qui docet : Quies est Hierusalem ; Possessio est Siloh : qui dicit :
" Quies est Siloh : *Quia non venistis hactenus ad quietem:* Possessio est
" Hierusalem : *Numquid avis discolor hæreditas mea mihi?* Qui dicit :
" Possessio est Siloh : *Facta est mihi hæreditas mea quasi leo in Silva.*
" Quies est Hierusalem : *Hæc est requies mea in sæculum seculi*," &c.

How, then, did the first Hebrew readers of this epistle understand the expressions, Σιὼν ὄρει, καὶ πόλει Θεοῦ ζῶντος, Ἱερουσαλὴμ ἐπουρανίῳ?

They, doubtless, understood them as referring to those celestial abodes where the King Messiah dwells (Ps. ii. 6, ואני נסכתי כלי על ציון הר קדשי), and which are at present accessible to the Church below, by the wings of faith, and the privilege of the "communion of Saints," even that "*Jerusalem which is above*," and "*is free*," and "*which is the mother of us all*." Gal. iv. 26. This is that "holy hill" concerning which David writes, Ps. iii. 4, "I cried unto the Lord with my voice, "and He heard me out of his holy hill." And again, Ps. xv., "Lord, "who shall abide (מי יגור, or, *sojourn*) in thy tabernacle? who shall "dwell in thy holy hill? He that walketh uprightly," &c. And again, Ps. xxiv., "Who shall ascend into the hill of the Lord? or who " shall stand in his holy place? He that hath clean hands and a pure "heart," (נקי כפים ובר לבב), &c. See also Ps. xliii. 3, xlviii. 1, 2 (2, 3), lxviii. 15, 16 (16, 17), xci. 2—9; Is. ii. 2, 3, viii. 18, xi. 9, xiv. 13. " For thou hast said in thine heart, I will ascend into heaven, I will "exalt my throne above the stars of God, I will sit also upon the "mount of the congregation (בהר מועד), in the side of the north." (Compare Ps. xlviii. 2 (3). "I will ascend above the heights of the "clouds, I will be like the Most High (לעליון), yet shalt thou be brought "down to hell" (אל שאול, εἰς ᾅδην, LXX.), Is. xxiv. 23, xxv. 6, xxvi. 1, xxvii. 13, xxix. 8, lvi. 7, lvii. 13, lxii. 1, &c., lxv. 25, lxvi. 20; Joel ii. 32 (iii. 5); Joel iii. 17 (iv. 17); Micah iv. 1, 2, 7; Zech. viii. 3. Here, then, we have abundant examples of the spiritual signification of the words of Hebrews xii. 22. In Isaiah ii. 3, and Micah iv. 2, it is foretold that, in Messiah's days, "the law shall go forth out of Zion," not from Sinai. The following extract from the *Yalkut Shimoni* on Isaiah, § 296, c. 1, l. 34, &c., illustrates the belief of the Rabbinic Jews that Messiah would promulgate a new law.

עתיד הק"בה להיות יושב בגן עדן ודרש וכל צדיקים יושבים לפניו וכל פמליא של מעלה עומדים על רגליהם, והםה ומזלות מימינו של הק"בה ולבנה וכוכבים משמאלו והק"בה יושב ודורש תורה חדשה שעתיד ליתן על יד משיח.

"The Holy One, blessed be He, will sit in the garden of Eden and "expound. And all the righteous (or *saints*) shall sit before Him, and "all the families of the upper regions will stand on their feet, and the "sun and the constellations shall be on his right hand, viz., of the "Holy One, blessed be He, and the moon and the stars on his left "hand. And the Holy One, blessed be He, shall sit and expound a "new law, and will give it by the hand of Messiah."

So also Rabbi Hezekiah, in the *Midrash Koheleth*, chap. ii. :—

כל תורה שאת לומר בעולם הזה הבל היא לפני התורה של עולם הבא:

"Every law which one learns in this life, is vanity, in comparison of "the law of the world to come." The gloss upon which is, לפני התורה של משיח in comparison of the law of the Messiah. See Herm. Witsii, *Dissert. de seculo hoc et futuro*, printed at length in Meuschen's *Nov. Test. ex Talmude illustr.*, p. 1178. The Hebrews are thus reminded, that their lot is fallen in Messiah's days, in which the new law and the better covenant is promulgated, and the former law and covenant, having waxed old, are ready to vanish away. In the *Baba Bathra*, f. 75, 2, the following occurs,—" What means Is. iv. 5, "'*And upon her assemblies*,' מקראיה. Raba answered, R. Jochanan "said, Not as the Jerusalem of this world, is the Jerusalem of the world "to come. Anyone that it pleases to go up, goes up to the Jerusalem of "this world. But into the Jerusalem of the world to come, none go up, "except המוזמנים, who are prepared (or invited) to it," &c. Schoettgen observes, "In like manner as they (the Rabbis) believed that there was "a tabernacle in heaven, they asserted that there was a heavenly "Jerusalem, which is called in Hebrew ירושלים של מעלה, in Chaldee "ירושלים דלעילא, in Greek ἡ ἄνω Ἱερουσαλήμ, Galat. iv. 26, and Ἱερου-"σαλήμ ἐπουράνιος, Hebr. xii. 22" He proceeds to give the following illustrations of his assertion :—"The מדרש הנעלם in the *Sohar Chadash*, "fol. 19, 3, Rabbi Judah said, The Holy One, Blessed be He, made a "Jerusalem above according to the pattern of the Jerusalem below, "and swore that He would not enter it, until the Israelites should have "entered the Jerusalem below, as He saith in Hos. xi. 9, *The Holy One "in the midst of thee, and I will not enter into the city*. And seven bands "of ministering angels guard it round about, and at each gate there is "a band of such angels ; but those gates are called the gates of Righte-"ousness (or justice), which are so prepared that through them the "souls of the just may enter.—*Tanchuma*, fol. 39, 2, makes a similar "statement. Kimchi, also, on the passage above cited of Hosea, says "the same, but at the same time produces an objection from Ps. cxxii. 3, "which, however, he does not answer.—I will adduce the following "additional specimens. The מדרש הנעלם, fol. 22, 3, on the words, "*Melchisedeck King of Salem*, says, וו ירושלים של מעלה, 'This is the "'Jerusalem which is above,' *ibid.*, fol. 23, 1, and which is also "repeated in the *Yalkut Rubeni*, fol. 72, 3, 'When David died the "'upper angels (angeli superni) refused to give him admission through "'the gates of the heavenly Jerusalem, and so he had to abide outside. "'But on the day on which the temple was completed, The Holy One, "'Blessed be He, called Michael, one of the chiefest Holy ones, and "'appointed him and two others with him, to be ἐπίτροποι, *i.e*, guardians "'of those Israelites who had prepared a fixed habitation for the throne

"'of his glory. And He commanded Michael to admit David his
"'anointed through the gates of the heavenly Jerusalem, and to
"'associate him with the other patriarchs.' *Ibid.*, fol. 25, 2, 'The
"'same guardians which guard the heavenly Jerusalem, also guard
"'the one below.' Rashi, on Ezek. xlviii. 35, says, בירושלים של מעלה
"'מהתחי קרא בתוך יחזקאל, The 'Scripture speaks concerning the heavenly
"'Jerusalem, at the end of Ezekiel.' The Jews assign the locality of
" this heavenly Jerusalem, to that heaven which is called זבול. *Chagiga*,
" fol. 12, 2. זבול 'in which Jerusalem, the temple and altar are built,
"' and Michael the great Prince stands, and offers sacrifice in it.'"
Schoettgen, *Horæ Hebr.*, tom i., pp. 1210, 1211.—The word זבול signifies
" habitation," and occurs in 1 Kings viii. 13, " an house *to dwell in*,"
lit. " house *of habitation*," 2 Chron. vi. 2, "an house *of habitation*," and
also Is. lxiii. 15, "Look down from heaven, and behold from *the
" habitation* of thy holiness and of thy glory."—The words of the
passage under consideration would, therefore, suggest to the minds of
the Hebrew readers, the "heavenly" or "high places," τὰ ἐπουράνια
(Eph. i. 3, 20, ii. 6, iii. 10, vi. 12), where Christ sits at the right hand
of God, the dwelling-place of the angels, and the holy and happy abodes
of departed saints, where they rest from their labours and enjoy the
fruition of God's presence, whilst waiting for the morning of the resurrection. This Jerusalem, doubtless, it was that our Saviour described
(Matt. v.) as being " the City of the Great King," and which St. John
beheld in Apocalyptic vision, in all its beautiful and endearing proportions. Rev. iii. 12, xxi. 2, 10. And to this Mount Sion (Rev. xiv. 1)
and City of the living God, the Heavenly Jerusalem, believers can and
do come by the anticipation of faith, for their " citizenship πολίτευμα
" (Phil. iii 20) is in heaven"; they are " fellow-citizens with the saints,
" and of the household of God." Συμπολῖται τῶν ἁγίων, καὶ οἰκεῖοι τοῦ
Θεοῦ. Ephes ii. 19. And this agrees also with what St. Paul asserts,
Ephes. ii. 6, καὶ συνήγειρε, καὶ συνεκάθισεν ἐν τοῖς ἐπουρανίοις ἐν Χριστῷ
Ἰησοῦ.—The following remarkable illustration is quoted by Schoettgen
(tom. ii., p. 620) from the *Sohar* on Deut., fol. 110, col. 438 :—

וראי משה שירותא הוה בצולמא למהוי שלים בכלא :

" *Apud omnes in confesso est, Mosen initium fuisse in mundo, ut
" homines essent perfecti in omnibus......Propterea Moses fuit initium fuit
" in mundo. Quod si vero dicas: Quisnam est consummatio? Respon-
" deo: Rex Messias. Per hunc enim talis perfectio in mundo inventa est,
" qualis omnibus generationibus nondum fuit. Illo tempore perfectio
" invenietur in supernis et inferioribus, et omnes* עולמין (universes), *mundi
" erunt in consociatione una; propterea Scriptura dicit,* Zachar. xiv. 9.
" *Illo tempore Dominus erit unus, et nomen ejus unum.*"—The Christian

reader cannot fail to observe an almost startling parallelism between the above cited passage from the *Sohar*, and the words of Ephes. i. 10, εἰς οἰκονομίαν τοῦ πληρώματος τῶν καιρῶν, ἀνακεφαλαιώσασθαι τὰ πάντα ἐν τῷ Χριστῷ, τά τε ἐν τοῖς οὐρανοῖς, καὶ τὰ ἐπὶ τῆς γῆς, ἐν αὐτῷ. Again, *ibid.*, p. 621, "Tanchuma in *Jalkut Simeoni* II., fol. 57, 2, ad verba "Jesa. lxvi. 23, *Et fiet singulis mensibus et Sabbathis*, &c. Quomodo "autem fieri potest, ut omnis Israël singulis Sabbathis et noviluniis "Hierosolymam veniat? Respondit R. Levi: Hierosolyma tanto erit "spatio, quantum terra Israël implet, et terra Israël, quantum totus "terrarum orbis." The following extract from the Jerusalem Gemara (*Megillah*, cap. i., col. 911, 913, Ugol. Thes., vol. 18) singularly illustrates the subject in hand:—

את חני תני מנוחה וו שילה . נחלה וו ירושלם. את הני תני מ:וח וו ירושלם . נחלה וו שילה. מאן דאמר מנוחה וו שילה כי לא באהם עד עתה אל המנוח. החלה וו ירושלם. היינו צנוע נחלתי לי . כאן דאמר נחלה וו שילה היתה לי נחלתי כאריה ביער . ט:וחה וו ירושלם. ואת מנוחתי עדי עד וגומר :

"Est qui docet: Quies: hæc est Siloh: *Possessio* est Hierusalem: "Est qui docet: Quies est Hierusalem: possessio est Siloh: Qui dicit: "Quies est Siloh: *Quia non venistis hactenus ad quietem: Possessio* est "Hierusalem: *Numquid avis discolor hæreditas mea mihi?* Qui dicit: "Possessio est Siloh: *Facta est mihi hæreditas mea quasi leo in silva.* "Quies est Hierusalem: *Hæc est requies mea in sæculum seculi.*"

Verse 22.—And to ten thousands (an innumerable company) of angels,[1] and to the general (or *joyful*) assembly and Church of the firstborn,[2] whose names are written (*or* enrolled) in (the) heavens.

[1] Καὶ μυριάσιν ἀγγέλων, πανηγύρει. This is the pointing adopted by J. C. Wolfius, who, nevertheless, writes:—" Ita libri editi plerique; "Boeclerus tamen, sublata στιγμῇ post ἀγγέλων, legit, καὶ μυριάσιν "ἀγγέλων πανηγύρει. Hoc modo accepit Athanasius, tom. i., p. 986, et Ori-"genes contra Celsum, ita allegans, καὶ μυριάδων ἀγγέλων πανηγύρει. Pro "hac interpunctione......pugnat Rev. Raphelius in Herodoteis, pag. 639, "propterea, quod ceteris orationis hujus partibus singulis particula καὶ "praefigitur. Quemadmodum vero paulo ante πόλει Θεοῦ ζῶντος et "Ἰερουσαλὴμ ἐπουρανίῳ per appositionem junguntur, ita hic quoque "usu venire idem censet, ut sensus sit: *Accessistis ad myriadas Ange-*"*lorum conventum.* Recte hæc dici existimo. Interim Beza et Erasmus "Schmidius vocem πανηγύρει proxime cum vocibus καὶ ἐκκλησίᾳ con-"jungunt; quod et fieri vult Cl. Polemanus in Exercitat. vi. Program-"matica de Pleonasmis, pag. 18." Professor Stuart does not propose

to read μυριάδων with Origen, but yet he adopts Dr. Knapp's pointing, e.g., "Καὶ μυριάσιν, ἀγγέλων πανηγύρει, *and to myriads*, the joyful *company* " *of angels*. So, beyond all reasonable doubt, this clause is to be pointed ; " for πανήγυρις is not to be joined (as some later critics have joined it) " with ἐκκλησίᾳ κ.τ.λ. The structure of the whole paragraph demon- " strates this ; for each separate clause of it (in vers. 18, 19, 22—24) is " commenced by καὶ, and continued (where any addition is made to it) " by nouns in apposition, without any conjunctive particle before " them," &c. The Vulgate, however, reads, "et multorum millium " Angelorum frequentiam, et ecclesiam primitivorum," whilst Luther has "und zu der Menge vieler tausend Engel, und zu der Gemeine " der Erstgebornen." The rendering of the Authorized English Version, after all, appears to be the most natural and preferable, "and to an " innumerable company of angels, to the general assembly and Church " of the firstborn ;" and so Wesselius reads, "ad panegyrin et ecclesiam " primogenitorum." (*Fasc. Diss.*, p. 443.)—Dean Alford adopts the punctuation καὶ μυριάσιν, ἀγγέλων πανηγύρει καὶ ἐκκλησίᾳ πρωτ. κ.τ.λ. He contents himself with " following Delitzsch's note in the main," and has very little original to say upon the subject. His remark, however, that the probable key to the insertion of the words κριτῇ Θεῷ πάντων, is the Κύριος κρινεῖ τὸν λαὸν αὐτοῦ of chap. x. 30, is a very just one. (See note 1, on p. 157.)—Dr. Ewald translates, "*zehntausen-* "*den von Engeln, in Festversammlung.*" Doubtless the Writer to the Hebrews had before his mind the words of Deut. xxxiii. 1, 3, " The " Lord came from Sinai, and rose up from Seir unto them ; he shined " forth from mount Paran, and he came with ten thousands of saints " (מרבבת קדש, σὺν μυριάσι Κάδης, LXX., cum eo sanctorum millia, " *Vulg.*): from his right hand *went* a fiery law for them (ἐκ δεξιῶν " αὐτοῦ ἄγγελοι μετ' αὐτοῦ, LXX.). Yea, he loved the people ; all thy " saints (כל קדשיו, πάντες οἱ ἡγιασμένοι) are in thy hand ; and they sat " down at thy feet (והם הכו לרגלך, *procubuerunt ad pedes tuos*, Gesenius) ; " *every one* shall receive of thy words (ישא מדברתיך, ἐδέξατο ἀπὸ τῶν " λόγων αὐτοῦ νόμον, LXX.)." In this passage we have the clue to the majestic grouping together of the "ten thousands of angels, and the " joyful assembly and Church of the firstborn." Compare also Ps. l., which commences, " The mighty God (אל אלהים, Θεὸς θεῶν, LXX.), *even* " the Lord, hath spoken, and called the earth from the rising of the " sun unto the going down thereof. Out of Zion, the perfection of " beauty, God hath shined. Our God shall come, and shall not keep " silence : a fire shall devour before him (אש לפניו תבאל), and it shall be " very tempestuous round about him. He shall call to the heavens " from above, and to the earth, that he may judge his people. Gather "my saints (הסידיו, τοὺς ὁσίους αὐτοῦ) together unto me; those that have made a covenant with me by sacrifice." Dr. Gill observes :—"The Targum, Kimchi, and R. O. Gaon interpret this Psalm of the day of Judgment, and Jarchi takes it to be a prophecy of the future redemption by their expected Messiah......ver. 1 (*The mighty God, &c.*). In the Hebrew text it is *El Elohim*, which Jarchi renders the *God of gods;* that is, of angels who are so called, Ps. viii. 5, and xcviii. 7," &c.—The Targum of Onkelos renders Deut. xxxiii. 2, 3, as follows :— "The Lord was revealed from Sinai, and the brightness of his glory appeared to us from Seir. He was revealed in his power upon the mountain of Pharan, and with him were ten thousand saints," &c. The Targum of Palestine adds a variety of amplifications not contained in the Hebrew text. "The Lord was revealed at Sinai, to give the law unto his people of Beth Israel, and the splendour of the glory of his Shekinah arose from Gebal to give itself to the sons of Esau; but they received it not. It shined forth in majesty and glory from mount Pharan to give itself to the sons of Ishmael, but they received it not. It returned and revealed itself in holiness unto his people of Beth Israel, and with him ten thousand times ten thousand holy angels. He wrote with his own right hand, and gave them his law and his commandments, out of the flaming fire. And whatever hath befallen to the nations (hath been done), because He loved his people of Beth Israel, and all of them He hath called to be saints." So also the Jerusalem Targum :—"The Lord was revealed from Sinai to give the law unto his people of Beth Israel. He arose in his glory upon the mountain of Seir to give the law to the sons of Esau ; but after they found that it was written therein, Thou shalt do no murder, they would not receive it. He revealed himself in his glory on the mountain of Gebala, to give the law to the sons of Ishmael, but when they found that it was written therein, Ye shall not be thieves, they would not receive it. Again did he reveal himself upon mount Sinai, and with Him ten thousands of holy angels ; and the children of Israel said, All that the Word of the Lord hath spoken we will perform and obey. And He stretched forth his hand from the midst of the flaming fire, and gave the law to his people." (Etheridge's Targums, *in loco.*) Very noteworthy is it, that both these Targums allude to the rejection of the law by the descendants of the two first born sons (Heb. xii. 23), Ishmael and Esau, as though the Targumists moved in the same atmosphere of thought as the Writer to the Hebrews, who distinguishes between the firstborn by natural descent, and the "firstborn that are written or enrolled in heaven." But to return to the subject of the Hebrews' approach to the "innumerable company of angels." R. David

Kimchi in his Commentary on Zechariah (iii. 7) :—"Thus saith the
"Lord of hosts ; If thou wilt walk in my ways, and if thou wilt keep
"my charges, then thou shalt also judge my house, and shalt also keep
"my courts, and I will give thee places to walk amongst those that
"stand by (ונתתי לך מהלכים בין הצמדים האלה)," thus explains the concluding clause of the verse, "They were the angels, who stand and
"endure for ever ; and this means, thou shalt walk amongst them, *i.e.*,
"his soul, when it should be separated from his body. The Targum
"of Jonathan says, ' In the resurrection of the dead I will receive thee,
"'and give thee feet to walk amongst these seraphs.' "—The English
translators have fairly rendered the words under consideration by
"an innumerable company." The רבבת of Deut. xxxiii. 2, like the
μυριάδες of the LXX., are often used to signify a number infinitely
great. B. Scheidius, in his *Loca Talmudica*, p. 228 (Menschen), quotes
the following from the Talmudical Tract *Chagiga*, f. 13, 2, in reference
to Dan. vii. 10 :—" Singulis diebus creantur angeli ministerii ex fluvio
"Dinur, et dicunt Canticum et cessant, quia dicitur Thren. III., 23.
"*Nova, singulis matutinis, magna est fides tua.*"—Gesenius makes the
equivalent of πανήγυρις, עצרה, or oftener עצרת, *concio populi ad dies
festos agendos*. But although the two Hebrew words occur ten times
in the Old Testament, in Amos v. 21 alone is בעצרתיכם translated
ἐν ταῖς πανηγύρεσιν ὑμῶν in the LXX. Ewald observes on the words,
"*und zu zehntausenden von Engeln in Festversammlung*, wie sie
"zwischen jenem höchsten Himmel wo das himmlische Jerusalem ist
"und der Erde in der Mitte wie eine niedere rein himmlische Gemeinde
"jenen Berg umringen, nach Ps. lxviii. 18 (17), f., Deut. xxxiii. 3,
"Dan. vii. 10." For Philo's opinion on this subject see note 2, p. 311,
chap. xii. 24, on the words καὶ πνεύμασι δικαίων τετελειωμένων.

² Ἐκκλησίᾳ πρωτοτόκων ἐν οὐρανοῖς ἀπογεγραμένων. These "firstborn"
are those who did not, like Esau (verse 16), sell τὰ πρωτοτόκια, for any
worldly advantage. They are enrolled in heaven as citizens of the
New Jerusalem, even as it is written in Ps. lxxxvii. 3, "Glorious things
"are spoken of thee, O city of God......5. And of Zion it shall be said,
"This and that man was born in her : and the Highest himself shall
"establish her (יאמר איש ואיש ילד בה והוא יכוננה עליון). 6. The Lord shall
"count, when he writeth up the peoples (compare Dan. xii. 1), that
"this *man* was born there (יהוה יספר בכתוב עמים זה ילד שם)—Κύριος διηγήσε-
"ται ἐν γραφῇ λαῶν, καὶ ἀρχόντων τούτων τῶν γεγενημένων ἐν αὐτῇ.)" Dr.
Phillips (*in loc.*) observes on בכתוב עמים, that the Syriac has translated
the two words by "*in the book of the people.* The Chaldee has expressed
"the signification more largely : ספרא די בכתבין ביה חושבן כל עממיא, *The
"book in which are written the numberings of all the people.*" The above

passage of Ps. lxxxvii. casts a flood of light upon these words of the Writer to the Hebrews, and removes all difficulty from the interpretation of ἐν οὐρανοῖς ἀπογεγραμμένων. It was a phrase with which the persecuted Hebrews were perfectly familiar. A parallel passage is found in Isaiah iv. 2, 3 : " In that day shall the branch of the Lord be "beautiful and glorious, and the fruit of the earth *shall be* excellent "and comely for them that are escaped of Israel (לפליטת ישראל). And " it shall come to pass, that *he* that is left in Zion, and he that remaineth " in Jerusalem, shall be called holy, *even* every one that is written to " life in Jerusalem " (כל הכתוב לחיים בירושלם, πάντες οἱ γραφέντες εἰς ζωὴν ἐν Ἱερουσαλήμ, LXX.). The Targum renders the first clause of verse 2, בעדנא ההוא יהי משיחא דיי להדוה וליקר, " In that time shall the Messiah of " the Lord be for a joy and for a glory." Kimchi says that this shall be " a day of salvation when the Redeemer shall come," יום התשועה בא הגואל, and explains the " branch of the Lord " of the Messiah, in accordance with Jer. xxiii. 5, whilst the Babylonian Gemara (*Sanhedrin*, col. 911, *Ugol. Thes.*, vol. xxv.) interprets verse 3 of the Resurrection—

תנא רבי אליהו צדיקים שעתיד הקב״ה להחיותן אינן חוזרי׳ לעפרן שנאמר והיה הנשאר בציון והנותר בירושלים קדוש יאמר לו כל הכתוב לחיים בירושלים מה קדוש לעולם קיים אף הם לעולמים קיימין :

" A disciple of Elias taught, It shall come to pass that the just whom " the Holy One, Blessed be He, shall quicken, shall not return to dust. " For it is said (in Isaiah iv. 3), *And it shall come to pass that he that is* " *left in Zion, and remaineth in Jerusalem, shall be* every one called holy, " every one that is written to life. As the Holy One lives for ever, so " likewise they shall also live for ever." Another mention of God's book is found in Exod. xxxii. 32, 33 in immediate connexion with the giving of the Decalogue : " Yet now, if Thou wilt forgive their sin— " and if not, blot me, I pray thee, out of thy book which Thou hast " written (מספרך אשר כתבה, ἐκ τῆς βίβλου σου, ἧς ἔγραφας, LXX.). And " the Lord said unto Moses, Whosoever hath sinned against me, him " will I blot out of my book (מספרי)." The Targum of Jonathan or Palestine paraphrases the above as follows :—" But now if thou wilt " forgive their sin, forgive ; but if not, blot me, I pray, from the book " of the just, in the midst of which Thou hast written my name," &c. A similar allusion is made in Ezek. xiii. 9, " And mine hand shall be " upon the prophets that see vanity and that divine lies. They shall " not be in the assembly of my people, neither shall they be written in " the writing of the house of Israel " (בסוד עמי לא יהיו ובכתב בית ישראל לא יכתבו). In St. Luke x. 20 we read how our Lord bid his disciples to rejoice because their names were " *written in heaven* " (ὅτι τὰ ὀνόματα ὑμῶν ἐγράφη ἐν τοῖς οὐρανοῖς). In Philipp. iv. 3, St. Paul makes use of similar language, ὧν τὰ ὀνόματα ἐν βίβλῳ ζωῆς. Some excellent remarks on the above subject are to be found in J. A. Danzii, *Programma de spiritu ardente in Esaiæ* iv. 4, *coll. Act.* ii. 2, printed at length on pp. 787—794 of Meuschen's *Nov. Test. ex Talmude illustr.* See also J. Wesselii, *Fasc. Dissertationum*, pp. 491, 493 (*Groningæ*, 1756, 4to.). See also the Dissertation (sect. 11, p. 244) by the same author, *De silentio Scripturæ mystico in historia Malchisedeki ad Ps. cx.* 4, contained in his *Diss. Sacr. Leidens.* Lugd. Bat., 1721, 4to.—And now with respect to πρωτοτόκων, I cannot help feeling that there is a reference back to the πρωτοτόκια of verse 16. The birthright that Esau renounced was twofold. He rejected the honour of being the head of the chosen Family and the ancestor of the Messiah ; secondly, as being the eldest son, the priesthood belonged to him. This honour he also parted with for a mess of pottage. He renounced this religious privilege and distinction, and cast scorn upon the promises of blessing which would have been transmitted, through himself, to the whole world. The Targum of Jonathan or Palestine (see note 2 on p. 282) describes Esau as saying to Jacob, " Behold, I am going to die, and in another world I shall have no life, " and what then to me is the birthright, or the portion in the world to " come of which thou speakest." And again, " And Esau scorned the " birthright, and the portion of the world that cometh ;" whilst the Jerusalem Targum says that " Esau despised the birthright and vilified the " portion in the world that cometh, and denied the Resurrection of the " dead." The Targum of Onkelos paraphrases the words of Exodus xxiv. 5, " And he (Moses) sent young men of the children of Israel " (וישלח את נערי בני ישראל), which offered burnt-offerings," &c., as follows : " And he sent the firstborn sons of Israel," &c., whilst the Targum of Palestine explains the reason why Moses did so : "And he sent the " firstborn of the sons of Israel, for until that hour had the firstborn " had the (office of performing) worship, the Tabernacle of Ordinance " not (as yet) being made, nor the priesthood given unto Aharon," &c. (See Etheridge's Targums, *in loc.*) Now what was the promise to the people of Israel immediately before the giving of the law on Mount Sinai ? It was, that they should be a KINGDOM OF PRIESTS AND AN HOLY NATION. See Exod. xix. 1—6. Had, then, the converts to Christianity forfeited their title to this glorious birthright, as their unbelieving brethren asserted they had ? Just the reverse. They did stand in the "congregation of the righteous," עדת צדיקים, spoken of in Ps. i. 5 ; they were acknowledged members of the " Church of "the Firstborn, whose names are written in heaven ! " To the superiority of the believer's priesthood over Aaron's, the Writer of this Epistle alludes in chap. xiii. 10 : " We have an altar, whereof "they have no right to eat which serve the tabernacle." To the exercise of their priestly functions he refers, in verse 15, "By him, therefore, let us offer the sacrifice of praise to God continually," &c. The kingdom he speaks of as already given to them in chap. xii. 28, "Wherefore we, receiving a kingdom which cannot be moved, let us "have grace, whereby we may serve God with reverence and godly "fear; for our God is a consuming fire." The very words of this concluding exhortation call to mind the conditions upon which the priestly kingdom was to be held by the children of Israel, and the fiery manifestation of Jehovah upon the Mount of God, which immediately followed. "Now, therefore, if ye will obey my voice indeed, and keep my covenant, then ye shall be a peculiar treasure unto me above all people, "for all the earth is mine. And ye shall be unto me a kingdom of "priests," &c. These words of Exod. xix. 6 are cited by St. Peter (1, ii. 9) :—" But ye are a chosen generation, a royal priesthood, an holy "nation, a peculiar people; that ye should show forth," &c. So also St. John, Rev. i. 5 : "And from Jesus Christ......the first-begotten "from the dead (ὁ πρωτότοκος ἐκ τῶν νεκρῶν)......and hath made us kings "and priests unto God." This also is the burden of the song of the elders, Rev. v. 10. We see, therefore, that the Writer to the Hebrews yet moves, so to speak, in a Sinaitic atmosphere. He still clothes his ideas in the phraseology of Old Testament Scripture, at once so familiar and so sacred to his readers. He shows them that they have obtained the spiritual birthright, of which their unconverted brethren have fallen short. It is a birthright for which they may well be content to suffer the loss of all things. As the Jewish father could not disinherit the son of his less-favoured spouse, and convey the right of primogeniture to the son of his favourite wife, so the whole Jewish hierarchy was powerless to alienate from the believers that spiritual birthright which was God's peculiar gift. (Compare Exod. iv. 22, 23.)

It is His alone to give the birthright, as well as the kingdom; as He of old preferred Jacob before Esau, and transferred from Reuben the kingdom to Judah, and the birthright to Joseph; even as it is written, 1 Chron. v. 1, 2, "Now the sons of Reuben, the firstborn of Israel "(בכור ישראל), for he was the firstborn (הבכור), but.........his birthright "(בכרתו) was given unto the sons of Joseph, the son of Israel, and the "genealogy is not to be reckoned after the birthright (ולא להתיחש לבכרה). "For Judah prevailed above his brethren, and of him came the chief "ruler (ולנגיד ממנו), but the birthright was Joseph's (והבכרה ליוסף)." And so also it is said, in Jer. xxxi. 9, "I am a father to Israel, and Ephraim "is my firstborn." Wesselius observes (*Fascic. Dissertat.*, p. 496. *Groningae*, 1756. 4to.), "Plures natura Primogeniti fuerunt rejecti, ut

"Cain, Ismael, Esavus, Ruben, qui typi fuere et exempla rejectionis
"legalium Judæorum, omniumque qui ex operibus justificari volunt
"coram Deo. Verum per liberrimam Dei gratiam, quidam fratres natu
"minores primogenitis prælati sunt, v.g. Isaacus, Jacobus, &c., qui
"non natura, sed electione divina facti Primogeniti, fuere typi vestri,
"O Hebræi, omniumque credentium, et hæredum æternæ salutis."
The translators of the London Jews' Society's Hebrew New Testament
have translated, לעדת וּלקהלת הבכורים הכתובים בשמים. Wolfius (*Cur. Phil.*,
tom. iv., p. 791, *in loc.*) writes:—"Πρωτοτόκων ἐν οὐρανοῖς ἀπογεγρ.
"Phrasis hæc apud Judæos etiam exstat. Sic in *Jalkut* Rubeni, fol.
"49, 2, ad Genes. xxvii. 18, כי נשמת יעקב היה בכור בשמים, *Nam anima*
"*Jacobi fuit primogenita in Cœlis.* Ita R. Joseph Albo, lib. עקרים, fol.
"147, col. 1, Justos perfectos dicit נכתבים ונחתמים לחיי עולם הבא, *scriptos*
"*esse et obsignatos inter vivos sæculi futuri.* Videtur ea respici ad
"morem, quo primogenitorum nomina in tabulis genealogicis describi
"solebant." See also Num. iii. 12, 13:—"And I, behold I have taken
"the Levites from among the children of Israel, instead of all the first-
"born that openeth the matrix among the children of Israel: therefore
"the Levites shall be mine. Because all the firstborn are mine; *for* on
"the day that I smote all the firstborn in the land of Egypt, I hallowed
"(הקדשתי לי) unto me all the firstborn in Israel. Both man and beast,
"mine shall they be. I am the Lord." For information on the subject
of the primogeniture, and of the law of firstlings, the reader may
consult Selden, *De Successionibus ad leges Ebræorum*, lib. i., cap. v.;
Reland's *Antiq. Sacr.* (Utrajecti, 1721, 8vo.), p. 342; T. Goodwin's
Moses et Aaron (Francofurti ad Mœnum, 1710, 8vd.), pp. 39, 40, 74,
848—864; Philo, *De Præmiis Sacerdotum* (Works, Mangey's Edition,
tom. ii., pp. 233, 234); and *De Humanitate*, ibid., p. 391; as also the
Treatise *Bechoroth*, Mishna Surenh., vol. 5, pp. 155—191.

Verse 23.—And to God the Judge of all,[1] and to the spirits of just men made perfect.[2]

[1] Καὶ κριτῇ Θεῷ πάντων. Alford has exercised a wise discretion in retaining the translation of our Authorized Version, although he does not seem to be aware of the reason why it should be so retained. The words are designed to convey two ideas to the Hebrews. *First,* they are in antithesis to what has been already adduced in verses 18—21 respecting the restrictions that were placed upon the approach to Sinai, at the giving of the Decalogue. Let the unbelieving Jews taunt these despised converts with having surrendered their part in the covenant of legality. Their fathers, who received the Law, and heard the voice of

God speaking out of the fire, were compelled to stand afar off, and quaked. The believers in Jesus need no more stand afar off. They are brought nigh by the blood of Christ. They are "come to God, the "Judge of all." It is "God that justifieth; who is he that con- "demneth ?" Thus is the position of the Christian Israelite contrasted with that of those who were yet under the beggarly elements of the law, and who could only approach once a-year, by the vicarious embassage of the High Priest, into the presence of the Shechinah.

But, *secondly*, the afflicted Hebrews are reminded that the God to whom they have perpetual access, is the JUDGE OF ALL. He heard the groaning of their fathers in Egypt ; and the Writer has already consoled them (x. 30) with the prophetic consolation spoken by Moses (Deut. xxxii. 36. See note 1 on p. 157), "The Lord shall judge his people "—and, "shall not the Judge of all the earth do judgment ?" (השפט כל הארץ לא יעשה משפט. Gen. xviii. 25.) Ewald, usually so happy in his translation, seems to miss some of the force of καὶ κριτῇ Θεῷ πάντων in his rendering, *und dem Richter-Gotte Aller*. Preferable is Luther's version, *Und zu Gott dem Richter über Alle*, the circumstances of whose times bore no faint resemblance to those of the hunted-down Hebrew converts to Christianity in the Apostolic age.

Wesselius (*Fasc. Dissertat.*, p. 500) would read, *And to the Judge, the God of all;* and says, " Justificationis beneficium exprimit Apostolus " his verbis, καὶ Κριτῇ Θεῷ πάντων, ET AD JUDICEM DEUM OMNIUM, " scilicet *accessistis*. Vulgatus habet *et Judicem omnium Deum*: Beza, " *et Judicem universorum Deum*. Belgæ ; *Ende tot Godt den Rechter* " *over alle*, quasi heic esset quædam *Hypallage*, seu verborum trajectio, " et vox πάντων ad vocem Κριτῇ, non ad vocem Θεῷ referri deberet. Sed " ejusmodi vocum transpositio absque ulla necessitate heic statuitur. " Sensus enim emerget satis aptus et emphaticus, si vocum ordinem in " Græco textu servemus. Figuram quandam Grammaticam heic esse " haud diffiteor, sed illa non est *Hypallage*, verum *Ellipsis* articuli " præpositivi τῷ, ut plene legatur, καὶ Κριτῇ τῷ Θεῷ πάντων. Quæ " ellipsis articuli præpositivi, qui pronominis demonstrativi vel relativi, " τοῦ אשר apud Hebræos, vim sæpe habet, Græcis auctoribus, etiam " Sacris, perquam familiaris est. Vide Noldium, p. 109, 110, et " Glassium in *Grammat. S. Lib.*, Tract ii., *Cap.* 2 et 22. Atque adeo " Verba hæc Græca ita verti possunt, *et ad Judicem, qui est Deus* " *Omnium*." Professor Stuart entirely misses the Writer's meaning in applying the words to the judgment of a "future world." He translates, *and to the Judge, the God of all*, and says, "Κριτῇ designates Him " before whose tribunal all must appear that enter a future world." The Writer is addressing *present* consolation to the Hebrews. He does

not say, *ye shall come*, but *ye have come*, προσεληλύθατε, " to God the
" Judge of all." He encourages them with the assurance that very
presently their avengement shall proceed from God himself.

² Καὶ πνεύμασι δικαίων τετελειωμένων. Ewald excellently renders these
words, *Und zu den Geistern vollendeter Gerechten* (which I would venture
to translate, *and to the spirits of just men whose course is run*), and adds,
" Derer die der irdischen Gemeinde jezt entnommen, dennoch stets mit
" ihrem unsterblichen Geiste an ihr den lebendigsten Theil haben, um
" sie seufzen und klagen, und um sie sich freuen und frohlocken, wie das
" Apoc. vi. 9—11, vii. 9—17, so malerisch beschrieben wird," *i.e.*, " of
" those who have been removed from the earthly Community, but who
" yet, with their immortal spirit, take the liveliest part in her, and who
" sigh and complain on her behalf, and rejoice and exult over her, as is
" so graphically depicted in Rev. vi. 9—11, vii. 9—17." (*Das Sendschr.
a.d. Hebr.*, p. 144.) It is observable that both these passages of the
Apocalypse depict the condition of those who have attained to the
martyr's palm. These are they who have attained to the REST THAT
REMAINETH, but are not yet fully glorified, τοῦ Θεοῦ περὶ ἡμῶν κρεῖττόν
τι προβλεψαμένου, ἵνα μὴ χωρὶς ἡμῶν τελειωθῶσι (Chap. xi. 40). Stuart,
again, makes but a sorry hand at the interpretation of the passage,
e.g., " *and to the spirits of the just men made perfect*, i.e., exalted to a
" state of final reward." How this could take place, before the resurrection of the body, the learned Professor does not proceed to explain.
Philo (*De Confusione Linguarum*, p. 431, Works, Mangey, tom. i.)
beautifully illustrates his belief upon the subject of the disembodied
souls of the just in the following words:—" God being ONE himself,
" has around Him innumerable auxiliary powers (δυνάμεις ἀρωγοὺς). By
" these powers, that world which is incorporeal, and mentally dis-
" cernible (νοητὸς), is compacted together, the archetype of the one that
" we see (τοῦ φαινομένου), which is made up of invisible forms, as this
" world is of visible bodies." Philo proceeds to say that, in admiration
of their endowments, some have not hesitated to call such spiritual
existences gods:—" Moses, entering into the intention of these latter,
" exclaims, *O Lord, O Lord, thou King of the gods* (Deut. x. 17), in order
" to intimate the superiority of the Ruler over his subjects. For there
" exists in the air a most holy choir (ἔστι δὲ κατὰ τὸν ἀέρα ψυχῶν ἀσωμάτων
" ἱερώτατος χορὸς) of disembodied souls, associated with the celestial
" (ὀπαδὸς τῶν οὐρανίων); for the Divine oracles are wont to call these
" latter souls *angels*. This entire host, ordered throughout in its several
" ranks, does suit and service to the Captain that so ordered it."

The writer of the Wisdom of Sol. (iv. 13) uses the word τελειωθεὶς,
in reference to Enoch, in the same signification as the writer to the

Hebrews—τελειωθεὶς, ἐν ὀλίγῳ ἐπλήρωσε χρόνους μακρούς·—I have failed to discover any allusion to the technical Rabbinical expression צדיקים גמורים, *Justi perfecti*, in these words of the writer to the Hebrews, although Schoettgen prefaces a long disquisition (*Hor. Hebr.*, tom. i., pp. 993—1003) upon the subject with the following words :—" Judæis " quam sæpissime in ore sunt צדיקים גמורים, *Justi perfecti*. Quum ergo "Apostolus eosdem hic memoret, operæ pretium erit illis parumper "immorari." It is true that Schoettgen remarks that the Sohar Exod., fol. 71, col. 283, speaks of the spirits of the just, רוחין דצדיקייא, *Spiritus justorum* in paradiso, " cum quibus Deus se oblectat." But the Jewish idea of a צדיק גמור is that of a perfectly righteous man. And so Buxtorf defines the term in his Chaldee and Rabbinical Lexicon, col. 451 :— " *Justus absolutus*, id est, שהיה רחוק מעבירה כל ימיו, *qui longe remotus fuit* " *a transgressione omnibus diebus suis*, ut scribit R. Salom. in Sanhed., " cap. Chelek, fol. 99, 1." The *Yalkut Rubeni*, fol. 30, 4 (See Schoettg., tom. 1, p. 996) says, " Messias portat peccata Israelitarum וגם צדיקים " גמורים סובלים יסורים, nam et justi perfecti aliquas passiones pro Israelitis "sustinent." It is certain that the Writer to the Hebrews would give no countenance to the Jewish figment that it was possible for any man to live altogether without sin, far less to make atonement for another. In Ps. cxxxviii. 8, David writes, יהוה יגמר בעדי, " The Lord will perfect " *that which* concerneth me"; and, in Philipp. iii. 3, St. Paul disclaims the notion that he was already perfect, οὐχ ὅτι ἤδη ἔλαβον, ἢ ἤδη τετελείωμαι. The word τετελειωμένων, *perfected*, if used in a theological sense, would refer to the operation of God's justifying grace, and not to any human works, merits, or deservings. It would signify " justified," " made "perfect." Alford lays stress on the word πνεύμασιν, as if the Writer would have written, *to just men made perfect*, had they not been waiting in a disembodied state, for the final consummation of the Resurrection. But then, surely, the Writer would have said, πνεύμασιν δικαίων τετελειωμένοις. The Dean adds, with a strange forgetfulness of the article of the Creed, *I believe in the communion of saints*, κοινωνία ἁγίων : " They are not sleeping, they are not unconscious, they are not absent " from us : they are perfected, lacking nothing except—and that is our " defect, because we are as yet imprisoned in an unspiritual body— " communion with us."—Bishop Pearson on the Creed (*Art.*, Comm. of Saints) writes, " *The saints of God are in communion with all the* " *saints departed out of this life and admitted to the presence of God.* " Jerusalem sometimes is taken for the Church on earth, sometimes for " that part of the Church which is in heaven, to show that, as both are " represented by one, so both are but one City of God. Wherefore thus " doth the Apostle speak to such as are called to the Christian faith,

" Ye are come unto Mount Sion, and unto the city of the living God,
" the heavenly Jerusalem, and to an innumerable company of angels,
" and to the general assembly and Church of the firstborn, which are
" written in heaven, and to God the Judge of all, and to the spirits of
" just men made perfect, and to Jesus the Mediator of the New
" Covenant (Heb. xii. 22—24).—Indeed, the communion of saints, in
" the Church of Christ, with those that are departed, is demonstrated by
" their communion with the saints alive. For if I have communion
" with a saint of God, as such, while he liveth here, I must still have
" communion with him when he is departed hence, because the founda-
" tion of communion cannot be removed by death. The mystical union
" between Christ and his Church, the spiritual conjunction with the
" members to the Head is the true foundation of that communion
" which one member hath with another, all the members living and
" increasing by the same influence which they receive from Him. But
" death, which is nothing else but the separation of the soul from the
" body, maketh no separation in the mystical union, no breach of the
" spiritual conjunction; and, consequently, there must be the same
" communion, because there remaineth the same foundation."—The
translators of the London Jews' Society's Hebrew New Testament,
avoiding the word נמורים, have ואל רוחות הצדיקים הנשלמים.

Wesselius (*Fasc. Diss.*, pp. 511, 512), who strongly opposes the
opinion of Schoettgen and Lightfoot, viz., that the Writer to the
Hebrews uses the phrase πν. δικ. τετελ. as the equivalent to the Rabbinical formula צדיקים גמורים, says:—" Verum hoc probari deberet, quod
' Rabbini *Justos in hac vita*, etiam vocaverint SPIRITUS JUSTORUM.
" Vel SPIRITUS *Justos Consummatos;* si nempe probare volunt Paulum
" *imitatum* fuisse phrasin Rabbinorum. Sed hoc non probarunt viri
" docti. Unde, si ex illorum hypothesi, hoc dictum Paulinum, ex
" antiquorum Rabbinorum phrasi, explicandum sit, certe non aliis
" hominibus *in hac terra* existentes *Justiores*, qui nunquam *Spiritus
" Justorum* a Rabbinis dicuntur; sed *pios, vita hac* jam *functos*, et quoad
" *animas* in Paradiso viventes ante resurrectionem corporum eorum,
" intelligere heic debemus. Veteres enim Judæi *Animas* Piorum a
" corporibus *separatas*, SPIRITUS JUSTORUM appellarunt. In libro
" Sapientiæ cap. iii., 1. Δικαίων δὲ ψυχαὶ JUSTORUM *vero* ANIMÆ *sunt
" in manu Dei, ut minime eos attingant cruciatus.* Et in *Cantico* Græco
" *Trium Juvenum*, vers. 36, aut in *Adjectionibus* ad Danielem, cap. xii.
" 86. *Benedicite Domino* πνεύματα καὶ ψυχαὶ δικαίων. *Spiritus et animæ
" justorum.* Similiter Talmudicos, aliosque Judæos animas piorum
" *separatas* vocare *Spiritus* aut *Animas Justorum*, uno atque altero
" exemplo comprobarunt Doct. Hasæus, l. c. § 12, et D'Outrein in *cap.*

"xii. 24 *ad Hebr.*, p. 238.. Nec pluribus testimoniis opus erit, postquam
"adscripsero verba R. Meir in libro *Avodath Hakkodesch*, a Clar.
"*Dassorio* in *Diatriba de Resurrectione* mortuorum, p. 64 ; atque a Doct.
"Hasæo, l. c. § 11, p. 110, laudata. *Rabbini nostri, si mentionem faciant*
"*animarum corporibus carentium, non memorant* Justos, *sed* Spiritus
"Justorum, *vel* Animas Justorum. Quando autem loquuntur de seculo
"*futuro post resurrectionem, ubi corpus et corporeitas est, Memorant*
"Justos."

Verse 24.—And to Jesus, Mediator of a new covenant,[1] and to a blood of sprinkling that speaketh better things than that of Abel.[2]

[1] Καὶ διαθήκης νέας μεσίτῃ 'Ιησοῦ. If the Levitic priesthood be abolished, if it be superseded by a high priesthood belonging to one of the tribe of Judah, then of necessity the Mosaic covenant is abrogated also. The Levitic priesthood was an *indispensable* feature of the Mosaic covenant— εἰ μὲν οὖν τελείωσις διὰ τῆς Λευϊτικῆς ἱερωσύνης ἦν, (ὁ λαὸς γὰρ ἐπ' αὐτῇ νενομοθέτητο) τίς ἔτι χρεία, κατὰ τὴν τάξιν᾽ Μελχισεδὲκ ἕτερον ἀνίστασθαι ἱερέα, καὶ οὐ κατὰ τὴν τάξιν 'Ααρὼν ͵λέγεσθαι ; chap. vii. 11—the new covenant must therefore have commenced to run from the date of the abrogation of the Levitic priesthood. But why is the Mediator of the New Covenant mentioned here in connexion with the blood of sprinkling ? Are the words merely a redundant amplification of what has gone before ? Or do they follow, in orderly sequence, upon what has been previously spoken ? A glance at Exod. xxiv. 1, will show that they are the legitimate complement of all that has been already adduced. In Exod. xx. 19, it is related how the children of Israel besought Moses to undertake the office of mediator : " And they said unto Moses, Speak thou
" with us, and we will hear ; but let not God speak with us lest we die."
Moses accepted the task, and received on their behalf all the injunctions which are contained in Exod. xx. 22, &c.—Exod. xxiii. These words, with the Ten Commandments, were written by Moses in a book (Exod. xxiv. 7) which was, doubtless, the *"Book of the Covenant."* After Moses had completed the above-mentioned signal discharge of his mediatorship, and had committed the words to writing and rehearsed them to the people, we read, Exod. xxiv. 1 : " And he (Jehovah) said
" unto Moses, Come up unto the Lord, thou, and Aaron, Nadab, and
" Abihu, and seventy of the elders of Israel ; and worship ye afar off."
(מרהב והשתחויתם),—Καὶ Μωυσῇ εἶπεν, ἀνάβηθι πρὸς τὸν Κύριον σὺ καὶ 'Ααρὼν, καὶ Ναδὰβ καὶ 'Αβιοὺδ, καὶ ἑβδομήκοντα τῶν πρεσβυτέρων 'Ισραήλ· καὶ

προσκυνήσουσι μακρόθεν τῷ Κυρίῳ., LXX.) And in verse 2 it is added, "And Moses alone shall come near the Lord ; but they shall not come "nigh, neither shall the people go up with him." Here, then, we see that not only the people of Israel, but also Aaron and his sons, and also the seventy elders, were forbidden to accompany the mediator Moses into the presence of God. The latter, indeed, were favoured with the Vision of the Most High (verse 10) ; but it is plain from what follows, that Moses went *alone* to receive the Two Tables into the Mount of God. Before Moses went up "he took the book of the "covenant, and read in the audience of the people," and then he took the blood of the sacrifices (verses 5—8) and "sprinkled it on the people, "and said, Behold the blood of the covenant, which the Lord hath "made with you concerning all these words." We see, then, that the congregation, though actually sprinkled with the blood of the covenant, were not permitted to accompany their mediator into the presence of God. Far different is the position of the believing Hebrews to whom the Epistle is addressed. They *have* come to Jesus the Mediator of the New Covenant, and to "a blood of sprinkling" that gives immediate and perpetual access to God. The command is no longer, as in Exod. xix. 12, "And thou shalt set bounds unto the people round about" (והגבלת את העם סביב ; Καὶ ἀφοριεῖς τὸν λαὸν κύκλῳ., LXX.). But it is with them, even as St. Paul writes to the Ephesians (ii. 13, 14) :—Νυνὶ δὲ ἐν Χριστῷ Ἰησοῦ, ὑμεῖς οἱ ποτὲ ὄντες μακράν, ἐγγὺς ἐγενήθητε, ἐν τῷ αἵματι τοῦ Χριστοῦ. Αὐτὸς γάρ ἐστιν ἡ εἰρήνη ἡμῶν, ὁ ποιήσας τὰ ἀμφότερα ἕν, καὶ τὸ μεσότοιχον τοῦ φραγμοῦ λύσας. Well might the Writer to the Hebrews declare (viii. 6) Νυνὶ δὲ διαφορωτέρας τέτυχε λειτουργίας, ὅσῳ καὶ κρείττονός ἐστι διαθήκης μεσίτης, ἥτις ἐπὶ κρείττοσιν ἐπαγγελίαις νενομοθέτηται. These "*better promises*" were promises of forgiveness and acceptance, as we see from verses 10—12, commencing with the words ὅτι αὕτη ἡ διαθήκη, κ.τ.λ., and closing with the declaration ὅτι ἵλεως ἔσομαι ταῖς ἀδικίαις αὐτῶν. κ τ λ. And now, as Moses (Deut. xviii. 15—19) expressly refers to Christ (see Ewald, *Das Sendschr. a.d. Hebr.*, p, 131) in his Mediatorial capacity and resemblance to himself, and does so in immediate connexion with the request of the Israelites (Exod. xx. 19), "Speak thou "with us, and we will hear ; but let not God speak with us lest we die," let us briefly inquire what it was that Moses led the Israelites to expect from the Messiah, in his capacity as a Mediator. We have it on the authority of St. Peter (Acts iii. 22), not only that Moses was the author of this prophecy, but, also, that he wrote therein expressly of our Lord Jesus Christ. And again (Acts vii. 37) St. Stephen asserts, "This is "that Moses, which said unto the children of Israel, A prophet shall "the Lord your God raise up," &c. In Exod. xxxiii. 11 it is said,

"And the Lord spake unto Moses, face to face, as a man speaketh unto
"his friend." In Numbers xii. 6—8 it is written, "Hear now my words:
"If there be a prophet among you, I the Lord will make myself known
"unto him in a vision, *and* will speak unto him in a dream. My servant
"Moses *is* not so, who is faithful (נאמן, see Hebr. iii. 5) in all mine
"house. With him will I speak mouth to mouth, even apparently, and
"not in dark speeches; and the similitude of the Lord shall he behold."
(פה אל פה אדבר בו ומראה ולא בחידת ותמנת יהוה יביט.) Whilst the author of
the closing verses of the book of Deuteronomy assures us that up to his
days "There arose not a prophet since in Israel like unto Moses, whom
"the Lord knew face to face," &c. But Moses intimates to his people
that THE PROPHET shall arise at a similar juncture to that which
occurred at the giving of the law at Horeb. He implies, therefore,
that a new law will be published by this his Successor in the Mediatorship, and that to refuse obedience will be a sin, for which the Lord
will exact the extreme penalty of excision from amongst his people.
(See note 2 on pp. 37, 38.) In Deut. xviii. 1—8, Moses reminds the people
how God had provided for their religious instruction by the perpetual
ministrations of the house of Levi, and had endowed them with dues
for the proper maintenance of their ministry. He then prohibits them
from imitating the heathen, in having recourse to the arts of divination,
to witchcraft, and necromancy. The law that Moses had given them
would not require to be supplemented by any such aids, the offspring
of an unhallowed curiosity. The revelation already imparted would be
all-sufficient, until the first covenant should have waxen old and be
ready to vanish away. And then he adds, "For these nations which
"thou shalt possess, hearkened unto observers of times, and unto
"diviners, but as for thee the Lord thy God hath not suffered thee so
"*to do.* The Lord thy God will raise up unto thee a Prophet from the
"midst of thee, of thy brethren, like unto me; unto him shall ye hearken.
"According to all that thou desiredst of the Lord thy God in Horeb in
"the day of the assembly, saying, Let me not hear again the voice of
"the Lord my God, neither let me see this great fire any more, that I
"die not. And the Lord said unto me, They have well *spoken that
"which* they have spoken. I will raise them up a Prophet from among
"their brethren like unto thee, and I will put my words in his mouth,
"and he shall speak unto them all that I shall command him. And it
"shall come to pass that whosoever will not hearken unto my words
"which he shall speak in my name (בשמי), I will require *it* of him
"(אנכי אדרש מעמו)." We see, then, that the office of the New Mediator
was to stand between God and the people as Moses did, seeing God
face to face (Num. xii. 6—8), and to supplement the revelation already

given by such fresh discoveries of God's will as the Lord Jehovah should
" put into his mouth." Now, to whom can these words be applied
except to the Messiah of God, concerning whom the Almighty speaks
by the mouth of his prophet ! (Zech. xiii. 7.) גבר עמיתי, " the man that
" *is* my fellow." For the interpretation of this latter passage see
Kimchi's Commentary on Zechariah, translated by the late Dr. M'Caul,
pp. 169—177 —Philo (*Deterius potiori insdiatur*) seems to allude to the
promise of the Messiah in his Mediatorial capacity of interpreter of the
Divine will as predicted by Moses :—'Ἐκείνοις δ' ὥσπερ ἰατροῖς τὸ ὑγιάζον
τὰς ψυχῆς νόσους τε καὶ κῆρας ἀναδιδαχθεῖσι μέρος, ἐπέχειν ἀναγκαῖον,
μέχρις ἂν ὁ Θεὸς καὶ τὸν ἑρμηνέα ἄριστον κατασκευάσῃ, τὰς τοῦ λέγειν πηγὰς
ἀνομβρήσας, καὶ ἀναδείξας αὐτῷ. " It is a duty of necessity to give heed
" to those who, like physicians, are instructed in healing the maladies
" and misfortunes of the mind until God shall also have prepared the
" *best Interpreter*, having swelled high the fountains of utterance, and
" showed them to him." (Works, Mangey, tom. i., p. 200. See also
De Monarchia, lib. i., *ibid.*, tom. ii., pp. 221, 222, where Philo cites
Deut. xviii., and explains it in connexion with the prohibition to use
the occult sciences.)

² Καὶ αἵματι ῥαντισμοῦ κρείττονα λαλοῦντι παρὰ τὸν, or better, τὸ Ἄβελ.—
Wolfius observes on the reading παρὰ τὸν Ἄβελ, " Ita plerique codices.
" Alii habent παρὰ τὸ Ἄβελ. sed duo tantum, quos recitat Millius. Et
" sic quoque editiones Aldi, Frobenii, Colin. et Er. Schmidii. Eam
" lectionem, tanquam Græcis veteribus et Syro quoque receptam, præ-
" fert Grotius, ut scilicet eo rectius ad αἷμα referatur, quod B. Lutherus
" quoque in versione disserte expressit. Rectius vero communior lectio
" tenetur, quam etiam vindicat Jos. Hallett in Paraphrasi et Notis ad
" h.l. Ita supra xi. 4. *Abel adhuc* dicitur *loqui*." Now it is quite true that
in chap. xi. 4 Abel is said to speak, but he is said to do so figuratively
(see note 1 on pp. 175—179), δι' αὐτῆς ἀποθανὼν ἔτι λαλεῖται, *i.e.*, through
his faith which led to his martyrdom. And so Ewald explains xi. 4,
" *und durch ihn* den Glauben, wie noch einmal nachdrücklich hervorge-
" hoben wird, *redet er gestorben noch.*" So also Ewald renders the words
of xii. 24 in accordance with the reading τὸ ; " *und dem Besprengungs-
" blute das besseres redet als das Abel's.*" (See also note 1, p. 175, &c.)
Luther has " und zu dem Blut des Besprengung, das da besser redet, denn
" Abel's." The translators of the London Jews' Society's New Testament originally pointedly adopted the same reading; ואל דם הזאה המדבר
כיב כדם הבל. For my own part, I cannot help regarding τὸ as the correct
reading. Abel being dead, can only speak figuratively. He does so by
his faith, manifested by his bringing a vicarious sacrifice according to
the Divine will. He therefore speaks, not only by the blood of his
martyrdom, but also by the blood of his sacrifice, which latter obtained

testimony from God that it was acceptable and accepted. It was *then*, that God openly expressed his Divine selection of blood, to the exclusion of all other means of ransom, for the redemption of the soul. In the term "the blood of Abel," therefore, may be included the blood of all vicarious victims afterwards offered, in accordance with God's appointment, until the sacrifice of the death of Christ superseded them. The blood which Moses sprinkled (Exod. xxiv. 8) would be included under the same general designation, which would thus signify " blood vicariously shed, and presented as a sin-offering to God." It need scarcely be observed, that the blood of Jesus, the Mediator of the New Covenant, which testifies of forgiveness, speaks of better things than the blood of Abel's sacrifice, which declares that without shedding of blood there is no remission. But Abel himself is spoken of *as a martyr* by our Lord Himself (Matt. xxiii. 34, 35) :—" Wherefore, behold, I send " unto you prophets, and wise men, and scribes : and some of them ye " shall kill and crucify ; and some of them shall ye scourge in your " synagogues, and persecute them from city to city : that upon you may " come all the righteous blood shed upon the earth, from the blood of " righteous Abel unto the blood of Zacharias son of Barachias, whom ye " slew between the temple and the altar." Here, then, the blood of Abel as the protomartyr, is represented as crying for vengeance. (See note 1, p. 175.) As the Gospel according to St. Matthew was early in circulation amongst the converts from Judaism, they would be familiar with this prophetic declaration of Christ Himself, viz, that retribution for all their persecutions was at hand. The allusion, then, to the blood of Abel would form no unfitting complement to the κριτῇ Θεῷ πάντων of verse 23. (See note 1, p. 309.) The blood of Abel spoke of martyrdom and of retribution ; the blood of Jesus of forgiveness, of patient endurance, and of triumph. And this is the burden of the new song in heaven, Rev. v. 9, 10 :—Ἄξιος εἶ λαβεῖν τὸ βιβλίον, καὶ ἀνοῖξαι τὰς σφραγῖδας αὐτοῦ, ὅτι ἐσφάγης, καὶ ἠγόρασας τῷ Θεῷ ἡμᾶς ἐν τῷ αἵματί σου, ἐκ πάσης φυλῆς, καὶ γλώσσης, καὶ λαοῦ, καὶ ἔθνους. Καὶ ἐποίησας ἡμᾶς τῷ Θεῷ ἡμῶν βασιλεῖς καὶ ἱερεῖς· καὶ βασιλεύσομεν ἐπὶ τῆς γῆς.

Verse 25.—See that ye refuse not (βλέπετε μὴ παραιτήσησθε. See note 3, p. 294) Him that speaketh[1] (Videte ne recusetis loquentem. *Vulg.*) : for if they did not escape (ἔφυγον) who refused him that spake the Oracles of God on earth (τὸν ἐπὶ τῆς γῆς παραιτησάμενοι χρηματίζοντα),[2] much less shall we that turn away from Him that speaks to us from heaven (πολλῷ μᾶλλον ἡμεῖς οἱ τὸν ἀπ᾽ οὐρανῶν ἀποστρεφόμενοι).[3]

¹ Τὸν λαλοῦντα. Look to it that ye refuse not Him that is pleading with us by his blood, viz., Christ. By it He speaks to our gratitude. He sets before the eyes of our faith the better things (κρείττονα) assured to us in the New Testament. As though, by this voice of gentle intercession, He would say to the wavering Hebrew converts, "Will ye also "go away ?" (John vi. 67.) To this "Blood of the Covenant" the Writer has already alluded in chap. x. 29. Πόσῳ (δοκεῖτε) χείρονος ἀξιωθήσεται τιμωρίας ὁ τὸν υἱὸν τοῦ Θεοῦ καταπατήσας, καὶ τὸ αἷμα τῆς διαθήκης κοινὸν ἡγησάμενος ἐν ᾧ ἡγιάσθη, καὶ τὸ πνεῦμα τῆς χάριτος ἐνυβρίσας; Ewald defends the reading, παρὰ τὸ Ἄβελ, in verse 24, in these words :—" V. 24, ist für τὸν umso richtiger τὸ zu lesen (obgleich "auch Sin. jenes hat), da der Leser dann desto weniger in Gefahr "kommt das folgende τὸν λαλοῦντα v. 25 misszuverstehen." The London Jews' Society's New Testament renders the words thus :—ראו לבל תמאסו במדבר, in the earlier edition.

² Εἰ γὰρ ἐκεῖνοι οὐκ ἔφυγον τὸν ἐπὶ τῆς γῆς παραιτησάμενοι χρηματίζοντα. The Vulgate rendering of these words coincides with that of the authorized Angl. Version, *Si enim illi non effugerunt, recusantes eum qui super terram loquebatur:* "For if they escaped not who refused Him "that spake on earth." Luther has, "Denn so Jene nicht entflohen "sind, die sich weigerten, da er auf Erden redete." The London Jews' Society's Hebrew New Testament has, כי אם לא נמלטו אלה המאסים בארץ במדבר. Alford, though he translates, "For if they did not escape, "declining as they did Him who spake on earth," yet adopts the reading, οὐκ ἐξέφυγον ἐπὶ γῆς παραιτησάμενοι τὸν χρηματίζοντα, and excuses his translation by saying, "The construction is a trajection not "unusual with our Writer : cf. ch. ix. 15, 16, and ver. 11." Ewald (*Das Sendschr. a.d. Hebr.*, pp. 47, 48) adopts this reading; but, with a keener perception of what it implies, translates, "Den wenn Jene auf "Erden nicht entrannen nachdem sie den Gottesworte Redenden sich "verbaten." And again (*ibid.*, p. 145), "*Denn wenn Jene auf Erden,* "*noch mitten im Erdenleben, nicht entflohen.*" And again, pp. 173, 174, "xii. 25, haben die besten Handschriften das τὸν, ganz richtig, "vor χρηματίζοντα: allein desto mehr, muss man ἐπὶ γῆς, von der "irdischen Strafe verstehen welche jene Ungehorsamen, nach Num. "c. xvi. f., erreichte, und unter τὸν ἀπ' οὐρανῶν, nur den vom Himmel "kommenden jüngsten Richter verstehen." To my mind, the old reading, τὸν ἐπὶ τῆς γῆς παραιτ. κ.τ.λ., is the preferable one, although there cannot be two opinions as to whether Ewald or Alford renders οὐκ ἐξέφυγον ἐπὶ τῆς γῆς παραιτησάμενοι in the more scholarly manner. And now, let us inquire who is the speaker designated by τὸν χρηματίζοντα. The answer is supplied by verse 19. It was the voice of Jehovah

which the Israelites declined to hear; ἧς οἱ ἀκούσαντες παρῃτήσαντο μὴ προστεθῆναι αὐτοῖς λόγον. The suggestion of Chrysostom, followed by Carpzov, that it was Moses, is contrary to the context, and inadmissible.

Under τὸν χρηματίζοντα, the same personage is spoken of as the τὸν ἀπ' οὐρανῶν of the next clause. Ewald rightly identifies the latter with Him who shall be Judge of all things, *i.e.*, our Lord Jesus Christ; although the context demonstrates that no *immediate* allusion is here intended to "Judgment to come." The βλέπετε μὴ παραιτήσησθε τὸν λαλοῦντα points to a present, and not to a future speaker. Jesus at *present* speaks in tones of mercy, by his blood. The quotation from Haggai ii. 6, contained in verses 26, 27, primarily refers to the first coming of Christ, as the seventh verse, which immediately follows the quotation, proves: "For thus saith the Lord of Hosts, Yet once, it is a little while, and I will "shake the heavens, and the earth, and the sea, and the dry *land*. And "I will shake all nations, and the Desire of all nations shall come, and "I will fill this house with glory, saith the Lord of Hosts." He then (ὁ ἀπ' οὐρανῶν) that speaks at present, is Jesus in his Mediatorial capacity, διαθήκης νέας μεσίτης, to whom the Writer reminds his readers they have come. The Second Person in the Ever Blessed Trinity also it was who spake at Sinai; the SHECHINAH; the מלאך פניו, *the Angel of his Presence* of Is. lxiii. 9; מלאך הברית of Mal. iii. 1, and Exod. xxiii. 20 —23; "The angel" of Eccles. v. 6 (5); the archangel Michael (מיכאל *Who is as God*), concerning whom the Targum of Palestine (Exod. xxiv. 1) says, "And Michael, the Prince of Wisdom, said unto Moses " ....Come up before the Lord."—The Shemoth Rabba, the Sohar, R. Moses bar Nachman, Rabbi Bechai, all assert that wherever Michael is mentioned there the Shechinah is intended to be expressed. (See J. A. Danzii, *Schechina cum piis cohabitans*, pp. 733, 734. Meuschen.) This is that ANGEL whom St. Stephen speaks of in reference to Moses (Acts vii. 38), "This is he (Moses) that was in the Church in the "wilderness with THE ANGEL which spake unto him in the Mount Sina." Most astounding, therefore, is the explanation of τὸν χρηματίζοντα offered by Dean Alford *in loco*:—"It must be laid down as certain that "ὁ ἐπὶ γῆς χρηματίζων is God. Then if so, who is ὁ ἀπ' οὐρανῶν;. or, in "other words, who is ὁ λαλῶν, for these are manifestly the same? "Clearly not Jesus (!), for by οὗ ἡ φωνή, which follows, the voice of this "same speaker shook the earth at the giving of the law: and it can by "no ingenuity be pretended that the terrors of the law proceeded from "the Son of God; especially in the face of the contrast drawn here, "and in ch. ii. 2 ff." Surely the Dean overlooks the consequence of his own application of Hagg. ii. 6, as here quoted, to the last dread Judgment scene. I do not admit the suitability of the interpretation; but, on the Dean's own showing, the *far greater* "terrors" of the Day of Judgment must "proceed from the Son of God." Even Dean Alford would hardly be expected to deny that it is Jesus Christ who shall "come again to judge the quick and the dead"; and yet, wonderful to relate, the Dean does, by implication, deny this cardinal doctrine of Christianity :—" And it would be against all accuracy and decorum in " Divine things, to pass from the speaking of the God of Israel to that " of our Lord Jesus Christ, in the way of climax, as is here done, with " πολὺ μᾶλλον, 'much more shall not we escape.' Add to which, that if " Christ is to be understood as the subject of verses 26 ff., we shall " have Him uttering the prophetic words, ἔτι ἅπαξ κ.τ.λ., whereas, both " from our Writer's habit (!) of quoting prophecy [cf. ch. i. 1, iv. 7, " vi. 13, viii. 8, xi. 11], and from the context of the prophecy itself, " they must be attributed to the Father. How, then, are these diffi- " culties to be got over ? Simply by taking, as above, the speaker, in " both cases, to be God. In the first, as appealing from Mount Sinai " by his angels (!) ; in the second, as speaking from his heavenly throne, " through his exalted Son." A more miserable jumble of criticism than the above can hardly be imagined. Dr. Alford first says ὁ λαλῶν (τὸν λαλοῦντα), who must be Jesus (comp. verse 24), is the same as ὁ ἐπὶ γῆς χρηματίζων, and yet he immediately sets to work to disprove that which, by the declaration of Scripture, and the traditional consent of both Jews and Christians, is an undoubted fact. And yet, on Acts vii. 38, οὗτός ἐστιν ὁ γενόμενος ἐν τῇ ἐκκλησίᾳ ἐν τῇ ἐρήμῳ, μετὰ τοῦ ἀγγέλου τοῦ λαλοῦντος αὐτῷ ἐν τῷ ὄρει Σινᾶ, καὶ τῶν πατέρων ἡμῶν, ὃς ἐδέξατο λόγια ζῶντα, δοῦναι ἡμῖν, the Dean says :—" That Moses conversed with both " the Angel of the Covenant and our fathers, implies that he was the " *mediator between them;* as, indeed, ὃς ἐδέξατ. λογ. ζ. more plainly " declares." Either the Dean, writing on the Acts, was of a different mind to the Dean writing on the Hebrews, or else he ignored, or was unacquainted with the fact that the ANGEL OF THE COVENANT is the same as the SHECHINAH, the Second Person in the Ever Blessed Trinity. The above miserable blundering prepares us for the following statement, if possible, more unhappy than the foregoing :—" Thus it is true we lie " open to one objection, viz., that the giving of the Law is ever regarded " in the Old Testament as a speaking from heaven. So Exod. xx. 22, " ὑμεῖς ἑωράκατε, ὅτι ἐκ τοῦ οὐρανοῦ λελάληκα ὑμῖν : cf. Deut. iv. 36 ; Neh. " ix. 13. But this objection, though at first sight weighty, is by no " means decisive. The οὐρανός spoken of is surely nothing but the " material heaven, as apparent to the Israelites in the clouds and dark- " ness which rested on Sinai, and totally distinct from the οὐρανός here, " the site of our Lord's glorification, who is spoken of, ch. iv. 14, as "διεληλυθώς τοὺς οὐρανούς." It is to be regretted that the author of the "*Queen's English*" has omitted to explain how "*the material heaven*" could be "*apparent to the Israelites in the clouds and darkness which rested on Sinai*"! But if the Dean had adopted the advice which he gives to his readers, viz., to refer to Deut. iv. 36, he might have spared himself the trouble of writing such childish nonsense as he has done. There it is written, "Out of heaven he made thee to hear his voice "(Exod. xix. 16—18), that He might instruct thee: and upon earth He "shewed thee his great fire (*ibid.*, 18): and thou heardest his words "(Exod. xx. 2) out of the midst of the fire." (Deut. iv. 12.—See also my note on φωνῇ ῥημάτων, verse 19 of this 12th chapter.) Here we see that "the voice" like a trumpet, which the Israelites heard *from heaven*, was different from, and preceded the "voice of words," or *articulate enunciation*, which they heard *out of the fire*. For some further patent instances of the Dean's habitual carelessness in dealing with the facts of the Holy Scriptures, see the Rev. Josiah Forshall's preface to his edition of the *Gospel according to St. Mark*, Longmans, London, 1862, 8vo. Respecting the personality of the ANGEL OF THE COVENANT, see note 1, pp. 128—130, of this Commentary.

³ Ἡμεῖς οἱ τὸν ἀπ' οὐρανῶν ἀποστρεφόμενοι. These words, *taken apart from the context*, might rightly be translated, *We who turn ourselves away from Him who is from the heavens*.—In this case Dean Alford is right in his rendering:—"We who are turning away from Him (who "χρηματίζει) from (the) heavens." There is no antithesis intended here between Moses who was a mortal man, and Jesus who is Divine; nor yet between Moses speaking on earth, and the voice of God the Son, which, *at the last day*, shall be heard from heaven. The antithesis is between the blood of Abel, which now speaks of martyrdom, and cries for vengeance, and the blood of Jesus, which now speaks of reconciliation and of triumph. This, Jesus at present does ἀπ' οὐρανῶν, where, in accordance with the prophetic invitation of Ps. cx. 1, He sits at God's right hand expecting, until his enemies be made his footstool. Moses' commission, as coming to him directly from God, who spake to him face to face, was unequivocally ἀπ' οὐρανῶν. He spake no words of his own, but the very words of Jehovah himself. The Writer sets the legal enactments of the Divine law, delivered *on Sinai* (ἐπὶ γῆς) in terrible pomp, and with uncompromising rigour, over against the gentle pleadings of Christ *from heaven*. The blood of vicarious sacrifice, similar to that of Abel (see note 1, pp. 175—179), offered only a parabolic expiation for transgressions against the Mosaic Code. The blood of Jesus offers a sovereign, and perfect, and ever fresh atonement for all sin. If he was accounted guilty who sinned against the Dispensation of threatening, much more

is he deserving of punishment who, knowing the efficacy of Christ's blood, and at how dear a price our redemption was purchased, yet refuses to listen to the Diviner persuasives of Almighty love. Stuart rightly says, "that χρηματίζοντα is implied after τὸν, results from com-"mon grammatical usage." He would have said what was more to the purpose if he had said that it was *demanded* by the context.—The silly habit of taking it for granted that, because two texts have something *common in sound* (*e.g.*, the passage under consideration compared with John iii. 13, 31; vi. 38, &c.), they are therefore *identical in application*, has led to many grievous misinterpretations of the Word of God. The safest key to the unlocking of any Scriptural enigma is to be found in the *where*, the *when*, and the *to whom*; in other words, in the IMMEDIATE CONTEXT. Until these preliminary and indispensable helps have been used, we have no right to run up and down in search of what are popularly supposed to be "parallel passages." In this passage I venture to differ respectfully from so great an authority as Ewald, where he writes (p. 145):—"*Wieviel mehr* werden wir der gerechten Strafe nicht "entfliehen, *wir* Christen *die* wir also wenn wir ihm zu folgen uns "weigern den *vom Himmel* zum allgemeinen Weltgerichte kommenden "meiden (O welche Thorheit von dem sich abkehren zu wollen!), ihn "*dessen Stimme damals* bei der Stiftung des A. B.'s *die Erde erschüt-* "*terte*, der *aber jetzt verheissen hat*, durch den viel späteren Propheten "Hagg. ii. 6, *noch Einmahl werde ich nicht nur die Erde erschüttern* "*sondern auch den Himmel*." The passage of Haggai, just quoted, refers unquestionably to the first coming of Christ; and the *spiritual shaking* spoken of by the prophet was to be preliminary to, and synchronous with, the second temple, and the establishment of the Gospel dispensation. The Vulgate translates rightly, *qui de coelis loquentem avertimus*. So also Luther has "der vom Himmel redet." Wolfius, usually so sagaciously accurate in his renderings, writes *in loco*:—"Τὸν ἀπ' οὐρανῶν, scilicet *loquentem*, quod B. Lutherus in ver-"sione expressit, et Jo. Buxtorfius, nepos, in Dissertationibus varii "argumenti p. 101, subintelligi vult. Aeque bene vero subintellexeris "τὸν ἐρχόμενον, quem se appellat Dominus ipse John iii. 31, ὁ ἐκ τοῦ "οὐρανοῦ ἐρχόμενος, ἐπάνω πάντων ἐστί. Sic 1 Cor. xv. 47, ὁ κύριος ἐξ "οὐρανοῦ vocatur." The alternative reading, so readily offered here by Wolfius, affords an apt illustration of the danger of taking for granted the *coincidence* of passages of Scripture, because they happen to have a correspondence, more or less remote, in sound or in doctrinal application.

Verses 26—29.—Whose voice shook[1] the earth THEN (τότε, *at that time*, i.e., at the giving of the law on

Sinai).—But NOW (νῦν δὲ, *i.e.*, at the present crisis of transition, when the Ceremonial Law and the Jewish Polity are passing away, and there is a mighty shaking of the Gentile nations and their systems of religious belief,—) He has promised (Hagg. ii. 6), saying,[2] Yet once (ἔτι ἅπαξ, עוֹד אַחַת, *adhuc semel*, Vulg., *i.e.*, strictly *once*, and no more) I will shake (ἐγὼ emphat, וַאֲנִי, *i.e.*, Jehovah Himself, the ὁ λαλῶν of verse 25) not only the earth, but the heavens also. But the expression YET ONCE (τὸ δὲ, ἔτι ἅπαξ) indicates the setting aside (τὴν μετάθεσιν) of the things shaken (*i.e.*, the Levitic covenant and ritual, with its paraphernalia of symbolism, and its material pomp) as being made (ὡς πεποιημένων; compare ix. 11. Χριστὸς δὲ παραγενόμενος ἀρχιερεὺς τῶν μελλόντων ἀγαθῶν, διὰ τῆς μείζονος καὶ τελειοτέρας σκηνῆς οὐ χειροποιήτου, τουτέστιν, οὐ ταύτης τῆς κτίσεως; and again, verse 24, οὐ γὰρ εἰς χειροποίητα ἅγια εἰσῆλθεν ὁ Χριστὸς, ἀντίτυπα τῶν ἀληθινῶν) in order that the things which are not shaken may remain. Wherefore, (inasmuch as He has said YET ONCE) inasmuch as we are put in possession of (παραλαμβάνοντες) a kingdom (See Exod. xix. 6, "Ye shall be unto me a kingdom of priests"), which is unshakeable (*immobile*, Vulg., *i.e.*, the Gospel kingdom which we receive, shall endure until Christ's final Advent to Judgment. The present order of things shall not be disturbed until the end of the world), let us hold fast (the) grace (ἔχωμεν χάριν, *Gnade festhalten*, Ewald) by which we may serve God acceptably, with reverence and pious submission (μετὰ αἰδοῦς καὶ εὐλαβείας). For our God is a consuming fire. (Deut. iv. 24.)

---

[1] Τὴν γῆν ἐσάλευσε. Exod. xix. 18; וַיֶּחֱרַד כָּל הָהָר מְאֹד, "and the whole mount quaked greatly."—Ps. lxviii. 8; lxxvii. 18; cxiv. 7.

[2] Ἔτι ἅπαξ ἐγὼ σείω (וַאֲנִי מַרְעִישׁ) οὐ μόνον τὴν γῆν, ἀλλὰ καὶ τὸν οὐρανόν. We have here another example of the Writer's custom of quoting the leading words of a passage of Scripture and trusting to the memory of his readers to carry on the quotation. Any one acquainted with the

Talmudical writings will know how strictly this is in accordance with Jewish usage. The entire passage (Hagg. ii. 6, 7) reads thus in the Hebrew:— כי כה אמר יהוה צבאות עוד אחת מעט היא ואני מרעיש את השמים ואת הארץ ואת הים ואת החרבה : והרעשתי את כל הגוים ובאו חמדת כל הגוים ומלאתי את הבית הזה כבוד אמר יהוה צבאות —Διότι τάδε λέγει Κύριος παντοκράτωρ, ἔτι ἅπαξ ἐγὼ σείσω τὸν οὐρανὸν καὶ τὴν γῆν καὶ τὴν θάλασσαν καὶ τὴν ξηράν. Καὶ συσσείσω πάντα τὰ ἔθνη, καὶ ἥξει τὰ ἐκλεκτὰ πάντων τῶν ἐθνῶν· καὶ πλήσω τὸν οἶκον τοῦτον δόξης, λέγει Κύριος παντοκράτωρ. LXX.—" Quia " hæc dicit Dominus exercituum : Adhuc unum modicum est, et com- " movebo coelum, et terram, et mare, et aridam. Et movebo omnes " Gentes : et veniet DESIDERATUS cunctis Gentibus : et implebo domum " istam gloria, dicit Dominus," *Vulg.*—" Denn so spricht der Herr " Zebaoth : Es ist noch ein Kleines dahin, das ich Himmel und Erde, " und das Meer und Trockene bewegen werde. Ja alle Heiden will " ich bewegen. Da soll dann Kommen aller Heiden Trost : und ich " will dies Haus voll Herrlichkeit machen, spricht der Herr Zebaoth," *Luther.*—" For thus saith the Lord of hosts, Yet once, it *is* a little " while, and I will shake the heavens and the earth, and the sea, and " the dry *land.* And I will shake all nations, and the Desire of all " nations shall come : and I will fill this house with glory, saith the " Lord of hosts," *Authorised Vers.*—From the above it will be plain that the prophecy was spoken, not in reference to the coming of Christ to judgment, but in reference to his first advent, also predicted by Malachi iii. 1. This is made more evident still, by the verses that follow : " The silver *is* mine, and the gold *is* mine, saith the Lord of hosts. The " glory of this latter house shall be greater than of the former, saith " the Lord of hosts, and in this place will I give peace, saith the Lord " of hosts." The verb רעש in the Kal, signifies *to quake,* or *to tremble,* and in the Hiphil, *to make to shake.* In the above passage of Haggai is denoted, therefore, not only the abrogation of the Mosaic covenant and the Jewish polity, but also the shaking down of the long-cherished systems of Gentile idolatry and philosophy at the coming of Christ and by the preaching of Christianity. And in this sense only can it be used by the Writer to the Hebrews. He reminds his readers that they have seen the prophecy fulfilled, that the figurative declaration that God would shake the heavens, as well as the earth, has come to pass in the decay of the Mosaic system, which is ἐγγὺς ἀφανισμοῦ, *i.e.,* " ready to vanish away." He reminds them, further, that no similar "shaking" is to occur again. God promised that He would again, ONCE only, shake " the heavens," but by implication the religious system introduced at that shaking, would endure for ever, ἵνα μείνῃ τὰ μὴ σαλευόμενα. To them, therefore, had been fulfilled the promise made to the fathers in Exod. xix. 6. They had been put in possession of the "kingdom that cannot be shaken." How ungrateful, therefore, and how foolish would it be to follow the example of those who had already apostatised, οἱ τὸν ἀπ' οὐρανῶν ἀποστρεφόμενοι. We see, therefore, that the words of verses 25—29 still move, so to speak, in the Sinaitic atmosphere. They are words of reassurance. They are also words of warning. Fitly, therefore, does the Writer conclude his exhortation with the admonition to hold fast the grace—the promised gift of God—by which alone they can serve Him acceptably, μετὰ αἰδοῦς καὶ εὐλαβείας. Even the closing words of the chapter, Καὶ γὰρ ὁ Θεὸς ἡμῶν πῦρ καταναλίσκων, contains an allusion to Exod. xxiv. 17, "And the sight of the "glory of the Lord was like devouring fire (כאש אכלה) on the top of the "mount, in the eyes of the children of Israel." Compare also Heb. x. 27 with Mal. iv. 1—3, where it is predicted that the fires of the Day of Doom shall devour the adversaries, or wicked. "But unto you that "fear my name, shall the Sun of Righteousness arise.. ...And ye shall "tread down the wicked ; for they shall be ashes under the soles of "your feet in the day that I shall do *this*, saith the Lord of hosts." See also Zech. ii. 4, 5 (in the Heb. iii. 8, 9), "Jerusalem shall be "inhabited as towns without walls, for the multitude of men and cattle "therein. For I, saith the Lord, will be unto her a wall of fire round "about, and will be the glory in the midst of her" (חומת אש סביב לכבור אהיה בתוכה). The rendering which I have given of ἔτι ἅπαξ, עוד אחת, is confirmed by the testimony of the venerable book of Sohar (*Sohar Genes.*, fol. 34, col. 133), where it is said, "Wherefore the temple which "is built in this mountain by the hands of the HOLY ONE, BLESSED BE "HE, shall be established throughout all generations, as it is said in "Hagg. ii. 9, *The glory of this latter house shall be greater than of the "former.*" (Schoettg., tom. ii., p. 389. See also *ibid.*, pp. 75, 90, 113, 217, 494, 500, 964.) On p. 217 Schoettgen writes :—"Hagg. ii. 6, "*Adhuc parum est et commovebo coelum et terram.* Debarim Rabba, "sect. 1, folio 250, 1, *Loquitur de redemptione quæ ventura est Israelitis.* "*Quando?* Resp. *Eo tempore, quo Propheta dicit :* Adhuc parum est— "Raschi ad Sanhedrin, fol. 97, 2. R. Akiba (qui hæc verba, sed sine "expositione, adduxerat), *ea intelligit de Messia.*" And again, *ibid.*, 113, "Tikkune Sohar., c. 8, *Eo vero tempore, quo Deus S.B. templum ædificat,* "*sicut antea, q.d.* Psalm. cxlvii. 2 : Aedificans Jerusalem Dominus : "*illo, inquam tempore* (Esa. xxiv. 23) pudore suffundetur Sol, et pudefiet "Luna. *Quando vero id fiet ?* Resp. *Quando Rex erit Dominus Zebaoth* "(l.c. Jesaiæ) *Aedificium enim prius factum est per manus hominum,* "*propterea homines in illo potentiam suam exercere potuerunt :* Nisi "Dominus ædificaverit domum, frustra laborant, qui ædificant eam.

"*Porro quia ædificium posterius per manum Dei S.B. erectum est,* יהקים, "*firmum erit ; et propterea Scriptura dicit,* Hagg. ii. 9, Major erit gloria "templi hujus posterius, quam prioris. *In illo vero tempore, quo ædifi-* "*cium per manus Dei S.B. ædificabitur, superius et inferius, de Shechina* "*superiore et inferiore illud implebitur, quod scriptum est* Esa. xxx. 26. "Et erit splendor Lunae sicut splendor Solis ; *item* c. xxiv. 23. Et "pudore suffundetur Sol, et pudefiet Luna." It will be seen, on reference to pp. 6, 7 of Schoettgen (*ibid.*), and also to Danzius' treatise *Schechina cum piis cohabitans,* printed at length in Meuschen, that the name *Shechinah* was regarded by the most ancient Jewish authorities as an attribute of the Messiah. Schoettgen also observes, p. 964, *ibid.*, that Raschi explains "yet once, it is a little while, and I will shake "the heavens and the earth," by "*Messiah shall come.*" This is the interpretation also given by Rabbi Akiba, who flourished, as Dr. Henderson (*The book of the twelve* Minor Prophets, p. 355) remarks, before the time of Jerome. R. Akiba's exposition is found in the chapter entitled הלק of the treatise *Sanhedrin* of the Babyl. Gemara. כיצ מלכות אתן להם לישראל לאחר חרבן ולאחר אותו מלכות הנני מרעיש שמים וארץ ויבא משיח. "For a "little I will give the kingdom to Israel, after our desolation ; and after "the kingdom, behold, I will shake heaven and earth, and Messiah shall "come."—See also *Carminis R. Lipmanni Confutatio,* p. 619, in Wagenseil's *Tela ignea Satanæ.* R. Isaac, in the *Chizzuk Emunah,* pp. 289 — 291, unhesitatingly applies the words of Haggai to the Messiah, although he asserts that they do not refer to the second temple but to a later period, "after the destruction of the fourth chariot." He adds, "these "things are spoken, without doubt, of the expected Messiah, על המשיח "המקוה, who will be of the seed of Zerubbabel." It is easy, therefore, to discover whence the interpretation of the words ובאו חמדה כל הגוים, *and the* DESIRE OF ALL NATIONS *shall come,* proceeded. In spite of the Bishop of St. David's recent insinuation that it is a Christian gloss which misinterprets the passage, we see that it was the rendering of the ancient Jewish Doctors.

This same interpretation is given by the Vulgate :—"Et veniet "Desideratus cunctis gentibus." By Leo Juda :—"Et veniet qui "desideratur ab omnibus gentibus." By Dathe :—"Et deinde veniet "gentibus omnibus expetendus." And by Luther :—"Da soll dann "kommen aller Heiden Trost."—The LXX. has καὶ ἥξει τὰ ἐκλεκτὰ πάντων τῶν ἐθνῶν; but Augustine (*De Civit. Dei,* 18, 48) rightly observes that the LXX. gives the sense of the Hebrew :—"Tunc enim veniet "Desideratus cunctis gentibus, *sicut legitur in Hebræo*......Tunc etiam, "secundum Septuaginta interpretes (quia et ipse propheticus sensus est), "venient quæ electa sunt Domini de cunctis gentibus." Jerome, in his letter to Paulinus about the various books of the Old and New Testaments, uses the same words :—"Et veniet Desideratus cunctis gentibus"; and, in his Commentary on Haggai, "Hæc adhuc semel movebo : quod "factum cernimus in adventu Domini Salvatoris." To my own mind, the LXX. translates the Hebrew noun of multitude המדה as closely as the difficulty of finding an exact equivalent would permit. Τὰ ἐκλεκτὰ might be fairly rendered, having reference to the Hebrew word which it represents, *the dearest aspirations.* It is plain that the LXX. translators regarded המדה as a noun of multitude, and rendered it accordingly, by the nearest Greek equivalent. *The question is not one of grammatical construction, but of interpretation.* The ancient Jewish and Christian Doctors understood the words to apply to the Messiah. There is no reason whatever, therefore, why (upon the dictum of even a more accomplished theologian than the Bishop of St. David's) we should, in order to conciliate Jewish or Gentile objectors to the Christology of our Anglican Version, alter so reasonable and venerable a rendering as the DESIRE OF ALL NATIONS. Surenhusius (βίβλ. καταλλ., pp. 660—663) has some erudite observations on the subject of the quotation from Hagg. ii. 6, contained in Heb. xii. 26, 27.

CHAPTER XIII.

THE Writer having now concluded his commonitory and consolatory dissuasive from apostacy, which is contained in chaps. x. 19—39, xi., xii., proceeds to address some exhortations of a more personal nature to the Hebrew converts. He displays not only an acquaintance with their requirements from a controversial point of view, but a more familiar knowledge of the special circumstances of the particular community to which he is writing. He speaks as a friend to friends. He solicits their intercessions on his own behalf (verse 18). He hopes soon to see them again (verse 19). He prays that God would make them perfect in every good work (verses 20, 21). With all the delicate courtliness and urbanity that were such distinguishing attributes of St. Paul's letters, he craves their indulgence for having addressed this word of exhortation to them, but which, considering the magnitude and importance of the subject, he had condensed into as brief a space as possible (verse 22). He speaks of Timothy in the familiar and endearing character of a mutual friend and brother (verse 23). He sends greetings to all their spiritual rulers, and to all the saints, adding a kindly message of friendly good wishes from their Italian fellow-believers (verse 24). And then, with the eloquent conciseness of a tried and venerated friend, who was sure of his ground, and felt persuaded that his Epistle would meet with no halting welcome, he adds, by way of postscript, Ἡ χάρις μετὰ πάντων ὑμῶν. Ἀμήν.—How completely is the futile nonsense dissipated, by a perusal of this 13th chapter, of those who assert that the Writer purposely concealed his name from those whom he addressed, lest perchance it should give offence, or awaken a preliminary prejudice in the minds of the readers! The readers and the Writer perfectly understood each other. There could be no concealment in the matter. Circumstances are alluded to which were fresh in their mutual recollections. Doubtless, the original draft of the Epistle was endorsed with the name of the author, (who, I cannot doubt, was St. Paul,) or else the bearer was commissioned to announce its authorship immediately upon its delivery. I have already explained (p. 4) why it was that the Writer omitted the usual statement of his Apostleship at the commencement of his Epistle. To a *Gentile* Church it was *everything* to be assured that any letter addressed to it was the genuine production of an Apostle of the Lord Jesus Christ. Not so in the present case. The personal claims of Jesus of Nazareth to be the Divine Messiah, *i.e.*, the Christ of God, had to be re-asserted and re-established. Until this had been done, the statement of his Apostleship by the Writer would have been worse than valueless. The question at issue was not, *Is Paul to be considered as a genuine Apostle of Christ?* but simply this, *Had Jesus, who claimed to be the* Christ *or* Messiah, *any right to commission Apostles at all?* But that the Writer and his readers were well known to, and perfectly understood each other, does not admit of the shadow of a doubt. No man, unless he were an imbecile, would flatter himself that he could write a letter containing allusions and messages, such as those contained in this 13th chapter of the Epistle to the Hebrews, and yet that his readers would be contented to remain in the dark as to who wrote it. But this chapter sets the pretended intentional concealment of the author's name entirely at rest. The marvel is that any one, even in pursuit of some favourite theory, should have ever ventured to propound a statement so inconceivably silly.

Verses 1, 2.—Let brotherly love continue.[1] Be not forgetful of hospitality, for by it some have entertained angels unawares.[2]

¹ Ἡ φιλαδελφία μενέτω. Ewald translates, with forcible felicity, "Die Bruderliebe bleibe, der Gastfreundschaft vergesset nicht! Hatten "doch Einige durch diese, ohne es zu ahnen, Engel zu Gästen." Luther has, "Bleibet fest in der brüderlichen Liebe. Gastfrei zu sein vergesset "nicht; denn durch dasselbe haben Etliche, ohne ihr Wissen, Engel "beherberget." The Vulgate has, "Charitas fraternitatis maneat in "vobis. Et hospitalitatem nolite oblivisci, per hanc enim latuerunt "quidam, Angelis hospitio receptis." The London Jews' Society's New Testament has, אהבת האחים העמוד: את הכנסת הארחים אל תשכחו כי על ידי זאת אחדים בהעלם כהם אספו מלאכים. A distinguishing attribute of the Jewish nation has always been brotherly love, as manifested in a substantial shape towards their poorer brethren. The Rabbinical term for almsgiving is *Righteousness*. Buxtorf writes in his Chald. and Rabb. Lex., col. 1891, 1892, "צדקה, *Eleemosyna*, Rab. מלח ממון צדקה, *Sal* "*divitiarum est eleemosyna*. Hac si divitiæ salitæ sint, constantes "permanent, ut caro sale conservatur a corruptione: גדולה צדקה שמקרבת "גאולה, *Tam magna est eleemosyna, ut appropinquet redemptionem*. Hoc "si verum est, sequitur paucas eleemosynas jam mille sexcentis annis "Judæos dedisse: גדול העושה צדקה בסתר יתר ממשה רבינו, *Major est dans* "*eleemosynam in occulto, Mose doctore nostro*. Vide de necessitate, "utilitate, et præstantia Eleemosynæ, R. Bechai in *Cad Hakkemach*, "in literâ *Tzade*, et Majemon. in lib. *Jad*, par. 3, in הלכות מתנות עניים, "*Sepher Musar*, cap. 1. In Chagiga, fol. 5, 2, *legitur de R. Jannæo*, "*quod cum vidisset quendam eleemosynam dantem pauperi* בפרהסיא *publice*, "*dixerit ei*, כובב ולא יהבה ליה, *Satius fuisset tibi, ut nihil dedidisses ei.* "Convenit id aliquo modo cum doctrina Christi, Matt. vi. In Targum "אין לא יעביר מנהון צדקתא Nisi fecerit ex illis eleemosynam, Eccl. v. 9, 18, "et vii. 13, et ix. 10; Esth. ix. 22."—Φιλαδελφία in the present instance, I take it, signifies the loving offices of charity and brotherly kindness, as exhibited towards those of the same household of faith, and extending also to the indigent even of the unbelieving Jewish community, who might stand in need of relief. In those hard times, benevolence was apt to grow chill, and the fountains of compassion to be dried up. A real Christian Hebrew convert would never forget his nationality, but ought to be ready to assist even an unbelieving kinsman, did he stand in need of help. Φιλαδελφία would, therefore, somewhat differ from that φιλανθρωπία of which the Old Testament is so full, and concerning which Philo writes (*De Humanitate*, περὶ φιλανθρωπίας) in so admirable a strain, tom. ii., pp. 383–405. Consult also Josephus against Apion, lib. ii. 30. Ewald (*Das Sendschr. a.d. Hebr.*, p. 146) thus explains the expression φιλαδελφία:—"Die thätige Bruderliebe, "auch in Beziehung auf die Fremden, und das allgemeine Mitleid mit "allen Leidenden; und so heist est *die Bruderliebe*, die urchristliche

"Regung des Geistes gegen die Mitchristen," &c. Dr. Gill, *in loc.*, quotes the following from the Jerusalem Gemara, *Berachoth*, fol. 3, 3: —" He that dwells in this house, let him plant among you אהוה ואהבה, " brotherhood, and love (or brotherly love), peace and friendship."

² Τῆς φιλοξενίας μὴ ἐπιλανθάνεσθε. From brotherly love the Writer passes on to hospitality, or the entertaining of strangers. This latter manifestation of Christian courtesy and benevolence would not be unattended with danger, in those troublous days. To entertain a stranger might be equivalent to entertaining a spy. With graceful tact, therefore, the Writer reminds his readers that, in olden time, "thereby " some have entertained angels unawares," διὰ ταύτης γὰρ ἔλαθόν τινες ξενίσαντες ἀγγέλους. Gen. xviii., xix.; Judges xiii. 15. Dr. Gill writes, *in loco*, " It is an observation of a Jewish writer (R. Abraham Seba, in " *Tzror Hammor*, fol. 18, 4), ' From hence we learn how great is the " 'strength (or virtue) of the reception of travellers (or hospitality). " ' As the Rabbins of blessed memory say, *Greater is* (הכנסת אורחים) " ' *hospitali'y than the reception of the face of the Shekinah.*' And this is " said (T. Bab. *Sabbat.*, fol. 127, 1) to be one of the six things which a " man enjoys the fruit of in this world, and for which there remains a " reward in the world to come." Philo's remarks, which are too long for transcription, but will well repay perusal, are to be found in his treatise *De Abrahamo*, Works, *Mangey's Edit.*, tom. ii., pp. 16—18. I will content myself with the following extract, *ibid.*, pp. 17, 18:—
'Ἐγὼ δὲ οὐκ οἶδα τίνα ὑπερβολὴν εὐδαιμονίας καὶ μακαριότητος εἶναι φῶ περὶ τὴν οἰκίαν, ἐν ᾗ καταχθῆναι καὶ ξενίων λαχεῖν ὑπέμειναν ἄγγελοι πρὸς ἀνθρώπους, ἱεραὶ καὶ θεῖαι φύσεις, ὑποδιάκονοι καὶ ὕπαρχοι τοῦ πρώτου Θεοῦ, δι' ὧν, οἷα πρεσβευτῶν, ὅσα ἂν θελήσῃ τῷ γένει ἡμῶν προθεσπίσαι, διαγγέλλει. " I am quite unable to say what could be wanting in felicity and " blessedness to a house in which angels suffered themselves to be intro-" duced amongst men, and to partake of hospitality, holy and godlike " natures that they are, the ministers and lieutenants of the Most High " God, by whom, as it were, sending an embassage, He announces " whatsoever things He wishes to acquaint our race with, before they " come to pass."

Verses 3, 4.—Remember those that are in bonds,' as being bound with them. [Remember] those who are evil entreated (τῶν κακουχουμένων, *der an Ungemach leidenden*. Ewald), as being yourselves also in the body. Marriage is honourable in all men,² and the bed undefiled, but whoremongers and adulterers God will judge.

¹ Μιμνήσκεσθε τῶν δεσμίων κ.τ.λ. (See note 3, pp. 161, 162.) Ewald translates *Gedenket der Gefesselten als Mitgefesselte*, and rightly explains ὡς καὶ αὐτοὶ ὄντες ἐν σώματι, " *als solche die auch selbst im Leibe sind*, und "schon daher wissen Können, dass jeder Mensch, so lange er in dem "hinfälligen sterblichen Leibe wallet, unzähligen Übeln ausgesetzt ist," i.e., "and are therefore able to know that every man, as long as he goes "about in this frail and mortal body, is exposed to innumerable ills." Wolfius writes, *in loc.*, " Captivorum curam solicite habuisse Christianos "veteres, testis est Lucianus, de morte Peregrini, p. 762, observante "Elsnero."

² Τίμιος ὁ γάμος ἐν πᾶσι, καὶ ἡ κοίτη ἀμίαντος κ.τ.λ. Ewald understands these words as conveying a peremptory command : —" *Ehrenwerth die* "*Heirath in allem* (vgl. xiii. 18) ! Ist jemand verheirathet so sei seine " Heirath und Ehe durch und durch so wie es die Ehre fordert, *und das* "*Ehebett unbefleckt!* so dass er sich hütet irgend etwas der keuschen "Ehe widerstreitendes zu thun : *Hurer aber und Ehebrecher wird Gott* "*richten*, &c. Let marriage be honourable in everything (comp. xiii. "18). Is anybody married, then let his marriage and married life be "thoroughly such as honour demands, and the marriage bed unstained ! "Let him guard himself against doing anything repugnant to a chaste "married life ; but whoremongers and adulterers God will judge." Alford has, " Let your marriage (γάμος, elsewhere in New Testament "in the sense of a *wedding*, here has its ordinary Greek meaning) be "(held) in honour in all things, and your marriage bed be undefiled, "for fornicators and adulterers God shall judge." The Arabic translates ἐν πᾶσι, says Dr. Gill, "*every way*," and the Ethiopic version "*every where*." But the Vulgate has, " Honorabile connubium in "omnibus, et thorus immaculatus "; whilst Luther translates, "Die "Ehe soll ehrlich gehalten werden bei Allen (*i.e.*, in all men), und das "Ehebett unbefleckt." J. C. Wolfius, *in loc.*, writes:—"Γάμος de "conjugio dicit Arrianus Indic., viii. 6 ; Herod., lib. ix., p. 630 ; et "clarius Plutarchus, cujus sententia cum Paulina nostra egregie con-"spirat, in Amatorio, p. 750, γάμον καὶ σύνοδον ἀνδρὸς καὶ γυναικὸς, ἧς οὐ "γέγονεν, οὐδ᾽ ἔστιν ἱερωτέρα κατάζευξις. Vide Raphelium et Bosium. "Subintelligendum in hac sententia esse non *ἐστὶ*, quod Beza præter "alios voluit; sed potius *ἔστω*, plures monuerunt. Id poscunt impera-"tivi, qui in hoc capite hinc antecedunt, hinc sequuntur ; tum vera res "ipsa. Quis enim dixerit, conjugium apud omnes eo loco haberi, quo "hic haberi vult Paulus ? Lege plura in hanc sententiam apud Erasm. "Schmidium, et Hombergium. Colomesius, p. 148. Observat. Sacra-"rum similiter verti volebat Gallice : *que le mariage soit honorable entre* "*tous*. Et sic versio Montensis : *que le mariage soit traité de tous avec* "*honnetcté*. Hanc interpretationem à Malleti exceptionibus tuetur

" Arnaldus in Nova illius Versionis defensione, p. 311 seq. adductis ex
" ipsis Pontificiis Estio et Em. a Saa ὁμοψήφοις. In versionem N. T.
" Græco-Anglicani, quæ itidem τὸ ἐστὶ exprimit, ἀμίαντον prave con-
" vertit, recte animadvertit L. Twells in Examine illius Critico, Pt. i.,
" p. 150." The London Jews' Society's translators have, בכל הנשואים קרים.
The compilers of our Marriage Service, in the address to persons who
are about to enter into the estate of matrimony, have swerved slightly
from the translation of the Authorized Version, whilst they also vouch
for the Pauline authorship of the Epistle to the Hebrews ; e.g., " And
" is commended of St. Paul to be honourable *among all men*," not, as
in Hebr. xiii. 4, " *in all*." Schoettgen, on 1 Tim. iv. 3, *Forbidding to
marry*, &c., remarks :—" De Pharisais non constat, eos tale quid prohi-
" buisse, bene tamen de Essenis. R. Abraham Zacut in Sepher
" Juchasin, fol. 139, 2. *Secta quædam ex ipsis non ducunt uxores librorum
" causa, putant enim, nullam mulierem viro fidem integram servare.*" Josephus, *De Bell. Jud.*, lib. ii., 8, 2, writes, " There are three philosophical
" sects among the Jews. The followers of the first are the Pharisees;
" of the second, the Sadducees ; and the third sect, who pretend to a
" severer discipline, are called Essenes. These last are Jews by birth,
" and seem to have a greater affection for one another than the other
" sects have. These Essenes reject pleasures as an evil, but esteem
" continence, and the conquest over our passions to be virtue. They
" neglect wedlock, but choose out other persons' children, while they
" are pliable and fit for learning, and esteem them to be of their
" kindred, and form them according to their own manners. They do
" not absolutely deny the fitness of marriage, and the succession of
" mankind thereby continued," &c. (Τὸν μὲν γάμον καὶ τὴν ἐξ αὐτοῦ
διαδοχὴν οὐχ ἀναιροῦντες, τὰς δὲ τῶν γυναικῶν ἀσελγείας φυλασσόμενοι, καὶ
μηδεμίαν τηρεῖν πεπεισμένοι τὴν πρὸς ἕνα πίστιν.)—Philo's account of the
Essenes is to be found amongst the *Fragments*, Works, Mangey's Edit.,
tom. ii., p. 632, &c., and also *Liber quisquis virtuti studet* (*Ibid.*, p. 457),
where he computes their number at about 4,000. Porphyry gives a
fairly-drawn description of their peculiar tenets in his treatise against
the use of animal food.

What particular occasion gave rise to the Writer's speaking as he
does, in these third and fourth verses, must ever lack complete explana-
nation (see pp. 279, 280) ; but the warning contained in chap. xii. 16,
μή τις πόρνος κ.τ.λ., taken in connexion with the verses under consideration, seems to point to a laxity of moral conduct in some of the converts
that called for decisive animadversion.

Verses 5, 6.—Let your conversation be without the greed
of money [1] (ἀφιλάργυρος ὁ τρόπος, Nicht geldgierig die

Lebensart, *Ewald*); and be satisfied² with such things as you have (ἀρκούμενοι τοῖς παροῦσιν, sich begnügend mit dem Vorhandenen, *Ewald*; i.e., contenting yourselves with such things as are present to hand). For He himself has said, I WILL NEVER LEAVE THEE, NOR FORSAKE THEE.³ So that we do boldly say (ὥστε θαρροῦντας ἡμᾶς λέγειν), The Lord is my helper, and I will not be afraid of what man will do unto me.⁴

¹ Ἀφιλάργυρος. This word occurs only twice in the New Testament, viz., here, and in 1 Tim. iii. 3, "No striker, *not greedy of filthy lucre*."
² Ἀρκούμενοι κ.τ.λ. Compare 1 Tim. vi. 8. Ἔχοντες δὲ διατροφὰς, καὶ σκεπάσματα, τούτοις ἀρκεσθησόμεθα. J. C. Wolfius says, *in loc.*, "Παρὸν
" Græcis est, quod adest bonum, quodque præsens est, quamvis parvum
" et vile sit; et distinguitur ab alieno, itemque sumptuoso et magnifico.
" Ita vim vocis explicat, et locis Xenophontis ac Herodoti munit Raphe-
" lius, p. 325 et 644. Xenophon., *Memorab.*, lib. 1., p. 577, Στρατεύοιτο
" δὲ πότερος ἂν ῥᾷον, ὁ μὴ δυνάμενος ἄνευ πολυτελοῦς διαίτης ζῆν, ἢ ᾧ τὸ
" παρὸν ἀρκοίη; et *Conviv.*, p. 70, Οἷς μάλιστα τὰ παρόντα ἀρκεῖ."—The expression, Ἀρκούμενοι τοῖς παροῦσιν, seems to have been in common use amongst the Greeks. Bleek, as cited by Alford, gives the exact words, as used by Stobæus.—Surenhusius writes, *in loc.* (Βιβλ. Καταλλ., pp. 663, 664), "Ii inter Hebræos qui fidei suæ in Messiam confessionem
" ediderant, ab infidelibus suis consanguineis odio habebantur, et cum
" amissione bonorum, atque auxilii inopes exularent, alii de bonis suis
" aliis quicquam largiri detrectarent, alii amissas opes deplorarent,
" paupertatem ut onus miserum et grave in se suscipere renuerunt,
" monet hosce omnes Apostolus, ut præsentibus suis bonis contenti
" essent, et fiduciam suam in Deo collocarent, qui neminem derelinquit,
" sed ex rebus adversis liberat, et rem ita se habere ex aliquot Scripturæ
" locis confirmat, quando dicit, αὐτὸς γὰρ (nempe ὁ Κύριος) εἴρηκεν, *ipse
" enim* (nempe Dominus) *dixit*, Hebraice והוא אמר *ille enim dixit*, sub-
" audito nomine יהוה, quod Hebræi propter maximam illius sanctitatem
" exprimere solent per רחמנא vel יהוה," &c.
³ Αὐτὸς γὰρ εἴρηκεν, οὐ μή σε ἀνῶ, οὐδ' οὐ μή σε ἐγκαταλίπω. Philo, *De Confusione Linguarum* (Works, Mangey's Edit., tom. i., p. 430), writes:—Παγχάλεπον γὰρ ἀχαλίνωτον ἐαθῆναι ψυχὴν, ἀτίθασσον οὖσαν ἐξ ἑαυτῆς, ἣν μόλις ἡνίαις μετ' ἐπανατάσεως μαστίγων ἐστὶ κατασχόντα πραΰναι. Διόπερ λόγιον τοῦ ἵλεω Θεοῦ μεστὸν ἡμερότητος, ἐλπίδας χρηστὰς ὑπογράφον τοῖς παιδείαις ἐρασταῖς, ἀνήρηται τοιόνδε, Οὐ μή σε ἀνῶ, οὐδ' οὐ μή σε ἐγκαταλίπω. "It is a very pernicious thing to let the soul be unbridled,

"being of itself impatient of restraints, and with difficulty kept in "bounds by bridles and whips. Wherefore the oracle of the merciful "God, being full of gentleness, holds out hopes serviceable to the lovers "of discipline, and declares, I WILL NEVER LEAVE THEE, NOR FORSAKE "THEE." The difficulty attaching to this quotation lies in the fact that in the LXX. there is no passage possessing a *verbatim* correspondence with it. Mangey regards it, I think rightly, as taken from Josh. i. 5 : כאשר הייתי עם משה אהיה עמך לא ארפך ולא אעזבך— , "As I was with Moses, "I will be with thee, I will not fail (nor *desert*. See Gesen., *Lex*. "*Man*., art. רפה, Hiph.), nor forsake thee." The LXX. has, Οὐκ ἐγκαταλείψω σε, οὐδ' ὑπερόψομαί σε. It is not improbable that there existed in common use, amongst the Greek-speaking Jews, a popularized rendering of these words of promissory encouragement to Joshua, and which is used by the Writer to the Hebrews and by Philo. Their translation gives far more of the genuine ring of the Hebrew original than that of the LXX. The supposition of Bleek and Lünemann, that the author of the Epistle to the Hebrews made the quotation direct from Philo, is more than improbable; it is contrary to good taste and the reverence due to the sacred writings of the Bible. It is also utterly inconsistent with the prefatory words, αὐτὸς γὰρ εἴρηκεν. If the quotation is intended from Joshua, it is easy to understand how appropriately the Writer introduces it on the present occasion. The promise was given to Joshua, just after the death of Moses, and was designed to nerve him to face the novel dangers and difficulties of leading the children of Israel into the promised land. The converts to whom this Epistle was addressed stood then in an analogous position to their forefathers. The Mosaic dispensation had just expired. They were entering upon a new and untried Land of Promise. How consolatory, then, to be reminded that the God of their fathers was still with them; that the promise made to Joshua still held good as regarded themselves—"I will "never leave thee, nor forsake thee"!' Delitzsch believes that the expression was taken from the Alexandrian rendering of Deut. xxxi. 6, οὐ μή σε ἀνῇ οὐδ' οὐ μή σε ἐγκαταλείπῃ, and had become interwoven into some liturgical or homiletic portion of the services in the Hellenistic synagogue. But this latter is a mere conjecture, unsupported by any evidence. Bagster's (Vatican) rendering of Deut. xxxi 6 is, 'Ανδρίζου καὶ ἴσχυε, μὴ φοβοῦ, μηδὲ δηλιάσῃς, μηδὲ πτοηθῇς ἀπὸ προσώπου αὐτῶν, ὅτι Κύριος ὁ Θεός σου ὁ προπορευόμενος μεθ' ὑμῶν ἐν ὑμῖν, οὔτε μή σε ἀνῇ, οὔτε μή σε ἐγκαταλίπῃ (לא ירפך ולא יעזבך). Compare also the words of David to Solomon, 1 Chron. xxviii. 20, and Ps. xxvii. 9. Consult also Surenhusius, Βιβλ. Καταλλ., pp. 664, 665. The London Jews' Society's New Testament (Edit. 1867) has the exact words of Josh. i. 5, viz.,

¹ לא ארפך ולא אעזבך. Ewald (*Das Sendschr. a.d. Hebr.*, p. 174) writes :—"Bei "dem A. T. lichen Worte, v. 5, ist die Schwierigkeit dass sie Deut. xxxi. "6, 8, in der dritten Person von Gott ausgesagt werden: allein Jos. "i. 5, stehen sie in der ersten, und obwohl die LXX. hier jezt eine "andere Übersezung haben, so kann man doch nicht bezweifeln dass "unser Sendschreiber, ebenso wie Philon, sie von hier entlehnte, hier "also einst dieselbe Übersezung sich gefunden haben muss."

¹ Κύριος ἐμοὶ βοηθός, καὶ οὐ φοβηθήσομαι τί ποιήσει μοι ἄνθρωπος. This verbatim quotation of the LXX. version of Ps. cxviii. 6 (in the Greek, cxvii. 6) furnishes us with another authoritative reading of the Hebrew text. Dean Alford decides in favour of the Masoretic reading, against the punctuation of the received Greek Text of the New Testament, and also of the LXX., which point the verse thus :— יהוה לי ׃ לא אירא מה יעשה לי אדם. The Dean says, "*The Lord* (יהוה in the Psalm, and "probably used of the Father, as in other citations (!) in this Epistle, "*e.g.*, ch. vii. 21, viii. 8—11, x. 16, 30, xii. 5; and, without a cita-"tion, ch. viii. 2) *is my helper* (in the Heb. only יהוה לי) [*and* (not in "Heb.)], *I will not be afraid: what shall man do unto me?* (such is the "connexion both in Heb. and here): not, 'I will not be afraid what "'shall man do unto me,' as in the English Prayer-book after the "Vulgate, *non timebo quid faciat mihi homo*." Now, what shall we say to pointing the Greek as follows?—Κύριος ἐμοὶ βοηθός, καὶ οὐ φοβηθήσομαι: τί ποιήσει μοι ἄνθρωπος;—As the earliest MSS., both Hebrew and Greek, are without accents or punctuation, the sense of any given passage may entirely turn upon the opinion of the critic, provided, of course, that such opinion does not contravene any doctrinal statement of God's Word, or the obvious intention of the quotation. The truth is, that Dean Alford is feebly competent to decide upon any matter of the real "Higher Criticism"; and, finding that the Masoretic reading did not coincide with the New Testament punctuation, for fear that he might be considered by German experimenters upon the Word of God as unscholarly, he at once pronounces against the received reading of the Epistle to the Hebrews. In these days of superficial acquirements, to pass a slight upon any portion of the received text of the Greek Testament seems to entitle the propounder to be esteemed an advanced scholar! Dr. Alford knew, *or ought to have known*, that the older Hebrew MSS. are entirely without punctuation, and that very many of the discrepancies between the LXX. and the Hebrew text, turn entirely upon the difference of the points (see note 3, p. 213) and accents. In the present case, the only question for the student to decide is, *Which is the best pointing of the Hebrew and Greek Texts?* That adopted by the *Textus Receptus* is perfectly admissible. So also is

the Masoretic reading of the Hebrew text in Ps. cxviii. 6. Both readings, after all, come to very much the same thing. The texts differ only in the insertion of καί. There is not, therefore, the shadow of a valid objection against the reading of Ps. cxviii. 6 as given in the Epistle to the Hebrews and also in the LXX. The Hebrew Masoretic version points the words thus, *" The Lord is my helper* (or, Jehovah *is* "for me לִי יהוה), *I will not fear—What can man do unto me?"* The New Testament and the LXX. punctuate the very same words (translated from an unpointed and unaccented Hebrew MS.), *The Lord is my helper*, and *I will not fear what man can do unto me*. The Hebrew words יהוה לי לא אירא מה יעשה לי אדם, apart from the accents, *which do not belong to the original text*, are capable, with perfect grammatical propriety, of either construction. The *Textus Receptus* of the Greek Testament and the LXX. have decided in favour of *The Lord is my helper ;* and *I will not fear what man can do unto me*. Compare Ps. lvi. 4, 11, 12,—See also Surenhusius, Βίβλ. καταλλ., pp. 665, 666, and Ewald, *Das Sendschr. a.d. Hebr.*, p. 148. On p. 48 he translates, *" so " dass wir getrost reden,* der Herr ist mein Helfer : was wird Mensch " mir thun ? "

Verse 7.—Remember[1] your leaders, who spake to you the word of God, whose faith imitate, considering (attentively pondering, or reviewing) the end of their conversation.

[1] The verse reads in the received text, Μνημονεύετε τῶν ἡγουμένων ὑμῶν, οἵτινες ἐλάλησαν ὑμῖν τὸν λόγον του Θεοῦ ὧν ἀναθεωροῦντες τὴν ἔκβασιν τῆς ἀναστροφῆς, μιμεῖσθε τὴν πίστιν. The Vulgate has " Memen- " tote praepositorum vestrorum qui vobis locuti sunt verbum Dei : quorum " intuentes exitum conversationis, imitamini fidem."—The translators of the London Jews' Society's New Testament have זכרו את מנהליכם אשר דברו אליכם את דבר האלהים אשר התבוננו את מוצא התהלכותם ולכו בתבנית אמונתם ׃ Luther translates, " Gedenket an eure Lehrer, die euch das Wort " Gottes gesagt haben, welcher Ende schauet an, und folget ihrem " Glauben nach." Ewald renders, " Haltet in Andenken eure Vorsteher " als welche euch das Wort Gottes redeten, und ahmet zu deren Lebens- " ausgange, hinaufblickend ihre Treue nach." Now, although Ewald and many others take τὴν ἔκβασιν τῆς ἀναστροφῆς to mean " the termina- " tion of their earthly career," (Alford asserts off-hand, " it is plain " from what follows here, *e g.*, ἐλάλησαν and ἔκβασιν, that the course of " these ἡγούμενοι is past, and it is *remembering*, with a view to imitation, " that is enjoined "), I cannot help thinking that there is an immediate reference to what has just gone before, ἀφιλάργυρος ὁ τρόπος κ.τ.λ. The converts are exhorted to remember the temporal wants of their

pastors, who have devoted themselves to the ministry of the Word. (Compare Gal. ii. 10, μόνον τῶν πτωχῶν ἵνα μνημονεύωμεν.) In those troublous days of halting faith, of doubt, perplexity, and persecution, who so likely to be neglected and straitened in their temporal concerns as the pastors of the flock? And as Elijah (1 Kings xvii. 13, 14) directed the widow, "Fear not, go and do as thou hast said; but make "me thereof a little cake first, and bring it unto me, and after make "for thee and thy son. For thus saith the Lord God of Israel, The "barrel of meal shall not waste, neither shall the cruse of oil fail;" so the Hebrew converts are invited to bear in mind that the spiritual workman is worthy of his hire; that God has promised never to leave nor to forsake them, whatever they may spend in his service, and furthermore, that the end and object, the proposed result of all the labours (τῶν ἡγουμένων) of these rulers is, the salvation of the souls of their flock. Ewald's translation of τὴν πίστιν, ihre Treue, "their fidelity," appears scarcely in harmony with what has gone before, or with the immediate context. Again, ὦν ἀναθεωροῦντες τὴν ἔκβασιν τῆς ἀναστροφῆς, μιμεῖσθε τὴν πίστιν, is an invitation to ponder attentively the "manner of life," the self-sacrificing disinterestedness of these spiritual guides, and to imitate their faith. They set before themselves no earthly reward. They were marked out as the first victims, should any popular tumult or persecution arise. The ἔκβασις τῆς ἀναστροφῆς, the issue of their conversation, the end of their daily walk and calling, the termination of their earthly career (ἠκούσατε γὰρ τὴν ἐμὴν ἀναστροφήν ποτε ἐν τῷ Ἰουδαισμῷ, Gal. i. 13), would be, in all human likelihood, a martyr's crown. With such a prospect before their leaders, with such examples of holy self-abnegation before their eyes, how ignoble and unworthy must the undue caring for filthy lucre appear! I cannot, then, accept the assertion as a decisive one, that the Writer refers to those teachers who had already sealed their testimony with their blood, or that he has already referred to them in chap. ii. 3. The word ἔκβασις occurs only twice in the New Testament, viz., here and in 1 Cor. x. 13, "a way to "escape."

Verse 8.—Jesus Christ (is) the same [1] yesterday and to-day, and (also) for ever. (Jésu Christus gestern und heute ist derselbe, auch in die Ewigkeiten, *Ewald*.)

[1] Ἰησοῦς Χριστὸς χθὲς καὶ σήμερον ὁ αὐτός, καὶ εἰς τοὺς αἰῶνας. Here, again, we must not forget that the Writer is speaking, as a Jew, to Jews. The phrase Ἰησοῦς Χριστὸς would strike a very different chord in the minds of the Hebrews, to what it does in the minds of modern Christian readers. The word "Christ" they would understand as a designation of Deity, as a proper attribute of the Divine Messiah, con-

cerning whom it is written in Ps. cii., " I said, O my God, take me not
" away in the midst of my days : thy years *are* throughout all genera-
" tions. Of old (see Heb. i. 11, 12) hast thou laid the foundations of
" the earth : and the heavens *are* the works of thy hands. They shall
" perish, but thou shalt endure (ואתה תעמד) : yea, all of them shall wax
" old as a garment ; as a vesture shalt thou change them (see note 6,
" p. 22), and they shall be changed. But thou art the same (ואתה הוא,
" ὁ αὐτὸς εἶ), and thy years shall have no end." The above, then, is a
citation from the already quoted (chap. i. 10—12) words of Ps. cii.
The Hebrews are reminded that they stand under the protection of
Almighty Omniscience, and unchanging Power and Goodness. The
words contain an all-sufficient dissuasive against a niggardly small-
heartedness, as well as against a faithless questioning how their daily
necessities were to be supplied. They furnish an ample incentive to
trustful and devout exultation in the thought that the Divine ὁ Αὐτὸς
is their Protector and their God, even He concerning whom Isaiah
(ix. 6) wrote that his name should be called אבי עד, *Father of Eternity*
(see the late Dr. M'Caul's *Messiaship of Jesus*, pp. 183—185), and concerning whom Moses the man of God spake in Ps. xc. 1, 2, " Lord, thou
" hast been our dwelling-place in all generations. Before the mountains
" were brought forth, or ever thou hadst formed the earth and the
" world, even from everlasting to everlasting, thou *art* God." בטרם הרים
ילדו ותחולל ארץ ותבל ומעולם עד עולם אתה אל—Πρὸ τοῦ ὄρη γενηθῆναι καὶ
πλασθῆναι τὴν γῆν καὶ τὴν οἰκουμένην, καὶ ἀπὸ τοῦ αἰῶνος ἕως τοῦ αἰῶνος σὺ
εἶ, LXX. And again, verse 4, " For a thousand years in thy sight
" *are but* as yesterday when it is past, and as a watch in the night."—
כי אלף שנים בעיניך כיום אתמול כי יעבר ואשמורה בלילה—"Οτι χίλια ἔτη ἐν ὀφθαλμοῖς
σου, ὡς ἡ ἡμέρα ἡ ἐχθὲς ἥτις διῆλθε, καὶ φυλακὴ ἐν νυκτί, LXX. It may be
as well to remark that the tradition of the early Jewish Church, as
represented by the LXX. and by the Targum, coincides in ascribing
the 90th Psalm to the pen of Moses.—Compare also Mal. iii. 6, " I *am*
" the Lord, I change not ; therefore ye sons of Jacob are not consumed,"
and James i. 17, παρ' ᾧ οὐκ ἔνι παραλλαγή, ἢ τροπῆς ἀποσκίασμα.

Verse 9.—Be not carried about with divers and strange
doctrines.[1] For *it is* a good thing that the heart be
established with grace, not with meats, in which they
who walked were not profited (ἐν οἷς οὐκ ὠφελήθησαν οἱ
περιπατήσαντες).

[1] Διδαχαῖς ποικίλαις καὶ ξέναις μὴ περιφέρεσθε, κ.τ.λ.—Compare Eph.
iv. 14, κλυδωνιζόμενοι καὶ περιφερόμενοι παντὶ ἀνέμῳ τῆς διδασκαλίας.—
Jude 12, ὑπὸ ἀνέμων περιφερόμεναι.—If Jesus Christ be the same ὁ αὐτὸς,
in benevolent Omniscience and oversight of his people, his Gospel is

equally immutable in its teaching as to what we must do to be saved. We may neither add thereto nor diminish therefrom. It is a good and perfect gift, *complete* from the first, and we shall make no new discoveries, as to what is the will of God concerning us, in τῇ ἅπαξ παραδοθείσῃ τοῖς ἁγίοις πίστει, "the faith once delivered to the saints," Jude 3. The Writer, therefore, skilfully adapts his declaration that " Jesus Christ is the same yesterday, to-day, and for ever," and makes it the text, so to speak, of a brief exhortation against the mischievous teaching of those who would persuade his readers to return to a mistaken compliance with the graceless precepts of the ceremonial law. To go back to these ordinances as touching meats and drinks, &c., after having once broken loose from them, and to attach any real virtue to them from a justificatory point of view, or as procuring acceptance from God, would be to offer a direct affront to the freedom of the Gospel. Of these the Writer has already asserted (ix. 9, 10), that they could not give the conscience of the worshipper any real satisfaction, but were only enjoined μέχρι καιροῦ διορθώσεως, *until the time of Reformation.* In Acts xxi. 20 we learn that there were "many "thousands" of Jews that believed, and yet were zealous of the law. It was one thing to adhere *from the very beginning*, as Jewish patriots and citizens, to the civil and religious customs and constitution of their forefathers, and quite another, *after having accepted the Gospel in its simplicity*, to go back to the discarded and beggarly elements of the law, either as a means of justification, or to curry favour with their unbelieving brethren. In times of persecution there existed a very strong temptation to the baptised Hebrews to dissemble in this manner, and so St. Paul writes to the Galatians vi. 12, 13, " As many as desire " to make a fair show in the flesh (εἰπροσωπῆσαι ἐν σαρκὶ), they con-" strain you to be circumcised, only lest they should suffer persecution " for the cross of Christ. For neither they themselves who are cir-" cumcised keep the law, but desire to have you circumcised, that they "may glory in your flesh." Ewald (*Das Sendschr. a.d. Hebräer.*, pp. 148, 149) writes :—" Allein weil der Sendschreiber wohl " weiss dass die neuerdings aufgestandenen Irrlehrer auch diese " Gemeinde leicht stören, und ihr erstes einfachstes Bekenntniss " auf Christus trüben könnten, so knüpft er daran eine neue dem " gesammten Inhalte des Sendschreibens völlig entsprechende Ermah-" nung, sich durch sie nicht stören zu lassen, und leitet diese mit dem " Wahlspruche, v. 8, ein : *Jesu Christus gestern und heute derselbe und* " *in die Ewigkeiten!* so dass weder die wechselnden Zeiten noch die " wechselnden Lehren ihn in seiner ursprünglichen reinen Wahrheit " verändern können. Doch nun folgt sogleich die Warnung : *Durch* " *bunte und fremde Lehren lasset euch nicht verleiten!* Weil aber die

" gerade jezt zu fürchtenden Irrlehrer von dem einfachen Christenthume
" wieder zum Buchstabendienste des A. T.'s zurücklenken wolten, so wird
" zur Begründung der Warnung gesagt, *ist es doch schön dass durch*
" *Gnade* die durch Christus nach dem oben iv. 16, x. 29, xii. 15,
" gesagten den gebesserten Menschen jezt umsonst dargebotene göttliche
" Gnade *das Herz fest werde*, voll göttlicher Zuversicht und Heiterkeit
" werde, nicht *durch Speisen* die schon ix. 10, erwähnten wie sie im
" A. T. gesezlich vorgeschrieben sind und damals auch von zu ängst-
" lichen Christen gefordert wurden (vgl. die *Gesch. des V. Isr.*, vi., s.
" 505, f.), *mit welchen man sich nuzlos herumtrieb*, bis das Christenthum
" mit seiner unvergleichlich erspriesslicheren Versöhnung und Stärkung
" des Menschen erschien." The meaning of the Writer to the Hebrews
is, therefore, as follows:—" When the Gospel was first delivered to you,
" no commandments respecting abstinence from meats, as a religious
" duty, or distinctions in them, accompanied it. Any fresh doctrines
" that may be at present obtruded upon you by would-be improvers
" upon the faith, are worse than valueless. Christ's Gospel establishes
" and fortifies the heart WITH GRACE, and not with meats. Those who
" have all their lifelong devoted themselves to the observance of such
" ordinances, have not been one whit profited by them." We must not
forget that the vanity, the self-love, the national exclusiveness of the
Pharisaic Jew were sorely wounded by being put on an equality, even
in respect to meat and drink, with the Gentiles. The latter were
looked down upon as an inferior caste ; and we know how long it took
to wean even the Apostles (Acts x. 28, xi. 1—3) from such preconceived
notions. It was actually considered, in the Hebrew Christian community at Jerusalem, to be an extraordinary exhibition of God's mercy
that He should grant unto the Gentiles "repentance unto life"! (Acts
xi. 18.) When, therefore, these false teachers appealed to the ancient
prejudice and national pride of the Hebrew converts, the temptation
to return to their old habits was not without strong fascinations. When
their unbaptized kinsmen twitted them with placing themselves on a par
with the Gentiles, even in the matter of meat and drink, the taunt fell
with burning acerbity upon their lacerated souls. It reminded them
that they were renegades and outcasts, ceremonially unclean, outside
the pale of all former friendships and intimacies, and (as the unbelieving
Jews would urge) cut off from the proud privilege of partaking of the
holy things which were offered in sacrifice to the God of their fathers.
With his usual subtlety of perception, however, the Writer contrives,
in the tenth and following verses, to turn these taunts and sneers to
good account, and to remind the perplexed Hebrew converts that, in
this very particular, they stood on far higher ground than those who
reviled them and persecuted them.

CHAP. XIII., 10—12. 343

Verses 10—12.—We have an altar¹ whereof they have no right to eat who serve the tabernacle. For the beasts² whose blood is brought in for sin (περὶ ἁμαρτίας) to the Holy Places (τὰ ἅγια, i.e., the Holy of Holies. See ch. ix. 8, 12, 24, 25; x. 19) by the Highpriest, the bodies of the same are burned outside the camp³ (τούτων τὰ σώματα κατακαίεται ἔξω τῆς παρεμβολῆς). Wherefore Jesus also, in order that He might sanctify the people by his own blood, suffered outside the gate.

¹ Ἔχομεν θυσιαστήριον ἐξ οὗ φαγεῖν οὐκ ἔχουσιν ἐξουσίαν οἱ τῇ σκηνῇ λατρεύοντες. As observed in the preceding note, the Writer retorts upon those who insinuated that the Hebrew converts had relinquished their privileges of partaking of the sacrifices, that Christians possessed a privilege from which the Jewish hierarchy itself was debarred. They dared not to eat of the bodies of the beasts which were offered for sin on the Day of Atonement by the highpriest. These were confessedly the cardinal sacrifices of the entire year. The believer in Jesus, however, can draw near and partake by faith of the true Sacrifice of the body and blood of Christ, of which even the sacrifices of the Day of Atonement were only the type and prophetic representation. The rejoinder is a triumphant one, and unanswerably telling. Little need it matter to the desponding Hebrews that they were shut out from participation in the consecrated meats to which their unbaptized brethren attached so paramount an importance. Those who prided themselves on the Levitic ceremonial law were still deluding themselves with what had been under the first covenant σκιὰ τῶν μελλόντων ἀγαθῶν. They were hugging mere empty shadows to their bosoms, being willingly ignorant of the fact that, the Substance being come, the typical fore-shadowings of his ONE, perfect, and all-sufficient sacrifice, had lost even their symbolical value and sanctity. What then does the Writer intend by the expression, "an altar"? That he cannot intend to contradict his own assertion, ix. 25—28, is superfluous to state. He has there asserted, in the most unqualified terms, that Christ does not "offer Himself often, "as the highpriest entereth into the holy place every year, with blood "that is not his own. For then must he often have suffered, since the "foundation of the world; but now ONCE, at the consummation of the "ages, He has been manifested for the putting away of sin by the "sacrifice of Himself. And, just as it is appointed to men ONCE to die, "and after this the judgment (things which cannot be repeated), so, "also, Christ having been ONCE offered for the special object of bearing

"the sins of many, shall appear the second time to those that wait for Him, without sin (or sin-offering. See note 1, p. 138, &c.), to announce to them their salvation." So also, again, in chap. x. 10—15, "By the which will we are sanctified through the offering of the body of Jesus Christ ONCE for all (ἐφάπαξ). And every priest standeth daily ministering, and offering oftentimes the same sacrifices (τὰς αὐτὰς πολλάκις προσφέρων θυσίας), which can never take away sins. But He, having offered ONE sacrifice for sins, for ever hath sat down at the right hand of God.........For by ONE offering He hath perfected FOR EVER, those that are sanctified." With such a series of explicit statements before his eyes, he would be a bold man indeed who would venture to prove from the Epistle to the Hebrews, and from the fact that the author applies the term θυσιαστήριον to the Lord's-table, that he thereby intimated that the sacrifice of the Lord's death is actually and continually repeated, by the Christian Presbyter, whenever he consecrates the memorial elements of his Saviour's passion. Such an assumption is directly in the teeth of the leading argument of the Epistle. That the Christian altar is *primarily* the Cross upon which the Great Sacrifice was once offered, and, *secondarily*, the table upon which the sacramental symbols are placed, who will deny? But "the Body of Christ is given, taken, and eaten, in the Supper, only after an heavenly and spiritual manner. And the mean whereby the Body of Christ is received and eaten in the Supper, is FAITH." Were not this the case, what need was there for the Writer of the Epistle to the Hebrews to remind his readers of the privilege which they enjoyed above their unbelieving brethren? The "partaking of the Altar," of which he speaks, must needs be done after a spiritual fashion, and by a living faith. And as the faith of many amongst them had waxed cold, it was necessary to admonish and put them in mind how that they could, *by faith*, realise a far higher privilege than the most exalted member of the Jewish priesthood could ever aspire to. The highpriest dared not to eat of the flesh of the bullock or the goat offered by himself on the Day of Atonement. We can, by faith (*but by faith alone*), eat of the flesh and drink of the blood of their great antitype—even of Him whose "flesh is meat indeed," and whose "blood is drink indeed." Schoettgen (*Hor. Hebr.*, tom. ii., p. 644) has the following:—" Midrasch Tehillim ad Ps. cxxxiv. 2, fol. 74, 2, ad verba 2, Paral. ii. 3, מידום ואת כל ישראל. In æternum hoc erit inter Israël. *R. Giddel dixit ex sententia Raf: Intelligitur altare extructum, et Michael Princeps Magnus* "(See p. 320) *stat, et sacrificium in eodem offert.*" For a very curious extract from the Schemoth Rabba, respecting the table of the shewbread, see Schoettgen, *ibid.*, p. 612.

² ῟Ων γὰρ εἰσφέρεται ζώων τὸ αἷμα περὶ ἁμαρτίας εἰς τὰ ἅγια διὰ τοῦ ἀρχιερέως κ.τ.λ. Dr. Gill writes, *in loc.*, "Not the red heifer, Numb. "xix., nor the sin-offerings in general, Lev. vi. 30, nor those for the "priest and people, Lev. iv. 11, 12, and chap. xxi. 6, 7, 18, but the "bullock and goat on the Day of Atonement, Lev. xvi. 11—18, 27, "which were typical of Christ, in the bringing of their blood into the "Most Holy Place by the high priest for sin; and in the burning of "them without the camp: these beasts were slain, their blood was "shed, and was brought into the most holy place by the high priest, "and was sprinkled on the mercy-seat, and the horns of the altar of "incense; and by it atonement was made for the priest, his house, and "all Israel: which was a type of the death of Christ," &c. Compare Reland's *Antiq. Sacr. Vet. Hebr.*, Pt. iii., cap. ii.; *De Holocaustis*, cap. iii.; *De Sacrificiis piacularibus*. On pp. 328, 329, under the head "*Quæ comburebantur*," he writes:—"Quæ ex posteriori genere erant, "non in altari ut holocausta, sed extra castra, in loco cineris, vel stante "Templo, extra urbem, ἐν προαστείοις, uti Josephus scribit, dissecta in "partes comburebantur. Hæc erant omnia illa, quorum sanguis infere- "batur in Aedem Sacram, ubi spargebatur coram velo et ad cornua "altaris interioris, at reliquum effundebatur ad basin altaris exterioris "Levit. iv. 3, 12, Hebr. xiii. 11, ita tamen ut אימורים eorum ex corpore "extracta in altari exteriori adolerentur. Pellis ipsa non detrahebatur "his victimis Lev. i. 17, et quum altare carnem non nancisceretur, "etiam Sacerdotes jus in pellem non habebant. *Zevach.* xii. 2. "Confer Levit. x. 16, ubi Moses indignabatur hircum piacularem pro "peccato populi combustum fuisse, quum comedendus fuisset," &c.

³ Ἔξω τῆς παρεμβολῆς. Reland, in his chapter, *de Tabernaculo ejusque situ*, writes:—"Atque ita tria se quasi produnt castra. I. Dei, "sc. Tabernaculum cum atrio; II. Levitarum; III. Populi Israëlitici. "Quibuscum convenerunt, respectu sanctitatis, rerumque et personarum "quæ ad illa admittebantur discrimine, stante Templo tria hæc spatia. "I. Atrium magnum, quod complectebatur atrium Israëlitarum et "Sacerdotum. II. Atrium mulierum, spatium antemurale et mons "Templi. III. Urbs Hierosolyma, *Gem. Zevachim*, 116, 2, quam "traditionem confirmat scriptor *Ep. ad Hebr.*, xiii. 11, 12, qui extra "castra populi idem censet ac extra Hierosolymam." *Ant. Sacr. Vet. Hebr.*, Traject. Bat., 1712. 8vo., p. 17. Some curious matter on the subject is to be found in the Babylonian Gemara, *Sanhedrin*, chap. 6, col. 596—600; *Ugol. Thes.*, tom. 25.—For the New Testament use of the word παρεμβολή. See note 4, p. 236. Dr. Gill writes, *in loc.*, "*Suffered without the gate*," i.e., of Jerusalem. The Syriac version "reads, "without the city," meaning Jerusalem, which answered to

"the camp of Israel in the wilderness, without which the bodies of
"beasts were burnt on the Day of Atonement. For so say the Jews
"(*T. Bab. Zevachim*, fol. 116, 2; *Bamidbar Rabba*, § 7, fol. 188, 3, 4;
"Maimon. *Beth Habbechira*, c. 7, § 11)—'As was the camp in the
"' wilderness, so was the camp in Jerusalem ; from Jerusalem to the
"' mountain of the house was the camp of Israel ; from the mountain
"' of the House, to the gate of Nicanor, was the camp of the Levites ;
"' and from thenceforward the camp of the Shechinah, or the Divine
"' Majesty.' And so Josephus (*Antiq.*, iii. 10, 3) renders the phrase
"*without the camp*, in Lev. xvi. 27, by ἐν τοῖς προαστείοις, *in the suburbs*,
"that is of Jerusalem, where Christ suffered." The words of Josephus
are προσάγουσι δὲ δύο πρὸς τούτοις ἐρίφους, ὧν ὁ μὲν ζῶν εἰς τὴν ὑπερόριον
ἐρημίαν πέμπεται, ἀποτροπιασμὸς καὶ προσαίτησις τοῦ πλήθους παντὸς ὑπὲρ
ἁμαρτημάτων ἐσόμενος, τὸν δ' ἐν τοῖς προαστείοις εἰς καθαρώτατον ἄγοντες
χωρίον αὐτόθι σὺν αὐτῇ καίουσι τῇ δορᾷ, μηδὲν ὅλως καθύραντες. Συγκατακαίεται
δὲ ταῦρος οὐχ ὑπὸ τοῦ δήμου προσαχθείς, ἀλλ' ἐκ τῶν ἰδίων ἀναλωμάτων τοῦ
ἀρχιερέως παρασχόντος κ.τ.λ.—J. Rhenferdius (*Expiatio Anniversaria
Pont. Max. V. et N. Test.*, p. 1037, Meuschen) writes :—" Interea vero,
" dum Emissarius deportabatur, Pontifex ad juvencum suum et hircum
" populi redibat, et intestina exemta rite imponebat altari, corpora item
" dissecta aliis sacerdotibus tradebat efferenda et comburenda extra
" castra, Lev. xvi. 25, 27 ; Misn., cap. vi. 7......Corporis elati mysterium
" Apostolus explicat : 'Nam quorum animalium sanguis,' etc., Heb. xiii.
" 11, 12......Comburebatur autem corpus hirci extra castra *loco mundo*,
" in quo reliquorum sacrificiorum cineres deponebantur. Ita igitur et
" Christi passi, mortuique corpus *sepulchro novo conditum est, in quo
" nemo nuquam jacuerat.*" Joh. xix. 41.—J. C. Wolfius writes, *in loc.*,
" Pro πύλης codex unus, *Barberin*, legit πόλεως, quam vocem Tertul-
" lianus etiam adversus Judæos cap. ultimo exprimit, et recte quidem,
" quod ad sensum, judice Grotio.........Absit vero, ut auctoritate unius
" Codicis adducti, quicquam mutemus, cum sensus idem ex recepta
" lectione nascatur, quem Tertullianus non tam, quod aliter legerit,
" quam, quod aliud significari non possit, expressit." See also Surenhusius, Βίβλος Καταλλ., pp. 666—668.

The Writer, with that controversial sagacity
which is so distinguishing an attribute of St. Paul,
whilst fortifying his readers against the arguments
and the taunts of those who would reimpose upon
them the observance of peculiarities in meats and

drinks, seizes the opportunity to demonstrate a further and striking correspondence between the typical sacrifices of the Day of Atonement and Jesus the Great Antitype. They were taunted with having cut themselves off from participation in the sacrifices, and polluting themselves amongst the Gentiles, by eating meats that were ceremonially unclean. The answer is ready. We have an altar of which the High Priest himself has no power to eat. He dared not to partake of the flesh of the bullock and the goat whose blood he offered on the Day of Atonement. We can partake of His body and blood who was prefigured by these sacrifices. The Christian believer, therefore, stands immeasurably above the proudest Pharisee that makes his boast in the law. The bodies of these beasts above mentioned were *not eaten*, but were burned without the camp. Jesus, therefore, that he might complete the correspondence between himself and these typical representations suffered "without the gate." It was no accidental coincidence. It was a prophetic fulfilment of the Scriptures. The law of Moses prescribed that malefactors should thus suffer outside the city. (See p. 242.) Jesus was the true victim, and by the legal necessity of the Mosaic criminal law, He suffered outside the gate. Thus He proved Himself, in this minute resemblance, to be Him " of whom " Moses in the law, and all the prophets, did write." The Jews thought Him a malefactor, and He was content, whilst "fulfilling all righteousness," to bear " the reproach." Those who burned the bullock and the goat were accounted ceremonially unclean. The converts must also be content to bear the revilings of their adversaries, and to go forth to Jesus without the camp bearing his reproach; and therefore the Writer continues:—

Verse 13.—Let us therefore come forth to him without (ἔξω τῆς παρεμβολῆς) bearing his reproach (τὸν ὀνειδισμὸν αὐτοῦ φέροντες).

It must not be forgotten that our Lord, having been crucified, or "hanged on a tree," was regarded by the unbelieving Jews as being "accursed of "God"; Deut. xxi. 22, 23, "And if a man have "committed a sin worthy of death, and he be put "to death, and thou hang him on a tree, his body "shall not remain all night upon the tree, but "thou shalt in any wise bury him that day. For "he that is hanged is accursed of God (כי קללת "אלהים תלוי), that thy land be not defiled," &c. This was, doubtless, the reason why the Jews were so urgent upon Pilate, that after the Saviour's crucifixion, the bodies might be removed and buried before nightfall. Such, then, was the "reproach" which Jesus bore for us. Well might the Writer appeal to the gratitude of his readers, and exhort them to bear with contented resignation the reproach of their Master. But again, with his skilful and characteristic tenderness and tact, he reminds them that the reproach will not be for ever, and the trial will be brief. What if they do place themselves outside the camp? What if they are cut off from former associations, and their very

CHAP. XIII., 14. 349

names are cast out as unclean by their brethren? Have they not the words of Jesus himself (Matt. v. 10—12) to cheer them, " Blessed are they which " are persecuted for righteousness' sake : for their's " is the kingdom of heaven. Blessed are ye, when " *men* shall revile you, and persecute *you*, and shall " say all manner of evil against you falsely, for my " sake. Rejoice, and be exceeding glad : for great " is your reward in heaven : for so persecuted they " the prophets which were before you." And again (Luke vi. 20—23), " Blessed *be ye* poor : for yours " is the kingdom of heaven. Blessed *are ye* that " hunger now : for ye shall be filled. Blessed *are* " *ye* that weep now : for ye shall laugh. Blessed " are ye, when men shall hate you, and when they " shall separate you (ἀφορίσωσιν ὑμᾶς) *from their* " *company*, and shall reproach *you*, and cast out " your name as evil, for the Son of man's sake. " Rejoice ye in that day, and leap for joy : for, " behold, your reward is great in heaven : for in " the like manner did their fathers unto the " prophets." The self-sacrifice thus required would be greatly mitigated and their regrets rendered less poignantly keen, if the converts would bethink themselves of the primary condition of their pilgrimage (see verses 10—16), and so the Writer continues :—

Verse 14.—For we have not here a continuing city,[1] but we seek the one to come (τὴν μέλλουσαν ἐπιζητοῦμεν, Die zukünftige suchen wir, *Luther*).

[1] Οὐ γὰρ ἔχομεν ὧδε μένουσαν πόλιν κ.τ.λ. The meaning of these words is doubtless, " Jerusalem, whose gate has just been mentioned, verse 12

" (albeit it is the seat of the temple worship and the Levitic sacrifices,
" albeit it is the *Holy City*, and the 'joy of the whole earth' in the
" Jewish patriot's estimation), is not the cherished home of the Chris-
" tian pilgrim's desires. It is, at best, transitory, and only a resting-
" place for wayfaring men who lodge in it, for a little season, on their
" way home to their city out of sight, even that *Jerusalem which is above*,
" *which is the Mother of us all.*" (See note 1, pp. 298—302.) The suggestion
of Schoettgen and Michaelis, that this verse contains a prophetic intimation of the approaching destruction of Jerusalem, seems to me entirely
foreign to the argument. The antithesis lies between the terrestrial
distinction and advantages comprised in the citizenship of the material
Jerusalem, and the abiding consolations of the Jerusalem above. The
words are intended, 1st, as a *dissuasive* against undue regret on the
part of the converts at being thrust out from all that they once held
most honourable, sacred, and dear ; 2dly, as a *consolatory admonition*
as to the better hopes which they professed to entertain for eternity,
as their final rest and consolation, after the toils of their pilgrimage
should be ended. Turning away their eyes from the fading scenes of
earthly endearments, the Writer bids them to solace themselves by the
contemplation of their heavenly metropolis and home. Wolfius (*in loc.*)
wisely remarks :—" Mihi quidem πόλις μέλλουσα de oeconomia Novi
" Testamenti accipi non posse videtur, quæ tunc non amplius erat
" μέλλουσα, sed vere existebat, ita, ut qui eam iustar civitatis ingressi
" essent, non jam ξένοι et πάροικοι, sed συμπολῖται τῶν ἁγίων καὶ οἰκεῖοι
" τοῦ Θεοῦ appellari possent."—Stuart also (*in loc.*) well observes :—
" The design of our verse is to show the Hebrews, that it cannot be of
" any great importance should they be exiled from their dwelling-places,
" and the habitations of their Jewish kindred ; for in this world no
" habitation, no place of abode, can be μένουσα, *permanent, lasting*. By
" profession the Christians, like the patriarchs, were seeking πατρίδα
" ἐπουράνιον, and consequently πόλιν μέλλουσαν," &c.

Verse 15.—Through him (Jesus) therefore[1] (see verse 10, ἔχομεν θυσιαστήριον κ.τ.λ.), let us offer up a sacrifice of praise continually (διαπαντὸς) to God, that is the fruit of lips[2] confessing to His Name[3] (χειλέων ὁμολογούντων τῷ ὀνόματι αὐτοῦ).

[1] Δι' αὐτοῦ οὖν ἀναφέρωμεν θυσίαν αἰνέσεως κ.τ.λ. One of the main arguments running through the entire Epistle is this. Christ the Messiah having offered himself to God, without spot, a perfect and sufficient sacrifice for the sins of the whole world, the Levitic sacrifices

are superseded and must entirely cease. Daniel had intimated as much, chap. ix. 27. Schoettgen (*Hor. Hebr.*, tom. ii., p. 612) gives the following decisive proofs that the ancient Rabbinical Jews expected the sacrifices to cease in the days of Messiah :—" Sohar Exod., fol. 85, " col. 346. *Cum Israelitæ essent in terra sancta, per illos cultus et sacri-*"*ficia, quæ fecerunt, omnes morbos et pœnas ex mundo sustulerunt :* " השתא משיח מסלק לון מבני עלמא, *nunc autem Messias tollit eas a filiis* " *hominum, usque dum ex hoc mundo egrediuntur :* ומקבל עונשיה, *et reatum* " *ejus* (mundi scilicet) *in se suscipit, sicut jam diximus :*—Vajikra rabba, " sect. 9, fol. 153, 1, Tanchuma, fol. 55, 2. Pesikta sotarta, fol. 11, 1, " et Midrasch Tehillim ad Psalm. c. 2, fol. 36, 4. *R. Pinchas nomine* " *R. Levi, et R. Jochanan ex ore R. Menachem Galilæi dixerunt ;* " לעתיד לבא כל הקרבנות בטלין וקרבן תודה אינו בטל. Temporibus Messiæ omnes " sacrificia cessabunt, sed sacrificium laudis non cessabit : (In Midrasch " Tehillim vox לבא abest,) *q.d.* Jerem. xvii. 26. Et adducentes laudem " in domum Domini.—Tanchuma, fol. 48, 1, *Dixit Deus S.B. : In hoc* " *mundo peccata hominum expiata sunt per sacrificia : verum* לעלמא הבא, " *Ego peccata tua expio sine sacrificio* (ex animantibus facto), *q.d.* Jesa. " xliii. 25. Ego, ego deleo peccata tua propter me.—De vacca rufa " (see Hebr. ix. 13, σποδὸς δαμάλεως.) in specie locus pulcherrimus exstat " in *Baal hatturim* ad Numer. xix. 9, לא יצטרכו לאפר פרה, *Non amplius* " *habebunt opus cinere vaccæ rufæ, nam* deglutiet Dominus mortem in " æternum."—Schoettgen adds,—" Hæc autem verba Prophetæ de " Messia loqui, jam aliquoties adfuit.—De panibus propositionum. " Schemoth rabba, sect. 50, fol. 142, 3. *Dixit Deus S.B. ad Israelitas :* " *Vos fecistis mihi mensam,* אני מציל אתכם מן הערובה, *Ego absolvam vos,* " *ut non amplius illam instruere debeatis* (panibus et reliquis eo perti-" nentibus), *et ipse instruam vobis mensam* לעתיד לבא, temporibus Messiæ." In Levit. vii. 12 we read :—" If he offer it for a thanksgiving, then he " shall offer with the sacrifice of thanksgiving (וזבח התודה, LXX. vii. 2, " ἐπὶ τῆς θυσίας τῆς αἰνέσεως) unleavened cakes," &c. In 2 Chron. xxix. 31 זבחים.ותדות is translated θυσίας αἰνέσεως, and θυσίας καὶ αἰνέσεις. So also in 2 Chron. xxxiii. 16, וזבחי שלמים ותודה is rendered θυσίαν σωτηρίου καὶ αἰνέσεως. The Rev. Dr. Phillips (The Psalms in Hebrew with Commentary, vol. ii., pp. 453, 454) writes on Ps. cxvi. 13 כוס ישועות אשא, *I will take the cup of Salvation.* " This verse and the following " contain an answer to the question in the preceding one מה אשיב וגו'. " The cup of salvation is thought to allude to the Eucharistic offering ; " so Mendelsohn observes that *it is the cup of blessing, full of wine, used* " *in the Eucharistic sacrifice.* Some persons, however, deny that there " is any allusion to those sacrifices, as Hengstenberg, who observes, " ' Dieser Kelch ist eine blosse Fiction ;' *this communion cup is a mere*

"*fiction.* It is true, in the institution of the festival-offerings, there is
" nothing said of the cup ; yet in the feast of the Passover, for instance,
" we know from Matt. xxvi. 29, 30 that the cup of wine to drink, and
" the singing of a hymn were parts of the celebration. See Lightfoot's
"*Horæ Hebraicæ* on Matt. xxvi." Dr. Phillips might have made his
case much stronger had he observed, that under the term used by
St. Matthew, viz., ὑμνήσαντες, was probably included the singing of this
very Psalm cxvi. It was included in the "*Great Hallelujah*" which
comprised Ps. cxiii.—cxviii. These Psalms were sung at the Jewish
festivals, particularly at the Feast of Tabernacles and the Passover.
From all these considerations we are able to gather certainly, that it
was the belief of the ancient Rabbis that in Messiah's days all vicarious
sacrifices should cease, but that the *Sacrifice of Praise* should never
cease. What they understood by the figurative *Sacrifice of Praise*
agrees excellently well with the definition given by the Writer to the
Hebrews, τουτέστι καρπὸν χειλέων ὁμολογούντων τῷ ὀνόματι αὐτοῦ, as will
be apparent from the following quotation given by Schoettgen, *in loc.*
(*Hor. Hebr.*, tom. i., p. 1005) :—" Vajikra Rabba, sect. 9, fol. 153, 1, et
" Tanchuma, fol. 55, 2. *R. Pinchas, R. Levi, et R. Jochanan ex ore*
" *R. Menachem Galilæi dixerunt ;* לעתיד לבא כל הקרבנות בטלין וקרבן תודה אינו בטל.
" *Tempore Messiæ omnia sacrificia cessabunt, sed sacrificium laudis non*
" *cessabit. Omnes preces cessabunt, sed laudes non cessabunt,* q.d. Jerem.
" xxxiii. 1. Vox lætitiæ et gaudii, vox sponsi et sponsæ, vox dicen-
" tium : Laudate Deum Zebaoth, &c. *Hæc est confessio :* et adferentium
" laudem in domum Domini : *Hoc est Sacrificium laudis. Et sic David*
" *dicit,* Ps. lvi. 13. In me sunt, Domine, vota tua, solvam laudationes
" tibi. *Quia scribitur in plurali* תודות, laudationes, *intelligitur confessio*
" *et sacrificium laudis.—*Jalkut Rubeni, fol. 92, 2, ad verba Exod. xix.
" 12. Ederunt panem cum Jethro coram facie Domini : *Observanda*
" *sunt verba* לפני אלהים. Exinde discimus, quod quicunque sacrificium
" offert ברעותא דלביה, in mente, coram ipso Deus est."

² Καρπὸν χειλέων κ.τ.λ. In the Hebrew text of Is. lvii. 19 we read,
בורא ניב שפתים, *Creavi fructum labiorum.* Vulg. These words are not in
the LXX. But in Hosea xiv. 3 the LXX. translate פרים שפתינו, *the
calves of our lips,* by καρπὸν χειλέων. There is no necessity for supposing
that the LXX. interpreters *must necessarily* have had the reading פרי,
fruit, before them in the MSS. of Hosea from which they translated.
They gave a very intelligible paraphrase of an equally intelligible
Hebrew expression. Dr. Gill writes, *in loc.,* "The *Sacrifice of Praise*
" is so called, in allusion to the offering of the first-fruits under the
" Law, and to distinguish it from legal sacrifices ; and to show in what
" manner we are to praise God, namely, with our lips. In Hosea xiv. 3,

CHAP. XIII., 15. 353

"which is thought to be referred to here, it is *the calves of our lips:*
" *sacrifices of praise* being instead of *calves:* and the Apostle interprets
" it in great agreement with the Jewish writers. The Chaldee para-
" phrase explains it by כלי ספוה, *the words of our lips;* and so Jarchi,
" דברי שפתינו, *The words of our lips;* and Kimchi, וידוי שפתים, *the confession*
" *of our lips.*"

³ 'Ομολογούντων τῷ ὀνόματι αὐτοῦ. Through Jesus (δι' αὐτοῦ), the converts are exhorted to offer the *Sacrifice of Praise* to God the Father continually. With his usual subtlety of adaptation, the Writer contrives to blend exhortation with his words of encouragement. The desponding Hebrews were out of conceit with the simplicity of the Gospel. They could no longer partake, with their unbaptized brethren, of the sacrifices of the temple. They looked back with regret upon the festive splendours of the Mosaic ritual, from which they had for ever cut themselves off. Some of them were ashamed of the obloquy attaching to the profession of Christ, and gave no unwilling ear to those who would teach them to avoid the reproach of the Cross, by a renewed conformity with the Levitic ceremonial Law. The Writer has reminded them (verse 10) that "we have an altar," of which the high-priest himself has no power to eat. We can offer the *Sacrifice of Praise* continually to God; but the most acceptable form in which this Sacrifice can be offered is, "the fruit of lips confessing to his (Jesus') " name." A bold, cheerful, grateful, and trustful avowal of the name of Jesus, by word and deed, is the *Sacrifice of Praise* that is demanded of the Christian believers, especially in time of persecution. A hesitating, halting profession of Jesus and his Cross, is dishonouring to God the Father; but when the name of the Son is glorified, the Father accepts the tribute of devotion as an oblation acceptable to Himself. There is much in this passage of the Epistle to the Hebrews to bring to remembrance the tone and style of St. Paul's exhortations to the Philippian converts, especially when he writes (Phil. ii. 5—11), "Let this mind be
" in you, which was also in Christ Jesus. Who being in the form of
" God, thought it not robbery to be equal with God. But made Him-
" self of no reputation, and took upon Himself the form of a servant,
" and was made in the likeness of men. And being found in fashion as
" a man, He humbled Himself, and became obedient unto death, even
" the death of the Cross. (Comp. Hebr. xiii. 11—13.) Wherefore God
" also hath highly exalted Him, and given Him a name which is above
" every name. That at the name of Jesus every knee should bow, of
" *things* in heaven, and *things* in earth, and things under the earth ;
" and that every tongue should confess (καὶ πᾶσα γλῶσσα ἐξομολογήσηται)
" that Jesus Christ *is* Lord, to the glory of God the Father."

Verse 16.—But to do good, and to communicate forget not,[1] for with sacrifices such as these God is well pleased (εὐαρεστεῖται ὁ Θεός).

[1] Τῆς δὲ εὐποιίας καὶ κοινωνίας μὴ ἐπιλανθάνεσθε κ.τ.λ. The *Sacrifice of Praise*, without works of benevolence, and a consecrated charity accompanying it, would be a mere lip-service. This was the fault of the forefathers of these Jewish converts in the days of Isaiah (Is. xxix. 13—21), and also in the days of Ezekiel, who wrote concerning them (xxxiii. 31), " With their mouth they shew much love, *but* their heart "goeth after their covetousness." Our Lord himself reproved the evil generation of his day in the very words of Isaiah (Matt. xv. 1—9; Mark vii. 1—15). So the Writer to the Hebrews puts the converts in mind that the self-seeking sacrifices of formalism are but dead works in the sight of God. Compare Isaiah lviii. 1, &c. The word εὐποιΐα is found nowhere else in the New Testament. The phrase κοινωνία is used by St. Paul in the sense of a charitable collection, or contribution, in Rom. xv. 26; 2 Cor. viii. 4, ix. 13. Schoettgen (*Hor. Hebr.*, tom. i., pp. 1006—1008) gives many illustrations from the early Rabbinic writers respecting the value of good works, from which I select the following: —" R. Samuel ben David in (his book) חסד שמואל, fol. 41, 1, says:— " The man who commits sin nowadays, since we have no longer either a " temple or sacrifice, יעסוק בתפלה, ought to be diligent in prayer, שהיא " עבודה במקום קרבן, for such service as this takes the place of sacrifice " (Corban). And since sacrifice cannot be performed without a sanctuary, " לכן יעסוק בגמילות חסדים עם עניים, let such an one be diligent in works of " mercy to the needy, והוא כאלו עושה משכן והקריב קרבן, and he is as if he " built a sanctuary and brought a sacrifice." Consult also J. C. Wolfius, *in loc., Curæ Phil. et Crit.*, tom. iv., pp. 802, 803.

Verse 17.—Obey your rulers,[1] and submit yourselves, for they watch for your souls, as they that must give account (ὡς λόγον ἀποδώσοντες), so that they may do this with joy (μετὰ χαρᾶς), and not bemoaning (your unruly demeanour, καὶ μὴ στενάζοντες); for this is unprofitable (ἀλυσιτελὲς) for you.

[1] Πείθεσθε τοῖς ἡγουμένοις ὑμῶν, καὶ ὑπείκετε, κ.τ.λ. The Writer now urges upon the Hebrews the necessity of a ready obedience and wholesome discipline. In troublous times, like those in which they were

living, a schismatical spirit could not but produce disastrous results. If the leaders grew disheartened by the unruly and contentious demeanour of those committed to their charge, the enemies could not fail to be encouraged to fresh and more vigorous assaults. Union, in such evil days, was strength. The struggle that was before the Church would require the collective and united efforts of every several member of the community. The Writer points out under the words ἀλυσιτελὲς γὰρ ὑμῖν τοῦτο, that the evil results would fall with double weight upon the flock. If its leaders were discouraged by divisions within, how could they, with a good heart, frame their energies to face the perils from without. They were placed in the forefront of the battle. They were marked out as the first victims for the cruel hand of Rabbinic intolerance and persecuting zeal to strike down. Scandalous would it be, then, if, by the factious conduct of those committed to their charge, their ministry should be rendered more arduous, and their anxieties embittered by the disobedient conduct of those for whose souls they watched, with a single eye to the Great Account! Josephus (*Ant.* xx. 9, 1) has left us a short, but graphic description of the persecution which the Church at Judæa endured at the hands of the Sadducean High-Priest Ananus:

—" And now Cæsar, upon hearing the death of Festus, sent Albinus
" into Judæa, as procurator; but the King deprived Joseph of the high-
" priesthood, and bestowed the succession to that dignity on the son of
" Ananus, who was also himself called Ananus. Now the report goes,
" that this elder Ananus proved a most fortunate man ; for he had five
" sons, who had all performed the office of a highpriest to God, and he
" had himself enjoyed that dignity a long time formerly, which had
" never happened to any other of our highpriests ; but this younger
" Ananus, who, as we have told you already, took the highpriesthood,
" was a bold man in his temper, and very insolent; he was also of the
" sect of the Sadducees, who were very rigid in judging offenders, above
" all the rest of the Jews, as we have already observed. When, there-
" fore, Ananus was of this disposition, he thought he had now a proper
" opportunity [to exercise his authority]. Festus was now dead, and
" Albinus was but upon the road ; so he assembled the Sanhedrim
" of the Judges, and brought before them the brother of Jesus, who
" was called Christ, whose name was James, and some others; and
" when he had formed an accusation against them as breakers of the
" law, he delivered them to be stoned (καθίζει συνέδριον κριτῶν, καὶ
" παραγαγὼν εἰς αὐτὸ τὸν ἀδελφὸν Ἰησοῦ τοῦ λεγομένου Χριστοῦ (Ἰάκωβος
" ὄνομα αὐτῷ). καί τινας ἑτέρους, ὡς παρανομησάντων κατηγορίαν ποιησάμενος,
" παρέδωκε λευσθησομένους); but as for those who seemed the most
" equitable of the citizens,......they disliked what was done : they sent also

"to the King [Agrippa], desiring him to send to Ananus that he should
"act so no more, for that what he had already done was not to be
"justified: nay, some of them went also to meet Albinus, as he was
"upon his journey, and informed him that it was not lawful for Ananus
"to assemble a Sanhedrim without his consent: whereupon Albinus
"complied with what they had said, and wrote in anger to Ananus,
"and threatened that he would bring him to punishment for what he
"had done; on which King Agrippa took the highpriesthood from him,
"when he had ruled but three months."—*Whiston's Josephus.*

Whiston, in his note on this passage, observes that the Sadducees
were much more severe, and inexorable as judges, than the Pharisees.
Professed free-thinkers are usually more implacable adversaries to truth
than even religious bigots. Besides Christianity, with its doctrines of
supernaturalism, and the resurrection of the dead, was in immediate
conflict with the tenets of those who denied the existence of angel, or
spirit, or a future life. Sadduceeism had, so to speak, a direct and
personal quarrel with, and antipathy to, the religion of Jesus. Ma-
terialism and Christianity must evermore remain in irreconcileable
antagonism. The most impracticable adversary that the modern
missionary has to cope with is the Jew, who, having turned his back
upon the Hope of the Fathers, professes a nondescript philanthropy,
which is usually accompanied by an active antagonism and hostility to
every description of definite belief.

Verses 18, 19.—Pray for us;[1] for we are persuaded that
we have a good conscience, in all things wishing to walk
honestly.[2] But more especially (περισσοτέρως) do I
entreat you to do this in order that I may be the more
quickly restored to you.[3]

[1] Προσεύχεσθε περὶ ἡμῶν. St. Paul makes the same request, Col. iv. 3,
προσευχόμενοι ἅμα καὶ περὶ ἡμῶν; 1 Thes. v. 25, ἀδελφοὶ, προσεύχεσθε περὶ
ἡμῶν; 2 Thes. iii. 1, τὸ λοιπὸν προσεύχεσθε, ἀδελφοὶ, περὶ ἡμῶν. Alford,
as usual, following Delitzsch, would include others as well as the Writer
in the plural expression, "pray for us." He says, "Here, as elsewhere,
"it is probably a mistake to suppose that the first person plural indi-
"cates the Writer alone." Probably even Dean Alford would not have
ventured to make the same assertion in reference to chap. vi. 9,
πεπείσμεθα δὲ περὶ ὑμῶν ἀγαπητοὶ, τὰ κρείττονα καὶ ἐχόμενα σωτηρίας, εἰ καὶ
οὕτω λαλοῦμεν. And again, verse 11, ἐπιθυμοῦμεν δὲ ἕκαστον κ.τ.λ. Such
an evasion of a testimony in favour of the Pauline authorship of this
Epistle is more ingenious, than candid or scholarly.

² Πεποίθαμεν γὰρ ὅτι καλὴν συνείδησιν ἔχομεν, ἐν πᾶσι καλῶς θέλοντες ἀναστρέφεσθαι. Ewald (*Das Sendschr. a.d. Hebr.*, p. 151), after noticing that the Writer follows the example of St. Paul in asking for the prayers of his readers, says,—" Aber er kann hinzufügen was Paulus " in solchen Fällen für unnöthig hielt : *halten wir uns doch überzeugt* " *dass wir ein gutes Gewissen haben, da wir in allem wohl zu handeln* " *streben.*" Now it is singularly noteworthy that the words of St. Paul before the Jewish Sanhedrin (Acts xxiii. 1) bear, to say the least, a very strong resemblance to these words of the Epistle to the Hebrews. Ἄνδρες ἀδελφοί, ἐγὼ πάσῃ συνειδήσει ἀγαθῇ πεπολίτευμαι τῷ Θεῷ ἄχρι ταύτης τῆς ἡμέρας. Not a few of the readers of the Epistle may perchance have heard St. Paul's emphatic *apologia* for his manner of life pronounced, and have stood by when the high priest called aloud for somebody to smite him on the mouth. So again (Acts xxiv. 16), in his defence before Felix against the accusations of Tertullus and the elders of the Jews, St. Paul uses almost identical language ; ἐν τούτῳ δὲ αὐτὸς ἀσκῶ, ἀπρόσκοπον συνείδησιν ἔχειν πρὸς τὸν Θεὸν καὶ τοὺς ἀνθρώπους διαπαντός. So far, then, from there being anything un-Pauline in the above declaration of the Writer to the Hebrews, it contains a re-echo of the great Apostle's twice-repeated assertion before the rulers of his own nation. To the Hebrews it would recall recollections of two of the most stirring episodes in the career of St. Paul. It would remind them how, for the " Hope of the Fathers," he had been, once and again, tried for his life. It would assure them that in spite of his bonds (chap. x. 34) he still persisted unhesitatingly in the course he had adopted. That he saw nothing to regret in his choice. His inmost convictions were still serenely undisturbed. " Faith and a good " conscience " (1 Tim i. 19) he yet held to with undaunted, unfaltering resolution. Compare 1 Cor. iv. 4, οὐδὲν γὰρ ἐμαυτῷ σύνοιδα, "for " I have nothing on my conscience," erroneously rendered in the Authorised Version, " For I know nothing by myself." So also the expression ἀναστρέφεσθαι is strictly Pauline in its application. I say *in its application*, because I consider that the recent style of arguing, for or against the authorship, or genuineness, of portions of the Bible from the use, or rather the occurrence of a word more or less frequently, is pitiful and contemptible. In Gal. i. 13 we read, ἠκούσατε γὰρ τὴν ἐμὴν ἀναστροφήν ποτε κ.τ.λ. Any scholar who has written much, and upon a variety of subjects, must be perfectly conscious that his claim to the authorship of any particular writing of his own might, upon certain fixed *data*, be disproved from his other acknowledged productions. I am fully persuaded that the modern " criticism," based upon isolated words and expressions, is the weakest of all criterions for judging of the

authenticity of any writing. Far different is the inference reasonably to be drawn, from a correspondence of statement, upon a peculiar topic such as the one under discussion, between an author's acknowledged sayings and writings, and his reputed compositions. That the Epistle to the Hebrews is the work of St. Paul must, as the evidence at present stands, remain a matter of opinion, but it may yet be an opinion amounting to a fairly grounded certainty. The advocates of the Pauline origin of the Epistle are just as much entitled to entertain, and advance with a modest firmness, their convictions upon the subject, as the holders of an opposite theory. The sensitive impatience of contradiction, and the sweeping insinuations of credulity against all who may dare to differ from modern experiments upon the Word of God, betray to my mind a limited acquaintance with the literature of the subject, and a fear lest, after all, the pretended new discoveries may be found, upon examination, to rest upon a basis far less secure than their propounders would have us to believe, viz., upon the ill-supported authority of their own personal predilections.

² Ἵνα τάχιον ἀποκατασταθῶ ὑμῖν. Stuart writes :—" This seems "plainly to imply that the writer was detained from paying those a "visit whom he addressed, by some adverse circumstances, viz., either "by imprisonment, sickness, or some like cause. It also implies that "he is known to them, and they to him; for it indicates that he had "formerly been among them." See St. Paul's words to Philemon, verse 22, ἐλπίζω γὰρ ὅτι διὰ τῶν προσευχῶν ὑμῶν χαρισθήσομαι ὑμῖν.

Verses 20, 21.—But the God of peace,¹ who brought back again from the dead the great Shepherd of the sheep,² by the blood of the eternal covenant,³ our Lord Jesus, make you perfect in every good work, so that you may do his will (see chap. x. 36), working in you that which is well-pleasing in his sight, through Jesus Christ; to whom be the glory for ever and ever. Amen.

¹ Ὁ δὲ Θεὸς τῆς εἰρήνης κ.τ.λ. Ewald rightly sees a reference back to chap. xii. 14, εἰρήνην διώκετε μετὰ πάντων. But there is also, doubtless, a reference to the already quoted passage of Isaiah lvii. 19, בורא ניב שפתים שלום שלום לרחוק ולקרוב אמר יהוה, "I create the fruit of the lips. "Peace, peace to him that is near, and to him that is afar off, saith "the Lord." See note 2, p. 352. Compare St. Paul's words in 1 Thess. v. 23, αὐτὸς δὲ ὁ Θεὸς τῆς εἰρήνης κ.τ.λ. 2 Thess. iii. 16, αὐτὸς δὲ ὁ Κύριος τῆς εἰρήνης κ.τ.λ. Romans xv. 33, ὁ δὲ Θεὸς τῆς εἰρήνης κ.τ.λ. ;

xvi. 20, ὁ δὲ Θεὸς τῆς εἰρήνης κ.τ.λ. 2 Cor. xiii. 11, ὁ Θεὸς τῆς ἀγάπης καὶ εἰρήνης κ.τ.λ. Philipp. iv. 9, ὁ Θεὸς τῆς εἰρήνης κ.τ.λ. We have, then, ample authority for regarding the above as a Pauline formula. Compare also 1 Cor. vii. 15—17, ἐν δὲ εἰρήνῃ κέκληκεν ἡμᾶς ὁ Θεός. Here the Apostle asserts that "God hath called us in peace," and uses his assertion as a persuasive for Christians who may be married to heathens, if possible to continue to live with them, as offering to the unbeliever the one opportunity of becoming savingly acquainted with the power of Christianity. I would propose to punctuate verses 16, 17 as follows, τί γὰρ οἶδας, γύναι, εἰ τὸν ἄνδρα σώσεις; ἢ τί οἶδας, ἄνερ, εἰ τὴν γυναῖκα σώσεις, εἰ μὴ ἑκάστῳ ὡς ἐμέρισεν ὁ Θεός; " For how knowest thou, O " wife, if thou shalt save thy husband? or how knowest thou, O husband, " if thou shalt save thy wife, except in the way that God has provi- " dentially cast your lot?" i.e., in originally permitting your union as man and wife.

² Ὁ ἀναγαγὼν ἐκ νεκρῶν τὸν ποιμένα τῶν προβάτων τὸν μέγαν. Alford asserts, " the passage before the Writer's mind has been that in the pro- " phetic 63d chapter of Isaiah, where speaking of Moses it is said, ποῦ ὁ " ἀναβιβάσας ἐκ τῆς θαλάσσης τὸν ποιμένα τῶν προβάτων, where some " MSS. read ἐκ τῆς γῆς." The Hebrew of Isaiah lxiii. 11, reads, איה המעלם מים את רעה צאנו. Dean Alford, however, does not seem to be mindful that in Romans x. 7 we have the inspired authority of St. Paul for translating the עבר הים, "beyond the sea," of Deut. xxx. 13, of the *resurrection of the dead*. The Apostle thus paraphrases the words of Moses ; μὴ εἴπῃς ἐν τῇ καρδίᾳ σου, τίς ἀναβήσεται εἰς τὸν οὐρανόν; τοῦτ᾽ ἔστι Χριστὸν καταγαγεῖν· ἤ, τίς καταβήσεται εἰς τὴν ἄβυσσον; (מי יעבר לנו אל עבר הים—τίς διαπεράσει ἡμῖν εἰς τὸ πέραν τῆς θαλάσσης; LXX.) τοῦτ᾽ ἔστι, Χριστὸν ἐκ νεκρῶν ἀναγαγεῖν. Schoettgen (*Hor. Hebr.*, tom. ii., p. 665) quotes as follows from the *Tikkune Sohar*, c. 18, fol. 28, 1, in reference to the Messiah :—" Arise, O Faithful Shepherd, and open the house of " prophecy, which is in the House above, the most secret of all secret " things, where the mysteries of the Heavenly King are found: for " thou art as the Son of the house, the Son of that House," &c. The real clue to the words τὸν ποιμένα τῶν προβάτων τὸν μέγαν is to be found in Zech. xiii. 7, " Awake, O sword, against my Shepherd, and against " the man that is my fellow (על רעי ועל גבר עמיתי), saith the Lord of " hosts. Smite the Shepherd," &c. Dr. Henderson (*The Book of the Twelve Minor Prophets*, p. 434) well observes, *in loc.*:—" Not only is " the Messiah designated the Shepherd of Jehovah to indicate the " relation in which he stood to the Father in the economy of redemp- " tion, but he is described as גבר עמיתו, *the man of his union;* conjointly " or closely united to Him. The term translated *man* is not that usually

"employed in Hebrew, which in such construction would be merely "idiomatic, but גבר, *a strong*, or *mighty man*, one who is such by way "of eminence." For Christian readers the Messianic interpretation of Zech. xiii 7 is authoritatively fixed by Matt. xxvi. 31, Mark xiv. 27, but it is important to notice that R. Abarbanel, after giving two other interpretations, says,—" The third interpretation is, that the words *my* "*shepherd, the man my fellow*, are spoken of Messiah the son of Joseph." The subject is discussed at length in *R. D. Kimchi's Commentary on Zechariah, transl. with notes* by the late Dr. M'Caul, pp. 169—177. Dr. Phillips, in his Commentary on the Psalms, vol. i., p. 26, writes,— " In the ancient book Zohar there is a passage which shows in what " sense the author understood the intention of this Psalm, and of this " verse in particular (Ps. ii. 12). It is as follows :—

אנת הוא בר רעיא מהימנא תלך אמר נשקו בר ואנת הוא רבן דישראל רב לחתא רבן
דמלאכי השרת בר לעילה ברא דקב״ה ושכינה :

" *Thou art the Son, the Faithful Shepherd; of Thee it is said*, KISS THE " SON, *and Thou art the Lord of Israel, Master below, the Lord of the* " *ministering* angels, Son above, Son of the Holy One, Blessed be He, " and the *Shechinah*. Lubbi edition, fol. 87."—Philo (*De Agricultura*, Works, Mangey's Edit., tom. i., p. 308) writes on Ps. xxiii. 1 :—
Καθάπερ γάρ τινα ποίμνην, γῆν καὶ ὕδωρ καὶ ἄερα καὶ πῦρ, καὶ ὅσα ἐν τούτοις φυτά τε αὖ καὶ ζῶα, τὰ μὲν θνητὰ, τὰ τὲ θεῖα· ἔτι δὲ οὐρανοῦ φύσιν, καὶ ἡλίου καὶ σελήνης περιόδους, καὶ τῶν ἄλλων ἀστέρων τροπάς τε αὖ καὶ χορείας ἐναρμονίους, ὡς ποιμὴν καὶ βασιλεὺς ὁ Θεὸς ἄγει κατὰ δίκην καὶ νόμον, προστησάμενος τὸν ὀρθὸν αὐτοῦ λόγον, πρωτόγονον υἱόν, ὃς τὴν ἐπιμέλειαν τῆς ἱερᾶς ταύτης ἀγέλης, οἷά τις μεγάλου βασιλέως ὕπαρχος διαδέξεται. Καὶ γὰρ εἴρηταί που, Ἰδοὺ ἐγὼ εἰμι, ἀποστελῶ ἄγγελόν μου εἰς πρόσωπόν σου, φυλάξαι σε ἐν τῇ ὁδῷ. Λεγέτω τοίνυν καὶ ὁ κόσμος ἅπας, ἡ μεγίστη καὶ τελειωτάτη τοῦ ὄντος Θεοῦ ποίμνη, Κύριος ποιμαίνει με, καὶ οὐδέν με ὑστερήσει. " For as a flock, God rules (according to right and law) as " a Shepherd and King, the earth, the water, the air, and fire, and " whatever species are therein contained, whether animal, human, or " celestial. Besides these, He rules the natural course of the heavens, " the circuits of the sun and moon, and the harmonious motions and " revolutions of the other planets : but over them all He has placed his " Upright WORD, his FIRSTBEGOTTEN SON, who undertakes the over- "sight of this sacred flock, as if He were the lieutenant of some great " king. It was therefore said (Exod. xxiii. 20), *Behold*, I AM, *I will* " *send my Angel before thy face, to keep thee in the way*. Let, therefore, " the whole universe (that vastest and most perfect flock of the Self- " existent God) affirm, *The Lord is my Shepherd, I shall not want*."

³ 'Εν αἵματι διαθήκης αἰωνίου. Stuart translates, "Now, may the God "of peace that raised from the dead our Lord Jesus, who by the blood "of an everlasting covenant, has become the Great Shepherd of the "Sheep." Ewald writes, "Um des Neuen Bundes Blut, um den Preis "das er zur Stiftung des Neuen Bundes sein Blut hingab, *auferstehen* "*liess*." Ewald therefore considers ἐν to be equivalent to *in consideration of*. Alford also rightly asserts, "The expression itself can hardly "but be a reminiscence of Zech. ix. 11, Καὶ σὺ ἐν αἵματι διαθήκης σου "ἐξαπέστειλας δεσμίους σου ἐκ λάκκου οὐκ ἔχοντος ὕδωρ: and, if so, the "import of the preposition here will be at least indicated by its import "there. And there it is by virtue of, in the power of, the blood of thy "covenant, *i.e.*, of that blood which was the seal of the covenant "entered into with thee." See Kimchi's Commentary on Zechariah, transl. by the late Dr. M'Caul, *in loc*.

Verse 22.—But I entreat you, brethren, bear with the word of exhortation, for I have written to you in a brief form (διὰ βραχέων ἐπέστειλα,¹ *i.e.*, concisely, considering the importance and gravity of the subjects treated of).

¹ Διὰ βραχέων κ.τ.λ. "Ita Polybius, p. 71, Διὰ βραχέων καὶ κεφαλαι-"ωδῶς." Wolfius, *in loc*.—Ewald (*Das Sendschr. a.d. Hebr.*, p. 152) says:—"Er bittet die Leser *das* hier ihnen vorgelegte *Wort der Ermahn-* "*ung zu ertragen*, es nur nicht übel zu nehmen, und sogleich wieder "von sich zu weisen; habe er ihnen doch hier nur *in der Kürze ge-* "*schrieben*, den ungemein reichen und schweren Inhalt so kurz als "möglich zusammengedrängt; und könne demnach umsomehr hoffen "das sie das Sendschreiben nicht sofort von sich weisen." There is much in this graceful entreaty to remind one of the admirable tact and delicate courtesy exhibited in St. Paul's Epistle to Philemon, on behalf of Onesimus the runaway slave, whom he sends back to his master, with a plea for forbearance and Christian indulgence. See especially verses 8—10:—Διὸ πολλὴν ἐν Χριστῷ παρρησίαν ἔχων ἐπιτάσσειν σοι τὸ ἀνῆκον· διὰ τὴν ἀγάπην μᾶλλον παρακαλῶ, τοιοῦτος ὢν ὡς Παῦλος πρεσβύτης, νυνὶ δὲ καὶ δέσμιος Ἰησοῦ Χριστοῦ. Παρακαλῶ σε περὶ τοῦ ἐμοῦ τέκνου, ὃν ἐγέννησα ἐν τοῖς δεσμοῖς μου, Ὀνήσιμον. Comp. also Rom. xii. 1, 1 Cor. xvi. 15, 2 Cor. ii. 8, x. 1. Αὐτὸς δὲ ἐγὼ Παῦλος παρακαλῶ ὑμᾶς διὰ τῆς πραότητος καὶ ἐπιεικείας τοῦ Χριστοῦ. Eph. iv. 1; Phil. iv. 2.

Verse 23.—Know ye that our brother Timothy¹ has been set at liberty, with whom, if he come quickly, I will see you.

¹ Γινώσκετε τὸν ἀδελφὸν Τιμόθεον ἀπολελυμένον κ.τ.λ. J. C. Wolfius writes, "i.e., *a vinculis liberatum.* Millius quidem in Prolegom., § 69, "Timotheum potius ad certa quædam negotia *dimissum* dicit, unde sit "rediturus. Id vero putem contrariari · receptæ verbi significationi, "quæ in Actis Apostolicis frequens est. *Vide* Act. iii. 13, iv. 21, 23, &c." Ewald (*Das Sendschr a.d. Hebr.*, p. 49) takes the same view as Wolfius, and translates, "Seiet benachrichtigt dass unser Bruder Timotheus frei "ist, mit welchem ich, wann er bald genug kommt, euch sehen werde." On p. 152, *ibid.*, he says, "Wo er gefangen gesezt war, wussten die "Leser." Ewald's theory (*ibid.*, p. 6) is, that the Epistle was written to the Hebrew community at Ravenna (!), that Timothy had been imprisoned at Jerusalem, and that the Writer was waiting for Timothy, to join him at Cæsarea, where he would take ship, and proceed on his proposed visit to Ravenna. Ewald's suggestion has at least the recommendation of novelty. He pitches upon Ravenna on account of its easy access to Palestine :—" Wir können also etwa an Ravenna denken, "vonwo damals der häufigste und schnellste Verkehr mit Palästina "stattfand." *Ibid.*, p. 6. Stuart, on the other hand, translates, "Know "ye that our brother Timothy is sent away." Alford renders ἀπολελυμένον by *dismissed*, and observes that "ἀπολύειν does not occur in St. "Paul, but is frequent in St. Luke." Perhaps the more correct form of putting the case would be, "St. Paul has no occasion to use the word ἀπολύειν in his acknowledged epistles." If such occasion had arisen, he doubtless would have used it. Where Timothy was really imprisoned, there are absolutely no data for determining. Much that has been written upon the subject is mere futile conjecture. That he was nearer to the Writer of the Epistle than to those to whom it was addressed is exceedingly probable; but to attempt to fix upon any particular locality, and to argue from such premises, is simply guesswork.

Verses 24, 25.—Salute all your rulers, and all the saints. They of Italy salute you.¹ Grace be with you all.² Amen.

¹ Οἱ ἀπὸ τῆς Ἰταλίας. A vast amount of scientific nonsense has been written about these words. J. C. Wolfius, with sagacious brevity, observes, "i.e., *Itali.* Ita Herodotus : οἱ ἀπὸ Πελοποννήσου pro οἱ "Πελοποννήσιοι. Conf. Raphelii Herodoteas ad h.l. et Polybianas ad "Matt. xv. 1." A glance at the concordance will show that ἀπὸ is constantly used, with the substantive, in the Greek Testament, instead of an appellative adjective derived from the name of a place, *e.g.*, Matt. xxvii. 57, "A rich man of (ἀπὸ) Arimathea," Mark xv. 43, "Joseph of (ἀπὸ) Arimathea," John i. 44 (45), "Philip was of (ἀπὸ)

"Bethsaida," *ibid.*, 45 (46), "Jesus of (ἀπὸ) Nazareth," John xi. 1, "Lazarus of (ἀπὸ) Bethany," xix. 38, "Joseph of (ἀπὸ) Arimathea," xxi. 2, "Nathanael of (ἀπὸ) Cana," Acts vi. 9, Κυρηναίων καὶ Ἀλεξανδρέων, καὶ τῶν ἀπὸ Κιλικίας καὶ Ἀσίας, x. 38, "God anointed Jesus of "(ἀπὸ) Nazareth." But a very decisive example is found in Acts xvii. 13, "But when the Jews of Thessalonica (ὡς δὲ ἔγνωσαν οἱ ἀπὸ τῆς "Θεσσαλονίκης Ἰουδαῖοι) had knowledge that the word of God was "preached of Paul at Berea, they came thither also (i.e., *from Thessa-*"*lonica to Berea*), and stirred up the people." I take it, however, that under the term οἱ ἀπὸ τῆς Ἰταλίας were included the brethren who did not reside at Rome (see Acts xxviii. 13, 14, δευτεραῖοι ἤλθομεν εἰς Ποτιόλους. Οὗ εὑρόντες ἀδελφοὺς παρεκλήθημεν ἐπ' αὐτοῖς ἐπιμεῖναι ἡμέρας ἑπτά κ.τ.λ.), but, yet being on terms of friendly intercourse with St. Paul, were for brevity's sake designated, with the resident believers at Rome, under the general term οἱ ἀπὸ τῆς Ἰταλίας, *i.e.*, as Wolfius says, *the Italians.*

[2] Ἡ χάρις μετὰ πάντων ὑμῶν. There is nothing un-Pauline in this formula. It is expressed with even greater brevity in Coloss. iv. 18, ἡ χάρις μεθ' ὑμων, and also in 2 Tim. iv. 22. The identical words of Heb. xiii. 25 are found in Titus iii. 15.

The Subscription.—Written to the Hebrews from Italy by Timothy.[1]

[1] Πρὸς Ἑβραίους ἐγράφη ἀπὸ τῆς Ἰταλίας διὰ Τιμοθέου. Professor Stuart says,—" Like most of the other subscriptions to the Epistles, it is of no "authority. It is demonstrably erroneous here; for how could Timothy "write this Epistle when the author says, at its very close, that Timothy "was *then absent?* The author of this subscription, one is tempted "to think, had either read the Epistle with very little care or with "very little understanding of its contents." Without presuming to defend the authenticity of the subscription, I would venture to suggest that Timothy *may have been* the amanuensis of the greater portion of the Epistle, and yet have been prevented from finishing his task. The book of Deuteronomy contains in its last chapter an account of the death of Moses, and yet, in common with other credulous folks, I cannot divest myself of the antiquated notion (be it remembered, on the authority of the New Testament, Acts iii. 22, vii. 37) that Moses was the author of the book. It is not absolutely necessary to restrict the

meaning of ἐγράφη to the actual manual labour of writing. It may signify *was dispatched*. If the Epistle was written by St. Paul at Rome, it is within the bounds of possibility, that after all, Timothy may have been the bearer of the missive after his release. To my mind, it is always dangerous to speak, with certain assurance, either for or against any statement whatever, where there are absolutely no *positive data* to argue from. J. C. Wolfius writes with a more judicious cautiousness than Stuart :—" Subscriptionem hanc ab Apostolo non " esse profectam, multa sunt, quæ persuadeant. Primo enim a multis " Codd. abest ; deinde in aliis varie effertur," &c.

Having thus been permitted to see the completion of my task, the accomplishment of which has beguiled many an hour, in sickness and in health, I desire to express my great obligations to the numerous subscribers who have encouraged me to persevere in my efforts to accomplish it. May the Great Master of the Church condescend to look favourably upon my endeavour to elucidate this portion of his Holy Word, accepting the sincerity of the attempt, pardoning its infirmity, and overruling its errors. Amen!

C. A. MACINTOSH, Printer, Great New-street, London.

www.ingramcontent.com/pod-product-compliance
Lightning Source LLC
Chambersburg PA
CBHW032029220426
43664CB00006B/410